ECONOMICS

2 MACROECONOMICS
READINGS & PROBLEMS

Sixth Edition

ECONOMICS DEPARTMENT
University of Pennsylvania

GINN PRESS

ISBN 0–536–58176-2

BA 4409

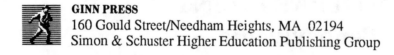 **GINN PRESS**
160 Gould Street/Needham Heights, MA 02194
Simon & Schuster Higher Education Publishing Group

COPYRIGHT ACKNOWLEDGMENTS

Contents

PART I:
READINGS

No One Has Starved—The Great Depression 1

The Intelligent Citizen's Guide to Inflation 4
    Robert M. Solow

Who Wins, Who Loses from Inflation? 20
    Joseph J. Minarik

The Postulates of the Classical Economics 26
    John Maynard Keynes

The Supply Side 34
    Lawrence R. Klein

On Theories of Unemployment 37
    Robert M. Solow

Tax Revision: Impact on Output and Employment 44
    Council of Economic Advisers

The Effectiveness of Temporary Changes in the Federal 50
Personal Income Tax
    Janice D. Halpern

Fiscal Policy 57
    Council of Economic Advisers

The Importance of Balancing the Budget 63
    Harry Flood Byrd

The Need for Balanced Federal Budgets _____ 74
        Maurice H. Stans

The Ricardian Approach to Budget Deficits _____ 79
        Robert J. Barro

Budget Deficits: Rhetoric and Reality _____ 89
        Robert Eisner

Of Money _____ 102
            David Hume

Money in Action _____ 105
            Lawrence S. Ritter
            and William L. Silber

Open Market Operations _____ 110
            Paul Meek

Should a Robot Replace the Federal Reserve? _____ 153
            Lawrence S. Ritter
            and William L. Silber

Lessons on Monetary Policy from the 1980s _____ 157
            Benjamin M. Friedman

Sequential Signals of Recession and Recovery _____ 171
            Victor Zarnowitz
            and Geoffrey H. Moore

Fiscal Policy _____ 185
            Milton Friedman

Has Fiscal Policy Been Oversold? _____ 192
            Milton Friedman

Is Monetary Policy Being Oversold? _____ 198
            Walter W. Heller

Rules and Roles for Fiscal and Monetary Policy _____ 207
            Arthur M. Okun

The Design of Macroeconomic Policy_____ 214
     Council of Economic Advisers

Rational Expectations—Fresh Ideas That Challenge Some_____ 217
Established Views of Policy Making
     Clarence W. Nelson

Rational Expectations and the Real World_____ 225
     Leonard Forman

The Effectiveness of Anticipated Policy _____ 229
     Martin Neil Baily

The Monetarist Controversy or, Should We Forsake _____ 237
Stabilization Policies?
     Franco Modigliani

Money Wage Inflation: The Endogeneity-Exogeneity_____ 252
Issue
     Michael L. Wachter
     and Susan M. Wachter

The Effect of Monetary Policy on the Economy _____ 261
     Council of Economic Advisers

Rational Expectations _____ 263
     Bennett T. McCallum

Inflation and Supply Side Economics _____ 270
     Martin Feldstein

Controls Are Not the Answer _____ 273
     C. Jackson Grayson, Jr.

Exchange Rates—How Flexible Should They Be?_____ 276
     Milton Friedman

A Defense of Fixed Exchange Rates_____ 283
     Henry C. Wallich

The Operation of Flexible Exchange Rates _____ 287
     Council of Economic Advisers

The Case Against Trying to Stabilize the Dollar _____ 292
      Martin Feldstein

The Case for Roughly Stabilizing the Real Value of the _____ 297
Dollar
      John Williamson

International Aspects of Fiscal and Monetary Policy_____ 302
      Council of Economic Advisers

Implications of the U. S. Current Account Deficit _____ 311
      David H. Howard

Distinguished Lecture on Economics in Government:_____ 320
Thinking About International Economic Coordination
      Martin S. Feldstein

Is Growth Obsolete? _____ 329
      William Nordhaus
      and James Tobin

The Case Against Economic Growth _____ 339
      Ezra J. Mishan

The Limits to Growth _____ 343
      Donella H. Meadows,
      Dennis L. Meadows,
      Jorgen Randers,
      and William W. Behrens III

Is the End of the World at Hand? _____ 349
      Robert M. Solow

Tax Policy and Economic Growth: Lessons from the_____ 358
1980s
      Michael J. Boskin

The United States and Economic Development_____ 363
      Council of Economic Advisers

Lessons from Korean Economic Growth _____ 380
      Susan M. Collins

Organizing Debt Relief: The Need for a New Institution _____ 383
    Peter B. Kenen

Cleaning up Third World Debt Without Getting Taken to _____ 394
the Cleaners
    Jeremy Bulow
    and Kenneth Rogoff

PART II:
PROBLEMS   405

Part III:
ANSWERS   445

PART IV:
SAMPLE EXAMS   460

"No One Has Starved"— The Great Depression

DULL mornings last winter the sheriff of Miami, Florida, used to fill a truck with homeless men and run them up to the county line. Where the sheriff of Fort Lauderdale used to meet them and load them into a second truck and run them up to *his* county line. Where the sheriff of Saint Lucie's would meet them and load them into a third truck and run them up to *his* county line. Where the sheriff of Brevard County would *not* meet them. And whence they would trickle back down the roads to Miami. To repeat.

It was a system. And it worked. The only trouble was that it worked too well. It kept the transients transient and it even increased the transient population in the process. But it got to be pretty expensive, one way or another, if you sat down and figured it all out—trucks and gas and time and a little coffee. . .

That was last winter.

Next winter there will be no truck. And there will be no truck, not because the transients will have disappeared from Miami: if anything, there will be more blistered Fords with North Dakota licenses and more heel-worn shoes with the Boston trade-mark rubbed out next winter than there were last. But because the sheriff of Miami, like the President of the U. S., will next winter think of transients and unemployed miners and jobless mill workers in completely different terms.

THE difference will be made by the Emergency Relief Act. Or rather by the fact that the Emergency Relief Act exists. For the Act itself with its $300,000,000 for direct relief loans to the states is neither an adequate nor an impressive piece of legislation. But the passage of the Act, like the green branch which young Mr. Ringling used to lay across the forks of the Wisconsin roads for his circus to follow, marks a turning in American political history. And the beginning of a new chapter in American unemployment relief. It constitutes an open and legible acknowledgment of governmental responsibility for the welfare of the victims of industrial unemployment.* And its ultimate effect must be the substitution of an ordered, realistic, and intelligent relief program for the wasteful and uneconomic methods (of which the Miami truck is an adequate symbol) employed during the first three years of the depression.

*A brief history of state and federal relief action will be found in Appendix A, page 84. . . here omitted.

There can be no serious question of the failure of those methods. For the methods were never seriously capable of success. They were diffuse, unrelated, and implanned. The theory was that private charitable organizations and semi-public welfare groups, established to care for the old and the sick and the indigent, were capable of caring for the casuals of a world-wide economic disaster. And the theory in application meant that social agencies manned for the service of a few hundred families, and city shelters set up to house and feed a handful of homeless men, were compelled by the brutal necessities of hunger to care for hundreds of thousands of families and whole armies of the displaced and the jobless. And to depend for their resources upon the contributions of communities no longer able to contribute, and upon the irresolution and vacillation of state Legislatures and municipal assemblies long since in the red on their annual budgets. The result was the picture now presented in city after city and state after state—heterogeneous groups of official and semi-official and unofficial relief agencies struggling under the earnest and untrained leadership of the local men of affairs against an inertia of misery and suffering and want they are powerless to overcome.

But the psychological consequence was even worse. Since the problem was never honestly attacked as a national problem, and since the facts were never frankly faced as facts, people came to believe that American unemployment was relatively unimportant. They saw little idleness and they therefore believed there was little idleness. It is possible to drive for blocks in the usual shopping and residential districts of New York and Chicago without seeing a breadline or a food station or a hungry mob or indeed anything else much more exciting than a few casuals asleep on a park bench. And for that reason, and because their newspapers played down the subject as an additional depressant in depressing times, and because they were bored with relief measures anyway, the great American public simply ignored the whole thing. They would still ignore it today were it not that the committee hearings and the Congressional debate and the Presidential veto of relief bills this last June attracted their attention. And that the final passage of the Emergency Relief and Construction Act of 1932 has committed their government and themselves to a policy of affirmative action which compels both it and them to know

definitely and precisely what the existing situation is.

IT SHOULD be remarked at this point that nothing the federal government has yet done or is likely to do in the near future constitutes a policy of *constructive* action. Unemployment basically is not a social disease but an industrial phenomenon. The natural and inevitable consequence of a machine civilization is a lessened demand for human labor. (An almost total elimination of human labor in plowing, for example, is now foreseeable.) And the natural and inevitable consequence of a lessened demand for human labor is an increase of idleness. Indeed the prophets of the machine age have always promised an increase of idleness, under the name of leisure, as one of the goals of industry. A constructive solution of unemployment therefore means an industrial solution—a restatement of industrialism which will treat technological displacement not as an illness to be cured but as a goal to be achieved—and achieved with the widest dispensation of benefits and the least incidental misery.

But the present relief problem as focused by the federal Act is not a problem of ultimate solutions but of immediate palliatives. One does not talk architecture while the house is on fire and the tenants are still inside. The question at this moment is the pure question of fact. Having decided at last to face reality and do something about

---

WHAT DO YOU DO?

You are a carpenter. Your last cent is gone. They have cut off the gas. The kid is white and stupid looking. You have always earned your own way before but you can't get a job now for love or money. What do you do?

In some, but by no means all, cities you can get a meal at the Salvation Army or the Municipal Lodging House merely by waiting a few hours in a breadline. But that's no use now. So you go to the cop. He pulls out his directory and sends you to one of the listed charitable societies. The society takes your name and gives you emergency aid if you need it. It then asks you a list of questions about your age, your nationality, your religion, and your need. Your answers to these questions will determine to which of the charities specializing in Jews, Catholics, Protestants, abandoned babies, homeless boys, sickly children, pregnant women, disabled veterans, and the like you should be sent. You draw the Episcopal Family Relief Society. The Relief Society clears your name through the central agency to see that you are not receiving help elsewhere and sends around within the next few days to visit your family, prepare a budget, detail a nurse (if there is one), and eventually to allot you $2 to $8 a week, depending on the locality and the funds available. If its funds are exhausted it asks you to wait. Meanwhile you register for work. You wait anyway.

•   •   •

You are a white collar man. You have a wife and two children. What do you do?

You do as the carpenter did . . .

it, what is reality? How many men are unemployed in the U. S.? How many are in want? *What are the facts?*

Twenty-five millions

THE following minimal statements may be accepted as true—with the certainty that they underestimate the real situation:

(1) Unemployment has steadily increased in the U. S. since the beginning of the depression and the rate of increase during the first part of 1932 was more rapid than in any other depression year.

(2) The number of persons totally unemployed is now at least 10,000,000.*

(3) The number of persons totally unemployed next winter will, at the present rate of increase, be 11,000,000.

(4) Eleven millions unemployed means better than one man out of every four employable workers.

(5) This percentage is higher than the percentage of unemployed British workers registered under the compulsory insurance laws (17.1 per cent in May, 1932, as against 17.3 per cent in April and 18.4 per cent in January) and higher than the French, the Italian, and the Canadian percentages, but lower than the German (43.9 per cent of trade unionists in April, 1932) and the Norwegian.

(6) Eleven millions unemployed means 27,500,000 whose regular source of livelihood has been cut off.

(7) Twenty-seven and a half millions without regular income includes the families of totally unemployed workers alone. Taking account of the numbers of workers on part time, the total of those without adequate income becomes 34,000,000 or better than a quarter of the entire population of the country.

(8) Thirty-four million persons without adequate income does not mean 34,000,000 in present want. Many families have savings. But savings are eventually dissipated and the number in actual want tends to approximate the number without adequate income. How nearly it approximates it now or will next winter no man can say. But it is conservative to estimate that the problem of next winter's relief is a problem of caring for approximately 25,000,000 souls. . . .

For nothing but estimates exists. No heritage from the fumbling of the last three years is more discouraging than the complete lack of statistics. The Director of the President's Organization on Unemployment Relief, Mr. Walter S. Gifford of the American Telephone & Telegraph Co., was forced to acknowledge before a subcommittee of the Senate in January, 1932, that he did not know, nor did his Organization know, how many persons were out of work and in need of assistance in the U. S. nor even how many persons were actually receiving aid at the time of his testimony. And more recently the Commissioner of Labor Statistics, Mr. Ethelbert Stewart, generally recognized as the government's foremost authority on unemployment, has been allowed to lose his office at the most critical period in American unemployment history

*I.e., persons "usually employed but now unemployed and seeking work" as defined in the census schedule. Criticisms of authoritative unemployment figures on the ground that they include a large percentage of "unemployables" are unfounded. "All census enumerations," says Commissioner Stewart, "have excluded the unemployables . . . the ne'er-do-wells were not counted . . ."

because, according to press accounts, the Secretary of Labor, Mr. Doak, was irritated by the Commissioner's correction of one of his over-optimistic statements.

Fortunately, however, the more important estimators agree among themselves and the total of 25,000,000 may fairly be accepted. . . .That is to say that the general situation can only be judged by the situation in the particular localities. But certain generalizations are possible. Of which the chief is the broad conclusion that few if any of the industrial areas have been able to maintain a minimum decency level of life for their unemployed. Budgetary standards as set up by welfare organizations, public and private, after years of experiment have been discarded. Food only, in most cases, is provided and little enough of that. Rents are seldom paid. Shoes and clothing are given in rare instances only. Money for doctors and dentists is not to be had. And free clinics are filled to overflowing. Weekly allowances per family have fallen as low as $2.39 in New York with $3 and $4 the rule in most cities and $5 a high figure. And even on these terms funds budgeted for a twelve-month period have been exhausted in three or four. While city after city has been compelled to abandon a part of its dependent population. "We are merely trying to prevent hunger and exposure," reported a St. Paul welfare head last May. And the same sentence would be echoed by workers in other cities with such additions as were reported at the same time from Pittsburgh where a cut of 50 per cent was regarded as "inevitable," from Dallas where Mexicans and Negroes were not given relief, from Alabama where discontinuance of relief in mining and agricultural sections was foreseen, from New Orleans where no new applicants were being received and 2,500 families in need of relief were receiving none, from Omaha where two-thirds of the cases receiving relief were to be discontinued, from Colorado where the counties had suspended relief for lack of funds . . . from Scranton . . . from Cleveland . . . from Syracuse . . . But the individual localities present their own picture:

New York City

ABOUT 1,000,000 out of the city's 3,200,000 working population are unemployed. Last April 410,000 were estimated to be in dire want. Seven hundred and fifty thousand in 150,000 families were receiving emergency aid while 160,000 more in 32,000 families were waiting to receive aid not then available. Of these latter families—families which normally earn an average of $141.50 a month—the average income from all sources was $8.20. Of families receiving relief, the allowance has been anything from a box of groceries up to $60 a month. In general, New York relief, in the phrase of Mr. William Hodson, executive director of the New York Welfare Council, has been on "a disaster basis." And the effects have been disaster effects. It is impossible to estimate the number of deaths in the last year in which starvation was a contributing cause. But ninety-five persons suffering directly from starvation were admitted to the city hospitals in 1931, of whom twenty died; and 143 suffering from

malnutrition, of whom twenty-five died. While visiting nurses and welfare workers report a general increase in malnutrition, and the clinics and medical relief agencies are so overcrowded they can give adequate relief to no one, although 75 per cent of persons applying to one relief agency had some form of illness. Housing is, of course, with the general lowering of standards and the doubling-up of families, worse even than it was during the boom. Relief expenditures for 1930 were something over $6,000,000; for 1931, more than $25,000,-000; and for the first four months of 1932 over $20,000,000, or $5,000,000 per month. But large as this latter figure is it must be compared with the wage and salary loss by reason of unemployment, which is at least $100,000,000 per month. The need, even with static unemployment figures, is cumulative, and $75,000,000 for the next twelve months is a low estimate.

Philadelphia

THE situation in Philadelphia was described by its Community Council in July, 1932, as one of "slow starvation and progressive disintegration of family life . . ." "Normal" unemployment in Philadelphia is 40,000 to 50,000. In April, 1931, 228,000 or 25.6 per cent of the city's normally employed were unemployed, and 122,000 or 13.7 per cent were on part time. Of the city's 445,000 families with employable workers, 210,000 had workers unemployed or on part time, about one in four had no worker employed on full time, and 12 per cent had *no* worker employed. Even the average person unemployed had been out of work for thirty-seven weeks and had had only a little over one week of casual or relief work during the period. By December, 1931, the number of unemployed had reached 238,000 with 43,000 families receiving relief and 56,000 families in which no one was at work. And by May, 1932, the total of unemployed was 298,000. In the following month the Governor of the state estimated that 250,000 persons in Philadelphia "faced actual starvation." Over the state at large the same conditions held. In June, 1931, 919,000 or 25 per cent of the normally employed in the state were unemployed, according to the "secret" report then submitted to the Governor, and the number had risen to 1,000,000 by December and to 1,250,000 in August, 1932. One hundred and fifty thousand children were in need of charity. Malnutrition had increased in forty-eight counties—27 per cent of school children being undernourished (216,000 out of a school population of 800,000). New patients in the tuberculosis clinics had doubled. And the general death rate and disease rate had risen. Only nine counties were well organized. Fifty-five gave cause for grave concern and nineteen were listed as distressed counties in dire need. Moreover, relief allowances have steadily dropped. Last December 43,000 of the 56,000 families in Philadelphia where no one was employed were receiving relief at the rate of $4.39 per week for families averaging 4.8 persons. By May the number of families receiving relief had risen to 55,000 and the amount of relief had dropped to $4.23, of which $3.93 was for food, being two-thirds of the minimum required for health. No provision is made for rents and the result is that the landlords of Philadelphia, like the landlords of the country at large, are compelled to choose between throwing their tenants into the streets or providing from their own pockets the shelter required. Outside of Philadelphia the weekly grant to a family is $3 or less in thirteen counties, and $3 to $4 in six more, while in some of the small steel towns it may be even lower. Funds in the counties are either exhausted or will be exhausted before November.

Detroit

RELIEF in Detroit was originally upon a boom-time, boom-extravagance basis with gross incompetence in the administration of funds, an embezzlement of $207,000, and doles of silk stockings and cosmetics. The resultant imminent bankruptcy forced a contraction of expenditures, and relief in May, 1932, with a greatly increased need, was only $859,925 as against $2,088,850 in January, 1931. There were 223,000 unemployed last November in the city and 410,000 in the state. In January the city was caring for 48,000 distressed families. This number was cut to 22,000 in April and relief was given at the rate of fifteen cents per day per person. In July under pressure of further shortage a further cut of 5,000 families totaling 20,000 persons was determined. Aid was to be denied to able-bodied persons who had been public charges for a year or more whether work was available for them or not, and childless couples and small families with no definite ties in Detroit were to be forced to leave the city. The resultant relief roll was expected to be 17,757 families, of whom 7,000 were dependent because of age or illness. The great majority on relief are laborers but Detroit also carries or has carried forty-five ministers, thirty bank tellers, lawyers, dentists, musicians, and "two families after whom streets are named." Riots, chiefly employment riots, have been fairly common with bloodshed in at least one. And enormous breadlines and the like are daily sights. No adequate statistics on public health in Detroit exist but it may safely be assumed to be at least as low as New York's.

Chicago

UNEMPLOYED in Chicago number somewhere between 660,000 and 700,000 or 40 per cent of its employable workers while the number for the state at large is about one in three of the gainfully employed. About 100,000 families have applied down to July for relief in Cook County. The minimum relief budget has been $2.40 per week for an adult and $1.50 per week for a child for food, with $22 to $23 per month to a family. But these figures have since been cut to $2.15 weekly for a man, $1.10 for a child. And persons demanding relief must be completely destitute to receive it. Rents are not paid by the relief agencies and housing in certain sections, unspeakably bad. While the situation of city employees is tragic. Teachers in May, 1932, had had only five months cash for the last thirteen months, 3,177 of them had lost $2,367,000 in bank failures, 2,278 of them had lost $7,800,000 in lapsed policies, 805 had borrowed $232,000 from loan sharks at rates adding up to 42 per cent a year, and 759 had lost their homes. (The city at one time undertook to sell for tax default the houses of its employees unable to pay taxes because of its own default in wages.) The vicissitudes of Chicago's relief funds are noticed in Appendix A. It is estimated that $35,000,000 will be spent in 1932 for an inadequate job and that an adequate job would cost $50,000,000.

The Intelligent Citizen's
Guide to Inflation

Robert M. Solow

Two broadly opposite frames of mind seem to dominate the current discussion of inflation. One says that we are beset by some utterly mysterious plague of unknown origin. If it is not stopped soon, it will cause unimaginable, or at least unspecified, disasters. The only hope is that some Pasteur or Jenner or Ehrlich will discover The Cure. The other view is that it is all quite simple. There is some one thing we have failed to do: control the money supply or balance the budget or legislate price controls or abolish the unions. As soon as we do it, the problem will then go away.

This essay is written in the belief that both these currents of opinion are wrong. I do not, however, have an alternative solution to offer. Indeed, I rather doubt that there is a Solution, in the sense of some policy that your average mixed capitalist economy can reasonably be expected to pursue which will drastically reduce the tendency to inflation, without substituting some equally damaging and intractable problem instead.

What I can hope to do is to explain the vocabulary and intellectual framework evolved by economists for discussing and analyzing inflation. By itself, this will contribute to clarity of thought—much, perhaps most, of current popular discussion is hopelessly confused. I hope to be able to go further than that, however. There are some positive statements one can reasonably make about the behavior of modern mixed economies. We know less than we would like to know, but much more than nothing. Where I verge on speculation, or where there are real differences of opinion within the economics profession, I will try to be honest about it.

What is inflation?

Inflation is *a substantial, sustained increase in the general level of prices*. The intrinsic vagueness of "substantial" is harmless. One would not want to use a heavyweight word to describe a trivial rise in the price level; granted, it will never be perfectly clear where to draw the line, but neither can it be important since only a word is at stake. "Sustained" is a little trickier. One would not want to label as inflationary a momentary (six-month? one-year?) upward twitch of the price level, especially if it is soon reversed. There is no point in being forced to describe mere short-term fluctuations in prices as alternating bouts of inflation and deflation. "Sustained" also carries some connotation of "self-perpetuating" and that raises broader questions. It is obviously important to know whether each step in an inflationary process tends to generate further inflation unless some "outside" force intervenes, or whether the inflationary process is eventually self-limiting. The answer need not be the same for all inflations, and it certainly depends on what you mean by "outside." So it is probably best not to incorporate this aspect as a part of the definition.

It is the notion of the "general price level" that will lead us somewhere. Economists make a sharp and important distinction between the system of relative prices and the general price level. Relative prices describe the terms on which different goods and services exchange for *one another;* the general price level describes the terms on which some representative bundle of goods and services exchanges for *money.* Imagine an economy in which the only goods produced are meat and vegetables, and first suppose that all exchange is barter; some people trade meat for vegetables with other people who want to trade vegetables for meat. If one pound of meat exchanges for three pounds of vegetables, then the relative price is established. But since there is no money, there is no such thing as the general price level. Notice that inflation is inconceivable in a barter economy. It would be logically contradictory for "all prices" to rise at the same time. Suppose that, because of a change in tastes or a natural catastrophe, one pound of meat should come to exchange for six pounds of vegetables. One could say that the price of meat (in terms of vegetables!) had doubled. But that is exactly the same thing as saying that the price of vegetables (in terms of meat!) had halved. A carnivorous farmer would find himself worse off; but a vegetarian rancher would be sitting pretty.

So inflation has intrinsically to do with money. Now let us introduce some greenbacks to serve as money in our meat-and-vegetables economy. Suppose meat goes for $1.50 a pound and vegetables for 50 cents a pound—i.e., one pound of meat for three of vegetables, as before. Now suppose that at a later time meat goes to $3.00 a pound and vegetables to $1.00. The relative price is unchanged. From most points of view the meat-and-vegetables economy goes along as if nothing has happened, and from most points of view nothing has. (Not quite nothing: A tradesman or a miser who happened to be sitting on a load of greenbacks at the time will have taken quite a beating.)

We can go a step further. Suppose the average daily diet consists of one pound of meat and one pound of vegetables (though very few individuals may actually consume exactly the average diet). We could agree to measure the general price level by the money cost of the average consumption bundle. In that case, we would say that the price level was 200 in the initial situation, and 400 after the price increases. (It is the custom to choose some year as "base year" and set its price level arbitrarily at 100. If the initial year is the base year, then the later price level would be 200.) In any case, we would certainly want to say that the general price level had doubled, and if it had doubled in exactly 12 months, we would say that the rate of inflation had been 100 per cent a year.

Since the prices of all goods and services had exactly doubled, it is no trick to say that the general price level had doubled. But we now have a routine that will take care of less obvious situations. Suppose meat goes from $1.50 to $2.40 a pound and vegetables from 50 cents to 60 cents. The price of meat has risen by 60 per cent, that of vegetables by 20 per cent. But the cost of the average consumption bundle rises from $2.00 to $3.00 (or the price index from 100 to 150). So we could say that the price level had gone up by 50 per cent. Notice also that this time relative prices have also changed: A pound of meat exchanges for four pounds of vegetables at the new prices. The vegetarian rancher gains at the expense of the carnivorous farmer, but *that is because of the change in relative prices.* In the case of "pure inflation," when *all* prices change *in the same proportion,* nobody loses (except owners of money) and nobody gains (except owers of money).[1]

Perhaps the simplest way to define inflation is as a loss in the purchasing power of money. That has the merit of emphasizing the fact that inflation is essentially a monetary phenomenon. But there is a possible semantic trap here. Some economists believe that the whole inflationary mechanism is primarily or exclusively monetary, in particular that the main or only cause of inflation is too rapid a growth in the supply of money. They may be right or they may be wrong. (I happen to think that doctrine is too simple by half.) But the mere fact that you can have inflation only in a monetary economy is neither here nor there, just as the fact that you can't have a drowning without water doesn't prove that the way to understand drowning is to study water. I will come back to this analytical question later.

Measuring inflation

In the real world there are thousands of goods and services, whose relative prices are changing all the time in complicated ways. The measurement of the general price level thus becomes a major statistical enterprise. But it is done, and generally according to the principles just described. In fact, the American reader is confronted with at least three separate indexes of the general price level: the Consumer Price Index (CPI), the Wholesale Price Index (WPI), and the GNP Deflator. Since there are some conceptual differences among them, and since they may occasionally say different things, it is worthwhile to understand exactly what each of them means.

The CPI (what is sometimes called the cost-of-living index) is produced and published monthly; it is closest in principle to the kind of price index described earlier. At intervals of a decade or more, the Bureau of Labor Statistics (BLS) conducts an expensive survey of the spending habits of families of different size, income, and other characteristics. From this survey it calculates the typical budget of a middle-income, urban wage-earner or clerical worker with a family of four. Then each month it actually prices out that budget in a number of cities around the country. If the cost of that bundle goes up or down by one per cent, the CPI goes up or down by one per cent.

That is certainly a reasonable and meaningful price index, but it does have some drawbacks. (Of course, any method of reducing all those thousands of price changes to a single number will have drawbacks.) It relates only to consumers; the prices of industrial machinery and raw materials could go sky-high, and the CPI would register that fact only later, when cost increases filtered down to retail prices. Moreover, the CPI relates only to some consumers—those middle-income, urban, wage-earning families of four. Old people, or poor people, or oil millionaires, who buy different bundles, may have different experiences. Finally, economists have a technical reservation. The CPI covers, as its concept dictates it should, everything consumers spend money on, including sales taxes, monthly mortgage payments, used cars, and so on. It reflects changes in state and local taxes, interest rates, used-car prices, etc. For some purposes, economists would prefer a price index confined to currently-produced goods and services. Certainly it matters whether a rise in the CPI reflects mainly higher sales taxes and interest rates or higher prices for food and clothing.

The WPI, also available monthly, is based on prices collected at the wholesale level. Its coverage is wide but rather peculiar, for several reasons. For one thing, it omits all services, medical care, house rents, etc. For another, it counts some prices over and over again, and thus gives them more weight than they deserve. For example, a change in the price of raw cotton will appear first as a crude material, then again as it is reflected in the price of cloth, then again as it is reflected in the price of clothing. This pyramiding overemphasizes crude material prices and can cause the WPI to behave quite erratically, especially when the prices of materials are changing. Its main utility is that, just because of its coverage of the early stages of fabrication, it often catches price developments early. The WPI, like the other indexes, is broken down into sub-indexes (in the case of the WPI, farm products, processed foods, industrial materials, various categories of finished manufactures, etc.), and these may be very informative.[2]

The GNP Deflator

The GNP Deflator is by and large the economists' favorite. Unlike the CPI, it covers only currently produced goods and services, and unlike the WPI, it avoids all double-counting. But it is constructed in a more complicated way. The Department of Commerce calculates every quarter the country's Gross National Product. This is essentially the value at current market prices of the current flow of newly produced final goods and services. (The force of "final" is that one omits goods and services which are immediately used up in the production of something else, because their value will be included in the value of the final product.) At the same time, Commerce also calculates the GNP "in constant prices." That is, it takes the current flow of final goods and services, but instead of valuing them at this quarter's prices, it values them at the prices of some fixed year, currently 1958. For instance, in 1973 the GNP in current prices was $1,295 billion, but the GNP in 1958 prices was $839 billion, because 1958 prices were lower than 1973 prices.

How much had prices risen between 1958 and 1973? The natural computation is $1,295/$839=1.54, for an increase of 54 per cent. If the 1973 flow of output valued in 1973 prices is 54 per cent higher than the *same* flow of output valued in 1958 prices, then the obvious inference is that the general level of prices must have risen by 54 per cent since 1958. So the general formula for the GNP Deflator in year X is: GNP in year X in current prices/GNP in year X in base-year prices. (Exercise: Convince yourself that the GNP Deflator for the base year itself is automatically 1.00 or 100, because in the base year GNP in current prices and GNP in base-year prices are the same quantity.)

Economists like this price index for the analysis of inflation not because it is obscure, but for the reasons I mentioned before: It eliminates double-counting, and it focuses on the pricing of currently produced goods, not existing assets. For that very reason, of course, it may not reflect exactly the experience of consumers. Another disadvantage is that the GNP Deflator is available only at quarterly intervals.[3]

All price indexes suffer from a common difficulty. Commodities change in character and quality. How can the BLS price the same consumer-bundle in 1955 and 1975 when many of the things consumers buy in 1975 did not exist, and so had no prices, in 1955? How can the Commerce statisticians value 1975 GNP in 1958 prices, when there were no 1958 prices for some of the items entering the 1975 GNP? If the price of an ordinary shirt rises 10 per cent in the course of a year, but simultaneously the wrinkle-resisting properties of the shirt are improved, how is one to decide how much of the 10 per cent represents the greater value of an improved product and how much represents pure price increase? The agencies do the best they can, but it is hardly a job that can ever be done perfectly. It used to be thought that there was systematic underallowance for quality improvements to such an extent that an annual rise of one or two per cent in the measured price level could be ignored as not being a true price increase; but no one knows for sure. Perhaps the best conclusion is that one ought not to attach great significance to small changes in price indexes.

This discussion of price indexes has given us another concept of absolutely fundamental importance for rational discussion. GNP in

FIGURE 1. *The Price Index, 1867-1973 (1929 Base)*

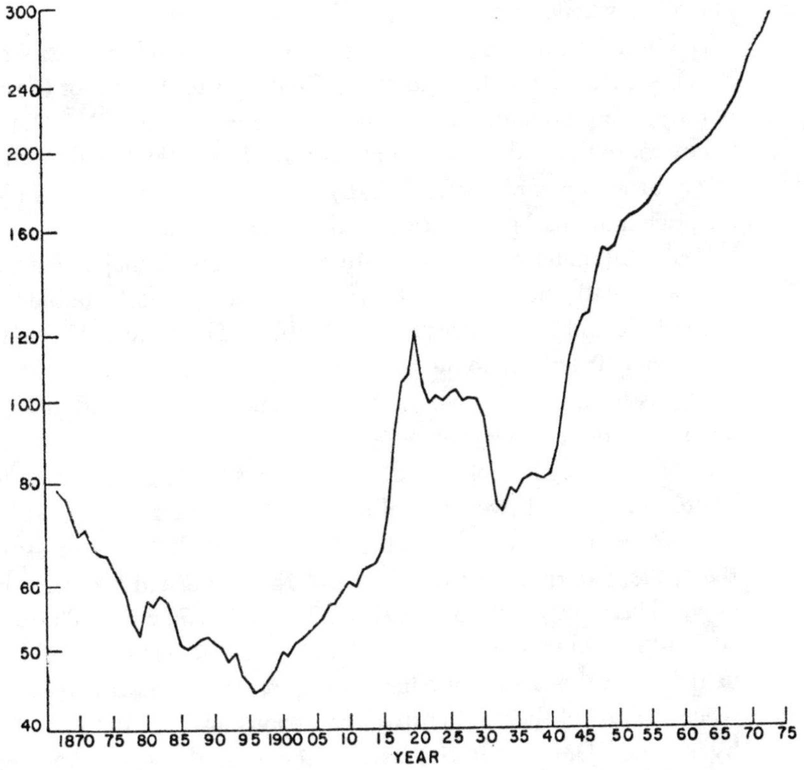

constant prices is in an important sense a "physical" concept. It is an attempt to measure the size of the flow of actual production in a way that is independent of inflationary and deflationary aberrations. When GNP in constant prices changes, it is because the production of goods and services has changed, not because prices have changed. In terms of my earlier example, the difference between the 1968 GNP of $707 billion in 1958 prices and the 1973 GNP of $839 billion in 1958 prices permits us to say that "aggregate output" rose by 18.7 per cent between those years. In the jargon, GNP in constant prices is called "real GNP" or "real aggregate output." We will be coming back to it.

The last 100 years

The two charts on the following pages show what has happened to the general price level since 1867. The price index used is the GNP Deflator.[4] Figure 1 shows the price index itself on what is called a logarithmic scale, to draw attention to the proportional changes that really matter. The base year is 1929=100. The fact that the price level in 1973 (291.5) is almost four times that in 1867 (78.0) is not to be taken as utterly precise, in view of the vast difference between the commodities making up the GNP in 1867 and those actually produced in 1973. But for orders of magnitude, the figures will do. Steep portions of the curve represent periods of more severe inflation; when the curve points downward, the price level was actually falling.

Figure 2 converts the price index into percentage rates of inflation and deflation; prices are rising when this curve is above the zero line, and falling when it is below.

The broad outlines of the history of the price level are easily read from the charts. From the end of the Civil War to the end of the 19th century, the predominant trend was deflationary. The GNP Deflator fell by more than 40 per cent between 1867 and 1896. Although the curve turned upward about then, by the eve of the First World War the price index had gone back up only to the level of 1873.

Really big inflationary bursts are associated with major wars, and their aftermath. Between 1914 and 1920, prices almost doubled. Between 1940 and 1948, prices almost doubled. The Korean War added only about 10 per cent to the price level. In the case of the Vietnamese War it is hard to know where to start; between 1966 and 1972, the index rose about 30 per cent.

But that is only half of it, and in some ways the less interesting half. There were at least two years of deflation after the First World War; by 1922 the index was back to the 1917-1918 level. The depression of the 1930's, like those of the 1870's and 1890's, pushed the price level down. The index, pegged at 100 in 1929, fell to 73.3 in 1933, rose to 80.3 in 1936, and stayed there until the eve of the Second World War in 1940. But the last minus-sign on Figure 2 appears briefly in 1949 when the first of the mild postwar recessions lowered the price index by a point. (On a quarterly basis one could find a somewhat bigger decline.) From 1950 on we have had a quarter-century without a dip in the general price level. The best one can find is the period beginning with the recession of 1958, running through the milder recession of 1960, and continuing during the slow return to approximate full employment at the end of 1965. During that interval, the Deflator rose at an average annual rate of about 1.5 percent. It is simply not

FIGURE 2. *Percentage Rates of Inflation and Deflation, 1870-1973*

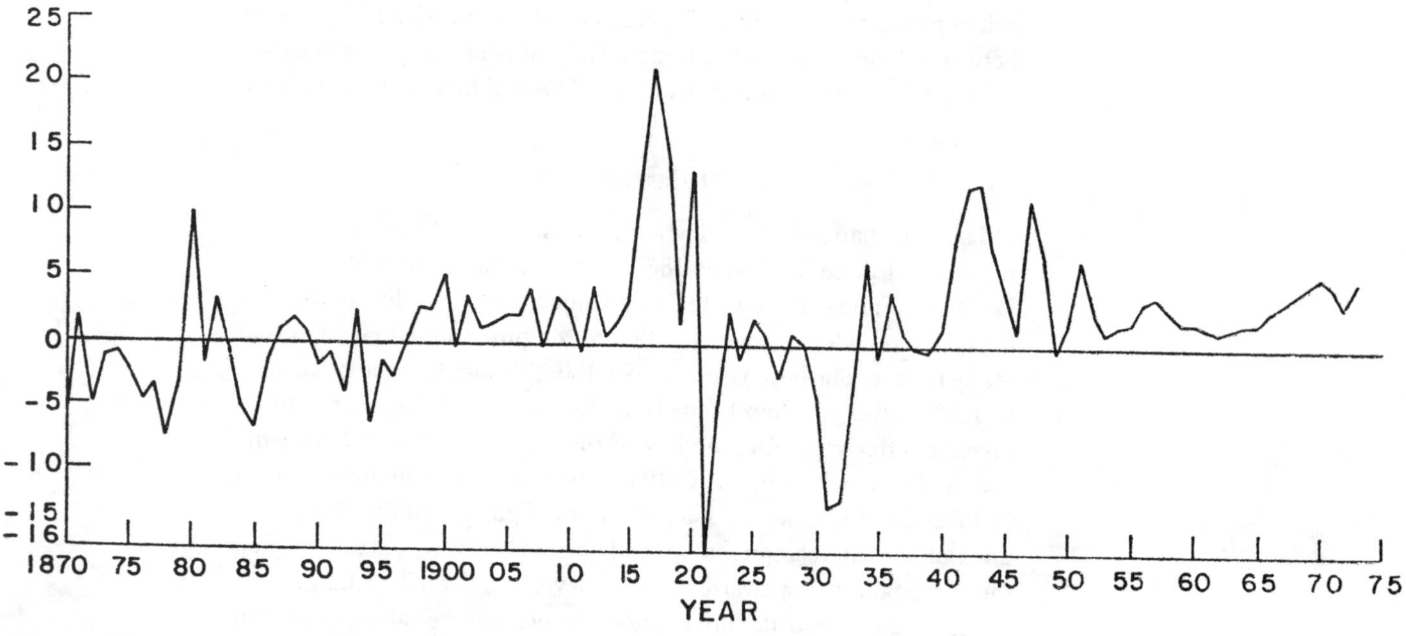

possible to know with any confidence what would have happened if the escalation of the war either had not occurred or had not been allowed to overheat the economy in the last years of the Johnson Administration.

Why is pure inflation a bad thing?

There seems to be universal agreement that rising prices are a cause for alarm and perhaps fear. Candidates for office accuse incumbents of having fostered inflation or failed to prevent it, and promise to eliminate it themselves. Incumbents announce that they are working on the problem. And surveys of public opinion show that very many ordinary people regard inflation of the price level as one of the most serious problems they face, or at least as an important background worry. Yet it is fair to say that public discussion offers no insight at all into the precise way in which a rising price level damages the current or prospective welfare of the representative citizen. Occasionally, the implied mechanism in the background makes no sense at all. Such a peculiar situation clearly deserves the most thorough investigation.

For the sake of clarity, let us first make an abstraction and think about a "pure" inflation, during which all prices rise at the same proportional rate—so many per cent per year—so that relative prices are unchanged throughout. Real inflations don't happen that way; but if we are to understand how and why inflation is a burden on society, we had better be able to understand the hypothetical special case of a pure inflation. After all, relative prices can change without any change in the general price level; we ought not to confuse the effects of the one with those of the other.

Well, then, who gets hurt in a pure inflation? If you think back to our meat-and-vegetables economy, it is hard to see how producers, including workers, suffer at all. So long as the prices of meat and vegetables, and wage rates in both industries, go up at the same percentage rate, every participant in the economy continues to have the same purchasing power over all goods and services as before. The inflation appears to have no "real" effects. The general point is that a person's economic welfare depends on the prices of the things he or she buys and sells, including labor and the services of property; if the prices of all those things go up or down in the same proportion, then economic welfare stays the same.

Now there is an optical illusion that clearly plays some role in popular discussions of inflation. Many people see no connection between the prices of the things they buy and the prices of the things they sell. The ordinary person works hard and feels that each year's wage increase is deserved. When it turns out that prices have also increased, so that all or part of the wage increase is illusory, the ordinary person regards that price rise—inflation—as a form of theft, a hand in his or her pocket. But of course, wages could not have increased had prices not increased. I cannot estimate how widespread this illusion may be, but there can hardly be any doubt that such an illusion does exist.[5]

If you want to know how the country as a whole is doing, then the course of the price level will not tell you. In narrowly economic terms, the proper measure of success is the flow of goods and services produced and made available to the society for consumption and other uses. The closest thing we have to look at is the real GNP, which we have already met. GNP in constant prices is the most comprehensive available measure of the performance of the economy in doing what it is supposed to do—the generation of want-satisfying commodities. It is far from perfect for reasons that involve the treatment of depreciation, environmental effects of economic activity, the organization of work, the "quality of life," governmental activity, and other things, but none of them has to do with inflation. So if inflation is a net burden to society, that ought to show up in a reduction of real GNP, or at least a slowing-down of its normal upward trend. But that is not what happens; in fact the opposite is more nearly true. Periods of prosperity are somewhat more likely to coincide with periods of inflation and periods of recession are somewhat more likely to coincide with intervals of stable or more slowly rising prices.[6]

Is the social cost of inflation a mirage? There is one earlier hint that needs to be followed up. In a monetary economy—the only kind that can have inflation—holders of cash see their real wealth eroded by a rising price level, even in a pure inflation. So do creditors who hold claims for payment fixed in money terms. Offsetting at least some of these losses are the gains of debtors, who can pay back in dollars of smaller purchasing power what they had borrowed and spent in dollars of higher real value. Perhaps the true social costs of inflation are to be found among the holders of money, or among cash creditors more generally.

Anticipated inflation

Another distinction—this time between anticipated and unanticipated inflation—is required for this analysis. So let us take the strongest case first: a pure inflation which is confidently and accurately expected by everyone in the economy. Suppose you lend me a dollar today and I agree to pay back $1.05 a year from today. Then we have agreed on an interest rate of five per cent annually. (You laugh, somewhat bitterly. But it's just an example.) If we both correctly expect the general price level to be quite steady during the next year, then that is all there is to it. You as lender and I as borrower are both willing to make the transaction at an interest rate of five per cent a year. Now imagine instead that we both confidently expect the general level of prices (which means each individual price and wage, since we are talking about a pure inflation) to be four per cent higher a year from now. I would be delighted to take your dollar today and pay you $1.05 in a year. Why not? If meat is a dollar a pound today and will be $1.04 a pound in a year, then in effect you would be lending me a pound of meat today, and I would be obliged to pay you only 1.05/1.04 or about 1.01 pounds of meat next year. In *real* terms, you would be getting interest at one per cent a year, not five per cent. Of course for the same reasons that I would be pleased at the transaction, you would not be. In fact, if we were both prepared to make the deal at five per cent with stable prices, we ought both to be prepared to make the deal at nine per cent when we both confidently expect the price level to rise at four per cent a year; in the real purchasing power terms that matter, you will then be collecting interest at five per cent per year. In the professional jargon, the *real* rate of interest (five per cent) is the *nominal* or *money* rate of interest (nine per cent) less the expected rate of inflation (four per cent). Thus the very high interest rates of early 1974 have to be read against the substantial inflation of the same period. Real rates are not as high as nominal rates; in fact, they are lower by about the expected future rate of inflation—about which we can only guess. Of course, anyone who borrows long and is locked in at high interest rates is left holding the bag if the inflation should unexpectedly slow down or stop.

What follows? *If* the inflation is fully anticipated by everyone, *if* everyone has complete access to the capital markets, and *if* all interest rates are free to adjust to expectations about the price level, and do so quickly and smoothly, then borrowers and lenders will be able to protect themselves against inflation. Once again, the inflation would seem to have no real effects.

Well, not quite. Those qualifications are pretty strong. Obviously, we will have to consider the case of unanticipated inflation; but even before we get to that there are some important things to say. First of all, some assets bear no interest at all: the important ones are currency and balances in ordinary checking accounts. They constitute the money supply. It would be mechanically difficult for the Treasury to pay interest on currency. Commercial banks are restrained by law from paying interest on checking accounts. (They do the next best thing by providing financial services free of charge, or at a fee that diminishes with the size of balance; but that is hardly the same thing and cannot in any case serve the same purpose as a nominal interest rate in adjusting to expectations about rising prices.) So, even if the inflation is correctly anticipated, holders of currency and checking accounts will suffer (as they would symmetrically gain if deflation should ever come back into style). These losses to holders of money are not, so to speak, net losses to society, because there are corresponding gains to others. In the case of checking accounts, the gainer is the bank and its stockholders, who earn the higher nominal interest rates on their own assets and pay no interest—except for those free financial services—on deposit liabilities. In the case of currency, the U.S. Government, in the person of the Federal Reserve, is the issuer of the paper, but it is rather special paper, and a special kind of liability, and in any case not very important.

The "deadweight loss"

Since anticipated inflation redistributes to others part of the wealth of holders of money, it is natural that businesses and people should try to reduce their holdings of money when they expect prices to be rising. One can hardly do without any cash in the modern world, but nevertheless it is usually possible to substitute effort for liquidity. Corporations can buy relatively liquid short-term securities and try correspondingly harder to synchronize inflows and outflows of cash. Individuals can rely more on savings banks as a repository of funds, making correspondingly more frequent trips downtown to deposit and withdraw cash, and to transfer funds to a checking account just before large payments have to be made. Indeed they can, and the figures suggest that they do. It is true that this minimization of cash holdings costs time, trouble, and shoe leather. Clever comptrollers are thinking about cash management when they could be worrying about higher things. Moreover, and this is the point, these expenditures of time and effort are a real net burden to society, not merely a transfer to others. They are sometimes described as a "deadweight loss" to emphasize this. They are a true cost of inflation in the same sense that the maintenance of expensive police forces is a cost of crime. Some economists seem to regard these losses as the main social cost of pure inflation. But in that case, something very peculiar is afoot, because one finds it hard to believe that they amount to much. For *this* governments tremble and people cry on the pollster's shoulder? Even if you add in the computational difficulties of planning with changing prices, the discomfort that comes from not knowing whether your anticipations about future price levels are approximately right or dangerously wrong, it is hard to get excited.[7]

There is one other important "real" effect of anticipated pure inflation; it works through the tax system. Think of any progressive tax, a tax that takes a higher fraction of a higher income than of a lower income. Now let all prices, and thus all before-tax incomes, rise in the same proportion. Nobody's purchasing power has changed. But the general rise in nominal incomes will drive everyone into a higher tax bracket. If the general rise in prices amounted to X per cent, incomes after tax will rise by less than X per cent, because of the higher effective tax rate, and the government's revenues will rise by more than X per cent, for the same reason. So taxpayers suffer a loss in purchasing power after taxes, and their loss is the Treasury's gain. Our tax system is not as progressive in action as it is on paper, but nevertheless this effect is quite real. The sharpest case is that of someone whose income is low enough not to be taxable at all; pure inflation can push such a person into the taxable range and thus impose a loss of real income.

In summary, a perfectly anticipated pure inflation imposes a small deadweight loss on society, mostly through a waste of effort directed toward economizing on the holding of money; in addition, it redistributes wealth, from holders of cash and checking accounts to banks, and from everyone to the Treasury. Not good, one is tempted to say, but no worse than a bad cold. Real GNP, for all its faults, is the best measure we have of the current production of valued goods and services; that's the number to watch.

Unanticipated inflation

Now real-life inflations are not perfectly anticipated. Neither do they come as a complete surprise. But different people have different opinions about the future of the price level; not all of them can be right, and most of them can be wrong. The consequences of this fact are important, but still special. Interest rates cannot adjust to cushion both debtors and creditors from the effects of pure inflation. Some people will be caught with their pants down: those creditors who have locked themselves into long-term loans at interest rates that do not fully reflect the particular rate of inflation that happens, and borrowers who have agreed to pay high nominal interest rates in the expectation of faster inflation than actually materializes. Of course, for each of these unlucky lenders and borrowers, there is a lucky borrower or lender. Needless to say, when the losers include the broad class of pensioners whose expectations of a viable old age are dashed, it is not a trivial matter.

These gains and losses are not restricted to loans. *Anyone* who has concluded a long-term contract of any kind, stipulated in money terms, stands to gain or lose, depending on which side of the contract we are talking about and whether the rate of inflation turns out in fact to be higher or lower than had been expected when the terms of the contract were agreed. (If rapid inflation continues, we can expect to see more long-term contracts with renegotiation clauses, or with rates of payment explicitly tied to some index of prices. These are a form of insurance against windfall gains and losses from unexpectedly fast or slow inflation.)

Finally, it should be realized that many people, especially non-rich people, are more or less excluded from the benefits of higher nominal interest rates in an inflationary period. Small savers lack either the knowledge or the minimal stake needed to gain access to the sorts of assets whose yields will provide protection against inflation. The small saver is limited in practice to savings accounts and Series E government bonds. The rate on Series E bonds is not set by a market but is managed by the Treasury, and usually kept low enough to constitute a swindle on the non-rich. (One wonders what would happen if Secretaries of the Treasury were required by law to keep all their private wealth in Series E bonds.) The maximum deposit rate payable by savings banks is also limited by law, and by the peculiar role of those institutions as essentially nothing but mortgage lenders. Heaven does not protect the working girl.

The net result of all this is that imperfectly anticipated inflation—the only kind we have—generates massive redistribution of wealth between some borrowers and some lenders, some buyers and some sellers. From a very lofty point of view, these are still transfers, not a net burden on society as a whole. But that doesn't make them good. Moreover, in the public mind these transfers come to look like a net loss: The gainers attribute their gains to their own perspicacity, energy, and virtue; the losers attribute their losses to inflation.

"Impure" inflation

Pure inflation is an abstraction, though a necessary and useful one. If you can't understand the workings of pure inflation, you will never be able to understand what is actually happening. What is actually happening, of course, is a mixture: The general price level is rising, and at the same time relative prices are changing, sometimes drastically. The price indexes I described earlier are supposed to measure the pure inflationary component of the complicated set of price changes we experience. When I tell you that in the 12 months between June 1973 and June 1974 the CPI rose by 11.1 per cent, the WPI by 14.5 per cent, and the GNP Deflator by 9.7 per cent, I am saying something like: It is approximately as if there were a pure inflation of about 10 per cent, accompanied by a "pure" change in relative prices around a stationary level. In fact, I can add such information as this: The price of food went up by 14.7 per cent during the year, while rents went up by 4.7 per cent, so there was clearly a rise in the price of food relative to rental housing.

That is conceptually clear (though not quite as clear as I am pretending). The trouble is that what you observe and feel in the course of the year is the Total Experience, and it is by no means easy to sort out in one's mind the causes and consequences of a rising general level of prices and the causes and consequences of simultaneous changes in relative prices. This difficulty is complicated further by the fact that price movements are not synchronized. Even if, when all is said and done, the price of A and the price of B are both going to rise by X per cent, A may take off first and B only later. You would think that these timing differences would all come out in the wash, but they may actually have important independent consequences of their own.

The important thing to say about an inflation in which some prices and some incomes rise faster than others is that the *redistribution* of income can become both quite drastic and quite haphazard. It may be that real GNP is high and rising, so that the country as a whole is not being deprived of goods and services and the satisfactions they bring. But definable groups in the population may find their own standards of living deteriorating, either because the prices of the things they buy are rising faster than the average, or because the prices of the things they sell—including their labor—are rising slower than the average of all prices. And often enough it will appear to them that the inflation is the cause of their troubles, when in fact the real thief is the accompanying change in relative prices. Some economically and socially pointless or harmful redistributions can happen just because certain prices and incomes are less flexible than others and adapt sluggishly to a generally inflationary climate.

There are fewer valid univeral generalizations about these redistributions than one might think. The rhetorical commonplaces are not always true. It is often said that inflation is especially hard on the poor. One careful study by Robinson G. Hollister and John G. Palmer found that this was not the case in the inflationary episodes of the 1950's, and until 1967, if by "the poor" you mean those below the official poverty line (that is, pretty damn poor). Their figures show that a cost-of-living index weighted the way the poor spend their incomes rose no faster than, perhaps slightly less fast than, the official middle-income CPI. The sources of income that matter for the poor—mainly wages and salaries, Social Security benefits, and various forms of social assistance—just about kept pace with other forms of income in purchasing-power terms. And the poor have little wealth exposed to the risk of erosion. Hollister and Palmer conclude: ". . . because the relative position of the poor seems to improve during inflationary periods and overall real income gains per capita occur during such periods, the poor as a whole must be gaining both absolutely and relatively in economic well-being during periods in which inflationary processes operate."

But not all inflations are alike. Between 1947 and 1967, food prices rose a little more slowly than the CPI as a whole. In 1973, I hardly need tell you, food prices went up about three times as fast as the rest of the CPI. Poor people spend a larger fraction of their incomes on food than richer people do. Moreover, as it happens, food costs at home went up faster than restaurant prices in 1973, and hamburger faster than steak. It would not be surprising to find that the inflation of 1973 did contribute to a redistribution of income away from poor people.[8] . . .

Are we in a whole new ball game?

In trying to understand the accelerated inflation of the last few years, it is worth remembering that the same thing has been happening everywhere. Here, for instance, are the percentage rates of increase of the CPI for a number of advanced countries between Jan./Feb. 1973 and Jan./Feb. 1974:

COUNTRY	PERCENTAGE RATE OF INFLATION OF CPI
Japan	24.1
Denmark	14.6
United Kingdom	13.2
Italy	12.6
France	10.9
Switzerland	10.8
United States	9.7
Canada	9.3
Norway	8.7
Sweden	8.4
Austria	8.3
Netherlands	8.2
Belgium	7.9
West Germany	7.5

You will notice that the United States is somewhere around the middle of this league. A similar table compiled for 1970-71, say, would show rates of inflation centered around five per cent rather than 10 per cent.

By itself, the universality of inflation tells us very little. It could come about because all countries are exposed to the same forces, characteristic of modern advanced economies, or because the international trading and monetary system works to spread the impact of forces originating anywhere in the system, or because different countries happen to be inflating for different reasons, and find it easier to do so when others are doing the same. Or the explanation could involve elements of all these possibilities. I am going to concentrate on the first line of explanation; but I believe each of the other two has something to say. My main reason for insisting on the importance of these comparative figure is to warn that no entirely parochial account of the causes of inflation will do.

Modern mixed-capitalist economies seem to have an inflationary bias near full employment. That is a description, not an explanation, but it seems to summarize the situation. An economy that is running along moderately prosperously, but hardly straining its capacity to produce, will see its price level drift upward. In the good old days, the demands of war or the stimulus of excessively expansionary policy might bring an economy to flat-out operation and consequent inflation, but a return to more normal levels of demand would stabilize prices, and a touch of recession might bring on actual deflation. The trouble is that nowadays economics begin to inflate while they are showing no signs of excess pressure, and to reverse the price rise would appear to require longer and deeper recessions than seems reasonable or natural. The question is: Why should that be? Why, for instance, do so few prices ever actually fall?

Let me answer a question with a question. Is it possible that the price level was *more* stable on the average in the good old days because the economy was *less* stable on the average? More particularly, until very recently it was reasonable to fear that any momentary weakness in the economy might be the prelude to substantial and prolonged recession. Under those circumstances, businesses might see the wisdom of cutting prices early and often, to protect markets and market shares against competitors in their own and neighboring industries who would also be feeling the pinch of widespread market softness. The same fear might be expected to stiffen the resistance of employers to wage demands; a longish period of reduced sales and lowered prices is no time to bear the burden of higher wage costs, and discontent in the workplace is easier to handle when production has to be cut back anyway. To complete the circle, the danger of prolonged unemployment would induce workers to accept wage reductions, or at least reductions relative to long-term productivity gains. It is not hard to believe that the reality of major recessions and depressions would account for greater flexibility of prices and wages in the downward direction.[10]

If the threat of prolonged recession is absent, the situation is quite otherwise. There is less pressure to reduce prices when markets soften, if it is expected that they will soon improve. Similarly, there is less incentive to resist wage increases if prices are being maintained or even raised themselves; and if production will soon need to be increased, one is less likely to tempt strikes, ill will, and the reputation of being a lousy employer. Finally, when mass unemployment is unlikely workers are able more confidently to keep up the pressure for higher wages. . . .

[1] The smart kids in the class will now ask: If meat gets more expensive relative to vegetables, won't consumers buy less meat and more vegetables, and won't that change the make-up of the average consumption bundle, and what will that do to the price index? They can go on to the course in Index-Number Theory, but they will find it dull.

[2] For more on the WPI, and for a very informative and interesting article complementary to this one, I recommend "Inflation 1973: The Year of Infamy" by William Nordhaus and John Shoven in the May/June 1974 issue of *Challenge* magazine.

[3] There is another minor problem. The basis for putting a price on the output of governments—education, police services, "plumbers'" services, etc.—is pretty tenuous, though these are all part of the GNP. It is possible to produce a price index for privately produced GNP, nearly all of which is actually sold on a market.

[4] I owe the figures to Professor Benjamin Klein of the University of California at Los Angeles, who pieced them together from estimates made by Robert Gallman for 1874-1909 and Simon Kuznets for 1910-1946, and the official Commerce Department figures for 1947-1973. The earlier figures are based on very sketchy data.

[5] No one could make that mistake in the simple meat-and-vegetables economy. But the real world is more complicated. For instance, the timing of price and wage increases is irregular, with some temporary advantage from getting in early, and some loss from getting in late. Moreover, the normal experience is that standards of living rise as productivity improves. Then only part of a wage increase is eroded away by price increases, but even the loss of that part is felt as robbery.

[6] There is an exception to all this, but it need not concern us. Imagine a country which must import a large fraction of its basic necessities, like food and oil, and pay for them with exports of other commodities. Such a country may experience steady or rising real production, but if world food and oil prices are rising faster than the prices of its exports, its own standard of living could deteriorate. The United States is not in that position because it is so nearly self-sufficient; but of course it is hardly a hypothetical possibility for Japan and some European countries.

[7] In very rapid inflations—what are usually called "hyperinflations"—the losses from holding money are so great that one observes a genuine flight from the currency, whence come the stories from Germany in the 1920's of children meeting their fathers at the factory gate to bicycle madly into town and spend the day's pay before it has had a chance to depreciate further. In such cases there may be a return to barter. This kind of disorganization of the economy and society can be very costly, but it is not what we have to talk about. Even at relatively small rates of inflation, a little ingenuity can sometimes invent substitutes for the non-interest-bearing checking account—e.g., the NOW account.

[8] Poor people spend a larger fraction of their income on housing than rich people do, and a smaller fraction on transportation, especially automobile transportation. So the run-up in oil prices has more complicated effects: The rise in fuel oil prices hits the poor worse than the rich, but the rise in gasoline prices affects the rich more than the poor. Of course, all this is apart from the fact that any reduction in purchasing power is harder to take when you're poor.

[10] The same argument would work in reverse. Prices and wages would respond more quickly and amply upward when markets tighten. In fact, the knowledge that prices could easily rise or fall later would make it easier to let them fall or rise now. All that I need from this argument is an explanation of the fact that prices used sometimes to fall. If prices never fall, there is no way the price trend can ever be horizontal.

Who Wins, Who Loses from Inflation?

Joseph J. Minarik

No one doubts that inflation increases uncertainty, makes planning more difficult, and may inhibit long-run risk-taking. There is less agreement about the way inflation redistributes income. Who gains and who loses?

Various groups are sometimes considered winners in an inflationary economy: welfare recipients with their ever-rising benefits; workers with their generous wage contracts; wealthy people with their capital invested in inflation hedges. But each of these groups might reply that it is the victim, and make a convincing case: poor people on fixed incomes; the average consumer taking a beating at the supermarket; the rich man watching his money depreciate.

If the question were a matter of idle curiosity, we might not be greatly concerned. But as government fashions policies to stop inflation or cope with it while it lasts, the answer takes on importance. If we knew who was hurt most by inflation we could better decide how to ease its discomfort and how much we should give up to stop it.

One way to approach the question is to look at a typical household income and expenditure statement, to learn where people get their money and how they use it. Each source of income and each use of it can be expected to behave in a different way during inflation. A comparison of households at various income levels in terms of their sources and uses of income will help to explain who wins and who loses from inflation.

Income, spending, and inflation

Wages and salaries are the largest source of household income in the United States, having accounted for 64 percent of personal income in 1976. So the behavior of wages tells much of the story. Simply to observe wages during the recent inflationary period is not enough, however, for wage behavior is influenced by many things other than inflation.

The wage share of income in the corporate sector moves in a fairly predictable pattern when the unemployment rate fluctuates. When demand decreases, the proportion of workers laid off is not as great as the reduction in sales; this means that when unemployment goes up, profits fall faster than wages and the labor share of corporate income increases. If demand falls because government has tightened up on the economy to slow an inflation, the resulting increase in the labor share could easily be mistaken for a labor gain because of inflation. On the other side of the business cycle, firms have little rehiring to do when sales pick up, so the added revenue goes mostly into the profit share. If government stimulates the economy as inflation eases, the superficial conclusion would be that labor is hurt when inflation slows. The key point is that the labor share grows and then shrinks as demand falls and then rises, with or without inflation.

In short, the unemployment rate and the growth of the economy relative to its potential—not the inflation rate—are significant predictors of the labor share. It follows that labor's share is largely unaffected by inflation on the average, though individual wages may outpace or fall behind prices.

Interest income presents a different picture. Regulated bank interest rates tend to lag behind inflation, but unregulated interest rates increase when inflation accelerates, giving interest recipients sharply higher income flows in the short run. Consider a $1,000 bond whose yield increases from 5 to 7 percent because of a 2 percent increase in the inflation rate. While the interest rate increases by 2 percentage points, the interest income flow increases by 40 percent—from $50 to $70.

There are four drawbacks to a favorable balance sheet for the bondholder, however. First, the higher interest rate is not really a bonus to the bondholder. Over the course of a year, his $1,000 bond will depreciate in real value to only $980, so he needs the extra $20 of interest just to stay even. Second, interest rates do not increase for inflation instantaneously; so for some period of time there is a real loss to the bondholder. Third, when interest rates go up, the market prices of bonds go down, and the holder of a long-term bond cannot receive the new, higher yield unless he sells the bond at a precisely offsetting capital loss. Finally, even those who can cash in on higher interest rates are set back by the tax laws. The extra $20 of interest that replaced the depreciation of bond principal is considered income under the tax laws and is subject to tax. The bondholder is thus taxed not only on his interest but also, in effect, on part of his principal. From the standpoint of income flow, the interest income recipient looks like a big winner during inflation; but when the hidden balance sheet effects are taken into account, he is revealed as a big loser.

Stockholders are also hit by inflation. Even if real corporate sales remain unchanged, profits fall because corporate taxes increase faster than inflation as the result of a lag in corporate depreciation allowances behind real capital consumption. Consequently, firms have less after-tax profit to distribute as dividends, and lower real retained earnings to increase the underlying value, and ultimately the price, of corporate shares.

These effects are an average result. Some firms are helped by inflation; those that are financed largely by debt gain ground when they repay their loans with cheaper dollars. But most businesses are hurt, many of them seriously.

Social security benefits, food stamps, and certain other government transfer payments are explicitly indexed to inflation, and thus follow prices after a slight lag. The most prominent welfare program, aid to families with dependent children, is administered by the states; the best available evidence indicates that benefits in most states kept pace with prices through the recent burst of inflation. For other programs, including unemployment compensation, the evidence is less clear, though it suggests that some benefits may have lagged significantly behind prices.

Certain kinds of property income also appear to have risen more slowly than the price level. Rental income has lagged behind prices to a demonstrable degree. Private pension benefits typically are not indexed in any way and are rarely increased to make up for rises in the cost of living.

The *pattern* of price and cost increases can also be an important factor determining the impact of inflation on households. Until recently, inflation was usually defined as an increase in the general price level, with all prices rising at approximately the same rate. The inflation of 1973-75 demonstrated, however, that very rapid price increases may be concentrated in vital commodities such as food and fuel. Because low-income households spend a relatively large share of their budgets on those commodities, they were badly hurt. Since then, and except for an upsurge early in 1978 that diminished later in the year, the prices of food and fuel have increased less rapidly than those of other goods, reversing the earlier result.

Apart from such variations in the behavior of individual prices, households are affected in other ways by their commitment to long-term contracts, the most common being the home mortgage. Households whose budgets in part are contractually fixed by a mortgage suffer price increases only on the remainder of their regular expenses, and therefore are less vulnerable to inflation than other households.

A final item in the household budget that behaves differently from other prices is taxes. The federal income tax increases faster than the price level because exemptions and deductions usually do not increase in a given year, so every additional dollar of inflated income is taxed at the taxpayer's highest rate. The social security payroll tax increases in proportion to earnings up to the taxable ceiling, beyond which the tax remains fixed. Most federal excise, and most state and local sales taxes, are set as a fraction of the price of a product and thus increase with the price level; others are based on physical units and do not increase with inflation. State income taxes tend to outpace the price level, the margin depending on the progressivity of the tax. Local property taxes rise with the price level if assessments are kept current, rates are increased, or both. Since this tax is the most important local revenue source, city governments undaunted by California's example can be expected to keep the tax abreast of inflation.

The effects of inflation on various kinds of household income and expenditure now become clearer. In general, labor income keeps up with prices while transfer payments and property income tend to lag, especially when balance sheet effects (in the case of property income) are taken into account. On the expenditure side, households could be said to benefit from inflation in that rents lag behind the general price level and home mortgage payments are fixed. But household real income is reduced by income taxes that increase faster than money incomes.

A composite analysis

Now that the building blocks for an analysis of inflation's impact are identified, how can they be put together? One way is to take a sample of the population, calculate the effect of inflation on each member of the sample, and then show how different income classes fare. This is the method used here. The population sample is the Brookings 1970 MERGE file, a computer data base containing anonymous responses from a Census Bureau survey of households, combined with a large sample of unidentified tax returns from the Internal Revenue Service. The combined sample enables one to estimate the effects of economic phenomena such as inflation on an accurate cross section of the pop-

ulation, and to recalculate federal income tax liabilities that may be boosted by inflation.

When all the effects of a 2 percent increase in the actual inflation rate (say, from 6 to 8 percent) on a household's income and expenditures are quantified and then applied to the households in the 1970 MERGE file, we obtain measures of household real income before and after inflation. Two concepts of income are used. The first, called Census income, is a measure of the current cash income of the household as provided by the Census Bureau in its published statistics on poverty and income distribution. It includes wages, salaries, business income, interest, dividends, rents, royalties, pension benefits, government cash transfers, and private cash benefits. Taxes are not deducted.

The second measure is called accrued comprehensive income, or ACI. It is designed to reflect more accurately the whole range of household income by adding to Census income such additional items as income in kind (including employer-financed employee benefits and government in-kind transfers), balance sheet changes (such as depreciation of the cash value of bonds, the lagging of corporate retained earnings, and appreciation in home values), and taxes (including all federal, state, and local taxes on the household sector). The results

Figure 1

Effects of 2 Percent Increase in the Inflation Rate on Real Income

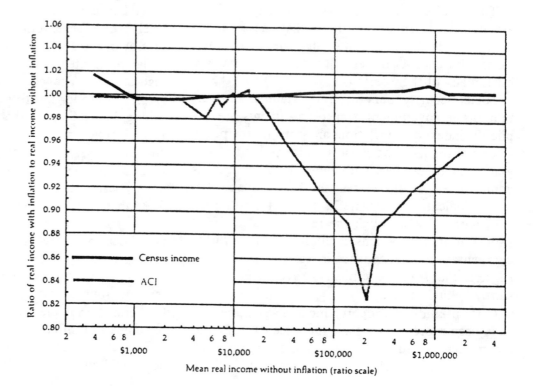

Ratio of real income with inflation to real income without inflation

Census income

ACI

Mean real income without inflation (ratio scale)

are displayed graphically as the ratio of real income after inflation to pre-inflation real income. Thus a value greater than 1.00 means that real income has been increased by inflation, while a value less than 1.00 means that real income has been reduced.

Figure 1 shows the results for a simulated 2 percent increase over the actual inflation rate of 1970 (when the CPI rose 5.9 percent). The Census income curve supports a fairly common belief about the effects of inflation: the rich get richer and the poor get poorer. At low-income levels (below $10,000), real income is reduced by slightly less than one-half of one percent, mostly because some transfer payments lag behind prices. At the middle-income levels (from about $10,000 to about $20,000), inflation has very little effect since most income here is in the form of wages and salaries, and homeowners benefit from contractually fixed mortgage payments. At upper-income levels, however, income flows are swelled by the rapid rise of interest rates, so these households appear to benefit from inflation by about one-half to one percent. The Census Bureau's income distribution statistics show a similar growth in the share of upper-income groups during the inflationary period from 1967 to 1972.

But this is only part of the story. Inflation affects forms of household income and wealth that are not included in the simple measure of household money income. When the income concept is broadened, as in the ACI curve in Figure 1, the results change dramatically. At the very lowest incomes, households for the most part are better off or unaffected by inflation: some losses due to lagging transfer payments occur, but they are offset by appreciation in home values. (Just over half of all households with incomes below $10,000 consisted of members owning their own homes in 1975.) Middle-income households are still mostly unaffected, since the burden of rising income taxes again is offset by home appreciation. The results for upper-income households are totally different under the ACI concept, however; greater real income taxes, lagging corporate retained earnings, and especially the depreciation of the face value of dollar-denominated interest-bearing securities combine to make upper-income households the big losers.

These results describe the effects of a 2 percent increase in the inflation rate in its first year. However, the consequences of a sustained inflation are equally significant. Figure 2 shows the effects on incomes in 1970 of a simulated 2 percent increase over the actual inflation rate each year from 1965 through 1970. When Census income is compared with the results in Figure 1, it can be seen that low-income households fare somewhat worse as a sustained inflation proceeds, with losses becoming as

Figure 2

Effects of 2 Percent Increase in the Inflation Rate during the Sixth Year

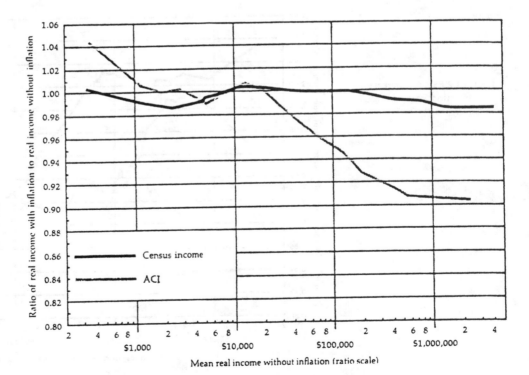

great as 1.3 percent and probably averaging about 0.6 percent. Middle-income households again fare well, benefiting from homeownership and keeping even through wage increases. Above about $25,000 of income, however, the gains recorded earlier become losses: the lag in dividends overcomes the rise in interest income, and the ultimate loss at the highest incomes is greater than that of the lowest. Thus even the limited apparent benefits of inflation to upper-income households are dissipated after a few years.

On the more revealing ACI basis in Figure 2, the sixth-year effects at low and moderate incomes differ only in detail from those of the first year, shown in Figure 1. Reduced real income is found in only a few low-income classes, leaving these households for the most part slightly better off. Middle-income households stay even. At upper incomes, the results are superficially different but the essence is the same: real income losses are substantial.

These diagrams show inflation's average effects, but at any given income level some households are better off and some worse off than the average. One group of people commonly identified as losers in inflation is the elderly, an assumption borne out by this analysis. At low- and middle-income levels the elderly are more adversely affected by inflation because their income is largely from property. At higher levels most income is from property regardless of age, and so the elderly fare little differently from other groups (see Figure 3).

Policy implications

Inflation has many consequences, of which the redistribution of income is only one. Yet the redistribution issue bears on all the policy decisions that affect or are affected by the rate of inflation, and it is worthwhile to consider how the findings presented here fit in.

So long as we have inflation, what should we do about it? Some people may feel that government should enact programs to undo the redistributional effects of inflation. They should recognize that the absence of such a program hurts mainly those with the highest incomes.

Low-income households as a group fare rather well. Some are demonstrably hurt by inflation—especially the elderly—but with social security and supplemental security income fairly effectively indexed, a measure of protection is in place. If the poor need help—and many would argue that they do—it is not because of inflation.

An effort to undo the redistributional effects of inflation would begin with indexation of the per-

Figure 3

Effects of 2 Percent Increase in the Inflation Rate on Aged and Non-Aged

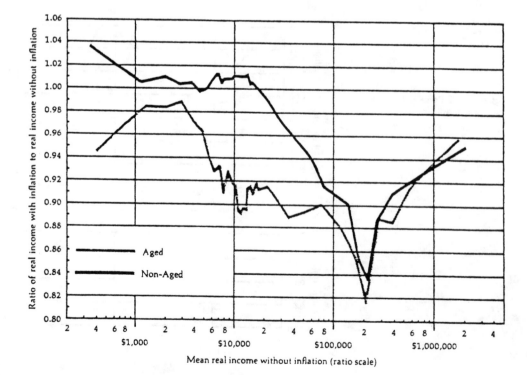

sonal and corporate income taxes, a difficult and potentially dangerous step. First, the complexity of the income taxes would increase enormously. Second, the effects on the tax system could far exceed what was intended. (Should debtors, for example, be taxed on inflationary gains realized through depreciation in the principal value of home mortgages?) Third, if income taxes are indexed, indexation may spread throughout the economy and reduce resistance to the momentum of inflation. Indexation of the tax system would only partly reduce the adverse impact of inflation on upper-income groups. It is hard to imagine how a government program could do the rest of the job.

The conventional anti-inflationary tools of budgetary and monetary restraint are often justified on the ground that inflation hurts the poor. But since contractionary policies increase unemployment and reduce real wages, thereby placing a disproportionate burden on low-income groups, it is clear from this analysis that the cure is far worse than the disease. At the same time, it should be no surprise that some recipients of property income advocate slower growth to combat inflation, even if that would reduce corporate profits. They apparently know that they have more to lose through inflation than they have to gain through faster growth.

JOSEPH J. MINARIK is a research associate in the Brookings Economic Studies program and a contributing author of *Setting National Priorities: The 1979 Budget*. The present study is based on an article in *Brookings Bulletin*, Summer 1978, and was supported by grants from the Department of Health, Education and Welfare and the National Science Foundation.

The Postulates of the Classical Economics

John Maynard Keynes

MOST treatises on the theory of Value and Production are primarily concerned with the distribution of a *given* volume of employed resources between different uses and with the conditions which, assuming the employment of this quantity of resources, determine their relative rewards and the relative values of their products.[1]

The question, also, of the volume of the *available* resources, in the sense of the size of the employable population, the extent of natural wealth and the accumulated capital equipment, has often been treated descriptively. But the pure theory of what determines the *actual employment* of the available resources has seldom been examined in great detail. To say that it has not been examined at all would, of course, be absurd. For every discussion concerning fluctuations of employment, of which there have been many, has been concerned with it. I mean, not that the topic has been overlooked, but that the fundamental theory underlying it has been deemed so simple and obvious that it has received, at the most, a bare mention.[1]

---

[1] This is in the Ricardian tradition. For Ricardo expressly repudiated any interest in the *amount* of the national dividend, as distinct from its distribution. In this he was assessing correctly the character of his own theory. But his successors, less clear-sighted, have used the classical theory in discussions concerning the causes of wealth. *Vide* Ricardo's letter to Malthus of October 9, 1820: "Political Economy you think is an enquiry into the nature and causes of wealth—I think it should be called an enquiry into the laws which determine the division of the produce of industry amongst the classes who concur in its formation. No law can be laid down respecting quantity, but a tolerably correct one can be laid down respecting proportions. Every day I am more satisfied that the former enquiry is vain and delusive, and the latter only the true objects of the science."

[1] For example, Prof. Pigou in the *Economics of Welfare* (4th ed. p. 127) writes (my italics): "Throughout this discussion, except when the contrary is expressly stated, the fact that some resources are generally unemployed against the will of the owners is ignored. *This does not affect the substance of the argument*, while it simplifies its exposition." Thus, whilst Ricardo expressly disclaimed any attempt to deal with the amount of the national dividend as a whole, Prof. Pigou, in a book which is specifically directed to the problem of the national dividend, maintains that the same theory holds good when there is some involuntary unemployment as in the case of full employment.

I

The classical theory of employment—supposedly simple and obvious—has been based, I think, on two fundamental postulates, though practically without discussion, namely:

I. *The wage is equal to the marginal product of labour.*

That is to say, the wage of an employed person is equal to the value which would be lost if employment were to be reduced by one unit (after deducting any other costs which this reduction of output would avoid); subject, however, to the qualification that the equality may be disturbed, in accordance with certain principles, if competition and markets are imperfect.

II. *The utility of the wage when a given volume of labour is employed is equal to the marginal disutility of that amount of employment.*

That is to say, the real wage of an employed person is that which is just sufficient (in the estimation of the employed persons themselves) to induce the volume of labour actually employed to be forthcoming; subject to the qualification that the equality for each individual unit of labour may be disturbed by combination between employable units analogous to the imperfections of competition which qualify the first postulate. Disutility must be here understood to cover every kind of reason which might lead a man, or a body of men, to withhold their labour rather than accept a wage which had to them a utility below a certain minimum.

This postulate is compatible with what may be called "frictional" unemployment. For a realistic interpretation of it legitimately allows for various inexactnesses of adjustment which stand in the way of continuous full employment: for example, unemployment due to a temporary want of balance between the relative quantities of specialised resources as a result of miscalculation or intermittent demand; or to time-lags consequent on unforeseen changes; or to the fact that the change-over from one employment to another cannot be effected without a certain delay, so that there will always exist in a non-static society a proportion of resources unemployed "between jobs". In addition to "frictional" unemployment, the postulate is also compatible with "voluntary" unemployment due to the refusal or inability of a unit of labour, as a result of legislation or social practices or of combination for collective bargaining or of slow response to change or of mere human obstinacy, to accept a reward corresponding to the value of the product attributable to its marginal productivity. But these two categories of "frictional" unemployment and "voluntary" unemployment are comprehensive. The classical postulates do not admit of the possibility of the third category, which

I shall define below as "involuntary" unemployment.

Subject to these qualifications, the volume of employed resources is duly determined, according to the classical theory, by the two postulates. The first gives us the demand schedule for employment, the second gives us the supply schedule; and the amount of employment is fixed at the point where the utility of the marginal product balances the disutility of the marginal employment.

It would follow from this that there are only four possible means of increasing employment:

    (*a*) An improvement in organisation or in foresight which diminishes "frictional" unemployment;

    (*b*) a decrease in the marginal disutility of labour, as expressed by the real wage for which additional labour is available, so as to diminish "voluntary" unemployment;

    (*c*) an increase in the marginal physical productivity of labour in the wage-goods industries (to use Professor Pigou's convenient term for goods upon the price of which the utility of the money-wage depends) ;

or (*d*) an increase in the price of non-wage-goods compared with the price of wage-goods, associated with a shift in the expenditure of non-wage-earners from wage-goods to non-wage-goods.

This, to the best of my understanding, is the substance of Professor Pigou's *Theory of Unemployment* —the only detailed account of the classical theory of employment which exists.[1]

II

Is it true that the above categories are comprehensive in view of the fact that the population generally is seldom doing as much work as it would like to do on the basis of the current wage? For, admittedly, more labour would, as a rule, be forthcoming at the existing money-wage if it were demanded.[2] The classical school reconcile this phenomenon with their second postulate by arguing that, while the demand for labour at the existing money-wage may be satisfied before everyone willing to work at this wage is employed, this situation is due to an open or tacit agreement amongst workers not to work for less, and that if labour as a whole would agree to a reduction of money-wages more employment would be forthcoming. If this is the case, such unemployment, though apparently involuntary, is not strictly so, and ought to be included under the

---

[1] Prof. Pigou's *Theory of Unemployment* is examined in more detail in the Appendix to Chapter 19 below.

[2] *Cf.* the quotation from Prof. Pigou above, p. 5, footnote.

above category of "voluntary" unemployment due to the effects of collective bargaining, etc.

This calls for two observations, the first of which relates to the actual attitude of workers towards real wages and money-wages respectively and is not theoretically fundamental, but the second of which is fundamental.

Let us assume, for the moment, that labour is not prepared to work for a lower money-wage and that a reduction in the existing level of money-wages would lead, through strikes or otherwise, to a withdrawal from the labour market of labour which is now employed. Does it follow from this that the existing level of real wages accurately measures the marginal disutility of labour? Not necessarily. For, although a reduction in the existing money-wage would lead to a withdrawal of labour, it does not follow that a fall in the value of the existing money-wage in terms of wage-goods would do so, if it were due to a rise in the price of the latter. In other words, it may be the case that within a certain range the demand of labour is for a minimum money-wage and not for a minimum real wage. The classical school have tacitly assumed that this would involve no significant change in their theory. But this is not so. For if the supply of labour is not a function of real wages as its sole variable, their argument breaks down entirely and leaves the question or what the actual employment will be quite indeterminate.[1] They do not seem to have realised that, unless the supply of labour is a function of real wages alone, their supply curve for labour will shift bodily with every movement of prices. Thus their method is tied up with their very special assumptions, and cannot be adapted to deal with the more general case.

Now ordinary experience tells us, beyond doubt, that a situation where labour stipulates (within limits) for a money-wage rather than a real wage, so far from being a mere possibility, is the normal case. Whilst workers will usually resist a reduction of money-wages, it is not their practice to withdraw their labour whenever there is a rise in the price of wage-goods. It is sometimes said that it would be illogical for labour to resist a reduction of money-wages but not to resist a reduction of real wages. For reasons given below (p. 14), this might not be so illogical as it appears at first; and, as we shall see later, fortunately so. But, whether logical or illogical, experience shows that this is how labour in fact behaves.

Moreover, the contention that the unemployment which characterises a depression is due to a refusal by labour to accept a reduction of money-wages is not clearly supported by the facts. It is not very plausible to assert that unemployment in the United States in 1932 was due either to labour obstinately refusing to

---

[1] This point is dealt with in detail in the Appendix to Chapter 19 below.

accept a reduction of money-wages or to its obstinately demanding a real wage beyond what the productivity of the economic machine was capable of furnishing. Wide variations are experienced in the volume of employment without any apparent change either in the minimum real demands of labour or in its productivity. Labour is not more truculent in the depression than in the boom—far from it. Nor is its physical productivity less. These facts from experience are a *prima facie* ground for questioning the adequacy of the classical analysis.

It would be interesting to see the results of a statistical enquiry into the actual relationship between changes in money-wages and changes in real wages. In the case of a change peculiar to a particular industry one would expect the change in real wages to be in the same direction as the change in money-wages. But in the case of changes in the general level of wages, it will be found, I think, that the change in real wages associated with a change in money-wages, so far from being usually in the same direction, is almost always in the opposite direction. When money-wages are rising, that is to say, it will be found that real wages are falling; and when money-wages are falling, real wages are rising. This is because, in the short period, falling money-wages and rising real wages are each, for independent reasons, likely to accompany decreasing employment; labour being readier to accept wage-cuts when employment is falling off, yet real wages inevitably rising in the same circumstances on account of the increasing marginal return to a given capital equipment when output is diminished.

If, indeed, it were true that the existing real wage is a minimum below which more labour than is now employed will not be forthcoming in any circumstances, involuntary unemployment, apart from frictional unemployment, would be non-existent. But to suppose that this is invariably the case would be absurd. For more labour than is at present employed is usually available at the existing money-wage, even though the price of wage-goods is rising and, consequently, the real wage falling. If this is true, the wage-goods equivalent of the existing money-wage is not an accurate indication of the marginal disutility of labour, and the second postulate does not hold good.

But there is a more fundamental objection. The second postulate flows from the idea that the real wages of labour depend on the wage bargains which labour makes with the entrepreneurs. It is admitted, of course, that the bargains are actually made in terms of money, and even that the real wages acceptable to labour are not altogether independent of what the corresponding money-wage happens to be. Nevertheless it is the money-wage thus arrived at which is held to determine the real wage. Thus the classical theory assumes that it is always open to labour to reduce its real wage by accepting a reduction in its money-wage. The postulate that there is a tendency for the real wage to come to equality with the marginal disutility of labour clearly presumes that labour itself is in a position to decide the real wage for which it works, though not the quantity of employment forthcoming at this wage.

The traditional theory maintains, in short, *that the wage bargains between the entrepreneurs and the workers determine the real wage*; so that, assuming free competition amongst employers and no restrictive combination amongst workers, the latter can, if they wish, bring their real wages into conformity with the marginal disutility of the amount of employment offered by the employers at that wage. If this is not true, then there is no longer any reason to expect a tendency towards equality between the real wage and the marginal disutility of labour.

The classical conclusions are intended, it must be remembered, to apply to the whole body of labour and do not mean merely that a single individual can get employment by accepting a cut in money-wages which his fellows refuse.

IV

We must now define the third category of unemployment, namely "involuntary" unemployment in the strict sense, the possibility of which the classical theory does not admit.

Clearly we do not mean by "involuntary" unemployment the mere existence of an unexhausted capacity to work. An eight-hour day does not constitute unemployment because it is not beyond human capacity to work ten hours. Nor should we regard as "involuntary" unemployment the withdrawal of their labour by a body of workers because they do not choose to work for less than a certain real reward. Furthermore, it will be convenient to exclude "frictional" unemployment from our definition of "involuntary" unemployment. My definition is, therefore, as follows: *Men are involuntarily unemployed if, in the event of a small rise in the price of wage-goods relatively to the money-wage, both the aggregate supply of labour willing to work for the current money-wage and the aggregate demand for it at that wage would be greater than the existing volume of employment.* An alternative definition, which amounts, however, to the same thing, will be given in the next chapter (p. 26 below).

It follows from this definition that the equality of the real wage to the marginal disutility of employment presupposed by the second postulate, realistically interpreted, corresponds to the absence of "involuntary" unemployment. This state of affairs we shall describe as "full" employment, both "frictional" and "voluntary" unemployment being consistent with "full" employment thus defined. This fits in, we shall find, with other characteristics of the classical theory, which is best regarded as a theory of distribution in conditions of full employment. So long as the classical postulates hold good, unemployment, which is in the above sense involuntary, cannot occur. Apparent unemployment must, therefore, be the result either of temporary loss of work of the "between jobs" type or of intermittent demand for highly specialised resources or of the effect of a trade union "closed shop" on the employment of free labour. Thus writers in the classical tradition, overlooking the special assumption underlying their theory, have been driven inevitably to the conclusion, perfectly logical on their assumption, that apparent unemployment (apart from the admitted exceptions) must be due at bottom to a refusal by the unemployed factors to accept a reward which corresponds to their marginal productivity. A classical economist may sympathise with labour in refusing to accept a cut in its money-wage, and he will admit that it may not be wise to make it to meet conditions which are temporary; but scientific integrity forces him to declare that this refusal is, nevertheless, at the bottom of the trouble.

Obviously, however, if the classical theory is only applicable to the case of full employment, it is fallacious to apply it to the problems of involuntary unemployment—if there be such a thing (and who will deny it?). The classical theorists resemble Euclidean geometers in a non-Euclidean world who, discovering that in experience straight lines apparently parallel often meet, rebuke the lines for not keeping straight—as the only remedy for the unfortunate collisions which are occurring. Yet, in truth, there is no remedy except to throw over the axiom of parallels and to work out a non-Euclidean geometry. Something similar is required to-day in economics. We need to throw over the second postulate of the classical doctrine and to work out the behaviour of a system in which involuntary unemployment in the strict sense is possible.

v

In emphasising our point of departure from the classical system, we must not overlook an important point of agreement. For we shall maintain the first postulate as heretofore, subject only to the same qualifications as in the classical theory; and we must pause, for a moment, to consider what this involves.

It means that, with a given organisation, equipment and technique, real wages and the volume of output (and hence of employment) are uniquely correlated, so that, in general, an increase in employment can only occur to the accompaniment of a decline in the rate of real wages. Thus I am not disputing this vital fact which the classical economists have (rightly) asserted as indefeasible. In a given state of organisation, equipment and technique, the real wage earned by a unit of labour has a unique (inverse) correlation with the volume of employment. Thus *if* employment increases, then, in the short period, the reward per unit of labour in terms of wage-goods must, in general, decline and profits increase.[1] This is simply the obverse of the familiar proposition that industry is normally working subject to decreasing returns in the short period during which equipment etc. is assumed to be constant; so that the marginal product in the wage-good industries (which governs real wages) necessarily diminishes as employment is increased. So long, indeed, as this proposition holds, *any* means of increasing employment must lead at the same time to a diminution of the marginal product and hence of the rate of wages measured in terms of this product.

[1] The argument runs as follows: n men are employed, the nth man adds a bushel a day to the harvest, and wages have a buying power of a bushel a day. The $n+1$th man, however, would only add ·9 bushel a day, and employment cannot, therefore, rise to $n+1$ men unless the price of corn rises relatively to wages until daily wages have a buying power of ·9 bushel. Aggregate wages would then amount to $\frac{9}{10}(n+1)$ bushels as compared with n bushels previously. Thus the employment of an additional man will, if it occurs, necessarily involve a transfer of income from those previously in work to the entrepreneurs.

The Supply Side

Lawrence R. Klein

I. The Meaning of Supply and Demand in a Macroeconomic Context

It is worth considering whether a new basic model should guide our thinking about performance of the economy as a whole. It is not that the macro models of the past twenty-five years or so have failed to serve us well. When we consider the state of our knowledge about the analytics of the economy at the end of World War II and the apprehensiveness with which we approached the modern era of expansion, it should be evident that we have come a long way professionally. Yet the economic problems of today seem to be intractable when studied through the medium of simplified macro models. The new system should combine the Keynesian model of final demand and income determination with the Leontief model of interindustrial flows. This is the motivation for my focusing attention on the supply side of the economy.

It is frequently said, in almost an offhand manner, that the theories of aggregate employment and output determination are demand models, that economic policy for overall direction of the economy is a policy of *demand* management. I would generally agree with these remarks, but not in every last detail, once the meaning of demand in these contexts is carefully pulled apart and analyzed. The *demand* aspects are possibly overstated.

It is, of course, true that demand for the *GNP* built up as the sum of demands by consumers, businesses, government, and foreigners (consumption, investment, public spending, and net exports) covers total demand in the economy and is composed of demands by the constituent parts. But demand by firms, and, in many cases by government, are not ends in themselves. Business demand is largely for goods to produce goods. The capital formation that results from business demand goes into the increment of capital stock, after allowance for capital consumption, and the capital stock becomes a factor input in the production function. The accumulation of capital contributes to the *supply* of goods and services. Indeed, investment *demand* now for new capital facilitates the implementation of the production process with the supply of factors of ever-increasing powers of productivity, thus making it possible to supply increasing amounts of goods and services with inputs that are increasing at a somewhat slower rate.

By focusing attention excessively on the "short run," in which the capital stock is timelessly held fixed by assumption only and not in reality, we have ignored the supply-side characteristics of investment demand. Students of today's business cycle commonly cite investment demand as the promising potential route to higher productivity in the relatively near future, thereby lessening inflationary pressure. In this respect, economic theoreticians have been myopic relative to the applied economic analysts in the world of affairs. Nevertheless, as we shall see, there is much more to the supply side than the transformation of investment into productive capital, and

*Presidential address delivered at the ninetieth meeting of the American Economic Association, New York City, New York, December 29, 1977.

the basic characterization of contemporary macroeconomics as demand analysis has a point.

III. Why Model Supply?

At the time of the Keynesian Revolution, there was a pervasive deficiency of demand throughout most of the world. The Keynesian policy development, building on that model, did, in my opinion, much good for the economy of the Western world, enabling us to come through an expansive era of more than twenty-five years without a recurrence of a Great Depression. That does not mean that this system of thought and policy formation did its work for all time in putting the world economy on a stable footing. It carried the situation only so far, and undoubtedly underestimated inflation potentials, leaving us now at the point where new systems of thought, drawing more on the supply side, are needed in order to develop policies that will be able to deal with the world's contemporary economic problems; hopefully, policies that will have as much longevity as the demand management policies of the last two to three decades. That should bring us nicely into the twenty-first century, which is about as far ahead as we might attempt to look at the present time.

The limits of demand management policies have become clearly visible in recent years. Let us look at the issues through the medium of specific problems, say the joint problems of too much unemployment and too much inflation. Policies of demand management alone have appeared to be adequate to deal with one or the other, but not both together. If demand is stimulated enough to bring down the unemployment rate to a full-employment minimum, there is danger of generating undue inflationary pressure as a side effect. Conversely, anti-inflationary policies of demand restriction run the danger of generating excessive unemployment while holding down the inflation rate.

How might supply-side policies be introduced to lower both the inflation and unemployment rates at the same time? It is conventionally thought that policies of aggregative demand stimulus through traditional fiscal and monetary policies might be able to bring down the $U.S.$ unemployment rate to about 5.5 percent. This is not a firm

point estimate, and is subject to error of at least one-half point above or below that figure, but it is not, in any case, a full-employment target figure.

One way, but not the only way, of getting to full employment without generating fresh inflationary pressure is to design a jobs program for about 1.0 million long-term, hard core unemployed. This jobs program cannot be described in full detail in the context of this presentation, but it is not to be viewed as an ordinary public jobs program. It is viewed as a job training program aimed at people who show signs of receptivity to training and enlisting the participation of employers who provide really productive jobs with potential for upward mobility. The 1.0 million target, spread over three years, is not purely indicative. It is meant to be plausible and necessary if full employment is to be reached by 1980-82 in the United States.

Apart from the fact that some public funds are to be spent on this program, it is not a typical demand management policy. It is aimed at increasing the supply of goods, at raising labor productivity, at sectors of the economy where job training can be accomodated or needed, and at sectors of the labor force.

In anticipation of criticism of this policy approach from the side of those who are strongly wedded to emphasis on demand management, I want to stress that a jobs program aimed at increasing productivity and reducing hard core unemployment is not a futile exercise in pushing some subsidized workers into the ranks of the employed while pushing others out. The program is intended to have balance; i.e., to be part of a larger program with corresponding support from the demand side. Such support could not be justified from the point of view of inflation potential unless steps are being taken to complement the effect with a jobs program and eventual lifting of productivity. Undue preoccupation with demand policies is not going to be adequate to meet the problems of the day, nor is pure emphasis on supply. Both sides of the economy must be coordinated in policy formation.

It should also be emphasized that demand policies of federal expenditures for public service employment appear to be inferior to private sector jobs programs of the type being mentioned here. In the former case, there is no long-term opportunity for those taken into the program and there is no contribution to national productivity. As long as job expenditures are going to be made, they ought, preferably, to be directed to an effort that promises to have some lasting benefit.

This example of the jobs program is one that fits the contemporary American economic scene and has been investigated with a *U.S.* model and data. The underlying idea, however, is meant to be much more general. It is that the whole industrial world is faced with a series of new supply-side economic problems. The problems of cyclical stabilization and reaching full employment without inflation will have to be dealt with as before, and the latter will require some degree of supply-side analysis in other economies as in the *U.S.* case, but a whole new range of economic issues looms on the horizon. These are development of new, greater energy supplies, protection of the environment, controlling the exhaustion of resources, enhancing agricultural supplies, balancing population development, and others of like nature. The juggling of

public budgets, the setting of tax rates, and the giving of a tone to money market conditions are not going to deal effectively with this new class of problems, from the viewpoints of influencing them in a favorable direction. Similarly, the demand oriented model is not going to provide much understanding of them.

REFERENCES

R. Frisch, "The Principle of Substitution: An Example of its Application in the Chocolate Industry," *Nordisk Tidsskrift for Teknisk Økonomi*, Sept. 1935, *1*, 21–27.

K. C. Hoffman and D. W. Jorgenson, "Economic and Technological Models for Evaluation of Energy Policy," *Bell J. Econ.*, Autumn 1977, *8*, 444–66.

Lawrence R. Klein, *A Textbook of Econometrics*, Evanston 1953.

S. Weintraub, "A Macroeconomic Approach to the Theory of Wages," *Amer. Econ. Rev.*, Dec. 1956, *46*, 835–56.

———, "The Micro-Foundations of Aggregate Demand and Supply," *Econ. J.*, Sept. 1957, *67*, 455–70.

On Theories of Unemployment

Robert M. Solow

There is a long-standing tension in economics between belief in the advantages of the market mechanism and awareness of its imperfections. Ever since Adam Smith, economists have been distinguished from lesser mortals by their understanding of and —I think one has to say—their admiration for the efficiency, anonymity, and subtlety of decentralized competitive markets as an instrument for the allocation of resources and the imputation of incomes. I think we all know this; for confirmation one can look at the results of a paper (James Kearl et al.) presented at the last annual meeting, reporting the responses of professional economists to a sort of survey of technical opinion. The propositions which generated the greatest degree of consensus were those asserting the advantages of free trade and flexible exchange rates, favoring cash transfers over those in kind, and noting the disadvantages of rent controls, interest rate ceilings, and minimum wage laws.

Views on these policy issues did not seem to represent mere conservative ideology: half of the respondents agreed and another 30 percent agreed "with provisions" that redistribution of income (presumably toward the poorest) is a legitimate function of government policy. The profession's reservations about rent control, interest rate ceilings, and minimum wage laws do not appear to reflect a rejection of the goals of those measures, but rather a feeling that nonprofessionals simply do not understand fully the consequences, often unexpected and undesired, of messing around with the market mechanism. Most of us are conscious of a conflict that arises in our minds

and consciences because, while we think it is usually a mistake to fiddle the price system to achieve distributional goals, we realize that the public and the political process are perversely more willing to do that than to make the direct transfers we would prefer. If we oppose all distorting transfers, we end up opposing transfers altogether. Some of us seem to welcome the excuse, but most of us feel uncomfortable. I don't think there is any very good way to resolve that conflict in practice.

Simultaneously, however, there is an important current in economics that focuses on the flaws in the price system, the ways that real markets fail because they lack some of the characteristics that make idealized markets so attractive. I think that outsiders, who tend to see economists as simple-minded marketeers, would be astonished to learn how much of the history of modern economic analysis can be written in terms of the study of the sources of market failure. The catalog runs from natural and artificial monopoly, to monopolistic competition, to the importance of public goods and externalities of many other kinds, to—most recently—a variety of problems connected with the inadequate, imperfect, or asymmetric transmission of information and with the likelihood that there will simply be no markets for some of the relevant goods and services.

Even the vocabulary can be revealing. Market "imperfection" suggests a minor blemish of the sort that can make the purchase of "irregular" socks a bargain. Market "failure" sounds like something more serious. To take a more subtle example, I mentioned that one kind of flaw in the system can be the absence of certain markets. The common generic term for the reason why markets are missing is "transaction costs." That sounds rather minor, the sort of thing that might go away in due course as accounting and information

*Presidential address delivered at the ninety-second meeting of the American Economic Association, December 29, 1979, Atlanta, Georgia. Like most people, I get by with a little help from my friends, in this case especially Paul Samuelson, George Akerlof, Arnold Kling, and James Tobin.

processing get cheaper. But some of the cases of missing markets really go much deeper. The fact that distant future generations can not participate directly in the markets for nonrenewable resources will not be remedied by improvements in communication. Nor are the residents of densely populated areas ever likely to be able to dicker effectively with the dozens or hundreds of sources of barely traceable pollutants whose health effects, if any, cumulate over many years.

There is a large element of Rohrschach test in the way each of us responds to this tension. Some of us see the Smithian virtues as a needle in a haystack, as an island of measure zero in a sea of imperfections. Others see all the potential sources of market failure as so many fleas on the thick hide of an ox, requiring only an occasional flick of the tail to be brushed away. A hopeless eclectic without any strength of character, like me, has a terrible time of it.

The tension between market efficiency and market failure is especially pointed in discussions of the working of the labor market, for obvious reasons. The labor market connects quickly with everything else in the economy and its performance matters more directly for most people than that of any other market. Moreover, the labor market's own special pathology, unemployment, is particularly visible, particularly unsettling, and particularly frustrating. The fuse leading from theory to policy in this field is short, and has been known to produce both heat and light throughout much of the history of economics.

Contemporary macro-economic theory, though apparently full of technical novelties, has revived many of the old questions in only slightly different form. One of the points I want to make is that underneath the theoretical innovations—some of which are interesting and important—the basic controversial issues that come to the surface are the same ones that occupied earlier literature. The most important among them is really the old tension between market efficiency and market failure. Should one think of the labor market as mostly clearing, or at worst in the process of quick return to market-clearing equilibrium? Or should one think of it as mostly in disequilibrium, with transactions habitually taking place at non-market-clearing wages? In that case presumably the wage structure is either not receiving any strong signals to make it

change in the right direction or is not responding to the signals it receives. My own belief in this case lies with the market-failure side. That is to say, I believe that what looks like involuntary unemployment is involuntary unemployment.

Of course that conclusion only leads to another question. If the labor market often fails to clear, we had better figure out why. There is no shortage of candidate hypotheses. Here I think it is worthwhile to insist on a commonplace: although it is natural for academic people to seek a single weighty Answer to a weighty Question, if only because it is so satisfying to find one, it is quite likely that many of the candidate hypotheses are true, each contributing a little to the explanation of labor-market failure. Now the second general point I want to make is one that I am surprised to hear myself making. While I find several of the candidate hypotheses entirely believable, I am inclined to emphasize some that might be described as noneconomic. More precisely, I suspect that the labor market is a little different from other markets, in the sense that the objectives of the participants are not always the ones we normally impute to economic agents, and some of the constraints by which they feel themselves bound are not always the conventional constraints. In other words, I think that among the reasons why market-clearing wage rates do not establish themselves easily and adjust quickly to changing conditions are some that could be described as social conventions, or principles of appropriate behavior, whose source is not entirely individualistic.

I said that I am a little surprised at myself. That is because I am generally stodgy about assumptions, and like to stay as close to the mainstream framework as the problem at hand will allow. In any case, I think that the unconventional elements in what I have to say are only part of the story. And I assure you that I am not about to peddle amateur sociology to a captive audience. All I do mean to suggest is that we may predispose ourselves to misunderstand important aspects of unemployment if we insist on modelling the buying and selling of labor within a set of background assumptions whose main merit is that they are very well adapted to models of the buying and selling of cloth. Far from advocating that we all practice sociology, I am pleasantly impressed at how much mileage you can get from the methods of conventional economic analysis if only you are willing to broaden the assumptions a little.

I

It might be interesting to have a history of the evolution of economic ideas about unemployment, and their relation both to the internal logic of the subject and to the parallel evolution of the institutions of the labor market. I am not sufficiently well read to provide that kind of survey. To make my point about the persistence of the market-efficiency market-failure tension, I took a short cut. I went back to reread Pigou's *Lapses from Full Employment*, a little book I remember having been assigned to read as a student just after the war. And that in turn sent me back to its parent book, Pigou's *Theory of Unemployment*. The Preface to *The Theory of Unemployment* is dated April 1933, after a decade of poor performance and relatively high unemployment in Great Britain, well into the Great Depression, and before the publication of the *General Theory*. The Preface to *Lapses from Full Employment* (another example of a revealing vocabulary) is dated November 1944, after five years of the war that put an end to the depression, and well after the appearance of the *General Theory*. That seemed like an interesting approach to the historical question, because current controversies in macro-economic theory are often described as a debate between "Keynesians" and others—"monetarists," "Classicals," or " equilibrium theorists" — and because Pigou, besides being a great economist, was in particular the embodiment of the Marshallian tradition, the leading figure in the "classical economics" that the Keynesian revolution was explicitly intended to overthrow.

Lapses makes interesting rereading. It emphasizes the money wage, whereas its predecessor was written almost entirely in terms of the real wage. The general macro-theoretic framework, in which the discussion of the labor market is embedded, clearly has an eye on Keynes. The underlying model could be *IS-LM* without doing much violence to the argument. There are little anachronisms: Pigou tends to think of the interest rate as being determined in the goods market (by Savings = Investment) and nominal income as being determined by the demand for money. Today we take simultaneity seriously, but the *General Theory* more or less speaks as if real output is determined in the goods market and the interest rate by liquidity preference. After what is to me a confusing description of a Keynesian low-level liquidity-trap

equilibrium, Pigou invokes the Pigou effect to explain why the low level might not be as low as all that and then, characteristically, remarks that none of it is very important in practice anyway. All this is relevant here only as background for the treatment of the labor market.

Pigou says the obvious thing first, and I agree that it is the first thing to say: if there is "thorough-going competition" among workers, then the only possible equilibrium position is at full employment. That is little more than a definition of equilibrium. He is aware that he is taking a lot of dynamics for granted. Expectations of falling wages could perversely reduce the demand for labor; and he discusses the possibility that under some conditions, with the interest rate at its practical floor, nominal wage rates and prices may chase each other down and thus prevent the real-wage adjustment needed for an increase in employment. (This is where the Pigou effect makes its appearance, of course.)

It is what comes next that interests me. It is obvious to Pigou, writing in 1944, that the labor market does not behave as if workers were engaged in thorough-going competition for jobs. With the common sense that seems somehow to have escaped his modern day successors, he wonders why it does not. And he discusses three or four of the institutional factors that a reasonable person would mention even now as obstacles to the classical functioning of the labor market.

First of all, he realizes that the labor market is segmented. Not everyone in it is in competition with everyone else. I am not referring here to the obvious fact that abilities, experience, and skills differ, so that unemployed laborers can not compete for the jobs held by craftsmen. That fact of life merely reminds us that "labor" is not a well-defined homogeneous factor of production. Even within skill categories or occupational groups, however, workers have ties to localities, to industries, to special job classifications, even to individual employers. These ties can be broken, but not easily. It is interesting to me that even the *Theory of Unemployment* of 1933 devotes a lot of space to the analysis of a labor market in which there are many "centers of employment"—to use the neutral term chosen by Pigou to describe segmentation of the labor market—between which mobility is absent or slow. Of course he observes that even in a completely segmented labor market, if there is thorough-going competition within segments, full employment will be the rule, although there may be wage differentials between centers of employment for otherwise identical workers. I think that the fact of segmentation is very important, not only because it limits the scope of competition but because its pervasiveness suggests—though it can not prove—that habit and custom play a large role in labor market behavior. From the prominence that he gives it, I gather that Pigou might have agreed.

A second factor, which has been more often discussed, is trade unionism. Pigou does not have very much to say about collective bargaining, but what he says makes sense.

> Of course, these agencies in their decisions have regard to the general state of the demand for labour; they will have no wish to set wage rates so high that half the people of the country are thrown out of work. Nevertheless, there is reason to believe that they do not have regard to demand conditions in such degree as would be necessary to secure, as thorough-going competition would do, the establishment of full employment.   [1945, p. 26]

Later on in the book, Pigou makes an observation that is not explicitly connected with collective bargaining. He does connect it with "actual life" however, and it fits organized workers very well, and perhaps others besides:

> In periods of expansion employers might be willing to agree to substantial advances in wage rates if they were confident that, when prosperity ended, they would be able to cancel them. They know, however, that in fact this will not be easy, that elaborate processes will have to be gone through, and that their work-people will put up a strong rear-guard action.... In periods of depression wage-earners, for precisely similar reasons, hold out against wage reductions, which they might be ready to concede if it were not for the difficulty that they foresee in getting them cancelled when times improve.... A widespread desire for 'safety first' helps to make wage rates sticky.
> [1945, p. 48]

These casual remarks raise more questions than they answer about the determination of nominal wages by collective bargaining. The first excerpt can be taken as a redefinition of full employment when the labor

market is not competitive; the second, however, advances an account of wage stickiness and is therefore on a different footing. It would help to explain the failure of the labor market to clear on any reasonable definition, and thus provide a connection between nominal demand and real output.

The third institutional factor mentioned by Pigou has also been the subject of much analysis, past and present: the provision of unemployment insurance. There are several channels by which the availability of unemployment compensation can add to the recorded amount of unemployment. The prolongation of search is only the most obvious. My own impression is that this is currently a significant factor.

The last comment of Pigou's that I want to cite is especially intriguing because it is so unlike the sort of thing that his present day successors keep saying. Already in the 1933 *Theory of Unemployment* he wrote: "...public opinion in a modern civilized State builds up for itself a rough estimate of what constitutes a reasonable living wage. This is derived half-consciously from a knowledge of the actual standards enjoyed by more or less 'average' workers.... Public opinion then enforces its view, failing success through social pressure, by the machinery of...legislation" (p. 255). A similar remark appears in *Lapses*. Such feelings about equity and fairness are obviously relevant to the setting of statutory minimum wages, and Pigou uses them that way. I think they also come into play as a deterrent to wage cutting in a slack labor market. Unemployed workers rarely try to displace their employed counterparts by offering to work for less; and it is even more surprising, as I have had occasion to point out in the past, that employers so rarely try to elicit wage cutting on the part of their laid-off employees, even in a buyer's market for labor. Several forces can be at work, but I think Occam's razor and common observation both suggest that a code of good behavior enforced by social pressure is one of them. Wouldn't you be surprised if you learned that someone of roughly your status in the profession, but teaching in a less desirable department, had written to your department chairman offering to teach your courses for less money? The fact that nominal wage rates did fall sharply during the early stages of the depression of the 1930's, and the fact that the Chrysler Corporation has been able to negotiate concessions from the UAW certainly show that wage rates are not completely rigid. But those very instances seem to me only to confirm the importance of social convention in less extreme circumstances. After all, people have been known to try to claw their way into a lifeboat who would never dream of cheating on a lift-line.

I think I have made the case that the most eminent representative of orthodox economics in the 1940's was fully aware of the many obstacles to "thorough-going competition" among workers, that is, of the many ways in which the labor market may "fail." In particular, one cannot under those circumstances expect the labor market always to clear. Pigou certainly drew that conclusion. He says, in the Preface to *Lapses*: "Professor Dennis Robertson...has warned me that the form of the book may suggest that I am in favour of attacking the problem of unemployment by manipulating wages rather than by manipulating demand. I wish, therefore, to say clearly that this is not so" (p. v).

Pigou clearly felt the tension between market efficiency and market failure. Nevertheless, he did not come down on the side of market failure, even after the 1930's. The very title of *Lapses from Full Employment* tells us that much. Evidently he concluded that the tendency of the capitalist economy to seek (and find) its full-employment equilibrium was strong enough so that departures from full employment could be regarded as mere episodes.

The modern classical school seems curiously remote from all this. When they try to explain how the equilibrium volume of employment can fluctuate as widely as actual employment does in business cycles, their only substitute for Pigou's high elasticity of demand is a high elasticity of supply (of labor) in the face of a perceived temporary opportunity for unusual gains, which in this case reflects wages that differ from average expected (discounted) future wages. In other words, People who give the vague impression of being unemployed are actually engaged in voluntary leisure. They are taking it now, planning to substitute extra work later, because they think, rightly or wrongly, that current real wages are unusually low compared with the present value of what the labor market will offer in the future. They may be responding to changes in real wages or to changes in the real interest rate.

It is astonishing that believers have made essentially no effort to verify this central hypothesis. I know of no convincing evidence in its favor,[3] and I am not sure why it has any claim to be taken seriously. It is hardly plausible on its face. Even if the workers in question have misread the future, they are merely mistaken, not confused or mystified about their own motives. It is thus legitimate to wonder why the unemployed do not feel themselves to be engaged in voluntary intertemporal substitution, and why they queue up in such numbers when legitimate jobs of their usual kind are offered during a recession.[4]

When they face the market-clearing issue at all, Pigou's successors take a rather abstract line. They regard it as inherently incredible that unexploited opportunities for beneficial trade should be anything but ephemeral—which means merely that they ignore all those human and institutional facts of which Pigou was aware. Or else they argue that one cannot believe in the failure of markets to clear without having an acceptable theory to explain why that happens. That is a remarkable precept when you think about it. I remember reading once that it is still not understood how the giraffe manages to pump an adequate blood supply all the way up to its head; but it is hard to imagine that anyone would therefore conclude that giraffes do not have long necks. At least not anyone who had ever been to a zoo. Besides, I think perfectly acceptable theories can indeed by constructed, as soon as one gets away from foolishly restrictive and inappropriate assumptions.

II

That brings me to the second and last general point I had hoped to make. Suppose one chooses to accept the apparent evidence of one's senses and takes it for granted that the wage does not move flexibly to clear the labor market. By the way, my own inclination is to go further and claim that commodity prices are sticky too, at least downward. But it is the persistence of disequilibrium in the labor market that I want to emphasize. How can we account for it?

There is, as I mentioned at the beginning, a whole catalog of possible models of the labor market that will produce the right qualitative properties. Since I have surveyed this literature elsewhere, I will just list a half-dozen possibilities now, with the reminder that they are not mutually exclusive alternatives.

(1) There is Keynes's idea that case-by-case resistance to wage reductions is the only way that workers can defend traditional wage differentials in a decentralized

labor market. The net result is to preserve the general wage level or its trend, but that is an unintended artifact.

(2) There is a complementary hypothesis about the behavior of employers that I have proposed myself: if employers know that aggressive wage cutting in a buyer's market may antagonize the remaining work force, hurt current productivity, and make it harder to recruit high-quality workers when the labor market tightens, they will be less inclined to push their short-run advantage.

(3) Pigou realized that widely held notions of fairness, enforced by social pressure or by legislation, might have to be part of any serious account of wage determination. George Akerlof has pursued this trail further, documented the prescription of codes of good behavior in manuals of personnel practice, and showed formally that such codes of behavior can be self-enforcing if people value their reputations in the community. Obviously there are no Emily Post manuals to consult as regards the behavior of laid-off workers, but you would certainly not be astonished to learn that self-esteem and the folkways discourage laid-off workers from undercutting the wages of their still-employed colleagues in an effort to displace them from jobs. Reservation wages presumably fall as the duration of unemployment lengthens; but my casual reading suggests that this pattern shows up more in a willingness to accept lower-paid sorts of jobs than in "thorough-going competition" for the standard job. The cost to the worker of this sort of behavior is diminished by the availability of unemployment insurance. It is worth remembering that the acceptance of lower-grade jobs is itself a form of unemployment.

(5) Wherever there is collective bargaining in our economy, the standard pattern, with few exceptions, is that wage rates are specified in the contract, and the employer chooses the amount of employment. This is not exactly simple monopoly, because the union cannot set the wage schedule unilaterally. To the extent that it can, another source of wage stickiness can be identified.

(6) As a last example, I recall Pigou's observation that wage changes may be seen by the parties as hard to reverse without a struggle whose duration and outcome cannot be foreseen. The resulting uncertainty causes employers to drag their feet when demand increases temporarily and workers to reciprocate when demand falls.

The result is wage stickiness in the face of fluctuating employment.

Only what Veblen called trained incapacity could prevent anyone from seeing that some or all of these mechanisms do indeed capture real aspects of the modern capitalist economy. Assessing their combined significance quantitatively would be a very difficult task, and I do not pretend to be able to do that. We are all interpreting this ink blot together. Obviously I would not be giving this particular talk if I did not think that wage stickiness is a first-order factor in a reasonable theory of unemployment.

To make my position plausible, I want to try to summarize the sort of general characteristics that the labor market should have if the particular mechanisms that I have enumerated are to be important. By the way, I have no reason to believe that my list is anything like exhaustive; you may think of others. Simply to narrow the field, I have deliberately left out of account factors relating specifically to age, sex, race, and other characteristics that normally form the basis for discussions of structural unemployment as distinct from cyclical unemployment.

The sort of labor market I have in mind is segmented. It often makes sense to think of an employer or definable group of employers as facing its own labor pool. Some members of the labor pool may be unemployed, but still belong to it. Although transportation, information, and transaction costs are possible sources of segmentation, they need not be among the most important. The buildup of firm-specific or industry-specific human capital may be more fundamental, and equally a kind of mutual knowing-what-to-expect that gives both parties in the labor market a stake, a rent, in the durability of the relationship. This point is close to the distinction between auction markets and customer markets made by Arthur Okun in a different context. The labor market, at least the "primary" labor market, is a customer market; this may be one of the important facts that differentiates the primary from the secondary labor market.

A second general characteristic is the availability of some nontrivial source of nonemployment income. The obvious one is unemployment compensation, but I imagine that fringe activity ranging from hustling to home maintenance can function in much the same way. I suppose in some societies the possibility of returning temporarily to farming is now as important as it once was here. The presence of a second earner in the family can make an obvious difference. One consequence is that it becomes easier to maintain a labor pool in the presence of fluctuating employment. In addition, as I mentioned a few moments ago, several of the specific sticky-wage mechanisms in my catalog depend for their operation on this characteristic.

Third, the stability of the labor pool makes it possible for social conventions to assume some importance. There is a difference between a long-term relationship and a one-night stand, and acceptable behavior in one context may be unacceptable in the other. Presumably most conventions are adaptive, not arbitrary, but adaptiveness may have to be interpreted broadly, so as to include pecuniary advantage but not be limited by it. Critics who deride the notion of "economic man" have a point, but usually the wrong point. Economic man is a social, not a psychological, category. There are activities in our culture in which it is socially acceptable and expected that individual pecuniary self-interest will be the overriding decision criterion: choosing a portfolio of securities, for example.[6] There are others in which it is not: choosing a mate, for example.[7] The labor market is more complicated than either, of course, and contains elements of both. Perhaps in nineteenth-century Manchester labor was bought and sold by "thorough-going competition" but I think that is unlikely to be a good approximation to contemporary wage setting. In particular, as I have emphasized, there is nothing in the data or in common observation to make you believe that moderate excess supply will evoke aggressive wage cutting on either side of the labor market.

[6]The emotion aroused by the case of South Africa strikes me as one of those extreme exceptions that proves the rule.

[7]In Gary Becker's defense, I should point out that he does not assume cash income to be the decisive motive in courtship.

REFERENCES

G. Akerlof, "The Case Against Conservative Macroeconomics: An Inaugural Lecture," *Economica*, Aug. 1979, *46*, 219–37.

C. Azariadis, "Implicit Contracts and Unemployment Equilibria," *J. Polit. Econ.*, Dec. 1975, *83*, 1183–202.

M. N. Baily, "Wages and Employment under Uncertain Demand," *Rev. Econ. Stud.*, Jan. 1974, *41*, 37–50.

K. Clark and R. Freeman, "How Elastic is the Demand for Labor," Nat. Bur. Econ. Res. work. Paper no. 309, Cambridge, Mass., Jan. 1979.

P. Diamond and E. Maskin, "Externalities and Efficiency in a Model of Stochastic Job Matching," working paper, Mass. Inst. Technology, forthcoming.

D. F. Gordon, "A Neo-Classical Theory of Keynesian Unemployment," *Econ. Inquiry*, Dec. 1974, *12*, 431–59,

R. Hal, "Labor Supply and Aggregate Fluctuations," Nat. Bur. Econ. Res. work. paper no. 385, Stanford, Aug. 1979.

D. Hamermesh, "Econometric Studies of Labor Demand and their Applications to Policy Analysis," *J. Hum. Resources*, Fall 1976, *11*, 507–25.

J. Kearl, C. Pope, G. Whiting and L. Wimmer, "A Confusion of Economists?," *Amer. Econ. Rev. Proc.*, May 1979, *69*, 28–37.

A. Okun, "Inflation: Its Mechanics and Welfare Costs," *Brookings Papers*, Washington 1975, *2*, 351–90.

A. C. Pigou, *The Theory of Unemployment*, London 1933.

_____, *Lapses from Full Employment*, London 1945.

R. Solow, "Alternative Approaches to Macroeconomic Theory: A Partial View," *Can. J. Econ.*, Aug. 1979, *12*, 339–54.

Tax Revision: Impact on Output and Employment

Council of Economic Advisers

Tax reduction will directly increase the disposable income and purchasing power of consumers and business, strengthen incentives and expectations, and raise the net returns on new capital investment. This will lead to initial increases in private consumption and investment expenditures. These increases in spending will set off a cumulative expansion, generating further increases in consumption and investment spending and a general rise in production, income, and employment. This process is discussed in some detail in this section. Tax reduction may also have financial effects associated with the increased budget deficit that it will initially produce. Since these effects—in the first instance, at least—depend on the methods used to finance the deficit, they are left for discussion in a later section dealing with monetary and debt management policy.

Initial effects: consumption

Effects on disposable income. The proposed reduction in personal income tax rates will directly add to the disposable income of households. In addition, the reduction in corporate tax rates will increase the after-tax profits of corporations as a result of which corporations may be expected to increase their dividend payments. The initial direct effect on the disposable income of households resulting from the entire program of tax reductions should be approximately $8½ billion, at current levels of income.

Consumer response to increase in disposable income. The ratio of total consumption expenditures to total personal disposable income has in each recent calendar year fallen within the range of 92 to 94 percent. Although there are lags and irregularities from quarter to quarter or even year to year, the change in personal consumption expenditures has in the past, after a few quarters, averaged roughly 93 percent of any change in personal disposable income. On this basis, the initial addition to consumer expenditures associated with tax reductions would be on the order of $8 billion, although all would not be spent at once.

Additions to after-tax incomes resulting from tax reduction are likely to be spent in the same way as other additions to income. The largest part of the proposed tax reduction will be reflected in reduced withholding of taxes from wages and salaries, and therefore in larger wage and salary checks; thus, it will be indistinguishable from additional income arising from wage or salary increases, greater employment, or longer hours of work. Similarly, part of the reduced corporate taxes will be passed along to stockholders in increased dividend checks. Stockholders will not be able to identify the source of their additional dividends. Tax reduction dollars carry no identifying label, and there is no reason to expect recipients to treat them differently from other dollars.

Recent experience with tax reduction demonstrates clearly that additions to disposable income from this source are spent as completely as any other additions. Taxes were reduced by about $4.7 billion on May 1, 1948, retroactive to January 1, with resulting large refunds in mid-1949. Again taxes were cut, net, by about $6 billion, effective January 1, 1954, with further cuts later that year. Table 8 shows that the percentage of disposable income spent by consumers remained within the normal range of quarterly fluctuation during the periods following the enactment of each of these tax reductions.

TABLE 8.—*Personal consumption expenditures as percent of disposable personal income during two postwar periods of tax reduction*

1948–49		1953–55	
Quarter	Percent	Quarter	Percent
1948: I	97.3	1953: IV	91.5
II	94.0	1954: I	91.8
III	92.6	II	92.8
IV	93.2	III	93.0
1949: I	93.9	IV	93.2
II	95.2	1955: I	94.5
III	95.7	II	93.5

Note.—Based on seasonally adjusted data.

Source: Department of Commerce.

It is sometimes suggested that tax reductions which add only a few dollars to the weekly pay check of the typical worker would do little good even if the money was spent, since the amounts involved would not be large enough to permit major expenditures—say on washing machines or automobiles. Instead, the money would be "frittered away" on minor expenditures and would do little good for the economy. But all purchases lead to production which generates income and provides employment. Therefore, the purpose of tax reduction is achieved when the proceeds are spent on any kind of goods or services.

Actually, of course, tax reduction which expands take-home pay even by a relatively small amount each week or month may induce recipients to purchase durable goods or houses of higher quality, since the increased income would permit them to handle larger monthly installment payments. It may even induce a rearrangement of expenditure patterns and thus bring about purchases of durable goods that would not otherwise be made.

Initial effects: investment

Investment is a more volatile element than consumption in national expenditure. The timing and magnitude of its response to tax changes is less predictable. But a cut in tax rates on business income will stimulate spending on new plants and new machinery in two ways. First, it will strengthen investment incentives by increasing the after-tax profits that businessmen can expect to earn on new productive facilities. Second, it will add to the supply of internal funds, a large part of which is normally reinvested in the business (though part of this effect may initially be offset by the proposed acceleration of corporate tax payments).

Since the largest part of business investment is made by corporations, the proposed cuts in the corporate income tax are especially significant. But investments of unincorporated businesses will also be encouraged by cuts in personal income tax rates, especially in the upper brackets.

Two important reforms affecting the taxation of business income designed to stimulate investment in plant and equipment were put into effect during 1962: the new depreciation guidelines and the investment tax credit. (For details of these changes, see Appendix A.)

Evidence to date clearly indicates that these measures are already stimulating some capital spending that would not otherwise have taken place. The impact of the 1962 actions and the 1963 proposals to reduce taxes on business will, of course, differ from company to company and industry to industry, depending in part on the adequacy of their internal funds and their levels of capacity utilization. Though the speed of response may vary, industry after industry will begin to feel pressure on its capital facilities and funds as markets for its products are expanded by the 1963 tax program.

Furthermore, there are many individual companies for which the supply of internal funds is a constraint on investment, and many others that do not have excess capacity. Moreover, it is estimated that some 70 percent of the investment in plant and equipment is for modernization and replacement rather than expansion, that is, it is designed to produce new or better products, or to reduce production costs rather than primarily to expand productive capacity. For this large segment of capital spending, the stronger inducement to invest provided by the business tax changes already adopted and those now proposed will translate much more readily into actual purchases of plant and equipment.

As production expands and existing capacity is more fully utilized, the depreciation guidelines and the investment tax credit and the new business tax reductions will provide an even stronger stimulus to investment.

Cumulative expansion: the consumption multiplier

Tax reduction will start a process of cumulative expansion throughout the economy. If the economy is already undergoing slow expansion, this cumulative process will be superimposed upon it. The initial increases in spending will stimulate production and employment, generating additional incomes. The details and timing of this process will vary from industry to industry. The first impact may be to draw down inventories rather than to expand production. But as inventories are depleted, retailers will quickly expand orders. As manufacturers' sales rise in response and their own inventories of finished goods decline, they will activate idle production lines, hire additional workers, place orders for materials and components. Thus the expansion will spread to other industries, leading to further expansion of production, employment, and orders.

Expanded sales mean increased profits. Increased employment means greater wage and salary income. Each additional dollar's worth of gross production necessarily generates a dollar of additional gross income.

But expansion does not proceed without limit. A considerable fraction of the value of gross production is shared with governments or becomes part of corporate retained earnings and does not become part of consumers' after-tax income. Some of the increase goes to pay additional excise and other indirect business taxes. Typically, when GNP is rising toward potential, corporate profits increase by about one-fourth of the rise in GNP. But a substantial part of this increase in profits is absorbed by Federal and State corporate income taxes, and another part is ordinarily retained by the corporations. Only the remainder is passed on to the households in dividend payments. Part of the additional wage and salary incomes associated with added production is absorbed by higher social security contributions. At the same time, increased employment means a drop in payments for unemployment insurance benefits.

When all of these "leakages" are taken into account, a little less than two-thirds of an additional dollar of GNP finds its way into the before-tax incomes of consumers in the form of wages, dividends, and other incomes.

Part is absorbed by personal taxes, Federal, State, and local. The increase in personal disposable income is 50 to 55 percent. Of this amount a small fraction—about 7 percent—is set aside in personal saving, and the remainder—about 93 percent—is spent on consumption, as indicated earlier. Thus, out of each additional dollar of GNP, initially generated by the tax cut, roughly half ends up as added consumption expenditure. But the process does not stop here.

The additional expenditure on consumption that is brought about by the rise in GNP generates, in its turn, further production, which generates additional incomes and consumption, and so on, in a continuous sequence of expansion which economists call the "multiplier process." The "multiplier" applicable to the initial increase in spending resulting from tax reduction, with account taken of the various leakages discussed above, works out to roughly 2. If we apply this multiplier only to the initial increase in consumption (about $8 billion), the total ultimate effect will be an increase in annual consumption—and in production (and GNP)—of roughly $16 billion. Lags in the process of expansion will spread this increase in GNP over time, but studies of the relationships between changes in disposable income, consumption, and production of consumer goods suggest that at least half of the total stimulus of an initial increase in disposable income is realized within 6 months of that increase.

Cumulative expansion: the investment response

Tax reduction will also have important cumulative indirect effects on investment in inventories and in fixed productive facilities. These effects are much more difficult to predict than the induced effects on consumption.

Inventory investment. The stocks of goods that businessmen wish to hold depend upon current and expected rates of sales and production and the volume of new and unfilled orders, as well as on price expectations and other factors. An expansion of aggregate demand can be expected to raise business inventory targets. Production for inventory will generate further increases in demand and income over and above the multiplier effects discussed above, and will in turn induce further increases in consumption spending.

Inventory investment is volatile, and induced inventory accumulation can add significantly to the expansionary effects of tax reduction within a few months. At the same time, it should be recognized that inventory investment is exceedingly difficult to forecast. As the increase in production and sales tapers off, stocks and the rate of inventory investment will be correspondingly adjusted.

Business investment in plant and equipment. A tax reduction large enough to move the economy toward full employment will also stimulate business investment in plant and equipment. General economic expansion will reinforce the initial stimulus to investment of cuts in business taxes. In the first place, narrowing the gap between actual and potential output—now estimated at $30–40 billion—will increase the utilization of existing plant and equipment. As excess capacity declines, more and more businesses will feel increasing pressure to expand capacity. At the same time, increases in the volume of sales and in productivity will raise corporate profits—in absolute terms, relative to GNP, and as a rate of return on investment. Internal funds available for investment will rise, while at the same time higher rates of return on existing capital will cause businessmen to raise their estimates of returns on new investment. When investment incentives are strengthened by rising demand, internal funds are more consistently translated into increased investment than when markets are slack.

Residential construction. The demand for housing depends on growth in the number of families, on the existing stock of houses, and on the cost and availability of mortgage credit. But housing demand also responds, to some extent, to changes in disposable income. Thus, tax reduction will have some direct effect on residential construction. And as production, employment, and income generally expand, the demand for new homes can be expected to increase further. This increase will, in turn, reinforce the other expansionary effects of tax reduction.

State and local government expenditures

State and local government units have found it difficult to finance the needed expansion of their activities. Given the present importance of income and sales taxes in State and local tax systems, government revenues at the State and local level expand automatically as GNP rises. The additional State-local revenues generated by economic expansion will assist these governments to meet their pressing needs. Moreover, since Federal tax liabilities are deductible under many State income tax laws, reduction in Federal tax rates will automatically generate some further addition to State-local tax revenues. Finally, a reduction in Federal taxes will enlarge the tax base available to State and local government units and may make it easier for them to raise rates or impose new taxes.

Undoubtedly, some of the added State-local tax revenues will be used either to retire existing debt or to reduce current borrowing rather than to increase expenditures. Whether the net result will be expansionary will depend upon whether the proportion of additional tax revenues spent on goods and services by State and local government units is greater or smaller than the proportion which would have been spent by the taxpayers from whom they collect the additional taxes. But whether or not the response of State and local government units is such as to strengthen the aggregate impact of Federal tax reduction on income and employment, the Federal tax program will ease, to some extent, the problems of these units in obtaining revenues needed to finance urgent public activities, such as education, transportation facilities, and urban development.

Summary of effects on GNP

Tax reductions for consumers will have initial direct effects on the demand for goods and services, as consumers raise their spending level to reflect their higher after-tax incomes. Corporate tax reductions and the lower tax rates applicable to the highest personal income brackets will stimulate investment directly, through raising the rate of return on new investments and providing additional funds for their financing. Some of the tax reforms will also have a directly stimulating effect on productive investment.

These direct or initial effects on spending would occur even if total output, employment, and incomes remained unchanged. But the increased spending cannot fail to increase total output, employment, and incomes. And as activity responds to the initially increased level of spending, cumulative impacts begin to develop in which the several elements interact to carry the expansion far beyond its initial point.

The higher incomes which consumers receive from the added production of both consumer and capital goods will lead to a further step-up in the rate of spending, creating further increases in incomes and spending. The same expansion process raises rates of capacity utilization, thereby interacting with the initial impact of tax reduction on business incomes to make investment both for modernization and expansion more profitable. This in turn generates higher consumer incomes and more spending, helping to provide the added demand which justifies the higher investment.

If there were no investment stimulus—either initially, or as a result of the cumulative process of expansion—we could expect that GNP would ultimately expand by about $16 billion. If the result were no more than this, the tax reduction would still be abundantly rewarding in terms of greater production, employment, purchasing power, and profits. What will really be given up to produce added output will be only unwanted idleness of workers (whose families have reduced neither their needs nor aspirations) and incomplete utilization of plant and machinery (which have continued to depreciate).

But the pay-off is much more than this purely consumption impact. There is also an investment impact, and each extra dollar of investment that is stimulated should bring roughly another dollar of added consumption and encourage still further investment.

A strong expansion can alter profoundly the whole climate within which investment decisions are made. If not at once, then somewhat later, subtle but significant changes in business attitudes occur in response to the trend in the economic outcome. We have referred earlier to the cautious investment attitudes that more than 5 years of slack markets have generated. This caution did not arise at once in mid-1957, when output first began to fall away from the track of potential expansion. It developed gradually, fed on itself, and in part helped to justify itself. The reverse can and will happen.

No one can pretend to estimate with precision the ultimate impact of a program so far-reaching as that which the President will propose: it would come into operation in stages extending from July 1, 1963 to January 1, 1965, and its effects would cumulate and spread into 1966 and beyond.

Our study of the program, and our tentative projections based upon it do, however, convince us that the program measures up to the challenge that the 1960's present to our economy: that it will surely set us on a path toward our interim employment target; and that it will lay the foundation for more rapid long-run growth.

The Effectiveness of Temporary Changes in the Federal Personal Income Tax

Janice D. Halpern

IN the past ten years, temporary changes in the Federal personal income tax have been considered frequently and used twice in attempts to smooth cyclical fluctuations in the economy. The rationale underlying the first episode, the 1968 income tax surcharge, was that the decrease in disposable income generated by the increase in individuals' tax obligations would force consumers to reduce their spending and alleviate the inflationary pressures caused by excess demand. The opposite rationale justified the second episode, the 1975 tax rebate. It was hoped that most of the rebate checks would be spent on consumer goods and that the increased demand would stimulate employment.

The extent to which such temporary changes in individuals' tax obligations can affect economic activity has been the subject of considerable controversy. Most economists agree that a strict interpretation of the most widely accepted theory of consumption behavior, the permanent income hypothesis, implies that explicitly temporary changes in the personal income tax have only a small effect on consumption. Nonetheless, many of these same people argue that in fact the 1968 surcharge and the 1975 rebate did affect customers' expenditures sufficiently to be considered a useful tool for stabilizing the economy.

This paper examines the controversy on the effectiveness of temporary changes in the personal income tax in influencing consumer expenditures.[1] Part I describes the permanent income and life-cycle theories of consumption and their implications concerning the ability of explicitly temporary tax changes to influence consumption. Part II considers several reasons why, despite the general applicability of the permanent income hypothesis, temporary tax changes may still have the desired impact in stimulating or restraining the economy. The evidence gathered to assess the impact of the 1968 sur-

charge and the 1975 tax rebate is reviewed in Part III. Part IV concludes that neither the 1968 surcharge nor the 1975 rebate has been shown to have had a sufficiently large or immediate impact to warrant relying on policies of this magnitude to alleviate ordinary cyclical fluctuations. However, policies that resulted in large changes in individuals' incomes might be useful at a time, such as a major war or depression, when a large adjustment in aggregate demand was needed.

I. Determinants of Consumer Expenditure

Economists agree that current income is an important variable in explaining an individual's consumption expenditures. However, since the early 1950s other factors have been increasingly recognized as having an influence on consumers' allocation of their disposable income between consumption and saving. The basis of the consumption sectors of almost all the large macroeconometric models used in forecasting today is either the life-cycle or the permanent income hypothesis of consumer behavior. Both theories contend that consumption decisions are based on the total resources available to an individual over his lifetime, not just his current income. According to the life-cycle hypothesis, initially developed by Ando and Modigliani, each consumer determines the lifetime consumption path based on his total available resources that will bring him the greatest satisfaction.[2] These resources include the present discounted value of his expected future income from his labor and assets as well as his current income. If this consumption plan calls for expenditure in some year that exceeds his income, he will draw down his savings or borrow in order to finance it. The purpose of savings, then, is "to enable the household to redistribute the resources it gets (and expects to get) over its life-cycle in order to secure the most desirable pattern of consumption over life."[3]

A related aspect of this view of consumption behavior which has similar implications is the permanent income hypothesis (PIH) developed by Milton Friedman.[4] This theory contends that an individual's income is composed of permanent and transitory components. The permanent component is income the consumer can expect to continue receiving in the future, while the transitory part, consisting of receipts like unexpected overtime and bonuses, is completely uncorrelated with future income. Consumers base their consumption expenditure only on the permanent component of their income, while saving almost all their transitory income.

Attempts have been made to test the permanent income hypothesis using data in which permanent and transitory income were thought to be clearly distinguished. In the 1950 U.S. Bureau of Labor Statistics Survey of Consumer Expenditures, income from an unexpected National Service Life Insurance dividend paid to some veterans of World War II was differentiated from all other income. The average size of this dividend was $175, or about 12 percent of 1950 average per capita disposable income.[5]

Several studies examined data from this 1950 survey to see how much of both dividend and regular income was spent for the consumption of nondurables and the purchase of consumer durables. Table 1 shows the average percentages of 1950 transitory (dividend) and permanent incomes spent on various consumer items, as estimated by three studies. Although these three authors' results are not strictly comparable, there is a fairly strong consensus that a significant portion of the windfall life insurance income was spent for consumption and consumer durables. In fact, two studies by Bodkin and Jones found that a larger fraction of this windfall income than of regular income was spent on both durable and nondurable goods. The third found that a lower, although still considerable, portion of windfall income was spent on current consumption, but that all the windfall income gain went into some form of consumer expenditure. In addition, receipt of this windfall may have stimulated additional spending, since this study shows that more than 100 percent of the windfall was spent. Neither Bodkin's nor Jones's results are consistent with the permanent income hypothesis, since they find that at least as much of the windfall as of regular income was spent on nondurable con-

sumption. Reid's results are less damaging to the PIH, but by showing that a large fraction of windfall income was spent on durables, she also lends support to the belief that a transitory increase in income will be spent.

Thus, these studies of windfall gains suggest that, contrary to what would be expected from the PIH, this transitory increase in income was largely spent. This suggests that if consumers treat the income generated by a temporary tax cut as a windfall gain, they will spend about the same proportion of it as they would of increases in their permanent income, and so "even a temporary tax cut would be effective in alleviating some of the hardships of a recession."[6]

One shortcoming of these studies is that they assumed than an individual's entire 1950 income except for the dividend was permanent, while much of it in fact may have been transitory. In addition, an individual with changing income may not be certain how much of an income increase or decrease experienced in any period is transitory. Thus, it can be argued that because this literature did not embody an accurate formulation of permanent income, it cannot be used to reject the PIH. Current consumption models, especially those using aggregate time-

TABLE 1
Percentage of Transitory and Permanent Income Spent on Various Components of Consumer Expenditure, Three Studies

Author	Consumer Expenditure Category	Percentage of Permanent Income Spent	Percentage of Transitory Income Spent
Bodkin	C	75	97
	C'	56	72
Jones	F	14	25
	H	7	9
	K	10	11
Reid	C_{fa}	10	62
	C_0	83	58

C = consumption including purchase of consumer durables
C' = consumption excluding purchase of consumer durables
F = food expenditure
H = housing expenditure
K = clothing expenditure
C_{fa} = furniture and automobile expenditure
C_0 = all other consumer expenditure

SOURCES: Ronald Bodkin, "Windfall Income and Consumption," *American Economic Review*, September 1959, p. 602; Robert C. Jones, "Transitory Income and Expenditures on Consumption Categories," *American Economic Review, Papers and Proceedings*, May 1960, p. 584; and Margaret G. Reid, "Consumption, Savings and Windfall Gains: Reply," *American Economic Review*, June 1963, p. 444.

series data, have represented permanent income as a function of current and several past years' actual disposable income. This implies that an individual averages out yearly fluctuations to discover any trend in his income that might help him predict his income in future years. (All the studies discussed in Part III rely on this kind of specification.)

Even this formulation, however, may be too simple to correctly represent the way consumers estimate their permanent income since it assumes all changes in disposable income have the same impact on permanent or expected future income. In fact, changes in disposable income caused by changes in taxes may have a very different impact on an individual's permanent income estimate than changes in pre-tax earnings. Since a permanent reduction in taxes will increase disposable income in the year in which it is effective and in all subsequent years, its effect will eventually be translated into an equal increase in permanent income even if an individual takes account of income received in several past years in estimating his permanent income.[7] However, if consumers believe a tax change to be temporary from the beginning, it may be heavily discounted in their calculations of permanent income. While some impact might be expected since total lifetime resources will be slightly higher or lower than without the tax change, the impact should be small.[8]

II. Qualifications of the Permanent Income Hypothesis

Even if, as most people believe, the permanent income or life-cycle hypothesis correctly explains consumption decisions, several reasons still exist why temporary tax changes can be expected to be effective in stimulating or restraining consumer expenditures. Some of these factors may also help explain why the windfall studies previously discussed showed that so much of the life insurance dividend was spent for consumer goods.

The most important reason to expect some impact from a temporary tax change is that the life-cycle and permanent income hypotheses are designed only to explain the purchase of non-durable goods and services and the flow of services (or use) from durable goods. The purchase of durable goods is an investment decision, made on the basis of many of the same factors that affect an individual's decision to buy stocks or real property. However, while income spent on consumer durables is, by definition, income that

is saved, it has an impact on the economy similar to that of income spent to purchase food or clothing. Thus, if most of a tax rebate were "saved" through investment in consumer durables, it would stimulate the economy significantly. Likewise, if a surcharge led to a significant reduction in the purchase of durable goods, aggregate demand could be sufficiently restrained to ease inflationary pressures.

III. Evidence from 1968 and 1975

As can be seen from the preceding discussion, theory alone cannot resolve the debate over the impact of temporary tax changes. Resolution of this controversy thus depends on an examination of the data that have been collected on the state of the economy before and after the imposition of the 1968 surcharge and the 1975 rebate.

The 1968 Surcharge

In 1968 a temporary income tax surcharge was enacted in an attempt to reduce demand in an economy overheated because of large deficit-financed expenditures for the Vietnam War. Between the middle of 1965 and the end of 1967, a $25 billion rise in defense spending combined with a $23 billion expansion of civilian programs caused Federal expenditures to far exceed tax revenues. As a result, Federal budgetary policy during this period was extremely expansionary. The rate of inflation accelerated considerably, while the unemployment rate dropped from 4.5 percent in 1965 to 3.8 percent in 1966 and 1967, the lowest rate since 1948.

The 1968 temporary income tax surcharge was proposed because "in [the] absence of fiscal restraint. . . the economy would be subject to serious inflationary pressures, or serious financial stringency."[11] It was hoped that an increase in tax liabilities would reduce consumer demand and at least decelerate the rate of inflation. The law provided for a 10 percent surcharge on Federal corporate income taxes retroactive to January 1, 1968, and a 10 percent personal income tax surcharge retroactive to April 1, 1968. Table 2 presents estimates of the impact of the surcharge on Federal personal income tax payments. Tax payments increased sharply in the first two quarters of 1969 because the surcharge was retroactive to 1968. This led to an increase in final tax payments to compensate for underwithholding in 1968.

TABLE 2
Tax Payments Resulting from the Tax Surcharge, 1968–1970
(billions of dollars, seasonally adjusted annual rate)

	Personal Tax Payments		
Year and quarter	Current dollars	1958 dollars	As a percentage of disposable income
1968:3	6.1	5.1	1.0
1968:4	7.1	5.9	1.2
1969:1	10.7	8.8	1.8
1969:2	10.9	8.9	1.8
1969:3	7.1	5.7	1.1
1969:4	7.3	5.8	1.1
1970:1	5.0	3.9	.8
1970:2	5.0	3.9	.7
1970:3	0.4	0.3	(a)

(a) less than 0.5 percent.

SOURCE: Arthur M. Okun, "The Personal Tax Surcharge and Consumer Demand, 1968–70," *Brookings Papers on Economic Activity,* 1:1971, p. 171.

TABLE 4
Percentage Change from Preceding Period in Selected Economic Variables and the Savings Rate, 1968:1–1970:2 (annual rates)

Year and Quarter	GNP in 1958 dollars	Disposable Income in 1958 dollars	Personal Consumption Expenditures in 1958 dollars	Savings Rate
1968:1	13.0	7.1	10.0	7.1
1968:2	7.0	5.1	8.3	7.6
1968:3	4.7	2.1	11.1	6.1
1968:4	1.1	2.2	5.3	6.5
1969:1	3.8	0.6	6.4	5.6
1969:2	1.8	2.2	6.8	5.3
1969:3	1.4	6.6	6.7	6.5
1969:4	−2.2	1.5	7.1	6.3
1970:1	−1.5	3.9	8.8	6.7
1970:2	0.2	7.0	5.3	6.5

SOURCE: Author's calculations from data in *The Economic Report of the President,* various years.

Table 3 shows the distribution of total personal income from 1967 to 1970 among consumer outlays (consumption, interest payments and transfers to foreigners), savings, and tax and nontax payments. Between the first quarter of 1968 and the end of 1969, the percentage of personal income paid in taxes rose by 1.9 points, while consumption and savings fell by 1.2 and 0.6 percentage points, respectively. Moreover, as Table 4 shows, the savings rate dropped dramatically from 7.1 to 6.3 percent during this period. A quick look at the data, therefore, suggests that most of the surcharge revenues came out of savings, as the permanent income hypothesis predicts.

The economy during this period did not manifest any overwhelming improvement. Real GNP growth slowed, but instead of slowing consumer expenditures grew more quickly in 1968 and 1969 than in 1967 and became an increasingly large fraction of disposable income. In addition, the surcharge did not reduce the rate of increase in consumer prices, which rose from 3.0 percent in 1967 to 4.7 percent in 1968 and 6.1 percent in 1969 before slowing to 5.5 percent in 1970, the year the surcharge finally expired.

TABLE 3
Percentage of Total Personal Income Distributed among Personal Outlays, Personal Savings, and Personal Tax and Nontax Payments, 1967:1–1970:4

	Personal Outlays	Personal Savings	Personal Tax and Nontax Payments
1967:1	80.5	6.4	13.2
1967:2	81.0	6.0	13.0
1967:3	80.3	6.5	13.2
1967:4	79.9	6.7	13.4
1968:1	80.4	6.2	13.4
1968:2	79.8	6.5	13.6
1968:3	80.2	5.1	14.7
1968:4	79.7	5.2	15.0
1969:1	79.9	4.5	15.6
1969:2	79.7	4.5	15.8
1969:3	79.1	5.6	15.3
1969:4	79.2	5.6	15.3
1970:1	79.2	5.9	14.9
1970:2	78.6	6.7	14.7
1970:3	78.9	7.1	14.0
1970:4	78.7	7.2	14.1

SOURCE: *Survey of Current Business, Business Statistics 1971*, p. 7.

The 1975 Rebate

Even though considerable doubt existed as to whether the 1968 surcharge had been effective, the recessionary conditions of 1974 led Congress to legislate a temporary tax reduction in an attempt to stimulate the economy. The Tax Reduction Act of 1975 consisted of a one-time rebate of $8 billion paid out in the second quarter of 1975 and a $12 billion reduction in tax withholding at an annual rate beginning in May. Although the second part of the tax program was legislated as temporary, it was generally expected to become permanent and was in fact reenacted at the end of the year. The rebate was enacted to provide a quick stimulus to an economy in which real GNP had fallen by 6.6 percent between the fourth quarter of 1973 and the first quarter of 1975. The rebate provided approximately a 3 percent increase in disposable income in the second quarter of 1975, or a 0.7 percent increase in annual 1975 income.

As shown in Table 5, the economy showed considerable improvement beginning in the second quarter of 1975. Real GNP increased substantially throughout 1975 and 1976, as did real consumption expenditures and disposable income. The savings rate rose in the rebate quarter and averaged a fairly high 7.4 percent for the year.

Studies by Juster, Modigliani and Steindel, and Blinder have attempted to evaluate the effectiveness of the 1975 tax cut in stimulating expenditures.[14] Juster's examination of the response of personal savings to the tax rebate showed no evidence that savings rose more in the quarters after the rebate checks were received than would have been predicted if no rebate had been voted. Thus, he concluded that the extra income must have been used for consumption. Modigliani and Steindel found that the rebate had a positive impact on consumption but that the impact was quite slow. They concluded, however, that because of the imprecision of their estimates "one cannot reasonably reject the hypothesis either that by the end of the first year the proportion spent was negligible, or that it was nearly as large as the rebate."[15] Blinder constructed a complicated model of consumer expenditure which was based on the PIH but which distinguished income collected through temporary taxes from other income. While he was unable to obtain precise estimates of the impact of temporary taxes, his results suggested that in the first year a rebate, such as that of 1975, would be 10 to 50 percent as effective as a permanent tax cut of the same magnitude, while a two-year change in rates would be 20 to 60 percent as effective. Like Modigliani and Steindel, however, he found that much of the impact of the 1975 rebate came in the second year, with peak effects coming in the fourth quarter of 1976 and the first quarter of 1977.

None of these studies is definitive and none is above criticism on either theoretical or methodological grounds.

IV. Conclusion

Economists are far from unanimous as to the usefulness of temporary personal income tax changes in stabilizing the economy. Proponents argue that such policies can moderate cyclical fluctuations by stimulating or restraining consumer purchases for the brief period necessary to get the economy back on its steady growth path. Since no permanent adjustment in the level of government expenditures or revenues is desired, a permanent reduction in taxes is unwarranted. Opponents argue, however, that the explicitly temporary changes in disposable income resulting from temporary tax changes will have no effect on consumption since consumption expenditures are determined primarily by per-

TABLE 5
Percentage Change from Preceding Period in Selected Economic Variables and the Savings Rate, 1974–1977:2 (annual rates)

Year and Quarter	GNP in 1972 dollars	Disposable Income in 1972 dollars	Personal Consumption Expenditures in 1972 dollars	Savings Rate
1974	−1.4	1.8	−0.9	7.3
1975:1	−9.6	−2.5	4.7	6.4
1975:2	6.4	20.4	7.1	9.4
1975:3	11.4	−5.5	5.1	7.0
1975:4	3.0	5.2	6.5	6.7
1976:1	8.8	5.2	7.3	6.3
1976:2	5.1	2.9	4.1	6.0
1976:3	3.9	1.3	3.5	5.4
1976:4	1.2	4.9	8.3	4.6
1977:1	7.3	3.1	5.0	4.1
1977:2	6.0	7.1	1.7	5.3

SOURCE: Author's calculations from data in *The Economic Report of the President*, 1976–1978.

manent income which is not affected by temporary changes in income tax liabilities.

Several reasons have been suggested to explain why policies such as the 1968 income tax surcharge and 1975 tax rebate might be expected to have the desired impact on the economy, even though the permanent income hypothesis correctly describes consumer behavior. Consumers may mistake temporary changes for permanent ones, or may simply ignore small changes in their income. Credit constraints on a large proportion of consumers, or their decisions to spend most of an unexpected income gain on investment in consumer durables, could also cause temporary adjustments in disposable income to have a significant impact on the economy.

A group of studies that tried to test the permanent income hypothesis by examining consumers' expenditures out of an unexpected life insurance dividend indirectly supported the position of those who advocate the effectiveness of temporary tax changes. These windfall studies showed that a large portion of the dividend was spent on both durable and nondurable goods. One should, however, be careful about generalizing from these particular studies. For one thing, they all examined the same example of transitory income, the 1950 life insurance dividend, and unquantifiable variables (such as pent-up demand from World War II) may have affected individuals' propensities to spend out of this dividend. Studies of Israeli data showed that only about 17 percent of unanticipated West German restitution payments was spent. It has been suggested that since the average restitution payment was much larger than the average dividend, these results may be reconciled through the proposition that the propensity to spend out of windfall income declines as the size of the windfall increases.[16] Since the 1975 rebate was even smaller than the average life insurance dividend, this implies that a large part of it would be spent. However, an economy-wide tax rebate plan, widely promoted in advance as a policy to increase consumption to fight a recession, may have a different impact from a windfall benefit received with no expectation as to whether it will be saved or spent.

Observers of the economy after the 1968 surcharge was levied found little indication that it was effective. The principal variable it was meant to affect, the inflation rate, continued to increase until 1970, as did real consumer expenditures. Two studies that examined the surcharge more closely estimated that its impact was at most half as large as that which might have been expected from a permanent tax increase. A cursory examination of the economy after the 1975 tax rebate suggested that it was more successful in affecting economic activity since real GNP began to grow rapidly. However, the saving rate also rose, and two studies of the rebate's effectiveness found that while its impact was significant, it was quite slow. This suggests that rebate checks originally were saved and then spent slowly during the next six quarters, and that the rapid increase in real GNP that occurred in the middle of 1975 would probably have happened even without the rebate. Survey data collected during this period showed that between February and May of 1975, consumer confidence in the economy increased dramatically.[17] Juster found that an increase in consumer confidence significantly reduces savings and increases consumption.[18] This suggests that the rebate's principal impact may have been in boosting consumer confidence and thereby stimulating consumer spending.

Thus, our experience with these two temporary tax policies shows that policies of this magnitude can be expected to have at most half and perhaps as little as one-tenth as great an effect on consumer expenditure as equivalent permanent tax policies. Both the surcharge and the rebate, however, caused very small changes in disposable income. The surcharge never reduced disposable income more than 2 percent in any quarter, while the rebate amounted to a 3 percent increase in disposable income for the second quarter of 1975. Policies leading to larger changes in disposable income might be expected to have a much more significant impact on consumers, especially since credit constraints would become binding on an increasing portion of the population as the income loss caused by a tax increase became larger. Reducing consumers' incomes substantially in order to alleviate a moderate inflation is unlikely to be politically feasible. However, under extraordinary circumstances, such as a war, when public opinion is more favorable to making collective sacrifices, a large temporary increase in Federal personal income taxes might be an extremely effective restraint on consumer spending. Similarly, during a severe depression when consumers have exhausted most of their savings, a large rebate might provide a considerable stimulus to consumer spending.

---

*Research Associate, Federal Reserve Bank of Boston. The author would like to thank Alicia Munnell and Stephen McNees for their helpful comments, and Joan Poskanzer for her editorial assistance.

[1] The larger question of whether a change in consumer expenditure can successfully moderate cyclical fluctuations in the economy is not considered.

[2] A. Ando and F. Modigliani, "The 'Life-Cycle' Hypothesis of Saving: Aggregate Implications and Tests," *American Economic Review,* Vol. 53, No. 1 (March 1963), pp. 55–84.

[3] F. Modigliani, "Savings Behavior: A Symposium," *Bulletin of the Oxford Institute of Statistics,* Vol. 19 (May 1957), p. 105.

[4] Milton Friedman, A *Theory of the Consumption Function,* (Princeton: National Bureau of Economic Research, 1957.)

[5] The dividend is similar to an income tax rebate in that it was explicitly a one-time occurrence, was delivered in the form of a single payment (rather than reduced withholding), and was received only a short time after it was announced.

[6] Ronald Bodkin, "Windfall Income and Consumption," *American Economic Review,* September 1959, p. 614.

[7] Those who criticize the effectiveness of a permanent tax cut contend that if government expenditures are maintained at the same level and financed by floating bonds, interest rates will rise and as a result, investment expenditure will be cut back, leaving total demand exactly where it was before.

[8] If a consumer plans to spend an equal amount in every year of his life and inflation and the real rate of interest are zero, a $50 per person rebate should lead to increased annual consumption of $50/N where N equals the number of years between the rebate's issue and an individual's death. For the economy as a whole, it has been estimated that if the pure version of the PIH holds, between 4 and 10 percent of the revenue collected through the 1968 surcharge would come out of consumption.

[10] James S. Duesenberry, *Income, Saving, and the Theory of Consumer Behavior,* (Cambridge, Mass.: Harvard University Press, 1949.)

[11] *1968 Economic Report of the President,* (Washington, D.C.: Government Printing Office, 1968) p. 82.

[13] See Alan S. Blinder and Robert M. Solow, "Analytical Foundations of Fiscal Policy," p. 108, in Alan S. Blinder, *et al, The Economics of Public Finance,* (Washington, D.C.: The Brookings Institution, 1974.)

[14] F. Thomas Juster, "A Note on Prospective 1977 Tax-Cuts and Consumer Spending," (University of Michigan Institute for Social Research: Processed), January 1977; Franco Modigliani and Charles Steindel, "Is a Tax Rebate an Effective Tool for Stabilization Policy?" *Brookings Papers on Economic Activity* 1:1977, pp. 175–209; and Alan S. Blinder, "Temporary Taxes and Consumer Spending," National Bureau of Economic Research, Working Paper No. 283, October 1978. A fuller description of the methodology and results of these three studies is presented in the Technical Supplement.

[15] Modigliani and Steindel, *"Is a Tax Rebate an Effective Tool?",* p. 199. Modigliani and Steindel also apply their analysis to the 1968 surcharge and conclude that it was about half as effective in curbing consumption as a permanent tax increase would have been.

[16] See Michael Landsberger, "Windfall Income and Consumption: Comment," *American Economic Review,* June 1966, pp. 534–39.

[17] Richard T. Curtin, ed., *Surveys of Consumers 1974–75,* (University of Michigan, Institute for Social Research, 1976) p. 214.

[18] Juster, "Tax Cuts and Consumer Spending."

Fiscal Policy

Council of Economic Advisers

The spending and revenue activities of the government comprise its fiscal policy. In fiscal 1989 (October 1988 to September 1989) total outlays of the Federal Government for purchases of goods and services, transfer payments, grants, and interest payments amounted to 22.2 percent of gross national product (GNP). Tax and other receipts were 19.2 percent of GNP, with a resulting budget deficit of 2.9 percent of GNP. Receipts were the same fraction of GNP in 1989 as they were 10 years before, but outlays were up by 1.6 percent of GNP over the same period. The sheer size of the Federal sector suggests that fiscal policy can shape aggregate economic activity, for the better or worse. Focusing only on the impact of fiscal policy on the level of GNP, however, understates the importance of fiscal policy.

THE IMPACT OF THE INSTRUMENTS OF FISCAL POLICY

Fiscal policy affects the economy in several ways. Government purchases of goods and services are a direct use of the productive resources of the economy, and change prices, profits, and the allocation of capital and labor. Taxes, transfer payments, borrowing, and interest payments shift funds among individuals and over time, and thereby alter incentives for work, saving, and investment. For example, income-support programs affect both the distribution of purchasing power and incentives to work. In some circumstances—for example, by reducing barriers to saving—this power of fiscal policy can improve economic performance. But poorly designed policies, such as a tax system with high marginal rates, reduce incentives for productive activity and lower the growth of national income.

In the short run, changes in government spending and revenues can significantly affect total output in the economy. For instance, increases in Federal consumption of goods and services directly boost the demand for firms' output. In the short run, firms meet this demand by producing more. But because government purchases do not increase the total productive resources in the economy, the increase will eventually diminish. After a period of time, prices begin to increase or increase more rapidly. Higher interest rates reduce domestic demand, and purchases by the private sector fall. The reduction in private purchases will occur primarily in interest-sensitive areas such as investment, and some types of investment may suffer more than others. As interest rates rise, exchange

58

rates also rise, reducing demand for exports and raising demand for imports. The effects of the increase in government purchases are offset by the decline in investment and net exports. Over the longer term, the decline in investment in turn reduces the productive potential of the economy.

Conversely, decreases in government spending can slow growth of total demand in the short run. For example, a reduction in government spending lowers the demand for goods and services. But again, this decline is short-lived. Soon investment and net exports will increase, offsetting the reduction in government purchases, and in the long term the higher level of investment will increase potential GNP.

Short-run changes in taxes paid by households have effects similar to changes in government purchases. To the extent that households do not save the extra funds available after a tax cut, their increased spending boosts the demand for goods and services. These increases in demand will raise production by firms and increase overall employment. Again, in the absence of an increase in the productive capacity of the economy, these increases will be short-lived.

Permanent reductions in tax rates are far more likely to expand long-run productive capacity than is a one-time tax rebate or credit. Reducing the tax-induced distortion of decisions to work, save, innovate, and invest will raise the resources devoted to production in the economy, permanently expanding total output.

THE DESIGN OF FISCAL POLICY

It is tempting to use fiscal policy in a reactive fashion, employing frequent discretionary changes in taxes and spending to alter economic activity temporarily and to counteract each aggregate fluctuation. This approach is fraught with so many difficulties that discretionary fiscal policy becomes inconsistent with ambitious goals for long-run growth. Fiscal responses to economic fluctuations should be credible and predictable. These characteristics reduce the distortionary effects of policy by aiding private-sector plans for saving and investment.

Automatic Stabilizers

During recessions, income tax receipts fall, even though tax rates are unchanged. In addition, income assistance payments (such as unemployment benefits and traditional welfare programs) rise. These kinds of systematic adjustments are called "automatic stabilizers." They are an important example of systematic policy and contribute to the predictability of short-run fiscal policy. They are clearly not discretionary, as they are embodied in legislation. Automatic stabilizers help to maintain individuals' purchasing power and mitigate the decline in aggregate demand. Studies show that, on average, disposable income falls by 40 percent of a fall in GNP. Historically, modifications to the features of automatic stabilizers undertaken for other reasons have also changed their responsiveness to economic conditions.

Systematic fiscal policies such as automatic stabilizers have distinct advantages over discretionary policies. For example, discretionary increases in spending provide a ready rationale for politically motivated increases in government programs. Also, because investors cannot undo the past, it may appear that discretionary tax increases levied on existing investments have no detrimental effect. Over time, however, continuous application of such policies would teach investors to expect tax increases, reducing the incentive to invest and harming economic efficiency.

Budgeting Rules and Targets for Government Saving

Sustained economic growth requires continued increases in the Nation's productive capital. Government policies, such as fiscal, monetary, regulatory, and legal policies, affect national saving and are thus an important determinant of both the funds available to finance investment and their cost.

By definition, when the Federal Government budget deficit increases, government saving falls. Only if other savers—households or businesses—increase their saving dollar for dollar is there no detrimental effect on national saving—the sum of household, business, and government saving. Empirical studies find that when government reduces tax collections, increased private saving does not fully offset the decline in government saving. When government consumption increases, private investment and net exports decline; private consumption may fall, but not sufficiently to offset the rise in government consumption. Thus, chronic budget deficits reduce national saving, leading to lower domestic capital formation and reduced net exports.

The actual deficit is influenced by current economic conditions. For example, the budget deficit increased during the early 1980s in part as a result of the economic downturn. Accurately gauging the long-run impact of the deficit requires adjusting the deficit for changes caused by economic fluctuations. (This adjustment is made by calculating the difference between receipts and expenditures that would occur under current law if economic activity were equal to some estimate of the economy's high-employment potential.) At the trough of the most recent recession, the cyclical component was about two-thirds of the actual budget deficit. In the last few years, however, the economy has been closer to its potential output, making the cyclical correction less important. Nonetheless, the deficit as a fraction of GNP has fallen from 5.3 percent in fiscal 1986 to 2.9 percent in fiscal 1989 (Chart 3-1).

In 1985, the Federal Government adopted, and in 1987 amended, the Balanced Budget and Emergency Deficit Control Act, more commonly known as Gramm-Rudman-Hollings (GRH). GRH was a visible response to the record of deficit spending. At its heart are targets for the maximum allowable budget deficit, with the ultimate goal, as amended, of balancing the budget by 1993. GRH includes a mechanical procedure, known as sequester, for cutting Federal spending whenever deficits are expected to exceed the allowable target by more than $10 billion, except in fiscal 1993. (See Box 3-1 for an explanation of the sequester in fiscal 1990.) GRH provides a predictable means to reduce Federal deficits, thus serving as a valuable rule for fiscal policy that reduces Federal borrowing.

In each year since the inception of GRH, the Federal deficit has exceeded the GRH target (Table 3-1). How can this happen? The most important reason is that a sequester can be implemented, if necessary, only in the first 2 weeks of a fiscal year. Thus, the GRH deficit can initially fall below the target, but rise later in the year through appropriations for new spending. For example, the fiscal 1989 budget deficit reflected the addition of large costs attributable

Chart 3-1

FEDERAL BUDGET DEFICIT AS PERCENT OF GNP. The budget deficit as a percent of GNP has declined substantially since 1986 as a result of deficit control measures.

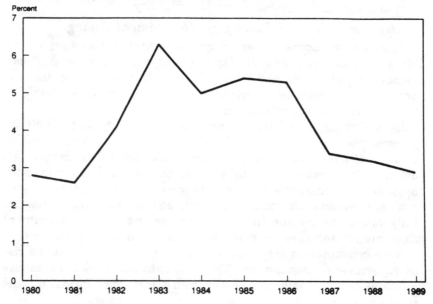

Percent

Note: Data are for fiscal years.
Source: Department of Commerce and Office of Management and Budget.

to the rescue plan for savings and loan institutions. In addition, some programs have been excluded from the deficit calculation so that the spending they entail does not count under GRH. Finally, the inherent difficulties of economic forecasting and technical budget projections can cause the actual deficit to differ from the GRH target, although there is no systematic direction to this effect.

When viewed from a broad perspective, GRH has provided valuable control over Federal spending. To some, the failure to match the targets exactly is an indictment of GRH. But this is a narrow view. A focus simply on the difference between GRH targets and annual budget deficits ignores important progress in controlling deficits. Since the adoption of GRH, the deficit has fallen steadily as a percentage of GNP. Moreover, deficits are far below the path projected prior to the adoption of GRH. One prominent study during 1985 projected that the unified deficit would reach $266 billion during fiscal 1989, more than $100 billion above the actual deficit. Further, the rate of Federal debt accumulation has stabilized—Federal debt held by the public rose from 26.6 percent of GNP in 1980 to 42 percent in 1986, but has remained at about this level since.

These improvements partly reflect better control over outlays. GRH has limited the ability to consider new spending programs or expand existing ones. Since GRH, the annual growth rate of real Federal outlays has fallen from an average of 4.7 percent for 1984 and 1985 to an average of 1.7 percent for 1986 through 1989. Controlling growth in Federal outlays is one part of sustained deficit reduction, and GRH has contributed to this process.

Although GRH has provided valuable control over deficits, it can still be improved. Currently, deficit targets may be circumvented too easily late in the fiscal year. The Administration has enunci-

Box 3-1.—The GRH Process: How It Worked in Fiscal 1990

Under GRH, the Administration reviews the budget and estimates the deficit. GRH allows for a $10 billion cushion or "margin of error" (except in 1993, when there is no margin of error), but if the projected deficit exceeds the target by more than this amount, the Administration calculates automatic spending cuts (or sequester) needed in each program to meet the GRH deficit target. If legislation does not achieve this reduction by the end of the second week of the fiscal year, the President orders a sequester.

For fiscal 1990, the GRH deficit target was $100 billion. In October 1989, the Administration estimated a deficit of $116.1 billion—$6.1 billion above the target plus "cushion." Hence a sequester designed to reduce outlays by $16.1 billion was brought into operation, and the President stated that he would continue with a sequester until a satisfactory budget reconciliation bill was passed.

To meet the target, total outlays had to be reduced by 1.4 percent. GRH splits these reductions evenly between defense and nondefense spending, thus requiring an $8 billion reduction in each. However, 35.4 percent of defense outlays and 73.7 percent of nondefense outlays (largely entitlements and interest payments) are exempt by law from a sequester. To achieve the $8 billion reduction, nonexempt nondefense programs had to be cut by 5.3 percent and nonexempt defense programs by 4.3 percent.

Under the Reconciliation Act, the President issued a revised order that required a sequester of 1.5 percent for defense programs and 1.4 percent for nondefense programs. The revised sequester was designed to achieve outlay reductions equivalent to keeping the original sequester in effect until early February 1990. Hence, the Administration established the important precedent of not restoring previously sequestered amounts after the sequester period.

ated a principle that any increased spending after the sequester period has passed must be fully offset elsewhere in the budget. This principle serves to buttress GRH and improve the credibility of efforts to reduce Federal deficits. Reforms to the GRH law itself could further increase control over deficits initiated in this way. For example, introducing a second sequester period later in the fiscal year would maintain the discipline of automatic reductions for a longer time period. Alternatively, it may be useful to require 60-percent majorities of the House and Senate to pass any legislation that increases the deficit after the sequester period is over. A related measure is the Administration's proposal to give the President enhanced rescission authority—the power to cancel unnecessary appropriations. These cancellations would be subject to a vote by the Congress to override the rescission.

GRH could also be modified to eliminate the practice of using surpluses in the Social Security trust funds to offset the operating

TABLE 3-1.—*GRH and Budget Deficits: The Record*

[Billions of dollars]

Fiscal Year	1985 Target	1987 Target	Actual Deficit	Actual as Percent of GNP
1986	171.9	171.9	221.2	5.3
1987	144.0	144.0	149.7	3.4
1988	108.0	144.0	155.1	3.2
1989	72.0	136.0	152.0	2.9
1990	36.0	100.0	NA	NA
1991	.0	64.0	NA	NA
1992	.0	28.0	NA	NA
1993	.0	.0	NA	NA

Sources: Department of the Treasury and Office of Management and Budget.

budget deficit. In fiscal 1989 there was a unified budget deficit of $152.0 billion. Social Security, however, had a surplus of $52.4 billion, indicating that the non-Social Security activities of the government had a deficit of $204.4 billion. As discussed below, the Administration proposes amending GRH as part of a program to protect the Social Security surpluses and reverse chronic Federal deficit spending. Balancing the non-Social Security budget will require additional control over Federal outlays. In exercising that control, care must be taken to ensure adequate funding for programs that contribute to economic growth and meet essential national needs, such as research and development, education, and reductions of drug abuse.

The Importance of Eliminating Chronic Government Borrowing

The Gramm-Rudman-Hollings law has served as an important rule for reducing Federal borrowing. An improved rule for long-run fiscal policy would not only reduce deficits but would commit the Federal Government to annual budget surpluses after 1993.

Raising the rate of government saving will lower interest rates and increase capital formation and growth, leading to higher incomes. A credible policy of increased government saving would accelerate the reduction in interest rates and the increase in investment. By expanding U.S. economic resources, greater government saving will make it easier for society to meet the full range of private and government obligations. Increasing government saving will also reduce net interest payments, which constituted 14.8 percent of Federal outlays in fiscal 1989, thus freeing these resources to address other budgetary needs.

The Importance of
Balancing the Budget

Harry Flood Byrd

Wednesday, May 4, 1955

Mr. BYRD. Mr. President, I ask unanimous consent to have printed in the CONGRESSIONAL RECORD the text of a speech I made today before the annual meeting of the United States Chamber of Commerce, at the Statler Hotel, Washington, D. C.

There being no objection, the address was ordered to be printed in the RECORD, as follows:

I am pleased to have this opportunity to speak on the subject: Is it important to balance the budget?

As I see it, balancing the budget without resorting to legerdemain or unsound bookkeeping methods is certainly in the category of our No. 1 problems.

Beginning with 1792, the first fiscal year of our Federal Government, and through 1916, federal deficits were casual and usually paid off in succeeding years. In this 124-year period there were 43 deficit years and 81 surplus years. As late as July 1, 1914, the interest-bearing debt was less than $1 billion.

In Andrew Jackson's administration the public debt was paid off in toto, an achievement in which President Jackson expressed great pride.

It can be said for this first 124 years in the life of our Republic we were on a pay-as-you-go basis. In that period I think it can be accurately said that we laid the foundation for our strength today as the greatest nation in all the world.

Then, in 1917, 1918, and 1919, World War I deficits aggregated $13 billion. Heavy current taxation in those years paid much of the war cost.

The next 11 years, from 1919 to 1931, were surplus years, and the war debt was reduced.

In 1932 Mr. Roosevelt came into office, and the most outstanding plank in his platform was to reduce Federal expenditures by 25 percent and to keep the budget in balance. He accused Mr. Hoover of "throwing discretion to the winds and indulging in an orgy of waste and extra-vagance." Mr. Hoover spent $4 billion in his last year, and the record shows that this spendthrift Hoover was the only President to leave office with fewer Federal employees than when he came in.

Mr. Roosevelt added more than $200 billion to the public debt during his administrations.

I took my oath as a Senator the same day Mr. Roosevelt took his as President--March 4, 1933. The first bill I voted on was the legislation recommended by President Roosevelt to redeem his economy pledge by re-ducing all expenditures 15 percent--a difference of 10 percent less than his original promise, it is true--but I thought this was a sub-stantial redemption of a campaign pledge, as such things go, and I enthusiastically supported him.

The title of the bill was "A bill to preserve the credit of the United States Government." Out debt was then about $16 billion. This economy program was shortlived--about 6 months--and the spending then began to steadily and rapidly increase.

Mr. Roosevelt presented 13 budgets and in every peacetime budget he promised a balance between income and outgo for the next year, but it turned out that next year never came. He was in the red all the way, and in every year of his administration a substantial deficit was added to the public debt.

There were eight Truman budgets. Three were in the black--those for fiscal year 1947, 1948, and 1951. Two resulted from war contract cancellations following the end of World War II and the third resulted from increased taxes for the Korean war before the war bills started coming due. Five Truman budgets were in the red.

Mr. Eisenhower has presented two budgets--both in the red but on a declining ratio. The Eisenhower deficit estimates for fiscal years 1955 and 1956 aggregate $7 billion as compared to the last Truman budget which alone contemplated a $9 billion deficit.

The cold facts are that for 21 years out of the last 24 years we have spent more than we have collected. In these 24 years we have balanced the budget in only 3; and these were more by accident than by design.

We must recognize that we have abandoned the sound fiscal policies strictly adhered to by all political parties and all Presidents for considerably more than a century of our existence. It is true that during these 21 deficit years we were engaged in World War II for 4 years and in the Korean war for 2 years. Yet, in the years when the pay-as-you-go system prevailed we also had quite a few wars.

It is the quarter of a century of deficit spending which now makes balancing the budget so imperative. Young men and women, born in 1930, have lived in the red virtually all their lives. Our acceptance of deficit spending for so long a period had weakened public resistance to the evils of this practice. Bad habits are hard to change.

Will the deficits become permanent and continue to pile debt upon debt until real disaster comes? If we cannot balance the budget in this day of our greatest dollar income, when taxes are near their peak, and when we are at peace, I ask, when can we?

It is disturbing these days to hear some economists argue the budget should not be balanced and that we should not begin to pay on the debt because, they allege, it will adversely affect business conditions. Have we yielded so far to the blandishments of Federal subsidies and Government support that we have forgotten our Nation is great because of individual effort as contrasted to state paternalism?

Today the direct debt of the Federal Government is $280 billion. Our debt is equivalent to the assessed value of all the land, all the buildings, all the mines, all the machinery, all the livestock-- everything of tangible value in the United States.

I think no one can deny we are mortgaged to the hilt. If we add to this Federal debt the debts of the States and localities, we have an amount in excess of $300 billion in direct public obligations.

This is 5 times as much as the total public debts in 1939. While public debt has increased fivefold since 1939 the gross national product--the output of our factories farms, etc.--increased less than fourfold. When debt increases at a pace faster than the increase in the value of all goods and services, the currency is diluted with consequent shrinkage in the purchasing power of the dollar.

But the direct debts I have mentioned are not all of our obligations. In addition, we have contingent liabilities totaling $250 billion which the Federal Government has guaranteed, insured, and otherwise assumed on a contingent basis. No one can predict to what extent this contingent liability will result in losses which must be paid by the Federal Government.

For example, $40 billion of this contingent liability is in some 40 Federal housing programs, and from recent disclosures of graft and windfall profits in the various public housing programs. It is evident that a substantial percentage of these contingent liabilities eventually may become a draft on the Treasury.

In addition to the $280 billion in direct Federal debt, and the $250 billion in contingent liabilities, we have on our hands a social-security system guaranteed by the Federal Government involving many millions of our citizens, which is no longer actually sound.

The ultimate cost of this system to the Treasury is still unestimated, but the fact remains that when the income from premiums imposed upon those who are covered in the system is no longer sufficient or available to pay the benefits, then regular tax revenue collected from those in and out of the system will be used to finance the deficiency.

EVILS OF DEFICIT SPENDING

Here are some of the evils of deficit spending:

The debt today is the debt incurred by this generation but tomorrow it will be debt on our children and grandchildren, and it will be for them to pay, both the interest and the principal.

It is possible and in fact probable that before this astronomi-cal debt is paid off, it it ever is, the interest charge will exceed the principal.

Protracted deficit spending means cheapening the dollar. Secretary Humphrey testified before the Finance Committee that the greatest single factor in cheapening the American dollar has been deficit spending.

Since I have been in the Senate, interest alone on the Federal debt has cost the taxpayers of this country more than $75 billion. At present rates, on the Federal debt at its present level, interest on it in the next 20 years will cost taxpayers upwards of $150 billion.

Since 1940 the Federal Government has borrowed and spent a quarter of a trillion dollars more than we have collected in taxes.

Year by year, nearly in direct ratio to deficit spending, the purchasing value of the dollar has declined. Beginning with a 100-cent dollar in 1940, the value of the dollar had declined to 52 cents in 1954.

As proof of the fact that deficit spending is directly responsible for cheapening the dollar, let me mention that in 1942, when we spent $19 billion in excess of revenue, the dollar in that 1 year declined 10 cents in value.

In 1943, another big deficit year, the dollar lost 5 cents more in value, and another 9 cents in 1946. From 1940 through 1952, an era of heavy deficit spending, the dollar lost 48 cents in value, or nearly 4 cents each year, and it is still slipping but in much lesser degree.

Some may regard these facts and figures lightly, but the loss of half the purchasing power of its money in 13 years should be a serious warning to any nation.

Cheapened money is inflation. Inflation is a dangerous game. It robs creditors, it steals pensions, wages, and fixed income. Once started, it is exceedingly difficult to control. This inflation has been partially checked but the value of the dollar dropped slightly again in the past year. It would not take much to start up this dangerous inflation again.

Public debt is not like private debt. If private debt is not paid off, it can be ended by liquidation, but if public debt is not paid off with taxes, liquidation takes the form of disastrous inflation or national repudiation. Either is destructive of our form of government.

Today the interest on the Federal debt takes more than 10 percent of our total Federal tax revenue. Without the tremendous cost of this debt our annual tax bill could be reduced 10 percent across the board.

The interest charge would be greater if much of the debt was not short-termed with lower interest rates. Should this debt be long-termed at the 3¼ percent paid on recent 30-year bonds, the interest would be nearly 15 percent of the Federal income. No business enterprise could survive such heavy interest out of its gross income.

FEDERAL GRANTS TO STATES

Since 1934 Federal grants to States have expanded enormously in both cost and functions. They slip in like mice and soon grow to the size of elephants. Every Federal grant elevates the control of the Federal Government and subordinates the control and authority of the States.

Nothing is more true than the rule that power follows the purse. When the Federal Government makes a grant it directs exactly the manner in which the funds are expended, even though the States partially contribute to the project. Time and time again I have seen the iron hand of the Federal bureaucracy with grants compel the States to do things they did not want to do.

Growth in Federal grants is indicated by the fact that in 1934, 21 years ago, the total of such grants was $126 million covering 18 programs. Now Federal grants total $3 billion for 50 programs. This is an increase of 300 percent in programs and 2,300 percent in cost.

These are the figures to date. As to additional grants for the future, President Eisenhower, in his address on the state of the Union, proposed to open up three Pandora's boxes of new Federal "handouts" to the States.

The proposals by the President, if adopted by Congress, would be the greatest increase in grants to States yet undertaken and the longest step yet to Federal paternalism.

Under the administration's road proposal, a "dummy" corporation, without assets and without income, would issue bonds for $21 billion, and Washington would take control of 40,000 miles of the best roads in the 48 States.

By legerdemain this $21 billion in Federal agency bonds would be declared as not Federal debt and would be excluded from the debt limitation fixed by Congress.

The interest would be $11.5 billion, or 55 percent of the funds borrowed.

It was proposed to pay the principal of these bonds and the interest on them with permanent indefinite appropriations, which would remove the corporation from annual appropriation control by Congress.

The proposal would abolish the policy established in 1916--39 years ago--requiring States to match Federal funds for roads.

The scheme was predicated upon pledging federally imposed gasoline taxes over a period of 30 years for the repayment of the bonds and the interest.

The Comptroller General of the United States, Mr. Joseph Campbell, recently appointed by President Eisenhower, said of this proposal:

"We (the General Accounting Office) feel that the proposed method of financing is objectionable, because *** the borrowing would not be included in the public debt obligations of the United States.*** It is our opinion that the Government should not enter into financial arrangements which might have the effect of obscuring financial facts of the Government's debt position."

We all want good roads. The people are willing to pay for good roads, but it is certainly not necessary practically to destroy the fiscal bookkeeping of our country in order to finance our road system.

These bonds would, of course, be a general obligation of the Government. There is no banker in the audience who would buy bonds of such a dummy Federal corporation without the guaranty of the Federal Government.

Should the gasoline tax be dedicated 30 years in advance for the payment of bonds issued to build roads then, by the same line of reasoning, other taxes could be dedicated for other specific purposes. If this were carried far enough there would be no funds for the more unglamorous but essential functions.

The second of the three administration State-aid proposals involved about $8 billion in direct appropriations and contingent liabilities for payments, grants, bonds, and guaranties to States for school construction. The last bastion of States rights and individual liberty lies in the education of our children.

Federal appropriations to public schools followed by the inevitable Federal control will strike a fatal blow at the grass-roots of our democracy.

I do not believe that there is a State or locality in the Union that cannot provide for the cost of its public school system if there is the will to do so.

It is impossible to estimate the cost of the President's third proposal. It was for a so-called Federal health payment program. It would be certain to cost millions of dollars annually and it could easily be the beginning of socialized medicine.

NO SUCH THING AS A FEDERAL GRANT

It is well for everyone to understand that there is no such thing as a Federal grant. All of the money goes to Washington and there it is subject to deducations for Federal administration. This money then goes back to the States less deductions, and the Federal Government tells us how to spend our own money.

Proposals have been advocated changing our budgetary system. The Secretary of the Treasury has not approved these proposals and I am certain he will not. But there are two budgetary proposals which recur with persistency, and I want to warn you of them.

First, there is the proposal for a cash budget. Those who advocate the cash budget are suggesting that the Government pay its routine bills with savings of the citizens who have entrusted protection of their old age and unemployment to the guardianship of the Federal Government. These trust funds were established from premiums paid by participants in social security, unemployment insurance, bank deposit insurance programs, etc. Not a cent of these funds belongs to the Government.

Second, some are advocating a capital budget which means that so-called capital expenditures should not be considered as current expenditures in the budget.

Those who advocate the so-called capital budget must start out with the fallacious assumption that the Government is in business to make a profit on its citizens. To my knowledge the Federal Government has never made a bona fide profit on any Government operation.

They must assume that debt contracted by a Federal agency is not a debt of the Federal Government and a burden on all of the taxpayers.

I am an old-fashioned person who believes that a debt is a debt just as much in the atomic age as it was in the horse and buggy days.

A capital budget must assume that Government manufacturing plants, such as atomic energy installations, are in commercial production for a profit, and that Government stockpiles are long-time investments for profit instead of precautions against emergencies when they would be completely expendable with no financial return.

Likewise, it must assume that the agriculture surplus program is primarily a long range investment deal instead of a prop for annual farm income to be used when needed on a year-by-year basis.

While the vastness and complexity of the Federal Government of the United States necessarily makes budgeting difficult, the so-called conventional budget currently in use offers the best approach to orderly financing with fullest disclosure.

What is needed for a better fiscal system is fuller disclosures of Federal expenditures and responsibility for them--not less, as inevitably would be the case with so-called cash and capital budgets.

With full disclosure of the Federal expenditure situation, the American people then would have an opportunity to decide whether they wanted to recapture control and bring the rate of spending into balance with the rate of taxing and thus reduce the tremendous Federal debt burden we are now bearing.

To recapture control we must first reduce unexpended balances in appropriations already made and rescind those which are nonessential. When we started this fiscal year unexpended balances in appropriations already made totaled about $100 billion, including $78 billion in appropriations enacted in prior years and $20 billion in authority to spend directly out of the public debt.

The situation is made even worse by the procedure under which Congress acts on appropriation bills. Not only has Congress lost control over the annual rate of expenditure, but once the President's budget is submitted in January, Congress never again sees it as a whole until after the appropriations are enacted. The first thing Congress does is to split the appropriation requests of the President into a dozen or more bills. Then it proceeds to consider them separately over a period of 6 months or more. In the consideration of these bills attention is given only to appropriations, and these may be spent over a period of years. An appropriation enacted in a year when revenue is high may actually be spent in a year when revenue is low. There is never an opportunity in Congress, in action on appropriation bills, to consider them in terms of annual expenditures in view of estimated revenue.

To correct such an intolerable situation, along with 48 other Senators, I have introduced legislation providing for a single appropriation bill which would set forth not only requested appropriations for the future but also unexpended balances available in prior appropriations. Ths resolution has three times passed the Senate but has not yet been acted on by the House.

It provides further that Congress write into the consolidated appropriation bill limitations on expenditures in the ensuing year from each appropriation. And beyond this it provides that in determining the expenditure limitations all proper consideration should be given the anticipated revenue, the cash position of the Treasury and the level of our Federal debt.

By this process, the Congress and the public would have the means of knowing our fiscal position and the facilities would be provided for balancing the budget with reduction in taxes and debt.

Along with this, I have introduced legislation giving the President the authority to veto items within appropriation bills, thus according him a double check on log-rolling which most of the governors in this country have used for years without abuse.

In short, I advocate one budget with full disclosure as to our expenditures, which fixes responsibility not only for the expenditures but also the administration of expenditure programs; I advocate a single appropriation bill in which Congress not only authorizes expenditures but controls them in a manner that can be considered in view of revenue. A budget is not a budget unless it has two sides, expenditure and income. And finally, I advocate an item veto for the President, who is elected to his office by all of the people.

With these provisions, I believe the budget can be balanced, the debt can be reduced and taxes can be lowered.

If, by budgetary and legislative procedure, we could recapture control of expenditures from the bureaucratic agencies, there are obvious places where they could be substantially reduced and eliminated without impairment of any essential function.

President Eisenhower has made a good start. The Truman budget for fiscal year 1953 totaled $74.3 billion. Estimates of the Eisenhower budget currently under consideration total $62.4 billion --a reduction of nearly $12 billion. Our tax income is $60 billion. Our deficits are decreasing, but we are not yet on a pay-as-you-go basis.

Most of the reduction has been in the military,and this is largely incident to the end of the Korean war.

The Secretary of the Treasury, Mr. Humphrey, for whom I have great admiration, and the able Budget Director, Mr. Hughes, are working diligently and making substantial progress toward sounder budgetary procedure and the elimination of waste in expenditures.

We are still practically at the peak of expenditures for domestic-civilian programs and proposals for more are coming forth in a steady stream.

In fact, expenditures for strictly domestic-civilian programs now total $24 billion, and this is more than 3 times the total cost of these programs in 1940, when we started the World War II buildup.

Even this is not the whole story on domestic-civilian expenditures, because these figures do not reflect the liabilities of the tremendous loan insurance and guarantee programs.

Nonessentials in these programs must be eliminated and this clearly can be done, as Mr. Hoover and his two fine Commissions on Government Organization have demonstrated in nearly 500 recommendations to date-- some of which have been adopted, while others still await aciton.

With the pressure for more and more Government which seems to characterize our times, I am convinced that such constant examination of Government as the Hoover Commission surveys has become a continuing necessity.

With budgetary disclosures and congressional control, under current circumstances and conditions, we should reject all new proposals for Federal spending innovations.

In fact, the budget for fiscal year 1956, beginning next July 1, could be reduced $5 billion by eliminating expenditures contemplated under new legislation and by eliminating increases in items under existing legislation. I would oppose all new proposals to invade the responsibilities of States, localities, and individuals and start immediately to liquidate many of the programs already in existence.

Beyond this, I would eliminate as rapidly as possible all foreign economic aid, and I would get military expenditures quickly in hand through control of unexpended balances.

So far we have spent nearly $40 billion for foreign economic assistance. And at this late date, after 10 years of post-war foreign aid, the President has proposed to increase foreign-aid expenditures in the coming year by nearly 10 percent, and he has asked Congress for new foreign-aid appropriations in amounts nearly 25 percent higher than were enacted during the past year.

We are still employing 562,158 civilians overseas. These people are employed all over the world, including 64 in Cambodia.

This foreign aid has got to stop sometime, and so far as I am concerned the time to stop so-called economic aid is past due.

No one favors a reduction of our present burdensome taxes more than I do. I sit on both sides of the table. As an individual, I pay substantial taxes on my business operations. As a member of the Senate Finance Committee I have the opportunity to hear testimony of those who protest exorbitant taxation.

But as anxious as I am as an individual for tax reductions. I am opposed patriotically to tax reduction which requires us to borrow and add to the public debt. It seems to me to be a certain road to financial suicide to continue to reduce taxes and then to borrow the money to make good this loss in revenue.

As things are now shaping up, there will be keen competition between the two political parties for tax reduction in the political year of 1956. If we reduce expenditures this is all well and good but, under political pressure, we should not yield to reducing taxes and still further unbalance the budget. Tax reduction should never be made a political football.

As chairman of the Senate Finance Committee, I opposed the $20-tax reduction to each individual as passed by the House of Representatives this year. This would have occasioned a loss of $2.3 billion to the Treasury, all of which would be added to the debt. It would have given a tax relief of only about 7 cents a day to each taxpayer and would have removed 5 million taxpayers completely from the tax rolls.

To borrow money to reduce taxes is not, in fact, a tax reduction. It is merely a postponement of the collection of taxes as, sooner or later, the taxes thus reduced will have to be paid with interest. There is only one sound way to reduce taxes and that is to reduce spending first.

At home we can get along without Federal usurpation of individual, local, and State responsibilities, and we can get along without Federal competition in business whether it be hotels, furs, rum, clothing, fertilizer, or other things.

The Bible says if thine eye offend thee pluck it out. I say if the Federal Government should not engage in such activities, we should first stop new invasions and then gradually, if not abruptly, eliminate the old intrusions. When we do these things we shall balance the budget, for lower taxes and reduced debt. There will be no further need for trick budgets and debt-ceiling evasions and hiding taxes. The Government will be honest in itself, and honest with the people.

A balanced budget could be in sight if (a) we do not increase spending, and (b) we do not reduce taxes. Assuming no further cut in taxes, on a 4-percent reduction in spending, in terms of the President's budget, would bring us to that highly desirable goal.

The Need for Balanced Federal Budgets

Maurice H. Stans

ABSTRACT: It should be the policy of the federal government to aim always for a balanced budget or financial stability will be upset. To balance the budget, action should be taken to reduce or end some federal programs which we have been acquiring in the past thirty years. The compensatory theory of federal spending has not been successful until now and offers little hope for the future unless there is control in the growth of federal spending. We should not initiate programs as temporary expedients during times of recession since they create great problems in future years. Although we must accept deficits when the country is in a national emergency, we should later create equivalent surpluses to offset deficits caused by the emergency. It is, therefore, necessary to pay as we go if we want to reduce the national debt and taxes. It is also necessary to plan for budgetary surpluses in good years if we do not want to extend inflation in the future.—Ed.

THE federal government should have a balanced budget; its expenditures, especially in times like these, should not exceed its income. Of this I am deeply convinced.

As a matter of fact, I find it difficult to understand why there are still some people who do not seem to agree. Even though I have now been an official of the government almost four years and know by hard experience that there are at least two sides to all public questions, on this one the facts speak eloquently for themselves. And the arguments that are marshalled in opposition to show that a balanced budget is unimportant —or that it can be safely forsaken for lengthy periods of time—certainly seem unsound. It is true that we as a nation have been extremely fortunate in maintaining our fundamental strengths thus far despite the heavy deficit spending of the past thirty years. But we cannot count on being lucky forever, and more and more the consequences of past profligacy are now catching up with us.

Let us look at some of the facts:

1. It is a fact that in 24 of the last 30 years the federal government has spent more than it has received.

2. It is a fact that last fiscal year the federal government had a deficit (12.5 billion dollars) larger than ever before in time of peace.

3. It is a fact that the federal government debt is now 290 billion dollars and that the annual cost of carrying that debt is more than 10 per cent of the budgeted income of the government—and has been going up.

4. It is a fact that our economy is operating at a higher rate of activity than it ever has before and that the standard of living it is producing for

all America is far beyond that of any other country in the world.

5. It is a fact that in times of high economic activity there is competition among business, consumers, and government for the productive resources of the country; if government, by indulging in high levels of spending in such times, intensifies that competition, it openly invites inflation.

6. It is a fact that with an unbalanced budget, federal borrowings to raise the money to spend more than income tend to add to the money supply of the country and therefore are inflationary.

7. It is a fact that the purchasing power of the dollar has declined more than 50 per cent in the last twenty years. Today we spend more than $2.00 to get what $1.00 would buy in 1939.

8. And finally, it is a fact that all too often in history inflation has been the undoing of nations, great and small.

True, there are many people who still feel that a bit of inflation is a tolerable, if not a good, thing. I think they fail to see that a bit of inflation is an installment on a lot of inflation—a condition in which nobody can hope to gain.

Those of our citizens who believe that inflation is not undesirable simply overlook the history of nations. Inflation is an insidious threat to the strength of the United States. Unless we succeed in exercising a tighter rein over it than we have been able to up to this point, I am afraid that we will all lose—as individuals, as a nation, and as a people.

In my view, the facts that I have recited clearly demonstrate the need for:

1. Containing federal expenditures within federal income—which means balancing the budget—in fiscal years 1960 and 1961.

2. Establishing the principle of a balanced budget—including some surplus for reduction of the national debt—as a fiscal objective for the prosperous years ahead.

These are the standards on which fiscal integrity for the nation should rest. These are the standards by which the force of inflation induced by reckless fiscal policy can be averted. Yet in 24 of the last 30 years we have not been able to attain them.

Let us look at some of the circumstances which have caused heavy federal spending in the past and have, perhaps, made us insensitive to the dangers of deficits.

LOOKING BACK

Over the last three decades the federal government has spent 264 billion dollars more than it has received. The six years in which there was an excess of income over expense produced negligible surpluses in relation to the deficits of the other years.

We need hardly be reminded of the cause of most of those deficits. In the earlier years it was depression; in the middle years it was war; in recent years it has been war again and then recession.

In the depression years it was not possible to balance the budget; while government services and costs were growing by popular demand, federal revenues declined as a result of economic inactivity. The efforts made to balance the budget by increasing tax rates in 1930 and 1932 and in 1936 to 1938 were apparently self-defeating.

As for the expenditure side of the budget, the decade of the 1930's produced a great deal of talk about "pump-priming" and "compensatory spending" —federal spending which would compensate in poor times for the decline in business and consumer demand and thus lend balance and stability to the economy. The theory was, of course, for the federal government to spend proportionately larger amounts during depression times and proportionately smaller amounts during good times—to suffer deficits in poor years and enjoy surpluses in prosperous years, with the objective of coming out even over the long pull.

Then, in the early 1940's came World War II. During the war years, the federal government's expenditures vastly exceeded its income, and huge further deficits were piled up. In retrospect, most students of wartime economic developments now agree that we did not tax ourselves nearly enough. We did not pay enough of the costs of war out of current income. We created a large debt while suppressing some of its inflationary consequences with direct economic controls, but the suppression was only temporary.

Depression and war, although major factors, were not the only reasons for increased federal expenditures and deficits during the past thirty years. It was more complex than that. In the 1930's the national philosophy of the responsibilities of the federal government underwent a major change. The country's needs for economic growth and social advancement were gradually given increased recognition at the federal level.

The aim of economic growth, of social advancement, and of "compensatory" economic stability became intertwined. Many federal activities of far-reaching implications were established in ways which affected federal expenditures for very long periods of time—if not permanently. Social security, greatly increased support for agriculture, rural electrification, aids to homeowners and mortgage institutions, public housing, public power developments like the Tennessee Valley Authority and other multipurpose water resource projects, and public assistance grants are just a few examples. All of them, however, remained as federal programs after World War II. And we were actually fighting in that war before federal spending for work relief could be stopped.

The immediate postwar period was marked by dramatic demobilization. Nevertheless, many of the major costs of war lingered on. The maintenance in the postwar period of even the reduced and relatively modest structure of our Armed Forces was far more costly than anything that existed in the way of the machinery of war prior to 1940. The war also left us with greatly increased expenditure commitments for interest on the public debt, for veterans, and for atomic energy. The Marshall Plan and the mutual security program followed in succession. It became obvious, next, that the cold war was going to be expensive. Then, with the Korean aggression, it became necessary to rearm and, even after the shooting stopped, the peacetime striking force and defensive machinery we had to maintain continued expenditures at levels that far

exceeded in cost anything we had earlier imagined.

Thus, the postwar growth of the budget has been partly in the area of national security, partly deferred costs of World War II, and partly the inheritance of activities and ways of thinking that characterized the depression of the 1930's. We have now learned that many of the programs the federal government initiated in the 1930's were neither temporary nor "compensatory" in character. Moreover, we have not only retained many of them, but we have also greatly expanded them in the postwar period. Since World War II we have seen large increases in federal expenditures for urban renewal, public health, federal aid for airports and highways, new categories and a higher federal share of public assistance grants, aid to schools in federally impacted areas, great liberalization in aid to agriculture, as well as new programs for science, education, and outer space.

THE PRESENT

What can we conclude from all of this?

It seems to me that in the first place we must recognize that the compensatory theory of federal spending has failed thus far and offers little hope for the future unless we exert a more forceful and courageous determination to control the growth of federal spending. The major spending programs which originated in the depression years have in most cases persisted in the following decades. A work relief project could be turned off when we started to fight a war, but most of the programs established in the 1930's developed characteristics of a far more permanent sort.

An example can be found in the program of the Rural Electrification Administration (REA). This program was started in 1936 when only a minority of farm families enjoyed the benefits of electricity. Today, 95 per cent of our farms receive central station electric service. We have invested 4 billion dollars in this program, at 2 per cent interest. Nonetheless, indications are that future demands for federal funds will be even greater as the REA cooperatives continue to grow.

The startling fact is that three out of four new users currently being added are nonfarm users. About one-half of REA electric power goes to industries, communities, or nonfarm families. The reasonable approach is that rural electric co-operatives should now be able to get some of their financing from other than government sources, especially for nonfarm purposes that compete with taxed private industry. Recognizing this, the President last year—and again this year—recommended that legislation be adopted to encourage co-operatives to switch from government to private financing, and his budget recommended a decrease in the funds for government loans. These proposals were not enacted by the Congress.

Inability to turn off expenditures is not all that is wrong with the compensatory theory of the prewar period. Initially, it dealt largely with the spending side of the fiscal equation whereas the income side now appears to be playing a more important part. Today—with corporate income tax rates at 52 per cent—any substantial reduction of corporate earnings produces an immediate proportionate and large loss to the federal treasury. Personal income taxes also respond, though less sharply, to a fall in national production and employment. Thus, when times take a turn for the worse, federal revenues decline promptly and substantially.

Couple this with enlarged social obligations in times of recession or depression—unemployment compensation, public assistance, and so on—and you have substantial leverage of a more or less automatic character for the production of federal deficits in times of depressed economic activity. To do more than this—to deliberately step up expenditures still more, for public works and other construction, as was done last year—runs grave risks. There is, first, the risk that an antirecession expenditure program cannot be turned off after the recession, but instead represents a permanent increase in the public sphere at the expense of the private. Second, it is difficult to start programs quickly, so the major impact may come long after the need for the economic stimulation has passed. Both of these risks mean that antirecession actions can

well represent an inflationary danger for the postrecession period. The danger is there even if, as some believe, positive governmental intervention is required to counter recessions. It is more grave, however, if—and I believe this was proved true in 1958–59—the economy is vigorous and resilient enough to come out of a temporary recession and to go on through a revival period to new prosperous peaks without any direct financial federal interference.

I think we may conclude that it is inevitable that our nation will be faced with large budgets in the years ahead. This is particularly true for the defense obligations which our country has assumed, for its international undertakings to provide economic and military assistance to other free nations, and as a result of many programs which have been started over the years—major programs for water resource development, agriculture, veterans' benefits, low-cost housing, airways modernization, and space exploration—all these and many others have taken on a permanent quality which makes it clear that federal budgets will be large budgets in our lifetimes.

There is still another conclusion which springs from this short recitation of the history of the last thirty years. It is that the federal government has asumed more and more reponsibility for activities which formerly were regarded as being under the jurisdiction of state and local governments. More and more the federal government has assumed responsibility for public assistance, housing, urban renewal, educational aid to areas with federal installations, and many other programs that are now supported by federal grants-in-aid to the states. All this, of course, contributes to the conclusion that these federal programs are not only large at the present time, but have a built-in durability—a staying power with which we must reckon as a fact of life.

I think these thoughts are well summarized in the words of Mr. Allen Sproul, former President of the New York Federal Reserve Bank, who recently said:

Government, in our day, touches upon the economic life of the community in an almost bewildering variety of ways, but its overall influence comes into focus in the consolidated cash budget and, in a subsidiary way, in the management of the public debt. When we abandoned the idea of taxation for revenue only and admitted, as we must, a more important role of Government in economic affairs, we thought up a tidy little scheme called the compensatory budget. This envisaged a cash budget balanced in times of real prosperity, in deficit in times of economic recession, and in surplus in times of inflationary boom. What we have got is a budget that may throw up a shaky surplus in times of boom, but that will surely show substantial deficits in times of recession. The bias, over time, is toward deficits, with only wobbly contracyclical tendencies.

Looking Ahead

It seems to me that as we move into another decade it will be essential to recognize that unless we have a more positive program for operating our federal government within its income, the forces that have gained such tremendous momentum in the past will perpetuate the tradition of deficits—to the great disadvantage of the country as a whole.

Assuming a continuous, but not uninterrupted, economic growth for the country, accompanied by ever-increasing, but not uninterrupted, growth of federal revenues, we should nevertheless expect that the growth of programs started in the past will have a strong tendency to absorb the expected additional revenues—unless aggressive controls are exercised by an alert administration and a statesmanlike Congress during those years.

On those occasions when the economy recedes from its way of growth, we must expect great leverage to be exerted toward the building up of additional deficits. We must learn to live with recession-induced deficits as a matter of necessity, but we should not take unneeded actions which mortgage our nation's future with both more debt and an inflationary potential.

Conclusions

It seems to me to follow from these facts and analyses that it should be the policy of the federal government to strive determinedly for a balanced budget at all times, for, clearly, if it does not, the forces at work to upset financial stability will surely prevail as a matter of momentum.

As we move into the next decade we have the lessons of the three past decades to guide us:

1. Federal programs persist and in most cases grow. As demand expands, the programs expand. It is extremely difficult to curtail them. Their growing costs—and a growing economy—must be reckoned with realistically. This means that actions should be taken to reduce or to end them as they accomplish the purposes for which they were initiated (eighteen such proposals were made in the President's budget message for the fiscal year 1960).
2. In times of recession, it is important to avoid doing things as temporary expedients which will become longer range programs and create major problems later on. We have plenty of these as carryovers from earlier days; we should avoid creating new ones for the years ahead.
3. We must, of course, learn to live with deficits when major national emergencies threaten or exist in our country. But we should resolve to create equivalent surpluses later on to offset such deficits.

The lesson is clear. We should pay as we go, and if we are to look for debt reduction or tax reduction on a sound footing—as we should—we must do more than this. We must plan for substantial budgetary surpluses in good years—or we will surely contribute to further dangerous inflation in the years ahead.

Maurice H. Stans, LL.D., Washington, D. C., is Director of the Bureau of the Budget. Formerly he was Financial Consultant to the Postmaster General and Deputy Director of the Bureau of the Budget. Mr. Stans was previously executive partner in the national accounting firm of Alexander Grant and Company. He is a member and former President of the American Institute of Accountants, member and former Director of the Illinois Society of Certified Public Accountants, and member of the National Association of Accountants, the American Accounting Association, the Federal Government Accountants Association, and the American Society for Public Administration.

The Ricardian Approach to Budget Deficits

Robert J. Barro

In recent years there has been a lot of discussion about U.S. budget deficits. Many economists and other observers have viewed these deficits as harmful to the U.S. and world economies. The supposed harmful effects include high real interest rates, low saving, low rates of economic growth, large current-account deficits in the United States and other countries with large budget deficits, and either a high or low dollar (depending apparently on the time period). This crisis scenario has been hard to maintain along with the robust performance of the U.S. economy since late 1982. This performance features high average growth rates of real GNP, declining unemployment, much lower inflation, a sharp decrease in nominal interest rates and some decline in expected real interest rates, high values of real investment expenditures, and (until October 1987) a dramatic boom in the stock market.

Persistent budget deficits have increased economists' interest in theories and evidence about fiscal policy. At the same time, the conflict between standard predictions and actual outcomes in the U.S. economy has, I think, increased economists' willingness to consider approaches that depart from the standard paradigm. In this paper I will focus on the alternative theory that is associated with the name of David Ricardo.

The Standard Model of Budget Deficits

Before developing the Ricardian approach, I will sketch the standard model. The starting point is the assumption that the substitution of a budget deficit for current taxation leads to an expansion of aggregate consumer demand. In other words, desired private saving rises by less than the tax cut, so that desired national saving declines. It follows for a closed economy that the expected real interest rate would have to rise to restore equality between desired national saving and investment demand. The higher real interest rate crowds out investment, which shows up in the long run as a smaller stock of productive capital. Therefore, in the language of Franco Modigliani (1961), the public debt is an intergenerational burden in that it leads to a smaller stock of capital for future generations. Similar reasoning applies to pay-as-you-go social security programs, as has been stressed by Martin Feldstein (1974). An increase in the scope of these programs raises the aggregate demand for goods, and thereby leads to a higher real interest rate and a smaller stock of productive capital.

■ *Robert J. Barro is Professor of Economics, Harvard University, Cambridge, Massachusetts; Research Associate, National Bureau of Economic Research, Cambridge, Massachusetts; Research Associate, Rochester Center for Economic Research, University of Rochester, Rochester, New York.*

The Ricardian Alternative

The Ricardian modification to the standard analysis begins with the observation that, for a given path of government spending, a deficit-financed cut in current taxes leads to higher future taxes that have the same present value as the initial cut. This result follows from the government's budget constraint, which equates total expenditures for each period (including interest payments) to revenues from taxation or other sources and the net issue of interest-bearing public debt. Abstracting from chain-letter cases where the public debt can grow forever at the rate of interest or higher, the present value of taxes (and other revenues) cannot change unless the government changes the present value of its expenditures. This point amounts to economists' standard notion of the absence of a free lunch—government spending must be paid for now or later, with the total present value of receipts fixed by the total present value of spending. Hence, holding fixed the path of government expenditures and non-tax revenues, a cut in today's taxes must be matched by a corresponding increase in the present value of future taxes.[1]

Suppose now that households' demands for goods depend on the expected present value of taxes—that is, each household subtracts its share of this present value from the expected present value of income to determine a net wealth position. Then fiscal policy would affect aggregate consumer demand only if it altered the expected present value of taxes. But the preceding argument was that the present value of taxes would not change as long as the present value of spending did not change. Therefore, the substitution of a budget deficit for current taxes (or any other rearrangement of the timing of taxes) has no impact on the aggregate demand for goods. In this sense, budget deficits and taxation have equivalent effects on the economy—hence the term, "Ricardian equivalence theorem."[2] To put the equivalence result another way, a decrease in the government's saving (that is, a current budget deficit) leads to an offsetting increase in desired private saving, and hence to no change in desired national saving.

Since desired national saving does not change, the real interest rate does not have to rise in a closed economy to maintain balance between desired national saving and investment demand. Hence, there is no effect on investment, and no burden of the public debt or social security in the sense of Modigliani (1961) and Feldstein (1974).

Theoretical Objections to Ricardian Equivalence

I shall discuss five major theoretical objections that have been raised against the Ricardian conclusions. The first is that people do not live forever, and hence do not care about taxes that are levied after their death. The second is that private capital markets are "imperfect," with the typical person's real discount rate exceeding that of the government. The third is that future taxes and incomes are uncertain. The fourth is that taxes are not lump sum, since they depend typically on income, spending, wealth, and so on. The fifth is that the Ricardian result hinges on full employment. I assume throughout that the path of government spending is given. The Ricardian analysis applies to shifts in budget deficits and taxes for a given pattern of government expenditures; in particular, the approach is consistent with real effects from changes in the level or timing of government purchases and public services.

In many cases it turns out that budget deficits matter, and are in that sense non-Ricardian. It is important, however, to consider not only whether the Ricardian view remains intact, but also what alternative conclusions emerge. Many economists raise points that invalidate strict Ricardian equivalence, and then simply assume that the points support a specific alternative; usually the standard view that a budget deficit lowers desired national saving and thereby drives up real interest rates or leads to a current-account deficit. Many criticisms of the Ricardian position are also inconsistent with this standard view.

Finite Horizons and Related Issues

The idea of finite horizons, motivated by the finiteness of life, is central to life-cycle models—see, for example, Franco Modigliani and Richard Brumberg (1954) and Albert Ando and Franco Modigliani (1963). In these models individuals capitalize only the taxes that they expect to face before dying. Consider a deficit-financed tax cut, and assume that the higher future taxes occur partly during the typical person's expected lifetime and partly thereafter. Then the present value of the first portion must fall short of the initial tax cut, since a full balance results only if the second portion is included. Hence the net wealth of persons currently alive rises, and households react by increasing consumption demand. Thus, as in the standard approach sketched above, desired private saving does not rise by enough to offset fully the decline in government saving.

A finite horizon seems to generate the standard result that a budget deficit reduces desired national saving. The argument works, however, only if the typical person feels better off when the government shifts a tax burden to his or her de. tndants. The argument fails if the typical person is already giving to his or her children out of altruism. In this case people react to the government's imposed intergenerational transfers, which are implied by budget deficits or social security, with a compensating increase in voluntary transfers (Barro, 1974). For example, parents adjust their bequests or the amounts given to children while the parents are still living. Alternatively, if children provide support to aged parents, the amounts given can respond (negatively) to budget deficits or social security.

The main idea is that a network of intergenerational transfers makes the typical person a part of an extended family that goes on indefinitely. In this setting, households capitalize the entire array of expected future taxes, and thereby plan effectively with an infinite horizon. In other words, the Ricardian results, which seemed to depend on infinite horizons, can remain valid in a model with finite lifetimes.

Two important points should be stressed. First, intergenerational transfers do not have to be "large;" what is necessary is that transfers based on altruism be operative at the margin for most people.[3]

Second, the transfers do not have to show up as bequests at death. Other forms of intergenerational transfers, such as *inter vivos* gifts to children, support of children's education, and so on, can work in a similar manner. Therefore, the Ricardian results can hold even if many persons leave little in the way of formal bequests.

One objection to Ricardian equivalence is that some persons, such as those without children, are not connected to future generations (see James Tobin and Willem Buiter, 1980, pp. 86ff.). Persons in this situation tend to be made wealthier when the government substitutes a budget deficit for taxes. At least this conclusion obtains to the extent that the interest and principal payments on the extra public debt are not financed by higher taxes during the remaining lifetimes of people currently alive. However, the quantitative effects on consumption tend to be small. For example, if the typical person has 30 years of remaining life and consumes at a constant rate, a one-time budget deficit of $100 per person would increase each person's real consumption demand by $1.50 per year if the annual real interest rate is 5 percent, and by $2.10 per year if the real interest rate is 3 percent.[4]

The aggregate effect from the existence of childless persons is even smaller because people with more than the average number of descendants experience a decrease in wealth when taxes are replaced by budget deficits. (In effect, although some people have no children, all children must have parents.) In a world of different family sizes, the presumption for a net effect of budget deficits on aggregate consumer demand depends on different propensities to consume out of wealth for people with and without children. Since the propensity for those without children tends to be larger (because of the shorter horizon), a positive net effect on aggregate consumer demand would be predicted. However, the quantitative effect is likely to be trivial. Making the same assumptions as in the previous example, a budget deficit of $100 per capita would raise real consumption demand per capita by 30 cents per year if the real interest rate is 5 percent, and by 90 cents if the real interest rate is 3 percent.

Imperfect Loan Markets

Many economists argue that the imperfection of private credit markets is central to an analysis of the public debt; see, for example, Robert Mundell (1971). To consider this argument, assume that a closed economy consists of two types of infinite-lived economic agents; those of group A who have the same discount rate, r, as the government (and are therefore willing to hold the government's debt), and those of group B who have the higher discount rate, $\tilde{r} > r$. The constituents of group A would include large businesses, pension funds, and some individuals. The members of group B, such as small businesses and many households, possess poor collateral; therefore, loans to these people imply large costs of evaluation and enforcement. It follows that the members of group B face higher borrowing rates (even after an allowance for default risk) than the government. Whether or not they are actually borrowing, the high discount rate $\tilde{r}$ for group B corresponds to a high rate of time preference for consumption and a high marginal return on investment.

Suppose that the government cuts current taxes and runs a budget deficit. Further, assume that the division of the tax cut between groups A and B—say fifty-fifty—is the same as the division of the higher future taxes needed to service the extra debt. Since those from group A experience no net change in wealth, they willingly hold their share of the extra public debt. For group B, where the discount rate $\tilde{r}$ exceeds r, the present value of the extra future taxes falls short of the tax cut. The members of this group are better off because the tax cut effectively enables them to borrow at the lower interest rate, r. This cut in the effective borrowing rate motivates the members of group B to raise current consumption and investment.

In the aggregate a budget deficit now raises aggregate demand, or equivalently, the aggregate of desired private saving increases by less than one-to-one with the government's deficit. It follows that the real interest rate r, which applies to group A and the government, must rise to induce people to hold the extra public debt. Hence there is crowding out of consumption and investment by members of group A. For group B, the opportunity to raise current consumption and investment means that the rate of time preference for consumption and the marginal return to investment would decline. That is, the discount rate $\bar{r}$ falls. Thus, the main effects are a narrowing of the spread between the two discount rates, r and $\bar{r}$, and a diversion of current expenditures from group A to group B. In the aggregate investment may either rise or fall, and the long-term effect on the capital stock is uncertain. The major change, however, is a better channeling of resources to their ultimate uses. Namely the persons from group B—who have relatively high values for rates of time preference and for marginal returns to investment—command a greater share of current output. In any event the outcomes are non-neutral, and in that sense non-Ricardian.

The important finding from the inclusion of imperfect loan markets is that the government's issue of public debt can amount to a useful form of financial intermediation. The government induces people with good access to credit markets (group A) to hold more than their share of the extra public debt. Those with poor access (group B) hold less than their share, and thereby effectively receive loans from the first group. This process works because the government implicitly guarantees the repayment of loans through its tax collections and debt payments. Thus loans between A and B take place even though such loans were not viable (because of "transaction costs") on the imperfect private credit market.

This much of the argument may be valid, although it credits the government with a lot of skill in the collection of taxes from people with poor collateral (which is the underlying source of the problem for private lenders). Even if the government possesses this skill, the conclusions do not resemble those from the standard analysis. As discussed before, budget deficits can amount to more financial intermediation, and are in that sense equivalent to a technological advance that improves the functioning of loan markets. From this perspective it is reasonable to find a reduced spread between various discount rates and an improvement in the allocation of resources. If the government really is better at the process of intermediating, more of this activity —that is, more public debt—raises perceived wealth because it actually improves the workings of the economy.

Uncertainty about Future Taxes and Incomes

Some economists argue that the uncertainty about individuals' future taxes—or the complexity in estimating them—implies a high rate of discount in capitalizing these future liabilities (Martin Bailey, 1971, pp. 157–58; James Buchanan and Richard Wagner, 1977, pp. 17, 101, 130; Martin Feldstein, 1976, p. 335). In this case, a substitution of a budget deficit for current taxes raises net wealth because the present value of the higher expected future taxes falls short of the current tax cut. It then follows that budget deficits raise aggregate consumer demand and reduce desired national saving.

A proper treatment of uncertainty leads to different conclusions. Louis Chan (1983) first considers the case of lump-sum taxes that have a known distribution across households. However, the aggregate of future taxes and the real value of future payments on public debt are subject to uncertainty. In this case a deficit-financed tax cut has no real effects. Individuals hold their share of the extra debt because the debt is a perfect hedge against the uncertainty of the future taxes. (This analysis assumes that private credit markets have no "imperfections" of the sort discussed earlier.)

Suppose now that future taxes are still lump sum but have an uncertain incidence across individuals. Furthermore, assume that there are no insurance markets for relative tax risks. Then a budget deficit tends to increase the uncertainty about each individual's future disposable income. Chan (1983, p. 363) shows for the "usual case" (of non-increasing absolute risk aversion) that people react by reducing current consumption and hence, by raising current private saving by more than the tax cut. Consequently, the effects on real interest rates. investment, the current account, and so on are the opposites of the standard ones.

The Timing of Taxes

Departures from Ricardian equivalence arise also if taxes are not lump sum; for example, with an income tax. In this situation, budget deficits change the timing of income taxes, and thereby affect people's incentives to work and produce in different periods. It follows that variations in deficits are non-neutral, although the results tend also to be inconsistent with the standard view.

Suppose, for example, that the current tax rate on labor income, τ_1, declines, and the expected rate for the next period, τ_2, rises. To simplify matters, assume that today's budget deficit is matched by enough of a surplus next period so that the public debt does not change in later periods. Because the tax rate applies to labor income, households are motivated to work more than usual in period 1 and less than usual in period 2. Since the tax rate does not apply to expenditures (and since wealth effects are negligible here), desired national saving rises in period 1 and falls in period 2. Therefore, in a closed economy, after-tax real interest rates tend to be relatively low in period 1—along with the budget deficit—and relatively high in period 2—along with the surplus.

Full Employment and Keynesian Models

A common argument is that the Ricardian results depend on "full employment," and surely do not hold in Keynesian models. In standard Keynesian analysis (which still appears in many textbooks), if everyone thinks that a budget deficit makes them wealthier, the resulting expansion of aggregate demand raises output and employment, and thereby actually makes people wealthier. (This result holds if the economy begins in a state of "involuntary unemployment.")

This result does not mean that budget deficits increase aggregate demand and wealth in Keynesian models. If we had conjectured that budget deficits made people feel poorer, the resulting contractions in output and employment would have made them poorer. Similarly, if we had started with the Ricardian notion that budget deficits did not affect wealth, the Keynesian results would have verified that conjecture. The odd feature of the standard Keynesian model is that *anything* that makes people feel wealthier actually makes them wealthier (although the perception and actuality need not correspond quantitatively). This observation raises doubts about the formulation of Keynesian models, but says little about the effect of budget deficits. Moreover, in equilibrium models that include unemployment (such as models with incomplete information and search), there is no clear interplay between the presence of unemployment and the validity of the Ricardian approach.

Empirical Evidence on the Economic Effects of Budget Deficits

It is easy on theoretical grounds to raise points that invalidate strict Ricardian equivalence. Nevertheless, it may still be that the Ricardian view provides a useful framework for assessing the first-order effects of fiscal policy. Furthermore, it is unclear that the standard analysis offers a more accurate guide. For these reasons it is especially important to examine empirical evidence.

The Ricardian and standard views have different predictions about the effects of fiscal policy on a number of economic variables. The next three sections summarize the empirical evidence on interest rates, saving, and the current-account balance.

Interest Rates

The Ricardian view predicts no effect of budget deficits on real interest rates, whereas the standard view predicts a positive effect, at least in the context of a closed economy. Many economists have tested these propositions empirically (for a summary, see U.S. Treasury Department, 1984). Typical results show little relationship between budget deficits and interest rates. For example, Charles Plosser (1982, p. 339) finds for quarterly U.S. data from 1954 to 1978 that unexpected movements in privately-held federal debt do not raise the nominal yield on government securities of various maturities. In fact, there is a weak tendency for yields to decline with innovations in federal debt.

Evans (1987a, Tables 4–6) finds for annual U.S. data from 1931 to 1979 that current and past real federal deficits have no significant association with nominal interest rates on commercial paper or corporate bonds, or with realized real interest rates on commercial paper. Over the longer period from 1908 to 1984, using monthly data, there is some indication of a negative relation between deficits and nominal or real interest rates (Evans, 1987a, Tables 1–3). Evans also explores the effects of expected future budget deficits or surpluses. He assumes that people would have expected future deficits in advance of tax cuts, such as in 1981, and future surpluses in advance of tax hikes. But interest rates turn out typically not to rise in advance of tax cuts and not to fall in advance of tax hikes.

Overall, the empirical results on interest rates support the Ricardian view. Given these findings it is remarkable that most macroeconomists remain confident that budget deficits raise interest rates.

Consumption and Saving

Many empirical studies have searched for effects of budget deficits or social security on consumption and saving. Most of these studies—exemplified by Levis Kochin (1974) and the papers surveyed in Louis Esposito (1978)—rely on estimates of coefficients in consumption functions. Basically, the results are all over the map, with some favoring Ricardian equivalence, and others not.

One such study, a comparison of saving in Canada and the United States, was carried out by Chris Carroll and Lawrence Summers (1987). They note that the private saving rates in the two countries were similar until the early 1970s, but have since diverged; for 1983–85 the Canadian rate was higher by about six percentage points. After holding fixed some macroeconomic variables and aspects of the tax systems that influence saving, the authors isolate a roughly one-to-one, positive effect of government budget deficits on private saving. That is, the rise in the private saving rate in Canada, relative to that in the United States, reflected the greater increase in the Canadian budget deficit as a ratio to GNP. Thus, as implied by the Ricardian view, the relative values of the net national saving rates in the two countries appeared to be invariant with the relative values of the budget deficits. These results are particularly interesting because the focus on relative performance in Canada and the United States holds constant the many forces that have common influences on the two countries. It may be that this procedure lessens the problems of identification that hamper most studies of consumption functions.

Recent fiscal policy in Israel comes close to a natural experiment for studying the interplay between budget deficits and saving.[7] In 1983 the gross national saving rate of 13 percent corresponded to a private saving rate of 17 percent and a public saving rate of −4 percent. In 1984 the dramatic rise in the budget deficit led to a public saving rate of −11 percent. (A principal reason for the deficit was the adverse effect of the increase in the inflation rate on the collection of real tax revenues.) For present purposes, the interesting observation is that the private saving rate rose from 17 percent to 26 percent, so that the national saving rate changed little; actually rising from 13 percent to 15 percent. Then the stabilization program in 1985 eliminated the budget deficit, along with most of the inflation, so that the public saving rate increased from −11 percent in 1984 to 0 in 1985–86 and −2 percent in 1987. The private saving rate decreased dramatically at the same time—from 26 percent in 1984 to 19 percent in 1985 and 14 percent in 1986–87. Therefore, the national saving rates were relatively stable, going from 15 percent in 1984 to 18 percent in 1985, 14 percent in 1986, and 12 percent in 1987. The main point is that this evidence reveals the roughly one-to-one offset between public and private saving that the Ricardian view predicts.

Concluding Observations

The Ricardian approach to budget deficits amounts to the statement that the government's fiscal impact is summarized by the present value of its expenditures. Given this present value, rearrangements of the timing of taxes—as implied by budget deficits—have no first-order effect on the economy. Second-order effects arise for various reasons, which include the distorting effects of taxes, the uncertainties about individual incomes and tax obligations, the imperfections of credit markets, and the finiteness of life. To say that these effects are second order is not to say that they are uninteresting; in fact, the analysis of differential taxation in the theory of public finance is second order in the same sense. However, careful analysis of these effects tends to deliver predictions about budget deficits that differ from those of standard macroeconomic models.

I have argued that empirical findings on interest rates, consumption and saving, and the current-account balance tend mainly to support the Ricardian viewpoint. However, this empirical analysis involves substantial problems about data and identification, and the results are sometimes inconclusive. It would be useful to assemble additional evidence, especially in an international context.

Although the majority of economists still lean toward standard macroeconomic models of fiscal policy, it is remarkable how respectable the Ricardian approach has become in the last decade. Most macroeconomists now feel obligated to state the Ricardian position, even if they then go on to argue that it is either theoretically or empirically in error. I predict that this trend will continue and that the Ricardian approach will become the benchmark model for assessing fiscal policy.

■ *I am grateful for support of research from the National Science Foundation. Also, I appreciate the high quality comments provided by the editors.*

87

[1]The calculations use the government's interest rate in each period to calculate present values, and assume perfect foresight with respect to future government expenditures and taxes. For further discussion see Ben McCallum (1984) and Robert Barro (1989).

[2]The term, Ricardian equivalence theorem, was introduced to macroeconomists by James Buchanan (1976). After Gerald O'Driscoll (1977) documented Ricardo's reservations about this result, some economists have referred to the equivalence finding as being non-Ricardian. But, as far as I have been able to discover, David Ricardo (1951) was the first to articulate this theory. Therefore, the attribution of the equivalence theorem to Ricardo is appropriate even if he had doubts about some of the theorem's assumptions. As to whether the presence of this idea in Ricardo's writings is important for scientific progress, I would refer to Nathan Rosenberg's (1976, p. 79) general views on innovations in the social sciences: "...what often happens in economics is that, as concern mounts over a particular problem...an increasing number of professionals commit their time and energies to it. We then eventually realize that there were all sorts of treatments of the subject in the earlier literature. ... We then proceed to read much of our more sophisticated present-day understanding back into the work of earlier writers whose analysis was inevitably more fragmentary and incomplete than the later achievement. It was this retrospective view which doubtless inspired Whitehead to say somewhere that everything of importance has been said before—but by someone who did not discover it." (This last point relates to "Stigler's Law," which states that nothing is named after the person who discovered it.)

[3]Philippe Weil (1987) and Miles Kimball (1987) analyze conditions that ensure an interior solution for intergenerational transfers. Douglas Bernheim and Kyle Bagwell (1988) argue that difficulties arise if altruistic transfers are pervasive. See Barro (1989) for a discussion of their analysis.

[4]The assumption is the real debt remains permanently higher by the amount of the initial deficit. For some related calculations, see Merton Miller and Charles Upton (1974, Chapter 8) and James Poterba and Lawrence Summers (1987, Section I).

[6]A colleague of mine argues that a "normative" model should be defined as a model that fits the data badly.
[7]I am grateful to Ed Offenbacker for calling my attention to the Israeli experience. The data, all expressed in U.S. dollars, are from Bank of Israel, 1987.

References

Ando, Albert and Franco Modigliani, "The 'Life Cycle' Hypothesis of Saving: Aggregate Implications and Tests," *American Economic Review,* March 1963, *53,* 55–84.

Bailey, Martin J., *National Income and the Price Level,* 2nd edition, New York: McGraw Hill, 1971.

Bank of Israel, *Annual Report.* Jerusalem, 1987.

Barro, Robert J., "Are Government Bonds Net Wealth?" *Journal of Political Economy,* November/December 1974, *82,* 1095–1117.

Barro, Robert J., "On the Determination of the Public Debt," *Journal of Political Economy,* October 1979, *87,* 940–971.

Barro, Robert J., "U.S. Deficits since World War I," *Scandinavian Journal of Economics,* 1986, *88,* no. 1, 195–222.

Barro, Robert J., "Government Spending, Interest Rates, Prices, and Budget Deficits in the United Kingdom, 1701–1918," *Journal of Monetary Economics,* September 1987, *20,* 221–247.

Barro, Robert J., "The Neoclassical Approach to Fiscal Policy," in Barro, Robert J., ed., *Modern Business Cycle Theory,* Cambridge: Harvard University Press, 1989.

Barsky, Robert B., N. Gregory Mankiw, and Stephen P. Zeldes, "Ricardian Consumers with Keynesian Propensities," *American Economic Review,* September 1986, *76,* 676–691.

Bernheim, B. Douglas, Andrei Shleifer, and Lawrence H. Summers, "The Strategic Bequest Motive," *Journal of Political Economy,* December 1985, *93,* 1045–1076.

Bernheim, B. Douglas and Kyle Bagwell, "Is Everything Neutral?" *Journal of Political Economy,* April 1988, *96,* 308–338.

Board of Governors of the Federal Reserve System, *Balance Sheets for the U.S. Economy, 1948–87,* Washington D.C., October 1988.

Brown, E. Cary, "Fiscal Policy in the 'Thirties: a Reappraisal," *Journal of Political Economy,* December 1956, *46,* 857–879.

Buchanan, James M., "Barro on the Ricardian Equivalence Theorem," *Journal of Political Economy,* April 1976, *84,* 337–342.

Buchanan, James M. and Richard E. Wagner, *Democracy in Deficit,* New York: Academic Press, 1977.

Carroll, Chris and Lawrence H. Summers, "Why Have Private Savings Rates in the United States and Canada Diverged?" *Journal of Monetary Economics,* September 1987, *20,* 249–279.

Chan, Louis K. C., "Uncertainty and the Neutrality of Government Financing Policy," *Journal of Monetary Economics,* May 1983, *11,* 351–372.

Council of Economic Advisers, *Annual Report,* Washington: U.S. Government Printing Office, 1962.

Darby, Michael, R., *The Effects of Social Security on Income and the Capital Stock,* American Enterprise Institute, Washington D.C., 1979.

Eisner, Robert and Paul Pieper, "A New View of the Federal Debt and Budget Deficits," *American Economic Review,* March 1984, *74,* 11–29.

Esposito, Louis, "Effect of Social Security on Saving: Review of Studies Using U.S. Time-Series Data," *Social Security Bulletin,* May 1978, *41,* 9–17.

Evans, Paul, "Interest Rates and Expected Future Budget Deficits in the United States," *Journal of Political Economy*, February 1987a, *95*, 34–58.

Evans, Paul, "Do Budget Deficits Raise Nominal Interest Rates? Evidence from Six Industrial Countries," *Journal of Monetary Economics*, September 1987b, *20*, 281–300.

Evans, Paul, "Do Budget Deficits Affect the Current Account?" unpublished, Ohio State University, August 1988.

Feldstein, Martin S., "Social Security, Induced Retirement, and Aggregate Capital Accumulation," *Journal of Political Economy*, September/October 1974, *82*, 905–926.

Feldstein, Martin S., "Perceived Wealth in Bonds and Social Security a Comment," *Journal of Political Economy*, April 1976, *84*, 331–336.

Hayashi, Fumio, "Tests for Liquidity Constraints: a Critical Survey and some New Observations," in Bewley, Truman F., ed., *Advances in Econometrics, Fifth World Congress*, Cambridge: Cambridge University Press, 1987.

Kimball, Miles S., "Making Sense of Two-Sided Altruism," *Journal of Monetary Economics*, September 1987, *20*, 301–326.

King, Mervyn A., "Tax Policy and Consumption Smoothing," unpublished, London School of Economics, April 1986.

Kochin, Levis A., "Are Future Taxes Anticipated by Consumers?" *Journal of Money, Credit and Banking*, August 1974, *6*, 385–394.

Kotlikoff, Laurence J., "Intergenerational Transfers and Savings," *Journal of Economic Perspectives*, Spring 1988, *2*, 41–58.

Kotlikoff, Laurence J. and Lawrence H. Summers, "The Role of Intergenerational Transfers in Aggregate Capital Accumulation," *Journal of Political Economy*, August 1981, *89*, 706–732.

McCallum, Ben T., "Are Bond-financed Deficits Inflationary? A Ricardian Analysis," *Journal of Political Economy*, February 1984, *92*, 123–135.

Miller, Merton H. and Charles W. Upton, *Macroeconomics, a Neoclassical Introduction*, Homewood, IL: Irwin, 1974.

Modigliani, Franco, "Long-run Implications of Alternative Fiscal Policies and the Burden of the National Debt," *Economic Journal*, December 1961, *71*, 730–755.

Modigliani, Franco, "The Role of Intergenerational Transfers and Life Cycle Saving in the Accumulation of Wealth," *Journal of Economic Perspectives*, Spring 1988, *2*, 15–40.

Modigliani, Franco and Richard Brumberg, "Utility Analysis and the Consumption Function: an Interpretation of Cross-Section Data," in

Kurihara, K. K., editor, *Post-Keynesian Economics*, New Brunswick: Rutgers University Press, 1954.

Modigliani, Franco and Merton H. Miller, "The Cost of Capital, Corporation Finance and the Theory of Investment," *American Economic Review*, June 1958, *48*, 261–297.

Mundell, Robert A., "Money, Debt, and the Rate of Interest," in Mundell, R. A., *Monetary Theory*, Pacific Palisades: Goodyear, 1971.

O'Driscoll, Gerald P., "The Ricardian Nonequivalence Theorem," *Journal of Political Economy*, February 1977, *85*, 207–210.

Pigou, A. C., *A Study in Public Finance*, London: Macmillan, 1928.

Plosser, Charles I., "Government Financing Decisions and Asset Returns," *Journal of Monetary Economics*, May 1982, *9*, 325–352.

Plosser, Charles I., "Further Evidence on the Relation between Fiscal Policy and the Term Structure," *Journal of Monetary Economics*, September 1987, *20*, 343–367.

Poterba, James M. and Lawrence H. Summers, "Finite Lifetimes and the Savings Effects of Budget Deficits," *Journal of Monetary Economics*, September 1987, *20*, 369–391.

Ricardo, David, "Funding System," in Sraffa, Piero, editor, *The Works and Correspondence of David Ricardo, volume IV, Pamphlets and Papers, 1815–1823*, Cambridge: Cambridge University Press, 1951.

Rosenberg, Nathan, *Perspectives on Technology*, Cambridge: Cambridge University Press, 1976.

Sahasakul, Chaipat, "The U.S. Evidence on Optimal Taxation over Time," *Journal of Monetary Economics*, November 1986, *18*, 251–275.

Siegel, Jeremy J., "Inflation-Induced Distortions in Government and Private Saving Statistics," *Review of Economics & Statistics*, April 1979, *61*, 83–90.

Tobin, James and Willem Buiter, "Fiscal and Monetary Policies, Capital Formation, and Economic Activity," in von Furstenberg, George M., editor, *The Government and Capital Formation*, Cambridge: Ballinger, 1980.

U.S. Treasury Department, *The Effect of Deficits on Prices of Financial Assets: Theory and Evidence*, Washington: U.S. Government Printing Office, 1984.

Weil, Philippe, "Love Thy Children: Reflections on the Barro Debt Neutrality Theorem," *Journal of Monetary Economics*, May 1987, *19*, 377–391.

Yotsuzuka, Toshiki, "Ricardian Equivalence in the Presence of Capital Market Imperfections," *Journal of Monetary Economics*, September 1987, *20*, 411–436.

Budget Deficits: Rhetoric and Reality

Robert Eisner

Whatever the real or imagined ills of the economy, the news media, most politicians and a fair proportion of the economics profession are quick to point to the culprit: "the budget deficit." No matter that few appear to know or care precisely what deficit they are talking about or how it is measured. No matter that few bother to explain in terms of a relevant model just how government deficits may be expected to impact the economy. No matter that few offer any empirical data to sustain their judgments.

So budget deficits cause inflation. Budget deficits raise interest rates. Budget deficits bring on the trade deficits. Budget deficits crowd out investment. Budget deficits are an irresponsible mortgage on the future. And budget deficits caused the October 1987 stock market crash and now threaten further financial cataclysms! Is there truth in any of these assertions? Or does it all depend?

Budget deficits do matter and their effects, contrary to Barro's "Ricardian equivalence theorem," can be substantial. As most economists have recognized for at least half a century, budget deficits can, however, be too small as well as too large. To know which, you have to measure them right. And you have to analyze their role in the world in which we live. Pure Walrasian and rational-expectation market-clearing models may prove more useful for academic advancement than for promotion of economic health.

I need not repeat many of the objections to the equivalence theorem raised by Bernheim and Gramlich and addressed by Barro in this symposium. However, there is one overriding objection that cannot be overstressed. We simply do not live in a Walrasian, market-clearing world, and all our economic agents—as opposed apparently to some economists—know it. Aside then from all the issues of uncertainty as to who might pay any future taxes occasioned by a current deficit, real world economic agents have no reason to assume that there will be any additional tax burden at all. With the existence of what, in the older vernacular, we used to call simply "less-than-full-employment"—the so-called "natural" (God-given?) rate of unemployment belongs perhaps with those who accept the doctrine of creationism—increases in current consumption need not involve any borrowing from the future or from any future generation of taxpayers. The consumption is supplied from otherwise unutilized resources. With the consumption then will come more, not less investment. The economy will move to a higher growth path. Extra taxes in the future, if there are to be any, may then readily be paid out of higher future incomes.

I believe there are serious problems with our fiscal policy. These relate to fundamental national priorities and the provision of public goods, now and for the future. But the current size of the federal deficit is not "our number one economic problem," if indeed it is a problem at all.

On Measures of Deficits, Government Liabilities and Assets

One might think it obvious that in order to talk about budget deficits, one must first have an accurate measure of their size. But the measurement of budget deficits has generally been a highly ignored issue. Here are some of the most fundamental problems.

First, the national income accounts measure of budget deficits, furnished by the Bureau of Economic Analysis, is a handier economic tool than the official "unified" budget. This measure focuses on current income flows and avoids some of the nonsense of counting sale of real or financial assets as "receipts" (or as offsets to expenditures) and the purchase of financial assets as "outlays." Such sales and purchases are essentially portfolio changes, having no first-order effect on the net debt or net worth of government or the private sector. The unified budget and the NIA budget can differ by nontrivial amounts. In fiscal 1985 the deficit on a national income accounts basis was indeed $28 billion less than the unified budget deficit. The difference was only $7 billion in fiscal 1986 and $1 billion in 1987 but was $11.7 billion in 1988.

Second, while what goes on within the beltway is important, Washington is not the only seat of government in the United States. Along with the fiscal 1988 federal deficit of $141.5 billion on a national income accounts basis, there was a state and local government aggregate *surplus* of $54.4 billion. It would certainly seem in order to take this into account, if only because the federal deficit was swollen by grants-in-aid to state and local governments totalling $108.6 billion. Including the non-federal surpluses knocks the total government deficit for fiscal 1987 down to $87.1 billion, or about 1.8 percent of GNP.

Third, the federal accounts make no distinction, in the expenditures contributing to a "deficit," between current expenses and investment. Most of the large corporations in the United States would find themselves in deficit if they had to include capital expenditures rather than depreciation charges in their profit and loss statements.[2] The Office of Management and Budget classified $127 billion of projected "Federal, investment outlays" for fiscal 1988 as expenditures on physical assets and another $80 billion of non-physical investment, for education, training, research, and development (*Special Analyses*, p. D-3). If we were to substitute a reasonable estimate of capital consumption for these $207 billion of investment expenditures, we would reduce the measure of the federal deficit by another $70 billion or so. With similar adjustments for state and local budgets, particularly if we were to capitalize the vast expenditures for education and include in the national income account budget only the depreciation of human capital, the entire government budget deficit would disappear. And with it would have to go the oft-repeated charge that our budget deficits mean that we are reckless with our future. Our public policy may well be mortgaging the next generation, but it is not "the deficit" that is doing it.[3,4]

Indeed, there is only one way in which we can allow today to injure tomorrow. That is to act today so that tomorrow has less productive capital, and that includes capital of all kinds—business plant, equipment, and inventories *and* government, household and nonprofit institution tangible capital, and human and intangible capital in all sectors. The impact of budget deficits—and budget deficit reduction—on intertemporal distribution then comes back smack to their impact on net investment, on *all* net investment.

We may get some perspective by sober study of federal balance sheets on the one hand and estimates of the *nation's* capital stock on the other. First, as seen in Table 1, despite year after year of deficits by official, conventional measure, from 1945 to 1980 the net worth of the federal government *rose* from a negative $44 billion to a positive $382 billion. The values of its tangible assets of land, structures, equipment and inventories and of its financial assets of gold, securities, mortgages and loans had grown more than its liabilities. Indeed, even ignoring real assets, the federal "net debt,"[5] the excess of liabilities over financial assets, had grown only from $230 billion to $441 billion, far less relatively than the more than 400 percent increases in prices over this period. It is true, however, that net worth turned down again after 1980 as deficits soared—although accounting for the value of federal mineral rights under the land and offshore might still leave it positive (Boskin et al., 1985).

Table 1

Federal Government Consolidated Balance Sheet:
Liabilities and Tangible and Financial Assets

Item	Year and Amount (Billions of Dollars)			
	1945	1960	1980	1984
Tangible assets	186.2	205.8	822.5	1,118.0
Reproducible assets	179.3	187.4	648.1	915.2
Land	6.8	18.4	174.4	202.8
Financial assets	102.8	124.7	720.9	887.4
Total assets	289.0	330.4	1,543.4	2,005.4
Total liabilities	332.6	331.8	1,161.6	2,063.3
Net debt (total liabilities minus financial assets)	229.8	207.1	440.7	1,175.9
Net worth	−43.7	−1.3	381.8	−57.9

Including Federal Reserve and credit agencies, based on market or replacement values.
Source: Eisner (1986), Table 3.3, p. 29.

After the dramatic increases in debt taken out to finance the fighting of World War II, the history of U.S. debt until the early 1980s was one of major reduction in its relevant, *relative* magnitude. The gross federal debt as a ratio of GNP, shown in Table 2, actually fell from 110 percent at the end of 1945 (and 114 percent at the end of 1946) to 26 percent in 1980, before rising to its current level of about 42 percent. And net federal debt per capita fell, in constant 1982 dollars, from $8639 at the end of 1945 to $2219 in 1980, before rising to something over $6000 currently.

The bottom line, though, should be the capital or wealth of the nation. Table 3 provides an estimate of $23.7 trillion (at the end of 1981) for total capital, of which government and government enterprise capital comprised $2.7 trillion or 9.4 percent.

The largest portion of the total by far, some $14.6 trillion or 61.6 percent, is accountable, however, to households. And most of that is the intangible or human capital attributable chiefly to government-financed education.[6]

The Real Deficit and Growth, Employment and Inflation

The issues of substituting depreciation for federal investment expenditures, including state and local budgets in the total deficit calculation, and examining net national worth are major. But rather than trying now to manufacture all of the figures

Table 2
Measures of the Federal Debt

Year	Gross Federal Debt Held by Public		Net Debt per Capita
	Billions of Dollars	*% of GNP*	*1982 Dollars*
1945	232.2	110.2	8,639
1946	241.9	113.9	7,227
1960	237.2	46.0	3,576
1970	284.9	28.1	2,815
1980	715.1	26.2[a]	2,219
1984	1,312.6	34.5	4,496
1986	1,746.1	40.9	5,963
1987	1,888.1	41.3	
1988	2,050.0	41.8	
Change, 1945–1980	+ 479.9	− 84.0	− 6,420
Change, 1980–1984	+ 597.5	+ 8.3	+ 2,277
Change, 1984–1986	+ 433.5	+ 6.4	+ 1,467
Change, 1986–1988	+ 303.9	+ 0.9	

Adapted and updated from Eisner (1986), Tables 2.3 and 2.5, pp. 18–19, 21.
[a] Percent of third quarter GNP for this and subsequent years. For years up to 1970, where fiscal years ended June 30, percents were of corresponding calendar year GNP.

relevant to those issues, I should like to focus at this point on a simpler but crucial measure: the otherwise unadjusted federal budget deficit, itself, corrected for inflation.

As Paul Pieper and I have indicated in a series of papers—starting with Eisner and Pieper (1984)—and as I have elaborated in *How Real Is the Federal Deficit?* (Eisner, 1986) and elsewhere—we must look at the *real* deficit. This means, for many critical purposes, a measure of the deficit that corresponds to real changes in the government's debt, and hence to changes in the public's perception of the value of its holdings of that debt.

The change in the real value of the net federal debt may be viewed as the sum of three components: the nominal deficit exclusive of offsetting changes in financial assets and liabilities; changes in the nominal market value of existing financial assets and liabilities due to changes in nominal interest rates; and changes in the real values due to changes in the general level of prices (inflation). When we add these "interest effects" and "price effects" to the federal budget surplus (or subtract them from the deficit) we get a measure of the *real deficit*. The real deficit corresponds to the change in the real value of the net government debt, which it should be noted is not at all the nominal deficit divided by a price deflator. That measure, the real value of the nominal change, appears to be an arithmetic construct devoid of economic content.

Table 3
Capital Stocks, 1981

Component of Capital	Billions of Current Dollars
Business	6,085.9
Tangible	5,528.9
Intangible (R & D)	557.0
Nonprofit	248.2
Government	2,220.4
Government enterprise	476.3
Household	14,626.0
Tangible	3,949.7
Intangible (human)	10,676.3
Total	23,746.4

Source: Eisner (1985), Table 13, p. 47.

The real deficit, until the last six years of the Reagan Administration, was very different from the nominal one that drew all the attention. As shown in Table 4, the $153 billion of nominal deficits during the four Carter years, from 1977 through 1980, were actually surpluses totaling $72 billion. Rising prices, reducing the real value of the dollar, was serving as an inflation tax on the holders of government obligations. Rising interest rates, in part associated with *rising* rates of inflation, further reduced the market value of outstanding debt. In effect, measures of the official, nominal deficit include in expenditures nominal rather than real interest payments. They fail to impute as offsetting receipts the component of nominal interest payments which goes only to compensate holders of Treasury debt for their capital losses, and the Treasury's gains.

The nominal *high-employment* deficits, which averaged 0.53 percent of GNP from 1977 through 1981, correspond to real high-employment surpluses averaging 1.76 percent. All this suggests the need for some substantial revision of economic history and perhaps of the economic theory inspired by a misreading of the facts. In the words of Robert Lucas and Thomas Sargent (1981, pp. 295–296), the lesson of the 1970s was that "massive government budget deficits and high rates of monetary expansion" were accompanied not by decreasing unemployment but by *growing* unemployment *and* growing inflation. It was indeed the failure of the Keynesian paradigm in this regard to which Lucas (1981, p. 2) points as the motivation for his own search for a new macroeconomic model.

But viewing the real budget surpluses we are led rather to conclude that it was aggregate demand, in the face of the inflationary supply shocks of soaring petroleum prices and rising raw material prices on world markets, that failed after all. These exogenous forces brought on an inflation tax that reduced the real value of private wealth in the form of government debt, aggravating a loss due to the lower market

Table 4

Nominal and Real Budget Surplus or Deficit on National Income Account, Billions of Dollars, and Nominal and Real High-Employment Budget as Percent of GNP

| | Surplus or Deficit | | | |
| | Actual Billions of Dollars | | High-Employment As Percent of GNP | |
Year	Nominal	Real	Nominal	Real
1977	− 45.9	− 0.6	− 1.06	1.30
1978	− 29.5	32.9	− 0.73	2.15
1979	− 16.1	32.1	− 0.08	1.91
1980	− 61.2	7.6	− 0.65	1.97
1981	− 64.3	− 18.3	− 0.11	1.45
1982	− 148.2	− 177.2	− 1.06	− 2.01
1983	− 178.6	− 101.2	− 1.72	0.62
1984	− 175.8	− 154.1	− 2.51	− 1.92
Totals				
1977−80	− 152.7	72.0		
1981−84	− 566.9	− 450.8		
Means				
1977−81	− 43.4	10.7	− 0.53	1.76
1982−84	− 167.4	− 144.2	− 1.76	− 1.10

Derived from Eisner (1986), Table B.7, p. 192, and Table 8.3, p. 87.

values associated with rising interest rates. It was then relatively tight fiscal policy, combined with the new tight monetary policy initiated in 1979, both continued through the first half of 1982, which brought us to 10.7 percent unemployment by December of that year.

What is the appropriate underlying theory? Going back to Pigou, Haberler, Lange and Patinkin, increased real holdings of government obligations by the private sector—money or interest-bearing—create an excess demand for goods. This must drive up output or prices or both. In the somewhat more recent formulation of Modigliani's life cycle theory of consumption, they enter as an increase of wealth in the individual's budget constraint. As he or she tries to maximize lifetime utility or welfare, the increased wealth is allocated to present and future needs and thus serves to generate increases in current and planned future consumption.

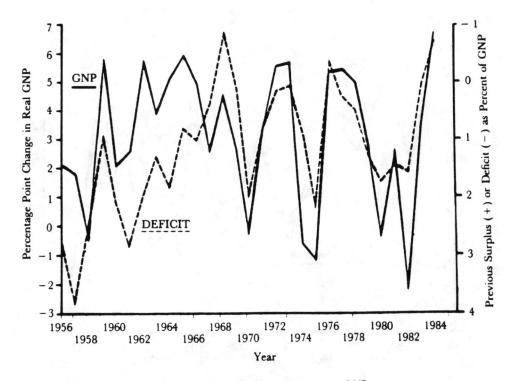

Fig. 1. Adjusted Deficit and Change in GNP

Whether this increased demand can be effected in real goods depends upon whether the economy is capable of increased production. And this comes back to the issue that provoked modern macroeconomics half a century ago, and which remains critical to any policy decisions today. That is the issue of unemployment and unused resources. If there is no involuntary unemployment and there are no idle resources, increased demand cannot generate more output; it can only bring higher prices. This is apparently the world of Milton Friedman (1968) and then Lucas, although they allow for various short run real effects as economic agents are slow or asymmetrical in their assimilation of information. But if you doubt that somehow our economy has generally been at its "natural rate" of employment, you may not be shocked to learn that real structural budget deficits have over the last several decades proved stimulatory to the economy.

And that is exactly the fact. As Figure 1 makes abundantly clear, the greater the real or inflation-adjusted high-employment federal deficit from 1955 to 1983, the greater was the next year's increase in GNP. The less the deficit, or the more the surplus, the less was the subsequent increase in GNP, or the more the GNP tended to decline. And since more rapid increases in output are associated with declines in unemployment, and less rapid increases (or decreases) with increases in unemployment, a corresponding close fit is seen between the curves in Figure 2 for the adjusted budget surplus and subsequent changes in unemployment.

But that is only part of the story. Budget deficits have not only been related positively to growth of GNP as a whole, but also to growth of its components of both consumption and investment. We may note in Table 6 that each percentage point of real high-employment deficit was associated with growth of consumption the next year amounting to 0.642 percentage points of consumption. It was also associated with growth in gross private domestic investment equal to 1.383 percentage points of GNP.

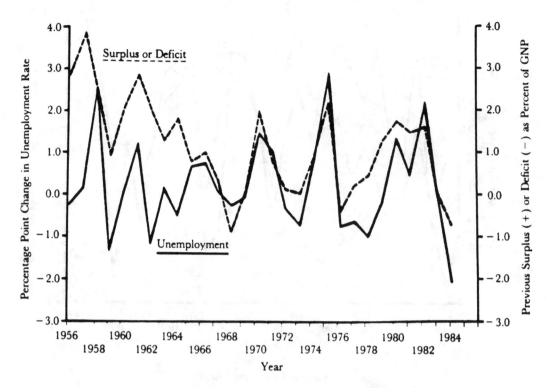

Fig. 2. Adjusted Surplus and Change in Unemployment

The evidence is thus that deficits have not crowded out investment. There has rather been "crowding in." And this should come as no surprise except to those devotees of "the new macroeconomics" who have embraced the old Euclidian world where employment and output are fixed (at those nefarious "natural" rates). We are in fact not only on the rising slope of the infamous Laffer curve but also on the rising slope of the curve for investment implicit in Lange's old (1938) article on the optimal propensity to consume.[11] Where more resources are available, and perverse monetary policy does not raise interest rates so as to preclude their use, more consumption may indeed be expected to be associated with more investment. The life cycle model, as we have noted, and Friedman's permanent income theory as well, both imply that deficits will bring more consumption now and in the future. This should lead rational producers to try to produce more to meet current consumption demand but also to undertake more investment to provide the capital to produce more in the future.

Real *gross* private domestic investment as a percent of real GNP was 18.0 percent in 1979 and exactly the same figure, 18.0 percent, in 1987, despite a 3.8 percentage point move in the National Income Account federal budget, from a surplus of 0.4 percent of GNP to a deficit of 3.4 percent. Over the same period, however, net exports, which essentially account for net foreign investment, moved from +0.1 percent of GNP to −3.5 percent. The move to real structural budget deficit had something to do with this, by stimulating the economy and thereby increasing our imports. But in 1983, when the recession-swollen deficit was 5.2 percent of GNP, net exports were only −0.6 percent—and gross private domestic investment was down to 15.4 percent of GNP.

The large move to negative net exports and negative foreign investment from 1983 to 1987 is very largely accountable to the one-third previous rise, from 100.8 to

132.0, in a trade-weighted index of the real exchange rate for the dollar. The fall in the dollar since early 1985 has increased the value of U.S. assets abroad, thus offsetting the negative foreign investment. If the Federal Reserve were to permit the dollar to fall further, our measured foreign investment, and hence net saving, would increase with the stimulation to our exports. And we would have a further gain in the dollar value of our mainly foreign-currency denominated foreign assets and in the dollar earnings from those assets.

The evidence that budget deficits have caused a decline in correctly measured national saving, even as a percent of GNP, is thus doubtful indeed.[16] And in terms of a comprehensive measure of national saving, including public investment in infrastructure, education and research, misguided efforts to reduce the budget deficit are by far the greatest threat to investment in our future.

A New View of the Past, and Balance for the Future

What has been going on and where do we go from here? First, budget deficits did not contribute to the inflation of the 1970s, which reached its peak in 1981. This stemmed from the supply shocks in petroleum and world markets for agricultural products, not a surge in demand. The inflation tax converted supposed deficits into substantial real surpluses until the latter half of 1982. It was large structural surpluses, along with tight money, that brought us the worst recession since the great depression of the 1930s and an unemployment rate of 10.7 percent by December 1982.

It was then the huge swing to real deficit in the latter half of 1982, along with the switch to easier money, and the continued deficits thereafter which sparked our substantial economic recovery. It may of course be noted, as was probably reflected in the earlier regression results, that the large deficits were accompanied by a sharp reduction in the rate of inflation as well as interest rates.

What does that indicate now? To begin, with all of the nonsense in current calculations of the deficit, "balance" in the conventional sense makes no sense. At the 1988 inflation rate of 4 percent, for example, the inflation tax on the $2,100 billion of our current federal debt held by the public implies that nominal balance would be a real surplus of $84 billion. The federal government would be reducing the real value of its debt, and the assets of the public in the form of that debt, by $84 billion per year, with all that this would imply for consumption, portfolio adjustment, investment, output and employment.

A much better concept of balance, in a growing economy such as ours, with or without inflation, would be one in which the debt-income ratio were constant. The necessary and sufficient condition for this, of course, is that the debt grow at the same rate—no faster or slower—as income. I offer this not as an iron-clad imperative, regardless of circumstances, but rather as a rule of thumb which would, one may note, be equally appropriate for an individual or a corporation.

For the federal government, with GNP growing at about 7.5 percent per year, the debt could then grow at 7.5 percent per year. With the gross federal debt at $2100 billion, this comes to an increase in debt, and hence a nominal current deficit, of $157 billion. It may be noted that this "balanced deficit" is almost exactly the actual nominal deficit of $155 billion for fiscal year 1988 and is exceeded only trivially by the gloomier projections, without further reductions, for 1989. And if we take into account state and local government budgets, we find that for total government we are in substantial surplus. Despite all the furor, total government debt is currently a declining ratio of GNP.[17]

This rule of balance should not be engraved in stone—or in the Constitution. Even this measure should at times show a deficit, at times a surplus. It depends on the shape of the economy, on associated monetary policies and on relative needs for public and private investment. At least until the reductions legislated in late 1987 and early 1988, the nation's current federal deficits did appear large for the long run. They implied an increasing ratio of federal debt-to-GNP. Over the long run, it might have been argued then, the federal deficits should be brought down. But that judgment should depend on what is happening to state and local governments. And most fundamentally, it should depend on how much of the nation's resources are being devoted and should be devoted to private versus public investment.

If public investment in the education and health of America, in the nation's stock of basic scientific and technological knowledge and in its collective resources and infrastructure are to be increased, continued large nominal deficits may well be in order, and even large real deficits.

It is tempting to suggest, recalling Abba Lerner's old principle of "functional finance," that nominal deficits will never cause permanent real deficits that are too large. If an economy has unemployed resources, a large nominal deficit will increase aggregate demand, both real and nominal, until it reaches full (or "natural") employment. At that point (if not before), inflation will have risen, and will keep rising until the inflation tax, reducing the real value of existing government debt, is sufficient to bring the rate of increase in the real value of that debt—the real deficit—down to equality with the rate of growth in real GNP. Any still greater nominal deficit will then only raise the rate of inflation but not the rate of increase in the real value of government debt and hence not the real deficit. There is hence no further increase in real consumption, and no crowding out of investment, even at full employment. There will, however, be crowding out of investment if the monetary authority acts to reduce the inflation by tightening credit and raising interest rates.

If we are not facing a full-employment, excess-demand inflation, the case for nominal and real deficit reduction, despite what has apparently become dominant conventional wisdom among politicians, press and pundits and, I must confess, considerable numbers of economists, is shaky indeed. If deficits are to be reduced, a prime concern should be avoidance of a recession, and this, as Keynes argued a half century ago, is not to be accomplished by lopping off a boom. Too many of us have allowed our targets of full employment to recede with the political winds and misguided concern for inflation. We may take comfort that, from the 10.7 percent official measure of December 1982, unemployment had declined (as of November 1988) to 5.4 percent. But whatever happened to that "full employment" target of 4 percent unemployment? The unemployment rate was 3.5 and 3.4 percent twenty years ago.

At this time, therefore, the prime aggregate policy instrument should be monetary policy, and it should be more stimulatory. Significant and sustained increases in the monetary base would lower interest rates and encourage a further decline in the dollar.[18] Both gross private domestic investment and exports would thus increase. Not

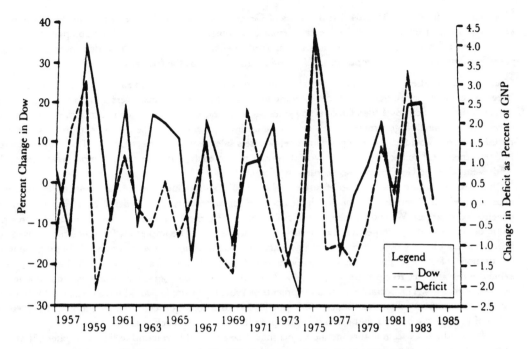

Fig. 3. Changes in Dow Industrials and Price-Adjusted Deficit

only would the U.S. trade deficit finally come down, but the nominal budget deficits themselves would be reduced. Lower interest rates would contribute directly; each percentage point drop would save the Treasury over $20 billion in annual interest payments within two or three years, as the debt is rolled over.[19] And the stimulus to the economy would further reduce the deficit as tax revenues rise and unemployment benefit payouts decline.

And what about the stock market? Those who have trumpeted budget deficits as the cause of share price declines would do well to think again. I have for some time now been gleefully passing out copies of charts such as Figure 3 and regressions from my 1986 book showing that increases in deficits were strongly correlated with *in*creases in the Dow. Of course, I can add that the October 1987 crash followed immediately on the news that "the deficit" had declined from $221 billion in fiscal 1986 to $148 billion in 1987. Further *reductions* in the deficit might bring new, dismal reverberations on Wall Street!

■ *I am grateful for valuable comments and suggestions by the editors, Timothy Taylor, Joseph E. Stiglitz and Carl Shapiro. I have benefitted as well from the financial support of a series of National Science Foundation grants, including the current SES-8707979.*

■ *Robert Eisner is William R. Kenan Professor of Economics, Northwestern University, Evanston, Illinois.*

[2]For example, from 1970 to 1984, the liabilities of General Motors grew 546 percent, from $4.3 billion to $27.9 billion, and those of IBM 530 percent, from $2.6 billion to $16.3 billion. Both companies have of course been eminently profitable and neither reported "deficits." The gross federal debt over this period grew 361 percent, to the accompaniment of myriad warnings about the federal deficit.

[3]Sales of public assets of land and mineral rights and other acts of "privatization," if accomplished at bargain basement prices, have the effect of adding to the burden of future taxpayers even as they reduce the current official deficit. By Federal accounting rules we could indeed reduce the deficit to zero by the simple expedient of selling off government assets on a lease-back arrangement. In the initial years the government rental payments could easily be kept enough below assets sales receipts to meet Gramm-Rudman balanced budget targets. Of course, the rental payments would mount each year as more and more assets are sold. And eventually the Government would run out of assets to sell!

[4]It has been suggested that a comprehensive budget should also include the vast amounts of "contingent expenditures" or commitments, of which prospective social security and Federal employee retirement benefits loom largest. We should then, in principle, take their present value and offset them by the present value of corresponding prospective tax receipts. Certainly, it would be important for economic analysts to keep these contingency obligations, which have varying amounts of immediacy, in mind. Including them in calculations of "the budget deficit," however, would appear to be fraught with mischief. Projected expenditures and tax receipts are subject to wide variation with demographic, economic and, not least, legislative changes. The Social Security amendments of 1982, for example, would have created a fiscal 1983 surplus of some $1.3 trillion (see Eisner, 1986, pp. 36–38), as a consequence of the reduction in the present value of prospective benefits and increase in the present value of prospective taxes.

It would hardly seem that economic agents should be expected to respond to the same extent, if at all, to such changes in uncertain prospects as they would to changes in their assets of explicit government debt. And empirical investigation generally confirms that (see Eisner, 1983, *inter alia*). Very few Americans, except perhaps some of those at the point of retirement, have the vaguest notion of their future Social Security benefits. It is probably most reasonable to assume that they act as if, in the aggregate, their net wealth in contingency obligations is zero, that is, that the government will periodically adjust taxes to benefits. On this assumption, which may be taken as one of "equal ignorance," contingency obligations contribute nothing, one way or the other, to the general budget deficit.

[5]The Federal government and its associated credit agencies are lenders as well as borrowers. To the extent Federal expenditures are financing loans to small business, farmers, students or others, government debt held by the public is matched by the public's debt to the government.

[6]These capital estimates are all constructed on a cost basis, adjusted to current prices. The value of education reflects both market expenditures and the opportunity costs of students 14 years of age and older. A full description of sources and methods is to be found in Eisner (1989).

[17]The ratio of *deficit* to GNP, d, consistent with a constant debt-GNP ratio, b, is simply the product of that ratio and the rate of growth of GNP, g, thus expressed as $d = bg$. Hence, for b approximately equal to 0.42 and g at about 7.5 percent, we can maintain a deficit at 3.15 percent of GNP forever without raising the debt-GNP ratio.

[18]The curious notion that a more rapid growth in the quantity of money can only in the long run raise nominal interest rates and leave the real rate unchanged, again attributable to Friedman (1968), rests largely on the equally curious notion that we are always at that fully market-clearing, "natural," full-employment rate of output. If we are (and all agents know we are), then increases in demand as a consequence of a greater quantity of money can only raise prices. By a further leap of imagination—or of assumption—increases in the quantity of money (or the monetary base) somehow entail equiproportionate increases in all obligations and claims denoted in money, including the very government debt created quite independently by budget deficits. Alternatively, money neutrality in the face of Federal Reserve open market operations can be rescued by unreserved acceptance of Barro-Ricardian equivalence; since government debt is not viewed as a private asset, substitution of money for that debt merely adds equivalent amounts to private wealth and proportionately increases nominal spending. For those not fully committed to the equivalence theorem, the proposition that increasing the money supply, in the manner in which this actually occurs in our economy, will have no real effects would appear to be as preposterous as the assumption that since there is some rate of taxation so high that it will kill off all taxable income, we are, in fact, in the current United States economy, on the falling portion of the Laffer curve so that lower tax rates will actually raise tax revenues.

[19]The real deficit would of course rise temporarily as the *falling* interest rates would raise the market value of outstanding government debt. Once interest rates reached their lower value, both the nominal and real deficits would be less.

References

Boskin, Michael J., M. S. Robinson, T. O'Reilly, and P. Kumer, "New Estimates of the Value of Federal Mineral Rights and Land," *American Economic Review*, December 1985, *5*, 923–936.

Dilullo, Anthony J., "U.S. International Transactions, Second Quarter 1988," *Survey of Current Business*, Sept. 1988, *68*, 33–38.

Eisner, Robert, "Social Security, Saving and Investment," *Journal of Macroeconomics*, Winter 1983, *5*, 1–19.

Eisner, Robert, "The Total Incomes System of Accounts," *Survey of Current Business*, Jan. 1985, *65*, 20–25.

Eisner, Robert, *How Real Is the Federal Deficit?* New York: The Free Press, A Division of Macmillan, 1986.

Eisner, Robert, *The Total Incomes System of Accounts*, Chicago: University of Chicago Press, 1989.

Eisner, Robert and Paul J. Pieper, "A New View of the Federal Debt and Budget Deficits," *American Economic Review*, March 1984, *74*, 11–29.

Eisner, Robert and Paul J. Pieper, "Measurement and Effects of Government Debt and Deficits." In *Economic Policy and National Accounting in Inflationary Conditions*, *Studies in Banking and Finance*. Amsterdam: North Holland, 1987, pp. 116–144.

Eisner, Robert and Paul J. Pieper, "The World's Greatest Debtor Nation?," forthcoming, 1989.

Friedman, Milton, "The Role of Monetary Policy," *American Economic Review*, March 1968, *58*, 1–17.

Greenwald, Bruce C., and Stiglitz, Joseph E., "Financial Market Imperfections and Business Cycles," NBER Working Paper No. 2494, Cambridge MA, January 1988.

Lange, Oscar, "The Rate of Interest and the Optimal Propensity to Consume," *Economica*, February 1938, New Series *5*, 12–32. Reprinted in American Economic Association, *Readings in Business Cycle Theory*. Philadelphia: Blakiston, 1944; pp. 169–192.

Lerner, Abba, "Functional Finance and the Federal Debt," *Social Research*, 1943, *10*, 38–58.

Lucas, Robert E., Jr., *Studies in Business Cycle Theory*. Cambridge, Mass.: MIT Press, 1981.

Lucas, Robert E., Jr. and Thomas J. Sargent, "After Keynesian Economics." In Lucas and Sargent, eds., *Rational Expectations and Economic Practice*. Minneapolis: University of Minnesota Press, 1981, pp. 295–319.

Stiglitz, Joseph E., and Weiss, Andrew, "Credit Rationing and Its Implications for Macro-Economics," unpublished manuscript, 1988.

U.S. Government, Office of Management and Budget, *Special Analyses*, *Budget of the United States Government*, *Fiscal Year 1989*, Washington: Government Printing Office, 1988.

Of Money

David Hume

But notwithstanding this conclusion, which must be allowed just,
'tis certain, that since the discovery of the mines in America,
industry has increas'd in all the nations of Europe, except in
the possessors of those mines; and this may justly be ascrib'd,
amongst other reasons, to the encrease of gold and silver.
Accordingly we find, that in every kingdom, into which money
begins to flow in greater abundance than formerly, every thing
takes a new face; labour and industry gain life; the merchant
becomes more enterprizing; the manufacturer more diligent and
skillful; and even the farmer follows his plough with greater
alacrity and attention. This is not easily to be accounted for,
if we consider only the influence, which a greater abundance of
coin has in the kingdom itself, by heightening the price of
commodities, and obliging every one to pay a greater number of
these little yellow or white pieces for every thing he purchases.
And as to foreign trade, it appears, that great plenty of money
is rather disadvantageous, by raising the price of every kind of
labour.

To account, then, for this phenomenon, we must consider that tho'
the high price of commodities be a necessary consequence of the
encrease of gold and silver, yet it follows not immediately
upon that encrease; but some times is requir'd before the money
circulate thro' the whole state, and make its effects be felt on
all ranks of people. At first, no alteration is perceiv'd; by
degrees, the price rises, first of one commodity, then of another;
till the whole at last reaches a just proportion, with the new
quantity of specie, which is in the kingdom. In my opinion, 'tis
only in this interval or intermediate situation, betwixt the
acquisition of money and rise of prices, that the encreasing
quantity of gold and silver is favourable to industry. When
any quantity of money is imported into a nation, it is not at
first disperst into many hands; but is confin'd to the coffers
of a few persons, who immediately seek to employ it to the best
advantage. Here are a set of manufacturers or merchants, we shall
suppose, who have receiv'd returns of gold and silver for goods,
which they sent to Cadiz. They are thereby enabled to employ
more workmen than formerly, who never dream of demanding higher
wages, but are glad of employment from such good paymasters.
If workmen become scarce, the manufacturer gives higher wages,
but at first requires an encrease of labour; and this is willingly
submitted to by the artizan, who can now eat and drink better
to compensate his additional toil and fatigue. He carries his
money to market, where he finds evry thing at the same price as

formerly, but returns with greater quantity and of better kinds, for the use of his family. The farmer and gardner, finding, that all their commodities are taken off, apply themselves with alacrity to the raising of more; and at the same time can afford to take better and more cloths from their tradesmen, whose price is the same as formerly, and their industry only whetted by so much new gain. 'Tis easy to trace the money in its progress thro' the whole commonwealth; where we shall find, that it must first quicken the diligence of every individual, before it encrease the price of labour.

And that the specie may encrease to a considerable pitch, before it have this latter effect, appears, amongst other reasons, from the frequent operations of the French king on the money; where it was always found, that the augmenting the numerary value did not produce a proportional rise of the prices, at least for some time. In the last year of Louis XIV money was raised three sevenths, but prices augmented only one. Corn in France is now sold at the same price, or for the same number of livres, it was in 1683, tho' silver was then at 30 livres the mark, and is now at 50.[3] Not to mention the great addition of gold and silver, which may have come into that kingdom, since the former period.

From the whole of this reasoning we may conclude, that 'tis of no manner of consequence, with regard to the domestic happiness of a state, whether money be in a greater or less quantity. The good policy of the magistrate consists only in keeping it, if possible, still encreasing; because, by that means, he keeps a spirit of industry alive in the nation, and increases the stock of labour, wherein consists all real power and riches. A nation, whose money decreases, is actually, at that time, much weaker and more miserable, than another nation, who possesses no more money, but is on the encreasing hand. This will be easily accounted for, if we consider, that the alterations in the quantity of money, either on the one side or the other, are not immediately attended with proportionable alterations in the prices of commodities. There is always an interval before matters be adjusted to their new situation; and this interval is as pernicious to industry, when gold and silver are diminishing, as it is advantageous, when these metals are encreasing. The workman has not the same employment from the manufacturer and merchant; tho' he pays the same price for every thing in the market. The farmer cannot dispose of his corn and cattle; tho' he must pay the same rent to his landlord. The poverty and beggary and sloth, which must ensue, are easily forseen.

---

3.   These facts I give upon the authority of Mons. du Tot in his Reflections politiques, an author of reputation. Tho' I must confess, that the facts, which he advances on other occasions, are often so suspicious as to make his authority less in this matter. However, the general observation, that the augmenting the money in France does not at first proportionably augment the prices, is certainly just.

By the bye, this seems to be one of the best reasons which can be given, for a gradual and universal augmentation of the money, tho' it has been entirely overlook'd in all those volumes, which have been wrote on that question by Melon, Du Tot, and Paris de Verney. Were all our money, for instance, recoin'd, and a penny's worth of silver taken from every shilling, the new shilling wou'd probably purchase every thing that cou'd have been bought by the old; the prices of every thing wou'd thereby insensibly be diminished; foreign trade enliven'd; and domestic industry, by the circulation of a greater number of pounds and shillings, wou'd receive some encrease and encouragement. In executing such a project, 'twou'd be better to make the new shilling pass for twenty-four half-pence, in order to preserve the illusion, and make it be taken for the same. And as a recoinage of our silver begins to be requisite, by the continual wearing of our shillings and sixpences, 'tis doubtful, whether we ought to imitate the example in King William's reign, when the clipt money was raised to the old standard.

Money in Action

Lawrence S. Ritter
and William L. Silber

When the Federal Reserve increases the money supply by $1 billion, how does it know how much of an effect this will have on people's spending and thereby on GNP? Say we are in a recession, with GNP $20 billion below prosperity levels. Can the Federal Reserve induce a $20 billion expansion in spending by increasing the money supply by $2 billion? Or will it take a $10 billion—or a $15 billion—increase in the money supply to do the job? As we noted at the end of the previous chapter, if people always respond in a consistent manner to an increase in their liquidity (the proportion of money in their portfolio), the Federal Reserve will be able to gauge the impact on GNP of a change in the money supply. But if people's spending reactions vary unpredictably when there is a change in the money supply, the central bank will never know whether it should alter the money supply a little or a lot to bring about a specified change in spending.

Clearly, this is the key puzzle the Federal Reserve must solve if it is to operate effectively. After all, the central bank is not in business to change the money supply just for the sake of changing the money supply. Money is only a means to an end, and the end is the total volume of spending (GNP); when the chips are down, GNP will determine whether the overall economy is performing well or poorly.

How stable is the public's propensity to spend on goods and services out of increased liquidity? Does the public react to a change in the money supply predictably enough to allow the central bank to calculate the effect of its actions on GNP? Or is the reaction so unpredictable that the Federal Reserve can do no more than probe and pray?

The Missing Link

When the money supply increases, the recipients of this additional liquidity probably spend some of it on financial assets, such as stocks and bonds, and some on real goods and services, such as cars and TVs. The increased spending leads directly or indirectly to a higher GNP. Moreover, the funds move from the original recipients to the sellers of the various assets and products. Now *they* have more money than before, and if they behave the same way as the others, they too are likely to spend some of it. GNP thus rises further—and at the same time the money moves on to a still different set of owners who, in turn, may also spend part of it, thereby increasing GNP again.

Over a period of time, say a year, a multiple increase in spending and GNP could thus flow from an initial increase in the stock of money. Whether this expansion in GNP is large or small, relative to the change in the money supply that set it going initially, depends on two things: first, on how much of the new money is respent on *real* goods and services at each stage; and second, on how quickly the respending takes place. If a large fraction of the increased money is respent by each recipient soon after receiving it, GNP will expand a great deal relative to the increase in the stock of money. On the other hand, if a small fraction (or none) of the increased money is respent, or if it is held a long time at each stage, or if many financial transactions intervene, the expansion in GNP during the year will be quite small relative to the enlarged money supply.

This relationship between the increase in GNP over a period of time and the change in the money supply that brought it about is important enough to have a name: the velocity of money. Technically speaking, it is found, after the process has ended, by dividing the increase in GNP by the increase in the money supply that started it all.

We similarly can compute the velocity of the *total* amount of money in the country by dividing total GNP (not just the increase in it) by the total money supply. This gives us the average number of times each dollar turns over to buy goods and services during the year. In 1982, for example, with a GNP of $3,060 billion and a money supply of $454 billion, the velocity of money was 3,060 divided by 454, or 6.74 per annum. Each dollar, on the average, was spent about 6¾ times in purchasing goods and services during 1982.

With this missing link—velocity—now in place, we can reformulate the problem of the Federal Reserve more succinctly. The Federal Reserve controls the supply of money. Its main job is to regulate the flow of spending. The flow of spending, however, depends not only on the supply of money but also on that supply's rate of turnover, or velocity, and this the Federal Reserve does *not* have under its thumb. Since any given supply of money might be spent faster or slower—that is, velocity might rise or fall—a rather wide range of potential spending could conceivably flow from any given stock of money.

The *ideal* situation for the central bank is a stable velocity, or at least one that is changing slowly and predictably over time. If velocity is stable or predictable, or close to it, the Federal Reserve can induce almost any volume of spending it wants simply by adjusting the money supply to the known velocity. For example, the velocity of the total money supply is now close to 7. If an *addition* to the money supply also turns over about 7 times a year in the purchase of goods and services, then the Federal Reserve knows for sure that if it increases the money supply by a billion dollars the end result will be an increase in GNP of about $7 billion. In that case, the Federal Reserve has it made; monetary policy alone would be both necessary *and sufficient* to control aggregate spending.

At the other extreme, the *worst* situation from the point of view of the monetary authorities is if velocity fluctuates randomly or perversely. If velocity moves randomly up and down without rhyme or reason, it would be impossible to gauge the impact on GNP that might result from a change in the money supply. If movements in velocity are perverse, that would mean that every time the Federal Reserve increased the money supply by 10 percent, velocity would respond by falling 10 percent. Monetary policy would be impotent. Changes in the money supply would merely be offset by an opposite change in velocity, leaving spending (and therefore GNP) unaltered. The public would not be responding to changes in liquidity and would be deciding by itself how much it would spend, irrespective of the actions of the Federal Reserve. Under such circumstances, monetary policy would be close to useless as a tool of national economic policy.

Living with Velocity

The facts are that velocity is neither perfectly stable nor fully predictable. Unfortunately for the Federal Reserve, it does not operate in a world designed for its own convenience. With a money supply of about $500 billion today, a miscalculation of only 0.1 in velocity means a $50 billion swing in GNP. But all is not necessarily lost. While velocity is not fixed, neither do its movements appear random or perverse. If the Federal Reserve could discover the underlying determinants of fluctuations in velocity, it might still be able to coexist with such a moving target.

With that in mind, examining the past may provide a clue to developments in the future. The velocity of the money supply (M1) reached an annual peak of slightly over 4 times per year in 1918. It fell slightly during most of the 1920s and then regained that peak of 4 in 1929. Thereafter, during the Depression and World War II, velocity fell almost continuously to an all-time low of 2 in 1946. In that year GNP was about $210 billion and the money supply $105 billion; each dollar, on the average, was being spent only twice.

Since then, however, velocity has risen considerably. It rose to 2.5 by 1950; to 3 by 1955; 3.5 in 1960; reached 4 (the previous peak) in 1964; continued on upward, beyond its previous peak, to 4.5 in 1968; hit 5 in 1973; 6 in 1978; and now, still climbing, it is approaching a turnover rate of 7 times per annum. The increase since World War II has been steady and even, with only slight dips now and then, usually in recessions, to interrupt an otherwise unbroken upward climb.

But, of course, facts alone do not speak for themselves. Understanding requires interpretation. Why has velocity behaved this way, especially in the past thirty-five years? After World War II it was generally expected that velocity would accelerate somewhat. Unexpected, however, has been the magnitude of the increase and its duration.

Perhaps the main reason for the extent of the postwar rise in velocity has been the increasing attractiveness of financial assets *other than money*—bonds, stocks, savings and loan shares, money market mutual funds, and savings accounts in commercial banks—as prudent and desirable outlets in which to invest excess cash. These assets are often highly liquid, almost as liquid as money, and yet they pay relatively high rates of interest. Attractive yields on financial assets other than money have led more and more people to wonder why they should ever hold any idle cash aside from what they need for day-to-day transactions purposes. And traditional concepts about how much cash on hand is really necessary for doing business have also come under reexamination. If cash for day-to-day transactions purposes can be pared down, then some of it can be loaned out to earn more interest. The money that is put to work moves to borrowers who can use it for current purchases. As a result, a larger volume of current spending flows from the same stock of money.

Corporate treasurers, in particular, have found that it pays dividends to scrutinize their cash holdings intensively. Could they manage to get along with somewhat less in the till than they had previously thought of as "normal," and invest a portion in high-yielding certificates of deposit at commercial banks or in U.S. Treasury bills (short-term government securities)? Increasingly, the answer has been yes, and imaginative new techniques of cash management have been developed to facilitate the process (also some not so imaginative old techniques, such as becoming "slow payers" when bills come due).

This trend has not escaped the attention of consumers. They have learned to economize on money by substituting lines of credit at retail stores and financial institutions in place of cash reserves; in addition, the growing use of credit cards has drastically reduced household needs for day-to-day transactions money. What was formerly held in the form of checking accounts or currency, for emergency use or for current payments, now shifts to higher interest-bearing savings deposits.

In summary, it is clear that velocity has not been stable; however, neither has it fluctuated randomly or perversely. There is a pattern in the movements of velocity during the postwar period—a persistent long-run rise with minor short-run dips during recessions. Even though we may not be able to pinpoint all the specific determinants, we can still see broad cause-and-effect relationships.

Higher interest rates lead to an increase in velocity by inducing business firms and households to economize on money. They hold less, lend out the excess, and others (the borrowers) can then spend it. Once learned, techniques of cash management are not easily forgotten, so that even in recessions, when interest rates fall, velocity does not drop back very far.

Furthermore, the long-run upward trend in velocity over the past quarter century suggests that fundamental structural relationships between the money supply and the spending habits of the community are apparently in the process of transition. New payment methods are developing (credit cards are a prime example), as financial innovation occurs side by side with technological innovation in industry. Such financial innovation, however, rarely takes root overnight. Established payment habits are likely to change only gradually.

Thus, although velocity is not fixed, neither is it likely to change drastically in the short run. The Federal Reserve may be able to live with it, even though it is a moving target. By gaining further insight into what makes velocity move, the central bank might be able to establish a range of probabilities as to where velocity is likely to be tomorrow and the day after, and act on that basis. In other words, a morning line on velocity (not unlike the one your local bookie puts out on the races at Hialeah)—provided the odds are unemotionally calculated and continuously reassessed in the light of emerging evidence—might still enable the Federal Reserve to come out a winner.

Open Market Operations

Paul Meek

THE "GO-AROUND"

The time is early afternoon on a Wednesday in mid-June. The place is the trading room on the eighth floor of the Federal Reserve Bank of New York. The Manager of the Open Market Account for Domestic Operations gathers with his trading room officers to reaffirm the judgment reached earlier to buy about $1¼ billion of Treasury bills. The banking system has a clear need for additional reserves to meet the increased public demand for currency and deposits expected as the end of the quarter and July 4 approach. The markets for bank reserves and Treasury securities are functioning normally with prices moving narrowly. After a brief discussion, the Manager gives final approval to the planned operation.

The officer-in-charge at the Fed's Trading Desk turns to the ten officers and securities traders who sit before telephone consoles linking them to three dozen primary dealers in U.S. government securities. "We're going to ask for offerings of all bills for regular delivery," she says. Each trader knows this means delivery and payment will take place the next day. Each picks up the vertical strips on which the offerings will be recorded for the four dealers he will call.

Bill, one of the group, presses a button on his telephone console, sounding a buzzer on the corresponding console of a government securities dealer.

"John," Bill says, "we are looking for offerings of bills for regular delivery."

John replies, "I'll be right back." He turns and yells, "The Fed is in, asking for all bills for delivery tomorrow." Moments later information screens around the country and abroad flash the news. Salesmen begin ringing their customers to see if they have bills they want to offer. Meanwhile, John checks with the trading manager of his firm to see how aggressive he should be in pricing the firm's own securities.

Twenty minutes later John rings back. "Bill, I can offer you $15 million of bills maturing August 9 at 9.20 percent, $40 million September 13 bills at 9.42, $25 million of September 20's at 9.46 and another 25 at 9.44. I'll sell $75 million December 13's at 10.12 percent and another 100 at 10.09. I can offer $20 million of March 21's at 10.25 and 50 May 16's at 10.28. All for delivery tomorrow."

Bill reads back each of the offerings to double check, then says, "Can I have those firm?"

"Sure."

Within ten or fifteen minutes each trader has written the offerings obtained from his calls on preprinted strips. The officer-in-charge arrays the individual dealer strips on an inclined board placed atop a stand-up counter. A quick tally shows that dealers have offered $7.8 billion of bills for regular delivery—that is, on Thursday.

The officer and a colleague begin comparing rates across the different maturities, seeking those that are high in relation to adjoining issues. She circles any special bargains with a red pencil. With an eye on heavy existing holdings, she circles other propositions that offer yields on or above a yield curve she draws mentally through the more heavily offered issues. Her associate keeps a running total of the amounts being bought. When the desired volume has been circled and cross-checked, the individual strips are returned to the traders, who quickly ring up the dealers.

Bill says, "John, we'll take the $25 million of September 20's at 9.46, the 75 of December 13's at 10.12, and the 50 of May 16's at 10.28 for regular delivery. A total of $150 million. No, thanks, on the others."

Forty-five minutes after the initial entry, the follow-up calls have been completed. The Trading Desk has bought $1,304 million of Treasury bills. Only the paper work remains. The traders write up tickets, which authorize the accounting section to instruct the Reserve Bank's Government Bond Department to receive and pay for the specific Treasury bills bought.

On Thursday the Federal Reserve will take delivery of the purchased securities from the banks that handle deliveries for the dealers—the clearing banks for nonbank dealers. As authorized by these banks, it will deduct these securities from the book entry list of their holdings at the Federal

Reserve and add them to the System Open Market Account. In return, the banks will receive credit that day to the reserve accounts they maintain at their Federal Reserve Bank. The Federal Reserve's credits to these accounts will add about $1.3 billion to the reserves maintained by U.S. financial institutions at the Reserve Banks. (See toned area.)

The Trading Desk's market entry sparks discussion immediately in dealer firms, the foreign exchange market and other financial markets. Within minutes money market analysts give their opinions over electronic information screens as to whether the bill "go-around" signifies any change in the outlook for monetary policy. Was the Federal Reserve just supplying reserves in anticipation of the seasonal demands ahead? Or did its purchases seem aggressive, suggesting it might be trying to encourage more rapid growth of money and credit in the country?

Such questions can rarely be answered by analyzing a single Federal Reserve market operation. But they underscore how important the current thrust of monetary policy is to bankers, businessmen, and governments throughout the world. Open market operations can quickly affect the cost and availability of credit in the United States and foreign financial markets. Sustained Federal Reserve action can exert strong economic effects in the world economy.

Under the Federal Reserve Act, the System uses open market transactions in government and federal agency securities as its most flexible means of adding to, or reducing, the reserves which depository institutions maintain in relation to their deposits. Operations routinely seek to head off the stresses imposed on the monetary machinery by seasonal or sudden, and potentially reversible, shifts of

TABLE I

Federal Reserve Bank of New York		The Dealers' Clearing Banks	
Assets	Liabilities	Assets	Liabilities
1. Treasury Bills	2. Reserve accounts of the dealers' clearing banks	3. Reserve account at Federal Reserve	4. Demand Deposit accounts of dealers
+$1,304,000	+$1,304,000	+$1,304,000	+$1,304,000
1. Federal Reserve buys Treasury bills and...	2. Clearing banks transfer Treasury bills by wire, receiving credit to their reserve accounts	3. Clearing banks' reserve accounts increase and...	4. Clearing banks credit demand deposit accounts of dealers selling the Treasury bills

funds. But the overriding longer term objective of such operations is to foster the monetary and credit conditions conducive to a healthy economy. Under the law the System establishes growth rates for various measures of money and credit over each calendar year. Its ultimate goals are sustainable economic growth, high employment, reasonable price stability and viability in the nation's international accounts.

Federal Reserve purchases of securities supply reserves to the banking system; sales withdraw reserves. When the Manager purchased $1,304 million of Treasury bills on Wednesday June 13, he paid the securities dealers by crediting the reserve accounts of the banks handling the dealers' paper work, an action that created reserves that didn't exist before. Had he sold Treasury bills instead, he would have reduced the System's open market account holdings and extinguished bank reserves. The Federal Reserve derives this power to create or extinguish bank reserves from Congress, which has the Constitutional power to "coin money (and) regulate the value thereof" (Article 1, Section 8).

Assume the Manager purchased the Treasury bills from nonbank dealers. The dealers' New York clearing banks receive credit to their reserve accounts and they, in turn, credit the dealers' deposit accounts. (When bills are bought from a bank acting as a dealer, the dealer bank simply receives a credit to its reserve account.) The immediate effect of the day's open market purchases is a $1,304 million rise in Federal Reserve assets (Treasury bill holdings) and in Federal Reserve liabilities to clearing banks. Bank reserve balances rise $1,304 million while bank deposit liabilities to customers rise by a similar amount.

When nonbank dealers buy Treasury securities from the Fed, they usually arrange for their clearing banks to pay through a charge to each clearing bank's reserve account. The Reserve Bank delivers the securities through the government securities clearing arrangement. Dealer banks pay for System sales by authorizing direct deductions from their reserve accounts.

When the System adds to bank reserves through open market purchases, the additional reserves don't all remain in the New York City banks that handle securities for the nonbank dealers. To buy and hold government securities, these dealers normally borrow money from all around the country—from insurance companies, nonfinancial corporations, banks, state and local governments and others. In fact, they borrow 95 cents or more of every dollar used to buy securities, pledging the securities bought as collateral.

When the Federal Reserve bought securities from dealers on Wednesday, nonbank dealers had to repay their borrowings and redeem the securities before they could deliver them to the System Account. In effect, they repaid their loans that day with the proceeds of the sale to the System.

A large part of the increase in reserves moved the same day from the dealers' checking accounts over the Federal Reserve's wire network to the reserve accounts of banks in other cities. Perhaps $20 million went to Hartford by a dealer to pay off an insurance company loan, $15 million to Chicago to repay a manufacturer, $75 million to a San Francisco bank to redeem securities held by it, and so on. Thus, an addition to bank reserves spreads quickly across the country. The banks gaining reserves may also redistribute part of them temporarily by lending them in the federal funds market. ∎

COPING WITH MONETARY STRESSES

The monetary system in the United States, like that of most other countries, is a fractional reserve system. Virtually all depository institutions whose checkable deposits for customers exceed a certain size must maintain cash reserves equal to a specified fraction of those deposits. Savings and personal time deposits are free of reserve requirements while nonpersonal time deposits maturing in less than 18 months are subject to them.

Commercial banks, which offer demand deposits and make commercial loans, supplied almost three-quarters of checkable deposits in the United States at the end of 1984. Savings and loan associations and savings banks accounted for over 20 percent. Credit unions provided the remaining 5 percent. Commercial banks also held nearly three-quarters of the time deposits subject to reserve requirements. Savings and loan associations accounted for most of the remainder.

About 5,800 commercial banks were members of the Federal Reserve System at the end of 1984. The 4,800 banks chartered by the federal government—national banks—are required to be members. An additional 1,000 banks chartered by the states had chosen membership. Over 9,000 state-chartered banks were nonmembers, but they and the other depository institutions have access to the Federal Reserve's lending facility on equal terms with members.

Reserve requirements on checkable deposits at any depository institution are graduated on the basis of the deposits each institution has outstanding. In early 1985 banks belonging to the Federal Reserve System were free on the first $2.4 million of balances, were subject to a 3 percent requirement thereafter up to $29.8 million, and 12 percent on deposits in excess of this total. A 3 percent requirement remained on nonpersonal time deposits maturing in less than a year and a half—predominantly negotiable certificates of deposits (CDs). These requirements are being phased in for nonmember banks with the process scheduled for completion in 1987.

Institutions hold their required reserves either as cash in their own vaults or as deposits at the Federal Reserve Bank of their district. They must meet requirements for a two week period ending on alternate Wednesdays. Requirements for the checkable deposits are based on average deposits held for the two weeks ending on the preceding Monday. For nontransactions accounts, requirements are based on a two-week period ending 16 days earlier. Most of the smaller institutions are able to meet their requirements entirely with vault cash. As of September 1984 about 4,300 out of a total of 39,000 depository institutions had requirements in excess of vault cash, making it necessary to hold balances at Reserve Banks to meet their requirements. These so-called bound institutions account for about three-quarters of checkable deposits.

As profit-seeking enterprises, commercial banks, in particular, try to keep their reserves, which produce no income, close to the required minimum. Yet they also want to avoid reserve deficiencies, on which the Federal Reserve may levy a penalty charge.

Managing the reserve position of a depository institution can be a trying business. Most of its transactions and those of its depositors affect the institution's reserve position. Checks drawn by customers to pay out-of-town bills, for example, funnel back through its Reserve Bank and are charged against its reserve or clearing account. A bank or thrift institution loses reserves when it pays out vault cash or transfers funds by wire on behalf of its customers. And it is likely to lose reserves when it makes loans or buys securities. When the money and securities wires close down at 6:30 p.m. each day, a bank's reserve position reflects the net of reserves lost through such transactions, on the one hand, and the reserves brought in, on the other, by deposits of checks and currency, tax or other credits to the Treasury accounts the bank holds, and its sales of securities or other assets.

A bank or other depository institution can employ several lines of defense if reserves are lost to other institutions through the daily ebb and flow of transactions. It can seek to borrow reserves for one or more days from other institutions in the federal funds market. It can also sell short-term government securities or other "liquid"—readily marketable—assets, pulling reserves from the bank of the buyer. Or a bank can issue CDs as evidence of its promise to repay with interest in 7 days or longer. Alternatively, the larger banks can bid for funds in the Eurodollar market for periods ranging from overnight to several years.

Depository institutions have a final defense against unforeseen reserve losses in their privilege of borrowing from their district Reserve Bank. Usually, they borrow only for short periods on their own notes, secured by government securities or other acceptable collateral. Borrowers pay interest on such borrowing at the Federal Reserve's *discount rate*. In fact, many large institutions buy federal funds routinely from correspondent institutions in large volume to support their loan and investment activity. For them, reserve drains increase their need to purchase federal funds or adjust in other ways. For smaller institutions adjustment may take place initially by cutting back on federal funds sales or switching to the buy side of the market.

Open market operations enable the Federal Reserve System to manage the reserves of the monetary system as a whole, regulating the pressure on financial institutions to adjust their borrowing and lending operations. Individual banks or thrift institutions can meet their reserve requirements by drawing reserves from other issuers of checkable deposits. But, in the short run, financial institutions as a group can only pass around the reserves already in the monetary system—or borrow new reserves at the Federal Reserve discount window.

Open market operations allow the Trading Desk at the New York Reserve Bank to adjust the volume of reserves in the system before depository institutions borrow at the Federal Reserve—that is, to manage *nonborrowed reserves*. In this way the Fed can offset the reserve swings caused by the public's changing demand for cash and by other factors. By managing nonborrowed reserves in relation to estimated reserve requirements, the Fed can consciously adjust the pressure on banks to borrow from the 12 regional Reserve Banks and thereby affect the interest rate institutions pay each other when borrowing overnight—the federal funds rate. By adding more reserves than banks and others require, it can stimulate their expansion of money and credit. Conversely, the Fed can restrain that growth by holding back on reserves supplied in relation to the financial system's demand for them.

Through open market purchases, the System can replace the reserves lost when depository institutions withdraw cash from the Reserve Banks in anticipation of customer withdrawals—for example, before the Fourth of July. Later, when coin and currency are redeposited by merchants, open market sales by the Trading Desk can offset the reflow of cash back to the Federal Reserve.

Variations in the public's cash needs are reasonably predictable (Chart I). The biggest annual need for coin and

CHART I
The Effect of Changes in Currency in Circulation on Bank Reserves*

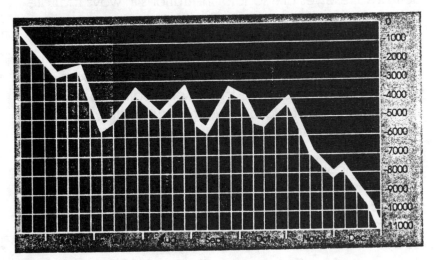

*Cumulative changes in daily averages

currency arises between early November and Christmas as the holiday shopping season builds to a climax. Banks and other depository institutions supply customers with pocket money from their own vaults. They obtain additional cash as needed from their district Reserve Banks, paying for it by drawing down their reserve accounts. If the Federal Reserve didn't offset such recurrent drains on reserves, banks would have to try to rebuild their reserve positions by buying funds from other banks—bidding up the federal funds rate—or by selling securities or calling short-term loans.

Such actions would put strong upward pressure on interest rates and could lead to serious market disturbances. Indeed, before the Federal Reserve System was established, financial strains of this type became so severe on a few occasions that they touched off financial panics that led to widespread bankruptcies and recessions in economic activity. A panic in 1907 set off the search for a system for assuring that currency could be expanded or contracted to meet the needs of the economy. That search contributed to the passage of the Federal Reserve Act in 1913.

Coin and currency now make up only a quarter of the nation's money supply. Households and business depend primarily on checkable deposits for making the stream of payments that keep the economy moving. The Federal Reserve provides a national check clearing system that facilitates these movements of funds. Each Reserve Bank credits a bank's reserve account for checks deposited by the bank and debits its account for checks drawn on it by its customers, which funnel back through the Reserve Bank.

The flow of checks around the country affects the non-borrowed reserves of financial institutions in ways that are hard to predict. Each Reserve Bank credits the reserve account of a bank sending checks for collection within a maximum of two business days. Yet three or more days may be needed to collect some of them from the bank on which they are drawn. As a result, the Reserve Banks often show on their books more dollars *due from* depository institutions, than dollars *due to* others, which have deposited checks for collection.

On a typical day in 1985, for example, *due from* items in process of collection totaled $8,249 million while deferred availability—*due to*—cash items totaled only $7,591 million. The amount by which the *due from* items exceeded the *due to* items—$658 million that day—is called Federal Reserve *float*. In effect, some institutions are credited before others are charged. Credits can also arise without offsetting debits in the routine processing of funds and securities over the Fed's wire transfer network.

Float can vary widely within a week or month as well as over the year, although variations are not as big a problem to the Trading Desk as a few years ago when float levels were higher. Float rises near the middle of each month as people and businesses pay their monthly bills (Chart II). This bulge provides the monetary system with substantial additional reserves for a brief period until float subsides

CHART II
The Effect of Changes in
Float on Bank Reserves*

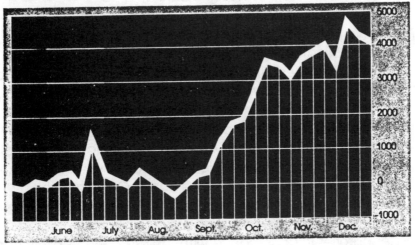

*Cumulative changes in daily
averages

along with check volume toward the end of the month. The Fed deducts these float credits in a subsequent reserve period so that banks no longer benefit, as they once did, from float. Still their variation during each period is a considerable source of uncertainty to the Trading Desk. In 1984 daily float range from –$0.7 billion to $5.3 billion. Bad weather, transportation tie-ups, or anything affecting check deliveries or the speed of processing can cause large daily changes in float.

During the Christmas season, the volume of checks written rises sharply. Check deliveries may be delayed as Christmas cards and packages flood the mails, superimposing a strong seasonal rise on the monthly pattern of float. To prevent the large swings in float from alternately expanding and reducing the supply of nonborrowed reserves, the Fed's Trading Desk engages in offsetting open market operations.

Changes in the deposits maintained at the Federal Reserve by the Treasury, foreign central banks, and international financial institutions also affect nonborrowed reserves. When such deposits rise, reserves are transferred from the banking system to these accounts. When the balances are drawn down to make payments, the reserve balances of depository institutions receiving payments increase.

The U.S. Treasury maintains its working balances at the Federal Reserve Banks. Government checks are drawn against these accounts and may be presented at any one of the Reserve Banks for payment. The public's payments for U.S. government securities are typically made to the Treasury's accounts at the Reserve Banks.

The Treasury seeks to keep its total balances at the Reserve Banks reasonably stable so that its operations will not complicate the Fed's job of managing nonborrowed reserves. To this end it maintains "tax and loan" accounts at financial institutions. A large part of the Treasury's tax and other receipts funnel into such accounts in the first instance. Each depository pays interest on its "note" to the Treasury. The Treasury then calls on these balances at a rate intended to offset the anticipated pace at which its checks will be presented at the Reserve Banks. Generally, the object is to hold the balances at the Federal Reserve around $3 billion. Depositories are classified as A, B, and C depositories in accordance with their size. The Treasury can make calls daily before 11 a.m. on the larger institutions, the C banks, and receive payment into its Federal Reserve accounts that same day if it so orders.

Forecasts of the Treasury balance are subject to sizable margins of error. It is not unusual to have the balance turn out $1 billion higher—or lower—than expected. The Treasury can take action the next day to bring the balance back to desired levels.

A more serious problem arises occasionally following major corporate and individual tax dates when Treasury receipts are particularly heavy. Each depository institution puts limits on the size of the Treasury note balances it will hold, since interest must be paid and collateral held. When balances exceed the limit, the excess is automatically remitted to the district Reserve Bank. When Treasury balances pile up in excess of the aggregate limits set by the depositories, balances at the Fed rise, draining reserves from the banking system. The Fed's Trading Desk has to compensate by injecting reserves—occasionally in very large size.

The System faces a never-ending task in counterbalancing the reserve pressures arising from fluctuations in the factors affecting nonborrowed reserves. As reserves shift, the open market Desk must be prepared to change from supplying to absorbing reserves, sometimes within the same two-week reserve period. The major swings in nonborrowed reserves are predictable, albeit with a sizable margin of error. Financial market participants must allow for these prediction errors as they try to evaluate the policy significance of daily open market operations.

The open market Desk is concerned with offsetting seasonal and more short-lived reserve strains through defensive operations. It must also track various measures of the money stock and credit to judge whether their growth is unfolding as the Federal Reserve desires. Operations have a dynamic as well as a defensive dimension.

Checkable deposits provide the principal means of payment for the transactions of everyday life in a complex society. But such deposits pay low rates of interest, if they pay any at all. There is every reason for depositors to economize on them, shifting surplus funds to higher paying time deposits or securities. An efficient monetary system will make it easy to shift between such assets and money as needed.

Operationally, the Trading Desk focuses on nonborrowed reserves in the two-week reserve maintenance period. Projections of the public's demands for checkable deposits serve as the basis for estimating the required reserves depository institutions will have to maintain. Adding to required reserves an allowance for excess reserves produces an estimate of the total reserves that will be demanded by the financial system in the reserve maintenance period at current interest rates. By deducting from this the amount of discount window borrowing the Fed wants to produce, one arrives at the level of nonborrowed reserves that the Desk seeks to achieve.

The public's demand for checkable deposits is highly variable in the short run. Businesses try to keep their checkable balances to a minimum, shifting out of short-term investments into deposits when large tax, payroll or other payments are due. In mid-June, for example, banks create billions of dollars of new demand deposits so that corporations may make their quarterly tax payments to the U.S. Treasury. Required reserves increase correspondingly, only to decline a few days later when the funds are transferred to the Treasury's note balances, which are free of reserve requirements.

Regular payroll disbursements lead to a similar need for reserves. In this case the decline in deposits is more gradual as people pay their bills and withdraw cash. Of course, big holiday demands for currency—for example, those beginning before July 4—can lead to large declines in deposits and required reserves.

The variability of checkable deposits in the short run make it hard to judge within a two-week reserve period whether money and credit are growing at the desired pace. One needs a longer perspective to have any confidence that their growth is on track—or off. Applying a seasonal adjustment procedure to the recurring patterns of behavior is essential.

The main seasonal movements in demands for credit and deposits are clear to the Federal Reserve and commercial bankers alike. As a rule, there is a pronounced upswing in bank loans to business in the last four months of each year. Agricultural crops move to market in summer and fall. More importantly, businesses are borrowing to build up inventories of materials and finished goods as they produce for the fall season and the Christmas rush. Later retail merchants use additional credit to carry merchandise until it is sold and consumers pay for it—often weeks or months later. Treasury borrowing also rises at this season because tax receipts typically are lower in the second half of the calendar year.

CHART III
The Effect of Changes in
Required Reserves on
Excess Bank Reserves*

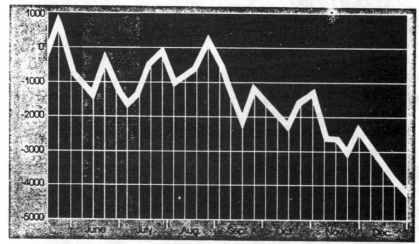

*Cumulative changes in daily averages

A rise in employment and incomes—and in working balances—is characteristic of the fall season. Rising deposits lead to an increase in the required reserves that financial institutions must hold (Chart III). In pre-Federal Reserve days, banks often had to sell liquid assets in volume to make room for the seasonal increase in loans and reserve requirements. Today, open market operations supply additional reserves in step with rising demands for credit and deposits. There is no need for interest rates to rise or fall with seasonal changes in economic activity.

The actual behavior of credit, deposits and interest rates each year reflects the interaction of depository institutions, their customers, and the Federal Reserve. The lending and funding decisions of banks and other financial institutions are influenced by present and prospective customer demands, the economic outlook, and perceptions of how readily the Federal Reserve may accommodate demands for money and credit. Most lenders project both the loan demand they are likely to face and the growth of their own deposits. The scale of federal deficits in relation to private credit demands will influence their thinking. They must judge whether all the credit demands they foresee can be accommodated within the rates of growth in the money stock and credit being sought by the Federal Reserve System. Interest rates will be expected to rise if money and credit demands prove excessive—or to fall if they are below the Fed's growth objectives.

Against this background, bankers will act on their individual readings of the evidence coming in. Suppose a bank's holdings of loans and securities are rising faster than its demand and savings deposits. It would then lose reserves to other banks and find itself borrowing larger and larger amounts in the federal funds market to meet its rising reserve requirements.

How the bank reacts depends on its expectations of loan demand and Fed policy. If management sees strong loan demand and forecasts a rapidly growing money supply, it may expect the Federal Reserve to hold back on supplying nonborrowed reserves in order to slow deposit and credit growth. Since interest rates would rise in that case, management might choose to sell domestic CDs or borrow in the Eurodollar market at current interest rates rather than risk having to roll over overnight borrowings at escalating rates. Conversely, if deposit growth were to outrun loan demand, the banker would be likely to buy additional securities, while stepping up efforts to lend more. Expectations of a sluggish economy or a more expansive

Fed policy would speed up such actions.

The Federal Reserve for its part follows closely the response of the money stock and credit to monetary policy, institutional decisions and customer demands. The Manager of the Open Market Account watches carefully how the money supply behaves. Each Thursday new seasonally adjusted data are available on the weekly level of M1—coin, currency and checkable deposits—as well as new projections of future growth. The Manager also receives revised estimates each week of the monthly behavior of M2. M2 consists basically of M1 plus time and savings deposits at banks and thrift institutions (excluding large negotiable CDs) plus accounts of money market mutual funds.

The Manager compares the new information with the growth rates desired over the calendar quarter by the Federal Open Market Committee (FOMC—see pages 18-19), a key policymaking body. Suppose the monetary aggregates appear to be expanding more rapidly than the FOMC desires while the economy is very strong. The FOMC would then typically instruct the Manager not to supply nonborrowed reserves to the full extent of the rise in demand for reserves because of M1 and M2 growth. Financial institutions would be left short of reserves, bid up the federal funds rate and be forced to borrow more at the Federal Reserve discount window. In time, the rise in interest rates and the resulting portfolio adjustments of depository institutions, businesses, and consumers should work to slow the growth in deposits and in required reserves.

Conversely, suppose money and credit growth fell short of the Federal Reserve's desires while economic activity appeared sluggish. The Manager would be expected to provide nonborrowed reserves more freely. Aggressive purchases of Treasury securities might even be in order. Such actions would contribute to a decline in interest rates on federal funds and other short-term assets. Financial managers should then increase their investments and lending activities over the months ahead, leading to an acceleration in money and credit growth.

Open market operations enable the Federal Reserve to defend flexibly against short-run reserve strains while still pursuing its longer term objectives for monetary and credit growth. Financial institutions and markets, given their preoccupation with interest rates, anxiously examine the Trading Desk's actions for possible clues to a shift in emphasis in reserve management. Their analysis starts with an appreciation of the role monetary policy plays in influencing economic activity. ▪

MONETARY POLICY AND THE ECONOMY

The Board of Governors of the Federal Reserve System and the 12 Reserve Banks have several means of implementing monetary policy. The Board sets reserve requirements, that is, the proportion of deposits that depository institutions must hold as reserves. Directors of the Reserve Banks initiate changes in the discount rate, subject to the review and determination of the Board of Governors. The Reserve Banks administer lending to depository institutions, making loans, which usually do not exceed 15 days.

The Federal Open Market Committee oversees the most flexible instrument of monetary policy—open market operations—to affect the reserves of depository institutions. The Chairman of the Board of Governors presides over eight meetings each year, in which he, his six fellow governors, and the 12 Reserve Bank presidents assess the economic outlook and plan monetary policy. The Committee proper—the voting members—includes the seven Governors of the Board, the president of the New York Reserve Bank, and four other Reserve Bank presidents, who serve in annual rotation. There is sometimes discussion as well at Committee meetings of the use of reserve requirements and the discount rate, although these are outside FOMC's purview.

Responsible to the Congress, the Federal Reserve is charged with fostering a healthy economy—one that provides employment for a growing work force, rising incomes, and stable domestic prices in a world of interdependent national economies. Under the Humphrey-Hawkins Act of 1978, FOMC members must set annual objectives for the growth of money and credit that are consistent with economic health. Then they must devise an operational strategy for pursuing these objectives, which are *intermediate* between the Trading Desk's short-run reserve targets and society's longer run economic goals.

In setting annual monetary objectives, policymakers are participating in a dynamic process whose direction and momentum are often unclear. The President's economic plans and budget proposals are important, but how businessmen and consumers will spend and save in the quarters ahead is more often the key to the economy's performance. The FOMC also has to estimate how the use of monetary policy instruments will affect money, credit and interest rates, and thereby influence the output of real goods and services. There is no escape from forecasting the future since the lags from Trading Desk action to the economy are long and variable.

In choosing an operating strategy, the Committee concentrates on the nonborrowed reserves of depository institutions. The Trading Desk can come reasonably close to such a target in a two-week reserve period. The FOMC also spells out for the calendar quarter the growth in various measures of money that it expects to be consistent with its annual objectives. Such guidelines provide the basis for having the Trading Desk change reserve pressure between meetings.

One approach to reserve targeting is to specify a growth path for nonborrowed reserves that is believed to be consistent with the specified objectives for money and credit growth. Then, if money starts to grow more rapidly than allowed by the path, the depository institutions will be forced to borrow more at the Reserve Banks than before. Such adjustment credit is available only temporarily to individual institutions, giving them time to meet their requirements by reducing assets or borrowing elsewhere. The banks bid up the federal funds rate and the rates paid to attract deposits, quickly affecting the terms on which they are ready to make loans. Holders of money and other financial assets redistribute their assets away from deposits paying little or no interest toward higher yielding assets, tending to reduce the growth in checkable deposits toward the rate desired. Conversely, a shortfall in money growth would tend to reduce bank demand for reserves, cut borrowing at the discount window, and lower interest rates. The resultant portfolio changes should tend in time to spur money and credit growth and quicken economic activity.

This procedure was used for three years beginning in October 1979. It provided important reassurance to the public and financial markets that the Federal Reserve would not underwrite a continuation of the inflation then raging. Reinforcing its automatic effects were judgmental changes in nonborrowed reserve objectives and in the discount rate. Monetary policy contributed to cutting the inflation rate sharply, albeit not without a big increase in interest rate volatility and a marked fall in economic output.

In 1982 the relationship between M1—coin, currency and checkable deposits—and the economy seemed to be breaking down. M1 continued to grow rapidly even though the economy was sliding into deep recession. Gradually, the FOMC relaxed its constraints on M1 growth. In late 1982 it disengaged from its automatic procedure for setting nonborrowed reserves—one which was closely tied to M1's behavior.

The FOMC's alternative strategy called for providing nonborrowed reserves consistent with a specified degree of pressure on banks, commonly measured by borrowing at the discount window. The objective typically called for increasing (or decreasing) the degree of reserve restraint depending on the behavior of the monetary aggregates and/or the economy. This judgment approach left some room for the federal funds rate to vary in response to changes in market expectations of future interest rates. It also meant that rates were less likely to fluctuate in response to short-term swings in the economy, demands for money and credit. Under this procedure resistance to undesirably rapid, or slow, money growth depend chiefly on the judgment of the policymakers.

The money market, the natural point of contact between the Federal Reserve and the financial system, is the channel through which it affects the economy. Broadly defined, the money market encompasses debt instruments maturing within one year. An international market for money and money substitutes provides a complex national economy—and the world as well—with a means for economizing the use of money. Businesses, financial corporations, households and governmental units minimize cash balances by investing in short-term interest-earning assets. These can be readily converted to cash with little risk of loss. The U.S. Treasury, banks, business corporations, and finance companies issue these short-term IOUs. They borrow in the money market to bridge differences between receipts and payments or to defer long-term borrowing to a more propitious time.

The Trading Desk at the New York Reserve Bank affects bank reserves and thereby the money market through its operations in Treasury securities. It can buy or sell a large volume of such issues, either outright or on a temporary basis, with minimal effect on prices. The stock-in-trade in this market ranges from Treasury bills falling due every

Thursday out to 30-year bonds. The daily volume in this "over-the-telephone" market is huge—several times that of the most active day of trading in all stocks listed on the New York Stock Exchange.

Primary dealers in government and federal agency issues stand ready to buy these securities from the issuers and customers for inventory and to sell to all comers from their own holdings. Nonbank dealers borrow from banks and others to finance their holdings, which can be 50 times as large as their capital. Naturally, they seek to borrow at a lower rate of interest than they earn on their holdings. Dealers also earn income from the spread between their purchase and sale prices. Fierce competition keeps these spreads close to $50 per million dollars on Treasury bills maturing in three months and correspondingly more on longer maturities. Dealers also seek trading profits from anticipating rate movements and arbitraging between different maturities, using both the cash market and contracts for future delivery traded on one of the futures exchanges.

Banks are at the heart of the money market. Customer deposits on their books and their own balances at the Reserve Banks are its lifeblood. In the federal funds market banks borrow or lend funds to each other or to other financial institutions for periods ranging from overnight to several months. Depository institutions borrow directly on their own name when they sell negotiable CDs or bankers' acceptances, and when they bid for funds in the Eurodollar market. Banks and other financial institutions use the money market also to acquire Treasury bills or business commercial paper as investments.

The large money market banks are as important to the money market as it is to them. They supply much of the credit that permits nonbank dealers in money market paper to buy and hold an inventory. When businesses or other banks who lend to dealers cut back on such loans, the money market banks fill the credit gap. The reserve positions of these banks reflect quickly the financial demands that appear elsewhere in the economy.

The market for bank reserves—the federal funds market—reflects immediately changes in the supply of nonborrowed reserves relative to the financial system's demands for them. If the Federal Reserve makes reserves more abundant, lower interest rates follow in short order. Holding back on reserves will lead to upward pressure on rates. Sustained changes in the federal funds rate are transmitted nearly one-for-one to Treasury bill, CD, and other money market rates.

The transmission of monetary policy to the capital market, which includes corporate shares as well as bonds maturing out to 40 years, is less predictable. Insurance companies, pension funds and others that invest in intermediate- and long-term securities seek rates of return that will outpace expected future inflation. In making investment decisions, such investors take into account recent experience with inflation and the magnitude of potential federal budget deficits as well as the credibility of the Federal Reserve's policies.

The FOMC's operating strategy calls for managing non-borrowed reserves to keep money and credit growth within the annual ranges it establishes. If reserves are provided at a rate less than is implied by the economy's demands for money and credit, a rise in interest rates follows, tending to slow monetary growth. Conversely, adding to reserves more rapidly than required reserves are growing, leads to lower interest rates and faster financial expansion. But how do these changes in the monetary and credit aggregates influence production, employment, and prices?

Some analysts, usually classified as monetarists, expect changes in the money supply itself to have a strong, and predictable, impact on economic activity. In their view, consumers and others increase spending on goods and services when money balances grow more rapidly than they desire. They also cut back on spending whenever money balances fall below a desired proportion of income. The actual interactions within the economy may be complex but the relation between money growth and economic activity is deemed sufficiently reliable that controlling the money supply is seen as assuring that the economy will behave as desired, in the absence of real shocks such as a rise in oil prices.

Other economists embrace the view that monetary targets are appropriate, but use more complex models of the economy to explain how financial flows and interest rates interact with monetary growth to affect the economy. They tend to see greater variation in the demand for money and are more willing to vary monetary targets at times to accommodate such variation. In this version monetary policy influences activity by affecting: (1) the net worth and spending of consumers, (2) the cost and availability of credit used to finance business spending and the capital outlays of state and local governments, and (3) supply and demand for housing. (See Chart IV). U.S monetary policy also exerts expansionary or restrictive effects on the world economy, which feed back to the demand for U.S. exports.

Consumers' own experience with the cyclical rise and fall in money growth and interest rates affects their actions. A sharp rise in interest rates may suggest that economic uncertainty and rising unemployment lie ahead, producing greater consumer caution. At other times, rapid money growth may lead consumers to step up spending in anticipation of inflation. In recessions, a sharp fall in interest rates and a rise in money supply growth may lead to expectations of economic recovery and increased spending. At other times the persistence of unemployment will tend to delay such a response.

The rise in interest rates that accompanies an economic expansion gradually undermines household wealth, adversely affecting spending. The value of holdings of stocks and bonds typically declines as rising short-term interest rates become increasingly attractive investment alternatives. Investment in housing is particularly affected when interest costs rise and credit availability declines. Initial down payments and monthly carrying costs rise significantly, squeezing many prospective buyers out of the market. Conversely, a fall in interest rates in a recession buoys the net worth of consumers and encourages spending. Greater availability of mortgage credit at lower rates also energizes the latent demand for housing which was crowded out in the preceding expansion.

Businesses depend heavily on the credit markets to finance the inventories and productive capacity needed to meet customer demands. Retained earnings and depreciation allowances provide only about three-fifths of their cash requirements. Business credit demands typically grow more rapidly than the economy in the expansive phase of the business cycle. If business people expect strong sales, they try to keep inventories ample so that sales are not lost because of shortages. Similarly, a strong economic outlook lends greater urgency to plans for additional capacity, which may require several years to complete. The longer an expansion continues, the greater the need for external financing.

Monetary policy has to allow short-term interest rates to rise rapidly enough during expansions to make inventory building an increasingly costly strategy. Managers, encountering pressure on profit margins, step up their efforts to contain costs in a competitive environment. Capi-

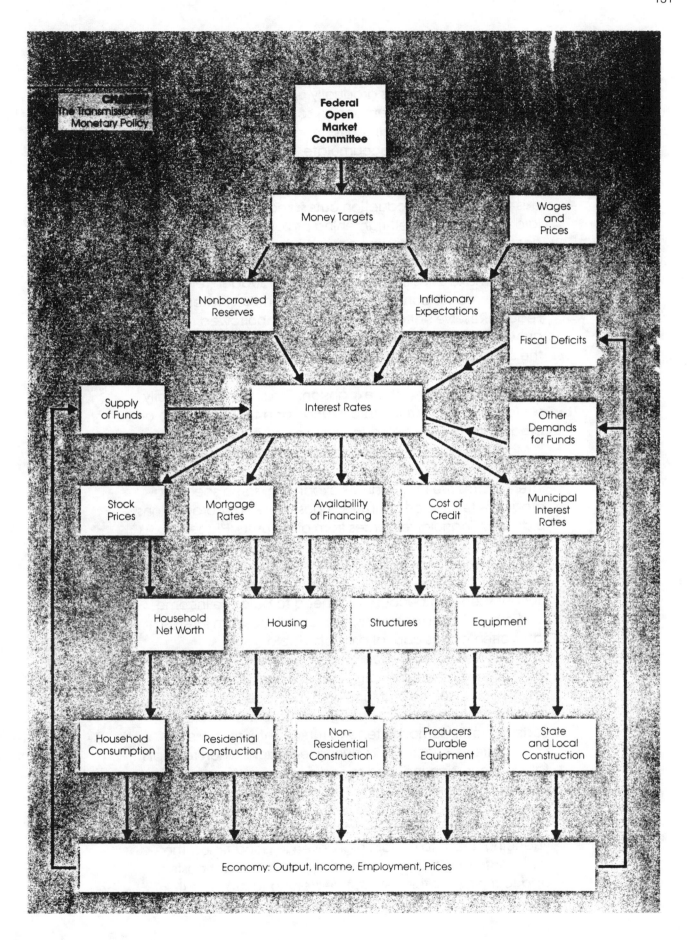

tal spending may also be affected by changes in the economic outlook. The very success of business in bidding away resources in the financial markets to finance inventories and capital outlays gradually undermines current consumption. Consumer demand at some point falls below the advance assumed in current production schedules. Unwanted inventories accumulate. High interest rates, which were tolerable as long as sales were rising, force a reduction in production so that sales can be met from existing stocks. As production cuts spread and workers are laid off, a general belt tightening prolongs the inventory correction and a recession ensues.

In a business slowdown, businessmen repay borrowings as they make sales from inventories. The sudden reversal of credit demands contributes to a fall in interest rates. The Federal Reserve's efforts to maintain nonborrowed reserve growth in the face of moderating credit demands works to the same end. Credit becomes readily available at declining rates to housing and other areas in which production was curtailed during the expansion. The stage is gradually set for an end to the inventory runoff and the restoration of production to the levels needed to meet current sales.

Monetary policy has a modest direct effect on the capital spending of state and local governments. As interest rates rise in a business expansion, some spending programs tend to be trimmed or postponed as corporations bid away financial resources from other users. Higher employment reduces support payments. Current state and local spending, however, often rises as tax receipts increase. Conversely, a recession enforces discipline on current spending because of a need to balance income and outgo. But in recessions, the fall in long-term interest rates often makes capital projects viable.

The discretionary spending and revenue decisions of the federal government are largely unaffected by monetary restraint or ease. The Treasury is a major independent force in financial markets, competing with other borrowers. Federal credit demands tend to run counter to those of other borrowers, increasing during recessions when receipts fall and recession-induced spending rises. In the past federal deficits typically fell in economic expansions when these factors reversed. However, the sharp rise in structural federal deficits in recent years has caused Treasury financing needs to remain high, even in good times. The rapidly growing debt and the steep rise in interest costs add to the size of the deficit, threatening to crowd out other borrowers. While heavy borrowing abroad has enabled capital spending to continue at a high level, this dependence on imported capital rather than domestic saving is not likely to be sustainable over the long haul.

U.S. monetary policy also affects interest rates and credit flows in international markets. The rates banks pay on their Eurodollar liabilities rise in step with domestic rates in economic expansions. As domestic credit demands increase, both U.S. and foreign banks draw funds from the rest of the world to make loans in the United States. So long as inflationary trends look favorable, the dollar tends to appreciate versus other currencies.

Other countries have to weigh the long-term benefit this means for their export sectors against the increase in the domestic currency cost of energy and other imports. If there is considerable slack in its economy, a country may welcome the stimulus from the U.S. expansion, maintaining its own monetary expansion as well. If instead it worries about growth becoming too rapid at home or the price pressures flowing from the depreciation of its currency, a country may choose a more restrictive monetary policy to maintain its existing exchange rate. The feedback on the demand for U.S. exports is a function of the policies that others pursue and the growth of their economies.

The explosive growth of the international banking system's loans to developing countries in the 1970s modified the responsiveness of the system to changes in the U.S. interest rates. The size of the debts to be serviced in an environment of reasonable price stability forced a much more disciplined approach to new credit extensions under the watchful eye of the International Monetary Fund. The credit-financed impetus to rapid world growth with accelerating commodity prices was reduced drastically. When U.S. interest rates rise, the increase in the interest burden on such countries provides a partial offset to the increase in exports to the United States. In time, an orderly resumption of capital flows should provide a basis for sustained growth in such countries.

When the U.S. economy weakens and the Federal Reserve continues to boost bank reserves, interest rates fall in U.S. and international markets. The dollar also tends to decline in terms of other currencies. Foreign governments may not welcome the resulting erosion in the competitive position of their export industries. The more the dollar declines, the more likely foreign authorities are to intervene in the exchange markets to stem the decline. Their monetary policies are likely to become more stimulative, in part to compensate for the fall in exports to the stagnating U.S.

economy. With domestic demand slack, U.S. exporters are likely to be more aggressive in both domestic and foreign markets. An improvement in U.S. net exports usually contributes to economic recovery. ∎

THE FOMC'S DECISIONS

The policy process in the Federal Open Market Committee centers on the Committee's annual objectives for money and credit growth, which are presented to the Congress twice each year. The FOMC undertakes in late January or early February a comprehensive review of the economic outlook and establishes the growth to be sought for various money and credit measures in the current calendar year. The Chairman of the FOMC, who is also Chairman of the Board of Governors, reports to the banking committees of the Congress in February. In July, after further FOMC consideration, he reports any revisions in the objectives for the current year, along with preliminary goals for the following year.

When Board members and Reserve Bank presidents meet early each year at the Board in Washington, they have in hand the staff's estimates of how some 40 key economic and financial variables will behave during the next two years. As a starting point, these forecasts assume monetary growth at the rates tentatively adopted the previous July. They draw on simulations of a complex economic model that specifies quantitatively the historical relationships among major economic sectors, which include those sketched in Chart IV. But the estimates presented are essentially judgmental, incorporating current information on how the federal budget and key economic sectors are likely to behave.

When the Committee meets, the staff presents its analysis of how the U.S. economy and balance of payments are expected to evolve over the current and following years. It sets forth the relation between its estimates of output, employment and prices and those of the Administration. The Director for Monetary and Financial Policy examines for the Committee alternative growth ranges for the monetary and credit aggregates from the fourth quarter of the year just ended to the fourth quarter of the current year. A key question is what rate of turnover of money, or income velocity, appears reasonable, taking into account recent behavior and past business cycle experience. The staff director discusses the longer term implications of the different growth alternatives being considered.

In discussing their choices, monetary policymakers weigh the likely response of the economy to the different alternatives. They usually address the likelihood that growth will turn out to be weaker, or stronger, than the outcome presented by the staff as most likely. Those who believe that interest rates provide the primary thrust of monetary policy give particular attention to the sectors most sensitive to interest rate changes. Those of a more monetarist persuasion are likely to be influenced strongly by the recent growth of money in either the M1 or M2 definitions. Each participant chooses among alternative annual monetary growth objectives in the light of the economic performance he sees as desirable within the range of possible outcomes.

Policymakers know how difficult it is to specify the relationship between money growth and nominal GNP, on the one hand, and the linkages between the Desk's operations on bank reserves and money growth, on the other. A participant may agree that the staff's projection of the economy over the next two years is both reasonable and desirable. Still he or she might conclude that money growth needs to be faster—for example, if money turnover is below normal because of the payment of interest on a rising proportion of checkable deposits. Another might agree basically with the staff's economic and monetary projections, but want to scale down growth objectives to reduce the likelihood that the economy will overheat and rekindle inflation.

The wide ranging discussion illustrates how hard it is to anticipate the results of decentralized decision-making in a flexible market economy. Yet when the voting members give the actual growth ranges they favor for the year, the Chairman can usually present ranges for growth in M1, M2, M3 and net credit that will command majority support. There is a collegial desire to be as united as possible in setting objectives for the year. Even after agreement, members may differ on the performance they expect from the economy.

Once the goals are set early in the year (or reviewed in July), the Committee turns to its operating strategy. Then and at other meetings during the year, participants discuss the economic outlook in detail after a staff presentation, as well as how the aggregates are behaving in relation to their objectives. The staff also reports on the U.S. balance of payments and international economic developments. The Manager for Foreign Exchange Operations, a senior officer of the New York Reserve Bank, reviews what has been happening in the foreign exchange markets, including intervention by foreign central banks or by the New York Bank's foreign exchange Trading Desk. He also comments on issues under discussion with foreign central banks. On occasion, he will report on present thinking at the U.S. Treasury, which takes the lead in formulating the international financial policy of the United States.

The Committee then takes up the instructions to be issued to the New York Reserve Bank for conducting open market operations until the next meeting. The Manager of the System Open Market Account for Domestic Operations reports on how the Committee's previous directive was implemented. He describes how the monetary aggregates have behaved relative to the Committee's quarterly and annual ranges. He notes any changes that have been made in the expected level of borrowing at the discount window in response to the behavior of the aggregates or the economy—and how borrowing has actually behaved during the period. The Manager also highlights developments in the money and bond markets during the interval, assessing market expectations of the economy and interest rates. After discussion, the Committee ratifies the operations conducted over the period.

The Director for Monetary and Financial Policy analyzes the emerging relationships among the various aggregates, noting changes since the last meeting. He reviews the options for the near term, which have previously been sent to the policymakers in the *blue book.* Typically, each option will specify a growth range for M1, M2, and M3 over the three months ending in a calendar quarter, as well as an associated amount of seasonal and adjustment borrowing at the discount window. The slower the growth rate indicated, the higher the initial borrowing level. Each option also includes a range for the federal funds rate. Should the rate move outside the range for a sustained period, the draft directive instructs the Manager for Domestic Operations to report to the FOMC Chairman who will decide on whether a consultation with the Committee is needed.

After the staff director gives his views on the alternatives, individual policymakers around the long table indicate which option or shading of options seems most appropriate to them. Each person's reading of the economy conditions his policy prescription. A vigorous economy will heighten concern about permitting overly rapid monetary growth. A weak outlook will strengthen support for relaxing the pressure on depository institutions. If monetary growth to date has been running on the high side, participants are likely to choose slower monetary growth over the quarter and for higher initial levels for discount window borrowing. Some participants expect changes in the pressure on banks to affect deposit growth only gradually over a period of months. Others look for a quicker feedback.

After extensive discussion, the Chairman develops a set of specifications that commands widespread support. He will also outline the conditions under which the degree of pressure to borrow at the discount window might be changed between meetings. If the economy were approaching full use of capacity, the Committee might choose to bias its response. It could call for increasing pressure promptly if money growth were above desired rates or the economy were gathering steam. In the contrary case, the directive might suggest maintaining existing pressure, unless the aggregates or the economy turned notably weak. Further discussion of the directive often leads to modifications and explanatory comments by the Chairman. A final vote approves the growth in M1, M2 and M3 desired for the calendar quarter, and the associated range for the federal funds rate. An understanding is also reached on the level of discount window borrowing expected initially. ∎

MANAGING THE ACCOUNT

After each FOMC meeting, the Manager of the System Open Market Account for Domestic Operations returns to New York with the responsibility for conducting operations until the next meeting. He presides over a finely tuned mechanism for assessing the pressures on reserve positions of depository institutions and on financial markets.

The Manager's task in each two-week interval is to aim for the level of *nonborrowed reserves* (NBR) that are believed consistent with the amount of seasonal and adjustment borrowing from the Federal Reserve that the FOMC has discussed. To arrive at the period's NBR objective, the Board staff first adds an estimate for the excess reserves likely to be needed in the financial system to its current estimate of required reserves to give estimated *total reserves* for the period. It then subtracts the indicated level of discount window borrowing to arrive at the NBR objective.

The projection of required reserves is the starting point. Financial institutions must meet these requirements over the two weeks ending on alternate Wednesdays. They are based principally on the reservable deposits held with these depositories over the two weeks that end on the preceding Monday.

The research staffs in Washington and New York built up their estimates of required reserves by forecasting both deposit behavior and the mix of deposits among banks subject to high and low ratios. Large banks report daily on their deposits while a stratified sample of other institutions report weekly. These help in making revised projections of required reserves during the two weeks. But even on the last day of the period, the Manager faces considerable uncertainty about required reserves because of the lags involved in reporting and checking deposit data.

Once the latest required reserve estimate is incorporated in a revised NBR objective, the Manager can compare it with the projections of nonborrowed reserves made each business day to see whether he needs to add or subtract reserves. This may sound a bit mechanical. In fact, a wide margin of error affects both the deposit and NBR estimates, and this introduces a need for judgment in daily decisions at the Desk. Every day of the two-week period brings new information on borrowing at the discount window the previous night. It also brings a report on nonborrowed reserves for the previous day as well as revised NBR estimates for the period. Several revisions of the NBR objective during the interval underscore the operational uncertainty with which the Manager must live.

The interbank market for reserves, the federal funds market, may provide clues as to the availability of reserves relative to reserve requirements. The Manager has a rough idea of the federal funds rate likely to be associated with the expected level of borrowing at the window. Whenever nonborrowed reserves fall significantly short of requirements, he expects the rate to come under upward pressure. If reserves are overly abundant, that should show up in a declining federal funds rate. Hence, the behavior of the reserves market provides a check on the validity of the reserve projections.

This information is not altogether reliable. The federal funds market is also significantly affected by the way bankers manage their reserve positions. Banks may bid up the rate because of collective caution before a long holiday weekend, demanding more excess reserves than the Manager expects. Conversely, if banks are willing to accumulate reserve deficiencies early in the two-week period, federal funds can trade at a lower rate than a given level of discount window borrowing might suggest. Accordingly, the Manager keeps close watch on how banks are managing their positions as he interprets reserve projections and the money market.

The Manager's pursuit of a NBR objective for each two-week period leaves considerable leeway for the federal funds rate and other market rates to flex. Market expectations, whether about money growth or the economy's behavior, can affect rates appreciably for days, even weeks, even when Federal Reserve operations are directed at stabilizing discount window borrowing. Market participants can initiate movements in rates. But they are sustainable only if incoming data justify market anticipations of economic developments or Federal Reserve action. Market participants frequently ascribe changes in the behavior of the federal funds rate to the monetary authorities, even when the Manager is holding to a steady reserve course. On occasion, the Manager may modify the timing or amount of his operations to resist unusually large movements in the federal funds rate, which might lead to significant misperceptions about the thrust of current policy.

Managing operations involves a good deal of judgment. The Manager watches developments in the markets for Treasury bills, bankers' acceptances, CDs, and Eurodollars, in which investors are exchanging cash for securities or securities for cash. The markets for longer term securities are also kept in view because the smooth flow of capital into investment is essential to the economy's growth. The orderly sale of securities by corporations and governmental units depends on the reliable availability of short-term credit to investment bankers and other securities dealers on reasonably stable terms. Like the government securities dealers, these depend on borrowed money to finance their inventories of salable securities.

The Manager must always be alert to the interaction between the short- and long-term credit markets. The forces set in motion by open market operations at the short end of financial markets typically exert a large part of their economic effects through the mortgage and other sectors of the capital market. The Manager's weekly written reports to the FOMC help keep Committee members informed about the transmission process and financial attitudes.

Each reserve period presents a new challenge to the Manager and his colleagues. Daily decision making relies on new information. Yet each day has much in common with every other day. Let's go back to that Wednesday in mid-June and follow the developments that led to the Fed's purchase of $1,304 million in Treasury bills.

On that day, as on all days, the Manager must bear in mind the directive adopted at the last meeting of the Committee. Suppose the directive adopted in May, after a review of economic conditions, called for growth in M1 from March to June at a 6 percent annual rate, for M2 growth at an 8 percent rate and for M3 growth at a 9 percent rate. Suppose further that the initial level of discount window borrowing associated with the desired degree of reserve pressure was indicated to be $1 billion. Suppose the directive also made an increase (decrease) in that level between meetings dependent on whether growth in the M's were above (below) the desired rate and whether the economy seemed stronger (weaker) than expected. Finally, let's assume that the FOMC set a range of 7 to 11 percent for the federal funds rate with the Manager instructed to consult with the Chairman if the rate seemed likely to move outside the range.

On last Thursday, the first day of the current two-week reserve period, the Manager had reviewed the behavior of the monetary aggregates with the Board's Director for Monetary and Financial Policy. At that time M1 appeared to be growing at a 5.4 percent annual rate from March through June while M2 was expanding at an 8.8 percent annual rate and M3 at a 9½ percent rate. Reports in recent weeks had suggested greater strength in the economy than had been expected at the time of the May meeting. But consultation with the Chairman indicated that no increase in reserve pressures was yet called for. Accordingly, the NBR objective for the current period had been drawn up to be consistent with discount borrowing at $1 billion. A review of past behavior suggested an allowance of $600 million be made for excess reserves in the first and third periods but that $700 million be allowed for the July 4 period because of seasonal factors.

The broad outline of the task facing the Manager on the

preceding Thursday is shown in Table II. Required reserves were estimated at $36,650 million for the two-week reserve maintenance period ending June 20. Given a borrowing level of $1 billion and assuming excess reserves of $600 million, the tentative NBR objective was $36,250 million (column (4)) ($36,650 + $600 – $1,000 = $36,250.) That day's New York staff forecast of nonborrowed reserves for the period was $35,050 million. Accordingly, there was an indicated need for the Desk to supply $1.2 billion of reserves

TABLE II
The Reserve Outlook-
June 7
(in millions of $)

Two-Week Reserve Period Ending	Path Assumptions			NBR Path (4)=(1)+ (2)-(3)	Projected Supply NBR (5)	Open Market Operations To Hit Path (6)=(4)-(5)
	(1) Required Reserves	(2) Excess Reserves	(3) Borrowing			
June 20	36,650e	600	1,000	36,250	35,050	+1,200
July 4	36,100e	700	1,000	35,800	34,375	+1,425
July 18	37,200e	600	1,000	36,800	33,850	+2,950

e = estimated

to the financial system. (A similar Board staff forecast suggested a reserve need of $1.6 billion.) New York estimates for ensuing periods suggested that NBR would need to be $1,425 million higher than now forecast in the July 4 period. In the reserve period ending July 18, the need for reserves would be about $3 billion as required reserves rose sharply and currency in circulation stayed high after the July 4 holiday.

Faced with a sizable reserve need stretching over several reserve periods, the Manager would normally think of buying Treasury bills outright in the market at some point. However, before the weekend he and his associates had been impressed with the general tautness in the money market. He had been expecting federal funds to trade around 10½ percent if borrowing from the Federal Reserve were $1 billion. Instead, demand for funds on Thursday and Friday had been insistent, with the rate rising to 11 percent each morning and trading a bit higher in the afternoons. It seemed likely that either NBR were somewhat lower than the staff was projecting or that banks were trying to accumulate larger excess reserve positions than had been allowed for in constructing the NBR objective.

Against this background the Manager had decided to supply a sizable amount of reserves on a temporary basis to add reserves early in the period where the demand seemed largest. On his instructions the Desk had made $2.8 billion of overnight repurchase agreements on Thursday and a similar amount of over-the-weekend agreements on Friday. While this pumped reserves into the first part of the period, it only added $800 million to the period average ($2.8 billion x 4 days/14). The expectation was that NBR would be $800 million higher for the two weeks ending June 20, leaving another $400 million still to be added if Thursday's New York forecast of NBR proved correct.

After the weekend the Desk learned that nonborrowed reserves had fallen about $500 million short of projected levels on Friday because of high Treasury balances at the Reserve Banks. Borrowing at the discount window had been $1,435 million over the weekend. Excess reserves had also been quite high, suggesting that money center banks had not been willing to run deficiencies in the first week of a settlement period.

Federal funds continued to trade around 11 percent and the Manager decided to temporize once more. The Desk made $2.1 billion of overnight repurchase agreements on Monday. On Tuesday the rate eased off to trade principally at 10¾ percent and the Manager took no action.

On Wednesday, the day of the bill "go-around," business got under way in the trading room a bit before 9 a.m. One of the traders had already been canvassing the federal funds brokers about activity the previous day. He calculates that the weighted average rate for overnight federal funds was 10.80 percent for Tuesday. Meanwhile, the news tickers have come alive, pounding out the overnight accumulation of financial news. Other securities traders begin scanning information screens for signs of early price changes in government securities from yesterday's close. They also flip through the pages of analysis being put up on the screens by money market economists. Once trading is under way they call traders in the various dealer firms to learn what is happening. The clerks also call selected dealers to get opening quotations on the full range of Treasury securities. These are posted on the large U-shaped board that laps around one end of the trading room.

Shortly before 9 a.m. two officers of the Securities Department hurry to a tenth floor conference room to meet with representatives of government securities dealer firms with whom the Desk trades. Fed officers in the open market area talk with the dealers on a rotating basis every business day. The dealers comment on market developments and interest rate trends, as well as commenting on the Treasury's financing needs and perhaps on their own firm's operations. The Trading Desk officers listen and ask questions, probing market expectations about the economic and interest rate outlook. The conversations, brief and to the point, are laced with market jargon, which speeds communication.

At the first session a senior partner of a large firm and the firm's economist are present. The partner comments extensively on the rapid growth in overseas demand for zero-coupon Treasury securities. These are created by dealers who sell at large discounts from par both the semiannual interest coupons and the principal amount (or corpus) of a long-term Treasury issue. (These separate interest and principal obligations are held in book entry form at Federal Reserve Banks and can be wired between Reserve Banks.) Because of strong demand for zeroes, the dealer expects active market interest in the new 20-year bond, which is to be sold shortly. He notes that yields may have to rise a bit further before dealers will be willing to take on the large volume of 2-, 4-, 7- and 20-year issues that the Treasury is selling around the end of the month. The firm's economist notes that the rise in the federal funds rate in recent days has made traders begin to wonder whether the Fed is allowing seasonal pressures to tighten the market for policy purposes. He gives his reasons for terming this conclusion premature.

The Desk officers are noncommittal on this matter, of course. After responding to several questions asked by Desk officers, the two dealer representatives depart at 9:15.

Entering the room next are the senior vice president in charge of dealer operations for a major New York City bank and his bill trader. They both express concern that the economy is stronger than most analysts are projecting. Their bank is expecting vigorous loan demand over the last half of the year and has been issuing 6-month CDs in size to reduce the bank's exposure to rising rates. While they see the firmer money market as a seasonal phenomenon, they do expect the Federal Reserve to have to tighten up in the course of the summer. The chief of trading believes investor interest in the coming Treasury issues will be good—at somewhat higher yields than now prevail. To limit the bank's own risk, he will bid in the auctions to get only a moderate amount for position beyond the issues already sold to customers beforehand in when-issued trading. The bill trader reports that bill rates have held steady in recent days despite the rise in financing costs. The market still expects the Fed's Desk to come in as a buyer before the month-end, as it has in most recent years.

After this meeting the officers walk down the tenth floor corridor to the Manager's office. There a telephone call is just coming in from an out-of-town dealer. He reports that there was sizable selling in the futures market yesterday, partly because of reports that a well-known investment manager had decided to sell $500 million of intermediate-term securities before the Treasury auctions began. Reportedly good buying from the Far East had helped give today's market a better opening tone. The dollar's strength in the exchange markets seemed consistent with this. Their own pension-fund customers appeared ready to commit a good portion of cash reserves to the coming 7- and 20-year issues. The customers were expecting the economy to slow in the last half and inflation to remain subdued, given the weakness in oil prices. Current yield levels offered high real rates of return relative to what they expected from common stocks. The up-tick in the funds rate was seen as seasonal, partly related to pre-funding of large CD maturities.

When the call ends at 9:45, the two officers return to the eighth floor trading room. There they learn from the traders that prices of Treasury coupon securities had moved ⅛ to ⅝ points higher at the opening, a carryover from moderate trading in London. Lately, however, profit-taking has brought prices back to about the level of last night's New York close. Bill rates are narrowly mixed. The federal funds market had opened with trading at 10⅝ percent and trading seems likely to continue there. Some analysts advise on the information screens that the Desk still has a reserve need to meet. Two of them thought multi-day repurchase agreements were likely while another looked for the Desk to buy Treasury bills.

At about 10:20 a.m. each day the Manager and Desk officers gather in the office of a vice president on the eighth floor to prepare for a daily telephone conversation with the representative of the Fiscal Assistant Secretary of the Treasury. They are joined by the research analyst responsible for making the daily reserve projections. She reports that non-borrowed reserves the day before had fallen about $250 million short of her estimates—not bad since misses of $1 to $2 billion often occur. She notes that required reserve estimates for the two-week maintenance period have been revised upward by $250 million by the Board staff on the basis of new data. Her own new estimate of nonborrowed reserves indicates that the Desk needs to add about $850 million to meet the upward revised objectives. (See Table III.)

TABLE III
The Reserve Outlook-
June 13
(in millions of $)

Two-Week Reserve Period Ending	Path (1) Required Reserves	Assumptions (2) Excess Reserves	(3) Borrowing	NBR Path (4)=(1)+ (2)-(3)	Projected Supply NBR (5)	Open Market Operations To Hit Path (6)=(4)-(5)
June 20	36,900e	600 (845)¹⁄	1,000 (1,230)¹⁄	36,500	35,650	+ 850
July 4	36,350e	700	1,000	36,050	34,550	+1,500
July 18	37,350e	600	1,000	36,950	33,900	+3,050

e=estimated
¹⁄=average period to date

The vice president places the call to the Treasury official, who is responsible for managing the Treasury's cash balance at the Federal Reserve. He gives the estimates of the net change his staff expects in the balance over the next three days. The vice president provides the corresponding New York staff estimates. The Treasury sees a shortfall of $500 million for tomorrow from the $3 billion balance customarily maintained. He suggests a corresponding call from its Class C note depositories into the Reserve Banks to meet the checks expected to be presented today and tomorrow. The funds will come from the note accounts maintained at 40 or so large institutions and will be in addition to the calls previously scheduled on similar accounts at medium-sized and smaller depositories. The Fed's projections indicate a drain of $1 billion for the two days. After discussion the Treasury officer decides to call 25 percent of the previous night's book balance at the "C" banks—about $750 million. On the Fed's estimates the balance tomorrow would be slightly below the $3 billion level assumed routinely in making the Desk's reserve projections.

The conversation over, the vice president informs the responsible section elsewhere in the Bank about the Treasury's action. By 11 a.m., in response to a Treasury wire, all of the Reserve Banks will have notified the "C" banks in their districts to transfer 25 percent of the Treasury's note balances with them at Tuesday's close to the regional Reserve Bank on Thursday. (If need be, the Treasury could make a special call for payment on the same day the banks are notified.)

These transfers will drain reserves from the affected banks on Thursday, but the payment for Treasury checks should restore an equivalent amount of reserves to the financial system. Even so, the "C" banks may find themselves net losers as the payment for Treasury checks presented to the Federal Reserve are apt to go to a much wider array of institutions. Any reserve imbalances can be quickly redressed through the federal funds market.

After the Treasury call, the Manager and other officers discuss the program of action for the day. The new reserve projections, to be received a bit later in final form, indicate a need of about $850 million. With the money market a touch more comfortable than before the weekend, there is general agreement that a market purchase of Treasury bills for regular—i.e., next day—delivery is appropriate. Since only half the period will be affected, a purchase of $1 to $1.5 billion of bills will add just half of the amount bought to average reserve positions for the two weeks, but add the full amount to later periods. A modest residual need would remain for the current period—subject to further revisions in the NBR objective and future errors in reserve projections. Since outright System purchases occur infrequently, the Manager checks with the Board's Director for Monetary and Financial Policy, who calls back shortly to confirm that the Chairman has no objection to the proposed operation. A senior Desk officer begins writing out the program the Desk plans to implement that day.

The scene moves to the trading room itself. There the Desk officer or senior staff person who is to report on the morning call is making notes on developments in the money and securities markets. One by one he talks to the traders responsible for following the various markets. Prices of Treasury coupon securities have continued to drift lower. Two or three dealers appear to be hitting bids through the brokers, which link the primary dealers. There is also selling pressure in bond contracts on the futures exchange in Chicago. Apparently, professionals are setting up short positions against the issues the Treasury is expected to sell soon. Treasury bill rates, on the other hand, are a bit lower. Dealer financing costs have eased with the decline in the federal funds rate. There is also reinvestment demand from holders of bills maturing after mid-month. They are buying for future delivery, anticipating a multibillion dollar bill paydown by the Treasury from incoming corporate tax receipts. Prices in the corporate and municipal markets are narrowly mixed in quiet trading.

Another trader recaps the money market for the reporting officer as the clock moves on toward 11 a.m. Federal funds, he notes, continue trading steadily at 10⅝ percent with supply and demand reasonably balanced. The major banks around the country report a collective need to buy about $16 billion in funds and have already bought $6 billion. Government securities dealers have a need to raise $14 billion through overnight or term repurchase agreements to finance their positions. They are finding good money from out-of-town banks, corporations and state governments at 10¼ to 10⅜ percent, well below the 10⅞ percent rate most commonly quoted by the New York banks.

The reporting officer also gets a briefing by phone from the foreign exchange Trading Desk on the seventh floor. This morning the dollar is somewhat stronger against the deutschemark and the yen. U.S. companies operating abroad are reported buying dollars to remit dividends. Also short covering is reported before the quarter-end statement publishing date, related partly to nervousness about the higher federal funds rate that prevailed before the weekend.

Meanwhile, another Desk trader is busy pulling together the data on reserves and bank positions that she will transmit to the Board staff and the research staff of the Reserve Bank whose president will participate in the coming conference call. Shortly before 11 a.m., a report arrives that gives the previous day's reserve positions, federal funds transactions, and discount window borrowings of eight New York City and seven major out-of-town banks. Clerks from the Research Department bring additional reports in rapid succession. The latest projection of nonborrowed reserves confirms the estimate given to the Manager at the time of the Treasury call, namely that nonborrowed reserves remain about $850 million below the revised NBR objective. Another report gives the distribution among major depository groups of excess reserves and borrowings at the discount window. Finally, a few minutes after 11 a.m., detailed data become available on positions held the previous day by the government securities dealers that report daily to the Federal Reserve.

The trader duly communicates this data by phone to her opposite numbers at the Board and the other Reserve Bank. In the course of this pre-call the Board staff passes along its estimate that NBR are still $1.1 billion below the new objective. This information is quickly passed to the senior officer who is writing the action program for the day.

That officer has already checked with another Desk specialist about the volume of outright buy and sell transactions in Treasury bills that the Desk is to execute for foreign accounts that day, either for cash or next-day delivery. Today such accounts are selling a net of $50 million for cash and $125 million for regular delivery. Since it fits the System's book to inject reserves, the officer includes provision in the program for the System to buy these bills directly from foreign accounts at the middle of the quoted market at noon. (These purchases will add about $90 million to reserves in the current period and $175 million to NBR in following periods.) He also incorporates the latest estimate of the bills to be sold routinely to foreign accounts under repurchase agreements (RPs) to meet the overnight investment orders of the foreign "RP pool." (The reserve projections made each morning assume that all such orders will be met by temporary sales from the System account.)

Just past 11 a.m. the Manager of the System Open Market Account enters the trading room. A Desk officer quickly brings him up to date on the latest market information, including the recent behavior of the dollar in the foreign exchange market. The senior officer writing the program reports that foreign accounts will be selling Treasury bills and notes that he has included the purchase of such bills in the program. The Manager reviews the program, adding a phrase to the stated rationale for the proposed purchase of bills in the market. The officer reporting on the call reads the program through to familiarize himself with the language. A few minutes later a secretary notifies the officers that the call is coming through. They and selected senior staff move to a nearby office to participate in the key telephone conversation that formalizes the day's plan.

"Washington and San Francisco are standing by," announces the telephone operator, completing the three-way hookup that enables the Manager to review developments with the Board staff and the FOMC member serving on the call. The Manager and his associates are joined at the New York end by an officer from the Foreign Department. Seated behind a telephone microphone on the large special desk, the reporting officer speaks:

"The Treasury market opened with prices of coupon issues rising in response to good foreign demand that appeared in London trading. Since the opening, however, prices have receded on profit-taking and dealer short sales and are now ¼ to ⅜ of a point below the levels of late yesterday. The approach of the Treasury's financing seems to be the chief influence, but there is also a little sensitivity to the possibility that the Fed might use this period of seasonal reserve pressures to tighten up a bit. Treasury bill rates are unchanged to 5 basis points lower, reflecting lower financing costs and advance reinvestment of proceeds expected from the bill maturing after the tax date. The corporate market is also drifting a bit lower in price in a subdued market, while municipal issues are in good demand with prices up by ¼ point or so."

The reporting officer goes on to cover briefly developments in the foreign exchange markets, including indications of any market intervention by foreign central banks. He touches on the reasons behind the previous day's reserve shortfall and brings everyone up to date on the money market, using information phoned in from the trading room as well as the rates displayed on a nearby information screen. He compares reserve projections with the Board staff to find the source of the differences in the two sets of projections of nonborrowed reserves. His speech is clear and concise, making use of the verbal shortcuts familiar to people operating in the money market.

The Board's staff Director for Monetary Policy gives the latest data on M1 and the staff's preliminary ideas of what that may do to the growth rates for M1, M2 and M3 for June. The San Francisco Reserve Bank president observes that the new numbers seem reasonably consistent with the desires incorporated in the May directive.

In conclusion, the reporting officer in New York reads the Manager's proposed program of buying $1 to $1.5 billion of Treasury bills in the market for delivery the next day. He also notes that the Desk plans to buy $50 million of bills from foreign accounts for immediate delivery and another $125 million for delivery the next day. He invites comments on the program. The San Francisco president asks whether the action is widely expected by the market. The reporting officer replies that it is generally anticipated over the next several days although not all analysts are projecting it for today. He thinks that the purchase will probably reduce latent fears that the tighter money market before the week-end could foreshadow a snugging up in the federal funds rate. The San Francisco president concurs that the purchase is appropriate in the light of the FOMC's instructions.

The call is usually completed soon after 11:30 a.m. A staff member at the Board promptly summarizes its contents in a memorandum sent to each Board member and a tele-gram sent to each Reserve Bank president.

The call over, the Manager briefs the assembled group on any of a variety of topics ranging from administrative or budget matters to his discussions with Treasury officials about the forthcoming financing. Other officers contribute reports of their individual discussions with dealers or with asset-liability managers of the major banks. A visiting officer from the Foreign Department may discuss the recent behavior of the foreign exchange markets. Shortly before each FOMC meeting, the Manager may ask the other officers to give him their thoughts on the appropriate course for monetary policy to be adopted at the meeting.

At times the officers from the unit charged with surveil-lance of the government securities market will join the Trading Desk group to keep everyone posted about dealer financial performance. Periodically, the officers will go over the operations of an individual dealer whose principals are coming in for lunch. These daily sessions are invaluable in keeping all participants informed of the main policy issues and market developments that are their collective responsibility.

Today, there is no immediate market entry by the Trading Desk since the program calls for the purchase of bills for delivery and payment the next day. The "go-around," which was described at the beginning of the booklet, gets under way at about 12:45 p.m. after all cash business for the day is out of the way. Within 45 minutes, give or take ten minutes, the operation is completed. The System has purchased $1,304 million of Treasury bills and bank reserves will rise the next day by a corresponding amount.

The Desk's entry did not, in fact, prove much of a surprise. The dealers offered bills at pretty much the rates prevailing before the announcement of System action. Treasury coupon prices did lift just a bit. Some traders took the bill purchase as reassurance that the Federal Reserve was not really promoting the higher federal funds rates that had prevailed before the weekend. A quick exchange of information among the dealers leads to estimates that the Desk bought perhaps $1.5 billion of bills. The operation appeared routine, certainly not on a scale that would suggest the Fed was trying to promote lower short-term interest rates.

Money market economists are on the screen within a few minutes, generally commenting that the bill "go-around" did not involve any change in the Desk's reserve objectives. On Thursday afternoon they will examine closely the reserve statistics that are published for signs that seasonal and adjustment borrowing for the week ended on Wednesday are within the usual range of variation. They will note the rise in Treasury bills bought for cash from foreign accounts, but the "go-around" will not show up in the data until next week since delivery is scheduled for Thursday.

These analysts are well aware that the federal funds rate, and indeed other interest rates, can swing back and forth for any given relationship between borrowing and the excess reserves in the financial system. Accordingly, much of their effort focuses on the outlook for economic activity and inflation over the months and quarters ahead. They weigh the same fundamental questions regarding the balance between monetary demand and capacity utilization that confront the Federal Open Market Committee. Every new economic number brings a marginal refinement in analysis. Changes in trend are quickly reflected in the market's outlook for rates. Surges in the economy will produce a rise in all interest rates automatically, usually well before the Desk's reserve objectives change. Conversely, a downward revision in expectations will cause an easing of rates.

This flexibility of market response provides some assurance to FOMC policymakers that interest rates will respond to incoming economic information in an appropriate direction—although not necessarily to the degree necessary. Policymakers must still decide whether to accept, or to reinforce, the market's expectations. Ultimately, the FOMC's success in pursuing its goals for money and the economy depend on how well it uses the flexible tool of open market operations to modify financial and real economic decisions at the margin in a timely fashion.

In the financial markets, analysts and participants alike will continue to examine every nuance of the Desk's operations against their analytical—or visceral—conviction of what the Fed ought to be doing. It is the daily challenge that gives zest to the game.

Tomorrow is another day . . .

Should a Robot Replace
the Federal Reserve?

Lawrence S. Ritter
and William L. Silber

Some Monetarists, most notably Milton Friedman, have abandoned countercyclical stabilization policy altogether. They never had any use for fiscal policy to begin with, and the issue of time lags in the impact of monetary policy has led them to jettison countercyclical monetary policy as well. In chapter 5, we noted that time lags do indeed make the implementation of monetary policy potentially hazardous.

"Countercyclical" monetary policy means leaning against the prevailing economic winds: easy money in recessions, to get the economy on the move again; tight money when there is a boom, to slow it down. In its most naive form, however, countercyclical monetary policy tends to ignore the complications bred by time lags.

Assume that the Federal Reserve forecasts a recession due six months from now. If the forecast is correct, and if a current expansion in the money supply would have an impact six months hence, well and good. But what if the Federal Reserve's crystal ball is not that clear, and it is more than a year before the main impact of today's monetary policy is reflected in the economy? Then the effects of today's expansionary monetary policy are likely to be felt *after* the economy has passed the trough and is already on its way up.

As the accompanying diagram illustrates, the impact of today's easy money may exacerbate tomorrow's inflation. Tight money will have similarly delayed effects; it may be imposed with the best of intentions, to curtail a boom, but its real impact, being long delayed, might accentuate a recession. Monetary policy is a destabilizer rather than a stabilizer!

On these grounds—the precarious nature of economic forecasting and the alleged length, variability, and unpredictability of the time lags involved—Friedman and some other Monetarists have given up on orthodox monetary policy. Friedman argues that the economy has been and is now inherently stable, and that it would automatically tend to

154

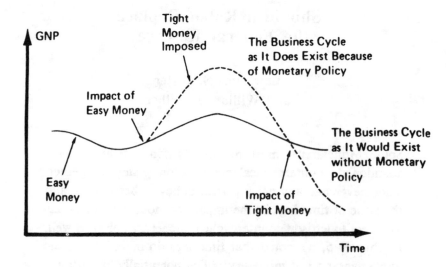

**Friedman's Alleged Perverse Effects of
Countercyclical Monetary Policy**

stay on a fairly straight course if only it were not being
almost continuously knocked off the track by erratic or un-
wise monetary policies. Conclusion: quarantine the central
bank. The best stabilization policy is no stabilization policy
at all. Hasn't it all been said before:

> They also serve who only stand and wait.
>
> JOHN MILTON

Rules Versus Discretion

What Professor Friedman proposes instead is that the Federal Reserve be instructed by Congress to follow a fixed
long-run rule: Increase the money supply at a steady and
inflexible rate, month in and month out, year in and year out,
regardless of current economic conditions. Set the money
supply on automatic pilot and then leave it alone.

The specific rule would depend on the definition of the
money supply adopted. Actually, the particular number itself
is not so important to Friedman as the restriction that once
it is decided upon it be left alone thereafter. No tinkering!

The constant growth rule is intended to keep prices stable
and employment high by allowing aggregate demand to grow
secularly at the same rate as the growth in the economy's real
productive capacity (due to growth in the labor force and
increased productivity). It is also supposed to compensate,
according to Friedman, for a long-term gradual downtrend

in velocity, although, in fact, velocity has done nothing but rise since the end of World War II, and from all indications will continue to do so.

Such a rule, it is claimed, would eliminate forecasting and lag problems and therefore remove what Friedman sees as the major cause of instability in the economy—the capricious and unpredictable impact of countercyclical monetary policy. As long as the money supply grows at a constant rate each year, be it 3, 4, or 5 percent, any decline into recession will be temporary. The liquidity provided by a constantly growing money supply will cause aggregate demand to expand. Similarly, if the supply of money does not rise at a more than average rate, any inflationary increase in spending will burn itself out for lack of fuel. Anyway, any discretionary deviations by the central bank would interfere with the natural course of the economy and only make matters worse.

The United States Congress has been impressed enough to come part of the way toward a Friedman-type rule, in preference to allowing the Federal Reserve to rely entirely on its own judgment and discretion. In March 1975, both the House of Representatives and the Senate passed House Congressional Resolution 133, which instructed the Federal Reserve to "maintain long-run growth of the monetary and credit aggregates commensurate with the economy's long run potential to increase production." It also required that the Fed report quarterly to Congress on its target monetary and credit growth rates for the upcoming twelve months. In November 1977, these provisions were incorporated into the Federal Reserve Act itself.

The Friedman position is based on a number of pillars, each supported by mounds of statistical evidence produced by Friedmanites. However, very little is really known about the length and variability of the time lags. Such evidence as there is, and there is not much, is extremely mixed, as we saw in chapter 5. There is no consensus among economists who have worked in the area.

It is ironic—or instructive—that in the final analysis the extremists from both camps, Monetarist and Keynesian, have collectively ganged up on the Federal Reserve. The extreme Monetarists want to shackle it, because their concern with time lags leads them to believe it is both mischievous and harmful. The extreme Keynesians want to subordinate it to fiscal policy, because they think it is either useless or lethal.

In the middle, squabbling but finding more common cause than they had thought possible, are the moderates: moderate Monetarists, who believe that the forecasting-lag problem is not so great as to negate all the potential stabilizing effects of monetary policy; and moderate Keynesians, who believe that monetary policy probably does change interest rates and/or the availability of credit and that those changes, along with fiscal policy, probably do influence spending decisions in the right way at more or less the right time. While one group concentrates mainly on the money supply and the other primarily on credit conditions, they are nevertheless in agreement that some form of countercyclical monetary policy is, on balance, beneficial.

It seems clear, after all is said and done, that central banking is still at least as much art as science. We simply do not yet know enough to legislate an eternal rule, or even a rule for the next six months, that the Federal Reserve must follow under any and all circumstances. When we do know that much, the Federal Reserve will know it too, and if they are rational they will follow it regardless of whether it has been enacted into law.

Meanwhile, for better or worse, we appear to have no alternative but to rely on our best knowledge and judgment in the formulation of monetary policy. We can only try to make sure that the decision-makers are able and qualified people with open minds and the capacity to learn from experience.

Lessons on Monetary Policy
from the 1980s

Benjamin M. Friedman

The half-decade running from mid-1982 to mid-1987 was a pretty good era for U.S. monetary policy, as these things go. A sharp easing of policy, beginning some time around midyear 1982, helped set in motion a recovery from the most severe business downturn the United States had experienced since the 1930s—a downturn that tight monetary policy earlier on had deliberately brought about in order to slow the alarming acceleration of prices. The recovery that ensued developed into a sustained expansion that continued without interruption through the end of 1987, thereby setting a new record for the longest recorded business expansion in U.S. peacetime experience. A fiscal policy based on unprecedentedly large (and continually growing) structural budget deficits was a major factor underlying this record-length expansion, but at least monetary policy did not stand in the way. Just as importantly, the severe 1981–82 recession served its intended purpose of substantially restoring price stability, and even after five years of expansion inflation remained modest by recent historical standards. At least as judged by these outcomes for the standard objectives of macroeconomic policy, U.S. monetary policy was a distinct success during these years.

Economists hoping to say something useful about monetary policy have had a tougher time. The quantitative relationships connecting income and price movements to the growth of familiar monetary aggregates, including especially the $M1$ measure of the money stock that had been the chief focus of monetary policy during 1979–82, utterly fell apart during this period.[1] Moreover, the collapse of these long-standing empirical regularities was not merely a matter of larger than usual quarter-to-quarter or year-to-year variances around longer-run benchmarks that otherwise continued to be reliable. Double-digit $M1$ growth, sustained on average over fully five years, repeatedly led prominent economists who had relied on these relationships in the past to offer widely publicized warnings of an imminent re-acceleration of prices. Yet the inflation rate fell dramatically, and then remained low. The presumption that "inflation is always and everywhere a monetary phenomenon" became progressively less compelling as a substantive rather than merely tautological description of the determination of prices.

Economists who preferred to think about monetary policy in different terms had no more success in fitting the major developments of this period into some alternative conceptual framework. Relationships connecting income and prices to the monetary

■ *Benjamin M. Friedman is Professor of Economics, Harvard University, Cambridge, Massachusetts.*

base, or to measures of credit, fell apart just as visibly as did those centered on $M1$. Although real interest rates declined somewhat from the record levels posted in 1981 and early 1982, they nevertheless remained historically high throughout the next five years. Yet the economy's rate of growth in after-inflation dollars was about average for post war business cycle expansions, and in this case the expansion continued on for five years without even a single negative quarter.

In the meanwhile, the rapidly changing structure of the U.S. international economic position brought importance of a whole new magnitude to complications that most economists addressing questions about U.S. monetary policy had acknowledged often enough in the past, but nonetheless had usually ignored in substance. The U.S. current account balance, which had frequently changed sign since World War II but had always remained trivially small in comparison to the economy's size, suddenly became large enough to matter in a domestic macroeconomic context. The dollar exchange rate therefore emerged as a primary focus of U.S. macroeconomic policy. In addition, just within these few years the steady string of mounting current account deficits transformed the United States from the world's largest creditor country to the largest debtor. The exchange rate therefore acquired a new importance in the U.S. financial markets as well.

In the eyes of many economists, the Federal Reserve System has been steering without a rudder ever since it effectively abandoned its commitment to monetary growth targets in 1982. The visible success of monetary policy during the past half-decade is therefore all the more puzzling. In fact, over the course of this period the Federal Reserve's conduct of monetary policy appears to have centered ever more closely on controlling short-term interest rates. Whether this development really means that U.S. monetary policy has now returned to the conceptual basis of a quarter-century ago, when short-term nominal interest rates (or their equivalent) were practically the only focus of the policy process, remains unclear. At the very least, it raises the issue of whether the blatant flaws that crippled this policy strategy in the past were inherent and unavoidable. The other side of the same question is what will happen if the Federal Reserve continues to pursue what is basically an interest rate strategy, if and when inflation again becomes a major problem.

The 1979–82 Experiment and Its Aftermath

The basic facts describing the conduct of U.S. monetary policy in recent years are well known, although their interpretation has been the subject of much disagreement. In October 1979, the Federal Reserve System announced that it was adopting a new policy strategy placing primary emphasis on reducing over time the growth of the money stock. Further, to gain better control over money growth the Federal Reserve would be implementing new operating procedures, based in the first instance on the stock of nonborrowed reserves rather than the federal funds rate or some other short-term interest rate. The bands within which the federal funds rate would be free to fluctuate in the interval between meetings of the Federal Open Market Committee were accordingly widened by more than an order of magnitude. Several more narrowly technical measures, designed in principle to enhance control over money growth, were also part of the overall package.

The immediate motivation underlying this dramatic move was the rapidly deteriorating inflation situation, together with growing concerns about the dollar exchange rate. The overall U.S. inflation rate, as measured by the GNP deflator, had risen from a post-recession low of 6.4 percent in 1976 to 8.9 percent in 1979. The comparable rise measured by consumer prices was from 4.8 percent to 13.3 percent, the highest rate since 1946. At the same time, dollar exchange rates declined between 1976 and 1979 by 16.4 percent on a trade-weighted basis (14.5 percent after correcting for differential inflation). Especially once the OPEC cartel announced yet another major hike in crude petroleum prices, fears of an uncontrollable inflation spiral or a precipitous decline in the dollar, or both, began to spread.

Although the Federal Open Market Committee had at least mentioned money growth targets in its formal policy directives ever since 1970, and had formally reported money growth targets to Congress since 1975, in practice there was little correspondence between the stated targets and actual money growth. Evidence from the 1970s shows that the Federal Reserve did systematically adjust the federal funds rate in the direction required to offset deviations of actual money growth from the targets, but that the magnitude of these adjustments was far too small to be effective for plausible estimates of the interest elasticity of money demand.[2] Perhaps more importantly, the Committee typically did not set the coming year's targets so as to make up for past deviations, but instead let bygones be bygones and so treated each year as independent of the past. As the years rolled on, the difference between actual and targeted money growth was usually positive, and the average difference was positive. As a result, the actual rate of $M1$ growth gradually drifted upward, from 4.9 percent per annum during 1965-69 to 6.1 percent per annum during 1970-74, and then 7.1 percent per annum during 1975-79 (although the fastest growth for any year during this period, 8.4 percent, occurred during 1972).

The effects of the new combination of policy strategy and policy tactics implemented in October 1979 were immediately visible, and they continued to be so for the next several years, although in some aspects they ran counter to the new policy's declared intent. At the most basic level, the Federal Reserve did carry through on its commitment to contain, and then reduce, the growth rate of the $M1$ money stock. The rate of $M1$ growth, measured from the fourth quarter of one year to the fourth quarter of the next (the same basis used for officially reporting money growth targets to Congress) had been 8.2 percent in 1978. The "gradualist" objective of reducing the money growth rate by one percent each year, until it reached a level consistent with price stability, would imply targets of roughly 7 percent for 1979, 6 percent for 1980, 5 percent for 1981, and so on.[3] Although $M1$ had grown at a 9.0 percent per annum rate in the first three quarters of 1979, with the sharp policy shift in the final quarter the growth for 1979 as a whole was 7.9 percent. A continuation of the new policy delivered 7.3 percent $M1$ growth in 1980, and 5.1 percent in 1981 (see Figure 1). For this three-year period viewed as a whole, the new policy did manage to achieve results roughly consistent with the objective of reducing the money growth rate by one percent per year.

Not surprisingly, delivering on this objective involved interest rates that were both higher on average and also more volatile.[4] Nominal interest rates immediately rose to record highs, and then declined sharply as the economy entered a recession and the Federal Reserve Board also imposed credit controls as authorized by President Carter under the Credit Control Act of 1969.[5] Nominal interest rates then rose to yet new record highs in 1981 after business began to recover and credit controls were no longer in effect. Interest rates were high in real terms as well. The difference between the three-month Treasury bill rate and the next quarter's inflation rate, which had averaged close to zero during the post World War II period up until then, fluctuated in the 4-8 percent per annum rage throughout 1981 and 1982. Short-run volatility of interest rates—month-to-month, day-to-day, and even within the trading day—increased by what for most measures were large multiples.

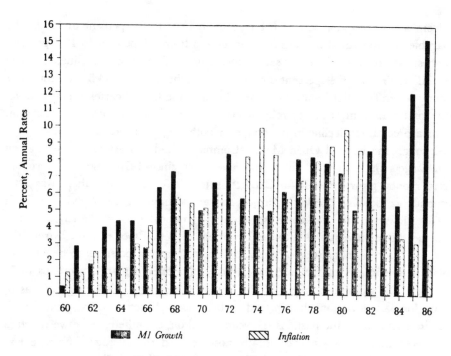

Fig. 1. Money growth and price inflation

The most striking respect in which the results of the new monetary policy did not correspond to its declared intent was that the short-run volatility of money growth increased sharply too. The Federal Reserve's success in gradually reducing the yearly $M1$ growth rate—8.2 percent in 1978, 7.9 percent in 1979, 7.3 percent in 1980, 5.1 percent in 1981—did not carry over to the quarterly growth rate, which varied in the immediate post-1979 period from a high of 21.1 percent per annum in 1980:$Q3$ to a low of *minus* 5.8 percent per annum in 1980:$Q2$, nor to any finer time calibration. The standard deviation of $M1$ growth from one quarter to the next jumped from 2.37 percent per annum during 1970:$Q1$–1979:$Q3$ to 6.64 percent per annum during 1979:$Q4$–1982:$Q2$ (although omitting the two back-to-back extreme quarters during the 1980 credit control episode, the increase was only to 3.00 percent per annum). Although the Federal Reserve had never formally acknowledged any commitment to stabilize money growth on a within-year basis, critics of monetary policy, both at the time and subsequently, focused on this increase in short-run volatility as casting doubt on the strength of the central bank's commitment to money growth targets in a broader perspective.

The monetary policy experiment that commenced in October 1979 ended almost as abruptly as it had begun. By the summer of 1982 the slowdown in U.S. business activity had developed into what was, by many measures, the most severe recession since the great depression of the 1930s. Unemployed labor, idle industrial capacity and business bankruptcies were all at post war record levels. At the same time, bank failures had also reached record levels, and there were increasing signs of fragility throughout the financial structure. In August 1982 an impasse over Mexico's ability to meet its dollar-denominated external obligations called widespread attention for the first item to the debt problems not just of Mexico but of developing countries throughout Latin America and sub-Saharan Africa.

Yet the demand for money balances continued to be strong. Following the 5.1 percent growth in 1981, the Federal Reserve had set a 2.5-5.5 percent target range for

$M1$ growth in 1982. The revised data now available show that actual $M1$ growth was within this range (4.6 percent per annum) during the first half of 1982; but the data available at that time showed $M1$ growth running consistently above the stated target range, despite continuing high interest rates and contracting real economic activity. In August the Federal Reserve allowed short-term interest rates to drop by almost three percentage points notwithstanding the emergence of still more rapid money growth. In October, within less than a week of the third anniversary of the announcement that had proclaimed the new dedication to money growth targets, Federal Reserve Chairman Paul Volcker publicly acknowledged that the $M1$ growth target was no longer in effect. With a further speed-up in the fourth quarter, $M1$ growth for the year 1982 came to 8.6 percent—above the target range, above the 1978 growth rate from which the program of cutting back on money growth had originally begun, and even above the postwar record growth rate set back in 1972.

The experience of the next five years largely continued the course set in the latter half of 1982. The yearly $M1$ growth rate was in double digits in each of 1983, 1985 and 1986 (see again Figure 1). For the five-year span ending at mid-1987, the average $M1$ growth was 10.8 percent per annum. Only in 1984 did actual money growth fall within the stated target range. In both 1983 and 1985 the Federal Reserve officially changed the target range at midyear, once the difference between actual and targeted $M1$ growth became obvious. In 1986 the Federal Reserve suspended its $M1$ target range without setting a new one. In 1987 the Federal Reserve simply set no target range for $M1$ growth at all.

Throughout the post-1982 period the Federal Reserve's official pronouncements continued to emphasize targets for broader monetary aggregates in place of $M1$, but it is not clear to what extent these measures genuinely guided monetary policy. Actual $M2$ growth did fall within the stated target range in every year between 1983 and 1986.[6] Actual $M3$ growth exceeded the stated target range in 1983 and 1984, but fell within it in 1985 and 1986. In 1987, until the October drop in stock prices, the Federal Reserve either instigated or accepted (depending upon one's perspective) rising market interest rates, and also raised the discount rate, despite the fact that both $M2$ growth and $M3$ growth were falling short of the stated target range; and the decline of market interest rates immediately after the stock market crash appeared to have little to do with money growth patterns in any direct way.

By contrast, short-term nominal interest rates since 1982 have resumed the smooth pattern characteristic of the pre-1979 era, thereby suggesting a renewed role for interest rates—as before—at the center of the monetary policymaking process. The standard deviation of the month-to-month change in the three-month U.S. Treasury bill rate, for example, had risen from .42 percent per annum between January 1970 and September 1979, to 1.54 percent per annum between October 1979 and September 1982. It dropped back to .32 percent per annum between October 1982 and June 1987. The standard deviation of the month-to-month change in the federal funds rate rose from .50 percent to 1.92 percent, and then fell to .38 percent, over the same three periods.

Although some of this return to interest rate smoothness on a month-to-month basis may simply have reflected the continuity of the business expansion and the absence of a re-acceleration of prices during this period, the pronounced stability of short-term interest rates over a substantial span of time more likely indicates the return to a monetary policy approach based on closely controlling interest rate movements. At the least, it presents a strong contrast to the behavior that the Federal Reserve has accepted for the monetary aggregates.

Collapse of the Money-Income and Money-Price Relationships

What makes this unusual record of monetary policy actions look so successful in retrospect is that the bizarre behavior of money growth in no way corresponded to the behavior of income or prices. The familiar relationships that had characterized prior experience simply disappeared.

Instabilities in the money-income relationship—or, in more sophisticated forms, the money demand function—had actually begun to become more pronounced as early as the mid-1970s, and their appearance had already spawned a substantial new body of empirical literature even before the new monetary policy experiment commenced in October 1979.[7] By 1980 the Federal Reserve System had already adopted a whole new set of definitions of the monetary aggregates, designed in part to overcome just such difficulties. A survey paper bearing the suggestive title "The Search for a Stable Money Demand Function: A Survey of the Post-1973 Literature," and including more than eighty references, was already in print in the *Journal of Economic Literature* before Paul Volcker acknowledged in October 1982 that the Federal Reserve was suspending its $M1$ growth target (Judd and Scadding, 1982.)

As Figure 2 makes clear, however, the instability that generated so much concern and research in the pre-1982 period was small stuff in comparison to what followed.

The figure plots the ratio of the $M1$ money stock to GNP for each quarter since the start of the redefined $M1$ series in 1959:$Q1$. Through the end of 1980, the $M1$-to-GNP ratio displayed the familiar downward trend of roughly 3 percent per annum that most students of the money-income relationship had come to see as inevitable in the post-war period, with a standard deviation around this trend of only .0044 (in comparison to a 1980:$Q4$ value of .1466). After 1980 the $M1$-to-GNP ratio not only experienced wider fluctuations but even reversed course. A simple extrapolation of the 1959-80 trend implies a ratio of .1007 by 1987:$Q2$ (the last quarter plotted). The actual value in 1987:$Q2$ was .1686, different from the trend extrapolation by more than 15 times the 1959-80 standard deviation.

Discussion of this phenomenon at the popular level has typically offered as an explanation the fact that "velocity" has declined. Because the so-called income velocity of money is nothing other than the ratio of GNP to money (the reciprocal of the ratio plotted in Figure 2), however, such explanations are completely empty of content. Given the definition of "velocity" in this context, the fact that velocity declined is simply identical to the fact that money grew rapidly while income did not. Saying that money growth outpaced income growth because velocity declined is like saying that the sun rose because it was morning.[8]

Two examples, both drawn from the same paper, readily illustrate the pitfalls that confronted anyone who continued to rely closely on straightforward money-income and money-price relationships during this period. First, Figure 3 is an expansion, both backward in time and forward, of a figure included in a paper by Milton Friedman (1984) in the *American Economic Review*. The figure plots the respective annualized quarter-to-quarter growth rates of GNP and, with a one-quarter lag, $M1$. The figure covers 1960:$Q1$–1987:$Q2$ and distinguishes three time intervals. The middle one, 1979:$Q4$–1983:$Q4$, is identical to that plotted by Friedman. It spans the period from the October 1979 inception of the new monetary policy experiment through what was presumably the most recent observation available as of his time of writing.

After pointing out that the correlation between these two series during 1979:$Q4$–1983:$Q4$ was .46, or .71 after eliminating the two quarters affected by the credit control episode, Friedman wrote, "Two things are notable about the relation

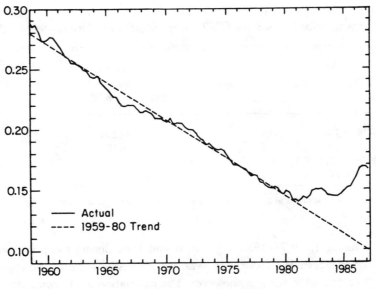

Fig. 2. Ratio of money to GNP

Note: The series plotted is the ratio of $M1$, as a quarterly average of monthly data (source: Board of Governors of the Federal Reserve System) to quarterly GNP at annual rates (source: U.S. Department of Commerce). Both series are seasonally adjusted.

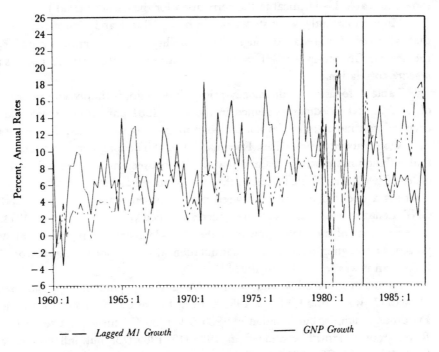

— — *Lagged M1 Growth* ———— *GNP Growth*

Fig. 3. Growth rates of GNP and lagged money

between money and income in these years: first, the lag is both shorter on the average and less variable than in earlier years, second, the relation is unusually close. I believe that both are a consequence of the exceptionally large fluctuations in $M1$ growth. The effect was to enhance the importance of the monetary changes relative to the numerous other factors affecting nominal income and thereby to speed up and render more consistent the reaction."

Table 1 summarizes the record of the GNP-to-lagged-$M1$ growth correlation and the variability of $M1$ growth for the three intervals shown in Figure 3. Money growth on a quarter-to-quarter basis (as used by Friedman in his paper) was certainly more

Table 1

Money growth volatility and the GNP-to-lagged-$M1$ correlation, 1960–1987

Sample	Standard deviation of M1 growth	Correlation between GNP growth and lagged M1 growth
1960:$Q1$–1979:$Q3$	2.87%	.47
1979:$Q4$–1983:$Q4$	6.16	.45
1979:$Q4$–1980:$Q1$, 1980:$Q4$–1983:$Q4$	4.18	.47
1984:$Q1$–1987:$Q2$	4.80	−.10

Data are seasonally adjusted at annual rates. Money data are quarterly averages.

variable during 1979:$Q4$–1983:$Q4$ than it had been during the prior two decades. The GNP-to-lagged-$M1$ correlation was not "unusually close" during 1979:$Q4$–1983:$Q4$ compared to the past, however. The correlation of .45 computed over these eleven quarters (Friedman reported .46) is essentially identical to that for the previous 79 quarters. Excluding 1980:$Q2$ and 1980:$Q3$ reduces the variability of money growth, but does not materially affect the GNP-to-lagged money correlation. (Subsequent data revisions have reduced the .71 correlation reported by Friedman to .47 as shown in Table 1—identical to the correlation for the earlier period.)

More importantly, what stands out in both Table 1 and Figure 3 is the changes that occurred after 1983. Although the variability of money growth remained high, the positive GNP-to-lagged-$M1$ correlation disappeared entirely. In its place is a small *negative* correlation.

Table 2, focusing on the money-price relationship, is simply an updated version of a table that Friedman presented in the same 1984 paper. The horizontal line in each column indicates entries not included in the original version. In describing the data shown above the two lines, Friedman wrote, "The long-period evidence suggests that inflation has much inertia and that the lag between money and inflation is of the order of two years. Table [2] shows that this relation has held in recent years as well. There is a one-to-one relation between movements in monetary growth, and in the GNP deflator two years later over successive two-year periods since 1971... The increased rate of monetary growth in the 1981-83 biennium suggests that we have passed the trough in inflation and that inflation will be decidedly higher from 1983 to 1985 than it was from 1981 to 1983."[11]

As the below-the-line entries in Table 2 show, quite the opposite happened. Growth of $M1$ during 1981:$Q3$–1983:$Q3$ was the fastest for any of the six biennia in Friedman's sample, but inflation in 1983:$Q3$–1985:$Q3$ turned out to be the lowest. Rapid money growth continued in 1983:$Q3$–1985:$Q3$, but inflation slowed still further in 1985:$Q3$–1987:$Q3$. The simple correlation between the two time series shown, calculated for the first five observations only, is .70. Calculated for all seven observations, the correlation is *minus* .23.

Other Money and Credit Aggregates

The breakdown of long-standing relationships to income and prices has not been confined to the $M1$ money measure. Neither $M2$ nor $M3$, nor the monetary base, nor the total debt of domestic nonfinancial borrowers has displayed a consistent relationship to nominal income growth or to inflation during this period.

Table 2
Rates of change in money and in inflation eight quarters later

| Period for money | Annual rate of change over eight quarters | | Period for deflator |
	M1	Deflator eight quarters later	
1971:Q3–1973:Q3	6.9%	9.5%	1973:Q3–1975:Q3
1973:Q3–1975:Q3	5.2	6.3	1975:Q3–1977:Q3
1975:Q3–1977:Q3	6.4	8.3	1977:Q3–1979:Q3
1977:Q3–1979:Q3	8.6	9.4	1979:Q3–1981:Q3
1979:Q3–1981:Q3	6.1	4.8	1981:Q3–1983:Q3
1981:Q3–1983:Q3	9.2	3.3	1983:Q3–1985:Q3
1983:Q3–1985:Q3	8.1	2.8	1985:Q3–1987:Q3

Data are seasonally adjusted.
Source: Friedman (1984), updated. (The entries above the lines differ from Friedman's because of subsequent data revisions, but the differences are slight.)

A Relationship That Did Hold Up

In sharp contrast to the collapse of relationships connecting the ultimate objectives of monetary policy to standard quantity measures of policy actions, the long-standing relationship between the two most prominent macroeconomic policy objectives—inflation and unemployment—remained intact during this period. The point is of some interest because one of the principal supposed merits widely claimed in favor of the use of publicly announced money growth targets for monetary policy was a potential lessening of the real costs of disinflation. The idea was that public knowledge of such targets would affect expectations in such a way as to minimize (according to some models, to eliminate altogether) the usual negative impact of disinflationary monetary policy on employment, output, incomes, and profits.

What this idea should have led one to predict about the real costs of the major disinflation achieved in the United States in the 1980s is far from clear. For almost three years beginning in October 1979, the Federal Reserve did approximately carry through on its widely publicized intention to reduce the yearly rate of money growth by one percent per year—that is, as long as everyone understood that "money" meant $M1$. Because the familiar claim that most measures of money move roughly together over time turned out to be false, however, anyone who watched $M2$ or $M3$ instead of $M1$ would have seen no evidence of monetary deceleration.[14] Moreover, on a within-year basis even $M1$ growth became not more regular but less after October 1979 (see again Table 1). After mid-1982 there was no reason for anyone to find the Federal Reserve's commitment to its stated money growth targets credible.

Regardless of whether any part of the policy experience of the 1980s constituted a good test for an effect of preannounced money growth targets in reducing the real costs of disinflation, it is clear that no such reduction occurred. Ten years ago, Arthur Okun (1978) surveyed a variety of econometric estimates of these costs, none of which incorporated any expectations effects due to reliance on preannounced money growth targets. Okun's survey indicated that the cost of each percentage point reduction in inflation achieved by monetary policy would be between two and six "point-years" of unemployment, with a median estimate of three point-years.[15] Table 3 shows the annual rate of change of the GNP deflator and the annual average unemployment rate beginning in 1978. The table also shows, for years beginning in 1980, the cumulative excess of the unemployment rate above 6 percent (the approximate average for the two prior years and a standard "full employment" benchmark.

The slowing of inflation from nearly 10 percent per annum in 1980-81 to roughly 3 percent per annum a half-decade later required approximately 14 point-years of unemployment—right at the lower end of the range implied by the econometric models Okun surveyed. Especially in light of the evidence suggesting that something like a third (and perhaps as much as a half) of this disinflation was a product of the 74 percent appreciation of the dollar's trade-weighted exchange rate between 1980 and early 1985—an appreciation which has been almost entirely reversed as of the time of writing—this result seems fully consistent with Okun's prediction.[16]

Everyone had always known that sufficiently tight monetary policy, maintained for a sufficiently long time, could halt even the most deeply rooted inflation. The reluctance to proceed in that fashion lay not in disbelief that such a policy would do its job, but in concern for the resulting real costs. What was new beginning in October 1979 was the willingness to bear those costs.

Vacuum at the Center?

It is difficult to escape the conclusion that there is now a conceptual vacuum at the center of the U.S. monetary policymaking process. The seemingly endless quest from various quarters to impose some kind of simple rule on the conduct of monetary policy is, at least for now, no longer a going concern. The interactions among money, income and prices during the 1980s—including the half-decade that followed the monetary targets experiment, even more than what happened during 1979–82—have under-

Table 3

Percentage rates of inflation and unemployment, 1978–1987

	Inflation rate	*Unemployment rate*	*Cumulative excess unemployment*
1978	7.3%	6.1%	—
1979	8.9	5.8	—
1980	9.0	7.1	1.1%
1981	9.7	7.6	2.7
1982	6.4	9.7	6.4
1983	3.9	9.6	10.0
1984	3.7	7.5	11.5
1985	3.2	7.2	12.7
1986	2.6	7.0	13.7
1987	3.2	6.5	14.2

Data for 1987 based on first half year only.

mined it both intellectually and practically. The claim that reliance on some kind of simple rule would open the way to costless disinflation is at best unproven, and for practical purposes doubtful. The notion that some kind of simple rule would adequately encompass the new complications due to the increased practical importance of the U.S. economy's openness is dubious at best. In retrospect, the contemptuous dismissal by some economists of the Federal Reserve's reluctance to adopt the monetary policy rules they had proposed—and the readily voiced assumption that that reluctance could have stemmed only from ignorance or a faulty set of objectives on the part of Federal Reserve officials, or perhaps even their self-aggrandizement at the public expense—stands as a sorry reminder that economists outside government can also make each of these errors.

The most powerful element of what has happened in this regard in the 1980s is the collapse of the longer-run relationship between money on the one side and income and prices on the other. In this decade the main event has been very different from the quarter-to-quarter or even year-to-year irregularity that was always the focus of debate about whether these relationships were stable before. Proponents of simple monetary policy rules in the past could and did claim that such rules failed to offset short-run economic fluctuations that policy could probably not hope to eliminate anyway, but that over longer horizons the anchor they provided would keep the economy on a steadier course than an alternative policy that attempted to achieve "fine tuning." With nominal GNP by mid-1987 more than 40 percent below the value implied by the long-run relationship to $M1$ which prevailed during 1959–80, the problem is no longer in the fine tuning but in the anchor itself.

The relevant issue here for policy purposes is not whether for any time interval there exists some abstract notion of "money" that conceptually bears a stable and reliable relation to income and prices, and that statisticians can seek to uncover after that interval ends, but whether policymakers can identify and measure that quantity substantially in advance of their need to base planning and operating decisions on it. Appeals to the tradition of the "quantity theory" are of no use in this context in the absence of a clear statement of what is the quantity and what is the theory. Especially in a world of institutions that increasingly blur the distinction between transactions balances and saving balances, being precise about either the theory or the quantity is ever more difficult. The continuing (indeed increasing) interest within the economics profession in some kind of constitutional constraint on monetary policy jars harshly againt the likelihood of what such constraints suggested (but not enacted) in years past would have meant in the 1980s.

Nor is the problem merely one of money (or credit) "targets." The more flexible idea that such variables as money and credit, which are endogenous to the monetary policy process in the short run, should be used as "information variables" to guide the initial setting and ultimate readjustment of whatever genuinely exogenous instrument the central bank is using, has always seemed highly attractive—at least to me. The information-variable approach to monetary policy makes no sense, however, in the absence of a reasonably compact set of variables that reliably provide information about the macroeconomic outcomes monetary policy is seeking to affect. After the experience of the 1980s, it is difficult to foresee any ready consensus on what that compact set of variables should be. Subsequent experience may provide a new basis for such a consensus, and new data to substantiate it; but that prospect remains a matter for the future, if not later still.

In the meanwhile, the Federal Reserve System has not ceased operations. Nor should it be inclined to do so, in light of the performance of both income and prices during the past half-decade. Five years of fairly steady economic growth, with inflation consistently lower than at any time since before the Vietnam War, represents no small achievement by today's standards. In the world of practical affairs, it is difficult to argue with success.

Notwithstanding the Federal Reserve's continuing formulation of money growth targets that it reports to Congress, as current law requires, and even notwithstanding the relatively high success rate in meeting the target for $M2$, it seems clear enough that the Federal Reserve System since mid-1982 has centered its monetary policy actions primarily around controlling short-term nominal interest rates.[21] In so doing, Federal Reserve decision makers have no doubt taken account of the movements of money (and perhaps credit, too); but they have also taken account of many other potential information sources, including longer-term asset prices and yields, dollar exchange rates, and numerous aspects of nonfinancial economic activity. More to the point, they have apparently proceeded in the absence of any well-articulated conceptual framework linking the interest rate as the chief policy instrument to the main macroeconomic policy objectives, or linking the associated large and diverse information base to either the policy instrument or the policy objectives. Although procedures differ in various details, the overall approach is strongly reminiscent of the practice of the 1950s and 1960s.[22]

It is therefore useful to ask why the policy approach followed at that time failed. The voluminous investigation of this question, both at the time and subsequently, supported three general conclusions: First, Federal Reserve officials systematically confused the level of interest rates as the instrument of monetary policy with the level of interest rates as an ultimate objective of monetary policy. As a result, they usually delayed too long before raising or lowering interest rate levels, and even then made changes of insufficient magnitude. Second, with no nominal quantity at the center of the policy process, the overall approach lacked an anchor to provide price stability. Although inflation was not therefore inevitable, there was little protection against it when various inflationary pressures arose. Third, once inflation did emerge, Federal Reserve officials (and many other people too) often failed to distinguish nominal from real interest rates. As a result, they often associated higher observed interest rates with a tighter policy stance even when the increase in nominal interest rates merely kept pace with, or even fell short of, rising inflationary expectations.

Are these three flaws inherent in the approach to monetary policy that the Federal Reserve System followed a quarter-century ago, and that it has apparently been following again since mid-1982? Or is it possible to design and implement monetary policy along these lines, albeit in a way that has learned from the still relatively recent past? Were the familiar failures of monetary policy under this approach in the past inevitable? Or does the experience of the last half-decade show that this kind of monetary policy can work, and work well? Research on these questions may be the best contribution economists concerned with U.S. monetary policy can now make.

■ *I am grateful to Kenneth Kuttner for research assistance; to Stanley Fischer, William Poole, Joseph Stiglitz and Timothy Taylor for helpful comments on a previous draft; and to the National Science Foundation and the Harvard Program for Financial Research for research support.*

---

[1]The $M1$ money stock consists of currency, checkable deposits (including both non-interest-bearing demand deposits and interest-bearing NOW accounts) and travelers checks; its value as of June 1987 was $747

billion. $M2$ consists of $M1$ plus a much larger quantity of savings-type accounts, including ordinary passbook accounts and certificates of deposit (in amounts up to $100,000), money market deposit accounts and money market mutual funds (both of which can have limited checking facilities), and overnight repurchase agreements and Eurodollars; its June 1987 value was $2.8 trillion. $M3$ consists of $M2$ plus institutionally oriented instruments like certificates of deposit in amounts over $10,000 and money market mutual funds used by institutional investors, as well as repurchase agreements and Eurodollars extending beyond overnight; its June 1987 value was $3.6 trillion.

[2] See, for example, De Rosa and Stern (1977) and Lombra and Moran (1980).

[3] The official $M1$ target range for 1979 was 5-8 percent.

[4] Increased short-run volatility of short-term interest rates, as a result of no longer accommodating temporary disturbances affecting money demand, is a straightforward implication of Poole's (1970) analysis of the money growth target strategy for monetary policy. Whether long-term interest rates should be expected to be more or less volatile is a more complicated question, however, involving changing risk factors and expectations of future inflation and interest rates.

[5] The 1969 legislation under which the Board acted was quite far reaching, empowering the Federal Reserve Board, whenever explicitly authorized by the President, to "prohibit or limit any extensions of credit under any circumstances the Board deems appropriate." In 1980 the Board proceeded under this authority to impose special reserve-type requirements on increases in certain kinds of consumer credit by all lenders (including non-banks), on increases in deposits at money market mutual funds, and on increases in non-deposit liabilities at banks that were not members of the Federal Reserve System.

[6] In 1983 the stated target range for $M2$ growth covered only part of the year.

[7] The standard reference to state first is the contrast between the findings in Goldfeld (1973) and Goldfeld (1976). The most widely read studies done at the time by the Federal Reserve's own staff include Enzler et al. (1976), Porter et al. (1979), and Simpson and Porter (1980).

[8] I owe the analogy to William Bennett.

[11] Friedman made the some prediction more forcefully in writings directed at broader audiences. In a column in the September 26, 1983 issue of Newsweek, for example, Friedman wrote, "Inflation has not yet accelerated. That will come next year, since it generally takes about two years for monetary acceleration to work its way through to inflation... The monetary explosion from July 1982 to July 1983 leaves no satisfactory way out of our present situation... The result is bound to be renewed stagflation—recession accompanied by rising inflation and high interest rates." A lengthy interview in the March 19, 1984, issue of Fortune indicated that Friedman "... also sees a strong possibility that by the end of [1984] inflation could reach an annual rate as high as 9%."

[14] For the five years 1978–82, the simple correlations among the fourth-quarter-over-fourth-quarter growth rates of the major M's were each negative: − .53 between $M1$ and $M2$, − .57 between $M1$ and $M3$, and − .12 between $M2$ and $M3$.

[15] A "point year" of unemployment is one percentage point of unemployment in excess of the rate that corresponds to "full employment," maintained for one year. Some writers—for example, Fischer (1985)—have focused on real output rather than unemployment, and have argued on that basis that the post-1980 disinflation involved smaller costs than Okun's survey implied. The focus of the evidence that Okun surveyed was the inflation-unemployment relationship, however. His translation of the cost estimate into foregone real output simply relied on the usual three-for-one "Okun's Law" relation, which has not held up during the 1980s.

[16] See, for example, Sachs (1985) for an analysis of the importance of the dollar's appreciation in the U.S. disinflation.

[21] See Wallich (1984) for a description in different but equivalent terms.

[22] See, for example, the descriptions given by Brunner and Meltzer (1964) and Guttentag (1966).

References

Brunner, Karl, and Allan H. Meltzer, *The Federal Reserve's Attachment to the Free Reserve Concept.* U.S. Congress, House of Representatives, Committee on Banking and Currency, Subcommittee on Domestic Finance, 88th Congress, 2nd Session. Washington: U.S. G.P.O., 1964.

DeRosa, Paul, and Gary H. Stern, "Monetary Control and the Federal Funds Rate," *Journal of Monetary Economics*, April 1977, *3*, 217–231.

Eichenbaum, Martin, and Kenneth J. Singleton, "Do Equilibrium Real Business Cycle Theories Explain Postwar U.S. Business Cycles?" In Fischer, ed., *NBER Macroeconomics Annual*. Cambridge: The MIT Press, 1986.

Enzler, Jared, Lewis Johnson, and John Paulus, "Some Problems of Money Demand," *Brookings Papers on Economic Activity*, 1976, No. 1, 261–278.

Fischer, Stanley, "Contracts, Credibility, and Disinflation," mimeo, National Bureau of Economic Research, 1985.

Friedman, Benjamin M., "Money, Credit, and Interest Rates in the Business Cycle." In Gordon, ed., *The American Business Cycle: Continuity and Change*. Chicago: University of Chicago Press, 1986.

Friedman, Benjamin M., "New Directions in the Relationship Between Public and Private Debt," *Science*, April 24, 1987, *236*, 397–403.

Friedman, Benjamin M., "The Roles of Money and Credit in Macroeconomic Analysis." In Tobin, ed., *Macroeconomics Prices and Quantities: Essays in Memory of Arthur M. Okun*. Washington: The Brookings Institution, 1983.

Friedman, Benjamin M., "Time to Reexamine the Monetary Targets Framework," *New England Economic Review*, March/April 1982, 15–23.

Friedman, Milton, "Lessons from the 1979–82 Monetary Policy Experiment," *American Economic Review*, May 1984, *74*, 397–400.

Goldfeld, Stephen M., "The Case of the Missing Money," *Brookings Papers on Economic Activity*, 1976, No. 3, 683–730.

Goldfeld, Stephen M., "The Demand for Money Revisited," *Brookings Papers on Economic Activity*, 1973, No. 3, 577–638.

Goldfeld, Stephen M., and Daniel E. Sichel, "The Demand for Money." In Friedman and Hahn, eds., *Handbook of Monetary Economics*. Amsterdam: North-Holland Publishing Company, forthcoming.

Guttentag, Jack M., "The Strategy of Open Market Operations," *Quarterly Journal of Economics*, February 1966, *80*, 1–30.

Judd, John J., and John L. Scadding, "The Search for a Stable Money Demand Function: A Survey of the Post-1973 Literature," *Journal of Economic Literature*, September 1982, *20*, 993–1023.

Lombra, Raymond, and Michael Moran, "Policy Advice and Policymaking at the Federal Reserve." In Brunner and Meltzer, eds., *Monetary Institutions and the Policy Process*. Amsterdam: North-Holland Publishing Company, 1980.

Okun, Arthur M., "Efficient Disinflationary Rules," *American Economic Review*, May 1978, *68*, 348–352.

Poole, William, "Optimal Choice of Monetary Policy Instruments in a Simple Stochastic Macro Model," *Quarterly Journal of Economics*, May 1970, *84*, 197–216.

Porter, Richard D., Thomas D. Simpson, and Eileen Mauskopf, "Financial Innovation and the Monetary Aggregates," *Brookings Papers on Economic Activity*, 1979, No. 1, 213–237.

Roley, V. Vance, "Money Demand Predictability," *Journal of Money, Credit and Banking*, November 1985, *17*, Part 2, 611–641.

Sachs, Jeffrey D., "The Dollar and the Policy Mix: 1985," *Brookings Papers on Economic Activity*, 1985, No. 1, 117–185.

Scholl, Russell B., "The International Investment Position of the United States in 1986," *Survey of Current Business*, June 1987, *67*, 38–45.

Simpson, Thomas D., and Richard D. Porter, "Some Issues Involving the Definition and Interpretation of the Monetary Aggregates." In *Controlling Monetary Aggregates III*. Boston: Federal Reserve Bank of Boston, 1980.

Solomon, Robert, "The United States as a Debtor in the Nineteenth Century," mimeo, The Brookings Institution, 1986.

Stock, James H., and Mark W. Watson, "Interpreting the Evidence on Money-Income Causality," mimeo, National Bureau of Economic Research, 1987.

Wallich, Henry C., "Recent Techniques of Monetary Policy," Federal Reserve Bank of Kansas City, *Economic Review*, May 1984, 21–30.

Sequential Signals of Recession and Recovery*

Victor Zarnowitz and Geoffrey H. Moore

I. Countercyclical Policy Triggers: The Problem and Its Setting

This paper describes a sequential procedure for identifying the beginning and ending dates of business cycle recessions as promptly and accurately as practicable. Its origin lies in a study in progress for the Economic Development Administration (EDA), U.S. Department of Commerce, which deals with the problem of designing and testing an efficient trigger formula for public works expenditures with the aid of a system of cyclical indicators. However, the proposed approach can be applied much more broadly to any temporary countercyclical policy program on the national level.

Federal policy programs of job creation through public works or public service employment have been repeatedly called *countercyclical* without in fact being so. Most such programs came into effect much too late to counter the cyclical *rises* in the national unemployment rate (which, of course, does not necessarily preclude their being appropriate for other reasons, e.g., because of relatively high *levels* of unemployment in the intended impact areas). In fact, public works programs were not enacted until 9–19 months after the cyclical decline in output had been reversed and that in employment nearly completed.[1] For the public service employment programs, the legislative and administrative lags have been considerably shorter, but not sufficiently so to produce significant countercyclical effects.[2] Moreover, no provision was made in any of the programs for effective cutoff dates related to signals of the progress of the recovery. In sum, the overall lags involved were such that the funds, instead of being spent to combat unemployment during recessions, were actually spent when the expansion of the national economy was already well under way.

The tardiness of policies designed to stimulate employment not only reduces their intended stabilizing (antirecession) effects but also induces some unintended destabilizing effects. Government expenditures are likely to contribute more to excess demand and inflationary pressures during a business expansion than during a business contraction. Ill-timed fiscal and monetary policies can, of course, have similar effects.

The success of any discretionary countercyclical policy action depends critically on its timeliness; in addition, it must also have a sufficient degree of flexibility. However, the accuracy of economic forecasts tends to deteriorate as the forecast span lengthens and is generally not adequate for predictions looking as far ahead as a year or more. But shorter predictions of slowdowns and recessions, based on the actual record of cyclical indicators with early timing characteristics rather than on forecasts of such series, can be shown to provide useful first-alert signals which, when combined with confirmatory signals from measures of aggregate economic activity, are capable of producing a timely and reliable "triggering" mechanism.

The main problem with recent public works programs as well as other policies intended to be countercyclical lies in the long lags with which they are *initiated and terminated*. Most of the total delay is accounted for by the recognition, legislative, and administrative lags—which would be eliminated if the programs were effectively triggered at the onset and at the end of a recession.[3] As noted, the time between the allocation of funds and the employment of half the workers to be employed is approximately 6–12 months, which is not unduly long, given the duration of high unemployment created by recent recessions. The solution, then, lies primarily in making the policy action timely by tying it to certain prespecified indicator values which reliably signal the beginning and end of a recession. The required flexibility can be obtained by advance preparation of a backlog of useful projects to be mobilized progressively according to schedules related to a sequence of increasingly reliable signals.[4]

This study relates only to the problem of optimal *timing* of public employment policies in the context of cyclical movements in the U.S. economy as a whole. It is recognized that the effectiveness of the programs depends also on their size, financing, organization, and still other factors (such as any displacement and spillover effects), but these matters lie outside the scope of the present paper.

The plan of the procedure consists in identifying certain signals from suitably smoothed rates of change in composite indexes of cyclical indicators, which normally occur in a predetermined sequence. The possibility of false alarms is reduced by using turning points first in the leading and then in the confirming indicators. Actions based upon the initial turning points should be of a limited and reversible nature, involving relatively small commitments of funds. When the initial points have been confirmed by the subsequent turning points, more definitive and substantial actions should be taken. The signals devised in this plan refer directly to business cycles as defined and dated by NBER, but they also make use of the concept of growth cycles, that is, alternating periods of above-average and below-average rates of growth in aggregate economic activity. Since a growth slowdown preceded each recent recession, signals of the former give some advance warning of business cycle peaks. At troughs, leads of this type are typically fewer and much shorter, but if the signals are somewhat late they are also less scattered and often easier to read.

In what follows, the rationale of the proposed strategy for using the cyclical indicators is outlined; the concept of the growth cycle and its relationship to the business cycle is explained; the procedures used and the results obtained thus far are presented and assessed; and some perspective is provided on the needs and the promise of further work.

II. Concepts and Procedures

The proper objective of countercyclical policy programs is to reduce the number of cyclically unemployed at times of overall slowdowns and recessions. This might seem to indicate that the policies should be initiated (discontinued) when the national unemployment rate rises above (falls below) some specified "high" level for some sufficiently long time. Indeed, triggering formulas based on unemployment statistics have received much attention in recent programs of direct employment stimulation by fiscal means. But here, as elsewhere, policy targets should not be confused with policy indicators. While the behavior of total unemployment is strongly influenced by business cycles, it is very difficult to separate the cyclical component of unemployment from the other components—frictional, structural, and institutional. The use of high-unemployment trigger formulas will inevitably cause the programs to be badly mistimed, that is, to lag behind recessions and be active during expansions when unemployment may be relatively high for reasons other than cyclical declines or deficiencies in aggregate demand.

An analysis of a variety of labor market indicators shows that they are strongly affected by cyclical changes in the economy, but also that most of them are either too sluggish or too irregular in their timing to produce useful signals for our present purposes. However, there is one promising option which is being explored in another study. This consists of combining several leading and trendless labor turnover series.[5]

The best of the options for a trigger formula, as currently considered, is a plan based on a comprehensive coverage of leading and confirming indicators of business expansions and contractions. There is ample evidence from a long series of studies that important and persistent timing sequences exist among series in each of the areas viewed as critical in business cycle theories. The tabulation below illustrates this in a general and selective way.[6]

Some of the main factors in business cycle theories:	Evidence from time series for the corresponding variables:
1. Interaction between investment and final demand, or between the investment and savings functions.	Large cyclical movements in business investment commitments (orders, contracts) lead total output and employment; smaller movements in investment expenditures coincide or lag.
2. Changes in the supply of money, bank credit, interest rates, and the burden of private debt.	Money and credit flows (rates of change) are highly sensitive, with typically early cyclical timing; market interest rates coincide or lag.
3. Changes in price-cost relations, in the diffusion, margins, and totals of profits, and in business expectations.	The profit variables all show large and unusually early cyclical movements, and so do stock price indexes. Unit labor costs contribute to this result by rising rapidly prior to and just after a business peak and falling prior to and just after a trough.

More specifically, series that represent early stages of production and investment processes (e.g., new orders for durable goods, housing starts, or permits) lead series that represent late stages (finished output, investment expenditures). Under uncertainty, less binding decisions are taken first, for example, hours of work are lengthened (shortened) before the work force is altered by new hirings (layoffs). Other timing sequences reflect important stock-flow relationships involving the demand for and supply of output and goods and services as influenced by changes in business fixed capital and inventories, money and credit.

For well-supported theoretical reasons, a selected group of indicators representing a whole set of these relationships has much greater predictive value over time than any of the individual indicators.[7] This insight led to the construction of composite indexes of leading, coincident, and lagging indicators which indeed, as a rule, outperform the individual indicators. These indexes incorporate series that represent different economic processes but have similar cyclical timing. The best indicators from each economic-process group are selected by means of a detailed scoring procedure incorporating several major criteria (economic significance, statistical adequacy, consistency of timing and conformity to the cyclical movements of the economy at large, smoothness, and currency). For each timing category (say, the leading series), the chosen indicators are combined into an index with weights provided by their overall performance scores.[8]

Our procedure uses the data from the leading and coincident composite indexes published by the U.S. Department of Commerce in *Business Conditions Digest (BCD)* each month. Cyclical peaks in the leading index often occurred early in the low-growth phases and anticipated the beginning dates of recessions by variable but, on the average, rather long intervals, whereas the troughs in the index led the beginning dates of recoveries by quite short intervals. Reliable signals from the indexes proper, when we take into account the need for some smoothing and confirmation, would occasionally be too tardy for the purpose on hand. To obtain more timely and dependable indications, we found it advisable to use rates of change in the composite indexes with the aid of simple smoothing and decision rules.[9]

One such rule that turned out to be effective is that of taking the ratio of the current month's index to the average of the 12 preceding months and expressing the resulting percentage change at a compound annual rate.[10] This is a smoothed 6-month rate, which involves the same loss of lead time as an ordinary 6-month change (where the current month is compared with the single month's figure 6 months earlier). The two are affected in the same way by any special factors that pertain to the current month, but the ratio that uses the 12-month centered moving average in the denominator is for this reason much less subject to erratic fluctuations than the ordinary rate of change over 6-month moving periods.[11]

Each of the composite indexes published in *BCD* contains a "target trend" of 3.3% per year (0.272% per month). The purpose is to make the long-run trend in each index the same and equal to the trend rate of growth in the economy as a whole from 1948 to 1975, so that any differences in the behavior of the indexes are due to short-run factors.[12] Accordingly, the average value of the annualized rate-of-change series derived from the indexes over a long period is in each case approximately 3.3%. Thus, when the 6-month smoothed rates of change described in the preceding paragraph are less than 3.3%, this means that the underlying index is rising at less than its long-term average rate. In the case of the leading index, this is an indication that a declining phase of the growth cycle is approaching; in the case of the coincident index, that it is probably under way. Likewise, when the annual rates of change come to exceed 3.3%, this means that an upswing in the growth cycle may be starting.

Growth cycles represent an important but not very familiar phenomenon which may require some additional explanation. They are movements in aggregate economic activity defined by the consensus of fluctuations in comprehensive indicators adjusted for their long-term trends. They are thus composed of specific cycles in the *deviations from trend* of time series representing output, income, trade, employment, and many other economic processes, and they differ from business cycles in that the latter are defined by the consensus of fluctuations in the *levels* of the same collections of comprehensive economic indicators.

A business cycle always involves at least one growth cycle, since in a contraction the short-term growth rate, being negative, is necessarily less than the long-term growth rate (which for an expanding economy is, of course, always positive—reflecting the growth of total resources and their productivity). A business cycle will involve more than one growth cycle on those occasions when its expansion contains one or more protracted low-growth phases (i.e., periods when the short-term growth rate, while remaining positive, falls below the trend rate for a year or so).[13] Consequently, there are some "extra" growth cycles in addition to those which stand in a one-to-one correspondence with business cycles. Since 1945 the U.S. economy has passed through seven recessions—the latest in the first half of 1980—and it has also witnessed three periods of below-average growth rate that did not encompass recessions.

Each of the seven expansions of the 1945–79 period decelerated before peaking and ending in a contraction; in other words, each of the recessions was preceded by a phase of positive but below-normal economic growth. The lags of business cycle peaks behind the starting dates of the low-growth phases lengthened substantially over this period, from 2–6 months for the first four of the peaks, which occurred in 1948–60, to 8–13 months for the last three, which have occurred since 1969. This development reflects several interrelated trends in an economy with an expanding government, intensified inflation, increasing role of services versus goods in national employment, and reduced rates of private investment and productivity.

Whereas the growth cycle peaks led the business cycle peaks, the growth cycle troughs (marking the transition from low- to high-growth phases) usually occurred at about the same time as the business cycle troughs. Occasionally, as in 1954, a growth cycle trough would follow a business cycle trough, that is, the recovery would start slowly, with the overall growth rate not getting up to the average level until some months later.

The NBER reference chronologies for growth cycles and business cycles, on which the above statements are based, are presented in the first two columns of tables 1 and 2 for the peaks and troughs, respectively. These lists of dates have been established by a close examination of time series of levels and deviations from trend for a broad set of comprehensive indicators of real economic activity.[14] It should be noted that the expansions of recent business cycles varied greatly in length but averaged about 50 months, that is, about 4½ times the mean duration of the contractions. In contrast, the growth cycles which emerge after elimination of the secular upward trend are nearly symmetrical, with high- and low-growth phases averaging 20 and 18 months. Such regularities are attractive to business-conditions analysts and increasingly recognized. Certainly, it is much easier to recognize a developing slowdown than to pinpoint the date of a future downturn, and this strong presumption is well supported by lessons from recent forecasts. Since most low-growth periods do end as recessions, the concept and measurement of growth cycles can help provide some advance warning of business cycle peaks. Even though a slowdown may not evolve into a recession, its recognition gives time for precautionary action. Similarly, it is more important to stop antirecession action when a rapid recovery is under way than when a recovery is proceeding slowly.

III. The Results: A Signaling System and Its Ex Post Record

The cyclical movements in the leading index tend to occur earlier than those in the coincident index. Figure 1 shows, in a hypothetical diagram, the smoothed rates of growth in the two series, which for simplicity will be called the "leading index rate" (L) and the "coincident index rate" (C).[15] Among the earliest signs that an ongoing expansion may start to decelerate is a decline in the leading index rate. This development is more decisively indicated when a sustained decline of the growth rate in the leading index puts it below the average 3.3% line. A similar decline in the coincident index rate, which would normally occur later, confirms the onset of a general slowdown (low-growth phase) and suggests an increased possibility of a business cycle recession. If the leading index rate then falls below zero and the coincident index rate falls below 3.3% (not necessarily in this order), the probability of recession is heightened. Finally, if the coincident index rate follows the leading index rate by turning negative, chances are high indeed that the slowdown is being succeeded by an actual decline in overall economic activity, that is, a recession.

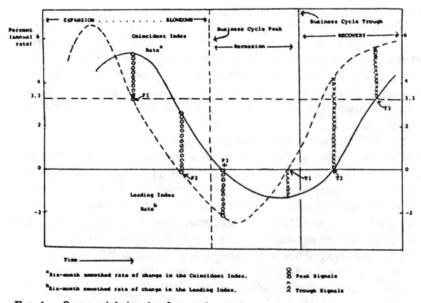

FIG. 1.—Sequential signals of recession and recovery: a schematic diagram.

TABLE 1   Three Signals of Recession: Timing at Business Cycle Peaks

Growth Cycle Peak	Business Cycle Peak	First Signal ($L < 3.3$; $C > 0$)	Second Signal ($L < 0$; $C < 3.3$)	Third Signal ($L < 0$; $C < 0$)	Lead ($-$) or Lag ($+$), in Months, at Business Cycle Peaks		
					First Signal	Second Signal	Third Signal
7/48	11/48	N.A.	N.A.	N.A.	...	...	...
3/51	None	2/51	7/51	...	...	...	...
3/53	7/53	6/53	8/53	9/53	-1	$+1$	$+2$
2/57	8/57	12/55	1/57	8/57	-20	-7	0
2/60	4/60	8/59	5/60	8/60	-8	$+1$	$+4$
5/62	None	5/62	...	...	...	...	...
6/66	None	6/66	2/67	...	...	...	...
3/69	12/69	6/69	11/69	1/70	-6	-1	$+1$
3/73	11/73	7/73	12/73	2/74	-4	$+1$	$+3$
12/78	1/80	7/78	6/79	10/79	-18	-7	-3
Average	...	...	...	...	-10	-2	$+1$

NOTE.—For full definitions of signals, see text. The following are regarded as false signals of a business cycle peak in constructing this table. First signal: a decline in the leading index rate below 3.3% in July 1977. Second signal: a decline in the coincident index rate below 3.3% in May–September 1956, October–November 1959, and April 1979. Third signal: a decline in the coincident index rate below zero in July 1956 and October–November 1959.

The expected sequence of signals at business cycle peaks, then, is when each of the following conditions is first observed:

First signal ($P1$): The leading index rate falls below 3.3%, while the coincident index rate is positive ($L < 3.3$; $C > 0$).

Second signal ($P2$): The leading index rate becomes negative, and the coincident index rate falls below 3.3% ($L < 0$; $C < 3.3$).

Third signal ($P3$): Both the leading index rate and the coincident rate become negative ($L < 0$; $C < 0$).

In figure 1, the vertical links between the two curves remind us that these signals involve prespecified positions or changes in both index rates. The business cycle peak is expected to occur in the vicinity of $P3$, that is, no more than a few months earlier or later than that signal.

This system of signals would have identified each of the six business cycle peaks from 1953 to 1980 (we do not have sufficient data available to check the 1948 peak). The average lead at business cycle peaks was nearly 10 months for the first signal, 2 months for the second signal. The third signal lagged the peak by an average of 1 month. As shown in table 1, the variation of the individual leads or lags around these averages was considerable, with long advance warnings before the 1957 and 1980 peaks, very short leads and lags in 1953, and intermediate situations in the remaining cases. However, sizable leads prevailed for the first signal, and even the third signal involved no long lags. It is important, too, that the sequence of the signals was maintained in each of the episodes covered.

The first two signals also identified two of the three growth cycle slowdowns that did *not* become business cycle recessions (the first signal alone identified all three), but the third signal ruled out each of these instances. In addition, the system produced four "false warnings" that were not associated with either slowdowns or recessions, but none of these would have done real harm. Of these cases (listed in table 1), two were single-month declines that related to the first or second signal only and were ruled out by the third. The other two were

TABLE 2   Three Signals of Recovery: Timing at Business Cycle Troughs

Growth Cycle Trough	Business Cycle Trough	First Signal ($L > 0$; $C < 0$)	Second Signal ($L > 3.3$; $C > 0$)	Third Signal ($L > 3.3$; $C > 3.3$)	Lead (−) or Lag (+), in Months, at Business Cycle Troughs		
					First Signal	Second Signal	Third Signal
10/49	10/49	8/49	1/50	3/50	−2	+3	+5
8/54	5/54	5/54	11/54	12/54	−0	+6	+7
4/58	4/58	5/58	9/58	11/58	+1	+5	+7
2/61	2/61	2/61	6/61	8/61	0	+4	+6
11/70	11/70	11/70	4/71	11/71	0	+5	+12
3/75	3/75	6/75	9/75	11/75	+3	+6	+8
7/80	7/80	9/80	12/80	2/81	+2	+5	+7
Average	...	...	...	...	+1	+5	+7

NOTE.—For full definitions of signals, see text.

caused by the major steel strikes in 1956 and 1959 and would have been recognized as such at the time.[16]

At the latest business cycle peak, which on June 3, 1980, was identified by the National Bureau of Economic Research as January 1980, the timing of the signals was as follows: first signal, July 1978, a lead of 18 months; second signal, June 1979, a lead of 7 months; and third signal, October 1979, a lead of 3 months.

In this instance the third signal, where both the leading and coincident index 6-month rates were negative for the first time, was interrupted in December 1979–January 1980, when the coincident rate turned positive for 2 months. In February 1980, it became negative again and remained negative through May. Hence the third signal either gave an advance warning 3 months before the January 1980 peak or a delayed warning of 1 month after the peak.

In interpreting these results, one must allow for the fact that data are not available instantaneously. The indexes are published initially by the Commerce Department toward the end of the month following the month to which they refer. For example, the May indexes were released June 30. Hence, in terms of availability, the dates in table 1 should be placed at least 1 month later.

At business cycle troughs, the signals we have selected are slightly different, occurring when each of the following conditions is first observed:

First signal ($T1$): The leading index rate rises above zero, while the coincident index rate is negative ($L > 0$; $C < 0$). This means that the first signal of a trough must follow the third signal of a peak.

Second signal ($T2$): The leading index rate rises above 3.3%, and the coincident index rate rises above zero ($L > 3.3$; $C > 0$).

Third signal ($T3$): Both the leading index rate and the coincident index rate exceed 3.3% ($L > 3.3$; $C > 3.3$).

These signals identified the end of each of the six business cycle recessions between 1949 and 1975, though with more of a lag than was true of the peak signals. The average timing of the three signals at the six business cycle troughs is as follows: first signal, zero months (i.e., no lead or lag); second signal, 5-month lag; and third signal, 8-month lag. The variation around these averages from one cycle to another is shown in table 2. There were no false signals of recovery in any instance in which the preceding business cycle peak had already been identified by the three peak signals.

We believe the lags of the signals at troughs are acceptable because at the beginning of recovery the level of activity is low (unemployment is at its cyclical peak levels), so that a program of public works expenditures may still be appropriate if it is tapering off and is discontinued after a brief period. While the third signal lags at business cycle troughs by 8 months on average, most of the cyclical expansion is yet to come. In fact, in none of the six instances would aggregate economic activity as measured by the coincident index have regained its previous peak level by the time the third signal was reached.[17] Hence the 8-month lag means that recovery is well under way and not likely to be

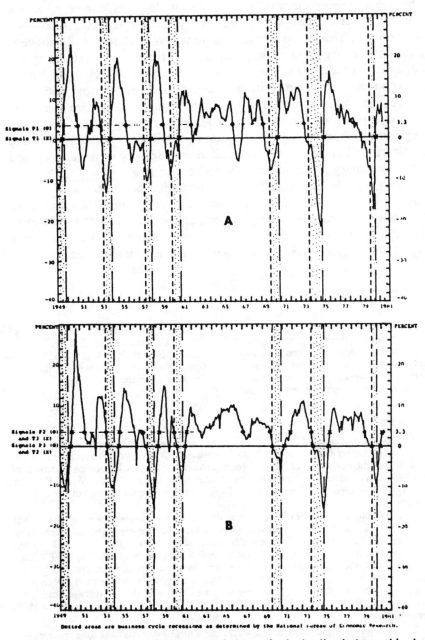

FIG. 2.—Six-month smoothed rates of change in the leading index and in the coincident index. A, The leading index rate. B, The coincident index rate.

aborted but has not reached a point where capacity utilization has become a problem.

Figure 2 displays the behavior of the 6-month smoothed rates of change in the leading index and in the coincident index relative to the business cycle peak and trough dates. The crossings of the 3.3% trend line and of the zero baseline—which underlie the signals of these dates as listed in tables 1 and 2—are identified. This allows a visual assessment of the workings of the procedure.

One way to evaluate the set of signals here is to count the number of months during business recessions when the signals would have operated in the appropriate way—and likewise during business expansions. Table 3 does this for the third signal and shows that it operated in the correct direction nearly 85% of the time between 1949 and 1980. The signal of recession was "on" for about 8½ years, compared with a total of about 5 years accounted for by the six recessions covered (since 1953). The record shows that these errors were heavily concentrated at the beginning of expansions and (to a lesser extent) at the beginning of recessions. The recession signal was always "off" before the economy recovered to its previous peak level (see text and n. 17 above). In terms of public works expenditures, these are the most tolerable types of error. A brief delay in turning them off at the beginning of an expansion means that they will be concentrated during a part of the business cycle when economic activity is most depressed and inflationary pressures are apt to be receding.

This record is very different from the actual performance of public works expenditures in the past, where a major problem has been that they have been concentrated in periods of high activity rather than low. The set of signals described in this paper should make possible a significant improvement on past performance in this respect.

*The research underlying this paper was supported by a grant to the Center for International Business Cycle Research from the Economic Development Administration. The EDA bears no responsibility for the content. Earlier versions of this paper were presented at the annual meeting of the American Economic Association in Denver on September 5, 1980, and at the annual meeting of the Illinois Economic Association in Chicago on October 31, 1980. We are indebted to Steven McNees, John Myers, and David Woolford for helpful comments, and to Chantal Dubrin and J. Rao for efficient research assistance.

1. Thus the Accelerated Public Works Program was enacted in September 1962, that is, 19 months after the end of the 1960–61 business cycle contraction as dated by the NBER. For the Public Works Impact Program (August 1971), the lag behind the trough of the 1969–70 recession was 9 months. The enactment of the Local Public Works Program in July 1976 followed by 16 months the NBER reference date for the end of the 1973–75 contraction.

2. The Public Employment Program was created by the Emergency Employment Act in July 1971, 8 months into the recovery from the 1969–70 recession. The Comprehensive Employment and Training Act (Title VI) was enacted in December 1974—13 months after the business cycle peak, but 3 months before the trough as dated by NBER. It is estimated that about 6 months elapsed between the allocation of funds and the employment of half the number of workers (half the direct jobs to be created) under these programs. The lags with which the policies take effect are, on the average, longer for public works, where the half-life is of the order of 1 year. See Vernez and Vaughan 1978, pp. 48–59.

3. While it is true that some public works (new large projects) have long implementation lags, others (renovations and small new projects) take much less time to complete. Public employment service programs have relatively short outside lags, with the best results showing 60%–70% of the peak number of jobs filled in 6 months (as shown for EEA in 1971–72 and CETA VI in 1974–75 by Vernez and Vaughan [1978], p. 56).

TABLE 3   Countercyclical Record of the Third Signal

A. Business Cycle Recessions

Business Cycle		Third Signal		Total (5)	Months of Recession			% of Total		
					Third Signal Correct (6)	Third Signal Incorrect		Third Signal Correct (9)	Third Signal Incorrect	
Peak (1)	Trough (2)	Peak (3)	Trough (4)			at Beginning (7)	at End (8)		at Beginning (10)	at End (11)
11/48	10/49	N.A.	N.A.	11	...	...	...	...	...	...
7/53	5/54	9/53	12/54	10	8	2	0	80	20	0
8/57	4/58	8/57	11/58	8	8	0	0	100	0	0
4/60	2/61	8/60	8/61	10	6	4	0	60	40	0
12/69	11/70	1/70	11/71	11	10	1	0	91	9	0
11/73	3/75	2/74	11/75	16	13	3	0	81	19	0
1/80	7/80	10/79	2/81	6	6	0	0	100	0	0
Total				61*	51	10	0	84	15	0

B. Business Cycle Expansions

Business Cycle		Third Signal		Total (5)	Months of Expansion			% of Total		
					Third Signal Correct (6)	Third Signal Incorrect		Third Signal Correct (9)	Third Signal Incorrect	
Trough (1)	Peak (2)	Trough (3)	Peak (4)			at Beginning (7)	at End (8)		at Beginning (10)	at End (11)
10/49	7/53	3/50	9/53	45	40	5	0	89	11	0
5/54	8/57	12/54	8/57	39	32	7	0	82	18	0
4/58	4/60	11/58	8/60	24	17	7	0	71	29	0
2/61	12/69	8/61	1/70	106	100	6	0	94	6	0
11/70	11/73	11/71	2/74	36	24	12	0	67	33	0
3/75	1/80	11/75	10/79	58	47	8	3	81	14	5
Total				308	260	45	3	84	15	1

C. Business Cycle Recessions and Expansions

Cols. 5	Cols. 6	Cols. 7	Cols. 8	Cols. 9	Cols. 10	Cols. 11
369	311	55	3	84	15	1

NOTE.—Col. 5 is the interval between the dates in cols. 1 and 2. Column 6 is the interval between the dates in cols. 1 and 3. Column 7 is the interval between the dates in cols. 3 and 2. Column 8 is the interval (if any) from the date in col. 4 to the date in col. 2. The false signals in 1956 and 1959 listed in the note to table 1, which were associated with strikes, are ignored in this table.

*Excluding 1948–49.

4. Note the following passage from an early, authoritative document: "Within limits, expenditures for public works can be timed to serve the interests of stability, but only if a reservoir of engineering studies and blueprints for specific projects has been prepared well in advance of need" (Council of Economic Advisers 1954, p. 123).

5. The composite index of "marginal employment adjustments" compiled by the Bureau of Economic Analysis (BEA) of the U.S. Department of Commerce includes the average workweek, accession rate, and layoff rate (all in manufacturing) and the average initial claims on state unemployment insurance. Two of these series (the workweek and the layoff rate) are components of the BEA index of 12 leading indicators used in the procedure described in the text below. For a modified version of the employment adjustment index, see Moore 1981.

6. This is of necessity but a starkly condensed list which groups together several types of explanations, e.g., (1) includes accelerator-multiplier models, hypotheses stressing autonomous investment, disturbances, lags, innovations, etc.; (2) covers both the older theories that assign a central role of fluctuations in bank credit and interest rates and the current monetarist theories; and (3) refers to the roles of cost-price imbalances, volatility of prospective rates of return, and expectational errors. Nor is this tabulation in any sense exhaustive. For an overview of business cycle literature with references, see Zarnowitz (1972), pp. 1–38. For a bibliography of indicator studies, see Zarnowitz (1972) and Moore (1980), pp. 329–33.

7. Careful observation led to an acceptable working definition of business cycles as a recurrent but not periodic sequence of cumulative expansions and contractions which spread unevenly over the myriad of processes and participants that constitute a market economy yet are sufficiently synchronized to show up as fluctuations in the overall aggregates of real income, output, employment, and trade. The historical movements display certain well established and important (but far from immutable) regularities along with many unique features of the individual processes and cycles. There are plausible hypotheses that are not necessarioy mutually exclusive, but there is no unified theory that has succeeded in explaining all that seems essential about business cycles. Thus, prediction cannot reliably depend on any single presumptive chain of cause and effect. The composition of factors which influence the course of the economy can and does vary from one business cycle to another, so some indicators may work better in one environment, others in a different environment. To increase the chances of getting true signals, it is therefore advisable to construct indexes from data of historically tested usefulness, with diversified economic coverage. It is also important and helpful that, in such indexes, much of the independent measurement error and other noise in the included series are smoothed out.

8. The series are also subjected to a standardization procedure designed to put them on an equal basis and to prevent the more volatile series from dominating the index. Further, trend adjustments are used, as noted later in this paper. For detail on the construction, record, and predictive value of the composite indexes of cyclical indicators, see Zarnowitz and Boschan 1975a, 1975b; U.S. Department of Commerce, Bureau of Economic Analysis 1977; Vaccara and Zarnowitz 1978 (pp. 41–50), 1979; Moore 1979 (pp. 401–36).

9. Another technique with a good claim to be considered is the use of trend-adjusted indexes, again after smoothing. But trend estimation is often difficult and uncertain, especially near the end of a series, and this is precisely where attention must be focused in a signaling system.

10. This is done by raising the ratio to the 12/6.5 power (the average of the 12 preceding months is located 6.5 months before the current month).

11. In fact, the smoothed 6-month change at annual rate was found to compare favorably with a simple 12-month change, i.e., the popular "same month year ago" comparisons. The latter series, while slightly smoother, lagged behind the former by 1 or 2 months at nearly every turn.

12. Specifically, the trends are made equal to the average of the long-term trends in the four components of the index of roughly coincident indicators (number of employees on nonagricultural payrolls; index of industrial production; personal income less transfer payments in constant dollars; manufacturing and trade sales in constant dollars). For each of these monthly series, a loglinear trend is computed by converting the percent change from the centered initial cycle average (1949–54) to the centered terminal cycle average (1970–75) into a monthly rate by the compound interest formula. For further details, see U.S. Department of Commerce, Bureau of Economic Analysis 1977 (pp. 74–76), 1979 (p. 157). The target trend will be reestimated each time a new trough-to-trough cycle is completed in the four coincident indicators. Frequent updating of the target trend rate is not practicable, but this should not cause any serious errors because the change in the secular trend of the economy is gradual and small in the short run.

13. Theoretically, business cycle contractions could likewise be interrupted by high-growth phases, but there are no instances of this sort in recent history, and none would be expected in times when all recessions are relatively short. In the seven completed business cycles of the post–World War II period (1945–80), the contractions ranged in length from 6 to 16 months and averaged 10 months.

14. The series represent aggregate output, employment and unemployment, income, and sales; all are in constant dollars or physical units or quantity index numbers. The trends are estimated by interpolation between segments determined with the aid of ratios to long (75-month or 25-quarter) centered moving averages; they are estimated so as to cut through and contain no significant elements of the short cyclical movements in the series. Various composite and diffusion indexes based on the same set of indicators are used as well. For further deta. and applications, see Zarnowitz and Boschan 1977 (pp. 34–38); Zarnowitz and Moore 1977.

15. The rates of growth actually used in this paper are smoothed 6-month changes in annualized form, as described in the text above. Of course, these indexes, like any others built from real economic indicators, contain much "noise," i.e., short erratic movements, which are entirely disregarded in figure 1.

16. The coincident index rate was below 3.3% for 5 months in 1956 and was negative in 1 month. In 1959, it was below 3.3% (and negative) for 2 months.

17. The following tabulation compares the lags of the third signal with those involved in the recovery of the coincident index to its previous peak level.

Business Cycle Trough	Lag of Third Signal (Months)	Lag of Recovery in the Coincident Index (Months)
Oct. 1949	5	8
May 1954	7	12
April 1958	7	13
Feb. 1961	6	9
Nov. 1970	12	13
March 1975	8	24
Average	8	13

18. The main reason for the large revisions in the preliminary index is that it is constructed from only 10 of the 12 components. The figures for the two components (net business formation and net change in inventories on hand and on order in 1972 dollars) are not yet available. These figures are added to the index 1 month later in the first revision (however, lately the figures for the net business formation have lagged 2 months). The preliminary coincident index is based on three of the four components (the figures for manufacturing and trade sales in 1972 dollars are added 1 month later in the first revision).

19. The content and method of constructing the composite indexes of cyclical indicators were altered in several aspects by the compiling agency in 1976. See U.S. Department of Commer. Bureau of Economic Analysis (1977), for more information.

20. See Zarnowitz and Moore 1981.

21. The standard deviation of the irregular component of the leading index rate is 0.91%; the corresponding statistic for the coincident index rate is 1.00%.

22. During much of the 1973–74 recession (through September 1974), the CPI rate continued on an upward course, largely reflecting the earlier "supply shocks" of sharp rises in prices of imported oil and other materials. Such a long and large increase in the inflation rate during a period of business contraction was then, and still is, unique in U.S. business cycle history.

References

Council of Economic A. iers. 1954. *Annual Report*. Washington, D.C.: Government Printing Offic.

Moore, Geoffrey H. 1979. The forty-second anniversary of the leading indicators. In William Fellner (ed.), *Contemporary Economic Problems 1979*. Washington, D.C.: American Enterprise.

Moore Geoffrey H. 1980. Why the leading indicators really do lead. In G. H. Moore (ed.), *Business Cycles, Inflation and Forecasting*. Cambridge, Mass.: Ballinger, for the National Bureau of Economic Research.

Moore, Geoffrey H. 1981. A new leading index of employment and unemployment. *Monthly Labor Review* 104 (June): 44–47.

U.S. Department of Commerce, Bureau of Economic Analysis. 1977. *Handbook of Cyclical Indicators: A Supplement to Business Conditions Digest*. Washington, D.C.: Government Printing Office.

U.S. Department of Commerce, Bureau of Economic Analysis. 1979. *Business Conditions Digest* 19 (March): iii–iv.

Vaccara, Beatrice N., and Zarnowitz, Victor. 1978. How good are the leading indicators? *1977 Proceedings of the Business and Economic Statistics Section*. Washington, D.C.: American Statistical Association. Pt. 1, pp. 41–50.

Vaccara, Beatrice N., and Zarnowitz, Victor. 1979. Forecasting with the index of leading indicators. Cambridge, Mass.: NBER Working Paper 244 (May).

Vernez, Georges, and Vaughan, Roger. 1978. *Assessment of the Countercyclical Public Works and Public Service Employment Programs.* R-2214-EDA. Santa Monica, Calif.: Rand Corp.

Zarnowitz, Victor. 1972. The business cycle today: an introduction. In Victor Zarnowitz (ed.), *The Business Cycle Today.* New York: National Bureau of Economic Research.

Zarnowitz, Victor, and Boschan, Charlotte. 1975a. Cyclical indicators: an evaluation and new leading indexes. *Business Conditions Digest* (May), pp. v–xxii.

Zarnowitz, Victor, and Boschan, Charlotte. 1975b. New composite indexes of coincident and lagging indicators. *Business Conditions Digest* (November), pp. v–xxiv.

Zarnowitz, Victor, and Boschan, Charlotte. 1977. Cyclical indicators. In *Interaction in Economic Research, 57th Annual Report.* New York: National Bureau of Economic Research (September), pp. 34–38.

Zarnowitz, Victor, and Moore, Geoffrey H. 1977. The recession and recovery of 1973–76. *Explorations in Economic Research* 4 (Fall): 471–557.

Zarnowitz, Victor, and Moore, Geoffrey H. 1981. The timing and severity of the recession of 1980. *NBER Reporter* (Spring), pp. 19–21.

Victor Zarnowitz

University of Chicago and National Bureau of Economic Research

Geoffrey H. Moore

Rutgers University

Fiscal Policy

Milton Friedman

Ever since the new deal, a primary excuse for the expansion of governmental activity at the federal level has been the supposed necessity for government spending to eliminate unemployment. The excuse has gone through several stages. At first, government spending was needed to "prime the pump." Temporary expenditures would set the economy going and the government could then step out of the picture.

When the initial expenditures failed to eliminate unemployment and were followed by a sharp economic contraction in 1937–38, the theory of "secular stagnation" developed to justify a permanently high level of government spending. The economy had become mature, it was argued. Opportunities for investment had been largely exploited and no substantial new opportunities were likely to arise. Yet individuals would still want to save. Hence, it was essential for government to spend and run a perpetual deficit. The securities issued to finance the deficit would provide individuals with a way to accumulate savings while the government expenditures provided employment. This view has been thoroughly discredited by theoretical analysis and even more by actual experience, including the emergence of wholly new lines for private investment not dreamed of by the secular stagnationists. Yet it has left its heritage. The idea may be accepted by none, but the government programs undertaken in its name, like some of those intended to prime the pump, are still with us and indeed account for ever-growing government expenditures.

More recently, the emphasis has been on government expenditures neither to prime the pump nor to hold in check the specter of secular stagnation but as a balance wheel. When private expenditures decline for any reason, it is said, governmental expenditures should rise to keep total expenditures stable; conversely, when private expenditures rise, governmental expenditures should decline. Unfortunately, the balance wheel is unbalanced. Each recession, however minor, sends a shudder through politically sensitive legislators and administrators with their ever present fear that perhaps it is the harbinger of another 1929–33. They hasten to enact federal spending programs of one kind or another. Many of the programs do not in fact come into effect until after the recession has passed. Hence, insofar as they do affect total expenditures, on which I shall have more to say later, they tend to exacerbate the succeeding expansion rather than to mitigate the recession. The haste with which spending programs are approved is not matched by an equal haste to repeal them or to eliminate others when the recession is passed and expansion is under way. On the contrary, it is then argued that a "healthy" expansion must not be "jeopardized" by cuts in governmental expenditures. The chief harm done by the balance-wheel theory is therefore not that it has failed to offset recessions, which it has, and not that it has introduced an inflationary bias into governmental policy, which it has done too, but that it has continuously fostered an expansion in the range of governmental activities at the federal level and prevented a reduction in the burden of federal taxes.

In view of the emphasis on using the federal budget as a balance wheel, it is ironic that the most unstable component of national income in the postwar period is federal expenditure, and the instability has not at all been in a direction to offset movements of other expenditure components. Far from being a balance wheel offsetting other forces making for fluctuations, the federal budget has if anything been itself a major source of disturbance and instability.

Because its expenditures are now so large a part of the total for the economy as a whole, the federal government cannot avoid having significant effects on the economy. The first requisite is therefore that the government mend its own fences, that it adopt procedures that will lead to reasonable stability in its own flow of expenditures. If it would do that, it would make a clear contribution to reducing the adjustments required in the rest of the economy. Until it does that, it is farcical for government officials to adopt the self-righteous tones of the schoolmaster keeping unruly pupils in line. Of course, their doing so is not surprising. Passing the buck and blaming others for one's own deficiencies are not vices of which governmental officials have a monopoly.

Even if one were to accept the view that the federal budget should be and can be used as a balance wheel—a view I shall consider in more detail below—there is no necessity to use the expenditure side of the budget for this purpose. The tax side is equally available. A decline in national income automatically reduces the tax revenue of the federal government in greater proportion and thus shifts the budget in the direction of a deficit, and conversely during a boom. If it is desired to do more, taxes can be lowered during recessions and raised during expansions. Of course, politics might well enforce an asymmetry here too, making the declines politically more palatable than the rises.

If the balance-wheel theory has in practice been applied on the expenditure side, it has been because of the existence of other forces making for increased governmental expenditures; in particular, the widespread acceptance by intellectuals of the belief that government should play a larger role in economic and private affairs; the triumph, that is, of the philosophy of the welfare state. This philosophy has found a useful ally in the balance-wheel theory; it has enabled governmental intervention to proceed at a faster pace than would otherwise have been possible.

How different matters might now be if the balance-wheel theory had been applied on the tax side instead of the expenditure side. Suppose each recession had seen a cut in taxes and suppose the political unpopularity of raising taxes in the succeeding expansion had led to resistance to newly proposed governmental expenditure programs and to curtailment of existing ones. We might now be in a position where federal expenditures would be absorbing a good deal less of a national income that would be larger because of the reduction in the depressing and inhibiting effects of taxes.

I hasten to add that this dream is not intended to indicate support for the balance-wheel theory. In practice, even if the effects would be in the direction expected under the balance-wheel theory, they would be delayed in time and spread. To make them an effective offset to other forces making for fluctuations, we would have to be able to forecast those fluctuations a long time in advance. In fiscal policy as in monetary policy, all political considerations aside, we simply do not know enough to be able to use deliberate changes in taxation or expenditures as a sensitive stabilizing mechanism. In the process of trying to do so, we almost surely make matters worse. We make matters worse not by being consistently perverse — that would be easily cured by simply doing the opposite of what seemed at first the thing to do. We make matters worse by introducing a largely random disturbance that is simply added to other disturbances. That is what we seem in fact to have done in the past — in addition, of course to the major mistakes that have been seriously perverse. What I have written elsewhere in respect of monetary policy is equally applicable to fiscal policy: "What we need is not a skillful monetary driver of the economic vehicle continuously turning the steering wheel to adjust to the unexpected irregularities of the route, but some means of keeping the monetary passenger who is in the back seat as ballast from occasionally leaning over and giving the steering wheel a jerk that threatens to send the car off the road." [1]

For fiscal policy, the appropriate counterpart to the monetary rule would be to plan expenditure programs entirely in terms of what the community wants to do through government rather than privately, and without any regard to problems of year-to-year economic stability; to plan tax rates so as to provide sufficient revenues to cover planned expenditures on the average of one year with another, again without regard to year-to-year changes in economic stability; and to avoid erratic changes in either governmental expenditures or taxes. Of course, some changes may be unavoidable. A sudden change in the international situation may dictate large increases in military expenditures or permit welcome decreases. Such changes account for some erratic shifts in federal expenditures in the postwar period. But they by no means account for all.

Before leaving the subject of fiscal policy, I should like to discuss the view, now so widely held, that an increase in governmental expenditures relative to tax-receipts is necessarily expansionary and a decrease contractionary. This view, which is at the heart of the belief that fiscal policy can serve as a balance wheel, is by now almost taken for granted by businessmen, professional economists, and laymen alike. Yet it cannot be demonstrated to be true by logical considerations alone, has never been documented by empirical evidence, and is in fact inconsistent with the revelant empirical evidence of which I know.

The belief has its origin in a crude Keynesian analysis. Suppose governmental expenditures are raised by $100 and taxes are kept unchanged. Then, goes the simple analysis, on the first round, the people who receive the extra hundred dollars will have that much more income. They will save some of it, say one-third, and spend the remaining two-thirds. But this means that on the second round, someone else receives an extra $66 2/3 of income. He in turn will save some and spend some, and so on and on in infinite sequence. If at every stage one-third is saved and two-thirds spent, then the extra $100 of government expenditures will ultimately, on this analysis, add $300 to income. This is the simple Keynesian multiplier analysis with a multiplier of three. Of course, if there is one injection, the effects will die off, the initial jump in income of $100 being succeeded by a gradual decline back to the earlier level. But if government expenditures are kept $100 higher per unit of time, say $100 a year higher, then, on this analysis, income will remain higher by $300 a year.

This simple analysis is extremely appealing. But the appeal is spurious and arises from neglecting other relevant effects of the change in question. When these are taken into account, the final result is much more dubious: it may be anything from no change in income at all, in which case private expenditures will go down by the $100 by which government expenditures go up, to the full increase specified. And even if money income increases, prices may rise, so real income will increase less or not at all. Let us examine some of the possible slips 'twixt cup and lip.

In the first place, nothing is said in the simple account about what the government spends the $100 on. Suppose, for example, it spends it on something that individuals were otherwise obtaining for themselves. They were, for example, spending $100 on paying fees to a park which paid the cost of attendants to keep it clean. Suppose the government now pays these costs and permits people to enter the park "free." The attendants still receive the same income, but the people who paid the fees have $100 available. The government spending does not, even in the initial stage, add $100 to anyone's income. What it does is to leave some people with $100 available to use for purposes other than the park, and presumably purposes they value less highly. They can be expected to spend less out of their total income for consumer goods than formerly, since they are receiving the park services free. How much less, it is not easy to say. Even if we accept, as in the simple analysis, that people save one-third of additional income, it does not follow that when they get one set of consumer goods "free," two-thirds of the released money will be spent on other consumer goods. One extreme possibility, of course, is that they will continue to buy the same collection of other consumer goods as they did before and add the released $100 to their savings. In this case even in the simple Keynesian analysis, the effect of the government expenditures is completely offset: government expenditures go up by $100, private down by $100. Or, to take another example, the $100 may be spent to build a road that a private enterprise would otherwise have built or the availability of which may make repairs to the company's trucks unnecessary. The firm then has funds released, but presumably will not spend them all on what are less attractive investments. In these cases, government expenditures simply divert private expenditures and only the net excess of government expenditures is even available at the outset for the multiplier to work on. From this point of view, it is paradoxical that the way to assure no diversion is to have the government spend the money for something utterly useless—this is the limited intellectual content to the "filling-holes" type of make-work. But of course this itself shows that there is something wrong with the analysis.

In the second place, nothing is said in the simple account about where the government gets the $100 to spend. So far as the analysis goes, the results are the same whether the government prints extra money or borrows from the public. But surely which it does will make a difference. To separate fiscal from monetary policy, let us suppose the government borrows the $100 so that the stock of money is the same as it would have been in the absence of the government expenditure. This is the proper assumption because the stock of money can be increased without extra government expenditure, if that is desired, simply by printing the money and buying outstanding government bonds with it. But we must now ask what the effect of borrowing is. To analyze this problem, let us assume that diversion does not occur, so in the first instance there is no direct offset to the $100 in the form of a compensating drop in private expenditures. Note that the government's borrowing to spend does not alter the amount of money in private hands. The government borrows $100 with its right hand from some individuals and hands the money with its left hand to those individuals to whom its expenditures go. Different people hold the money but the total amount of money held is unchanged.

The simple Keynesian analysis implicitly assumes that borrowing the money does not have any effects on other spending. There are two extreme circumstances under which this can occur. First, suppose people are utterly indifferent to whether they hold bonds or money, so that bonds to get the $100 can be sold without having to offer a higher return to the buyer than such bonds were yielding before. (Of course, $100 is so small an amount that it would in practice have a negligible effect on the required rate of return, but the issue is one of principle whose practical effect can be seen by letting the $100 stand for $100 million or $100 ten-million.) In Keynesian jargon, there is a "liquidity trap" so people buy the bonds with "idle money." If this is not the case, and clearly it cannot be indefinitely, then the government can sell the bonds only by offering a higher rate of return on it. A higher rate will then have to be paid also by other borrowers. This higher rate will in general discourage private spending on the part of would-be borrowers. Here comes the second extreme circumstance under which the simple Keynesian analysis will hold: if potential borrowers are so stubborn about spending that no rise in interest rates however steep will cut down their expenditures, or, in Keynesian jargon, if the marginal efficiency schedule of investment is perfectly inelastic with respect to the interest rate.

I know of no established economist, no matter how much of a Keynesian he may regard himself as being, who would regard either of these extreme assumptions as holding currently, or as being capable of holding over any considerable range of borrowing or rise in interest rates, or as having held except under rather special circumstances in the past. Yet many an economist, let alone non-economist, whether regarding himself as Keynesian or not, accepts as valid the belief that a rise in governmental expenditures relative to tax receipts, even when financed by borrowing, is *necessarily* expansionist, though as we have seen, this belief implicitly requires one of these extreme circumstances to hold.

If neither assumption holds, the rise in government expenditures will be offset by a decline in private expenditures on the part either of those who lend funds to the government, or of those who would otherwise have borrowed the funds. How much of the rise in expenditures will be offset? This depends on the holders of money. The extreme assumption, implicit in a rigid quantity theory of money, is that the amount of money people want to hold depends, on the average, only on their income and not on the rate of return that they can get on bonds and similar securities. In this case, since the total stock of money is the same before and after, the total money income will also have to be the same in order to make people just satisfied to hold that money stock. This means that interest rates will have to rise enough to choke off an amount of private spending exactly equal to the increased public expenditure. In this extreme case, there is no sense at all in which the government expenditures are expansionary. Not even money income goes up, let alone real income. All that happens is that government expenditures go up and private expenditures down.

I warn the reader that this is a highly simplified analysis. A full analysis would require a lengthy textbook. But even this simplified analysis is enough to demonstrate that any result is possible between a $300 rise in income and a zero rise. The more stubborn consumers are with respect to how much they will spend on consumption out of a given income, and the more stubborn purchasers of capital goods are with respect to how much they will spend on such goods regardless of cost, the nearer the result will be to the Keynesian extreme of a $300 rise. On the other side, the more stubborn money holders are with respect to the ratio they wish to maintain between their cash balances and their income, the closer the result will be to the rigid quantity theory extreme of no change in income. In which of these respects the public is more stubborn is an empirical question to be judged from the factual evidence, not something that can be determined by reason alone.

Before the Great Depression of the 1930's, the bulk of economists would unquestionably have concluded that the result would be nearer to no rise in income than to a $300 rise. Since then, the bulk of economists would unquestionably conclude the opposite. More recently, there has been a movement back toward the earlier position. Sad to say, none of these shifts can be said to be based on satisfactory evidence. They have been based rather on intuitive judgments from crude experience.

In co-operation with some of my students, I have done some fairly extensive empirical work, for the U.S. and other countries, to get some more satisfactory evidence.[2] The results are striking. They strongly suggest that the actual outcome will be closer to the quantity theory extreme than to the Keynesian. The judgement that seems justified on the basis of this evidence is that the assumed $100 increase in government expenditures can on the average be expected to add just about $100 to income, sometimes less, sometimes more. This means that a rise in government expenditures relative to income is not expansionary in any relevant sense. It may add to money income but all of this addition is absorbed by government expenditures. Private expenditures are unchanged. Since prices are likely to rise in the process, or fall less than they otherwise would, the effect is to leave private expenditures smaller in real terms. Converse propositions hold for a decline in government expenditures.

These conclusions cannot of course be regarded as final. They are based on the broadest and most comprehensive body of evidence I know about, but that body of evidence still leaves much to be desired.

One thing is however clear. Whether the views so widely accepted about the effects of fiscal policy be right or wrong, they are contradicted by at least one extensive body of evidence. I know of no other coherent or organized body of evidence justifying them. They are part of economic mythology, not the demonstrated conclusions of economic analysis or quantitative studies. Yet they have wielded immense influence in securing widespread public backing for far-reaching governmental interference in economic life.

[1] *A Program for Monetary Stability*, (New York: Fordham University Press, 1959), p. 23.

[2] Some of the results are contained in Milton Friedman and David Meiselman, *The Relative Stability of the Investment Multiplier and Monetary Velocity in the United States, 1896–1958* (forthcoming publication of Commission on Money and Credit).

Has Fiscal Policy Been Oversold?

Milton Friedman

. . . The key source of misunderstanding about the issue of monetary policy, in my opinion, has been the failure to distinguish clearly what it is that money matters for. What I and those who share my views have emphasized is that the quantity of money is extremely important for nominal magnitudes, for nominal income, for the level of income in dollars—important for what happens to prices. It is not important at all, or, if that's perhaps an exaggeration, not very important, for what happens to real output over the long period.

I have been increasingly impressed that much of the disagreement about this issue stems from the fact that an important element in the Keynesian revolution in economics was the notion that prices are an institutional datum determined outside the system. Once you take that view, once you say that prices are somehow determined elsewhere, then the distinction between nominal magnitudes and real magnitudes disappears. The distinction between magnitudes in dollars and magnitudes in terms of goods and services is no longer important.

That is why the qualifications we have always attached to our statements about the importance of money tend to be overlooked. We have always stressed that money matters a great deal for the development of nominal magnitudes, but not over the long run for real magnitudes. That qualification has tended to be dropped and a straw man has been set up to the effect that we say that money is the only thing that matters for the development of the economy. That's an absurd position, of course, and one that I have never held. The real wealth of a society depends much more on the kind of institutional structure it has, on the abilities, initiative, driving force of its people, on investment potentialities, on technology—on all of those things. That's what really matters from the point of view of the level of output. But, how many dollars will that be valued at? When you ask that question, that's where money matters.

Let me turn more directly to the topics assigned for this session. Is fiscal policy being oversold? Is monetary policy being oversold? I want to stress that my answer is yes to both of those questions. I believe monetary policy is being oversold; I believe fiscal policy is being oversold. What I believe is that fine tuning has been oversold. And this is not a new conclusion. I am delighted to attest to the correctness of Walter's statement that many of our views have not changed over time. It so happens that the facts haven't been inconsistent with them, and, therefore, we haven't had to change them over time.

Just this past week I was reading proof on a collection of technical essays of mine written much earlier that is going to appear next year (1969), and I came across a paper I gave to the Joint Economic Committee in 1958. I would like to quote from that paper, written ten years ago, some sentences which expressed my view at that time, and which still express my view today, on the issue of fine tuning, rather than on the separate issues of monetary and fiscal policy.

I said: "A steady rate of growth in the money supply will not mean perfect stability even though it would prevent the kind of wide fluctuations that we have experienced from time to time in the past. It is tempting to try to go farther and to use monetary changes to offset other factors making for expansion and contraction. . . . The available evidence . . . casts grave doubts on the possibility of producing any fine adjustments in economic activity by fine adjustments in monetary policy—at least in the present state of knowledge. . . . There are thus serious limitations to the possibility of a discretionary monetary policy and much danger that such a policy may make matters worse rather than better."

I went on: "To avoid misunderstanding, it should be emphasized that the problems just discussed are in no way peculiar to monetary policy. . . . The basic difficulties and limitations of monetary policy apply with equal force to fiscal policy."

And then I went on, "Political pressures to 'do something' in the face of either relatively mild price rises or relatively mild price and employment declines are clearly very strong indeed in the existing state of public attitudes. The main moral to be drawn from the two preceding points is that yielding to these pressures may frequently do more harm than good. There is a saying that the best is often the enemy of the good, which seems highly relevant. The goal of an extremely high degree of economic stability is certainly a splendid one. Our ability to attain it, however, is limited; we can surely avoid extreme fluctuations; we do not know enough to avoid minor fluctuations; the attempt to do more than we can will itself be a disturbance that may increase rather than reduce instability. But like all such injunctions, this one too must be taken in moderation. It is a plea for a sense of perspective and balance, not for irresponsibility in the face of major problems or for failure to correct past mistakes." [1]

Well, that was a view that I expressed ten years ago, and I do not believe that the evidence of the past ten years gives the lie to that view. I think that the evidence of the past ten years rather reinforces it, rather shows the difficulties of trying to engage in a very fine tuning of economic policy. I would emphasize today even more than I did then my qualifications with respect to monetary policy because thanks fundamentally, I think, to the difficulties that have been experienced with fiscal policy and to the experience of other countries, there has been an enormous shift in opinion.

Walter says we all know that money matters; it's only a question of whether it matters very much. His saying that is, in itself, evidence of the shift in opinion. Before coming up here today I reread the reports of the Council of Economic Advisers that were published when he was chairman of the Council.[2] I do not believe that anybody can read those reports and come out with the conclusion that they say that money matters significantly. While there was some attention paid to money in those reports, it was very limited.

There has been a tremendous change in opinion on this subject since then. And I am afraid that change may go too far. I share very much the doubts that Walter expressed about the closeness of the monetary relations. There is a very good relation on the average. But the relation is not close enough, it is not precise enough, so that you can, with enormous confidence, predict from the changes in the money supply in one quarter precisely what's going to happen in the next quarter or two quarters later.

Indeed, that's the major reason why I'm in favor of a rule. If I thought I could predict precisely, well then, to go back to the statement I quoted from, I would be prepared to make fine adjustments to offset other forces making for change. It's precisely because we don't know how to predict precisely that you cannot in fact use monetary policy effectively for this purpose. So I emphasize that my basic view is that what has been oversold is the notion of fine tuning.

Yet, fiscal policy has, in my view, been oversold in a very different and more basic sense than monetary policy—to turn to the main subject assigned to me. I believe that the rate of change of the money supply by itself—and I'm going to come back to those two words "by itself"—has a very important effect on nominal income and prices in the long run. It has a very important effect on fluctuations in nominal and real income in the short run. That's my basic conclusion about changes in the stock of money.

Now let's turn to fiscal policy. I believe that the state of the government budget matters; matters a great deal—for some things. The state of the government budget determines what fraction of the nation's income is spent through the government and what fraction is spent by individuals privately. The state of the government budget determines what the level of our taxes is, how much of our income we turn over to the government. The state of the government budget has a considerable effect on interest rates. If the federal government runs a large deficit, that means the government has to borrow in the market, which raises the demand for loanable funds and so tends to raise interest rates.

If the government budget shifts to a surplus, that adds to the supply of loanable funds, which tends to lower interest rates. It was no surprise to those of us who stress money that enactment of the surtax was followed by a decline in interest rates. That's precisely what we had predicted and what our analysis leads us to predict. But—and I come to the main point—in my opinion, the state of the budget by itself has no significant effect on the course of nominal income, on inflation, on deflation, or on cyclical fluctuations.. . .

I'd like to call your attention to some items in that list which are relevant to the particular issue of the potency of fiscal and monetary policy.

I'm going to run over them very hastily. Some sixteen years ago, I wrote an article that compared the Civil War to World War I and World War II. The particular question I asked was, "Do you get a better understanding of what happened to prices during those three wars by looking at what was happening to monetary magnitudes, or by looking at what was happening to fiscal magnitudes?" [5] The answer was completely unambiguous. And nobody has since produced any evidence contradicting that analysis. It turns out that you get a very clear, straight-forward interpretation of price behavior in those three wars by looking at monetary magnitudes; you do not get an explanation by looking at fiscal magnitudes.

Second, Walter Heller was kind enough to comment on the studies that Anna Schwartz and I have done under the auspices of the National Bureau of Economic Research. We have studied the relation between monetary magnitude and economic magnitudes over the course of a hundred years, roughly a century. During that period, fiscal policy changed enormously. At the beginning of that period, the government budget was negligible. In the period since World War II, the government budget has been mammoth. And yet we found roughly the same kind of a relationship between monetary and economic magnitudes over the whole of that one-hundred-year period.

If fiscal policy were playing a dominant influence, it

should have introduced more variability, as Walter properly said it should have, into the relation between money and income in the later part than in the earlier; but as far as we can see, it's a homogeneous universe.

Third, some years back David Meiselman and I published a study directed specifically at the question, "Do monetary magnitudes or autonomous expenditure magnitudes give you a better interpretation of the movements in nominal income over short periods of time?" [6] That article produced a great controversy and a large number of replies and counterreplies.[7] It's a matter of biblical exegesis to trace through the thrusts and counterthrusts of that controversy though I am sure it would be good for all your souls to do so.

But one thing that came out of that controversy is that everybody agreed that the monetary magnitudes did have an important and systematic influence. The complaint that was made against us was the one that Walter makes tonight, that we had gone too far in denying that the autonomous magnitudes exerted an influence.

The most recent study is one by the Federal Reserve Bank of St. Louis,[8] which Walter was good enough to refer to as an unofficial arm of the Chicago School—well, we ought to have one out of twelve anyway. It is an extremely thorough and very fascinating study in which they have related quarter-to-quarter changes in GNP to changes in monetary totals over prior quarters and also to changes in governmental expenditures and taxes. They have been very thorough. Anything that anybody suggested to them which might be wrong with what they initially did, they have tried out. As a result, they have tried out many of the possible permutations and combinations. They have tried the high-employment budget and they have tried other budget concepts. But I'll refer to their findings about the high-employment budget.

What they have done is to try to see whether the monetary or the fiscal magnitudes play a more consistent and systematic role in explaining the course of GNP change over the period 1952 to 1968. That is the right period because Walter Heller is right in pointing to the Federal Reserve-Treasury Accord of 1951 as marking a distinct change in the role of monetary policy and its possibility.

Let me quote their summary conclusion. They say, "This section tested the propositions that the response of economic activity to fiscal actions relative to monetary actions is (I) larger, (II) more predictable, and (III) faster." [9]

Let me repeat this more explicitly. The proposition they tested was that the response of economic activity to fiscal action was larger, more predictable, and faster than the response of the economy to monetary action. "The results of the tests," they say, "were not consistent with any of these propositions. Consequently, either the commonly used measures of fiscal influence do not correctly indicate the degree and the direction of such influence, or there was no measurable net fiscal influence on total spending in the test period."[10] To put it in simpler terms, what they found—far from there being a proven efficiency of fiscal policy—was that, as a statistical matter, the regression coefficients of the high-employment budget surplus or deficit, if the monetary variables are held constant, were not statistically significant.

HAS FISCAL POLICY BEEN OVERSOLD?
Milton Friedman

1. Milton Friedman, "The Supply of Money and Changes in Prices and Output," *The Relationship of Prices to Economic Stability and Growth*, 85th Cong., 2nd Sess., Joint Committee Print (Washington, D. C., U. S. Government Printing Office, 1958), pp. 241–256, quotation from pp. 255–256. To be reprinted in Milton Friedman, *The Optimum Quantity of Money and Other Essays* (Chicago, Ill.: Aldine Publishing Co., 1969).

2. Contained in the 1962, 1963, and 1964 *Economic Report of the President*, (Washington, D. C.: U. S. Government Printing Office, 1962, 1963, 1964).

5. "Price, Income, and Monetary Changes in Three Wartime Periods," *American Economic Review* (May, 1952), pp. 612–625. To be reprinted in *The Optimum Quantity of Money and Other Essays, op. cit.*

6. Milton Friedman and David Meiselman, "The Relative Stability of Monetary Velocity and the Investment Multiplier in the United States, 1897–1958," *Stabilization Policies* (Commission on Money and Credit, Englewood Cliffs, N. J.: Prentice-Hall, 1963), pp. 165–268.

7. Donald D. Hester, "Keynes and the Quantity Theory: A Comment on the Friedman-Meiselman CMC Paper," and Milton Friedman and David Meiselman, "Reply to Donald Hester," *The Review of Economics and Statistics*, XLVI (November, 1964), pp. 364–377; Albert Ando and Franco Modigliani, "The Relative Stability of Monetary Velocity and the Investment Multiplier," Michael De Prano and Thomas Mayer, "Tests of the Relative Importance of Autonomous Expenditures and Money," and Milton Friedman and David Meiselman, "Reply to Ando and Modigliani and to De Prano and Mayer," *American Economic Review*, LV (September, 1965), pp. 693–792.

8. Leonall C. Anderson and Jerry L. Jordan, "Monetary and Fiscal Actions: A Test of Their Relative Importance in Economic Stabilization," *Review*, Federal Reserve Bank of St. Louis, November, 1968, pp. 11–23.

9. *Ibid.*, p. 22.

10. *Ibid.*, p. 22

Is Monetary Policy Being Oversold?

Walter W. Heller

My intent today is neither to praise nor to bury that towering iconoclast Milton Friedman, for to praise him and his works would absorb far too much of my limited time, and to bury him is, in a word, impossible. . . .

At the outset, let's clarify what is and what isn't at issue in today's discussion of fiscal-monetary policy, both inside and outside this hall. When we do this, I'm afraid that the lines may not be drawn quite as sharply as the journalists, who love a fight and drama, would have us believe with their headlines like "Is Keynes Defunct?" But have no fear. There will be plenty of grist for the mill of today's dialogue!

The issue is *not* whether money matters—we all grant that—but whether *only* money matters, as some Friedman-ites, or perhaps I should say Friedmanics, would put it. Or really, whether only money matters *much*, which is what I understand Milton Friedman to say—he is more reasonable than many of the Friedmanites.

It's important in this connection, too, to make clear that the economic policy of the 1960's, the "new economics" if you will, assigns an important role to *both* fiscal and monetary policy. Indeed, the appropriate mix of policies has often been the cornerstone of the argument: It was, for example, early in the 60's, when we feared that tight money might stunt recovery, might thwart the expansionary impact of the 1962–64 income tax cuts. It was again, in 1966, when in strongly urging a tax increase, we put heavy emphasis on avoiding the ill effects of imposing too much of the burden of restraint on Federal Reserve policy. It was once again, in 1967–68, when we sought the surtax in considerable part to insure against a repetition of the monetary crunch of 1966. And it will be in the future, when full employment surpluses in the federal budget may be the only defensible way to buy the monetary ease that commitment to rapid economic growth implies. In short, to anyone who might fear that the "new economics" is all fiscal policy, the record offers evidence, and the new economists offer assurance, that money *does* matter.

With that straw man removed, we can identify the real monetary issues with which the monetarists confront us: First, should money supply be the sole or primary guide to Federal Reserve policy? Should it, at the very least, be ranged side by side with interest rates and credit availability in the Fed's affections? Second, should we rely on the Federal Reserve authorities to adapt monetary policy flexibly to changing economic events and to shifts in fiscal policy, or should we instead not only enthrone money supply but encase it in a rigid formula specifying a fixed increase of 3, 4, or 5 per cent a year? In other words, should we adopt the Friedman rule and replace Bill Martin at the Fed with an exponential curve—or would we simply be throwing him one?

Again, in the fiscal field, the issue is not *whether* fiscal policy matters—even some monetarists, perhaps in unguarded moments, have urged budget cuts or tax changes for stabilization reasons. The issues are *how much* it matters, and how heavily we can lean on discretionary changes in taxes and budgets to maintain steady economic growth in a dynamic economy: Is the close correlation of activist fiscal policy and strong expansion—which has brought our economy into the narrow band around full employment—a matter of accident or causation? Does a fair balancing of the successes and shortcomings of active fiscal policy suggest (a) that we should now take refuge in rigid fiscal rules like the lock-stop tax cuts espoused by Barry Goldwater and Milton Friedman, or rather (b) that we need to modify our fiscal institutions—especially our procedures for cutting or boosting taxes—to step up their speed and precision, especially in dealing with inflation?

Pervading these operational issues is a basic question of targets, as yet not answered in any conclusive way by either analysis or evidence. Should the target be, as the Phillips-curve analysis suggests, somewhat less unemployment in exchange for somewhat more price creep? Or is this trade-off illusory, as the adherents of the classical real-wage doctrine are now reasserting? To hark back to words and men of the past—Is a little inflation like a little pregnancy? Or was Sumner Slichter prophetic when he said that if we wanted to live with steady full employment and brisk growth, we also had to—and could—live with a little chronic inflation, with a price creep of 2 per cent or so a year?

Summing up the key operational issues, they are: Should money be king? Is fiscal policy worth its salt? Should flexible man yield to rigid rules? You will note that I purposely cast these issues in a show-me form to put both the monetarists and the new economists on their mettle.

Let me review with you the factors that say "stop, look, and listen" before embracing the triple doctrine that only money matters much; that control of the money supply is the key to economic stability; and that a rigid fixed-throttle expansion of 4 or 5 per cent a year is the only safe policy prescription in a world of alleged economic ignorance and human weakness and folly.. . .

Now, turning to doubts, unresolved questions, and unconvincing evidence, I group these into eight conditions that must be satisfied—if not completely, at least more convincingly than they have been to date—before we can even consider giving money supply sovereignty, or dominance, or greater prominence in economic policy. These conditions center on such questions as: Which money-supply indicator do you believe? Can one read enough from money supply without weighing also shifts in demand and interest rates —that is, don't both quantity *and* price of money count? Don't observed variations in monetary time lags and velocity cast serious doubt on any simple relation between money supply and GNP? Can a rigid monetary rule find happiness in a world beset with rigidities and rather limited adjustment capabilities? That is, is the rigid Friedman rule perhaps a formula made in heaven, that will work only in heaven?. . .

The first condition is this: the monetarists must make up their minds which money-supply variable they want us to accept as our guiding star—M_1, the narrow money supply, just currency and bank deposits; M_2, adding time deposits; or perhaps some other measure like the "monetary base?" And when will the monetarists decide? Perhaps Milton Friedman has decided; but if he has, his disciples do not seem to have gotten the word.

Let me give you an example. Last spring, M_1 (the money stock) was all the rage. It spurted for four months in a row, from April through July. But when that slowed down, most of the alarmists switched horses to M_2 (money plus time deposits), which quite conveniently began rising sharply in July. And listen to the latest release from the St. Louis Federal Reserve Bank—the unofficial statistical arm of the Chicago School—which very carefully throws a sop to all sides: "Monetary expansion since July has decelerated as measured by the money stock, accelerated as measured by money plus time deposits, and remained at about an unchanged rate as measured by the monetary base. As a result, questions arise as to which monetary aggregate may be currently most meaningful in indicating monetary influence on economic activity."[2] Precisely.

It doesn't seem too much to ask that this confusion be resolved in some satisfactory way before putting great faith in money supply as our key policy variable.

Second, I would feel more sympathetic to the money-supply doctrine if it were not so one-track-minded about money stock—measured any way you wish—as the *only* financial variable with any informational content for policy purposes. . . .

Or, if we look at 1967 *only* in terms of the money stock, it would appear as the easiest-money year since World War II. M_1 was up 6 per cent, M_2 was up 12 per cent. Yet there was a very sharp rise in interest rates. Why? Probably because of a big shift in liquidity preference as corporations strove to build up their protective liquidity cushions after their harrowing experience the previous year—their monetary dehydration in the credit crunch of 1966. Again, the behavior of interest rates is vital to proper interpretation of monetary developments and guidance of monetary policy. Interest rates are endogenous variables and cannot be used alone—but neither can money stock. Either interest rates or money stock, used alone, could seriously mislead us.

I really don't understand how the scarcity of any commodity can be gauged without referring to its price—or, more specifically, how the scarcity of money can be gauged without referring to interest rates. It may, strictly speaking, be wrong to identify any market interest rate as the price of money. In the U. S., no interest is paid either on demand deposits or on currency. But this is quibbling. The point is that a change in the demand for money relative to the supply, or a change in the supply relative to demand, results generally in a change in interest rates.[4] To insist that the behavior of the price of money (interest rates) conveys no information about its scarcity is, as Tobin has noted, an "odd heresy."

Third, given the fluctuations in money velocity, that supposedly inexorable link between money and economic activity has yet to be established. We should not forget this, however sweet the siren song of the monetarists may sound. We should not forget the revealing passage from that monumental Friedman-Schwartz volume, *A Monetary History of the United States,* that makes my point:

. . . the observed year-to-year change in velocity was less than 10 per cent in 78 out of 91 year-to-year changes from 1869, when our velocity figures start, to 1960. Of the 13 larger changes, more than half came during either the Great Contraction or the two world wars, and the largest change was 17 per cent. Expressed as a percentage of·a secular trend, velocity was within the range of 90 to 110 in 53 years, 85 to 115 in 66 years. of the remaining 26 years, 12 were during the first 15 years, for which the income figures are seriously defective, and 17 during the Great Contraction and the two wars.[5]

Clearly, velocity has varied over time—some might say "greatly," others "moderately." Let me sidestep a bit and say, for purposes of this discussion, "significantly." For I would remind you that the income velocity of money rose roughly 28 per cent during the 1960–68 period. Had velocity been the same in 1968 as it was in 1960, nominal GNP would have been not some $860 billion, but only $675 billion.

What Friedman and Schwartz report, then, about the behavior of velocity suggests that there are other factors —strangely, such fiscal actions as tax cuts or budget changes come to mind—that influence the level of economic activity. Velocity has changed, as it were, to accommodate these other influences and will go on doing so, I have no doubt, in the future.

The observed changes in velocity underscore the broader point I was hinting at a moment ago: The Friedman-Schwartz study did not find anything like a. near-perfect correlation—a rigid link—between money and economic activity. And such correlation as they did find was based on complex and often quite arbitrary adjustments of their raw data. . . .

Fourth, it would help us if the monetarists could narrow the range on *when* money matters. How long *are* the lags that have to be taken into account in managing monetary policy? Here, I quote from Professor Friedman's tour de force, *A Program for Monetary Stability:*

In the National Bureau study on which I have been collaborating with Mrs. Schwartz we found that, on the average of 18 cycles, peaks in the rate of change in the stock of money tend to precede peaks in general business by about 16 months and troughs in the rate of change in the stock of money to precede troughs in general business by about 12 months. . . . For individual cycles, the recorded lag has varied between 6 and 29 months at peaks and between 4 and 22 months at troughs.[7]

So the Friedman-Schwartz study found a long average lag, and just as important it would seem, a highly variable lag. But why this considerable variance? No doubt there are several possible answers. But again, the most natural one is that the level of economic activity, or total demand for the nation's output, is influenced by variables other than the stock of money—possibly even by tax rates and federal spending and transfer payments!

Suppose I told you that I had checked and found that in repeated trials, it required from 100 to 300 feet for a car going so and so many miles an hour to stop. That is quite a range. But would you be surprised? I think not. You would simply remind me that the distance it takes a car to stop depends, among other things, on the condition of the road surface. If I had allowed for the condition of the road surface, I would not have ended up with such a wide range of stopping distances.

Just so. If Professor Friedman and Mrs. Schwartz had taken account of other variables that influence total demand, or if they had estimated the lag of monetary policy using a complete model of the U. S. economy, they would not have found the lag of monetary policy to be quite so variable. Again, then, one correctly infers that their findings are quite consistent with fiscal policy mattering, and mattering a great deal. Nor is it necessarily relevant, as some have suggested, that in the middle of the nineteenth century, the government sector was relatively small. Variables other than changes in tax rates and government expenditures and transfers can "distort" the money-income lag.

Professor Friedman has also used this finding of (a) a long average lag and (b) a highly variable lag in support of his plea for steady growth of the money supply. With so long an average lag, the argument goes, forecasters are helpless; they cannot see twelve or fifteen months into the future with any accuracy. And even if they could, they would be at a loss to know how far ahead to appraise the economic outlook. But I doubt that he can properly draw this inference from his finding of a long and highly variable lag.

It seems to me misleading to estimate a discreet lag as the Friedman-Schwartz team did. It's reasonable to suppose, given the research findings of other investigators, that the effect of a change in monetary policy cumulates through time. To begin, there's a slight effect; and as time passes, the effect becomes more pronounced. But insofar as the feasibility of discretionary monetary policy is at issue, what matters *most* is whether there is some near-term effect. If there is, then the Federal Reserve can influence the economy one quarter or two quarters from now. That there are subsequent, more pronounced, effects is not the key question. These subsequent effects get caught, as it were, in subsequent forecasts of the economic outlook, and current policy is adjusted accordingly. At least this is what happens in a non-Friedmanic world where one enjoys the benefits of discretionary policy changes.

Lest I leave any doubt about what I infer from this: if there is a near-immediate effect from a change in policy, then discretionary monetary policy does not impose an unbearable burden on forecasters. For six or nine months ahead, they can do reasonably well. But given the too-discreet way Friedman-Schwartz went about estimating the lag of monetary policy, I see no way of determining the shape of the monetary policy lag. Until they know more about the shape of this lag, I don't see how they can insist on a monetary rule.

Fifth, I'd be happier if only I knew which of the two Friedmans to believe. Should it be the Friedman we have had in focus here—the Friedman of the close causal relationship between money supply and income, who sees changes in money balances worked off gradually, with long lags before interest rates, prices of financial and physical assets, and, eventually, investment and consumption spending are affected? Or should it be the Friedman of the "permanent-income hypothesis," who sees the demand for money as quite unresponsive to changes in current income (since current income has only a fractional weight in permanent income), with the implied result that the monetary multiplier is very large in the short run, that there is an immediate and strong response to a change in the money stock?

Sixth, if Milton's policy prescription were made in a frictionless Friedmanesque world without price, wage, and exchange rigidities—a world of his own making—it would be more admissible. But in the imperfect world in which we actually operate, beset by all sorts of rigidities, the introduction of his fixed-throttle money-supply rule might, in fact, be destabilizing. Or it could condemn us to long periods of economic slack or inflation as the slow adjustment processes in wages and prices, given strong market power, delayed the economy's reaction to the monetary rule while policy makers stood helplessly by.

A seventh and closely related concern is that locking the money supply into a rigid rule would jeopardize the U. S. international position. It's quite clear that capital flows are interest-rate sensitive. Indeed, capital flows induced by interest-rate changes can increase alarmingly when speculators take over. Under the Friedman rule, market interest rates would be whatever they turned out to be. It would be beyond the pale for the Fed to adjust interest rates for balance-of-payments adjustment purposes. Nor is it clear that by operating in the market for forward exchange (which in any event Milton would presumably oppose) the system could altogether neutralize changes in domestic market rates.

Milton has heard all of this before, and he always has an answer—flexible exchange rates. Parenthetically, I fully understand that it's much easier to debate Milton in absentia than in person! Yet, suffice it to note that however vital they are to the workings of his money-supply peg, floating exchange rates are not just around the corner.. . .

Eighth, and finally, if the monetarists showed some small willingness to recognize the impact of fiscal policy—which has played such a large role in the policy thinking and action underlying the great expansion of the 1960's—one might be a little more sympathetic to their views. This point is, I must admit, not so much a condition as a plea for symmetry. The "new economists," having already given important and increasing weight to monetary factors in their policy models, are still waiting for signs that the monetarists will admit fiscal factors to theirs.

The 1964 tax cut pointedly illustrates what I mean. While the "new economists" fully recognize the important role monetary policy played in facilitating the success of the tax cut, the monetarists go to elaborate lengths to "prove" that the tax cut—which came close to removing a $13 billion full-employment surplus that was overburdening and retarding the economy—had nothing to do with the 1964–65 expansion. Money-supply growth did it all. Apparently, we were just playing fiscal tiddlywinks in Washington.

It seems to me that the cause of balanced analysis and rational policy would be served by redirecting some of the brilliance of Friedman and his followers from (a) single-minded devotion to the money-supply thesis and unceasing efforts to discredit fiscal policy and indeed all discretionary policy to (b) joint efforts to develop a more complete and satisfactory model of how the real world works; ascertain why it is working far better today than it did before active and conscious fiscal-monetary policy came into play; and determine how such policy can be improved to make it work even better in the future.

In a related asymmetry, as I've already suggested in passing, some Friedmanites fail to recognize that if fiscal policy actions like the 1964 tax cut can do no good, then fiscal policy actions like the big budget increases and deficits associated with Vietnam can also do no harm. Again, they should recognize that they can't have it both ways.

Now, one could lengthen and elaborate this list. But enough—let's just round it off this way: if Milton Friedman were saying that (as part of an active discretionary policy) we had better keep a closer eye on that important variable, money supply, in one or more of its several incarnations

—I would say well and good, by all means. If the manifold doubts can be reasonably resolved, let's remedy any neglect or underemphasis of money supply as a policy indicator relative to interest rates, free reserves, and the like. But let's not lock the steering gear into place, knowing full well of the twists and turns in the road ahead. That's an invitation to chaos.. . .

2. "U.S. Financial Data, week ending November 6, 1968," Federal Reserve Bank of St. Louis, p. 1.

4. This was not only Keynes's view; it is, I believe, Milton Friedman's. Indeed, his formulation of the monetary process—of the process whereby a change in the supply of money works its potent magic—reads remarkably like Tobin's, or for that matter, like Keynes's. See, for example, his "Money and Business Cycles," p. 60. This paper was written with Mrs. Schwartz, and appeared in the February, 1963 issue of the *Review of Economics and Statistics*.

5. Milton Friedman and Anna Jacobson Schwartz, *A Monetary History of the United States: 1867–1960* (Princeton, N.J.: Princeton University Press, 1963), p. 682.

7. Milton Friedman, *A Program for Monetary Stability* (New York: Fordham University Press, 1959), p. 87.

Rules and Roles for Fiscal and Monetary Policy

Arthur M. Okun*

When economists write text books or teach introductory students or lecture to laymen, they happily extol the virtues of two lovely handmaidens of aggregate economic stabilization — fiscal policy and monetary policy. But when they write for learned journals or assemble for professional meetings, they often insist on staging a beauty contest between the two. And each judge feels somehow obliged to decide that one of the two entries is just an ugly beast. My remarks tonight are in the spirit of bigamous devotion rather than invidious comparison. Fiscal policy and monetary policy are both beautiful; we need them both and we should treat them both lovingly.

THE GENERAL ECLECTIC CASE

In particular, both fiscal and monetary policy are capable of providing some extra push upward or downward on GNP. In fact, if aggregate stimulus or restraint were all that mattered, either one of the two tools could generally do the job, and the second — whichever one chose to be second — would be redundant. The basic general eclectic principle that ought to guide us, as a first approximation, is that either fiscal or monetary policy can administer a required sedative or stimulus to economic activity. As every introductory student knows, however, fiscal and monetary tools operate in very different ways. Monetary policy initially makes people more liquid without adding directly to their incomes or wealth; fiscal policy enhances their incomes and wealth without increasing their liquidity.

In a stimulative monetary action, the people who initially acquire money are not simply given the money; they must part with government securities to get it. But once their portfolios become more liquid, they presumably use the cash proceeds to acquire alternative earning assets, and in so doing they bid up the prices of those assets, or equivalently, reduce the yields. Thus prospective borrowers find it easier and less expensive to issue securities and to get loans; and investors who would otherwise be acquiring securities may be induced instead to purchase real assets such as capital goods. Also, because market values of securities are raised, people become wealthier, if in an indirect way, and may hence increase their purchases of goods and services. Thus many channels run from the easing of financial markets to the quickening of real economic activity.[1]

A stimulative fiscal action is appropriately undertaken when resources are unemployed; in that situation, an action such as expanded government purchases, whether for good things like hospitals or less good things like military weapons, puts resources to work and rewards them with income. The additional cash received by some people is matched by reduced cash holdings of those who bought government securities to finance the outlay. But the securities buyers have no income loss to make them tighten their belts; they voluntarily traded money for near money. In contrast, the income recipients become willing to spend more, and thus trigger a multiplier process on production and income. So, while fiscal and monetary routes differ, the ultimate destination — the effect on national product — is the same, in principle.

Indeed, the conditions under which either fiscal tools or monetary tools, taken separately, have zero effect on GNP are merely textbook curiosities rather than meaningful possibilities in the modern U.S. economic environment. For stimulative monetary policy to be nothing more than a push on a string, either interest rates would have to be just as low as they could possibly go, or investment and consumption would have to show zero response to any further reduction in interest rates. The former possibility is the famous Keynesian liquidity trap, which made lots of sense in describing 1936, but has no relevance to 1971. With prime corporations paying 8 percent on long-term bonds, interest rates are still higher than at any time in my lifetime prior to 1969.[2] There is plenty of room for them to decline, and, in turn, for states and localities, homebuyers and consumer installment credit users, as well as business investors, to be encouraged to spend more by lower costs of credit.

The opposite extreme, impotent fiscal policy, is equally remote. Fiscal policy must exert some stimulative effect on economic activity (even when the monetary policy makers do not accommodate the fiscal action at all) unless the velocity of money is completely inflexible so that no economizing on cash balances occurs. Though the money supply does not rise in a pure fiscal action, spending will tend to rise unless people are totally unable or unwilling to speed up the turnover of cash. And money holders do economize on cash to a varying degree — they do so seasonally and cyclically, and they do so dependably in response to changes in the opportunity cost of holding money. The holder of zero-yielding cash is sacrificing the opportunity to receive the going interest rates of earning assets. The higher interest rates are, the more he sacrifices; and hence, economic theory tells us, the more he will economize on his holdings of cash.

And the facts confirm the theory. The negative relationship between the demand for money and the rate of interest is one of the most firmly established empirical propositions in macroeconomics.[3] So a pure fiscal stimulus produces a speedup in the turnover of money and higher interest rates, and more GNP.

The fact that people do economize on cash balances in response to rises in interest rates demonstrates the efficacy of fiscal policy. Anybody who reports that he can't find a trace of fiscal impact in the aggregate data is unreasonably claiming an absolutely inflexible velocity of money — a vertical liquidity preference function[4] — or else he is revealing the limitations of his research techniques rather than those of fiscal policy.

A few other artful dodges, I submit, make even less sense. Try to defend fiscal impotence on grounds of a horizontal marginal efficiency schedule — that means investment is so sensitive to return that even the slightest interest variation will unleash unlimited changes in investment demand. Or make the case that people subjectively assume the public debt as personal debt and feel commensurately worse off whenever the budget is in deficit. Or contend that businessmen are so frightened by fiscal stimulation that their increased demand for cash and reduced investment spoils its influence.[5] Or use the argument that Say's law operates even when the unemployment rate is 6 percent.[6] It's a battle between ingenuity and credulity!

The eclectic principle is terribly important, not because it answers any questions, but because it rules out nonsense questions and points to sensible ones. It warns us not to get bogged down in such metaphysical issues as whether it is really the Fed that creates inflation during wartime. Every wartime period has been marked by enormous fiscal stimulus, and yet that fiscal fuel-injection could have been neutralized by some huge amount of pressure on the monetary brakes. In that sense, the Fed could have been sufficiently restrictive to offset the stimulus of military expenditures. Anyone who chooses to blame the resulting inflation on not slamming on the monetary brakes, rather than on pumping the fiscal accelerator, can feel free to exercise that curious preference. Take another example: Did the expansion following the tax cut in 1964-65 result from monetary policy? Of course it did, the eclectic principle tells us. If the Fed had wished to nullify the expansionary influence of the tax cut, surely some monetary policy would have been sufficiently restrictive to do so. There is no unique way of allocating credit or blame in a world where both tools can do the stabilization job.

SIDE EFFECTS AS THE CENTRAL ISSUE

So long as both tools are capable of speeding up or slowing down demand, the decisions on how to use them and how to combine them must be made on the basis of criteria other than their simple ability to stimulate or restrain. Nor do we typically get any help by considering *how much* work monetary or fiscal tools do, because usually the right answer is, "as much as needed," providing the shift in policy is large enough. In more formal terms, two instruments and one target produce an indeterminate system.

Of course, there are two basic targets of stabilization policy: price stability and maximum production. But the two tools will not serve to implement those two goals simultaneously. A pen and a pencil are one more tool than is needed to write a letter, but the second tool can't be used to mow the lawn. In the same way, fiscal and monetary policy can both push up aggregate demand or push down aggregate demand, but neither can solve the Phillips curve problem. Subject to minor qualifications,[7] the fiscal route to a given unemployment rate is neither less nor more inflationary than the monetary route to that same unemployment rate.

We can have the GNP path we want equally well with a tight fiscal policy and an easier monetary policy, or the reverse, within fairly broad limits. The real basis for choice lies in the many subsidiary economic targets, beside real GNP and inflation, that are differentially affected by fiscal and monetary policies. Sometimes these are labeled "side effects." I submit that they are the main issue in determining the fiscal-monetary mix, and they belong in the center ring.

Composition of output. One of the subsidiary targets involves the composition of output among sectors. General monetary policy tools, as they are actually employed, bear down very unevenly on the various sectors of the economy. Homebuilding and state and local capital projects are principal victims of monetary restraint. Although the evidence isn't entirely conclusive, it suggests that monetary restraint discriminates particularly against small business. In the field of taxation, we agonize about incidence and equity. The same intense concern is appropriate in the case of monetary restraint and, in fact, increasing concern is being registered in the political arena. In the 1969-70 period of tight money, many efforts (such as Home Loan Bank and Fannie Mae operations) were made to insulate housing from the brunt of the attack. But the impact on home-building was still heavy. Moreover, there is considerable basis for suspicion that these actions defused — as well as diffused — the impact of monetary restraint. A more restrictive monetary policy, as measured in terms of either monetary aggregates or interest rates, is required to accomplish the same dampening effect on GNP if the sectors most vulnerable to credit restraint are shielded from its blows.

The concern about uneven impact may be accentuated because, in 1966 and again in 1969-70, monetary restraint hit sectors that rated particularly high social priorities. But that is not the whole story. Any unusual departure of monetary policy from a "middle-of-the-road" position may lead to allocations that do not accord with the nation's sense of equity and efficiency. For example, in the early sixties, it was feared that a very easy monetary policy might encourage speculative excesses in building because some financial institutions would be pressured to find mortgage loans in order to earn a return on their assets.

In the last few years, some economists — most notably, Franco Modigliani — have argued that monetary policy may have a significant impact on consumption through its influence on the market value of equity securities and bonds[8] in addition to its more direct impact through the cost and availability of installment credit. In my view, the jury is still out on this issue. On the one hand, it's easy to believe that a huge change, say, $100 billion, in the net worth of the American public, such as stock market fluctuations can generate, could alter consumer spending in relation to income by a significant amount like $3 billion, even though that change in wealth is concentrated in a small group at the very top of the income and wealth distribution. On the other hand, previous empirical work on this issue came up with a nearly unanimous negative verdict.[9] In 1966 and 1969, however, the timing of stock market declines and the sluggishness in consumer demand seemed to fit fairly well with the hypothesis. One would like to believe the wealth hypothesis because it would suggest that monetary policy has broad and sizable effects on consumption, especially on that of high-income consumers; monetary restraint would then be revealed as less uneven and less inequitable. But before embracing that judgment, one should wait for more decisive evidence.

Interest rates and asset values. Another major consideration in monetary policy is its effects on interest rates and balance sheets. Some economists may argue that the only function of interest rates is to clear the market and the only sense in which rates can be too high or too low is in failing to establish that equilibrium. Every Congressman knows better! Interest rates are a social target. That is the revealed preference of the American public, reflected in the letters it writes to Washington and the answers it gives to opinion polls. And this is no optical illusion on the part of the citizenry. They have the same good reasons to dislike rising interest rates that apply to rising prices — the haphazard, redistributive effects. And they are concerned about *nominal* interest rates just as they are concerned about prices. It is not clear that such major groups as businessmen or workers are particularly hurt or particularly helped by tight money (or by inflation), but the impacts are quite haphazard in both cases. The resulting lottery in real incomes strikes most Americans as unjust.

The largest redistributive effect of tight money, like that of inflation, falls on balance sheets rather than income statements. People care about their paper wealth and feel worse off when bond and equity prices nose dive. Even though society is not deprived of real resources when security prices drop, it is hard to find gainers to match the losers. Although Alvin Hansen stressed the social costs of distorted, fluctuating balance sheets in the 1950's[10], this issue gets little attention from economists. But it never escapes the broader and keener vision of the American public.

Financial dislocation. A restrictive monetary policy may also have important, dislocating effects on the financial system. The key function of a financial system is to offer people opportunities to invest without saving and to save without investing. If people want risky assets, they can acquire them beyond the extent of their net worth; if they wish to avoid risk, they can earn a moderate return and stay liquid. The trade of funds between lovers of liquidity and lovers of real assets produces gains to all. "Crunch" and "liquidity crisis" are names for a breakdown in the functioning of the financial system. Such a breakdown deprives people of important options and may permanently impair their willingness to take risks and to hold certain types of assets. To the extent that very tight money curbs an inflationary boom by putting boulders in the financial stream, a considerable price is paid. And to the extent that extremely easy money stimulates a weak economy by opening the flood gates of speculation, that too may be costly.

Balance of payments. The pursuit of a monetary policy focused single-mindedly on stabilization goals would have further "side effects" on the balance of payments, to the extent that it changes international interest rate differentials and hence influences capital flows. There are strong arguments for fundamental reforms of the international monetary system — especially more flexible exchange rates — that would greatly reduce this concern. But those reforms are not on the immediate horizon; nor is the United States prepared to be consistently passive about international payments.[11] Meanwhile, the external deficit casts a shadow that cannot be ignored in the formulation of fiscal-monetary policies.

Growth. A final consideration in the mix of stabilization tools is the long-run influence of monetary policy on the rate of growth of our supply capabilities. An average posture of relatively easy money (and low interest rates) combined with tight fiscal policy (designed especially to put a damper on private consumption) is most likely to produce high investment and rapid growth of potential. That becomes relevant in the short-run because the long-run posture of monetary policy is an average of its short-run swings. If, for example, the nation relies most heavily on monetary policy for restraint and on fiscal policy for stimulus, it will unintentionally slip to a lower growth path. The contribution of extra investment to growth and the value of the extra growth to a society that is already affluent in the aggregate are further vital issues. Recently, enthusiasm for growth-oriented policies has been dampened by the concern about the social fallout of rapid growth and by the shame of poverty, which calls for higher current consumption at the low end of the income scale. Nonetheless, the growth implications of decisions about the fiscal-monetary mix should be recognized.

In the light of these considerations, there are good reasons to avoid extreme tightness or extreme ease in monetary policy — even if it produces an ideal path of real output. Tight money can be bad medicine for a boom even if it cures the disease, just as amputation of the hand is a bad remedy for eczema. The experience of 1966 provides an object lesson. Judged by its performance in getting GNP on track, the Federal Reserve in 1966 put on *the* virtuoso performance in the history of stabilization policy. It was the greatest tight-rope walking and balancing act ever performed by either fiscal or monetary policy. Single-handedly the Fed curbed a boom generated by a vastly stimulative fiscal policy that was paralyzed by politics and distorted by war. And, in stopping the boom, it avoided a recession. To be sure, real GNP dipped for a single quarter, but the unemployment rate did not rise significantly above 4 percent; the 1967 pause was as different from the five postwar recessions, including 1970, as a cold is different from pneumonia. Moreover, inflation slowed markedly in the closing months of 1966 and the first half of 1967. What more could anyone want? Yet, you won't find the 1966 Fed team in the hall of fame for stabilization policy. In the view of most Americans, the collapse of homebuilding, the disruption of financial markets, and the escalation of interest rates were evils that outweighed the benefits of the nonrecessionary halting of inflation. The Fed itself reacted by refusing to give an encore in 1967-68, accepting renewed inflation as a lesser evil than renewed tight money.

*The views expressed are my own and are not necessarily those of the officers, trustees, or other staff members of the Brookings Institution.

1. There is general agreement between Keynesians and monetarists regarding the mechanism for transmitting monetary changes. See Milton Friedman and Anna J. Schwartz, "Money and Business Cycles," in Friedman, *The Optimum Quantity of Money and Other Essays* (Aldine, 1969), pp. 229-34. Reprinted from *Review of Economics and Statistics*, Vol. 45 supplement (February 1963), pp. 59-63.
2. Even when any reasonable allowance is made for inflation, it is hard to view today's *real* rates as low by historical standards.
3. See Okun, *The Political Economy of Prosperity* (Brookings Institution, 1970), p. 58, and the bibliography on pp. 146-47 for a list of articles reporting empirical results confirming this relationship.
4. For discussion of a model implying the existence of a vertical liquidity preference function, see Leonall C. Andersen and Jerry L. Jordan, "Monetary and Fiscal Actions: A Test of Their Relative Importance in Economic Stabilization," Federal Reserve Bank of St. Louis, *Monthly Review* (November 1968).
5. See Roger W. Spencer and William P. Yohe, "The 'Crowding Out' of Private Expenditures by Fiscal Policy Actions," in Federal Reserve Bank of St. Louis, *Monthly Review*, Vol. 52, No. 10 (October 1970), pp. 17-24.
6. See "Interest Rates and the Demand for Money," Chapter 7 in Milton Friedman, *The Optimum Quantity of Money*. Reprinted from *The Journal of Law and Economics*, Vol. 9 (October 1966), pp. 71-85. So far as I can see, Friedman is invoking Say's Law.
7. An unbalanced composition of demand among regions and industries means more inflationary pressure at a given overall utilization rate. Thus, particularly concentrated excess demands (e.g. for defense goods or for new homes) may harm the cause of price stability. But the degree of balance cannot be uniquely linked to fiscal-monetary choices.
8. See Franco Modigliani, "Monetary Policy and Consumption — The Linkages Via Interest Rate and Wealth Effects in the Federal Reserve-MIT-Penn Model" (paper prepared for the Federal Reserve Bank of Boston Conference at Nantucket, Massachusetts, June 1971; offset), esp. part I.3. For earlier discussions of the effects of monetary policy as it operates in the Federal Reserve-MIT-Penn Model, see the following: Robert H. Rasche and Harold L. Shapiro, "The FRB-MIT Econometric Model: Its Special Features," in American Economic Association, *Papers and Proceedings of the Eightieth Annual Meeting, 1967* (American Economic Review, Vol. 58, May 1968), pp. 123-49; Albert Ando and Franco Modigliani, "Econometric Analysis of Stabilization Policies," in American Economic Association, *Papers and Proceedings of the Eighty-first Annual Meeting, 1968* (American Economic Review, Vol. 59, May 1969), pp. 296-314; Frank de Leeuw and Edward Gramlich, "The Federal Reserve-MIT Econometric Model," *Federal Reserve Bulletin*, Vol. 54 (January 1968), pp. 11-40; de Leeuw and Gramlich, "The Channels of Monetary Policy," *Federal Reserve Bulletin*, Vol. 55 (June 1969), pp. 472-91.

9. See John J. Arena, "The Wealth Effect and Consumption: A Statistical Inquiry," *Yale Economic Essays*, Vol. 3 (Fall 1963), esp. pp. 273-84 and "Postwar Stock Market Changes and Consumer Spending," *Review of Economics and Statistics*, Vol. 47 (November 1965), pp. 379-91; Saul H. Hymans, "Consumption: New Data and Old Puzzles," *Brookings Papers on Economic Activity* (1:1970), pp. 121-26.

10. See, for example, *The American Economy* (McGraw-Hill, 1957), pp. 53-55.

11. On the question of a passive stance, see Lawrence B. Krause, "A Passive Balance-of-Payments Strategy for the United States," *Brookings Papers on Economic Activity* (3:1970), pp. 339-60; and Gottfried Haberler and Thomas D. Willett, *A Strategy for U.S. Balance of Payments Policy* (American Enterprise Institute, February 1971).

The Design of Macroeconomic Policy

Council of Economic Advisers

The power of monetary and fiscal policies to affect the economy has led some to advocate discretionary policymaking, with frequent changes in policy instruments, such as tax rates or expenditure programs, to influence near-term economic conditions. Indeed, a strong endorsement of discretionary policy was eloquently put forth in the 1962 *Annual Report of the Council of Economic Advisers* as a way to achieve the goals of the Employment Act of 1946—"maximum employment, production, and purchasing power." That *Report* argued that "discretionary policy is essential" and recommendations constituting a "far-reaching innovation in discretionary fiscal policy" were made.

In contrast, recent economic research and practical experience, while supporting the view that macroeconomic policy has powerful effects, lead to the conclusion that discretionary macroeconomic policies can be detrimental to good economic performance. Instead, policies should be designed to work well with a minimum of discretion, with a clear focus on the longer term, and with allowance for future contingencies. Government should credibly commit to follow such policies consistently. As argued below, this approach to policy design can best achieve the Nation's economic goals.

ADVANTAGES OF SYSTEMATIC POLICIES

In its extreme form, discretionary policy involves frequently reacting to short-term developments, with little attempt to consider and communicate intentions for future actions. Such a shortsighted policy approach gives little weight to the benefits of outlining a contingency plan and committing to that plan. For this reason, discretionary macroeconomic policies can actually be counterproductive. Most businesses and many households are forward-looking; expectations of future tax rates, inflation rates, and government spending programs affect their decisions. Frequent unanticipated government actions cause uncertainty for the private sector and interfere with long-term business and household planning.

Without commitment to a clear plan, strong incentives exist to change policies in an attempt to achieve short-term gain. Economists refer to this incentive as "time inconsistency," because policymakers have a natural incentive to alter previously adopted policies or to follow "inconsistent" policies. Such policy changes can have detrimental long-term effects. For example, programs of fiscal stimulus can lead, over time, to long-run government spending that exceeds the level implied by an assessment of the costs and benefits of the programs themselves. Analogous problems exist for monetary policy. For example, an incentive exists to employ short-term monetary policy to boost output above sustainable levels. Such actions can lead to increased inflation over a longer term. Because inflation takes more time to develop than the rise in economic activity, it may not be adequately taken into account in the public policy process.

The drawbacks to discretionary policy go beyond these disadvantages. Experience has shown that the ability of discretionary macroeconomic policies to move the economy in the right direction at the right time is quite limited. First, assessing the current state of the economy is difficult because economic data are subject to appreciable errors and are generally available only after a considerable lag. Second, economic forecasting is difficult and quite imprecise, limiting the ability of policymakers to anticipate swings in the economy. Third, even if economic fluctuations are forecast correctly, determining the appropriate policy measures is difficult because the economy responds somewhat unpredictably to changes in fiscal and monetary policy. Finally, lags between a policy action and its ultimate effect on the economy imply that timely implementation of a discretionary change in policy frequently may not be possible. To be sure, discretionary policy changes might partly offset unusually large and sustained economic fluctuations. But, in general, the ability of discretionary macroeconomic policies to contribute to economic stability is quite limited.

The alternative to discretionary policies might be called systematic policies. A systematic policy specifies, as clearly as possible, *a plan for the instruments of policy*, be they the Federal budget, the growth rate of the monetary aggregates, or tax rates. For a systematic policy to improve economic performance, it must of course be well designed. In some cases a systematic policy might be very simple and specific, such as a promise not to raise marginal tax rates or a law that sets a target for the budget deficit for several years into the future. In the 1960s and 1970s, a rule that specified a fixed growth rate of the money supply was proposed and might have been appropriate; changes in the financial sector in the 1980s, however, have rendered such a simple rule unworkable. In other cases it is appropriate and possible to specify contingencies for future policy actions, such as indexing tax brackets for inflation according to a numerical formula, or stating the conditions under which a budget target could be suspended.

However, the concept of a systematic policy is much broader than a simple or even complex numerical formula for policy. In some cases it may not be possible to be so precise about a policy plan or its contingencies, and some judgment in interpreting or implementing the plan is necessary. Even in such cases, a systematic policy has significant advantages over a discretionary policy if it places some discipline or general guidelines on future changes in the policy instruments, and if policymakers commit to this discipline. Moreover, even the most carefully designed systematic policies may need to be revised occasionally in view of significant changes in economic structure.

IMPORTANCE OF CREDIBILITY

Economic research and policy experience have led to a growing awareness of the importance of the *credibility* of policymakers to carry out a stated policy. Various definitions of policy credibility have been offered, but the following seems most useful: an announced policy is credible if the public believes that it will be implemented, and acts on those beliefs even in the face of occasional contradictory evidence. Policy credibility is not an all-or-nothing concept, and in many situations credibility can only be achieved gradually.

Policy credibility will often lead to economic performance that is superior to that in which policy is not credible. The more credible the policy, the more likely it is to improve performance. A credible disinflation plan initiated by the monetary authorities will bring down inflation more quickly and with less chance of recession than a plan with little credibility. For example, a billion-dollar stabilization fund for Poland, recently established by a group of industrial economies, is designed to lend credibility to the Polish disinflation plan by providing financial backing to help the Polish government stabilize the exchange rate. This will reinforce other policies to reduce inflation and promote external trade.

In addition, credibility can help resolve problems arising from unpredictable shifts in the structural relationships between the policy instruments and the state of the economy. Such changes can make it quite difficult for the public to assess the appropriateness of macroeconomic policies when the policy rules are complicated. If the public is confident that appropriate policies are being followed, households and businesses can plan for the future, which promotes saving, investment, and economic growth.

A NEW RULE FOR FISCAL POLICY

Since the mid-1980s, fiscal policy in the United States has been guided by the Gramm-Rudman-Hollings law, which has served as a fairly systematic rule for budget policy. As part of the fiscal policy agenda for 1990, the Administration is proposing an innovative new rule for fiscal policy, one that would be an unprecedented step in U.S. fiscal policy. The proposed new Social Security Integrity and Debt Reduction Fund would ensure that projected future surpluses in Social Security are not spent for other purposes, but rather are used to build reserves needed to help provide Social Security benefits in the future. As discussed in detail below, payments into the fund would be used to reduce government debt and decrease the legacy of deficit spending passed on to future generations. This policy rule would also increase the supply of savings, lower interest rates, and increase resources in the future. Committing such a strong rule to law will increase the credibility of the policy, which will speed up the reduction in interest rates and more quickly enhance investment and economic growth.

Rational Expectations—Fresh Ideas That Challenge Some Established Views of Policy Making

Clarence W. Nelson

"Monetary policy cannot systematically stimulate the economy to lower unemployment rates."

That startling claim is one of the consequences of a new view of economic policy that has been termed, "rational expectations." This new view attacks widely held beliefs about how the economy works and challenges many prevailing theories about what economic policy can achieve.

These new ideas are so fundamentally important to the current predicament facing our nation's economy and to the future course of national economic policy that policy makers — and the general public affected by policy makers' choices — need to understand the logic and evidence that support the rational expectations view.

But most recent work in the theory and in the analysis of past economic experience — including major contributions made by the Research Department of this Bank — has been too technical to be understood by a more general audience. Hopefully this article will explain the essential ideas of the rational expectations challenge in fairly simple language. By doing that, we hope to encourage discussion of rational expectations among elected officials, policy makers, and a wider public.

We'll begin by briefly defining what we mean by "rational expectations" and by identifying the kind of policy to which it applies. Our discussion will then address the following points:

(I)   Why traditional views about how economic policy works are wrong,
(II) why rational expectations is a valid view of the world,
(III) what happens when current methods of policy making are used in a rational expectations world, and
(IV) in the light of rational expectations ideas, what can macroeconomic policy really hope to achieve?

"Rational expectations": what it means.

When the term "rational expectations" first appeared in an economic journal article in 1961, it was given a specific technical meaning connected with economic models. In an everyday, practical sense rational expectations is simply an assumption about people's behavior. The assumption claims that people make economic deci-

sions in a way that tends to take into account all available information bearing significantly on the future consequences of their decisions. And they tend to use that information in a way so as not to repeat their past mistakes. The information we're talking about can include, among other things, knowledge about government policy actions already taken and about strategies or approaches government policy makers regularly take when economic signals begin to change. So, rational expectations attributes to people a reasonably thorough, broad-view approach to appraising the future on matters that are going to make a big dollars-and-cents difference to them.

Put that way, there's certainly nothing startling about the rational expectations idea. Most of us have believed all along that rationality in that sense is a reasonable thing to attribute to economic decision makers — business people, labor leaders, workers, investors, or consumers. What is startling is that the ideas underlying current policy views deny such rationality. Current views about how policy achieves its effects depend on people *failing* to act in their own best interests. When we recast the decision-making process to allow people to act with "rational expectations," policy no longer has the same effects. And that's the heart of the problem we're examining in this article.

The importance of expectations in decision making.

All economists agree that people's beliefs about the future affect their decisions today. Employers and employees negotiate wage contracts with some picture in mind about what will happen to the cost of living or to other related wage rates over the life of a contract. Consumers deciding whether to purchase a car have expectations about future income, job prospects, future cash outlays, and perhaps sources of credit in an emergency — if only to judge whether the automobile installment payments can be met. Similarly, a business firm deciding whether to invest in new factories must form expectations about such things as future sales, future labor and other input costs, and future tax rates.

According to the rational expectations view, people use in the best way possible whatever information they have; and they do not tend to repeat previous errors. People are forward looking, and prospective government actions play an important part in their picture of the future. The myriad of commercially available newsletters, analytical reports, and forecasting services reminds us that forecasting government actions has become big business. And even though people must make plans in an environment of considerable uncertainty (and, therefore, are likely to make some mistakes), they do learn to avoid repeatedly misusing information that will bear on their future. That's because the economic process rewards those who make good forecasts and penalizes those who don't.

Types of policies under question.

We should emphasize that the kind of policy making we're looking at embraces attempts to manage, or influence, demand for goods and services in order to smooth out the business cycle. Sometimes these kinds of policies are called *demand management* policies, *aggregate demand* policies, or simply *countercyclical* policies. (We'll use these terms interchangeably.)

Virtually everyone who reads the newspapers is aware of the continuing public discussion of these policies. Government choices regarding how much it will spend in relation to how much it will tax, when used as deliberate countercyclical measures, are called *fiscal* policies. Decisions by the Federal Reserve to increase or decrease bank reserves, directed similarly, are called *monetary* policies. When the federal government deliberately takes action to spend more than it taxes away from businesses and individuals, fiscal policy is said to be *expansionary*. When the Federal Reserve acts to increase bank reserves — a kind of starter kit for expanded money and credit growth in the private economy — monetary policy is said to be *expansionary* and is viewed to be either a complement to expansionary fiscal policy or a stimulus in its own right. Both of these types of economic policy are commonly thought to be potent ways to help get a weak economy moving again.

I. What's wrong with traditional views of the policy process?

Since rational expectations ideas have developed as criticism of some prevailing ways of viewing the economy and the role of policy, the case for rational expectations is, to a large extent, the case against these current views. The traditional views we're talking about are those claiming that routinely applied fiscal and monetary stimulus in times of recession, and restraint in times of boom, will improve the general performance of the economy over the longer term and make people, on the whole, better off. What we want to show in the next few sections is that people's expectations, when formed "rationally," will generally frustrate government's attempts to successfully pursue activist demand management policies.

We'll do this by outlining the process through which activist policies are widely believed to get results and show how they depend on people behaving in ways inconsistent with their own best interests. Next we'll offer a rational expectations version of the policy process as a more realistic representation of people's decision making and indicate how that representation seems

consistent with some evidence from recent experience. We think the rational expectations view is persuasive.

Two stories of how activist countercyclical fiscal and monetary policies are believed to work will be traced out. In the first story policy has its effect through the labor market and hinges on the way labor reacts to changes in wages and prices. The other story has policy working via financial markets and hinges on the way changes in interest rates induce (or discourage) new investment. These two perceptions of the channels connecting policy with the economic outcome aren't mutually exclusive; they could easily be combined into a single, more general story. The stories, though, are often told separately, and since some of our readers will be more familiar with one or the other it will be useful to consider each of them in turn. The two perceived policy channels we are about to consider probably contain the essence of what most legislator's and policy maker's views depend on in order for activist policies to get results.

Story one: policy that takes effect through wage decisions.

Central to some widely held views of the policy process are wage-setting decisions in the labor market. This story, a rather standard Keynesian one, depends very much on labor *not* rationally forming expectations about future conditions at the time wage contracts are set.

We start with an economy in recession. Government policy makers want to stimulate hiring and producing by private business firms. They know the way to get business firms to expand *more* than already planned is to take policy actions that will cause business to see additional profit opportunities. So government increases the amount of money it spends for goods and services relative to the amount of money it draws in from the private economy in the form of taxes. And it creates money to pay for the difference. Prices move up as business experiences the effects of added spending for its products. All this time labor is not supposed to look ahead to the end of the story with its promise of rising prices, and so it continues to work at very nearly the same old wage. That's what creates new profit opportunities for business— prices for business output go up, but its major input cost, wage rates for labor, does not. The outcome: business expands, and as it does it hires more labor.

In this scenario, workers go along with unchanged wage rates in the face of prospectively higher prices. They find themselves in the peculiar situation of offering more labor at lower "real-wage rates," that is, wage rates measured in terms of the amount of goods they'll buy. That shortsightedness on the part of labor is crucial if this channel for policy action is to work as claimed. For if workers bargained for their wages in full anticipation that prices would rise, or if wages were "indexed" to automatically follow general price level increases, then that perceived policy channel would fail to work.

This simplified Keynesian story does no particular violence to the mechanism many policy activists believe enables government to start the economic ball rolling. It requires that workers in the labor market be oblivious to (or largely tolerant of) the prospect that an unchanging wage along with a rising general price level will progressively erode the amount of real goods and services their wages will buy. Since that kind of decision making hardly seems rational, it's easy to guess the forthcoming rational expectations criticism.

First, the process will work only if labor does not, in the course of its wage-bargaining and job-seeking behavior, anticipate the consequent general rise in prices. It's clear that fiscal and monetary policies deliberately attempting to stimulate total dollar spending in the economy would not be able to operate through this price- and wage-setting disparity if those policies were fully predicted or expected. That's because labor wouldn't willingly or knowingly enter into a contract that dooms workers to a shrinking real income when no changes in technology or productivity have occurred that force upon the whole of the economy—owners and managers of business as well—such a real loss in living standards. And in the absence of that kind of self-diminishing agreement, business would have no net expansion in profit opportunities to exploit.

Second, any policy process that operates by fooling people—as this Keynesian mechanism certainly requires—may work the first time, but cannot be expected to go on fooling people repeatedly. That's axiomatic from the rationalists' point of view. Any logical story of the policy process must grant labor in general and workers in particular at least reasonable acumen when it comes to making commitments affecting their personal economic interests. That much is granted to other actors in the story, of course. Our conclusion then is that the activist policy process we've been describing will not bring about any overall real expansion in the private economy—*unless it catches people by surprise.*

Some indications of labor market response to prospective inflation. One of the arguments supporters of activist countercyclical policy make against the rational expectations view starts with the observation that labor frequently locks itself into contracts by fixing the course of wages for as much as three years into the future. That fact, plus perhaps some slowness on the part of workers in recognizing what's happening to prices in general, means there's a built-in delay in wage adjustments. But, so the story goes, product prices can respond quickly to a policy stimulus, and therefore temporary profit opportunities, at least, can be created by policy action. That provides incentive for business to expand, if only temporarily, and thus some potency is retained by activist policy.

That fragile loophole cannot be relied on in the pursuit of any systematic countercyclical policy. Contracts are periodically rewritten and can certainly take into account any earlier misreading of government policy strategy on the practical principle of "once burned, twice cautious." One possible response by labor to being caught short in midcontract because of unpredictable policy moves by government is simply to shorten the contract period the next time. That course

Figure 1. Percent of Workers Under Contract Covered by Cost-of-Living Escalation

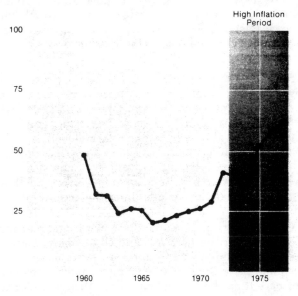

Source: Monthly Labor Review

was pointed out in 1971 by United Auto Workers President Leonard Woodcock when he said, ". . . if labor contracts can be torn up based upon the stroke of a pen [a reference to the Wage-Price Freeze on August 15, 1971], then obviously we can no longer in the future negotiate contracts for any longer than one year."

An alternative response by labor is to stay with longer-term contracts but base them on a better forecast of inflation. In fact, the closer labor can come to having wages fully adjusted for changes in cost-of-living indexes, the closer it comes to making a "perfect" forecast. That situation, from labor's point of view, would be the ultimate in rational expectations and would obviously frustrate the Keynesian policy mechanism described earlier.

A telling illustration of the way labor has moved to protect its real earnings in the recent environment of high price inflation is the data on the percentage of workers covered by cost-of-living clauses in their contracts. We've plotted that data in Figure 1. It suggests that labor is in fact responding in a "rational" way to government's continuing failure to deliver on its announced policy goals for containment of inflation.

Story two: countercyclical policy that takes effect by way of interest rate channels.

Now let's look at another commonly held notion of how monetary-fiscal stimulus makes things move. This one operates through a different market, the market for investment funds, and seems to depend on a kind of shortsightedness by suppliers of funds regarding their prospective "real" interest earnings. The earnings-versus-inflation discrepancy that policy appears to exploit here parallels labor's "illusion" about its wage in the first story. According to this policy story, policy makers' actions to expand the rate of money growth will influence business expansion decisions and consumer spending decisions through interest rates.

The story goes as follows.

Start with the perception that the economy is in, or going into, a recession. Policy authorities act to expand the money supply growth rate. The Federal Reserve does this by stepping up its buying of securities from the public (through a network of dealers in New York). By that deliberate action the public ends up with a flow of new cash, and banks end up with a flow of new reserves that enable them to expand loans to businesses, if they can find customers, by several times the amount of the new reserves.

Other things being equal, the buying action of the Fed drives securities *prices* up, and that means interest rates are driven down on those securities. The subsequent action by banks seeking to make loans at a faster pace than they would have done otherwise, or to buy bonds in greater volumes than they would have done otherwise, helps move still other interest rates down.

In the next step, business firms expand investment in new production facilities. One way to imagine why they would do so is to consider interest on borrowed business funds as simply another cost of doing business, just as wages for labor inputs are a cost of doing business. As expectations adjust to the prospect of lower interest costs, some investment possibilities not previously viewed as profitable will suddenly appear profitable—expected revenues don't change, but expected costs go down because the interest cost component has gone down. Thus, plant and equipment investments are undertaken, new workers are hired, and new output is produced.

The last step in the story simply recognizes that the added new workers start some new spending of their own, which further raises demand, causing additional businesses to expand their output, and so on. Thus, national product expands by some multiple of the initial investment stimulus, and we've succeeded in bringing about large real effects on the economy through small changes in monetary policy.

Once this process gets underway (plant expansion, new hiring, and all that), the increased private spending would, just as in the first story, likely bring forth some mixture of price increases and real quantity increases in the flow of goods and services. This story seems even to allow wage rates to be bid up approximately in line with prices as expansion moves along. The prospect of wage rate increases can be a part of business firms' expectations — as long as the necessary capital funds have been or can be acquired through borrowing at bargain interest rates.

Interest rate responses to monetary-fiscal actions appear to be the crucial link in the story we've just told. Interest rate responses also seem to provide the main channel through which monetary policy actions affect employment and output in the large macroeconometric models of the United States economy currently used by government to assist in determining policies and by business to assist in determining its strategies. The large multi-equation "MPS" model developed by the Federal Reserve, Massachusetts Institute of Technology, University of Pennsylvania, and the Social Sciences Research Council has five directly defined channels that depend on interest rate movements. Some dozen different interest rates appear in the equations to help generate quarter-by-quarter predictions of total spending for such categories as consumer durables, automobiles, producers' durable equipment, and residential construction. The interest rate linkage seems also to be a key part of the looser and more generalized anecdotal story that you might get if you asked some policy makers how their decisions affect the economy.

In the rational expectations view, however, those stories are wrong. The interest-rate-link story doesn't take a broad enough perspective and doesn't adequately accommodate the way people rationally form their expectations. While it's undeniable that Federal Reserve action to buy securities and expand bank reserves results in bidding interest rates down, that response is temporary and fleeting. The point is that rational lenders and investors, who look ahead to later chapters of the story, see that any Federal Reserve push to expand money growth rates will ultimately raise the growth in the general price level. Foreseeing that outcome, lenders won't want to tie up funds in long-term loans at rates of interest which they had calculated to be acceptable under an outdated view of future inflation. If they were to commit their funds with no upward adjustment of their lending rate, they would be agreeing to accept a lower rate of return in terms of the goods and services they would subsequently be able to buy. And nothing in the outlook has changed that should lead them to want to do that.

Instead, they would add an "inflation premium" to the interest rates they are willing to settle for — a little insurance policy against the heightened prospects for inflation. And interest rate levels finally settled on in the financial markets have got to reflect that premium. Finally, if the long-term interest rates relevant for business capital expansion go up by the full amount of expected inflation, as the rationalists argue would occur with any foreseen inflation, all costs — including interest as a cost — will go up proportionately to the expected price rise so that nothing will have changed in terms of exploitable profit opportunities. In short, when policy moves are anticipated or quickly sensed in market signals, this financial market channel to policy results we've been describing won't work either.

So what's the evidence that interest rates don't behave as the conventional policy view would argue they should? Any simple look at the relationship between money growth and interest rate levels in the historical record is bound to ignore a lot of other factors also influencing how those two things behave. Yet the fact

Figure 2a. Interest Rate vs. Money Growth for OECD Countries

Nov. 1976 short term interest rates vs. rate of money growth Nov. 1976 over Nov. 1975

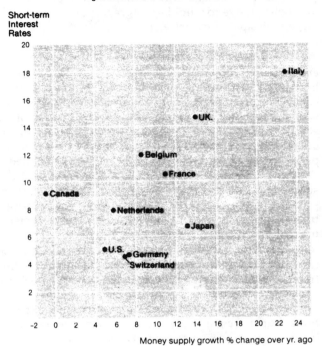

Source: Federal Reserve Bank of New York

Figure 2b. Interest Rate vs. Money Growth

Quarterly average U.S. data 1954 through 1977

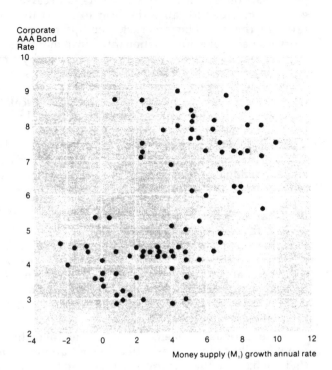

that economic data just don't show high rates of money growth regularly associated with low levels of interest rates must, at the very least, raise doubts about the dependability of that perceived route for policy actions.

You can look at experience across countries [Figure 2a] or over a period of time within the United States [Figure 2b] and see that *higher* interest rates, not lower, appear, if anything, to go along with higher rates of money expansion — probably reflecting higher actual and expected inflation rates.

To sum up, the rational expectations view argues that conventionally perceived policy channels — whether operating through wage costs, interest costs, or any other market-responsible variable — are wrong because they depend on having people behave contrary to their own clear best interests, repeatedly neglecting important information they have or can have about any systematically applied policy.

II. How valid is rational expectations as a representation of people's behavior?

Some critics argue that rational expectations demands too much wisdom and perceptiveness of people to be believable. But the validity of rational expectations does not require that *every* consumer or worker or business manager be the "complete seer" of future prices and other economic events. For example, in the case of wage bargaining by organized labor, only the union leadership actually engaged in the bargaining process — not each and every rank-and-file member — need have an informed view about what government policy is and what its consequences for future price levels are likely to be. Today's union leadership, as we pointed out in our review of policy channels in the previous section, does, in fact, acknowledge its concern about prospective "real" earnings. Small agricultural enterprises or commodity dealers need not have specialized resources of their own to forecast supply and demand movements and the effects of government policies. All they need do to learn what the experts are expecting in future market situations is pick up the newspaper, or the phone, and check on quoted futures prices — or subscribe at modest price to one of many private newsletters. In the case of small borrowers and investors, the information possessed by large and sophisticated borrowers and suppliers of funds becomes very quickly and widely reflected in publicized interest rates. Studies have shown that financial markets, including the stock markets, are efficient users of information in the sense that prices quickly adjust to reflect expert information on all the factors — government policy included — bearing on future profitability.

Clearly the major industrial and commercial firms in the economy have a crucial financial stake in correctly forecasting how they will be affected by changes in government policy. Any actions they take, because of changed expectations, in product or resource markets will quickly carry the message of their reappraisal to other participants, large and small, on both sides of the market.

Finally, when wage rates of a particular firm get out of line with other firms competing for the same labor pool, reaction by only a few workers is necessary, in general, in order to cause the firm to adjust its wage rates to the prevailing market. Perhaps none of the workers need take direct action if the firm monitors the market and adjusts its salary structure, as many firms do, using projections based on market surveys. Such surveys will reflect what's happening at the more responsive firms, including the effects of escalator provisions and other union bargaining results. In sum, the rational expectations argument is that information about the likely future is transmitted in the marketplace in the same way as information about the present. A given individual or firm need not be the "complete seer" of the future any more than of the present.

III. What happens to activist macro policy in a rational expectations world?

In earlier sections we reviewed arguments for disbelieving that macro policy actions can work the way conventional perceptions say they do, and we presented reasons for thinking that the kind of world policy makers must deal with is something very close to a rational expectations world.

The serious problem, then, is the following: If people really do behave as rational expectations models their behavior, then many existing beliefs about the

results policy can achieve are incorrect. As we've abundantly stressed already, macro policy initiatives that people anticipate will be frustrated by the changes people will then make in their plans. More particularly, any policy move to stimulate aggregate spending will be largely dissipated by price rises.

An illustration of the effects of rational expectations on economic policy.

Econometric models are constructed of mathematical equations, often designed to be solved on computers in a way capable of simulating the future course of an economy. Results can then be cranked out quarter-by-quarter to produce numerical forecasts of employment, prices, or whatever economic variables are contained in the model. It's now a commonplace that models of this sort — some with as many as several hundred equations — have since the mid-1960s become increasingly important information bases for business decision making and for government policy decision making.

Conventional policy transmission channels, such as the wage illusion described in section I, are also built into traditional econometric models often used as a basis for evaluating alternative policy actions. Those models, of course, were not designed to reflect rational expectations, but there generally is a way to impose on them a form of rational expectations. *When that's done, the revised macro model reveals that activist economic policy does not have much of an impact on the economic outcome — apart from what it does to prices.*

Conventional policy stimulus in a slack economy.

There is a widely held view that says, if the economy is operating with a great deal of slack, or "excess capacity," any policy-spending stimulus will have little effect on prices and will mainly result in an increased real quantity of output. Only when the economy nears "capacity" output, claims that view, will extra stimulus spending fail to bring forth much new physical output and instead be largely dissipated on price increases. Neither economic theory nor empirical evidence supports that view.

There is no compelling theoretical reason to believe that some kind of critical point exists in the economy's overall scale of operation that abruptly distinguishes price-quantity responses taking place above that point from those taking place below. That doesn't mean that physical constraints or bottlenecks might not occur at the individual plant or industry level to temporarily block output increases from occurring in response to stronger demand. But for the economy as a whole, substitution possibilities are enormous, so spending can shift to other lines or services where bottlenecks or constraints will not, in general, be reached at the same time. Thus, the economic concept of aggregate production suggests only gradual transition of cost, price, and profitability relationships over the full range of operating levels for the economy as a whole.

The observed Phillips relationship (see, for example, Figure 3), which does not in general exhibit a sharp bend, provides a rough, practical verification that such is the case. And that ought to indicate, to those who still

Figure 3.
Generalized Employment-Inflation Upswing for U.S. since mid-sixties
(Plotted points are semiannual averages)

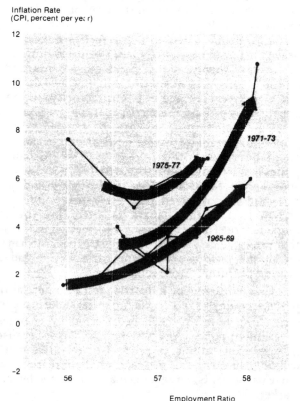

Inflation Rate
(CPI, percent per year)

1971-73

1975-77

1965-69

Employment Ratio
(percent of total employment to non-institutional population 16 and over)

believe in an exploitable Phillips curve, that the policy maker gets no "free ride" as the economy expands from its low points in relative operating levels.

There is further empirical evidence to that point: one of our studies [2], using data for the United States economy, has shown that the reported capacity utilization rate does not help explain inflation rates when the effects of other factors bearing on price changes are analytically separated out. That is, whatever the cause of price level changes, that cause doesn't appear to act any differently when excess capacity is high than when it is low.

It's true that a government monetary or spending stimulus sometimes will be dissipated nearly totally in price increases. At other times it will bring forth greater physical quantities of goods and services but *only* when accompanied by an increase in prices. The determining factor between these two alternatives has nothing to do with "capacity utilization," but instead depends on whether or not the stimulus has been *anticipated* by people who make buy-and-sell decisions in the economy.

In summary, there is no activist policy — at any level of excess capacity — that does not bring forth price increases at the same time it causes output expansion, and nowhere does the relative amount of output vs. price response change greatly as "excess capacity" is used up.

IV. Some conclusions: given the new view — what can macroeconomic policy really do?

The policy view built around rational expectations ideas does not argue that monetary actions by the Federal Reserve and fiscal actions by Congress and the Administration can't have an effect on production and employment. They can and do, but only when they surprise people.

As we've repeatedly emphasized, a crucial distinction required by the new view is that between policy actions that are expected and policy actions that are surprises — only the latter cause people to alter their expectations about opportunities for gain and hence to adjust their planned behavior.

In the case of policy actions that are expected, the new view argues there is neither an empirical nor theoretical basis for believing they can be exploited by policy makers for any beneficial real effect. Included in this category are predictable policies such as the Federal Reserve's traditional "leaning against the wind" (which is to say being "extra" restrictive in supplying reserves when the economy approaches high operating rates and being "extra" liberal when the economy has begun to slump), as long as that leaning is done consistently. The only economic effect of expected policy actions, if on the stimulus side, would be to boost general inflation.

Policy actions that come as a surprise to people, on the other hand, will, in general, have some real effects. Policy surprises cause people to change their plans, because the expectations on which they based those plans have been jolted. In the technical literature, much of the defense of activist policy against the rational expectations attack has hinged on preserving ways in which surprise could continue to provide workable leverage for the policy maker, even though decision agents are granted rational expectations. We've already discussed a few of these arguments — for one, the idea that people lock themselves into contracts on prices or wages. This, activists argue, enables policy makers to use surprise when needed, by catching people in midcontract, to foster a particular policy objective. We pointed out in section II why that argument is faulty. Another activist idea is that government policy makers have better information or superior knowledge about how the economy works, and so they can take an action that people won't catch on to, at least for a long enough time to enable some policy results. The premise about superior knowledge in the government sector is clearly faulty, and section II talked a bit about the efficiency of private sector information.

These arguments are at best attempts to patch up questionable policy theory by finding special conditions under which the policy of "surprise" can be routinely used by government to smooth out swings in the business cycle. Rationalists doubt, at one level of questioning, that stabilization efforts based on surprise really give the policy maker much to work with. To the extent surprise policy involves a deliberate strategy of fooling people (in the sense that had the people only known the truth they wouldn't have done what the government's action got them to do) it may easily work the first time, but then fail to be effective the second or third time because people have escalated their awareness of what government is likely to do in any given situation. And unless the "surprise-that-works" is later repeated, under similar conditions and in a consistent and logical way, it is not possible to distinguish government policy making from a random, or even perverse, game.

At a deeper level, rationalists doubt that it would be wise, or fair, for the government to attempt "policy by surprise" even if policy makers were sufficiently resourceful to invent unendingly new surprise ways to boost the money supply and government spending.

One of the most important ideas emerging from the new view, as we pointed out in section III, is that the "business cycle" might at last be adequately explained as a property of a properly working market economy. In such a view, individuals are thought to react to profit incentives and to imperfectly extract information about those incentives from changes in price signals that are in part useful information and in part meaningless "noise." An economic system doing the most efficient possible job of reading the information being reflected in price signals will still experience some irreducible business cycle swings. That's because the economic process contains inherent mechanisms that convert random shocks on prices into a more persistent, short-term misreading of changing profit opportunities. When misread by enough people, that action can stimulate a cumulative swing in output that will continue until the misreading is realized and retrenchment sets in. Random shocks to prices and markets are always with us. Some arise from natural catastrophes or man-made embargos, but Lucas [3] argues that an important source of shocks to prices may have been erratic "surprise" actions by policy makers themselves.

The new view conjectures that some amount of cyclical swing in production and employment is inherent in the *micro* level processes of the economy that no government *macro* policies can, or should attempt to, smooth out. *Expected* additions to money growth certainly won't smooth out cycles, if the arguments in this paper are correct. *Surprise* additions to money growth have the potential to make matters worse. That's because surprise policies, and the prospect of other future surprise policies, lead to greater uncertainty in people's expectations about future prices, wages, and interest rates — and those are prime ingredients in people's ongoing decision making. These new theories say the information value of price signals is *eroded* by erratic and unpredictable government policy action. Given the importance to an efficiently working market economy of information conveyed by prices, the potential of activist general demand policy to do costly mischief must be considered a serious one. Government's potential to systematically exploit surprise shocks is drastically limited in a rational expectations world.

The road ahead . . .

If it's true that traditionally perceived activist policy goals are unattainable through macroeconomic policy channels, what goals should guide monetary and fiscal policy? What should monetary policy try to do?

One strategy that seems consistent with the significant, though largely negative, findings of rational expectations would have monetary policy focus its attention on inflation and announce, and stick to, a policy that would bring the rate of increase in the general price level to some specified low figure. To be sure, merely to announce such a policy at this point in time would be a "surprise" — perhaps a rather large one given the past history of policy — and is therefore likely to have, for a period of time, some effects on the planned level of output and employment. But there's no way to avoid some lurching when a trajectory is changed. After a period of adjustment, so we've argued here, a steady and consistent pursuit of some publicly known, modest growth for the money supply would not have detrimental effects on employment levels because the general price level impact of monetary policy would be built into people's expectations.

Given that sort of primary dedication to a lower inflation path, the general objective of monetary policy suggested by rational expectations ought to be elimination or reduction of uncertainty about the future general price level — to make it as predictable and dependable as possible around some low average rate of growth. That course, rationalists argue, would do more than any alternative macro policy posture to contribute to long-term steady economic growth and high employment rates.

While we might have reasonable confidence in the wisdom of that general strategy, the rational expectations view can offer little on the question of how best to implement such a policy operationally. That's one of the unfinished tasks for research. In the meantime, the broader issues we've raised are topics for deep reflection and debate by those responsible for designing and controlling the economic policies of this nation. That's a responsibility that ought also to concern informed citizens who, after all, will reap the benefits of good policies and pay the costs of poor ones.

References Cited

[1] Anderson, Paul A. "Rational Expectations Forecasts From Nonrational Models, *Journal of Monetary Economics*, forthcoming.

[2] Bryant, John, James Duprey, and Thomas Supel. Unpublished memorandum, November 14, 1977, Federal Reserve Bank of Minneapolis.

[3] Lucas, Robert E., Jr. "Understanding Business Cycles," Carnegie-Rochester Conference Series on Public Policy, Volume 5, supplement to *Journal of Monetary Economics*, North Holland Publishing Company, 1977.

[4] Muench, Thomas J., Arthur J. Rolnick, Neil Wallace, and William Weiler. "Tests for Structural Change and Prediction Intervals for the Reduced Forms of Two Structural Models of the U.S.: The FRB-MIT and Michigan Quarterly Models." *Annals of Economic and Social Measurement*, Vol. 3, No. 3 (July 1974):491-519.

[5] Samuelson, Paul A., and Robert M. Solow. "Problem of Achieving and Maintaining a Stable Price Level," *American Economic Review*, Vol. 50, No. 2 (May 1960):177-222.

[6] Sargent, Thomas J. "A Classical Macroeconometric Model for the United States," *Journal of Political Economy*, Vol. 84, No. 2 (April 1976):207-37.

Rational Expectations and the Real World

Leonard Forman

There is a large number of economists who now hold that an activist stabilization policy is both superfluous and self-defeating, because there is supposedly no permanent or long-run tradeoff between unemployment and inflation. This position has been considerably bolstered by the research conducted by exponents of the rational expectations hypothesis, or REH.

The REH assumes not only that economic agents use all available and relevant information in forming their expectations, and that they process this information intelligently. It implies an even stronger assumption, namely, that except for random, non-economic disturbances, people have perfect foresight. Such a view suggests a world where events repeat themselves in logical time. And here we come to the real issue posed by the rational expectations hypothesis. Proponents of the REH have constructed theories which deny the very notion of historical time, and of uncertainty—which exists in a world of nonrepetitive events occurring in *historical* time. They embrace only the concept of risk—which exists in a world of repetitive events in *logical* time. Thus they expect economic agents to behave, in forming their expectations, in a way which scarcely ever occurs in practice.

This point of view has profound implications for model-building and economic theory, and also for policy. It has often been suggested that because the market is a self-regulating mechanism, policy-makers are thereby liberated from the onerous task of having to choose between the two evils of unemployment and inflation. If you add the REH to that view, you go even further, and conclude that stabilization policy is its own worst enemy. For under REH, economic agents are presumed to be able to anticipate the effects of policy decisions, and respond so as to offset the expected results. A model built on this assumption will therefore imply that there is not even a short-run tradeoff between unemployment and inflation, let alone the long-run tradeoff. In a world where people are forming their expectations through the scientific application of probability analysis to decision-making, perhaps that might be the case. But that is not the real world. Psychologists and sociologists have shown how unreal it is in their research. But modern economic theorists tend to ignore this work, preferring to rely on what Keynes called "introspection and heroic abstraction" in order to maintain the purity of the competitive model.

Risk and uncertainty

Keynes and Knight, in their writings, made a fundamental distinction between the concepts of risk and uncertainty. They were concerned with the effect of uncertainty on decision-making in a production-monetary economy set in historical time.

While risk is a statistical concept which can be quantified through the application of the probability calculus, uncertainty cannot be measured. Uncertainty implies that the future is *unpredictable*. It cannot be described in terms of probability. As Douglas Vickers suggested in a recent article in the *Journal of Post Keynesian Economics*, to use probability distributions to determine economic outcomes—that is, to replace the concept of uncertainty with the concept of risk—is to assume that most people have knowledge that they are actually unlikely to possess. Risk and probability imply a sampling of repetitive events and a specified outcome occurring with a given frequency. Most real world decisions, however, are not capable of being repeated. They are unique in terms of the events which necessitated a decision and the changes in physical and psychological states which result from that decision. According to Keynes "The one-way traffic of human history allows no repetition of the kind of experiments that change man's ideas. They are self-destructive experiments."

Since the future is logically unknowable, the choice of future alternatives is fundamentally uncertain. Probabilities cannot be calculated by sampling the future. Consequently, problems of uncertainty are incapable of being reduced to problems involving risk.

As Keynes pointed out, uncertainty pervades economic life because the economy exists in historical, not in logical, time. The economic system is indeterminate because history is indeterminate. The problem is "to make rational dispositions in the face of an uncertain future. It is a problem that is unsolvable. But, decisions need to be made. Usually present conditions and majority opinion are assumed to be a serviceable guide to the future. But such opinions are flimsy, without solid foundation, subject to sudden and violent change." Decisions which affect the future cannot possibly depend strictly on probability calculations, because the basis for making these calculations does not exist.

The operational meaning of the REH

Departures from the secular growth rate are the result of changes in discretionary expenditures by households, government, and the business sector. The decision to increase or decrease such expenditures depends primarily on one's view of the future. Because of uncertainty—the unpredictability of future events—expectations are continuously revised on the basis of new information. More important, such expectations or anticipations are often wrong. It is the deviation between an expectation of future economic activity and the actual unfolding of that future which causes a continuous revision in discretionary expenditures. The cyclical turbulence we observe in the economy is often the result of disappointed expectations.

Because of the obvious importance of uncertainty in economic decision-making, economists need to build macroeconomic models which describe more accurately the way in which expectations are formed. Whether the assumption of rational expectations fulfills this need and improves on the conventional assumption of adaptive expectations is a hotly debated question. Certainly, the REH does not imply that information is rationally used, but that economic agents form expectations of future activity by computing the expected (mean) values of those economic variables which are to be forecasted. The argument assumes that these expectations, which are generated by computing subjective probabilities, are equivalent to the forecasts based on objective probabilities (that is, frequency calculations or sampling experiments) which are generated from economic theory.

As Ben Friedman describes the process in a recent article in the *Journal of Monetary Economics*, "economic agents not only observe or know in advance the values of certain economic variables but also draw on the basis of these values inferences which are identical to the inferences of the processes which generate the actual outcomes." In other words, economic agents in the REH world have an economic model, have knowledge of the actual probability distributions which govern the behavior of the model, believe it to be accurate, know the true coefficients, and know how to solve them. Furthermore, they have a consistent set of forecasts with regard to the future values of the exogenous variables and error terms in the model.

The classical implications—the absence of an inflation-unemployment trade-off and the ineffectiveness of stabilization policies—emerge in rational expectations models because those models strongly require complete adjustment between expected and realized values. Typically, the deviation of output from its long-run trend depends on the deviation between current and expected price. By assumption, the information necessary to compute the expected values is available. Uncertainty is eliminated by taking the mathematical expectations (mean values) of *known* probability distributions and using the resulting certainty equivalents in forecasting. The unknown is reduced to perfect foresight. It is no surprise that such models yield the classical properties: by assumption the deviation between actual and expected price is ruled out. Economic agents are never fooled by policy-makers, since anticipations are always realized. As Friedman points out, such models should be viewed as long-run equilibrium models in which all adjustments are completed. Long-run equilibrium solutions provide a conceptual glimpse of an economy which

The Effectiveness of Anticipated Policy

Martin Neil Baily

Rational expectations theorists argue that private economic decisions are altered when the decision-makers anticipate monetary and fiscal policy actions. Martin Baily agrees with this view, but suggests that the implication of it is not necessarily to offset systematic policy. He argues first that the economy has become much more stable since the advent of active stabilization policies. He then describes some changes in the response of the private sector to business-cycle fluctuations. These changes may actually assist the goals of policy by making the private economy itself more stable.

WILL THE INITIATION OF active macroeconomic stabilization policies change the behavior of the private sector? If so, what will these changes be? And what are their implications for the design and effectiveness of stabilization policy?

Whether people anticipate policy and whether this matters are widely debated questions at present. The underlying issue is whether the sum of individual actions serves to maximize welfare in the absence of coordinating actions from a central authority. If the only cause of the business cycle is surprise events and if the private economy can itself act quickly to restore full-employment equilibrium following any initial shock, then policy actions are probably at best unnecessary and at worst undesirable. In such a context, it is natural to think of the private sector acting to minimize the impact of policy, to counteract its intent, just as most people minimize their liability for income taxes.

Post-Keynesian models often cite random shocks as the initiators of the business cycle, but stress the inability of the private economy to restore full employment in the short run. In this context it is more natural to think of the private sector welcoming the impact of policy and perhaps even reinforcing its effects. Since the view of the business cycle taken here is in the post-Keynesian tradition, the conclusions, not surprisingly, differ from those derived from more classical assumptions.

The rationality of expectations is the aspect of recent classical models that has received the most attention. But other assumptions are more crucial to the findings about policy, and they are much harder to accept. In particular, flexibility of prices is required in order that equilibrium be restored quickly after some disturbance.[1] To the extent that stickiness of wages or prices is caused by illusion or arbitrariness, rational expectations should rule it out. However, recent theories of wage and price setting and long-standing theories of imperfect markets have provided at least the beginnings of a reconciliation of rationality and stickiness. The persistence of wage and price inflation through recessionary periods is a fact to which theory must adapt.

THE CLIMATE OF GREATER STABILITY

The Federal Deposit Insurance Corporation is a remarkable institution. Prior to its existence, bank failures and runs on banks were very common. Since it came into being it has rarely had to pay out. Other things have not been equal, of course, but the fact that deposits are insured changes the behavior of depositors in a way that induces greater stability in the banking system. Fears of a run on the bank can become self-fulfilling as depositors scramble to withdraw funds. Even if an individual knows for a fact that a bank is basically sound, he is not being irrational to hurry to the teller's window for his money once the rush starts.

The analogy to the existence of stabilization policy is not exact, but it has some validity. If everyone believes that major depression and runaway inflation can be controlled, these events become less likely. A recession will not induce the same panicky cutbacks in investment or employemnt; an inflation will not induce the same flight from money and financial assets.

Deposit insurance aims at averting bank failures, but stabilization policy attempts to go beyond this—to smooth output fluctuations. The more stable the economic environment the fewer the economic resources that have to be devoted to contingency planning, to adjusting schedules, and to designing for flexibility. For example, a production process that may be the least-cost one when operations are near capacity may be a very high-cost one when capacity is underutilized. Greater stability of demand then permits the use of the least-cost process. Furthermore, when private individuals are risk averse, stabilization yields a tremendous gain. If the overall economic environment can be made less uncertain, a general gain in welfare will result.

Is there any sign that stabilization policy has actually produced greater stability? The Employment Act of 1946 marked an important turning point. It expressed the political will to avoid recession or depression, and the Keynesian revolution in macroeconomic theory held that stabilization policy could be the instrument of that will. The figure simply plots the rate of growth of real gross national product for the period 1901–76 while Table 1 gives some means and standard deviations for the GNP gap, unemployment, and inflation. The broad outlines of the story are familiar. But the change in the amplitude of cyclical fluctuations is surprisingly dramatic. The impact of the 1946 act is not seen immediately, but from about 1948 on the change is clear from the figure. The figure also reveals that the magnitude of the swings in the Great Depression were not so unusual as one might have thought. It is the sequence of three successive sharp downturns that marks off this period. Serious instability is evidenced even as late as 1946 itself, when the abrupt reduction in war-related expenditure resulted in a 12 percent decline in real GNP.

Table 1 shows that the standard deviation of GNP around its trend and the standard deviation of the unemployment rate are both higher in all early periods than they were in all later ones.[2] Some of the

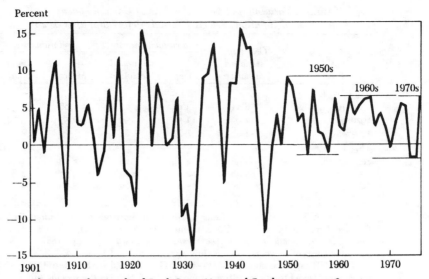

Percent

The Rate of Growth of Real Gross National Product, 1901–76
SOURCES: U.S. Bureau of the Census, *Historical Statistics of the United States: Colonial Times to 1970*, Pt. 1 (Government Printing Office, 1975), Series F3; *Economic Report of the President*, January 1977, p. 188; *Survey of Current Business*, vol. 57(July 1977), Table 1.2.

difference may be attributable to greater errors in the data for the earlier periods, but the general picture is the same even without relying on such data. For example, Schumpeter gives evidence of sharp booms and slumps going back all through the nineteenth century.[3] These swings appeared to last for several years and were not perceived as uncorrelated movements around a full-employment equilibrium.

The rate of inflation, as measured by the consumer price index, has also varied less in the postwar period. But the average rate of inflation has been higher, especially in the years 1966–76. Price stability has not been achieved.

Table 1 and the figure give only crude evidence. But for what it is worth, it is consistent with the view that the Keynesian revolution taught us how to stabilize the real variables of output and unemployment but not how to combine low and stable unemployment with price stability. The same figures present a challenge to anyone trying to make the case that policy can and should control the price level, but has no influence on real variables.

It is important to make a full accounting of the changes that took place in the way economic policy is made. Before World War II it was thought that raising taxes to balance the budget in a recession and allowing "unsound" banks to fail were both neutral or laissez-faire policies. Understanding how to avoid destabilizing the economy and enacting social programs that automatically stabilized it were both at least as important as was learning how to use discretionary policy.

Finally, two qualifications are in order. First, the postwar period has not been uniformly stable. The erosion of confidence during 1973–75 was an important reversal of trend. Second, cyclical instability is by no means the only form of serious uncertainty for firms; shifts in comparative advantage are another. The point remains that one major source of instability has been ameliorated.

TABLE 1. *Variability of GNP, the Rate of Unemployment, and
the Rate of Inflation, Selected Periods before and after 1946*

Period	GNP gap,[a] standard deviation	Unemployment rate		Inflation rate[b]	
		Mean	Standard deviation	Mean	Standard deviation
Before 1946					
1900–16, 1920–29	6.21	4.95	2.23	1.06	4.56
1920–41	12.99	11.52	7.59	−0.57	5.74
1900–45	13.58	7.77	6.51	1.86	6.11
After 1946					
1948–61	3.38	4.79	1.29	2.14	2.68
1962–73	2.46	4.74	0.88	3.37	1.84
1966–76	2.26	5.25	1.66	5.54	2.56
1946–76	3.56	4.95	1.34	3.84	3.60

SOURCE: U.S. Bureau of the Census, *Historical Statistics of the United States:
Colonial Times to 1970*, Pt. 1 (Government Printing Office, 1975), Series F3, D9,
D87, E135; *Economic Report of the President, January 1977*, pp. 188, 221, 242;
Survey of Current Business, vol. 57 (July 1977), p. S-8 and Table 1.2.

[a] The GNP gap is defined as (GNP—trend GNP)/trend GNP, where trend GNP
is computed from fitting a logarithmic time trend to GNP over the specific subperiod.
Values are for real GNP.

[b] The inflation rate is measured by the consumer price index.

HOW HAS THE BUSINESS COMMUNITY REACTED TO THE CHANGED CLIMATE?

A review of the business press from 1946 to the present was
undertaken.[4] The aim was to assess the evolving attitudes of the
business community to the overall climate of greater stability and to
the economic problems of the 1970s. Three phases will be distinguished. The first is from 1948 until the beginning of the 1960s
(leaving aside the immediate postwar years); the second from the
beginning of the 1960s through 1971; the third since 1971.

Even as early as 1946, the business community showed considerable awareness of the aims of stabilization policy and the mechanisms by which it might work. In 1946, *Business Week* discussed in
detail the Employment Act and the formation of the Council of Economic Advisers. However, the general tone throughout this period
was very cautious. There was great fear of budget deficits, a mistrust
of government intervention of any kind, a fear of letting inflation get
out of hand, and a general skepticism about whether policy really
could do anything to help smooth the cycle. The independence of
the Federal Reserve was viewed as extremely desirable, largely
because its governors were trusted to resist the inflationary printing
press more than was the Treasury, which was viewed as too political.

The second phase of the postwar period covered the activist and
generally expansionist policies followed during the 1960s. In its
March 17, 1962, issue, *Business Week* commented: "John F. Kennedy is beginning to show what kind of President he intends to be.
. . . He will be a president who intervenes overtly and systematically in areas of the United States economy that, in theory at least,
always operated on their own. . . . All modern presidents have
intervened in the economy to some extent. The distinctive thing
about the Kennedy brand of intervention is that it has been accepted
as a conscious and consistent policy." The rapid growth with low

inflation in the mid-1960s was to a considerable extent attributed to the activist policy measures. Even the skeptics, who had been given to frequent complaints about the "Keynesian nonsense," began to speak of a consensus concerning the benefits of using fiscal and monetary policies to control the economy.

The third phase, beginning in 1971, is the hardest one to characterize. Clearly, there has been a change in the climate since the 1960s in terms of both policymaking itself and the reactions to it. Policymakers have displayed much more concern with inflation, and the confidence of businessmen in the desirability of policy has waned. But expectations have not returned to what they were in the old days. In the 1970s, there remains a view that the path of the economy is governed by an interaction between the endogenous economy and policy actions and that policy has tremendous importance. "The fundamental cause of recession and high unemployment is not . . . history, but inflation. Inflation can cause recession in two basic ways. *The first (and most common) has to do with government actions,* while the second . . . [is that] if inflation is virulent enough, it will cause recession directly, by draining purchasing power enough to retard consumption significantly."[5]

The current decade is a complex time for policymaking, and a simple story will not suffice to explain it. The main theme has been the fight against inflation, by mild recession, by controls, and by tolerating a very high level of unemployment. The business press reveals an almost obsessive concern with predicting policy. Nevertheless, they made some wrong guesses. When sales began to fall in 1973–74, the business community did not quite believe policymakers would sit on their hands and allow a deep recession. Once it became clear that they would, however, the consensus developed (correctly) that the recovery would be slow. The fear of inflation would (and did) restrain any powerful measures toward stimulus.

Any review of this kind is necessarily subjective. But the division into three reasonably distinct phases seems justified. The 1940s and 1950s were a period of learning about what policy can do—for both the private sector and the policymakers. During the 1960s, people had considerable confidence in stabilization policy and a belief that it was a major factor in determining output. Policy shifted emphasis in the 1970s, and a good deal of enthusiasm was lost, but it was still seen as a major factor in determining output.

THE EFFECT OF CHANGING ATTITUDES ON BUSINESS decisions

Evidence confirms that the changes in business attitudes described above were reflected in shifts in business behavior.[6] A given fluctuation in output or sales has induced different responses in three important decisions variables of firms—employment, inventories, and investment—depending upon the postwar phase in which it occurred.

What signs of the changes in the expectational environment would be expected? If policy has smoothed cyclical fluctuations, increased the probability of a return to full employment, and reduced the probability of extreme outcomes, firms will view a given short-run change in output as less likely to persist or intensify. The adjustment of employment and investment to short-run movements in output will, therefore, be less complete. Firms will be more willing to take a long view. Despite a downturn, they will continue to invest; and they will tend more to hold onto their workers. Similarly, they will react less to upturns. Output changes will still have an impact, but it will become less pronounced.

THE RESPONSE OF EMPLOYMENT

When an individual firm is struck by a downturn or an upturn in demand, the way it reacts depends importantly on whether the change is expected to continue, intensify, or be reversed in the near future. The firm can react with some combination of three actions: laying off or hiring workers, varying hours of work per worker, and increasing or decreasing inventories. Each element of the decision costs something. Hiring, firing, and training costs are incurred directly by firms when employment is varied. Income uncertainty and the disutility of overtime are costs faced by workers when either employment or hours are varied. They become costs for the firm to the extent that firms must compensate workers for them with higher base wage rates or overtime premiums.

Holding inventories allows a gap between production and sales, but at the cost of interest expenses and storage charges. Firms may also hold excess labor rather than piling up unsold inventories. This labor hoarding may take the form of payment for more hours than employees actually provide or of requiring less intense effort from employees during downturns.

Quarterly data on output and employment for the private non-farm economy were examined over various periods between 1948 and 1976. The response of employment to output is strikingly different during the period 1948–61 than it is in later periods. The size of the response is different and, to a lesser extent, so is the speed. In the 1948–61 period, employment changed roughly one for one with output, allowing for a year to adjust. Most of the adjustment of employment occurs in the current and the following quarter. The results after 1961 look very different. The adjustment of employment to output changes is significantly less than equi-proportional. The response of employment in the same and the following quarter, in particular, is dramatically reduced.

These findings are, therefore, consistent with the view that once firms had learned of the amelioration of the business cycle (i.e., after 1961), they were more willing to retain employees in the face of an output decline. They expected that business would pick up again fairly quickly and the workers would be needed again.

It was noted earlier that the 1970s marked a shift in policy toward fighting inflation. In 1975, firms expected an extended recession. Retaining employees other than those required for current production needs looked less desireable in 1975 than in the 1960s. The findings for the period including the 1975 recession do show a return to a somewhat more complete adjustment of employment to output.

THE RESPONSE OF INVENTORIES

An efficient firm compares the costs of varying employment with the cost of using inventories to adjust the gap between sales and production in the short run. If firms after 1961 are varying employment less in response to a given output variation compared with earlier years, as the preceding section suggested, then they are changing behavior at the employment-output margin, and consistent change at the inventory-sales margin can be expected.

Furthermore, any change since 1948 in the relation between a distributed lag of past sales and firms' expectations of future sales also should show up. Specifically, a short-run increase in sales will raise expected sales by a smaller amount after 1961. Similarly, a fall in sales will lower expected sales by less.

To examine this, the relation between business inventories and final sales is considered. Again, there are substantial differences between the 1948–61 period and the later periods.

The descriptive picture does look consistent with the changes described above. After 1961, firms take a longer view when incorporating information about current and past sales into an expected sales estimate. And they are more willing to meet increases or decreases in sales by inventory adjustment (thereby reducing the extent of employment changes following a change in product demand).

THE RESPONSE OF ORDERS FOR PRODUCERS DURABLES

The accelerated resonse of investment to changes in output has been seen as a major determinant of the business cycle and as a potentially important source of dynamic instability in the economy. The simple accelerator says that the level of investment depends upon the change in real output. Growth in output then stimulates a high rate of investment demand, which feeds back to induce further growth in output. In most econometric work the simple accelerator is assumed to be softened in its effects by lags and by the impact of changes in the cost of capital. If producers' expectations have altered because of the existence of stabilization policy, then the parameters of the accelerator will alter. Producers will not change their desired stock of capital as much in response to short-run fluctuations in output.

The MIT-Penn-SSRC Quarterly Econometric Model estimates new orders for producers' durable equipment using a flexible accelerator equation. The way in which the parameters of this equation have changed over time was examined. After 1961, the amount of "acceleration" was markedly lower than in earlier years. That is to say, a given change in business output induced a smaller and slower response in orders for new equipment after 1961. As was true for employment, the period including the 1975 recession does show some erosion of confidence.

CONCLUSION

Two main strands run through recent thinking concerning the interactions between stabilization policy and private economic behavior. The first is that private economic behavior will be altered by the existence of active policy. The second is that policy will become ineffective if it is anticipated. This paper has offered support for the first of these ideas and has disagreed with the second. The results generally indicate that the shortrun response of the economy has become more stable. When the private sector anticipates stabilizing policies, the task of those policies is made easier, not harder. Rather than abandoning the use of monetary and fiscal policy to keep the economy on an even keel, we urgently need to find ways of combining a stable GNP with price stability.

1. The concept of price flexibility has to be defined relative to some time period. It is asserted here that the price level (or the rate of inflation) responds so sluggishly when there is deficient aggregate demand that it would take several years for the economy to restore equilibrium on its own (even assuming there is a stable adjustment). This is a period long enough for policy to be effective.

2. The "standard deviation" is a measure of variability. The larger it is the more the particular series has fluctuated.

3. Joseph A. Schumpeter, *Business Cycles: A Theoretical, Historical, and Statistical Analysis of the Capitalist Process*, vols. 1 and 2 (McGraw-Hill, 1939).

4. Two Yale undergraduates, Jon Friedman and Kathy Sheehan, surveyed *Business Week* and the *Commercial and Financial Chronicle* for me. Their reports were supplemented by some reviewing of my own.

5. Irwin L. Kellner, "Quarterly Business Conditions Analysis," *Business Report* (Manufacturers Hanover Trust, June 1977). (Emphasis added.)

6. In the paper from which this extract is drawn, the evidence presented is econometric. Only a summary of the findings is given here.

The Monetarist Controversy or, Should We Forsake Stabilization Policies?

Franco Modigliani

In recent years and especially since the onset of the current depression, the economics profession and the lay public have heard a great deal about the sharp conflict between "monetarists and Keynesians" or between "monetarists and fiscalists." The difference between the two "schools" is generally held to center on whether the money supply or fiscal variables are the major determinants of aggregate economic activity, and hence the most appropriate tool of stabilization policies.

My central theme is that this view is quite far from the truth, and that the issues involved are of far greater practical import. There are in reality no serious analytical disagreements between leading monetarists and leading nonmonetarists. Milton Friedman was once quoted as saying, "We are all Keynesians, now," and I am quite prepared to reciprocate that "we are all monetarists"—if by monetarism is meant assigning to the stock of money a major role in determining output and prices. Indeed, the list of those who have long been monetarists in this sense is quite extensive, including among other John Maynard Keynes as well as myself, as is attested by my 1944 and 1963 articles.

In reality the distinguishing feature of the monetarist school and the real issues of disagreement with nonmonetarists is not monetarism, but rather the role that should probably be assigned to stabilization policies. Nonmonetarists accept what I regard to be the fundamental practical message of *The General Theory*: that a private enterprise economy using an intangible money *needs* to be stabilized, *can* be stabilized, and therefore *should* be stabilized by appropriate monetary and fiscal policies. Monetarists by contrast take the view that there is no serious need to stabilize the economy; that even if there were a need, it could not be done, for stabilization policies would be more likely to increase than to decrease instability; and, at least some monetarists would, I believe, go so far as to hold that, even in the unlikely event that stabilization policies could on balance prove beneficial, the government should not be trusted with the necessary power.

What has led me to address this controversy is the recent spread of monetarism, both in a simplistic, superficial form and in the form of growing influence on the practical conduct of economic policy, which influence, I shall argue presently, has played at least some role in the economic upheavals of the last three years.

In what follows then, I propose first to review the main arguments bearing on the *need* for stabilization policies, that is, on the likely extent of instability in the absence of such policies, and then to examine the issue of the supposed destabilizing effect of pursuing stabilization policies. My main concern will be with instability generated by the traditional type of disturbances—demand shocks. But before I am through, I will give some consideration to the difficult problems

*Presidential address delivered at the eighty-ninth meeting of the American Economic Association, Atlantic City, New Jersey, September 17, 1976. The list of those to whom I am indebted for contributing to shape the ideas expressed above is much too large to be included in this footnote. I do wish, however, to single out two lifetime collaborators to whom my debt is especially large, Albert Ando and Charles Holt. I also wish to express my thanks to Richard Cohn, Rudiger Dornbusch, and Benjamin Friedman for their valuable criticism of earlier drafts, and to David Modest for carrying out the simulations and other computations mentioned in the text.

raised by the newer type of disturbance—supply shocks.

I. The Keynesian Case for Stabilization Policies

A. *The General Theory*

Keynes' novel conclusion about the need for stabilization policies, as was brought out by the early interpreters of *The General Theory* (for example, John Hicks, the author, 1944), resulted from the interaction of a basic contribution to traditional monetary theory—liquidity preference—and an unorthodox hypothesis about the working of the labor market—complete downward rigidity of wages.

Because of liquidity preference, a change in aggregate demand, which may be broadly defined as any event that results in a change in the market clearing or equilibrium rate of interest, will produce a corresponding change in the real demand for money or velocity of circulation, and hence in the real stock of money needed at full employment. As long as wages are perfectly flexible, even with a constant nominal supply, full employment could and would be maintained by a change of wages and prices as needed to produce the required change in the real money supply—though even in this case, stability of the price level would require a countercyclical monetary policy. But, under the Keynesian wage assumption the classical adjustment through prices can occur only in the case of an increased demand. In the case of a decline, instead, wage rigidity prevents the necessary increase in the real money supply and the concomitant required fall in interest rates. Hence, if the nominal money supply is constant, the initial equilibrium must give way to a new stable one, characterized by lower output and by an involuntary reduction in employment, so labeled because it does not result from a shift in notional demand and supply schedules in terms of real wages, but only from an insufficient real money supply. The nature of this equilibrium is elegantly captured by the Hicksian *IS-LM* paradigm, which to our generation of economists has become almost as familiar as the demand-supply paradigm was to earlier ones.

This analysis implied that a fixed money supply far from insuring approximate stability of prices and output, as held by the traditional view, would result in a rather unstable economy, alternating between periods of protracted unemployment and stagnation, and bursts of inflation. The extent of downward instability would depend in part on the size of the exogenous shocks to demand and in part on the strength of what may be called the Hicksian mechanism. By this I mean the extent to which a shift in *IS*, through its interaction with *LM*, results in some decline in interest rates and thus in a change in income which is smaller than the original shift. The stabilizing power of this mechanism is controlled by various parameters of the system. In particular, the economy will be more unstable the greater the interest elasticity of demand for money, and the smaller the interest responsiveness of aggregate demand. Finally, a large multiplier is also destabilizing in that it implies a larger shift in *IS* for a given shock.

However, the instability could be readily counteracted by appropriate stabilization policies. Monetary policy could change the nominal supply of money so as to *accommodate* the change in real demand resulting from shocks in aggregate demand. Fiscal policy, through expenditure and taxes, could *offset* these shocks, making full employment consistent with the initial nominal money stock. In general, both monetary and fiscal policies could be used in combination. But because of a perceived uncertainty in the response of demand to changes in interest rates, and because changes in interest rates through monetary policy could meet difficulties and substantial delays related to expectations (so-called liquidity traps), fiscal policy was regarded as having some advantages.

B. *The Early Keynesians*

The early disciples of the new Keynesian gospel, still haunted by memories of the Great Depression, frequently tended to outdo Keynes' pessimism about potential instability. Concern with liquidity traps fostered the view that the demand for money was highly interest elastic; failure to distinguish between the short- and long-run marginal propensity to save led to overestimating the long-run saving rate, thereby fostering concern with stagnation, and to underestimating the short-run propensity, thereby exaggerating the short-run multiplier. Interest rates were supposed to affect, at best, the demand for long-lived fixed investments, and the interest elasticity was deemed to be low. Thus, shocks were believed to produce a large response. Finally, investment demand was seen as capriciously controlled by "animal spirits," thus providing an important source of shocks. All this justified calling for very active stabilization policies. Furthermore, since the very circumstances which produce a large response to demand shocks also produce a large response to *fiscal* and a small response to *monetary* actions, there was a tendency to focus on fiscal policy as the main tool to keep the economy at near full employment.

C. *The Phillips Curve*

In the two decades following *The General Theory*, there were a number of developments of the Keynesian system including dynamization of the model, the stress on taxes versus expenditures and the balanced budget multiplier, and the first attempts at estimating the critical parameters through econometric techniques and models. But for present purposes, the most important one was the uncovering of a "stable" statistical relation between the rate of change of wages and the rate of unemployment, which has since come to be known as the Phillips curve. This relation, and its generalization by Richard Lipsey to allow for the effect of recent inflation, won wide acceptance even before an analytical underpinning could be provided for it, in part because it could account for the "puzzling" experience of 1954 and 1958, when wages kept rising despite the substantial rise in unemployment. It also served to dispose of the rather sterile "cost push" – "demand pull" controversy.

Acceptance of the Phillips curve relation implied some significant changes in the Keynesian framework which partly escaped notice until the subsequent monetarists' attacks. Since the rate of change of wages decreased smoothly with the rate of unemployment, there was no longer a unique Full Employment but rather a whole family of possible equilibrium rates, each associated with a different rate of inflation (and requiring, presumably, a different long-run growth of money). It also impaired the notion of

a stable underemployment equilibrium. A fall in demand could still cause an initial rise in unemployment but this rise, by reducing the growth of wages, would eventually raise the real money supply, tending to return unemployment to the equilibrium rate consistent with the given long-run growth of money.

But at the practical level it did not lessen the case for counteracting lasting demand disturbances through stabilization policies rather than by relying on the slow process of wage adjustment to do the job, at the cost of protracted unemployment and instability of prices. Indeed, the realm of stabilization policies appeared to expand in the sense that the stabilization authority had the power of choosing the unemployment rate around which employment was to be stabilized, though it then had to accept the associated inflation. Finally, the dependence of wage changes also on past inflation forced recognition of a distinction between the short- and the long-run Phillips curve, the latter exhibiting the long-run equilibrium rate of inflation implied by a *maintained* unemployment rate. The fact that the long-run tradeoff between unemployment and inflation was necessarily less favorable than the short-run one, opened up new vistas of "enjoy-it-now, pay-later" policies, and even resulted in an entertaining literature on the political business cycle and how to stay in the saddle by riding the Phillips curve (see for example, Ray Fair, William Nordhaus).

II. The Monetarists' Attack

A. *The Stabilizing Power of the Hicksian Mechanism*

The monetarists' attack on Keynesianism was directed from the very beginning not at the Keynesian framework as such, but at whether it really implied a need for stabilization. It rested on a radically different empirical assessment of the value of the parameters controlling the stabilizing power of the Hicksian mechanism and of the magnitude and duration of response to shocks, given a stable money supply. And this different assessment in turn was felt to justify a radical downgrading of the *practical relevance* of the Keynesian framework as distinguished from its *analytical validity*.

Liquidity preference was a fine contribution to monetary theory but in practice the responsiveness of the demand for money, and hence of velocity, to interest rates, far from being unmanageably large, was so small that according to a well-known paper by Milton Friedman (1969), it could not even be detected empirically. On the other hand, the effect of interest rates on aggregate demand was large and by no means limited to the traditional fixed investments but quite pervasive. The difficulty of detecting it empirically resulted from focusing on a narrow range of measured market rates and from the fact that while the aggregate could be counted on to respond, the response of individual components might not be stable. Finally, Friedman's celebrated contribution to the theory of the consumption function (1957) (and my own work on the life cycle hypothesis with Richard Brumberg and others, reviewed by the author, 1975) implied a very high short-run marginal propensity to save in response to transient disturbances to income and hence a small short-run multiplier.

All this justified the conclusion that (i) though demand shocks might qualitatively work along the lines described by Keynes, quantitatively the Hicks mechanism is so strong that their impact would be *small* and *transient*, provided the stock of money was kept on a steady growth path; (ii) fiscal policy actions, like other demand shocks, would have *minor* and *transitory* effects on demand, while changes in money would produce *large* and *permanent* effects on money income; and, therefore, (iii) the observed instability of the economy, which was anyway proving moderate as the postwar period unfolded, was most likely the result of the unstable growth of money, be it due to misguided endeavors to stabilize income or to the pursuit of other targets, which were either irrelevant or, in the case of balance of payments goals, should have been made irrelevant by abandoning fixed exchanges.

B. *The Demise of Wage Rigidity and the Vertical Phillips Curve*

But the most serious challenge came in Friedman's 1968 Presidential Address, building on ideas independently put forth also by Phelps (1968). Its basic message was that, despite ap-

pearances, wages were in reality perfectly flexible and there was accordingly *no* involuntary unemployment. The evidence to the contrary, including the Phillips curve, was but a statistical illusion resulting from failure to differentiate between price changes and *unexpected* price changes.

Friedman starts out by reviving the Keynesian notion that, at any point of time, there exists a unique full-employment rate which he labels the "natural rate." An unanticipated fall in demand in Friedman's competitive world leads firms to reduce prices and also output and employment along the short-run marginal cost curve—unless the nominal wage declines together with prices. But workers, failing to judge correctly the current and prospective fall in prices, misinterpret the reduction of nominal wages as a cut in *real* wages. Hence, assuming a positively sloped supply function, they reduce the supply of labor. As a result, the effective real wage rises to the point where the resulting decline in the demand for labor matches the reduced supply. Thus, output falls not because of the decline in demand, but because of the entirely voluntary reduction in the supply of labor, in response to erroneous perceptions. Furthermore, the fall in employment can only be temporary, as expectations must soon catch up with the facts, at least in the absence of new shocks. The very same mechanism works in the case of an increase in demand, so that the responsiveness of wages and prices is the same on either side of the natural rate.

The upshot is that Friedman's model also implies a Phillips-type relation between inflation, employment or unemployment, and past inflation,—provided the latter variable is interpreted as a reasonable proxy for expected inflation. But it turns the standard explanation on its head: instead of (excess) employment causing inflation, it is (the unexpected component of) the rate of inflation that causes excess employment.

One very basic implication of Friedman's model is that the coefficient of price expectations should be precisely unity. This specification implies that whatever the shape of the short-run Phillips curve—a shape determined by the relation between expected and actual price changes, and by the elasticity of labor supply with respect to the perceived real wage—the long-run curve *must be vertical*.

Friedman's novel twist provided a fresh prop for the claim that stabilization policies are not really needed, for, with wages flexible, except possibly for transient distortions, the Hicksian mechanism receives powerful reinforcement from changes in the real money supply. Similarly, the fact that full employment was a razor edge provided new support for the claim that stabilization policies were bound to prove destabilizing.

C. *The Macro Rational Expectations Revolution*

But the death blow to the already badly battered Keynesian position was to come only shortly thereafter by incorporating into Friedman's model the so-called rational expectation hypothesis, or *REH*. Put very roughly, this hypothesis, originally due to John Muth, states that rational economic agents will endeavor to form expectations of relevant future variables by making the most efficient use of all information provided by past history. It is a fundamental and fruitful contribution that has already found many important applications, for example, in connection with speculative markets, and as a basis for some thoughtful criticism by Robert Lucas (1976) of certain features of econometric models. What I am concerned with here is only its application to macro-economics, or *MREH*, associated with such authors as Lucas (1972), Thomas Sargent (1976), and Sargent and Neil Wallace (1976).

The basic ingredient of *MREH* is the postulate that the workers of Friedman's model hold rational expectations, which turns out to have a number of remarkable implications: (i) errors of price expectations, which are the only source of departure from the natural state, cannot be avoided but they can only be short-lived and random. In particular, there cannot be persistent unemployment above the natural rate for this would imply high serial correlation between the successive errors of expectation, which is inconsistent with rational expectations; (ii) any attempts to stabilize the economy by means of stated monetary or fiscal rules are bound to be totally ineffective because their effect will be

fully discounted in rational expectations; (iii) nor can the government successfully pursue *ad hoc* measures to offset shocks. The private sector is already taking care of any anticipated shock; therefore government policy could conceivably help only if the government information was better than that of the public, which is impossible, by the very definition of rational expectations. Under these conditions, *ad hoc* stabilization policies are most likely to produce instead further destabilizing shocks.

These are clearly remarkable conclusions, and a major *re*discovery—for it had all been said 40 years ago by Keynes in a well-known passage of *The General Theory*:

> If, indeed, labour were always in a position to take action (and were to do so), whenever there was less than full employment, to reduce its money demands by concerted action to whatever point was required to make money so abundant relatively to the wage-unit that the rate of interest would fall to a level compatible with full employment, we should, in effect, have monetary management by the Trade Unions, aimed at full employment, instead of by the banking systems. [p. 267]

The only novelty is that *MREH* replaces Keynes' opening "if" with a "since."

If one accepts this little amendment, the case against stabilization policies is complete. The economy is inherently pretty stable—except possibly for the effect of government messing around. And to the extent that there is a small residual instability, it is beyond the power of human beings, let alone the government, to alleviate it.

III. How Valid Is the Monetarist Case?

A. *The Monetarist Model of Wage Price Behavior*

In setting out the counterattack it is convenient to start with the monetarists' model of price and wage behavior. Here one must distinguish between the model as such and a specific implication of that model, namely that the long-run Phillips curve is vertical, or, in substance, that, in the long run, money is neutral. That conclusion, by now, does not meet serious objection from nonmonetarists, at least as a first approximation.

But the proposition that other things equal, and given time enough, the economy will eventually adjust to any indefinitely maintained stock of money, or nth derivative thereof, can be derived from a variety of models and, in any event, is of very little practical relevance, as I will argue below. What is unacceptable, because inconsistent with both micro and macro evidence, is the specific monetarist model set out above and its implication that all unemployment is a voluntary, fleeting response to transitory misperceptions.

One may usefully begin with a criticism of the Macro Rational Expectations model and why Keynes' "if" should not be replaced by "since." At the logical level, Benjamin Friedman has called attention to the omission from *MREH* of an explicit learning model, and has suggested that, as a result, it can only be interpreted as a description not of short-run but of long-run equilibrium in which no agent would wish to recontract. But then the implications of *MREH* are clearly far from startling, and their policy relevance is almost nil. At the institutional level, Stanley Fischer has shown that the mere recognition of long-term contracts is sufficient to generate wage rigidity and a substantial scope for stabilization policies. But the most glaring flaw of *MREH* is its inconsistency with the evidence: if it were valid, deviations of unemployment from the natural rate would be small and transitory—in which case *The General Theory* would not have been written and neither would this paper. Sargent (1976) has attempted to remedy this fatal flaw by hypothesizing that the persistent and large fluctuations in unemployment reflect merely corresponding swings in the natural rate itself. In other words, what happened to the United States in the 1930's was a severe attack of contagious laziness! I can only say that, despite Sargent's ingenuity, neither I nor, I expect, most others at least of the nonmonetarists' persuasion are quite ready yet to turn over the field of economic fluctuations to the social psychologist!

Equally serious objections apply to Friedman's modeling of the commodity market as a perfectly competitive one—so that the real wage rate is continuously equated to the *short-run* marginal product of labor—and to his treatment of labor as a homogenous commodity traded in an auction market, so that, at the going wage, there never is any excess demand by firms or excess supply by workers. The inadequacies of this model as a useful formalization of present day Western economies are so numerous that only a few of the major ones can be mentioned here.

Friedman's view of unemployment as a voluntary reduction in labor supply could at best provide an explanation of variations in labor force—and then only under the questionable assumption that the supply function has a significantly positive slope—but cannot readily account for changes in unemployment. Furthermore, it cannot be reconciled with the well-known fact that *rising* unemployment is accompanied by a fall, not by a *rise* in quits, nor with the role played by temporary layoffs to which Martin Feldstein has recently called attention. Again, his competitive model of the commodity market, accepted also in *The General Theory*, implies that changes in real wages, adjusted for long-run productivity trend, should be significantly negatively correlated with cyclical changes in employment and output and with changes in money wages. But as early as 1938, John Dunlop showed that this conclusion was rejected by some eighty years of British experience and his results have received some support in more recent tests of Ronald Bodkin for the United States and Canada. Similar tests of my own, using quarterly data, provide striking confirmation that for the last two decades from the end of the Korean War until 1973, the association of trend adjusted real compensations of the private nonfarm sector with either employment or the change in nominal compensation is prevailingly positive and very significantly so.

If, in the process, vacancies rise above a critical level, or "natural rate," firms will endeavor to reduce them by outbidding each other, thereby raising the rate of change of wages. Thus, as long as jobs and vacancies remain above, and unemployment remains below, some critical level which might be labeled the "noninflationary rate" (see the author and Lucas Papademos, 1975), wages and prices will tend to accelerate. If, on the other hand, jobs fall below, and unemployment rises above, the noninflationary rate, firms finding that vacancies are less than optimal —in the limit the unemployed queuing outside the gate will fill them instantly—will have an incentive to reduce their relative wage offer. But in this case, in which too much labor is looking for too few jobs, the trend toward a sustained decline in the rate of growth of wages is likely to be even weaker than the corresponding acceleration when too many jobs are bidding for too few people. The main reason is the nonhomogeneity of labor. By far the largest and more valuable source of labor supply to a firm consists of those already employed who are not readily interchangeable with the unemployed and, in contrast with them, are concerned with protecting their earnings and not with reestablishing full employment. For these reasons, and because the first to quit are likely to be the best workers, a reduction of the labor force can, within limits, be accomplished more economically, not by reducing wages to generate enough quits, but by firing or, when possible, by layoffs which insure access to a trained labor force when demand recovers. More generally, the inducement to reduce relative wages to eliminate the excess supply is moderated by the effect that such a reduction would have on quits and costly turnover, even when the resulting vacancies can be readily filled from the ranks of the unemployed. Equally relevant are the consequences in terms of loss of morale and good will, in part for reasons which have been elaborated by the literature on implicit contracts (see Robert Gordon). Thus, while there will be some tendency for the rate of change of wages to fall, the more so the larger the unemployment—at least in an economy like the United States where there are no overpowering centralized unions—that tendency is severely damped.

And whether, given an unemployment rate significantly and persistently above the noninflationary level, the rate of change of wages would, eventually, tend to turn negative and decline without bound or whether it would tend to an asymptote is a question that I doubt the empirical

evidence will ever answer. The one experiment we have had—the Great Depression—suggests the answer is negative, and while I admit that, for a variety of reasons, that evidence is muddied, I hope that we will never have the opportunity for a second, clean experiment.

In any event, what is really important for practical purposes is not the long-run equilibrium relation as such, but the speed with which it is approached. Both the model sketched out and the empirical evidence suggest that the process of acceleration or deceleration of wages when unemployment differs from the noninflationary rate will have more nearly the character of a crawl than of a gallop. It will suffice to recall in this connection that there was excess demand pressure in the United States at least from 1965 to mid-1970, and during that period the growth of inflation was from some 1.5 to only about 5.5 percent per year. And the response to the excess supply pressure from mid-1970 to early 1973, and from late 1974 to date was equally sluggish.

B. *The Power of Self-Stabilizing Mechanisms: The Evidence from Econometric Models*

There remains to consider the monetarists' initial criticism of Keynesianism, to wit, that even without high wage flexibility, the system's response to demand shocks is small and short-lived, thanks to the power of the Hicksian mechanism. Here it must be acknowledged that every one of the monetarists' criticisms of early, simpleminded Keynesianism has proved in considerable measure correct.

With regard to the interest elasticity of demand for money, post-Keynesian developments in the theory of money, and in particular, the theoretical contributions of William Baumol, James Tobin, Merton Miller, and Daniel Orr, point to a modest value of around one-half to one-third, and empirical studies (see for example, Stephen Goldfeld) are largely consistent with this prediction (at least until 1975!). Similarly, the dependence of consumption on long-run, or life cycle, income and on wealth, together with the high marginal tax rates of the postwar period, especially the corporate tax, and leakages through imports, lead to a rather low estimate of the multiplier.

Last but not least, both theoretical and empir-

244

ical work, reflected in part in econometric models, have largely vindicated the monetarist contention that interest effects on demand are pervasive and substantial. Thus, in the construction and estimation of the MIT-Penn-Social Science Research Council (MPS) econometric model of the United States, we found evidence of effects, at least modest, on nearly every component of aggregate demand. One response to money supply changes that is especially important in the MPS, if somewhat controversial, is via interest rates on the market value of all assets and thus on consumption.

There is, therefore, substantial agreement that in the United States the Hicksian mechanism is fairly effective in limiting the effect of shocks, and that the response of wages and prices to excess demand or supply will also work *gradually* toward eliminating largely, if not totally, any effect on employment. But in the view of nonmonetarists, the evidence overwhelmingly supports the conclusion that the *interim* response is still of significant magnitude and of considerable duration, basically because the wheels of the offsetting mechanism grind slowly. To be sure, the first link of the mechanism, the rise in short-term rates, gets promptly into play and heftily, given the low money demand elasticity; but most expenditures depend on long-term rates, which generally respond but gradually, and the demand response is generally also gradual. Furthermore, while this response is building up, multiplier and accelerator mechanisms work toward amplifying the shock. Finally, the classical mechanism—the change in real money supply through prices—has an even longer lag because of the sluggish response of wages to excess demand.

These interferences are supported by simulations with econometric models like the MPS. Isolating, first, the working of the Hicksian mechanism by holding prices constant, we find that a 1 percent demand shock, say a rise in real exports, produces an impact effect on aggregate output which is barely more than 1 percent, rises to a peak of only about 2 percent a year later, and then declines slowly toward a level somewhat over 1.5 percent.

These results, which are broadly confirmed by other econometric models, certainly do not support the view of a highly unstable economy in which fiscal policy has powerful and everlasting effects. But neither do they support the monetarist view of a highly stable economy in which shocks hardly make a ripple and the effects of fiscal policy are puny and fast vanishing.

IV. The Record of Stabilization Policies: Stabilizing or Destabilizing

A. *Was Postwar Instability Due to Unstable Money Growth?*

At this point, of course, monetarists will object that, over the postwar period, we have *not* had a constant money growth policy and will hint that the observed instability can largely be traced to the instability of money. The only way of meeting this objection squarely would be, of course, to rerun history with a good computer capable of calculating 3 percent at the helm of the Fed.

A more feasible, if less conclusive approach might be to look for some extended periods in which the money supply grew fairly smoothly and see how the economy fared. Combing through our post-Korean War history, I have been able to find just two stretches of several years in which the growth of the money stock was relatively stable, whether one chooses to measure stability in terms of percentage deviations from a constant growth or of dispersion of four-quarter changes. It may surprise some that one such stretch occurred quite recently and consists of the period of nearly four years beginning in the first quarter of 1971 (see the author and Papademos, 1976). During this period, the average growth was quite large, some 7 percent, but it was relatively smooth, generally well within the 6 to 8 percent band. The average deviation from the mean is about .75 percent. The other such period lasted from the beginning of 1953 to the first half of 1957, again a stretch of roughly four years. In sharp contrast to the most recent period, the average growth here is quite modest, only about 2 percent; but again, most four-quarter changes fell well within a band of two percentage points, and the average deviation is again .7. By contrast, during the remaining 13-year stretch from mid-1957 to the end of 1970, the variability of money growth was roughly twice as large if measured by the average deviation of four quarter changes, and some five times larger if measured by the percentage deviation of the money stock from a constant growth trend.

How did the economy fare in the two periods of relatively stable money growth? It is common knowledge that the period from 1971 to 1974, or from 1972 to 1975 if we want to allow a one-year lag for money to do its trick, was distinctly the most unstable in our recent history, marked by sharp fluctuations in output and wild gyrations of the rate of change of prices. As a result, the average deviation of the four-quarter changes in output was 3.3 percent, more than twice as large as in the period of less stable money growth. But the first stretch was also marked by well above average instability, with the contraction of 1954, the sharp recovery of 1955, and the new contraction in 1958, the sharpest in postwar history except for the present one. The variability of output is again 50 percent larger than in the middle period.

To be sure, in the recent episode serious exogenous shocks played a major role in the development of prices and possibly output, although the same is not so readily apparent for the period 1953 to 1958. But, in any event, such extenuating circumstances are quite irrelevant to my point; for I am not suggesting that the stability of money was the major cause of economic instability—or at any rate, not yet! All I am arguing is that (i) there is no basis for the monetarists' suggestion that our postwar instability can be traced to monetary instability—our most unstable periods have coincided with periods of relative monetary stability; and (ii) stability of the money supply is not enough to give us a stable economy, precisely because there are exogenous disturbances.

B. *The Overall Effectiveness of Postwar Stabilization Policies*

But even granted that a smooth money supply will not produce a very stable world and that there is therefore room for stabilization policies, monetarists will still argue that we should nonetheless eschew such policies. They claim, first, that allowing for unpredictably variable lags and unforeseeable future shocks, we do not know enough to successfully design stabilization policies, and second, that the government would surely be incapable of choosing the appropriate policies or be politically willing to provide timely enforcement. Thus, in practice, stabilization policies will result in destabilizing the economy much of the time.

This view is supported by two arguments, one logical and one empirical. The logical argument is the one developed in Friedman's Presidential Address (1968). An attempt at stabilizing the economy at full employment is bound to be destabilizing because the full employment or natural rate is not known with certainty and is subject to shifts in time; and if we aim for the incorrect rate, the result must perforce be explosive inflation or deflation. By contrast, with a constant money supply policy, the economy will automatically hunt for, and eventually discover, that shifty natural rate, wherever it may be hiding.

This argument, I submit, is nothing but a debating ploy. It rests on the preposterous assumption that the only alternative to a constant money growth is the pursuit of a very precise unemployment target which will be adhered to indefinitely no matter what, and that if the target is off in the second decimal place, galloping inflation is around the corner. In reality, all that is necessary to pursue stabilization policies is a rough target range that includes the warranted rate, itself a range and not a razor edge; and, of course, responsible supporters of stabilization policies have long been aware of the fact that the target range needs to be adjusted in time on the basis of forseeable shifts in the warranted range, as well as in the light of emerging evidence that the current target is not consistent with price stability. It is precisely for this reason that I, as well as many other nonmonetarists, would side with monetarists in strenuous opposition to recent proposals for a target unemployment rate rigidly fixed by statute (although there is nothing wrong with Congress committing itself and the country to work toward the eventual achievement of some target unemployment rate through *structural* changes rather than aggregate demand policies).

Clearly, even the continuous updating of targets cannot guarantee that errors can be avoided altogether or even that they will be promptly recognized; and while errors persist, they will result in some inflationary (or deflationary) pressures. But the growing inflation to which Friedman refers is, to repeat, a crawl not a gallop. One may usefully recall in this connection the experience of 1965–70 referred to earlier, with the further remark that the existence of excess employment was quite generally recognized at the time, and failure to eliminate it resulted overwhelmingly from political considerations and not from a wrong diagnosis.[3]

There remains then only the empirical issue: have stabilization policies worked in the past and will they work in the future? Monetarists think the answer is negative and suggest, as we have seen, that misguided attempts at stabilization, especially through monetary policies, are responsible for much of the observed instability. The main piece of evidence in support of this contention is the Great Depression, an episode well documented through the painstaking work of Friedman and Anna Schwartz, although still the object of dispute (see, for example, Peter Temin). But in any event, that episode while it may attest to the power of money, is irrelevant for present purposes since the contraction of the money supply was certainly not part of a comprehensive stabilization program in the post-Keynesian sense.

When we come to the relevant postwar period, the problem of establishing the success or failure of stabilization policies is an extremely taxing one. Many attempts have been made at developing precise objective tests, but in my view, none of these is of much value, even though I am guilty of having contributed to them in one of my worst papers (1964). Even the most ingenious test, that suggested by Victor Argy, and relying on a comparison of the variability of income with that of the velocity of circulation, turns out to be valid only under highly unrealistic restrictive assumptions.

But though the search for unambiguous quantitative tests has so far yielded a meager crop, there exists a different kind of evidence in favor of Keynesian stabilization policies which is impressive, even if hard to quantify. To quote one of the founding fathers of business cycle analysis, Arthur Burns, writing in 1959, "Since 1937 we have had five recessions, the longest of which lasted only 13 months. There is no parallel for such a sequence of mild—or such a sequence of brief—contractions, at least during the past hundred years in our country" (p. 2). By now we can add to that list the recessions of 1961 and 1970.

There is, furthermore, evidence that very similar conclusions hold for other industrialized countries which have made use of stabilization policies; at any rate that was the prevailing view among participants to an international conference held in 1967 on the subject, "Is the business cycle obsolete?" (see Martin Bronfenbrenner, editor). No one seemed to question the greater postwar stability of all Western economies—nor is this surprising when one recalls that around that time business cycle specialists felt so threatened by the new-found stability that they were arguing for redefining business cycles as fluctuations in the *rate of growth* rather than in the *level* of output.

It was recognized that the reduced severity of fluctuations might in part reflect structural changes in the economy and the effect of stronger built-in stabilizers, inspired, of course, by the Keynesian analysis. Furthermore, the greater stability in the United States, and in other industrialized countries, are obviously not independent events. Still, at least as of the time of that conference, there seemed to be little question and some evidence that part of the credit for the greater stability should go to the conscious and on balance, successful endeavor at stabilizing the economy.

V. The Case of Supply Shocks and the 1974–76 Episode

A. *Was the 1974 Depression Due to Errors of Commission or Omission?*

In pointing out our relative postwar stability and the qualified success of stabilization policies, I have carefully defined the postwar period as ending somewhere in 1973. What has happened since that has so tarnished the reputation of economists? In facing this problem, the first question that needs to be raised is whether the recent combination of unprecedented rates of inflation as well as unemployment must be traced to crimes of commission or omission. Did our monetary and fiscal stabilization policies misfire, or did we instead fail to use them?

We may begin by establishing one point that has been blurred by monetarists' blanket indictments of recent monetary policy: the virulent explosion that raised the four-quarter rate of inflation from about 4 percent in 1972 to 6.5 percent by the third quarter of 1973, to 11.5 percent in 1974 with a peak quarterly rate of 13.5, can in no way be traced to an excessive, or to a disorderly, growth of the money supply. As already mentioned, the average rate of money growth from the beginning of 1970 to the second half of 1974 was close to 7 percent. To be sure, this was a high rate and could be expected sooner or later to generate an undesirably high inflation —but how high? Under any reasonable assumption one cannot arrive at a figure much above 6 percent. This might explain what happened up to the fall of 1973, but not from the third quarter of 1973 to the end of 1974, which is the really troublesome period. Similarly, as was indicated above, the growth of money was reasonably smooth over this period, smoother than at any other time in the postwar period, staying within a 2 percent band. Hence, the debacle of 1974 can just not be traced to an erratic behavior of money resulting from a misguided attempt at stabilization.

Should one then conclude that the catastrophe resulted from too slavish an adherence to a stable growth rate, forsaking the opportunity to use monetary policy to stabilize the economy? In one sense, the answer to this question must in my view be in the affirmative. There is ample ground for holding that the rapid contraction that set in toward the end of 1974, on the heels of a slow decline in the previous three quarters, and which drove unemployment to its 9 percent peak, was largely the result of the astronomic rise in interest rates around the middle of the year. That rise in turn was the unavoidable result of the Fed's stubborn refusal to accommodate, to an adequate extent, the exogenous inflationary shock due to oil, by letting the money supply growth exceed the 6 percent rate announced at the beginning of the year. And this despite repeated warnings about that unavoidable result (see, for example, the author 1974).

Monetarists have suggested that the sharp recession was not the result of too slow a monetary growth throughout the year, but instead of the deceleration that took place in the last half of 1974, and early 1975. But this explanation just does not stand up to the facts. The fall in the quarterly growth of money in the third and fourth quarters was puny, especially on the basis of revised figures now available: from 5.7 percent in the second to 4.3 and 4.1—hardly much larger than the error of estimate for quarterly rates! To be sure, in the first quarter of 1975 the growth fell to .6 percent. But, by then, the violent contraction was well on its way—between September 1974 and February 1975, industrial production fell at an annual rate of 25 percent. Furthermore, by the next quarter, monetary growth had resumed heftily. There is thus no way the monetarist proposition can square with these facts unless their long and variable lags are so variable that they sometimes turn into substantial leads. But even then, by anybody's model, a one-quarter dip in the growth of money could not have had a perceptible effect.

B. *What Macro Stabilization Policies Can Accomplish, and How*

But recognizing that the adherence to a stable money growth path through much of 1974 bears a major responsibility for the sharp contraction does not per se establish that the policy was mistaken. The reason is that the shock that hit the system in 1973–74 was not the usual type of demand shock which we have gradually learned to cope with, more or less adequately. It was, instead, a supply or price shock, coming from a cumulation of causes, largely external. This poses an altogether different stabilization problem. In particular, in the case of demand shocks, there exists in principle an ideal policy which avoids all social costs, namely to offset completely the shock thus, at the same time, stabilizing employment and the price level. There may be disagreement as to whether this target can be achieved and how, but not about the target itself.

But in the case of supply shocks, there is no miracle cure—there is no macro policy which can both maintain a stable price level and keep employment at its natural rate. To maintain stable prices in the face of the exogenous price shock, say a rise in import prices, would require a fall in all domestic output prices; but we know of no macro policy by which domestic prices can be made to fall except by creating enough slack, thus putting downward pressure on wages. And the amount of slack would have to be substantial in view of the sluggishness of wages in the face of unemployment. If we do not offset the exogenous shock completely, then the initial burst, even if activated by an entirely transient rise in some prices, such as a once and for all deterioration in the terms of trade, will give rise to further increases, as nominal wages rise in a vain attempt at preserving real wages; this secondary reaction too can only be cut short by creating slack. In short, once a price shock hits, there is no way of returning to the initial equilibrium except after a painful period of both above equilibrium unemployment and inflation.

There are, of course, in principle, policies other than aggregate demand management to which we might turn, and which are enticing in view of the unpleasant alternatives offered by demand management. But so far such policies, at least those of the wage-price control variety, have proved disappointing. The design of better alternatives is probably the greatest challenge presently confronting those interested in stabilization. However, these policies fall outside my present concern. Within the realm of aggregate demand management, the only choice open to society is the cruel one between alternative feasible paths of inflation and associated paths of unemployment, and the best the macroeconomist can offer is policies designed to approximate the chosen path.

In light of the above, we may ask: is it conceivable that a constant rate of growth of the money supply will provide a satisfactory response to price shocks in the sense of giving rise to an unemployment-inflation path to which the country would object least?

C. *The Monetarist Prescription: Or, Constant Money Growth Once More*

The monetarists are inclined to answer this question affirmatively, if not in terms of the country's preferences, at least in terms of the preferences they think it should have. This is evidenced by their staunch support of a continuation of the 6 percent or so rate of growth through 1974, 1975, and 1976.

Their reasoning seems to go along the following lines. The natural rate hypothesis implies that the rate of inflation can change only when employment deviates from the natural rate. Now suppose we start from the natural rate and some corresponding steady rate of inflation, which without loss of generality can be assumed as zero. Let there be an exogenous shock which initially lifts the rate of inflation, say, to 10 percent. If the Central Bank, by accommodating this price rise, keeps employment at the natural rate, the new rate of 10 percent will also be maintained and will in fact continue forever, as long as the money supply accommodates it. The only way to eliminate inflation is to increase unemployment enough, above the natural rate and for a long enough time, so that the cumulated reduction of inflation takes us back to zero. There will of course be many possible unemployment paths that will accomplish this. So the next question is: Which is the least undesirable?

The monetarist answer seems to be—and here I confess that attribution becomes difficult —that it does not make much difference because, to a first approximation, the cumulated amount of unemployment needed to unwind inflation is independent of the path. If we take more unemployment early, we need to take less later, and conversely. But then it follows immediately that the specific path of unemployment that would be generated by a constant money growth is, if not better, at least as good as any other. Corollary: a constant growth of money is a satisfactory answer to supply shocks just as it is to demand shocks—as well as, one may suspect, to any other conceivable illness, indisposition, or disorder.

D. *Why Constant Money Growth Cannot Be the Answer*

This reasoning is admirably simple and elegant, but it suffers from several flaws. The first one is a confusion between the price level and its rate of change. With an unchanged constant growth of the nominal money stock, the system will settle back into equilibrium not when the rate of inflation is back to zero but only when, in addition, the price level itself is back to its initial level. This means that when inflation has finally returned back to the desired original rate, unemployment cannot also be back to the original level but will instead remain above it as long as is necessary to generate enough deflation to offset the earlier cumulated inflation. I doubt that this solution would find many supporters and for a good reason; it amounts to requiring that none of the burden of the price shock should fall on the holder of long-term money fixed contracts—such as debts—and that all other sectors of society should shoulder entirely whatever cost is necessary to insure this result. But if, as seems to be fairly universally agreed, the social target is instead to return the system to the original rate of inflation—zero in our example—then the growth of the money supply cannot be kept constant. Between the time the shock hits and the time inflation has returned to the long-run level, there must be an additional increase in money supply by as much as the price level or by the cumulant of inflation over the path.

A second problem with the monetarists' argument is that it implies a rather special preference function that depends only on cumulated unemployment. And, last but not least, it requires the heroic assumption that the Phillips curve be not only vertical in the long run but also linear in the short run, an assumption that does not seem consistent with empirically estimated curves. Dropping this last assumption has the effect that, for any given social preference, there will be in general a unique optimal path. Clearly, for this path to be precisely that generated by a constant money growth, would require a miracle—or some sleight of the invisible hand!

criticism has had a salutary effect on reassessing what stabilization policies can and should do, and on trimming down fine-tuning ambitions. But their contention that postwar fluctuations resulted from an unstable money growth or that stabilization policies decreased rather than increased stability just does not stand up to an impartial examination of the postwar record of the United States and other industrialized countries. Up to 1974, these policies have helped to keep the economy reasonable stable by historical standards, even though one can certainly point to some occasional failures.

The serious deterioration in economic stability since 1973 must be attributed in the first place to the novel nature of the shocks that hit us, namely, supply shocks. Even the best possible aggregate demand management cannot offset such shocks without a lot of unemployment together with a lot of inflation. But, in addition, demand management was far from the best. This failure must be attributed in good measure to the fact that we had little experience or even an adequate conceptual framework to deal with such shocks; but at least from my reading of the record, it was also the result of failure to use stabilization policies, including too slavish adherence to the monetarists' constant money growth presciption.

We must, therefore, categorically reject the monetarist appeal to turn back the clock forty years by discarding the basic message of *The General Theory*. We should instead concentrate our efforts in an endeavor to make stabilization policies even more effective in the future than they have been in the past.

VI. Conclusion

To summarize, the monetarists have made a valid and most valuable contribution in establishing that our economy is far less unstable than the early Keynesians pictured it and in rehabilitating the role of money as a determinant of aggregate demand. They are wrong, however, in going as far as asserting that the economy is sufficiently shockproof that stabilization policies are not needed. They have also made an important contribution in pointing out that such policies might in fact prove destabilizing. This

[3]Friedman's logical argument against stabilization policies and in favor of a constant money growth rule is, I submit, much like arguing to a man from St. Paul wishing to go to New Orleans on important business that he would be a fool to drive and should instead get himself a tub and drift down the Mississippi: that way he can be pretty sure that the current will eventually get him to his destination; whereas, if he drives, he might make a wrong turn and, before he notices he will be going further and further away from his destination and pretty soon he may end up in Alaska, where he will surely catch pneumonia and he may never get to New Orleans!

REFERENCES

L. C. Andersen and K. M. Carlson, "A Monetarist Model for Economic Stabilization," *Fed. Reserve Bank St. Louis Rev.*, Apr. 1970, *52*, 7–25.

———— **and J. L. Jordan,** "Monetary and Fiscal Action: A Test of Their Relative Importance in Economic Stabilization," *Fed. Reserve Bank St. Louis Rev.*, Nov. 1968, *50*, 11–23.

V. Argy, "Rules, Discretion in Monetary Management, and Short-Term Stability," *J. Money, Credit, Banking*, Feb. 1971, *3*, 102–22.

W. J. Baumol, "The Transactions Demand for Cash: An Inventory Theoretic Approach," *Quart. J. Econ.*, Nov. 1952, *66*, 545–56.

R. G. Bodkin, "Real Wages and Cyclical Variations in Employment: A Reexamination of the Evidence," *Can. J. Econ.*, Aug. 1969, *2*, 353–74.

Martin Bronfenbrenner, *Is the Business Cycle Obsolete?*, New York 1969.

A. F. Burns, "Progress Towards Economic Stability," *Amer. Econ. Rev.*, Mar. 1960, *50*, 1–19.

J. T. Dunlop, "The Movement of Real and Money Wage Rates," *Econ. J.*, Sept. 1938, *48*, 413–34.

O. Eckstein and R. Brinner, "The Inflation Process in the United States," in Otto Eckstein, ed., *Parameters and Policies in the U.S. Economy*, Amsterdam 1976.

R. C. Fair, "On Controlling the Economy to Win Elections," unpub. paper, Cowles Foundation 1975.

M. S. Feldstein, "Temporary Layoffs in the Theory of Unemployment," *J. Polit. Econ.*, Oct. 1976, *84*, 937–57.

S. Fischer, "Long-term Contracts, Rational Expectations and the Optimal Money Supply Rule," *J. Polit. Econ.*, forthcoming.

B. M. Friedman, "Rational Expectations Are Really Adaptive After All," unpub. paper, Harvard Univ. 1975.

Milton Friedman, *A Theory of the Consumption Function*, Princeton 1957.

————, "The Role of Monetary Policy," *Amer. Econ. Rev.*, Mar. 1968, *58*, 1–17.

————, "The Demand for Money: Some Theoretical and Empirical Results," in his *The Optimum Quantity of Money, and Other Essays*, Chicago 1969.

———— **and A. Schwartz,** *A Monetary History of the United States 1867–1960*, Princeton 1963.

S. Goldfeld, "The Demand for Money Revisited," *Brookings Papers*, Washington 1973, *3*, 577–646.

R. J. Gordon, "Recent Developments in the Theory of Inflation and Unemployment," *J. Monet. Econ.*, Apr. 1976, *2*, 185–219.

J. R. Hicks, "Mr. Keynes and the "Classics"; A Suggested Interpretation," *Econometrica*, Apr. 1937, *5*, 147–59.

John Maynard Keynes, *The General Theory of Employment, Interest and Money*, New York 1935.

R. G. Lipsey, "The Relation Between Unemployment and the Rate of Change of Money Wage Rates in the United Kingdom, 1862–1957: A Further Analysis," *Economica*, Feb. 1960, *27*, 1–31.

M. Lovell, "Why Was the Consumer Feeling So Sad?," *Brookings Papers*, Washington 1975, *2*, 473–79.

R. E. Lucas, Jr., "Econometric Policy Evaluation: A Critique," *J. Monet. Econ.*, suppl. series, 1976, *1*, 19–46.

————, "Expectations and the Neutrality of Money," *J. Econ. Theory*, Apr. 1972, *4*, 103–24.

M. Miller and D. Orr, "A Model of the Demand for Money by Firms," *Quart. J. Econ.*, Aug. 1966, *80*, 413–35.

F. Modigliani, "Liquidity Preference and the Theory of Interest and Money," *Econometrica*, Jan. 1944, *12*, 45–88.

————, "New Development on the Oligopoly Front," *J. Polit. Econ.*, June 1958, *66*, 215–33.

————, "The Monetary Mechanism and Its Interaction with Real Phenomena," *Rev. Econ. Statist.*, Feb. 1963, *45*, 79–107.

————, "Some Empirical Tests of Monetary Management and of Rules versus Discretion," *J. Polit. Econ.*, June 1964, *72*, 211–45.

————, "The 1974 Report of the President's Council of Economic Advisers: A Critique of Past and Prospective Policies," *Amer. Econ. Rev.*, Sept. 1974, *64*, 544–77.

————, "The Life Cycle Hypothesis of Saving Twenty Years Later," in Michael Parkin, ed., *Contemporary Issues in Economics*, Manchester 1975.

—— and A. Ando, "The Relative Stability of Monetary Velocity and the Investment Multiplier," *Amer. Econ. Rev.*, Sept. 1965, *55*, 693–728.

—— and ——, "Impacts of Fiscal Actions on Aggregate Income and the Monetarist Controversy: Theory and Evidence," in Jerome L. Stein, ed., *Monetarism*, Amsterdam 1976.

—— and R. Brumberg, "Utility Analysis and the Consumption Function: Interpretation of Cross-Section Data," in Kenneth Kurihara, ed., *Post-Keynesian Economics*, New Brunswick 1954.

—— and L. Papademos, "Targets for Monetary Policy in the Coming Years," *Brookings Papers*, Washington 1975, *1*, 141–65.

—— and ——, "Monetary Policy for the Coming Quarters: The Conflicting Views," *New Eng. Econ. Rev.*, Mar./Apr. 1976, 2–35.

J. F. Muth, "Rational Expectations and the Theory of Price Movements," *Econometrica*, July 1961, *29*, 315–35.

W. D. Nordhaus, "The Political Business Cycle," *Rev. Econ. Stud.*, Apr. 1975, *42*, 169–90.

A. M. Okun, "Inflation: Its Mechanics and Welfare Costs," *Brookings Papers*, Washington 1975, *2*, 351–90.

D. O'Neill, "Directly Estimated Multipliers of Monetary and Fiscal Policy," doctoral thesis in progress, M.I.T.

L. Papademos, "Optimal Aggregate Employment Policy and Other Essays," doctoral thesis in progress, M.I.T.

Edmond S. Phelps, "Money-Wage Dynamics and Labor-Market Equilibrium," *J. Polit. Econ.*, July/Aug. 1968, *76*, 678–711.

—— et al., *Microeconomic Foundations of Employment and Inflation Theory*, New York 1970.

A. W. Phillips, "The Relation Between Unemployment and the Rate of Change of Money Wage Rates in the United Kingdom, 1861–1957," *Economica*, Nov. 1958, *25*, 283–99.

T. J. Sargent, "A Classical Macroeconomic Model for the United States," *J. Polit. Econ.*, Apr. 1976, *84*, 207–37.

—— and N. Wallace, "'Rational' Expectations, the Optimal Monetary Instrument, and the Optimal Money Supply Rule," *J. Polit. Econ.*, Apr. 1975, *83*, 241–57.

D. Starleaf and R. Floyd, "Some Evidence with Respect to the Efficiency of Friedman's Monetary Policy Proposals," *J. Money, Credit, Banking*, Aug. 1972, *4*, 713–22.

Peter Temin, *Did Monetary Forces Cause the Great Depression?*, New York 1976.

James Tobin, *Essays in Economics: Vol. 1, Macroeconomics*, Chicago 1971.

Money Wage Inflation:
The Endogeneity-Exogeneity Issue

Michael L. Wachter and Susan M. Wachter

Modern theories of wage inflation derive from the late 1950s, when the Phillips curve emerged in the literature to dominate, or influence, three alternative approaches to the topic.[1] The first approach is the neoclassical quantity theory of money, adjusted to explain wages instead of prices. In this model, wage inflation rates simply follow changes in the money supply. Most recently, this view has been sharpened into the accelerationist theory, which is discussed below. The second view is based on Keynes' "wage-rigidity" argument.[2] In the 1930s, Keynes argued that money wage rates were relatively sticky, especially on the down side.

The third approach builds on the Phillips curve notion, which argued that wage inflation rates were essentially determined by the unemployment rate. This view differs from the quantity theory approach in that the latter would not allow any real variables, such as unemployment, to influence the money wage rate (at least in the long run).

The Phillips Curve

The debate is most easily developed for expositional purposes within the framework of the Phillips curve apparatus. The original Phillips curve position developed during the 1950s, first in England and then in the United States.[3] Advanced as an empirical observation, it argues three important points. First, and contrary to the standard textbook treatment of supply and demand, prices in general, and wages in particular, should be expected to increase even in the face of unutilized capacity or unemployment. Positive unemployment rates are associated with positive inflation rates, as shown in Figure 1. Second, the slope of the wage inflation-unemployment trade-off is convex. Third, the Phillips curve trade-off is stable. Indeed, the original British test of the model found an important degree of stability over several decades. It is this last hypothesis which has been subject to considerable disagreement.

The finding of inflation at positive unemployment rates and the existence of a convex slope for the Phillips curve are justified by a number of arguments. Most importantly, the unemployment rate in the Phillips curve is really introduced as a proxy for "excess supply," the supply of workers minus the demand for workers. Unemployment, however, only describes the individuals who are actually seeking jobs. Covering the supply side, it ignores the demand side or the

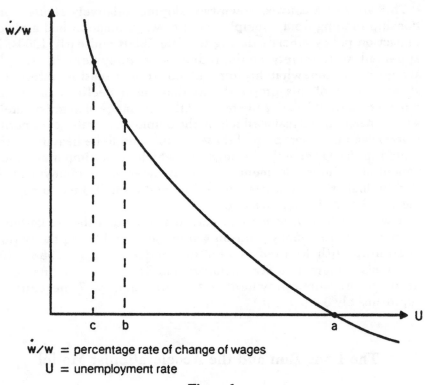

$\dot{w}/w$ = percentage rate of change of wages
U = unemployment rate

Figure 1.

number of jobs which are unfilled. That jobs can be unfilled while workers are unemployed is a consequence of mismatches between workers and jobs. These mismatches can involve occupations or skills, industries, or geographical locations. As an extreme case, an unemployed laborer in Boston cannot fill a vacancy for a surgeon in San Francisco.[4]

Specifically, the number of job vacancies grows disproportionately to the number of unemployed as aggregate demand increases. As unemployment declines to low levels, the unemployment pool is *increasingly composed of unskilled workers* who are difficult to place, young workers who have high turnover rates (as they search to find an occupation or firm they might be interested in staying with), workers in general who are between jobs, and individuals who seek only part-time or intermittent work. But increases in excess aggregate demand create numerous *new skilled jobs*, and jobs for those who want steady work, as well as lower-skilled and part-time jobs. In terms of Figure 1, at points to the left of point b, for example, the number of unemployed skilled workers is relatively small. Consequently, most jobs created by a demand expansion will remain unfilled and become job vacancies. Small reductions in unemployment to the left of point b are thus associated with large increases in job vacancies and this change will cause a significant rise in wage inflation. In other words, the true measure of tightness in the labor market—which includes job vacancies—is seriously understated by measured unemployment. To compensate for this, the Phillips curve is drawn as a convex curve with an increasingly steep slope at lower levels of measured unemployment.[5]

This view of a convex, downward-sloping, relatively *stable* relationship running from unemployment to wage inflation had a major impact on policy officials during the late 1950s and early 1960s. It appeared as if society could reduce unemployment by simply accepting a somewhat higher but constant inflation rate. The attractiveness of this proposal was that small declines in unemployment, once it had already reached the low range of approximately 4 to 4.5 percent, had major effects on the employment rates of minority workers and the poor. Both of these groups tend to be heavily represented in the lower-skilled categories, which are an important component of the unemployment pool at low rates of unemployment. A slightly higher inflation rate seemed indeed a small price to pay for the social gains in employment.

It was this theory, at least in part, that provided the background support for the Kennedy-Johnson war on poverty. During the period beginning with Kennedy's election and ending in 1968 with Johnson's full term in office, monetary and fiscal policy engineered a drop in the unemployment rate from nearly 7 percent to approximately 3.3 percent.[6]

The Long Run and the Accelerationist Model

Contrary to policy expectations, the Phillips curve turned out to be highly unstable. More specifically, as the government attempted to hold unemployment at a low level, the Phillips curve shifted upward. An explanation for this inflationary behavior of the economy during the late 1960s and early 1970s was offered in the context of a neoclassical, accelerationist model.[7]

One basic feature of the model is that, in the long run, there is no trade-off between inflation and unemployment; the long-run Phillips curve is vertical. There exists, at any one moment in time, a single unemployment rate, often termed the "natural" unemployment rate, which represents the equilibrium rate for the economy. For example, in Figure 2 the equilibrium rate is denoted by the vertical Phillips curve U_E. This "natural" or "noninflationary" unemployment rate, U_E, is not zero. It includes structural unemployment, which occurs when a worker's productivity, and hence the wage offered to him by an employer, is lower than the wage at which he wishes to work, or, in the presence of minimum wage laws, the wage at which he can work. It also includes frictional unemployment, which occurs when vacancies in some sectors balance unemployment in others. It is argued that these forms of unemployment cannot be reduced through expansive monetary and fiscal policy, except temporarily, and then at a cost of continuously increasing inflation rates. Thus, if unemployment is set by the monetary and fiscal authorities below U_E, inflation will be constantly increasing, while if it is set above U_E, the rate of inflation will fall continuously.

The mechanism through which this process occurs involves the changing of inflationary *expectations*. It is argued that the downward-sloping Phillips curve of Figure 1 is only a short-run trade-off, and that it is predicated on the prevalence of a certain level of inflationary expectations in the economy. When inflationary expectations shift, so does the short-run Phillips curve. As shown in Figure 2, each short-run curve crosses the vertical line U_E at the point where

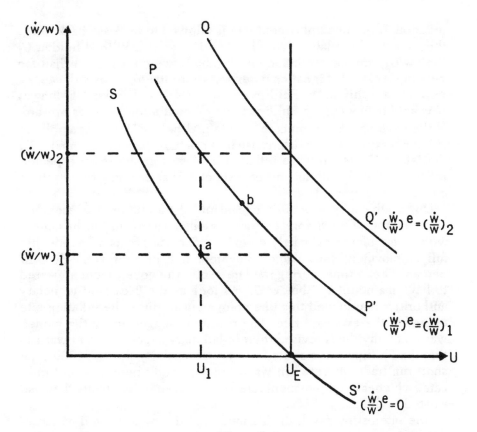

Figure 2.

the rate of wage inflation (or price inflation) is equal to the expected rate of wage (or price) inflation. For example, assuming, to begin with, no inflationary expectations, the economy will operate along the Phillips curve denoted by SS', which goes through U_E at the zero inflation level. If the economy is at U_E on SS', wage inflation will remain at the zero rate. To the left of the U_E line on the Phillips curve, the actual rate of inflation, $\dot{w}/w$, is greater than the anticipated rate, $(\dot{w}/w)^e$. Thus, if monetary and fiscal authorities expand aggregate demand so that unemployment moves temporarily below U_E, to U_1, for example, actual inflation will rise above the expected zero inflation rate to $(\dot{w}/w)_1$. Eventually, however, the expected inflation must adjust to the now positive inflation rate, and if $(\dot{w}/w)_1$ is maintained long enough, this will become the new expected inflation rate. As the expected rate of wage inflation increases, the short-run Phillips curve shifts upward to the right. In fact, it will continue to shift until the expected rate of inflation has increased enough so that it is equal to the actual rate of inflation, denoted $(\dot{w}/w)_1$, and the new short-run Phillips curve is now PP'. As PP' indicates, inflation will continue at the expected level $(\dot{w}/w)_1$ even when actual unemployment is equal to the equilibrium level of unemployment, U_E, at which there is no excess demand in labor markets.

The crucial result in this model, then, is that in order to stop the inflation rate from increasing above $(\dot{w}/w)_1$, once $(\dot{w}/w)_1$ becomes anticipated, the fiscal and monetary authorities must allow unemployment to increase from U_1 back to U_E. At U_E, zero excess demand again prevails and the expected rate is equal to the actual rate of wage inflation. If the unemployment rate is allowed to increase back to U_E, the new steady inflation rate of $(\dot{w}/w)_1$ is reached. With U held at U_1 (below U_E), the new inflation rate is $(\dot{w}/w)_2$, which is greater than the new higher level of inflationary expectations $(\dot{w}/w)_1$. This will cause a new upward shift in the Phillips curve to (QQ') and, indeed, as long as U is held below U_E, the Phillips trade-off continuously shifts upward. If the government attempts to maintain U below U_E (for example, at U_1), it necessitates a persistent rise in the actual wage inflation rate. To the left of U_E, actual wage inflation is always greater than expected inflation. The result magnifies expectations, causing the Phillips curve to shift upward.

During the long economic expansion of the 1960s, the economy was, in terms of the theory, operating along a short-run Phillips curve with $(w/w)^e$ of approximately 4 percent. (This suggests a "reasonable full employment" at an unemployment rate of approximately 5.15 percent.) For a time, during the late 1960s, the government appeared to have maintained U below U_E. As long as the fiscal and monetary authorities maintained this unemployment posture, the inflation rate exceeded the expected rate. The result, as suggested by the model, was that individuals revised their inflationary expectations upward so that the Phillips curve shifted upward as well. By the late 1960s, the short-run trade-off between wage inflation and unemployment indicated a higher unemployment rate for any given inflation rate than had existed in the early 1960s.

One interesting result of this model, which was viewed as somewhat of a puzzle when it first occurred in the early 1970s, is that inflation and unemployment increase together. Although this phenomenon appears to defy the downward-sloping short-run Phillips curve, this is not the case. For example, suppose the economy was at point a on Figure 2 when Nixon first entered office. As is well known, by then the policy makers had decided to slow down the economy in order to reduce the inflation rate. The problem was that the Phillips curve was in the process of shifting upward, catching up to the high inflation rates of previous years, at the time that unemployment was increasing. The result was that the economy followed a path from a to, for example, point b. The concurrent observation of increasing inflation and unemployment is not surprising.

In the accelerationist model, as in the standard downward-sloping Phillips curve, wages are basically endogenous. It is the level of aggregate demand which pushes the system. The difference between the two models is that when the long-run curve is downward-sloping (the predominant view of the 1960s), the government has a choice of unemployment-inflation rate combinations, in the long run and in the short run. In the accelerationist model, aggregate demand policies cannot alter the unemployment rate in the long run. The rate of inflation is determined by the level of inflationary expectations which, in turn, mirrors *past* aggregate demand conditions.

Neoclassical Explanations of the Short-run Trade-off

The accelerationists and traditional Phillips curve theorists disagree on the possibility of a permanent unemployment-inflation trade-off, but agree that a short-run trade-off does exist.[8] They have different views, however, on the explanation behind the short-run trade-off. Generally, in the accelerationist view, the mechanism which allows unemployment to vary in the short run is the transitory deviation between the expected and actual inflation rates. A crucial role is played by the inflationary expectations held by workers looking for jobs or by suppliers of services in general. The view is that these suppliers (including workers as suppliers of labor) are fooled by the inflation. While they can easily see that their wages are rising during an inflation, it is more difficult for them to judge that the overall wage or price level is rising as well. Hence, workers, for example, believe that their relative or real wages are rising and this encourages them to accept employment that they would not otherwise accept. This leads to the observation that falling unemployment is correlated with above-average rates of inflation (in other words, with actual inflation greater than perceived inflation).[9]

These theories place a fair amount of stress on the uncertainty of workers with respect to the current distribution of wages across jobs and across goods. This uncertainty exists because "it is costly to gather information." The lack of information involves the present, rather than the past or the future. A problem with this analysis is that it seems unlikely that the costs of gathering information about the present are so high that workers' perceptions are likely to stray far from the actual events. For example, a worker need not search over all possible jobs to gain a relatively clear perception of his wage possibilities.

There are alternative mechanisms which can explain the existence of a short-run Phillips curve and do not depend on the price deception of workers.[10] In fact, the devleopment of an institutionally oriented wage determination theory which can be used to support a model of exogenously determined wages (as discussed in the following section) can also be used to explain wage rigidities and the existence of a short-run Phillips curve.

This explanation, as will be seen below, is a neoclassical one which, in some ways, bridges the gap between the traditional Phillips curve and the accelerationist approaches. As in the original statement of the Phillips curve model, the lagged responsiveness of wages and prices to market pressure causes sectoral imbalances with vacancies in some sectors and unemployment in others. In the presence of these sectoral imbalances, changes in aggregate demand will generate a short-run Phillips curve. As in the accelerationist model, the lag in price adjustment is only a short-term phenomenon, and prices will eventually be adjusted with employment returning to normal. Thus again, only a short-run Phillips curve is entailed.[11]

There are a number of explanations for a lag in the reaction of wages and prices to market pressures. The traditional example is the labor union which bargains with a firm and sets a three-year contract. Although the contract allows for wage increases each year of the contract, the size of each increase is predetermined. Unions and firms may thus be viewed as forming expectations about likely labor market conditions over the fixed term of the contract. Clearly, the union wants at least to maintain its wage position relative to nonunionized workers or to other unions, but it does not want to "guess" too high because of the layoffs that may result. Management, of course, faces a similar problem, but from another perspective. Unlike the previous case, in which individuals were uncertain about the current distribution of wages and prices, the uncertainty in the bargaining model covers future labor market conditions.

Similar examples are easy to find on the product market side as well. Most business fixed investment requires long lead times between ordering the capital and its installation. In general, contracts are for a fixed price, perhaps allowing for some flexibility to cover a limited number of contingencies. Here again, buyers and sellers must make forecasts about the future and build these predictions into the contracts.[12]

The fixed contract, however, is only the proverbial tip of the iceberg. Most firms, whether or not they are unionized, follow a wage pattern in which wages do not respond immediately to market conditions. The rationale is inherent in the desire for an ongoing relationship between firms and their work forces. This arises, in a sense, because jobs, largely as a result of on-the-job training, tend to be highly specific to a given firm. As a consequence, these jobs do not have a direct demand and supply component in the external labor market. Rather, the jobs are part of the internal labor market of the firm, interconnected through a series of promotion ladders. Once workers are promoted, they receive a wage higher than the one which they could receive by quitting and starting at the entry level of a new firm. External market wages have their greatest impact on the firm through controlling the flow of new entrants to the firm, as well as by influencing the quit rate of new workers who have not yet received promotion increases. Because firms, for reasons of organizational efficiency, attempt to maintain their internal wage structures intact, external wage pressures on new workers will, over time, tend to spread throughout the firms.[13]

The importance of these labor market institutions is that they create a kind of inertia in the system. Changes in aggregate demand alter the rate of wage inflation, but these effects filter through a complex set of institutional arrangements of labor union contracts and internal labor market forces. Again, it should be stressed that this rigidity is not based on workers searching out information on the current distribution of wage offerings. Rather, due to complex institutional factors, prices and wages do not adjust rapidly to market pressures.

Because of the existence of lags in the wage and price adjustment process, output and employment (rather than wages and prices) adjust in response to changes in aggregate demand. This adjustment allows the unemployment rate to differ in the short run from its long-run equilibrium level and to vary with inflation in a manner which generates a short-run Phillips curve.

To illustrate, assume zero excess demand, $U = U_E$, and no inflationary expectations, $(\dot{w}/w)^e = 0$. Thus inflation is zero, with prices and wages falling in sectors with unemployment, and rising in sectors with vacancies. Eventually, prices and wages adjust so that these markets return to equilibrium with no unemployment or vacancies. In a growing, dynamic economy, however, new disequilibrium conditions continuously arise so that there is an ongoing amount of frictional unemployment and vacancies in the economy. In this setting, if the government expands aggregate demand, prices and wages rise at a faster rate in the sectors with vacancies, and the decline in prices and wages slows in the sectors with unemployment. Furthermore, in the sectors with unemployment, the increase in demand results in increased output and declines in unemployment. A Phillips curve is then observed.[14]

These various expectational, union contract, and internal labor market models provide an explanation for the distinction between the short- and long-run Phillips curves of Figure 2. A broad neoclassical model would encompass all of these elements. Their relative importance needs to be empirically determined.

A major result of analyzing the institutional framework of the labor (and product) markets is that a strong *prima facie* case is developed for long lags in the response of wage inflation to aggregate demand pressures. The exact length of the lags is ultimately an empirical question, but the institutional features suggest a fairly long lag. In addition to the potentially long adjustment process for unions and the internal labor market, the expectational element may generate considerable wage rigidity. For example, Milton Friedman, in originally developing the expectational framework for the accelerationist model, suggested that expectational lags could spread over decades. Thus, individuals' anticipations of inflation in the 1950s were still affected by the deflationary experience of the 1930s. In 1975, the inflation trend over the entire postwar period had to enter into the calculation of expectations.

[1] A. W. Phillips, "The Relation Between Unemployment and the Rate of Change of Money Wage Rates in the United Kingdom, 1862-1957," *Economica* 25 (November 1958): 283-299.

[2] John Maynard Keynes, *The General Theory of Employment, Interest, and Money* (London: Macmillan & Co., 1936).

[3] The literature on the Phillips curve is extensive. Much of the U.S. Phillips curve work follows the framework first adopted by George L. Perry, *Unemployment, Money Wage Rates, and Inflation* (Cambridge: Massachusetts Institute of Technology Press, 1966). The original Phillips curve for the U.S. was estimated by Paul A. Samuelson and Robert M. Solow, "Analytical Aspects of Anti-Inflationary Policy," *American Economic Review* 76 (August 1962): 379-414. For the theory of a long-run trade-off, see James Tobin, "Inflation and Unemployment," *American Economic Review* 52 (March 1972): 1-18.

[4] On the nonconvexity of the Phillips curve, see Albert Rees, *The Economics of Work and Pay* (New York: Harper & Row, 1973).

[5] The sectoral imbalance argument was advanced by Charles L. Schultze, "Recent Inflation in the United States," Joint Economic Committee Study Paper No. 1 (Washington, D.C.: Government Printing Office, September 1959). A second argument used to explain the finding of a convex Phillips curve is that wages are "sticky" in a downward direction. When unemployment is very high, there is excess supply in almost all occupational, geographical, and industrial labor markets. The tendency of money wages not to decline, or to decline only slightly, causes the Phillips curve to become very flat at high rates of unemployment.

[6] For a discussion of the Phillips curve in policy making, see *The Annual Report of the Council of Economic Advisors* (Washington, D.C.: Government Printing Office, mid-late 1960s).

[7] The current version of the accelerationist argument was advanced by Milton Friedman, "The Role of Monetary Policy," *American Economic Review* 58 (March 1968): 1-17. The model was developed in Edmund S. Phelps et al., *Microeconomic Foundations of Employment and Inflation Theory* (New York: Norton, 1970). For earlier statements of certain aspects of the model, see John R. Hicks, *The Theory of Wages* (London: Macmillan & Co., 1932), and see especially, William Fellner, "Demand Inflation, Cost Inflation, and Collective Bargaining," in Phillip D. Bradley, ed., *The Public Stake in Union Power* (Charlottesville: University of Virginia Press, 1959).

[8] This is not uniformly the case. Thomas J. Sargent and Neil Wallace, "'Rational' Expectations, the Optimal Monetary Instrument, and the Optimal Money Supply Rule," *Journal of Political Economy* 83 (April 1975): 241-257, argue (in a "super-neoclassical" model) that there is no downward-sloping Phillips curve in the short or the long run.

[9] Cf. Robert E. Lucas, Jr. and Leonard A. Rapping, "Real Wages, Employment, and Inflation," *Journal of Political Economy* 77 (September 1969): 257-305.

[10] A modern Keynesian view which combines a short-run Phillips curve and the absence of a neoclassical long-run trade-off is found in Axel Leijonhufvud, *On Keynesian Economics and the Economics of Keynes* (New York: Oxford University Press, 1968).

[11]See Stephen A. Ross and Michael L. Wachter, "Wage Determination, Inflation, and the Industrial Structure," *American Economic Review* 63 (September 1973): 675-692.

[12]For further discussion, see Arthur M. Okun, "Inflation: Its Mechanics and Welfare Costs," *Brookings Papers on Economic Activity* 2 (1975): 351-390.

[13]The internal labor market construct was developed in the 1950s. See John T. Dunlop, "The Tasks of Contemporary Wage Theory," in S. W. Taylor and F. C. Pierson, eds., *New Concepts in Wage Determination* (New York: McGraw-Hill, 1957), pp. 117-139. For a recent exposition, see Peter Doeringer and Michael Piore, *Internal Labor Markets and Manpower Analysis* (Lexington, Mass.: Heath, Lexington, 1971).

[14]It is not stable, however. Once the inflation is anticipated, it continues at the anticipated rate when labor markets are in balance, $U = U_E$. If U is maintained below U_E, inflation will continue to increase as in the accelerationist model.

The Effect of Monetary Policy on the Economy

Council of Economic Advisers

When the economy is operating near its long-term potential, an expansionary monetary policy raises real GNP and lowers unemployment temporarily. Wages and prices do not adjust immediately in response to a monetary expansion, but eventually they do adjust, and inflation begins to increase. If inflation increases to a level that instigates a subsequent sharp monetary tightening, a recession could be the ultimate result.

In the 1960s, many believed that the unemployment rate could be reduced permanently if only a higher rate of inflation was accepted. This belief was based largely on a negative relationship in historical data between the rate of inflation and the unemployment rate. Such historical data in the United States and other countries seemed to indicate that when inflation was higher, unemployment was lower, and *vice versa*. But the experience of the 1970s, with simultaneously rising inflation and unemployment (stagflation), and that of the 1980s, with inflation and unemployment both falling, cast grave doubt on any such simple relationship.

Since the late 1960s, economists have become increasingly convinced that a correct explanation of the relationship between inflation and unemployment depends critically on *expectations* of inflation. If expectations of inflation are low, workers will not demand large wage increases to compensate for the expected erosion of their real earnings caused by inflation. Businesses' costs of production will not rise rapidly, and increases in their product prices can be relatively low. Under these circumstances, a moderate increase in inflation may lead temporarily to lower unemployment.

Consequently, monetary policy under certain circumstances is able to reduce unemployment in the short run. An unexpected monetary expansion will produce a money-induced pickup in demand that will stimulate firms to expand employment, produce more, and raise prices.

Soon, however, people will notice the pickup of inflation. Firms will have incorporated it into their price increases; workers will add it to wage demands, eliminating the fall in real wages and leading to a return of the unemployment rate to its initial level. Because it is not possible for people to be "fooled" indefinitely about the rate of inflation, higher inflation cannot permanently lower the unemployment rate.

Moreover, under certain circumstances, higher inflation may not reduce unemployment at all. Suppose the central bank showed a persistent tendency to try to lower short-term unemployment below the level associated with realization of peoples' expectations of inflation—that is, below the nonaccelerating inflation rate of unemployment or NAIRU. (The concept of the NAIRU is explained in Chapter 5.) This tendency would be noticed and would foster higher inflation expectations. To the extent people correctly anticipate this behavior, even the temporary boom that a monetary expansion would otherwise produce would be thwarted.

Rational Expectations

Bennett T. McCallum

The monetarist views of Milton Friedman follow two lines. The first is that monetary rather than fiscal policy is of primary importance in determining the stability of the real economy in the short run and inflation in the longer run. Second, because the private economy is basically stable and because policymakers are inept or overly concerned with the next election, it is better to stick to a constant growth rate of money and not to try and stabilize output and employment.

A new critique of active stabilization policy, that is sympathetic to Friedman but goes far beyond his view, has been developed by rational expectations theorists. They argue that even monetary policy is powerless to alter real output and employment if that policy is anticipated. To the extent that the private sector forsees policy actions it will offset them. The following selection by Bennett McCallum describes the new ideas.

EVER SINCE THE "Keynesian Revolution" in the 1930s and 1940s, it has been widely agreed that a major responsibility of any national government is to utilize monetary and fiscal policy actively in an effort "to promote maximum employment, production, and purchasing power," as stated in the United States Employment Act of 1946. Most economists, in other words, have accepted what Franco Modigliani terms "the fundamental message of [Keynes's] *General Theory:* that a private enterprise economy using an intangible money *needs* to be stabilized, *can* be stabilized, and therefore *should* be stabilized by appropriate monetary and fiscal policies."

There have been recent developments in macroeconomic theory, however, that suggest that the activist stabilization policies favored by Keynesians will be unsuccessful—not because of inept behavior on the part of policymakers, but for more fundamental reasons.

These developments have resulted from a revised conception of the way in which individual economic agents—consumers, workers, and firms—form their expectations about future values of economic variables relevant for current behavior. The revised conception is usually referred to as the hypothesis of rational expectations.

EXPECTATIONAL BEHAVIOR

It is perhaps obvious that individual agents' expectations of future economic conditions are important determinants of their current choices. Thus, for example, firms may base the current month's employment decisions partly on product demand conditions expected to prevail next month (and/or in months following), while labor union leaders and firms are influenced at wage-negotiation time by the amount of inflation expected for the next year or two. Similarly, consumers will be more willing to borrow funds at a given rate of interest (say, 15 percent) in order to purchase durable goods if they expect 10 percent inflation over the next year, than they would be if they anticipated no inflation.

Furthermore, agents' expectations change from month to month and year to year as business conditions change. So for an economist's model—i.e., his view of the economy—not to be misleading, it must incorporate a representation of expectational behavior that is itself not flagrantly incorrect. This is, of course, as true for large quantitative models embodying sophisticated econometric research as it is for other types of models, formal or informal.

At present, however, virtually all econometric models used for macroeconomic forecasting and for governmental policymaking rely, often implicitly, on representations of expectational behavior that are naive in the extreme. In these models, expected future values of any given variable are usually taken to depend only on the past behavior of that single variable, and with a relationship that is assumed to be unchanging over time and unrelated either to market conditions or to policy stimuli. For example, the value of the consumer price index expected to prevail a month or a year hence is represented in such models as a particular weighted average or extrapolation of values of this index actually observed in recent months or years. The models ignore the fact that the government has recently taken policy actions which will certainly affect next month's value of this index. More generally, the type of expectational behavior assumed for agents in these models neglects various factors that (according to the models themselves) would be useful in forming expectations. So, within the models, agents' expectational *errors*—discrepancies between expected and actual values—are apt to be systematically related to past values of other variables or even the expectational variable itself.

Moreover, the same sort of extrapolative expectational relation is also present in most noneconometric models, formal or informal. Consequently, naive expectational behavior is implicitly assumed in most macroeconomic analyses and forecasts.

A drastically different view of expectational behavior is, however, rapidly winning support in the economics profession. This view, expressed as the hypothesis of *rational expectations*, presumes that individual economic agents use all available and relevant information in forming expectations and that they process this information in an intelligent fashion. It is important to recognize that this does not imply that consumers or firms have "perfect foresight" or that their expectations are always "correct." What it does suggest is that agents reflect upon past errors and, if necessary, revise their expectational behavior so as to eliminate regularities in these errors. Indeed, the hypothesis suggests that agents *succeed* in eliminating regularities involving expectational errors, so that the errors will on average be unrelated to available information. In statistical terms, the errors are assumed to be uncorrelated with known values of all relevant variables. Thus, according to the hypothesis, expectational errors may often be large, but will not be systematically related to variables observable at the time of expectation formation.

Although the rational expectations hypothesis (or more briefly, REH) has become rather widely accepted among leading economic theorists, many economists have failed to embrace the notion. The two most common objections voiced by critics of REH are: (1) it is unrealistic to assume that people or firms process information as intelligently as the hypothesis presumes; (2) it is also unrealistic to assume that agents use information on all relevant variables in forming expectations. The point of the second objection is that information collection is difficult and costly, so it must be unprofitable to obtain data on *every* relevant variable, since some will be of negligible value to the forming of expectations. But this point is not actually an objection to REH but rather to applications in which informational costs are neglected for the sake of simplicity. In fact, the point is entirely consistent with the basic idea behind REH: that expectations are formed optimally, that is, so as to equate marginal costs and benefits of expectational activities. The first point, however, is a genuine objection to the rationality hypothesis, not merely a misunderstanding. But it is an objection that seems poorly founded. All theories or models are "unrealistic" in the sense of being extremely simplified descriptions of reality; they must be simple to serve their purpose. Like a map, a useful theory reflects only the aspects of reality that are important for the purposes at hand. So the true issue is: of all the simple expectational assumptions conceivable, which one should be embodied in a macroeconomic model to be used for stabilization analysis? REH advocates contend that the assumption should avoid the implication that there are unexploited possibilities in the economy for huge speculative profits (this would be the implication if expectations were formed by naive extrapolations), since the actions of thousands of entrepreneurs seeking such profits should guarantee that sizable opportunities will soon be exploited. But the REH, by assuming that *all* possibilities are exploited, accomplishes precisely this in a reasonably simple way.

EVALUATING POLICY ALTERNATIVES

Let us now consider an implication of the rational expectations theory for the usefulness of macroeconomic models of the type mentioned above—i.e., models that embody the presumption that expectations are not rational. It is obvious that, if expectational behavior is incorrectly represented, these models will provide inaccurate forecasts of future business conditions that are not as accurate as they might be. But this criticism is mild in comparison to one, eloquently put forth by Lucas, which concerns the models' usefulness in formulating policy.

In order to choose among different policy rules—in other words, patterns of monetary and fiscal behavior to be followed for a number of periods—a policymaking body first uses its preferred model in simulation exercises that predict what outcomes would result from the adoption of the contending rules. Then, given the various hypothetical outcomes, the authority selects the rule that yields the outcome considered most desirable (or least undesirable) in terms of its implied values of GNP, unemployment, inflation, and so on, over the near future. This procedure, which may be extremely complex, was highly regarded by the economics profession only a few years ago. But if the rational expectations hypothesis is correct, the procedure cannot be fruitfully applied with existing models. For the REH asserts that consumers, workers, and firms will perceive what sort of policy is being followed and take the effects of this policy into account when forming expectations. Thus, for example, agents will expect more inflation in the near future, and consequently will *act* differently, if the policymakers are in fact pursuing an "expansionary" policy, than they would under a regime of austerity. But that implies that the types of models being discussed—in which agents' expectations are explicitly or implicitly treated as naive extrapolations of past actual values—will systematically fail to take proper account of policy rule changes. Accordingly, the models' predictions will be incorrect and the policymakers' choice among contending policy rules will be based on erroneous presumptions about the consequences of the various policies.

This point seems simple enough, but its implications for the econometric modeling "industry" are tremendous. To a large and increasing extent, macroeconomic forecasting in business and government as well as academic institutions, is based on large-scale formal econometric models that fail to take policy changes into account. Thus, as Lucas stressed, their usefulness in policymaking is entirely undermined. Despite resistance from proprietors and users of these models, existing models will almost certainly be revised or supplanted in policymaking and policy-evaluating organizations. This will probably bring about substantial changes in forecasting models as well, since most of the large-scale models are intended by their proprietors to serve as tools for both forecasting and policy simulation.

And the point is, as our previous discussion was designed to suggest, relevant not only for policymaking based on formal econometric models, but for policymaking based on *any* model—formal or informal—that treats expectations as being formed in an extrapolative, nonrational manner. Thus it is probably quite relevant to actual policy decisions of the fiscal and monetary authorities of the United States and other industrial countries. Indeed, this new view may play an important role in helping us to understand why recent macroeconomic policy has been so distressingly unsuccessful. In any event, its basic validity has been accepted even by economists who are unpersuaded by other applications of the rational expectations hypothesis.

POLICY IMPLICATIONS

The implications of the REH for the way in which models are used to formulate policy are important, but its implications for policy itself are even more dramatic. It is this area that many commentators have in mind when they speak of the "rational expectations revolution" in macroeconomics, and it derives essentially from combining the REH with a second, older hypothesis—the "natural rate hypothesis" (NRH)—that had been widely accepted before the notion of expectational rationality gained prominence.

NRH concerns the relation between unemployment (or deviations of real aggregate output from capacity levels) and inflation rates—the famous "Phillips curve." In his oft-cited 1967 presidential address to the American Economic Association, Milton Friedman argued convincingly that any stable Phillips-type equation for the labor market should relate unemployment not to the rate of change of nominal wages, but to the rate of change of real or price-deflated wages. To suppose otherwise would be to assume a form of "money illusion" that is inconsistent with traditional economic theory. Friedman's hypothesis, which was independently put forth by Edmund Phelps, seemed startling at the time but subsequent studies provided enough empirical support that by the mid-1970s the economics profession had been almost universally converted to the NRH.

In this context, the importance of expectations behavior results from the fact that most wage agreements are made in nominal, not real, terms. Since it is real wages that are of concern to employers and workers, they respond by evaluating contemplated increases in nominal wages in relation to *expected* increases in prices. Thus the basic relationship posited by Friedman and Phelps is between the level of unemployment—a measure of excess supply in the labor market—and the proportionate change in the nominal wage rate less the proportionate change in the price level expected for the upcoming period (in other words, the expected inflation rate). The relationship is, of course, negative: for a given expected inflation rate, the greater the rate of unemployment, the smaller the increase in the nominal wage. Since the unemployment rate is itself negatively related to the excess demand for labor, the Friedman-Phelps relation is simply a specific case of the venerable law of supply and demand, which states that the (real) price of a commodity will tend to rise when demand exceeds supply at the prevailing price.

To describe the role of the Friedman-Phelps equation in a macroeconomic model, it will be useful to combine it with two additional equations. For a given level of capacity, the first relates the unemployment (negatively) to the level of real output, and the other relates output, via the production function and the demand for labor, to the real wage rate (again, negatively). Together, these two equations imply that the real wage will be positively related to the unemployment rate and, consequently, that the (proportionate) change in the real wage will be positively related to the change in the unemployment rate. Then by eliminating the proportionate change in the nominal wage from this last relation and the Friedman-Phelps equation, we obtain a relationship involving the current and most recent values of the unemployment rate, and the difference between the actual and expected rates of inflation. Solving for the current unemployment rate, we find that its value in any period (say, a month) is partly determined by its own most recent value—a feature that will be mentioned again—and partly by the *difference between the actual and expected rates of inflation*, i.e., the expectational error for the inflation rate. The effect of the previous unemployment rate is positive and that of the expectational error is negative. The equation we have developed represents one version of the NRH. Its crucial characteristic, which macroeconomists have accepted with near unanimity, is that it relates unemployment only to the *unexpected* portion of the inflation rate. In a steady, expected inflation, unemployment would tend to its "natural" level.

There are other ways of deriving basically similar NRH relations. Indeed, the most influential papers in the rational expectations literature have taken an approach in which expectational errors refer to misperceptions by individuals of current macroeconomic variables (caused by incomplete information) rather than mistakes in anticipating future values. The approach used in this paper was chosen primarily for its comparative simplicity.

We now come to the most dramatic implication of the rational expectations hypothesis for macroeconomic policy. Clearly, our NRH equation says that monetary and fiscal policies can affect the evolution of the unemployment rate only if they affect the expectational error for the inflation rate. According to the REH, however, such policies can have no *systematic* effects on the latter: with expectational rationality this expectational error, like all others, is random and uncorrelated with past values of all relevant macroeconomic variables. But policies, to the extent that they are systematic, are simply rules relating current values of variables controllable by policymakers to observed (hence, past) values of relevant variables. Thus the REH implies that expectational errors must be uncorrelated with the systematic portion of all control variables, which eliminates the only available route for influencing unemployment. In short, since the Federal Reserve and the Treasury cannot induce systematic expectational errors, they cannot exert any systematic influence on the evolution of the unemployment rate.

It should be emphasized that the foregoing does not imply that the policymakers' *actions* have no influence; unsystematic or erratic behavior on their part will induce expectational errors and fluctuations in the unemployment rate. But macroeconomic *policies*—sustained patterns of action or reaction—will have no influence because they are perceived and taken into account by private decision-making agents. Thus the adoption of a policy to maintain "full employment" will not, according to the present argument, result in values of the unemployment rate that are smaller (or less variable) *on average* than those that would be experienced in the absence of such a policy.

It should also be said that the result refers only to macroeconomic policies; it does not claim that minimum wage laws, conscription, or other microeconomic arrangements fail to affect unemployment. But it is nevertheless a stunning result, one that provides theoretical support for the view that the monetary and fiscal policymakers should not attempt to engage in activist countercyclical policies of the type associated with the term "fine tuning." Instead, it suggests that the Federal Reserve and the Treasury should strive to eliminate unsystematic fluctuations in variables under their control, such as the money stock and the level of government spending, since such fluctuations induce expectational errors and thereby increase the variability of unemployment.

FOCUS ON INFLATION

I have described recent developments in macroeconomic theory which suggest that activist monetary and fiscal policies will tend to be unsuccessful in stabilizing employment. The suggestion is not only that current understanding of the economy is inadequate for effective design of such policies but, more basically, that the behavior over time of unemployment, output, and other "real" variables will be virtually independent of the authorities' policy-rule choices. Thus, the main systematic effects of these choices will be on "monetary" variables—in particular, the general price level and its rate of change, the inflation rate. The clear implication is that, if the rational expectations and natural rate hypotheses are correct, monetary and fiscal policies should be designed to yield the sequence of price levels (or inflation rates) that is regarded as most desirable. In other words, the Federal Reserve and the Treasury should concentrate their attention on the prevention or reduction (if such is desired) of inflation, not of unemployment. There is no point in focusing policy choices upon variables, no matter how great their intrinsic importance, that cannot be systematically affected by these choices.

Inflation and Supply Side Economics

Martin Feldstein

The growing support for supply side policies is one of the few encouraging signs on the economic scene today. Washington's new concern with economic incentives, capacity expansion, and tax distortions is a welcome shift from the more limited and often inappropriate Keynesian economics that dominated the 1960's and 1970's. The obvious failure of the old approach -a decade of high unemployment, rising inflation and declining productivity-has stimulated Congress to seek new ideas. Stagflation promises to be the catalyst of a revolution in economic policy.

But there is a danger that supply side policies will be called on to do the impossible.

Although I support a supply side approach to unemployment and productivity, I am convinced that inflation will be tamed only by appropriate limits to demand. The widespread view that supply policies can eliminate inflation by increasing productivity is just wishful thinking. Productivity increases might make a small contribution to reducing inflation but the pursuit of a truly supply side approach to inflation would be irresponsible. It would not only fail to cure inflation but would also discrdeit the use of desirable supply side initiatives to aid capital formation and real growth.

Classroom Economics

Since nobody likes a recession, it is easy to see why many people are hoping to find an alternative to demand restraint. Experience shows that an effective monetary of fiscal contraction must raise unemployment until the excess of supply over demand lowers the rate of inflation. While some "rational expectations" theorists maintain that a properly anticipated cut in money supply growth could in principle eliminate inflation immediately without any increase in unemployment, the institutional structure of wage-setting and price-setting in the American economy implies that such claims belong only in the realm of classroom economics.

Although a steady and predictable deceleration of the rate of money growth can reduce the adverse unemployment effects of tighter money, some employment decline is inevitable. Unemployment is the price we must pay to undo more than a decade of inflationary policies.

How then can a supply side strategy fit into the process of reducing inflation? The basic supply side proposal calls for tax cuts designed to encourage saving and investment, particularly more realistic depreciation rules and lower personal tax rates on the income from savings. I certainly favor such changes. More investment is desirable and tax cuts are an effective way of stimulating it. The question is not whether these are good high-priority policies-they definitely are-but whether they are capable of significantly reducing inflationary pressures.

A sustained increase in investment would undoubtedly raise labor productivity and total output. If the productivity increase doesn't alter the rate at which wages rise, the rate of increase of unit labor costs would fall and competition among firms would put downward pressure on prices. This downward pressure on prices would be reinforced by an automatic change in monetary conditions. More specifically, the amount of money needed to finance transactions would automatically rise with the increase in total output that results from the productivity gain. With no change in the Fed's rate of monetary expansion, the increase in the demand for money would reduce the inflationary gap between money supply and money demand. This reduction in the excess supply of money and the direct downward pressure on prices resulting from lower unit labor costs would together cause a reduction in inflation with no increase in unemployment. That in essence is the supply side approach to inflation.

Unfortunately, this effect of productivity on inflation is not likely to be very large and is certainly not very reliable. An increase in productivity doesn't necessarily translate into a slowdown in unit labor costs. Instead, if the rise in productivity pushed wages up by an equal amount, there would be no direct change in unit labor costs. In this unfavorable situation, a rise in productivity would reduce inflation only because the increase in total output raises money demand. With no change in the growth of money supply, the increased money demand effectively tightens the net availability of money. Although this tighter money would eventually reduce inflation, the unemployment rate would rise in the process by just as much as it would have if the tight money condition had been achieved by a reduced money supply with no change in productivity.

The extent to which an increase in productivity growth reduces inflation without increasing unemployment therefore depends on the response of wage-setting to changes in productivity and in inflation. Economists don't know enough about this adjustment process to estimate the impact of a rise in productivity with any accuracy. But even a quite optimistic estimate implies that any feasible improvement in productivity will still leave the inflation rate unacceptably high.

The Joint Economic Committee recently illustrated its enthusiastic endorsement of a supply side approach to fighting inflation with a package of tax cuts that would raise the annual rate of real business fixed investment more than 15% by the end of the decade. But the net effect of this increased investment, according to the Data Resources study on which the JEC based its conclusions, would only be a 1.3 percentage point reduction in the inflation rate by 1990. It is certainly hard to reconcile this modest reduciton with the JEC's assertion that inflation can now be fought by supply side policies without the need to accept unemployment.

The more extreme followers of Arthur B. Laffer argue that inflation should be fought by using a large across-the-board tax cut to stimulate the supply of effort and output. Again the numbers make it clear that this can be no substitute for demand restraint. With demand rising at 10% a year, there is no way that supply can be induced to keep up. Moreover, an across-the-board tax cut that did much more than give back the extra tax revenue generated by inflation (or by cuts in government spending) would increase inflation, crowd out investment, or both. The misuse of the Laffer curve could do as much to raise inflation in the 1980's as the misuse of the Phillips curve did in the 1970's.

Even the most optimistic plausible estimates of potential productivity increases don't support a supply side approach to inflation. There is widespread agreement that the inflation rate is likely to be down to about 10% by year-end if there are no unexpected price shocks. Even if the rate of productivity growth could somehow return from the 1.5% rate to the 3% rate that we enjoyed before 1970, the underlying inflation rate would still remain about 7%.

A goal of a seven or eight percent inflation rate by 1985 or 1990 is unacceptably high. Moreover, a government decision not to use demand contractions to reduce inflation would encourage further increases in wage demands and would leave the economy vulnerable to any external inflationary shocks. It's clear that a supply side policy can play only a small part in reducing inflation. The primary emphasis must be on a policy of sustained monetary deceleration and fiscal restraint.

Effect of Consistent Policy

How bad must unemployment be in order to get inflation back to the one or two percent rate of the early 1960's? Simple extrapolations of the unemployment-inflation experience of the last 15 years have led some economists to the dire conclusion that a 10% unemployment rate for at least five years would be needed to eliminate inflation. But such extrapolations ignore the favorable effect on wage-setting and price-setting of a consistent policy and the expectation of several years without excess demand.

Since the unemployment cost of reducing inflation depends crucially on the credibility of such a policy, it is important that the government and the Fed remain steadfast now in their determination to fight inflation even as the unemployment rate continues to rise. The perception that the government would accept 8% to 9% unemployment-about two percentage points over the natural unemployment rate-for three or four years in order to eliminate inflation would almost certainly bring inflation down so fast that it would be unnecessary to pay such a high cost.

A policy of demand restraint to reduce inflation is not incompatible with supply side incentives to increase capital accumulation and productivity. Even while total output is temporarily limited, more of it can be devoted to expanding the capital stock. The Fed's current policy of tight money should be coupled with a restraint on government spending and a tax change to spur investment in plant and equipment. But supply side policies should not be given responsibility for the job of eliminating inflation.

Controls Are Not the Answer

C. Jackson Grayson, Jr.

I will make one clear assertion at the outset: Wage-price controls are not the answer to inflation.

And yet I will also make the following prediction: We will turn again in the United States, in desperation, to some form of controls over wages and prices —just as people have done over the centuries. And the answer will still be the same—they may make some short-term gains, but at the expense of the long-run welfare.

The lessons of history seem pretty clear. Centralized efforts to fight inflation were started before Christ was born. Rome, for example, fought inflation by various means for centuries. Finally, in A.D. 301, the emperor Diocletian imposed the first extensive price-wage control program. His edict (referred to as "commanded cheapness") set schedules for 76 different wage categories and for 890 different price categories (222 of which were for food!). The penalty for an offense was death. Thirteen years later, the program, in shambles, was abandoned. In the thirteenth century, the great Mongol, Kublai Khan, decreed maximum prices. And Medieval Europe had a "just price" code.

Not many people are aware of it, but the United States began some attempts at wage-price controls during its early years. The American Puritans imposed a code of wage and price limitations in 1636; those who violated the code were classed with "adulterers and whoremongers." The Continental Congress set price ceilings even before the Declaration of Independence. A few states enacted price control laws. Inflation became so severe that General George Washington complained in April 1779 that "a wagonload of money will scarcely purchase a wagonload of provisions." The attempts at control were sporadic, highly controversial, and not comprehensive. All efforts were largely abandoned by 1780.

Most modern nations have instituted wage-price controls during periods of war, but it was in Europe right after World War II that almost every nation tried some form of comprehensive peacetime controls (remembering the inflation that had torn apart European economies after World War I). Some European nations had succeeded with their "incomes policies" for a period of time. Some were started, stopped, and reinstated in another version. But none has lasted continuously.

Though specific "lessons" are difficult to transfer across international boundaries, and even difficult to use in one nation from one time to another, it might be helpful to look at a summary that I have made of European experiences with controls (see table).

These experiences were summarized succinctly by Lloyd Ulman and Robert Flanagan in their book, *Wage Restraint—A Study of Incomes Policies in Western Europe:* "Incomes policy, to generalize from the experience of the countries in this account, has not been very successful." My conclusions about the accomplishments of the Price Commission do not vary from that. Perhaps we did obtain some short-range impact on price-wage levels, but they were gained under special conditions (slack in the economy, followed by productivity gains from a highly stimulated economy, and cooperation of business and labor) and at the cost of some long-term negative results.

As a result of my sixteen months as a price controller, I can list seven ways that controls interfere (negatively) with the market system and hasten its metamorphosis into a centralized economy.

First, wage-price controls lead to distortions in the economic system, which can be minimized only in the short run. The longer controls are in effect, the harder it is to discern real from artificial signals. No matter how cleverly any group designs a control system, distortions and inequities will appear. It happened in European control programs; it started to happen in Phase II.

For instance, lumber controls were beginning to lead to artificial middlemen, black markets, and sawmill shutdowns. Companies trapped with low base-period profit margins were beginning to consider selling out to those with higher base period margins, sending their capital overseas, or reducing their operations. Elsewhere, instances of false job upgrading—actually "raises" in disguise—were reported on a scattered but increasing basis. To keep away from profit-margin controls, some companies were considering dropping products where costs, and thus prices, had increased. And shortages of certain products (such as molasses and fertilizer) were appearing because artificially suppressed domestic prices had allowed higher world prices to pull domestic supplies abroad.

Exceptions and special regulations can handle some of these distortions, but the task grows more difficult as each correction breeds the need for another.

Second, during a period of controls, the public forgets that not all wage-price increases are inflationary. In a freely competitive economy, wage and price increases occur because of real consumer demand shifts and supply shortages. The resulting wage and price increases signal to businesses, "make more," or to labor, "move here," or to the public, "use less."

Controls interfere with this signaling mechanism. An artificially suppressed price can eventually cause shortages; natural gas is an example. Similar examples can be found in the labor market, where suppressed wages do not attract labor to areas in which there are shortages of skills or workers. But with wage-price controls in place, the public believes that all increases are inflationary—almost antisocial—and the clamor is for no increases, or at least very small ones.

"You can eliminate the middleman, but not his function"—this old business saying applies equally to our economic system. We live in a world of scarce resources, and, as much as some would like to repeal the laws of supply and demand, it cannot be done. Some system must allocate resources, we hope to the most efficient use for society. If wage-price controls, other government regulatory rules, or business-labor monopolies prohibit the price system from performing its natural function, then another rationing sys-

General Lessons from European Incomes Policies

1. If either labor or business does not cooperate, a wage-price controls program will not work.
2. Incomes policies do not work for long. They erode with time.
3. Getting into controls is easier than getting out.
4. Rising profits drive wage demands up.
5. Neither business nor labor is very satisfied with any given distribution of their share of income at any given time. Both will seek to improve their share.
6. Voluntary incomes policies have been limited in success and in time. The tendency is toward mandatory policies.
7. Labor nearly always believes that the government figure for estimated productivity in setting wage guidelines is low. History shows that labor is generally right.
8. A wage "drift" occurs over time as business and labor cooperate to break many of the wage guidelines.
9. Efforts to restrain business and labor through education and exhortation have very limited success.
10. It is increasingly difficult to make incomes policies work as demand increases and unemployment decreases.
11. If prices are to be controlled, then so must wages be. The only exception is France, which has had a limited price control program but no wage control program.
12. Cost of living escalators accelerate inflation.
13. Less productive labor groups eventually demand comparability in wages with the more highly productive labor sectors, thereby eroding the wage guideline.
14. Expectations feed inflation.
15. Increasingly interdependent world trade can intrude upon and upset a nation's incomes policies.

tem (such as central planning and control) must be used. You can eliminate the price system, but not its function.

Third, during a control period, the public forgets what profits are all about. Even before the recent wage-price controls, the public believed profits were "too high," though they actually declined from 6.2 percent of GNP in 1966 to 3.6 percent in 1970, and increased only to 4.3 percent in the boom year of 1972. And with profit increases raised to the top of the news during the recovery of 1972 and early 1973, the negative public sentiment against profits increased. Why? The control system itself heightened the public's negative attitude toward profits at a time when capital regeneration, the fuel of the capitalist engine, was already alarmingly low.

Fourth, wage-price controls provide a convenient stone for those who have economic or political axes to grind, particularly those interested in promoting a centralized economic system. For example, in 1972 Ralph Nader argued that the control system should be used to prohibit automobile companies from raising their prices to reflect style changes. Others argued that price increases should not be given to companies that employ insufficient numbers of minorities or pollute the environment. Nor should wage increases go to uncooperative unions. And so on.

Fifth, wage-price controls can easily become a security blanket against the cold winds of free-market uncertainties. They tell people what the limits are; they help employers fight unions; and they provide union leaders with excuses to placate demands for "more" from their rank and file. The controlled become dependent on the controllers and want regulations continued in preference to the competition of a dynamic market. At the same time, the controllers themselves can become so enamored of their task that they don't want to let go.

The public begins to fear what will happen when controls are ended and seeks continuance. Witness the fears of moving from Phase II to Phase III, and the public (and congressional) pressure for the freeze to replace Phase III. Even Wall Street seemed terrified at the thought of returning to supply and demand in the market. It is much easier to get into controls than to get out.

Sixth, under controls, business and labor leaders begin to pay more attention to the regulatory body than to the dynamics of the marketplace. They inevitably come to the same conclusion, summed up by one executive: "We know that all of our sophisticated analysis and planning can be wiped out in the blink of a Washington controller's eye."

Seventh, and most dangerous, wage-price controls misguide the public. They draw attention away from the fundamental factors that affect inflation—fiscal and monetary policies, tax rates, import-export policies, productivity, competitive restrictions, and the like. The danger is that attention will become permanently focused on the symptom-treating control mechanism rather than on the underlying problems.

In summary, perhaps the most dramatic way I can underscore my views is to point out the recent example of Britain, where years of successive stop-go economic policies and various types of controls (including guideposts) have led that nation to where it is today, economically and politically in a crisis state with one of the lowest income growth rates of modern nations and raging inflation.

Controls are not the answer.

C. Jackson Grayson, Jr., is Dean of the School of Business Administration, Southern Methodist University. He was Chairman of the Price Commission during Phase II and is author of *Confessions of a Price Controller* (Dow Jones–Irwin, 1974).

Exchange Rates—How Flexible
Should They Be?

Milton Friedman

Mr. FRIEDMAN. Thank you, Professor Douglas—Senator Douglas.
Discussions of U.S. policy with respect to international payments
tend to be dominated by our immediate balance-of-payments difficulties. I should like today to approach the question from a different,
and I hope more constructive, direction. Let us begin by asking ourselves not merely how we can get out of our present difficulties but
instead how we can fashion our international payments system so that
it will best serve our needs for the long pull; how we can solve not
merely this balance-of-payments problem but the balance-of-payments
problem.

A shocking, and indeed, disgraceful feature of the present situation
is the extent to which our frantic search for expedients to stave off
balance-of-payments pressures has led us, on the one hand, to sacrifice
major national objectives; and, on the other, to give enormous power to
officials of foreign governments to affect what should be purely domestic matters.

Chairman DOUGLAS. May I say, so far, so good. I enjoyed that
100 percent.

Representative REUSS. It might be wise to stop there.

Mr. FRIEDMAN. Foreign payments amount to only some 5 percent
of our total national income. Yet they have become a major factor in
nearly every national policy.

I believe that a system of floating exchange rates would solve the balance-of-payments problem for the United States far more effectively
than our present arrangements. Such a system would use the flexibility and efficiency of the free market to harmonize our small foreign
trade sector with both the rest of our massive economy and the rest of
the world; it would reduce problems of foreign payments to their
proper dimensions and remove them as a major consideration in governmental policy about domestic matters and as a major preoccupation
in international political negotiations; it would foster our national
objectives rather than be an obstacle to their attainment.

To indicate the basis for this conclusion, let us consider the national
objective with which our payments system is most directly connected:
the promotion of a healthy and balanced growth of world trade, carried on, so far as possible, by private individuals and private enterprises with minimum intervention by governments. This has been
a major objective of our whole postwar international economic policy,
most recently expressed in the Trade Expansion Act of 1962. Success would knit the free world more closely together, and, by fostering
the international division of labor, raise standards of living throughout the world, including the United States.

Suppose that we succeed in negotiating far-reaching reciprocal
reductions in tariffs and other trade barriers with the Common

Market and other countries. To simplify exposition I shall hereafter refer only to tariffs, letting these stand for the whole range of barriers to trade, including even the so-called voluntary limitation of exports. Such reductions will expand trade in general but clearly will have different effects on different industries. The demand for the products of some will expand, for others contract. This is a phenomenon we are familiar with from our internal development. The capacity of our free enterprise system to adapt quickly and efficiently to such shifts, whether produced by changes in technology or tastes, has been a major source of our economic growth. The only additional element introduced by international trade is the fact that different currencies are involved, and this is where the payment mechanism comes in; its function is to keep this fact from being an additional source of disturbance.

An all-around lowering of tariffs would tend to increase both our expenditures and our receipts in foreign currencies. There is no way of knowing in advance which increase would tend to be the greater and hence no way of knowing whether the initial effect would be toward a surplus or deficit in our balance of payments. What is clear is that we cannot hope to succeed in the objective of expanding world trade unless we can readily adjust to either outcome.

Many people concerned with our payments deficits hope that since we are operating further from full capacity than Europe, we could supply a substantial increase in exports whereas they could not. Implicitly, this assumes that European countries are prepared to see their surplus turned into a deficit, thereby contributing to the reduction of the deficits we have recently been experiencing in our balance of payments. Perhaps this would be the initial effect of tariff changes. But if the achievement of such a result is to be sine qua non of tariff agreement, we cannot hope for any significant reduction in barriers. We could be confident that exports would expand more than imports only if the tariff changes were one sided indeed, with our trading partners making much greater reductions in tariffs than we make. Our major means of inducing other countries to reduce tariffs is to offer corresponding reductions in our tariff. More generally, there is little hope of continued and sizable liberalization of trade if liberalization is to be viewed simply as a device for correcting balance-of-payments difficulties. That way lies only backing and filling.

Suppose then that the initial effect is to increase our expenditures on imports more than our receipts from exports. How could we adjust to this outcome?

One method of adjustment is to draw on reserves or borrow from abroad to finance the excess increase in imports. The obvious objection to this method is that it is only a temporary device, and hence can be relied on only when the disturbance is temporary. But that is not the major objection. Even if we had very large reserves or could borrow large amounts from abroad, so that we could continue this expedient for many years, it is a most undesirable one. We can see why if we look at physical rather than financial magnitudes.

The physical counterpart to the financial deficit is a reduction of employment in industries competing with imports that is larger than the concurrent expansion of employment in export industries. So long as the financial deficit continues, the assumed tariff reductions create employment problems. But it is no part of the aim of tariff reductions to create unemployment at home or to promote employment abroad. The aim is a balanced expansion of trade, with exports rising along with imports and thereby providing employment opportunities to offset any reduction in employment resulting from increased imports.

Hence, simply drawing on reserves or borrowing abroad is a most unsatisfactory method of adjustment.

Another method of adjustment is to lower U.S. prices relative to foreign prices, since this would stimulate exports and discourage imports. If foreign countries are accommodating enough to engage in inflation, such a change in relative prices might require merely that the

United States keep prices stable or even, that it simply keep them from rising as fast as foreign prices. But there is no necessity for foreign countries to be so accommodating, and we could hardly count on their being so accommodating. The use of this technique therefore involves a willingness to produce a decline in U.S. prices by tight monetary policy or tight fiscal policy or both. Given time, this method of adjustment would work. But in the interim, it would exact a heavy toll. It would be difficult or impossible to force down prices appreciably without producing a recession and considerable unemployment. To eliminate in the long run the unemployment resulting from the tariff changes, we should in the short run be creating cyclical unemployment. The cure might for a time be far worse than the disease.

This second method is therefore also most unsatisfactory. Yet these two methods—drawing on reserves and forcing down prices—are the only two methods available to us under our present international payment arrangements, which involve fixed exchange rates between the U.S. dollar and other currencies. Little wonder that we have so far made such disappointing progress toward the reduction of trade barriers, that our practice has differed so much from our preaching.

There is one other way and only one other way to adjust and that is by allowing (or forcing) the price of the U.S. dollar to fall in terms of other currencies. To a foreigner, U.S. goods can become cheaper in either of two ways—either because their prices in the United States fall in terms of dollars or because the foreigner has to give up fewer units of his own currency to acquire a dollar, which is to say, the price of the dollar falls. For example, suppose a particular U.S. car sells for $2,800 when a dollar costs 7 shillings, tuppence in British money (i.e., roughly £1=$2.80). The price of the car is then £1,000 in British money. It is all the same to an Englishman—or even a Scotsman—whether the price of the car falls to $2,500 while the price of a dollar remains 7 shillings, tuppence, or, alternatively, the price of the car remains $2,800, while the price of a dollar falls to 6 shillings, 5 pence (i.e., roughly £1=$3.11). In either case, the car costs the Englishman £900 rather than £1,000, which is what matters to him. Similarly, foreign goods can become more expensive to an American in either of two ways—either because the price in terms of foreign currency rises or because he has to give up more dollars to acquire a given amount of foreign currency.

Changes in exchange rates can therefore alter the relative price of U.S. and foreign goods in precisely the same way as can changes in internal prices in the United States and in foreign countries. And they can do so without requiring anything like the same internal adjustments. If the initial effect of the tariff reductions would be to create a deficit at the former exchange rate (or enlarge an existing deficit or reduce an existing surplus) and thereby increase unemployment, this effect can be entirely avoided by a change in exchange rates which will produce a balanced expansion in imports and exports without interfering with domestic employment, domestic prices, or domestic monetary and fiscal policy. The pig can be roasted without burning down the house.

The situation is, of course, entirely symmetrical if the tariff changes should initially happen to expand our exports more than our imports. Under present circumstances, we would welcome such a result, and conceivably, if the matching deficit were experienced by countries currently running a surplus, they might permit it to occur without seeking to offset it. In that case, they and we would be using the first method of adjustment—changes in reserves or borrowing. But again, if we had started off from an even keel, this would be an undesirable method of adjustment. On our side, we should be sending out useful goods and receiving only foreign currencies in return. On the side of our partners, they would be using up reserves and tolerating the creation of unemployment.

The second method of adjusting to a surplus is to permit or force domestic prices to rise—which is of course what we did in part in the early postwar years when we were running large surpluses.

Again, we should be forcing maladjustments on the whole economy to solve a problem arising from a small part of it—the 5 percent accounted for by foreign trade.

Again, these two methods are the only ones available under our present international payments arrangements, and neither is satisfactory.

The final method is to permit or force exchange rates to change—in this case, a rise in the price of the dollar in terms of foreign currencies. This solution is again specifically adapted to the specific problem of the balance of payments.

Changes in exchange rates can be produced in either of two general ways. One way is by a change in an official exchange rate; an official devaluation or appreciation from one fixed level which the Government is committed to support to another fixed level. This is the method used by Britain in its postwar devaluation and by Germany in 1961 when the mark was appreciated. This is also the main method contemplated by the IMF which permits member nations to change their exchange rates by 10 percent without approval by the Fund and by a larger amount after approval by the Fund. But this method has serious disadvantages. It makes a change in rates a matter of major moment, and hence there is a tendency to postpone any change as long as possible. Difficulties cumulate and a larger change is finally needed than would have been required if it could have been made promptly. By the time the change is made, everyone is aware that a change is pending and is certain about the direction of change. The result is to encourage flight from a currency, if it is going to be devalued, or to a currency, if it is going to be appreciated.

There is in any event little basis for determining precisely what the new rate should be. Speculative movements increase the difficulty of judging what the new rate should be, and introduce a systematic bias, making the change needed appear larger than it actually is. The result, particularly when devaluation occurs, is generally to lead officials to "play safe" by making an even larger change than the large change needed. The country is then left after the devaluation with a maladjustment precisely the opposite of that with which it started, and is thereby encouraged to follow policies it cannot sustain in the long run.

Even if all these difficulties could be avoided, this method of changing from one fixed rate to another has the disadvantage that it is necessarily discontinuous. Even if the new exchange rates are precisely correct when first established, they will not long remain correct.

A second and much better way in which changes in exchange rates can be produced is by permitting exchange rates to float, by allowing them to be determined from day to day in the market. This is the method which the United States used from 1862 to 1879, and again, in effect, from 1917 or so to about 1925, and again from 1933 to 1934. It is the method which Britain used from 1918 to 1925 and again from 1931 to 1939, and which Canada used for most of the interwar period and again from 19__ to May 1962. Under this method, exchange rates adjust themselves continuously, and market forces determine the magnitude of each change. There is no need for any official to decide by how much the rate should rise or fall. This is the method of the free market, the method that we adopt unquestioningly in a private enterprise economy for the bulk of goods and services. It is no less available for the price of one money in terms of another.

With a floating exchange rate, it is possible for Governments to intervene and try to affect the rate by buying or selling, as the British exchange equalization fund did rather successfully in the 1930's, or by combining buying and selling with public announcements of intentions, as Canada did so disastrously in early 1962. On the whole, it seems to me undesirable to have government intervene, because there is a strong tendency for government agencies to try to peg the rate rather than to stabilize it, because they have no special advantage over private speculators in stabilizing it, because they can make far bigger mistakes than private speculators risking their own money, and because there is a tendency for them to cover up their mistakes by changing the rules—as the Canadian case so strikingly illustrates—rather than by reversing course. But this is an issue on which there is much difference of opinion among economists who agree in favoring floating rates. Clearly, it is possible to have a successful floating rate along with governmental speculation.

The great objective of tearing down trade barriers, of promoting a worldwide expansion of trade, of giving citizens of all countries, and especially the underdeveloped countries, every opportunity to sell their products in open markets under equal terms and thereby every incentive to use their resources efficiently, of giving countries an alternative through free world trade to autarchy and central planning—this great objective can, I believe, be achieved best under a regime of floating rates. All countries, and not just the United States, can proceed to liberalize boldly and confidently only if they can have reasonable assurance that the resulting trade expansion will be balanced and will not interfere with major domestic objectives. Floating exchange rates, and so far as I can see, only floating exchange rates, provide this assurance. They do so because they are an automatic mechanism for protecting the domestic economy from the possibility that liberalization will produce a serious imbalance in international payments.

Despite their advantages, floating exchange rates have a bad press. Why is this so?

One reason is because a consequence of our present system that I have been citing as a serious disadvantage is often regarded as an advantage, namely, the extent to which the small foreign trade sector dominates national policy. Those who regard this as an advantage refer to it as the discipline of the gold standard. I would have much sympathy for this view if we had a real gold standard, so the discipline was imposed by impersonal forces which in turn reflected the realities of resources, tastes, and technology. But in fact we have today only a pseudo gold standard and the so-called discipline is imposed by governmental officials of other countries who are determining their own internal monetary policies and are either being forced to dance to our tune or calling the tune for us, depending primarily on accidental political developments. This is a discipline we can well do without. See my article entitled "Real and Pseudo Gold Standards" which I will present later for inclusion in the record.

Chairman DOUGLAS. The article will be placed in the record at the end of your oral presentation.

Mr. FRIEDMAN. A possibly more important reason why floating exchange rates have a bad press, I believe, is a mistaken interpretation of experience with floating rates, arising out of a statistical fallacy that can be seen easily in a standard example. Arizona is clearly the worst place in the United States for a person with tuberculosis to go because the death rate from tuberculosis is higher in Arizona than in any other State. The fallacy in this case is obvious. It is less obvious in connection with exchange rates. Countries that have gotten into severe financial difficulties, for whatever reason, have had ultimately to change their exchange rates or let them change. No amount of exchange control and other restrictions on trade have enabled them to peg an exchange rate that was far out of line with economic realities. In consequence, floating rates have frequently been associated with financial and economic instability. It is easy to conclude, as many have, that floating exchange rates produce such instability.

This misreading of experience is reinforced by the general prejudice against speculation; which has led to the frequent assertion, typically on the basis of no evidence whatsoever, that speculation in exchange can be expected to be destabilizing and thereby to increase the instability in rates. Few who make this assertion even recognize that it is equivalent to asserting that speculators generally lose money.

Floating exchange rates need not be unstable exchange rates—any more than the prices of automobiles or of Government bonds, of coffee or of meals need gyrate wildly just because they are free to change from day to day. The Canadian exchange rate was free to change during more than a decade, yet it varied within narrow limits. The ultimate objective is a world in which exchange rates, while free to vary, are in fact highly stable because basic economic policies and conditions are stable. Instability of exchange rates is a symptom of instability in the underlying economic structure. Elimination of this symptom by administrative pegging of exchange rates cures none of the underlying difficulties and only makes adjustment to them more painful.

The confusion between stable exchange rates and pegged exchange rates helps to explain the frequent comment that floating exchange rates would introduce an additional element of uncertainty into foreign trade and thereby discourage its expansion. They introduce no additional element of uncertainty. If a floating rate would, for example, decline, then a pegged rate would be subject to pressure that the authorities would have to meet by internal deflation or exchange control in some form. The uncertainty about the rate would simply be replaced by uncertainty about internal prices or about the availability of exchange; and the latter uncertainties, being subject to administrative rather than market control, are likely to be the more erratic and unpredictable. Moreover, the trader can far more readily and cheaply protect himself against the danger of changes in exchange rates, through hedging operations in a forward market, than he can against the danger of changes in internal prices or exchange availability. Floating rates are therefore more favorable to private international trade than pegged rates.

Though I have discussed the problem of international payments in the context of trade liberalization, the discussion is directly applicable to the more general problem of adapting to any forces that make for balance-of-payments difficulties. Consider our present problem, of a deficit in the balance of trade plus long-term capital movements. How can we adjust to it? By one of the three methods outlined: first, drawing on reserves or borrowing; second, keeping U.S. prices from rising as rapidly as foreign prices or forcing them down; third, permitting or forcing exchange rates to alter. And, this time, by one more method: by imposing additional trade barriers or their equivalent, whether in the form of higher tariffs, or smaller import quotas, or extracting from other countries tighter "voluntary" quotas on their exports, or "tieing" foreign aid, or buying higher priced domestic goods or services to meet military needs, or imposing taxes on foreign borrowing, or imposing direct controls on investments by U.S. citizens abroad, or any one of the host of other devices for interfering with the private business of private individuals that have become so familiar to us since Hjalmar Schacht perfected the modern techniques of exchange control in 1934 to strengthen the Nazis for war and to despoil a large class of his fellow citizens.

Fortunately or unfortunately, even Congress cannot repeal the laws of arithmetic. Books must balance. We must use one of these four methods. Because we have been unwilling to select the only on that is currently fully consistent with both economic and political needs—namely, floating exchange rates—we have been driven, as if by an invisible hand, to employ all the others, and even then may not escape the need for explicit changes in exchange rates.

We affirm in loud and clear voices that we will not and must not erect trade barriers—yet is there any doubt about how far we have gone down the fourth route? After the host of measures already taken, the Secretary of the Treasury has openly stated to the Senate Finance Committee that if the so-called interest equalization tax—itself a concealed exchange control and concealed devaluation—is not passed, we shall have to resort to direct controls over foreign investment.

We affirm that we cannot drain our reserves further, yet short-term liabilities mount and our gold stock continues to decline.

We affirm that we cannot let balance-of-payments problems interfere with domestic prosperity, yet for at least some 4 years now we have followed a less expansive monetary policy than would have been healthy for our economy.

Chairman Douglas. We thank you for that, Professor Friedman.

Mr. Friedman. Even all together, these measures may only serve to postpone but not prevent open devaluation—if the experience of other countries is any guide. Whether they do, depends not on us but on others. For our best hope of escaping our present difficulties is that foreign countries will inflate.

In the meantime, we adopt one expedient after another, borrowing here, making swap arrangements there, changing the form of loans to make the figures look good. Entirely aside from the ineffectiveness of most of these measures, they are politically degrading and demeaning. We are a great and wealthy Nation. We should be directing our own course, setting an example to the world, living up to our destiny. Instead, we send our officials hat in hand to make the rounds of foreign governments and central banks; we put foreign central banks in a position to determine whether or not we can meet our obligations and thus enable them to exert great influence on our policies; we are driven to niggling negotiations with Hong Kong and with Japan and for all I know, Monaco, to get them to limit voluntarily their exports. Is this posture suitable for the leader of the free world?

Chairman Douglas. I do not wish to interrupt you, but I would like to say that I think many visits to Monaco are for a different purpose. [Laughter.]

Go ahead.

Mr. Friedman. It is not the least of the virtues of floating exchange rates that we would again become masters in our own house. We could decide important issues on the proper ground. The military could concentrate on military effectiveness and not on saving foreign exchange; recipients of foreign aid could concentrate on how to get the most out of what we give them and not on how to spend it all in the United States; Congress could decide how much to spend on foreign aid on the basis of what we get for our money and what else we could use it for and not how it will affect the gold stock; the monetary authorities could concentrate on domestic prices and employment, not on how to induce foreigners to hold dollar balances in this country; the Treasury and the tax committees of Congress could devote their attention to the equity of the tax system and its effects on our efficiency, rather than on how to use tax gimmicks to discourage imports, subsidize exports, and discriminate against outflows of capital.

A system of floating exchange rates would render the problem of making outflows equal inflows unto the market where it belongs and not leave it to the clumsy and heavy hand of Government. It would leave Government free to concentrate on its proper functions.

In conclusion, a word about gold. Our commitment to buy and sell gold for monetary use at a fixed price of $35 an ounce is, in practice, the mechanism whereby we maintain fixed rates of exchange between the dollar and other currencies—or, more precisely, whereby we leave all initiative for changes in such rates to other countries. This commitment should be terminated. The price of gold should be determined in the free market, with the U.S. Government committed neither to buying gold nor to selling gold at any fixed price. This is the appropriate counterpart of a policy of floating exchange rates. With respect to our existing stock of gold, we could simply keep it fixed, neither adding to it nor reducing it; alternatively, we could sell it off gradually at the market price or add to it gradually, thereby reducing or increasing our governmental stockpiles of this particular metal. In any event, we should simultaneously remove all present limitations on the ownership of gold and the trading in gold by American citizens. There is no reason why gold, like other commodities, should not be freely traded on a free market.

STATEMENT OF MILTON FRIEDMAN, PROFESSOR OF ECONOMICS, UNIVERSITY OF CHICAGO

A Defense of Fixed Exchange Rates

Henry C. Wallich

Flexible rates have achieved a high measure of acceptance in academic circles, but very little among public officials. This raises the question whether we have a parallel to the famous case of free trade: almost all economists favor it in principle, but no major country ever has adopted it. Does the logic of economics point equally irrefutable to flexible rates, while the logic of politics points in another direction?

The nature of the case, I believe, is fundamentally different. Most countries do practice free trade within their borders, although they reject it outside. But economists do not propose flexible rates for the States of the Union, among which men, money, and goods can move freely, and which are governed by uniform monetary, fiscal, and other policies. Flexible rates are to apply only to relations among countries that do not permit free factor movements across their borders and that follow, or may follow, substantially different monetary and fiscal policies. It is the imperfections of the world that seem to suggest that flexible rates, which would be harmful if applied to different parts of a single country, would do more good than harm internationally.

It is quite arguable that the Appalachian area would benefit if it could issue a dollar of its own, an Appalachian dollar which in that case would sell, probably, at 60 or 90 cents. Exports from that region would increase, and unemployment would diminish. A great many good things would happen, but we are also aware of what it would do to the economy of the United States—and, therefore, we do not propose that solution. The question is, Do we want to look upon the world as quite different from the United States, as hopelessly divided into self-contained units where cooperation and efforts to coordinate policies are doomed to frustration? In that case, flexible rates may be the best way to avoid a very bad situation. But should we not try to establish within the world something that begins to approximate the conditions that prevail within a country, in the way of coordination of policies, freer flow of capital and of goods and so try to achieve the benefits of one large economic area within the world? That is what we should try for.

Now to resume: The proponents of flexible rates argue, in effect, that flexible rates can help a country get out of almost any of the typical difficulties that economies experience. This is perfectly true. If the United States has a balance-of-payments deficit, a flexible exchange rate allows the dollar to decline until receipts have risen and payments fallen enough to restore balance. If the United States has unemployment, flexible rates can protect it against the balance-of-payments consequences of a policy of expansion. We would then have less unemployment. If the United States has suffered inflation and fears that it will be undersold internationally, flexible rates can remove the danger.

All of these advantages are quite clear.

Other countries have analogous advantages. If Chile experiences a decline in copper prices, flexible rates can ease the inevitable adjustment. If Germany finds that other countries have inflated while German prices have remained more nearly stable, flexible rates could help to avoid importing inflation. If Canada has a large capital inflow, a flexible rate will remove the need for price and income increases that would otherwise be needed to facilitate the transfer of real resources.

There are other adjustments, however, that must be made in all of these cases. If a country allows its exchange rate to go down, some price adjustments still remain to be made. Furthermore, each time a country makes this kind of adjustment, allowing its exchange rate to decline, other countries suffer. If the U.S. dollar depreciates, we undersell the Europeans. It could be argued that if the U.S. price levels go down instead of the exchange rate, we also undersell the Europeans, and if because of a declining price level we have unemployment we would be buying still less from them. Nevertheless, there is a difference. A price adjustment tends to be slow and is likely to be no greater than it need be and tends to be selective for particular commodities. In contrast, an exchange rate movement is unpredictable. It can be large—we could easily have a drop of 10 or 20 percent in an exchange rate. It comes suddenly. And it compels other countries to be on their guard.

Why, given the attractions of flexible rates, should one advise policymakers to stay away from them? Since the dollar problem is the concrete situation in which flexible rates are being urged today, it is in terms of the dollar that they must be discussed. In broadest terms, the reason why flexible rates are inadvisable is that their successful functioning would require more self-discipline and mutual forbearance than countries today are likely to muster. Exchange rates are two sided—depreciation for the dollar means appreciation for the European currencies. To work successfully, a flexible dollar, for instance, must not depreciate to the point where the Europeans would feel compelled to take counteraction. I believe that the limits of tolerance, before counteraction begins today are narrow and that a flexible dollar would invite retaliation almost immediately.

In the abstract, the European countries perhaps ought to consider that if the United States allows the dollar to go down, it is doing so in the interests of all-round equilibrium. They ought perhaps to consider that with a stable dollar rate the same adjustment might have to take place through a decline in prices here and a rise in prices there. In practice, they are likely to be alive principally to the danger of being undersold by American producers if the dollar goes down, in their own and third markets. The changing competitive pressure would fall unevenly upon particular industries, and those who are hurt would demand protection.

The most likely counteraction might take one of two forms. The Europeans could impose countervailing duties, such as the United States also has employed at times. They could alternately also depreciate European currencies along with the dollar or, what would amount to almost the same thing, prevent the dollar from depreciating. This might involve the European countries in the purchase of large amounts of dollars. If they are to peg the dollar, they could minimize their commitment by imposing a simple form of exchange control that the Swiss practiced during the last war. The Swiss purchased dollars only from their exporters, also requiring their importers to buy these dollars thereby stabilizing the trade dollar, while allowing dollars from capital movements—finance dollars—to find their own level in the market.

The large volume of not very predictable short-term capital movements in the world today makes such reactions under flexible rates particularly likely.

Chairman DOUGLAS. Is that not what has been done for the last 2 years or so by Great Britain and the Netherlands?

Mr. WALLICH. Yes, in mild form for securities; that is correct, sir. A sudden outflow of funds from the United States, for instance (because of the fear of budget deficits or many other things that could happen), would tend to drive the dollar down. As a result, American exporters could undersell producers everywhere else in the world. It seems unlikely that foreign countries would allow a fortuitous short-term capital movement to have such far-reaching consequences. It would not even be economically appropriate to allow a transitory fluctuation in the capital account of the balance of payments to have a major influence on the current account. Such a fluctuation should not alter the pattern of trade, because the situation is likely to be reversed. Other countries therefore would probably take defensive action to make sure that no industry is destroyed and after several years may have to be rebuilt because of the ups and downs of short-term capital movements.

It can be argued that under flexible rates the effects of such a movement would be forestalled by stabilizing speculation on a future recovery of the dollar. This is possible. It is possible also, however, that speculation would seek a quick profit from the initial drop in the dollar, instead of a longer run one from its eventual recovery. Then short-run speculation would drive the dollar down farther at first. In any case there is not enough assurance that speculators will not make mistakes to permit basing the world's monetary system upon the stabilizing effects of speculation.

In the case of countries which import much of what they consume, such as England, a temporary decline in the local currency may even be self-validating. If the cost of living rises as the currency declines, wages will rise. Thereafter, the currency may never recover to its original level.

This points up one probable consequence of flexible exchange rates: A worldwide acceleration of inflation. In some countries the indicated ratchet effect of wages will be at work. If exchange rates go down, wages will rise, and exchange rates cannot recover. In the United States the rise in the cost of imports would not be very important. But the removal of balance-of-payments restraints may well lead to policies that could lead to price increases. The American inflation of the 1950's was never defeated until the payments deficit became serious. Elsewhere, the removal of balance-of-payments disciplines might have the same effect. Rapid inflation in turn would probably compel governments to intervene drastically in foreign trade and finance.

Chairman DOUGLAS. The payment deficit as a means of checking price advances—are you welcoming that?

Mr. WALLICH. No, I do not, but I am aware, Mr. Chairman, that there is a choice to be made here—more employment or more stable prices. If we pursued more sensible policies and exerted a little more self-restraint, this choice would not be upon us. But if we insist on raising costs and raising prices in the presence of unemployment then this unpleasant choice must be made. As Mr. Friedman has said, it is quite clear that the discipline of the balance of payments has made for a more restrictive policy in this country than would have been followed in the absence of this discipline. It is quite conceivable that the absence of balance-of-payments disciplines would have strong inflationary effects in some countries. In that case governments would be compelled immediately to intervene drastically in foreign trade and finance; in other words, flexible exchange rates would contribute to their own extinction or to exchange control.

The prospect that flexible rates would greatly increase uncertainty for foreign traders and investors has been cited many times. It should be noted that this uncertainty extends also to domestic investment decisions that might be affected by changing import competition or changing export prospects. It has been argued that uncertainties about future exchange rates can be removed by hedging in the future market. This, however, involves a cost even where cover is readily available. The history of futures markets does not suggest that it will be possible to get cover for long-term positions. To hedge domestic investment decisions that might be affected by flexible rates is in the nature of things impracticable.

The picture that emerges of the international economy under flexible rates is one of increasing disintegration. Independent national policies and unpredictable changes in each country's competitive position will compel governments to shield their producers and markets. The argument that such shielding would also automatically be accomplished by movements in the affected country's exchange rate underrates the impact of fluctuations upon particular industries, if not upon the entire economy. That international integration and flexible rates are incompatible seems to be the view also of the European Common Market countries, who have left no doubt that they want stable rates within the EEC. The same applies if we visualize the "Kennedy round" under the Trade Expansion Act. I think if we told the Europeans that, after lowering our tariffs, we were going to cast the dollar loose and let it fluctuate, we would get very little tariff reduction. They would want to keep up their guard.

If the disintegrating effects of flexible rates are to be overcome, a great deal of policy coordination, combined with self-discipline and mutual forbearance, would be required. The desired independence of national economic policy would in fact have to be foregone—interest rates, budgets, wage and prices policies would have to be harmonized. If the world were ready for such cooperation, it would be capable also of making a fixed exchange rate system work. In that case, flexible rates would accomplish nothing that could not more cheaply and simply be done with fixed rates. It seems to follow that flexible rates have no unique capacity for good, whereas they possess great capacity to do damage.

A modified version of the flexible rates proposal has been suggested. This version would allow the dollar and other currencies to fluctuate within a given range, say 5 percent up and down. This "widening of the gold points" is believed to reduce the danger of destabilizing speculation. It might perhaps enlist speculation on the side of stabilization, for if the dollar, say, had dropped to its lower limit, and if the public had confidence that that limit would not be broken, the only movement on which to speculate would be a rise. The spectacle of a currency falling below par may induce, according to the proponents, a strong political effort to bring it back.

This proposal likewise strikes me as unworkable. For one thing, I doubt that people would have a great deal of confidence in a limit of 5 percent below par, if par itself has been given up. Political support for holding this second line would probably be less than the support that can be mustered to hold the first. For another, the execution of the plan would still require the maintenance of international reserves, to protect the upper and lower limits. But with fluctuating rates, dollar and sterling would cease to be desirable media for monetary reserves. International liquidity would become seriously impaired. A third objection is that under today's conditions, the complex negotiations and legislation required, in the unlikely event that the plan could be negotiated at all, could not go forward without immediate speculation against the dollar before the plan goes into effect.

It remains only to point out that, even in the absence of a high degree of international cooperativeness, a system of fixed exchange rates can be made to work. It can be made to work mainly because it imposes a discipline upon all participants, and because within this discipline there is nevertheless some room for adjustment. The principal sources of flexibility are productivity gains and the degree to which they are absorbed by wage increases. Wages cannot be expected to decline. But their rise can be slowed in relation to the rate of productivity growth, in which case prices would become more competitive relative to other countries. With annual productivity gains of 2 to 3 percent in the United States and more abroad, it would not take many years to remove a temporary imbalance.

STATEMENT OF HENRY C. WALLICH, PROFESSOR OF ECONOMICS, YALE UNIVERSITY

The Operation of Flexible Exchange Rates

Council of Economic Advisers

Floating Rates in Principle

The role of floating exchange rates can best be seen in the need for adjustment among national economies. All countries are continually subjected to shocks that lead both to internal imbalances (excessive or deficient utilization of domestic resources) and to external imbalances (foreign trade or capital flows at unsustainable levels). A system of flexible, market-determined exchange rates (or, in short, "floating" rates) allows more automatic external adjustment than a system of fixed parities, and thus leaves more scope for domestic macroeconomic policies to adapt to the changing requirements for internal balance.

External adjustment occurs as exchange rates move to equilibrate trade and net capital flows. More precisely, for a given change in official holdings, the rate will move to a level that either brings the value of goods and services exported and imported into balance or induces changes in private asset holdings to finance the discrepancy.

The equilibrating mechanism works on both the capital and current accounts. For a country incurring a large current account deficit, the currency depreciates to reduce the current account deficit by increasing the country's price competitiveness. That process, however, takes time. In the interim, currency movements will induce private holders of wealth to accumulate the country's assets to the extent necessary to finance the deficit.

The second feature of an idealized system of floating exchange rates can be seen as a consequence of the first. Because floating rates tend to assure external equilibrium, countries can enjoy greater independence of macroeconomic policies and performance. Under a regime of fixed exchange rates, the extent to which a country's macroeconomic policies could diverge from those of its trading partners was limited in important ways. Divergent policies would lead to trade imbalances, with expansionary countries moving toward deficit and restrictive countries toward surplus. There was no automatic mechanism to generate the needed capital movements to support the imbalances. Indeed, outflows of capital from countries pursuing relatively expansionary policies to countries pursuing restrictive policies sometimes exacerbated disequilibria in overall balance of payments positions. A country's freedom to engage in independent macroeconomic policies was thus constrained by its capacity to absorb or lose reserves.

Under a floating rate regime, however, wide divergences of macroeconomic policies would, in principle, be possible. For those countries pursuing rapid growth through expansionary macroeconomic policies or those accepting high inflation, the presence of a depreciating currency would allow the balance of payments to remain close to equilibrium.

Critiques of Floating Rates

For more than 5 years the major economies have functioned under a floating rate regime. The new regime has been successful in permitting the industrial economies to absorb shocks that were unprecedented in the post-war period. At the same time, overall economic performance and exchange market behavior have been much less satisfactory than was expected, leading many to wonder whether the exchange rate regime was at least partly responsible for the poor performance.

Critics have argued that floating rates have had four failings: they have not eliminated balance of payments disequilibria; they have not allowed the d_gree of policy independence that had been anticipated; they have proved inflationary; and they have introduced major new elements of instability and uncertainty to financial markets.

First, floating rates clearly have not eliminated current account surpluses and deficits. These deficits and surpluses have not, in general, fallen from the levels of the late 1960s and early 1970s and, on many occasions, some have been even higher.

Such an observation, however, does not imply a failure of floating rates to perform their adjustment function. The imbalances that have occurred have not usually resulted from floating per se, but from the greater divergence of macroeconomic performances and from the exceptionally large shocks to the international system, such as OPEC price rises and large increases in agricultural and commodity prices. Exchange rate changes have generally responded well to these deficits and surpluses and have helped to move economies back toward external equilibrium, even if not as quickly or as smoothly as originally hoped. A balance of payments equilibrium, moreover, does not necessarily require that the current (or trade) account should be balanced, only that the current or trade account deficit or surplus be willingly financed. In fact, deficits or surpluses on current account may well represent the equilibrating counterpart to structural or "autonomous" capital inflows or outflows.

In contrast, during the final years of the Bretton Woods system, balance of payments disequilibria that resulted at least partly from divergent macro-economic performances led to several serious and protracted balance of payments crises. Normal trade and investment patterns were disrupted as governments responded to these disequilibrium situations by imposing trade and capital controls and other emergency measures before they were finally forced to change their exchange rate parities.

A second cause of concern exists because floating has led to less policy independence than had been anticipated. To be sure, countries have been significantly more independent than in prior years, especially in the realm of monetary policies. A good example lies in the ability of Germany, during the early phase of the current expansion, to pursue a relatively restrictive monetary policy, while that of the United States was relatively expansionary.

Although independence has been greater than with fixed rates, it has by no means been complete under floating. There have been obvious limitations to policy flexibility, partly because exchange rate changes cannot insulate national economies from their partners' performance or from international economic shocks. We have learned that in an increasingly inter-dependent international economic system floating exchange rates do not free countries from the effects of their neighbors' economic policies and performances. Similarly, countries must recognize their responsibility to act in ways that do not inflict excessive adjustment costs on others.

The third major criticism of the floating rate system has been that it contains an inflationary bias. Two lines of argument have been presented to support this view: first, that floating generates inflation because it fails to impose needed discipline on the conduct of fiscal and monetary policies; second, that because of asymmetries and ratchets the increased inflationary pressures associated with depreciation are not matched by commensurate downward price pressures in countries whose exchange rates are appreciating. Thus, it is argued, the net effect of exchange rate changes is inflationary for the world as a whole.

Neither of these arguments is entirely convincing. Regarding the first argument—presumed lack of discipline—it is important to note that even without external pressures there are clearly powerful internal forces which oppose inflation. Recent experience in the United States and some countries of Europe, where large current account deficits and currency depreciations have led to quite restrictive economic policies, indicates the extent to which difficult stabilization policies will be undertaken even in a flexible exchange rate system.

Moreover, a regime of fixed rates allows inflation to spill over the borders. Price rises originating in one country spill over into other countries directly if exchange rates cannot shift. Indeed, to the extent that inflation originating in one country is shared by others when exchange rates are fixed, discipline in the conduct of fiscal and monetary policies may be weaker than under floating rates, where the full inflationary impact of inappropriate policies is felt domestically.

The evidence to support the second argument—that there are asymmetries in the effects of exchange rate changes on inflation—is mixed. While it is true that there exists considerable evidence of increasing downward rigidity in the levels of prices and wages in a number of countries, there is no comparable evidence that rates of inflation are less responsive to currency appreciation than to depreciation.

Finally, factors other than floating exchange rates provide a more compelling explanation for the high and persistent inflation in the industrial countries: slower productivity growth, excessive demand pressures, external shocks such as those created by OPEC, and structural changes and rigidities in domestic labor and product markets.

A final criticism of floating has been that it induces excessive volatility in exchange rate movements. Chart 11 presents the path of the trade-weighted dollar since 1970, using an index of dollar movements against the 10 major currencies, and 1972–76 total multilateral trade shares as weights. In addition to these longer-run swings in rates, it is certainly true that day-to-day movements in exchange rates have been larger in the float than in the preceding Bretton Woods era. It is difficult to determine whether these movements have been excessive. In a fixed rate system such as Bretton Woods, day-to-day variability is sharply reduced by the active intervention of central banks to keep the rate within a narrow range. Furthermore, for as long as the range remains credible, private actions tend to keep the rate within the range whenever transient factors lead to a rate movement to the upper or lower limit. Day-to-day variability is thus largely eliminated. On the other hand, the fixing of exchange rates while economic conditions are changing makes it likely that exchange rates will increasingly diverge from levels that would be consistent with underlying economic factors. Eventually the credibility of the range is challenged by market participants, and potentially disruptive speculative attacks can then occur until rates are forced to new, more appropriate levels.

In a floating rate system, day-to-day variability of exchange rates is inevitable as market participants respond to new information about economic developments that alters their perceptions about appropriate exchange rate patterns. Indeed, these day-to-day movements in principle constitute the means of accomplishing longer-run adjustment of exchange rates to changing economic circumstances. This fundamental role of exchange rate movements raises the question whether the observed short-run variability of exchange rates has been larger than was required to allow the necessary medium-term flexibility. This question is complex and has not been thoroughly addressed. A preliminary examination of recent experience and related studies by the Council of Economic Advisers has uncovered mixed evidence. In some cases, short-run variability over the last 5 years has been broadly commensurate with longer-run changes, while in other cases short-run changes have been less than might be consistent with the longer run. No cases of persistent, excessive volatility were found.

There is a sense in which the floating rate system itself may have led to excessive volatility—through the relaxed constraints on macroeconomic behavior. As noted above, a floating rate system allows greater divergence in macroeconomic experience. Unfortunately, when greater scope for divergent policies and performance is allowed, market uncertainty about appropriate exchange rates is also increased. The uncertainty, in turn, can cause market exchange rates to move in an erratic and disorderly fashion as market participants react, and overreact, to transitory bits of information and rumors.

Greater exchange rate noise and uncertainty are among the costs of a floating rate system. Achievement of greater stability in exchange rate markets is dependent on the closer and more effective coordination of macro-

Chart 11

Weighted-Average Exchange Value
of the U.S. Dollar

INDEX. MARCH 1973=100

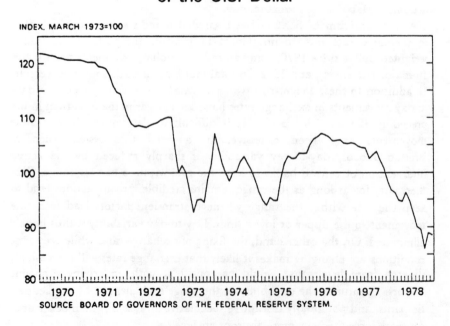

SOURCE BOARD OF GOVERNORS OF THE FEDERAL RESERVE SYSTEM.

economic policies among countries and on the continuing efforts of each country to sustain macroeconomic policies that are consistent with internal and external adjustment.

In general, however, the evidence, although not conclusive, does indicate that floating has worked well over the long run, especially considering the magnitude of the shocks to the international financial system. In fact, given these shocks, it is not clear that any system other than generalized floating would have been viable during the period. Exchange rate movements, while large, have broadly responded to economic fundamentals, have facilitated adjustment, and have tended to move the system toward rather than away from greater stability. If exchange rates are at present too volatile for some countries, steps to increase the coordination of macroeconomic policies could be helpful. Recognition of the current level of interdependence through improved coordination across countries may help to bring greater stability to the foreign exchange markets as well as to provide an international environment that is favorable to domestic policy goals.

The Case Against Trying to Stabilize the Dollar

Martin Feldstein

It is easy to understand why dollar stability has widespread political appeal. To businessmen, a fluctuating dollar means an uncertain competitive environment. Relatively small exchange rate fluctuations can eliminate previously profitable markets at home and abroad. To consumers, a declining dollar can mean inflation and a lower standard of living. And looking beyond economic self-interest, there is an atavistic nationalism that confuses the dollar and the flag, incorrectly regarding a strong dollar as a measure of national virtue and a declining dollar as an indication of national weakness.

Despite the popular support for the notion of a stable dollar, the analysis summarized in this paper implies that a stable dollar, if it could be achieved, would probably be undesirable and that the process of trying to stabilize the dollar would be economically harmful. A stable dollar would prevent desirable trade and capital adjustments, and induce unwarranted ones. The process of trying to stabilize the dollar would require diverting monetary and fiscal policies from their proper goals and thereby create more inflation, more unemployment, or an inferior rate of capital formation than would otherwise be possible.

There is, of course, nothing wrong with dollar stability if it happens to come about as a by-product of otherwise appropriate economic policies. That is not the issue that economists have in mind when they argue against trying to stabilize the dollar. The real issue is whether a stable exchange value of the dollar should be a separate target of economic policy and, to the extent necessary, other policy goals should be sacrificed in order to achieve dollar stability.

*Professor of Economics, Harvard University, Cambridge, MA 02138, and President of the National Bureau of Economic Research.

The appropriate exchange rate policy depends on the country and its economic circumstances. A small country within Europe that trades a major share of its GNP with its neighbors may find it appropriate to fix its exchange rate relative to its major trading partners even though that requires sacrificing the independence of its monetary policy and accepting German economic hegemony. Alternatively, even without important trade links, a country may choose to tie its currency to that of a low inflation country in order to achieve a monetary discipline and credibility that would not otherwise be possible. In considering the appropriate policy toward the dollar, it is important to recognize that U.S. trade is only 10 to 15 percent of GNP, that we can control our inflation rate through our own domestic monetary policy without an exchange rate anchor, and that the United States will not permit our monetary policy to be made in Frankfurt or Tokyo.

One final word of introduction is appropriate. Economists who oppose pursuing policies to stabilize the dollar are sometimes accused of favoring inflation or other inappropriate domestic policies. It is easy to understand the source of this misunderstanding. The major swings of the dollar during the fifteen years since the collapse of the Bretton Woods system can be traced primarily to the pursuit and subsequent corrections of inappropriate monetary and budget polices: the inflation of the 1970s followed by the anti-inflationary monetary policy at the beginning of the 1980s; the surge in actual and projected budget deficits in the early 1980s followed by a gradual decline in actual and projected budget deficits after 1985 (see my 1988a article). But the case against making dollar stability a separate goal of national economic policy should not be confused with condoning bad economic policies. An economist can be a firm advocate of sound domestic policies while still rejecting the notion of dollar stability as a separate goal of economic policy.

I. Capital Markets, Goods Markets, and Exchange Rates

Before looking at the consequences of trying to stabilize the dollar by explicit policy manipulation, consider how exchange rates naturally vary over time in response to supply and demand conditions in financial markets and in the international markets for goods and services.

Consider first the role of international capital markets. At any time there exist in each country desired levels of saving and investment corresponding to prevailing interest rates. If there were no opportunity to invest or borrow abroad, each country's domestic interest rate would adjust to bring saving and investment into balance. With completely integrated world capital markets, there would be a single world real interest rate that balanced worldwide saving and investment while the individual domestic saving and investment rates would in general be unequal. In practice, capital markets are less than perfectly integrated and real interest rates differ among countries. It nevertheless remains true that the saving rate in each country will not in general be equal to the desired level of investment at the interest rate prevailing in that country. If the desired level of domestic saving exceeds domestic investment, there will be a capital outflow; if desired saving is less than desired investment, capital will flow into the country.[1]

Since the capital flow is by definition equal to the current account balance which in turn is equal to the sum of the trade balance plus net international investment income, changing the capital flow in or out of the country requires a change in the trade balance. And since the trade balance is a function of the exchange rate, the only way in which a sustained change in the capital flow can be brought about is by a change in the exchange rate.

Of course, conditions in the markets for goods and services also affect the exchange rate. Any shift in the supply or demand for exports or imports (at given exchange rates) will alter the exchange rate. For example, if American consumers increase their demand for foreign products at the existing dollar exchange rate (because of a shift in tastes or an improvement in the relative quality of foreign products or a reduction in their foreign currency prices), the value of the dollar will fall in order to maintain the initial level

of the trade surplus or deficit and therefore the initial level of the international capital flow. Thus shifts in forces that influence the demand and supply of goods and services alter the exchange rate in a way that is directly linked to the equilibrium capital flow.

Since exchange rate changes play such a central role in balancing the supply and demand in capital markets and in the markets for goods and services, how can anyone believe that exchange rates could remain constant? The textbook answer is that exchange rate changes are not needed to achieve a capital flow between two countries if the products of the two countries are "perfect substitutes" (in the sense that the cross-price elasticity of demand is infinite). For example, an increased desire to invest in one country would put upward pressure on its local prices, thereby inducing an increase in net imports sufficient to maintain the initial level of demand. This increase in imports automatically entails a capital inflow equal to the desired increase in investment.

This "purchasing power parity" theory of fixed exchange rates is good textbook economics but only holds if the traded goods are perfect substitutes. Experience shows repeatedly that the demand elasticities of similar products produced in different countries are far from infinite even over rather long periods of time. As the experience of the 1980s confirms, imports and exports are slow to respond to changes in relative prices and therefore large departures of exchange rates from purchasing power parity are required to achieve significant shifts in trade balances, current account balances, and capital flows.

With all of this as background, I can now turn to the case against trying to stabilize the dollar. I will begin by explaining why a stable dollar, if it could somehow be achieved, would in general have undesirable effects on trade and capital flows. I then turn to the adverse effects of trying to stabilize the exchange rate.

II. Adverse Effects of Artificial Dollar Stability

Although shifts in saving and investment and in the supply and demand for internationally traded products might just happen to keep the dollar stable, such a singular coincidence can be ruled out as extremely unlikely. In general, the dollar will have to shift to achieve or maintain the desired net international capital flow described in the previous section.

It is important in this context to distinguish real and nominal exchange rates. Changes in nominal exchange rates are simply the changes in exchange rates quoted in the market, while changes in real exchange rates are those changes adjusted for differences in inflation rates between the home and foreign countries. Although it is of course the real exchange rates that influence patterns of trade and therefore the associated capital flows, popular discussions and official pronouncements do not make the distinction and therefore implicitly discuss the stabilization of nominal exchange rates. (See my 1988b article.)

Whenever domestic inflation rates differ among countries, the nominal exchange rates must change just to maintain the initial real exchange rates. The prices of tradable products in the United States are currently increasing at about 6 percent a year, while the corresponding price index in Japan is not increasing at all. Maintaining the real yen-dollar exchange rate therefore requires the nominal dollar-yen exchange rate to decline at a 6 percent annual rate.[2] Failure of the nominal dollar exchange rate to decline in this way would, all other things equal, lead to an increasing U.S. trade deficit and a more rapid accumulation of debt to the rest of the world.

Shifts in the nominal exchange rate that maintain a constant real exchange rate may provide nothing more than a first approximation to the required shift in the dollar's value. For example, the sharp increase in the world oil supply in 1988 that caused a fall in the dollar price of oil during the past year was of greatest help to those countries that are most dependent on imported oil. Thus Japan, which imports all of its oil and for which oil imports are a large part of total imports, was particularly benefited. The yen therefore had to rise relative to the dollar to prevent an increase in the Japanese trade surplus and a resulting unwanted additional capital outflow from Japan.

In addition to the shifts of the exchange rate that are needed to balance differences in inflation rates and to offset shifts in supply and demand in world product markets, the dollar has to shift to permit changes in desired levels of domestic saving and investment to be financed efficiently. The most obvious example of this in the 1980s was the dramatic decline in the U.S. saving rate caused by the surge in the budget deficit. Without an increased net capital inflow from the rest of the world, the U.S. net investment in plant and equipment, housing, and inventories would have had to decline by approximately one-third. In fact, the higher real U.S. interest rates attracted capital from abroad, inducing a rise in the real value of the dollar that caused an increased trade deficit that permitted the increased net capital inflow. Without the capital inflow, the decline of U.S. saving would have caused a substantial misallocation of worldwide investment with the productivity of capital significantly higher in the United States than abroad. Although the associated trade deficit had painful effects on some sectors of the American economy, the overall U.S. unemployment rate declined and total GNP rose throughout the period of the increasing trade deficit.

III. Dangers of Trying to Stabilize the Dollar

Trying to stabilize the dollar requires diverting monetary and fiscal policies from their proper roles. The result of such policy distortion can be a substantial sacrifice of the traditional goals of price stability, high employment, and an appropriate level of national capital accumulation.

Although currency market intervention is the most obvious tool of exchange rate manipulation, it is also the least effective. Experience continues to confirm that "sterilized intervention" (i.e., the buying and selling of foreign currencies with offsetting changes in government debt to keep the total money supply unchanged) has little or no effect on exchange rates (Maurice Obstfeld, 1988), and that any such effect is likely to last for only a few days or at most a few weeks. Some research suggests that even the modest impact of sterilized intervention exists only because financial markets interpret exchange market intervention as a "signal" that the government is prepared to shift monetary or fiscal policy to achieve the desired currency shift.

In contrast to the ineffectiveness of exchange market intervention, changes in monetary policy can alter nominal exchange rates in the long run and real exchange rates in the nearer term. Consider first the long-term effects of monetary policy on nominal exchange rates. An increase in the U.S. money supply eventually causes a corresponding rise in the U.S. price level. If the U.S. price level rises, a stable real exchange rate requires a proportionate fall of the nominal value of the dollar. This mechanism shows also how an expansionary monetary policy that raises the U.S. domestic price level can stabilize the nominal exchange rate when the real value of the dollar is rising.

It is important to emphasize, however, that the effect of an expansionary monetary policy on the real exchange rate is only transitory. An expansionary monetary policy can temporarily lower the real interest rate, causing the value of the dollar to decline. Since the prices of goods and services increase only with a lag, the initial nominal decline of the dollar is temporarily a real decline as well. Over time, however, the rise in domestic prices matches the fall in the dollar. There is a nominal dollar decline but no change in the real value of the dollar. In the long run, a shift in monetary policy can have only a monetary or nominal effect and cannot alter real values.

The experience in 1983 and 1984 illustrates the danger of trying to use monetary policy to stabilize the nominal value of the dollar when its real value is being increased by fundamental real factors. At that time, increases in the current and projected budget deficits were raising the dollar's real value. The rising dollar induced substantial pressure on the U.S. government from foreign as well as domestic sources to take steps to reverse the dollar's sharp rise. Although a contractionary fiscal policy would have been appropriate domestic policy at the time and would also have reduced the dollar's value, no fiscal action was taken. If the pressure had succeeded in inducing the U.S. administration to stabilize the dollar, the responsibility would have fallen to the Federal Reserve. An expansion of the money supply would have produced a temporary reduction in the real exchange rate and a sustained reduction of the nominal exchange rate. The important point is that, after a temporary period, the real exchange rate that influences trade would have been unaffected while the progress of the early 1980s in reducing inflation would have been reversed.

The futility and the danger of using monetary policy to stabilize the dollar is not just hypothetical. In the spring of 1987 the Federal Reserve began a policy of restricting the money supply and raising interest rates in order to support the value of the dollar. The two percentage-point rise in interest rates was one of the factors that precipitated the October stock market crash. Had the Fed not then explicitly abandoned the goal of supporting the dollar and allowed interest rates to decline, the American economy might well have slid into recession in 1988.

Although neither exchange market intervention nor monetary policy can have a sustained effect on the real value of the dollar, budget and tax policies could in principle be used to stabilize the real value of the dollar over a sustained period of time. As the experience in the early 1980s demonstrated, fiscal policies that reduce national saving raise real interest rates, thereby increasing the attractiveness of dollar securities and causing the dollar to rise. The opposite is true when fiscal policies increase the national saving rate.

It would, however, be a serious mistake to select otherwise inappropriate fiscal policies just to stabilize the dollar. At the present time, for example, the continued decline of the dollar could be delayed by fiscal actions that increase the real interest rate on dollar securities. But who would advocate an increase in the budget deficit or a tax change that penalizes private saving in order to stabilize the dollar?

One final word about the harmful effects of trying to stabilize the dollar. Although economists focus on real exchange rates, official pronouncements and policy decisions within the group of G-7 finance ministers are always in terms of nominal exchange rates. In a world in which nominal interest rates differ because of differences in inflation rates, the promise of nominal exchange rate stability is itself destabilizing. In 1988, U.S. interest rates exceeded corresponding Japanese rates by about four percentage points, approximately the difference in inflation rates. Portfolio investors who believed the G-7 assertions that the nominal dollar-yen exchange rate would nevertheless remain stable were induced to buy the higher yielding dollar securities. The result was a dollar increase of nearly 15 percent relative to the yen between January and October despite the evidence that the U.S. trade deficit and the Japanese trade surplus would remain very large unless the dollar fell further. When the credibility of the G-7 forecast evaporated in November, the dollar fell back to its January level. The counterproductive emphasis on nominal exchange rates does not reflect a lack of understanding on the part of the key G-7 finance ministers, central bankers, and advisors, but appears to be dictated by the political character of official efforts at exchange rate stabilization.

IV. Conclusion

Better domestic economic policies in the fifteen years since the collapse of the Bretton Woods system would have prevented the extreme fluctuations of the dollar's exchange value during those years. The pursuit of good policies here and abroad in the future should reduce the likelihood of such substantial exchange rate swings in the years ahead. But elevating exchange rate stability to a separate goal of economic policy would have serious adverse consequences. Trying to achieve that goal would mean diverting monetary and fiscal policies from their proper roles and thereby risking excessive inflation and unemployment and inadequate capital formation. And succeeding in the effort to achieve dollar stability would mean harmful distortions in the balance of trade and in the international flow of capital.

REFERENCES

Feldstein, Martin, (1988a) "Feldstein on the Dollar: Let the Market Decide," *The Economist*, December 5, 1988.

_____, (1988b) "Redefining Dollar Stability," *Wall Street Journal*, September 19, 1988.

_____ and Bachetta, Phillipe, "National Savings and International Investment," in John Shoven and B. Douglas Bernheim, eds., *The Economics of Savings*, Chicago: University of Chicago Press, forthcoming.

Obstfeld, Maurice, "The Effectiveness of Foreign-Exchange Intervention: Recent Experience," NBER Conference on International Policy Coordination and Exchange Rate Fluctuations, Kiawah Island, SC, October 27–29, 1988.

[1]The degree of capital market integration appears to be increasing over time but is still far from complete. See my forthcoming paper with Phillipe Bacchetta.

[2]The price indices used to convert nominal exchange rates to real exchange rates provide only a very imperfect measure of the changes in actual price competitiveness because of the impossibility of adequately reflecting changes in quality and the introduction of new products. These measurement problems raise serious doubts about any attempt to calculate purchasing power parity exchange rates.

The Case for Roughly Stabilizing the Real Value of the Dollar

John Williamson

The title of my paper implies the following five claims: 1) It is possible for macroeconomic policy to influence exchange rates in a substantive way; 2) It is desirable that macroeconomic policy target the exchange rate; 3) It is nevertheless desirable to leave substantial latitude for exchange rates to fluctuate around their target levels; 4) The target should be a real rather than nominal exchange rate; 5) The real value of the dollar was broadly appropriate when this paper was written (December 1988). The paper is devoted to explaining the basis for these five propositions.

I. The Controllability of Exchange Rates

The Jurgensen Report (1983) enthroned the view that sterilized intervention could have no significant influence on exchange rates as the conventional wisdom of the early 1980s. The subsequent success of the G-7, first in promoting a desired depreciation of the dollar following the Plaza and then in preventing overshooting following the Louvre, calls for a revision of this orthodoxy.

It is true that Martin Feldstein (1986) questioned whether the Plaza had any significant role in causing the dollar to depreciate. There is no way of answering this question with certainty since exchange rate models are quite unable to provide a convincing counterfactual, but two observations are in order. First, Feldstein's own counterfactual—that the dollar started a trend depreciation of 1.5 percent per month in March 1985 which was unaffected by the Plaza—is among the most unconvincing imaginable: it violates dramatically open-interest parity, the

theory that Feldstein's Council of Economic Advisers (1984) appealed to in order to explain how the markets expected the dollar's overvaluation to be unwound over a decade or so. Second, we now have the evidence, which Feldstein then lacked, that the G-7 broadly succeeded in stopping the dollar's decline when they decided that it had fallen far enough. In the 20 months subsequent to the Louvre it declined by an average of only 0.4 percent per month (as measured by the IMF's MERM index), which is little more than its trend rate of depreciation. The success of the bear squeeze mounted by the G-7 central banks in the first week of January 1988 in reversing the widespread belief that the dollar was entering a free fall is particularly noteworthy.

Hence my own judgment is now that sterilized intervention plus "jawboning" can have a substantial effect on exchange rates, and one that is not necessarily limited to the short run. Indeed, Paul Krugman (1987) has shown how the mere *expectation* of intervention at the edges of a wide zone can be expected to reduce exchange rate variability within the zone, even if the rate never actually reaches the edge of the zone and intervention never actually occurs.

None of this is to claim that intervention, with or without jawboning, is a particularly reliable instrument. In particular, it cannot be expected to hold an exchange rate that the market has decided is unrealistic: one-way bets will continue to attract an overwhelming response. When the authorities perceive that the market is questioning their target, they need to ask themselves whether the target remains appropriate. If not, it should be changed promptly (but modestly, so as to avoid forcing discontinuous changes in market rates). Otherwise, it should be defended by a convincing change in the short-term interest rate. Dutch experience in maintaining the guilder within the EMS

*Institute for International Economics, 11 Dupont Circle NW, Washington DC 20036. ©Institute for International Economics, all rights reserved; published with permission.

without capital controls shows that such a policy can be highly effective. Once the authorities have established their credibility, exchange rate management seems to require only occasional and short-lived changes in interest rates—always assuming that the target is indeed consistent with the fundamentals.

II. The Desirability of Targeting the Exchange Rate

Krugman (1988) has argued that the large exchange rate swings inherent in a floating regime tend to delink exchange rates from the real economy, and in the process to undermine the ability of exchange rate changes to influence the adjustment process. Exchange rate changes are such a useful mechanism that they should be hoarded for those occasions when they are needed to further an important social purpose, like promoting payments adjustment, not squandered on accommodating games played in the financial markets.

My own tendency has always been to base the case for treating the exchange rate as an intermediate target (rather than a residual) primarily on the high cost of exchange rate misalignments coupled with the overwhelming evidence that exchange rates become misaligned when neglected (whether benignly or malignly is a matter of opinion), rather than on the effects of volatility. To the extent that Krugman's "delinking" does not occur, the real exchange rate is the principal determinant of the division of domestic output between home and foreign markets, and of the distribution of domestic demand between home and foreign sources. A real exchange rate significantly out of line with that needed to sustain medium-run macroeconomic equilibrium therefore presents false signals to business that can misdirect investment or induce inappropriate closure of productive capacity, as well as generating inflationary or deflationary pressure. The costs of misalignments are serious: instances include the British struggle to maintain an overvalued pound in the mid-1960s, the German importation of inflation in the late 1960s and early 1970s, inflationary pressures in Britain in 1976 or the United States in 1978, the collapse of the Southern Cone stabilization plans in the early 1980s, the decimation of British manufacturing by the strong pound in Mrs. Thatcher's first three years, overexpansion of the tradable sectors in today's chronic surplus countries, and the rapid transformation of the United States into the world's largest debtor in the mid-1980s.

In some cases these misalignments developed through differential inflation leading fixed nominal exchange rates to become disequilibrium real exchange rates. In other cases they resulted from a choice of policy mix that drove a floating exchange rate away from long-run equilibrium. And in still other cases they were at least partly caused by a floating exchange rate responding to speculative pressures, which on occasion were justified but on other occasions appear to have been quite irrational. Whatever the cause, misalignments are costly.

Hence the conclusion that macroeconomic policy should take the exchange rate as an intermediate target. The exchange rate is, however, one of those variables to which the "$n-1$ problem" applies: a world of n currencies has only $n-1$ exchange rates, and thus only $n-1$ countries can pursue independent exchange rate policies. There are two alternative possible reactions to this situation. One is to pick a particular country, typically the largest, to play a passive or "nth currency" role. Postwar history does not suggest that this solution is either durable or satisfactory. The alternative is to seek international agreement on exchange rate targets. Thus, choice of the exchange rate as an intermediate target virtually dictates some degree of international macroeconomic policy coordination.

The minimal degree of coordination needed is agreement on exchange rate targets. But there are other variables beside exchange rates toward which $(n-1)$ considerations apply. In particular, excess or deficient demand in a single country can spill over into a temporary payments deficit or surplus, whereas generalized excess or deficient demand in the world necessarily causes inflation or unemployment. Hence the desirability of coordinating growth rates of demand as well as exchange rates, as proposed in the "blueprint" for policy coordination (see my study with Marcus Miller, 1987).

Policy coordination as practiced by the G-7 has not achieved anything like as much as the blueprint calls for, notably because of the defiance of its fiscal recommendations by the United States, Germany, and now Britain. The G-7's version of policy coordination must nonetheless be rated a distinct improvement over the controlled experiment in noncoordination that preceded it during the first Reagan Administration. Those were the years that witnessed the world's deepest postwar recession, the origin of the debt crisis, and the emergence of the massive payments imbalances that still hang like a sword of Damocles over the world economy. A simulation study by David Currie and Simon Wren-Lewis (1988) suggests that policy coordination on the lines of the blueprint would have led to a markedly less unsatisfactory outcome.

III. The Case for Wide Bands

While it is desirable to target exchange rates in order to avoid major misalignments, it is sensible to leave a rather wide band around the target within which the exchange rate will be free to fluctuate. There are three reasons for this.

First, monetary policy must be able to contribute to domestic stabilization. Even if world monetary policy is directed to world anticyclical policy and national fiscal policy is liberated from its present political strait-jacket, one will need some scope for national monetary policies to diverge from the world norm in the interests of national anticyclical policy. Since a credible medium-run exchange rate target reduces the response of the exchange rate to a rise in the short-term interest rate, a band of ± 5 percent or ± 10 percent can give substantial latitude to monetary policy.

Second, the band needs to be wide enough to accommodate changes in the central rate without forcing discontinuous changes in market rates and thus precipitating speculative crises. Changes in central rates may be needed to neutralize differential inflation, to offset trend factors that influence payments positions, and to promote payments adjustment in response to permanent real shocks. A band of ± 5 percent would appear adequate for these purposes provided that needed adjustments are made promptly.

Third, a wide band is needed to accommodate uncertainty regarding the correct level of the "fundamental equilibrium exchange rate" (FEER), the target central rate. As we emerge from a period of dramatic misalignments, caused by past neglect of exchange rates, it is particularly difficult to make estimates of equilibrium exchange rates with any accuracy. Hence I have suggested in the past (see my 1985 study) that target zones should initially be as wide as ± 10 percent. As the system succeeds in reducing the level of uncertainty, one might hope to narrow the bands to perhaps ± 5 percent.

IV. The Case for a Real Target

The case for adopting a real exchange rate target (i.e., *ceteris paribus* modifying the nominal target automatically to neutralize differential inflation) rests on the fact that the costs of misalignments stem from deviations of the *real* exchange rate from its FEER.

Of course, a real exchange rate target cannot provide a nominal anchor (Rudiger Dornbusch 1982; Charles Adams and Daniel Gros, 1987). A set of policy rules does need a nominal anchor in some form in order to preclude inflation accelerating as happened in the late 1960s and early 1970s. In the Williamson/Miller blueprint, the nominal anchor is provided by a rule for the target growth in domestic demand expressed in nominal terms. Simulation studies suggest that such a rule would have provided a perfectly adequate nominal anchor, assuming that monetary-fiscal policy had indeed been directed to its achievement. It has the great advantage over a nominal exchange rate target of spreading the burden of a disinflationary policy over both tradables and non-tradables, and thus of preventing the costly distortions that arise from misalignments.

The specification of the Louvre Accord in terms of nominal rather than real exchange rate stability was one of several flaws in its design. The commitment to nominal stability suggested to the markets in the late summer of 1987 that the German and Japanese inflation rates might be dragged up to the American level. It was to combat this perception that the Bundesbank felt it necessary to raise interest rates during the run-up to Black Monday.

V. The Dollar's FEER

I am presently making a new attempt to estimate the set of (real) exchange rates that could be expected to reconcile sustainable and satisfactory payments positions with "internal balance" in the medium term among the G-7 countries. I therefore hope that before long I shall be in a position to offer a more solid analysis with which either to substantiate or to modify the following remarks.

My present estimate is that the dollar's exchange rate, both in effective terms and vis-à-vis the two other major trading currencies (the Japanese yen and the deutschemark), was broadly satisfactory at the level reached at the end of 1987 and again prevailing in late 1988. That is, I believe that these rates could support a reduction of the U.S. current account deficit to a sustainable and satisfactory level of around $60 billion per year by the early 1990s in conjunction with additional policy actions that are desirable in their own right, plus trend changes in real exchange rates.[1]

The present consensus estimate is that on the basis of prevailing policies the U.S. current account deficit will bottom out at something over $100 billion in 1989 and then start rising again. I am dubious about the proposition that the trade deficit will start rising again after 1989: I agree with Peter Hooper (1988) in suspecting that the longer-run benefits from a major real depreciation, which require changes in investment, will by no means be exhausted.

The additional policy actions that I regard as called for are as follows:

1) A front-loaded four-year program of fiscal consolidation designed to eliminate the structural budget deficit in the United States by 1992. This should eliminate the present threat of overheating in the U.S. economy and create room for a further improvement in the real trade balance of the order of $80 billion. In addition to liberating capacity for a large trade improvement, the reduction in income to internal balance might in itself reduce imports and thus the trade deficit by $10 billion or $20 billion.

2) Continuing capacity growth in Japan and catch-up growth of 4 percentage point-years in Europe. According to the model of my colleague William Cline, this could be expected to improve the U.S. trade balance by some $14 billion by 1992. This is a minimum estimate as it makes no allowance for induced increases in imports by foreign-exchange-constrained developing countries.

3) Adjustment action by Korea and Taiwan adequate to reduce their joint surplus by around $30 billion, consisting of some combination of trade liberalization, increases in absorption, and real appreciation.

4) Debt reconstruction designed to reduce the negative resource transfer from the troubled debtor countries by at least $10 billion per year.

In addition, the dollar will need to depreciate at its trend rate of perhaps 1 percent per year, reflecting primarily the need to service the increasing external debt.

I would expect these actions together to achieve the needed adjustment in the U.S. current account, without any immediate further dollar depreciation beyond the level of late 1988, while keeping the economy at as high a level of activity as is prudent. Such an expectation is not certainty, and if the trade deficit persisted at an unsustainable level these actions would in due course have to be supplemented by a further above-trend real depreciation of the dollar. There is, however, no case for promoting a further immediate fall in the dollar.[2] Had such a policy been adopted a year ago, in place of the dollar stabilization sought by the G-7, U.S. inflation might well be a critical problem by now. Indeed, the economy might already have experienced the hard landing of collapsing confidence, the Fed might in consequence have been obliged to raise interest rates much further, and we might be on the brink of a recession. It is fortunate indeed that the siren song of aggressive unilateralism, an echo of the first Reagan Administration, was so decisively rejected in his second term. One hopes that the Bush Administration will be equally enlightened in regard to exchange rate policy and will finally acknowledge the need for decisive fiscal consolidation to complement stabilization of the dollar at a realistic level.

---

[1] C. Fred Bergsten (1988) calls for additional dollar depreciation as soon as the fiscal consolidation needed to release resources for the balance of payment is agreed. Our differing recommendations stem from a difference of view regarding the desirable target for the U.S. current account deficit: he seeks current account balance by 1992, a target that strikes me as both unattainable on political grounds and undesirable on welfare grounds.

[2] Space precludes treatment of the second-best issues of how the United States should react if the rest of the world fails to adopt appropriate policies to complement U.S. fiscal consolidation, or how the rest of the world should react if the United States fails to tackle its fiscal deficit.

REFERENCES

Adams, Charlesn, and Gros, Daniel, "The Consequences of Real Exchange Rate Rules for Inflation: Some Illustrative Examples," *IMF Staff Papers*, September 1987, *33*, 439–76.

Bergsten, C. Fred, *America in the World Economy: A Strategy for the 1990s*, Washington: Institute for International Economics, 1988.

Currie, David, and Wren-Lewis, Simon, "Evaluating the Extended Target Zone Proposal for the G-3," CEPR Discussion Paper No. 221, 1988.

Dornbusch, Rudiger, "PPP Exchange-Rate Rules and Macroeconomic Stability," *Journal of Political Economy*, February 1982, *90*, 158–65.

Feldstein, Martin, *New Evidence on the Effects of Exchange Rate Intervention*, NBER Working Paper No. 2052, 1986.

Hooper, Peter "Exchange Rates and U.S. External Adjustment in the Short Run and the Long Run," mimeo., Brookings Institution, 1988.

Krugman, Paul, "The Bias in the Band; Exchange Rate Expectations under a Broad-Band Regime," paper presented to a NBER Conference, December 1987.

_____, *Exchange-Rate Instability*, Cambridge, MA: MIT Press, 1988.

Williamson, John, *The Exchange Rate System*, Washington: Institute for International Economics, rev. ed., 1985.

_____ and Miller, Marcus, *Targets and Indicators: A Blueprint for the International Coordination of Economic Policy*, Washington: Institute for International Economics, 1987.

Council of Economic Advisers, *Economic Report of the President*, Washington: USGPO, 1984.

Jurgensen Report, *Report of the Working Group on Exchange Market Intervention*, Washington: U.S. Treasury, 1983.

International Aspects of Fiscal and Monetary Policy

Council of Economic Advisers

As discussed above, the internationalization of the U.S. economy has implications for monetary and fiscal policy. For example, there is a tendency for government deficits to crowd out net exports and for larger, more sensitive international capital flows to influence the effects of domestic policies on interest rates. This section analyzes the international dimension of economic policy considerations in more detail.

Linkages between the United States and the rest of the world led to some of the most visible and significant features of U.S. economic performance in the 1980s. There were wide swings in the value of the U.S. dollar. For example, it rose from 1.82 Deutsche marks per dollar (DM/$) in 1980 to more than 3.40 DM/$ in early 1985 before falling back to 1.76 DM/$ on average in 1988. The U.S. current account, which includes trade in both goods and services, plummeted from a surplus of $8 billion in 1981 to a record deficit of $144 billion in 1987—a deficit equivalent to 3.2 percent of U.S. GNP. This deficit reflected a $160 billion excess of merchandise imports over exports. Since this peak, the merchandise trade deficit has been cut more than 30 percent to an annualized level of $111 billion.

The fact that the United States has important connections to the rest of the global economy must be considered in the design of fiscal and monetary policy. These policies influence economic performance in part through their effects on exchange rates, on international capital flows, and on the trade balance. The United States accounts for more than one-quarter of total world production of goods and services. Not surprisingly, U.S. policy actions have implications for other industrialized economies and for developing economies. Policy actions taken by other countries, especially the larger ones, also influence U.S. economic performance. Growing recognition of mutual concerns and international economic linkages has heightened awareness of the potential benefits from enhanced international coordination of economic policies. A challenge for the 1990s is to use and improve the process for policy coordination developed in the 1980s to achieve sustained, noninflationary growth for the global economy.

INCREASED OPENNESS OF THE U.S. ECONOMY

The growing economic interdependence of the United States and other countries is reflected in expanding international trade and capital flows. U.S. imports of goods and services increased from less than 5 percent of total demand on average in the 1960s to more than 11 percent on average in the 1980s and 12.7 percent in 1988. This increased presence of foreign products has generated concern over the competitiveness of U.S. industries. What is not as frequently recognized is that U.S. exports of goods and services to other countries have also grown to record levels. Nearly 11 percent of domestic production was sold abroad during the 1980s, compared with just 6 percent on average during the 1960s. Through international trade, economic expansion in the rest of the world contributes to the health of the U.S. economy.

International financial markets have also grown dramatically over the past decade. Capital flows from abroad help to finance investment expenditures in the United States. These flows respond quickly in 24-hour financial markets to differences in short-term interest rates and other developments across countries. Because capital movements are sensitive to differences in policy, the globalization of financial markets has increased the interdependence of what were traditionally regarded as domestic policies.

Implications of Openness for Monetary and Fiscal Policies

International considerations do not alter the basic principle that credible, systematic monetary and fiscal policies can promote non-inflationary growth. The complex interactions among countries, however, should be taken into account in policy design.

U.S. policymakers must recognize that international linkages influence the effectiveness of their policy actions. The experience of 1980 to early 1985 provides an example. In a determined effort to bring inflation under control, the Federal Reserve, supported by the Administration, pursued firm anti-inflationary policies during 1980-82. Fiscal policy turned expansionary during the 1982 recession. These policies did contribute to the reduction of inflation and to strong economic growth in 1983 and 1984. However, they also contributed to rapid appreciation of the U.S. dollar (Chart 3-3) and a decline in net exports. First tight monetary policy and then declines in government and private saving relative to investment put upward pressure on interest rates in the United States. Partly in response to the resulting interest rate differentials, the dollar appreciated. Imports became relatively cheap, while U.S. exports became more expensive abroad. The resulting trade and current account deficits were the counterparts to the net capital inflows.

U.S. policy also affected the global economy. In particular, the U.S. economic recovery helped spur growth worldwide in the wake of the deep 1981–82 recession. At the same time, the increased demand for funds in international markets as the world economy recovered contributed to a rise in world interest rates, which added to the difficulties developing countries faced in meeting their external debt obligations.

EXTERNAL BALANCE AND EXCHANGE-RATE OBJECTIVES

To what extent should exchange-rate stability and external balance—current account and trade balance—be objectives of macroeconomic policy? The short answer is that both should be of concern to policymakers because, in an open economy, both are related to the fundamental objectives of economic growth and rising living

304

Chart 3-3

U.S. REAL EFFECTIVE EXCHANGE RATE. The real value of the U.S. dollar appreciated sharply in the first half of the 1980s before depreciating and then stabilizing at lower levels.

Index, March 1973=100

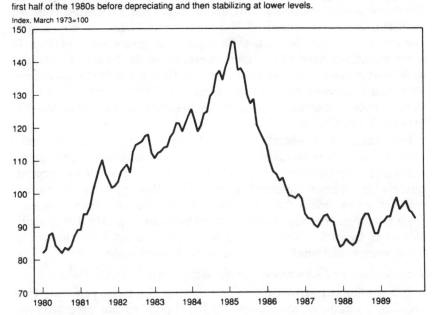

Note: Data are monthly.
Source: Board of Governors of the Federal Reserve System.

standards. Like price instability, current account imbalances and exchange-rate fluctuations—especially large, persistent misalignments—may jeopardize efficient resource allocation and, thus, economic growth.

External Imbalance

Current account deficits reflect an excess of investment over domestic saving. If that gap resulted from unusually strong investment, it would not generally be considered a problem. Inflows of foreign savings can contribute to higher investment, spurring economic growth and putting in place productive capacity to service the debt in the future without slowing the growth of domestic living standards. A reason for concern over the rise in the U.S. current account deficit from 1982 to 1987 was that it primarily reflected a decline in domestic saving. As saving has revived, the deficit has been cut by more than 30 percent since the mid-1987 peak.

An aggregate current account deficit implies that imports exceed exports in some sectors, and some of these sectoral trade imbalances are often large. Competitively priced imports may threaten domestic production and fuel pressures for protectionist trade policies, such as import tariffs or quotas. Yielding to these pressures impedes the efficient allocation of resources and harms consumers. Taken to an extreme, increased barriers to trade in one country result in a retaliatory trade war that can lead to worldwide recession. This danger provides a second reason for concern about large and persistent external imbalances.

Exchange Rates

Chart 3-3 shows the value of the dollar relative to currencies of the main U.S. trading partners since 1980. The graph shows both short-term volatility and sharp longer term swings in the value of the dollar. In asking whether policymakers should be concerned about exchange-rate changes, it is important to distinguish between the two.

Short-term volatility of the major currency-exchange rates has been much greater during the floating exchange-rate period since 1973 than during the previous two decades of the Bretton Woods System of fixed but adjustable rates. Although this fact is widely recognized, the problems associated with short-term volatility may be overstated. Exchange rates are the prices of assets (U.S. dollars relative to other currencies). Short-term interest rates and other asset prices, such as stock prices, are even more volatile than exchange rates. Furthermore, short-term volatility should not disrupt production decisions, such as where to purchase imported inputs, provided that longer term trends are predictable. Forward and futures markets can be used to hedge against short-run uncertainties. Also, empirical studies have found very little evidence that short-term exchange-rate volatility has a significant influence on the volume of international trade, once the influence of other factors (including real incomes and the relative prices of traded goods) is taken into account.

Concern about pronounced medium-term swings in exchange rates is based on the perception that they reflect misalignments relative to long-term, sustainable exchange-rate levels. Although there are disagreements about which exchange-rate level is appropriate to use as a benchmark, swings in the 1980s were so large that they were widely believed to represent misalignments. Unlike short-term variance, medium-term misalignments can have a profound effect on the allocation of resources. Large changes in the value of the dollar relative to the Japanese yen, for example, have led to large changes in prices of American goods relative to prices of Japanese goods. These large relative price movements, and uncertainty about how quickly they might be reversed, may complicate decisionmaking for both producers and consumers.

An appreciation of more than 60 percent, such as the U.S. dollar experienced in the mid-1980s, can erode the international competitiveness of domestic exporters and import-competing firms, putting firms out of business and generating unemployment. At the same time, goods and services produced abroad become bargains to domestic consumers, helping foreign firms to capture a larger share of the home market. Even if the appreciation is fully reversed within a few years, domestic firms may find it difficult to recapture the market share they held before the exchange-rate cycle. Macroeconomic policies that avoid large exchange-rate swings help to create an environment conducive to long-term growth.

MACROECONOMIC POLICY TOOLS

Monetary and fiscal policies influence external balances and exchange rates. For example, monetary policy can be used to maintain fixed exchange rates—at least temporarily. Monetary and especially fiscal policy can alter domestic saving and investment, and thus the current account balance. External balance and exchange rates are determined by a wide variety of factors, however, including policy and economic performance in other countries. Exchange-rate determination is especially complex. There is some tendency for high interest rates in the United States relative to those abroad to be associated with a stronger dollar. However, political events, credibility of policies, and news about economic performance at home or abroad also influence the value of the dollar. Furthermore, objectives of policymakers may come into conflict. A more expansionary monetary policy would tend to bring down the value of the dollar, but often with the cost of increased domestic inflation.

Exchange-Market Intervention

Policymakers can intervene directly in foreign exchange markets by buying and selling currencies. Following the dollar's peak in February 1985, policymakers used this tool more actively. However, the amounts of dollars sold or purchased by authorities are small relative to the total daily sales and purchases in the foreign exchange market, approximately $650 billion per day.

As a hypothetical example of foreign exchange intervention, suppose the dollar were overvalued. The Federal Reserve or the Treasury could sell dollars and purchase Deutsche marks in attempting to decrease the value of the dollar. When such actions are not permitted to affect the level of bank reserves, they are said to be "sterilized" intervention. The Federal Reserve can always sterilize any change in bank reserves through offsetting transactions in Treasury securities. If the Federal Reserve made no transactions to offset, or sterilize, the increase in bank reserves from a sale of dollars, the intervention would be called unsterilized. Unsterilized interventions, in effect, constitute monetary policy actions. The general practice of the Federal Reserve has been to sterilize intervention operations.

There is little disagreement that expansionary monetary policy tends to depreciate exchange rates. Most of the recent intervention by major central banks has been routinely sterilized, however, and some analysts have raised doubts about the effectiveness of sterilized intervention—at least as an instrument that produces lasting changes in exchange rates. Arguments in support of the effectiveness of sterilized intervention hinge largely on the fact that official transactions may signal the future course of domestic policy. If other market participants recognize, believe, and act in response to the signal, then sterilized intervention can be an effective tool for moving exchange rates.

What has been the actual experience with intervention in foreign exchange markets? Most studies have concluded that sterilized intervention is unlikely to be an effective tool for moving exchange rates in directions that are inconsistent with underlying fundamentals of policy and performance—except perhaps in the very short run. The effects are larger and more lasting if backed by other policy changes such as interest rate adjustments, which help to make the signal credible. Also, coordinated intervention by monetary authorities in more than one country seems to have a greater and more sustained effect on exchange rates than intervention by a single country alone.

INTERNATIONAL POLICY COORDINATION

Recognition of the increasingly integrated global economy and dissatisfaction with economic performance, including exchange-rate swings and persistent external imbalances, have precipitated calls for more consistent and compatible policies among major industrial countries. Since 1985, these countries have strengthened the process for international coordination of policies.

What Is Policy Coordination?

There is no single definition of international policy coordination. To some, the term has a rather lofty meaning: jointly determined policy actions in support of mutually agreed-upon objectives. However, national objectives will often differ substantially or conflict with one another. A more limited definition of policy coordination would be: a process through which national policies are modified in recognition that economic performance is interdependent.

Neither definition need imply that countries follow identical policies. Countries have different technologies, tastes, and political institutions. They may also be subject to different economic shocks. For example, many economists believe that a coordinated effort to reduce external imbalances while avoiding a slowdown in real growth worldwide would include fiscal contraction in the United States, which has a current account deficit, and an expansionary fiscal stance in Japan and West Germany, which have current account surpluses. Thus, even if countries adopt the same policy objective, actual policy settings are likely to differ.

Is Macroeconomic Policy Coordination a Good Idea?

The arguments in favor of policy coordination stress that the effects of one country's policies spill over to other countries. This spillover is especially true for the larger industrial economies, but even here, the linkages are stronger among some countries, such as those within Western Europe, than for others. However, policymakers may not take these spillover effects into account in weighing the costs and benefits of policy options. Coordination can improve domestic policy decisions by helping policymakers to consider the global implications of their actions. Small developing countries are likely to benefit greatly from policy coordination among the developed countries, if such coordination is successful in increasing world growth. At the same time, the most important aspect of promoting noninflationary growth in any one country is that it pursue sound domestic monetary and fiscal policies. Thus, macroeconomic policy coordination can also make a positive contribution by encouraging individual countries to pursue the proper credible and systematic policies at home.

International cooperation is important in other areas as well. In particular, agreement on rules for trade improve the functioning of the international trading system, with widespread benefits. The United States places a high priority on its active participation in the General Agreement on Tariffs and Trade, and is pursuing further international cooperation to advance mutual concerns about the environment.

What Is the Policy Coordination Process?

Since 1975, the leaders of the seven largest industrial economies (the United States, Japan, West Germany, France, the United Kingdom, Italy, and Canada) have met in annual economic summits to discuss economic issues of common concern. Over time, recognition of the growing integration of world goods and financial markets and shared concerns have led to the realization that further policy cooperation could be mutually beneficial.

The divergence of economic policies and performance among the major industrial countries after 1982 contributed to the sharp rise in the value of the dollar and to the emergence of large trade imbalances. In 1985, responding to shared concerns over these developments, finance ministers and central bankers from the United States, Japan, West Germany, the United Kingdom, and France (collectively called the G–5) met in New York. They agreed to work to strengthen the process for coordinating macroeconomic policies, to bring down the value of the dollar, and to reduce trade imbalances while maintaining noninflationary growth. In 1986, the G–5 together with Canada and Italy (the G–7) initiated regular meetings of their finance ministers and central bank governors. The purpose of these G–7 meetings is to promote more consistent and compatible economic policies among members so as to work toward sustained global growth with low inflation, reduced trade imbalances, and greater exchange-rate stability.

The policy coordination process that evolved during the 1980s has two main elements. First, the G–7 has instituted a regular, high-level dialogue on economic policy, performance, and objectives. Second, the G–7 has developed economic indicators to provide a framework for multilateral surveillance of their economies and to help monitor the international effects of national policies. This process is supplemented through frequent additional discussions in other forums, notably the International Monetary Fund, the Organization for Economic Cooperation and Development, and the Bank for International Settlements.

To What Extent Has Policy Coordination Been Useful?

To what extent has the G–7 process achieved its goals? Some observers note the continued fluctuations and last year's appreciation of the dollar and the persistence of trade deficits in the United States and surpluses in West Germany and Japan and conclude that policy coordination has been a failure. This view is extremely narrow and misleading. The economic policy coordination process has promoted more consistent and compatible policies among the major countries, helping to sustain the expansion of output and employment while reducing external imbalances. A regular dialogue on key economic policy issues now exists. The use of indicators has helped to focus their discussions on key linkages between economies. Further, the discussions have highlighted the importance of structural measures, such as lowering marginal tax rates, decreasing regulation, and reducing barriers to trade, to promote greater efficiency and openness, thereby facilitating noninflationary growth and adjustment of external balances.

Over the past decade, a substantial convergence in the longer term orientation of monetary policies among G–7 members has occurred. This convergence reflects increased mutual awareness among central bankers of the desirability of reducing inflation rates and moving toward price stability. As shown in Chart 3–4, this convergence has resulted in an overall reduction in the average inflation rate and the range of inflation rates among West Ger-

Chart 3-4

CONSUMER PRICES. During the 1980s consumer price inflation rates declined and converged among industrial countries.

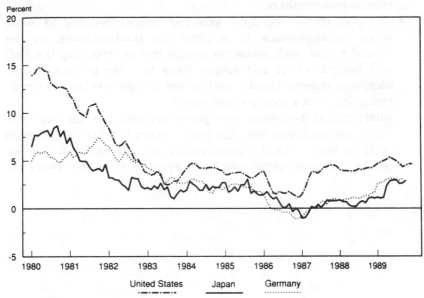

Percent

Note: Data are 12-month changes.
Source: Department of Commerce.

many, Japan, and the United States. With this awareness, there was also a common response to the indications of inflation resurgence in 1988. At the same time, international discussions have reflected concern that the effects of several countries responding together might result in too great a response. Such discussion is a natural part of the evolving policy coordination process and would have been more difficult just 15 years ago.

SUMMARY OF PRINCIPLES FOR INTERNATIONAL MACROECONOMIC POLICIES

The increased internationalization of the U.S. economy has important implications for monetary and fiscal policies and helps shape the principles that should form a basis for such policies.

- The United States is part of a global economy that is becoming increasingly integrated. This development implies both that policymakers must take international linkages into account when they design monetary and fiscal policies and that there are potential gains from working together.
- Credibility, highlighted in the previous discussions of monetary and fiscal policy, is equally important in this context. Consistently following appropriate policies, both in the United States and abroad, fosters an environment conducive to saving, investment, and economic growth.
- The ultimate objectives of monetary and fiscal policy are economic growth and rising living standards, *not* exchange-rate stability or current account balance per se. Nonetheless, reasonably stable exchange rates and sustainable external bal-

ances are important aspects of a healthy economy. Particularly when these variables get far out of line, they should be of concern to policymakers.

• The best means to adjust external imbalances and to avoid dollar misalignments is to alter the fundamentals. In the United States, such measures should include reducing the Federal budget deficit and taking steps to raise private saving. Sterilized intervention by itself is not an effective means for altering long-run exchange-rate levels.

• International macroeconomic policy coordination has had some important successes over the past 5 years but further progress could be made. The G-7 coordination process has been most effective in coordinating policies to respond to shared concerns.

Implications of the U. S. Current Account Deficit

David H. Howard

I n 1988, the United States recorded a deficit of about $135 billion on the current account of its balance of payments with the rest of the world.[1] This sum amounted to roughly $2\frac{3}{4}$ percent of GNP. The evolution of the U.S. current account is presented in Figure 1. Several conclusions can be drawn: $135 billion is a lot of money; $2\frac{3}{4}$ percent is a substantial portion of GNP; the decline in the current account was precipitous; and there are signs of a turnaround. The recent path of the U.S. current account deficit and the consequent accumulation of external debts have raised many interesting economic and policy questions. Some observers have pointed to the deficits and mounting debts and have predicted a large, sharp depreciation of the dollar in the future. Others have worried about the implications of the United States as the world's largest "debtor nation," references to the heavily indebted developing countries and the "debt crisis" have been voiced, as have been concerns about the growing foreign control implied by the growth in foreign claims on the United States.

The consensus forecast appears to be for little change in the nominal current account balance in the near term. However, based on current policies, mainstream assumptions about U.S. and foreign growth rates, and limited further currency realignments, many observers expect that within a few years the U.S. current account deficit will resume widening. The consensus forecast seems to be that a U.S. current account balance in the neighborhood of zero is not even a remote possibility in the near or not-so-near future.

As might be expected, the red ink recorded in the U.S. current account during the 1980s has affected markedly the country's net external asset position, since the excess of imports over exports had as a counterpart some type of credit transaction with foreigners. The exact level of net external assets in any particular year is not precisely known for a variety of reasons.[2] However, what is certain is that the cumulated U.S. current account deficit of nearly $700 billion for the 1983–1988 period seriously eroded the U.S. net external asset position, and probably transformed the United States from a substantial net creditor nation into a substantial net debtor. Indeed, the consensus forecast for the U.S. current account indicates that U.S. net external assets will continue to fall steeply for at least the next few years. The official estimate of the net external asset position (the "net international investment position") at the end of 1987—negative $368 billion—was about 8 percent of 1987 GNP.

It is useful to put the recent U.S. experience in perspective. As shown in Figure 1, the size the 1983–1988 current account deficits as a proportion of GNP is

■ *David H. Howard is Deputy Associate Director of the Division of International Finance, Board of Governors of the Federal Reserve System, Washington, DC.*

unprecedented (by a wide margin) since 1948. Data reported in Eichengreen (1987) indicate that the deficits have no historical precedent in the United States going back as far as 1890. However, the scale of the present U.S. current account deficit, but not necessarily the circumstances associated with it, does have precedents in other countries' experiences. Leaving aside the history of current accounts in developing countries as irrelevant to an advanced industrial country like the United States, there are many instances in which an industrial country's current account deficit has been on the order of 2 to 4 percent of its GNP or GDP. For example, in the five-year period, 1975–1979, Canada's current account deficit averaged over 2 percent of GDP; in 1974, the British and Italian deficits were 4 percent of GDP, and in some of the smaller industrial countries, annual deficits have been well in excess of 4 percent of GNP or GDP.[3]

Thinking about the Implications: Analytical Framework

The implications of a current account deficit depend in part on what caused the deficit in the first place and how the economy adjusts in response—for example, how the deficit is eventually closed. The U.S. current account balance is a general equilibrium phenomenon: it is jointly determined with other endogenous variables in the world economy. The usual proximate determinants of the current account balance —chiefly the terms of trade and relative rates of growth of economic activity—are themselves endogenous variables. Analysis of the current account deficit requires that the fundamental causes as well as the proximate causes be identified. Moreover, spillovers involving other markets and foreign economies must be taken into account. In the present exercise—analyzing the implications of the historically very large U.S. current account deficit—the general equilibrium nature of the problem is not just a theoretical fine point. Anticipating the discussion of the next section of the paper, the conclusion of most economists who have studied the issue is that the U.S. current account deficit is largely the product of the macroeconomic policy mix pursued by the United States and its major trading partners during the 1980s. Reducing the deficit probably, although perhaps not necessarily, would involve a significant reversal of those particular policy choices. Since changes in macroeconomic policies have consequences for the entire world economy—not just the U.S. balance of payments—it is imperative that the entire world economy be incorporated in the analysis.

The economics literature provides several lines of approach for thinking about current account balances. The conventional method—at least in the empirical literature—entails an eclectic model in which trade flows are essentially determined by prices and income flows, supplemented with judiciously and pragmatically chosen additional variables. These explanatory variables are for the most part only the proximate determinants of trade flows, and the trade equations are explicitly or implicitly considered to be a component of a more complete empirical model of the economy. In fact, one approach to modeling the current account involves an econometric model of the entire world economy, consisting of linked individual country models.

Another empirically oriented approach to thinking about current account balances focuses on one aspect of the general equilibrium problem by manipulating the national income accounts to arrive at the identity:

$$(1) \qquad\qquad X - M \equiv S - I,$$

where X and M represent exports and imports of goods and services, respectively, and S and I denote domestic (including the public sector) saving and investment,

Figure 1

U.S. Current Account Relative to GNP

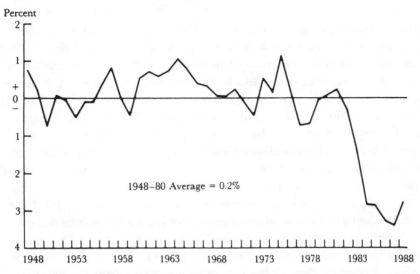

Source: Bureau of Economic Analysis, Department of Commerce.

respectively. Expressed in this manner, it is natural to view the current account [approximately $(X - M)$] as being reflective of a country's saving-investment behavior and imbalances. For example, in terms of this identity, the U.S. current account deficit can be thought of as being the result of a shortfall in U.S. saving, in which case the level of domestic investment is being supported by flows of foreign saving (equal to the negative of the current account balance). However, viewed in this manner, it is also easy to lose sight of the fact that equation 1 is an identity with no causal significance, and that all four variables are endogenously determined as part of a general equilibrium outcome for the entire international economy. The current account $X - M$ and the saving-investment balance $S - I$ are actually functions of many variables, including importantly income, the exchange rate, and the interest rate. The equilibrium external balance is determined by the intersection of the $X - M$ and $S - I$ functions. Thus, the actual external balance can reflect changes in export and import behavior as well as changes in domestic saving and investment behavior.

Another strand of the economics literature can also be brought to bear on the question of the U.S. current account deficit. The classic Diamond (1965) overlapping generations growth model of public debt provides an analysis of the implications of funding a public sector deficit by borrowing abroad. The open economy aspects of the Diamond model are more fully articulated in Persson (1985). One of the Persson's conclusions is particularly interesting (p. 82): "The adjustment towards the higher external debt implied by a higher public debt was shown to involve an extended period of current account deficits following an initial government budget deficit." Persson's explanation of this result essentially involves the use of foreign saving flows (and therefore current account deficits) to supplement domestic saving both during the initial period of the government deficit and during subsequent periods, when domestic saving is depressed by taxes used to service the higher public debt. In fact, Persson's analysis of the interaction between the public sector and current account deficits is similar to that underlying the more-or-less conventional view in official and international financial circles of the relationship between the U.S. budget and current account deficits (the so-called "twin deficits").

Causes of the Current Account Deficit

The explanation of the behavior of the U.S. current account during the 1980s that emerges from the empirical literature is one in which the fundamental cause is the macroeconomic policy mix pursued in the United States and its major trading partners. At the beginning of the decade, the anti-inflation stance of U.S. monetary policy drove real interest rates and the dollar upward. However, the dollar's strength had little effect on the current account since the ensuing U.S. recession dampened the demand for imports. Starting in about 1982, the strongly expansionary course of U.S. fiscal policy began to impart additional upward impetus to U.S. interest rates and the dollar while at the same time fostering a recovery in U.S. economic activity and U.S. demand for imports. The result was a sharp deterioration in the current account in 1983–1984, which was exacerbated by the restrictive posture taken by fiscal authorities in the major foreign industrial countries and the economic problems of the heavily indebted developing countries.[5] The widening of the U.S. current account deficit meant that foreigners in effect were financing more and more of the U.S. government budget deficit, thereby allowing the U.S. private sector to maintain higher levels of consumption and investment expenditures than it otherwise could have.[6]

Steps toward tightening U.S. fiscal policy, starting in 1985, appear to have played a role in reversing the course of the dollar and the current account. Another instrumental factor seems to have been financial market concerns about the longer-run sustainability of the U.S. external position and the recognition that at some point some adjustment would be necessary, a topic that is discussed in the next section of the present paper.

The attempts to *quantify* the various causes of the U.S. current account deficit are, of course, rough, and as one might expect, the results are far from unanimous across models. Nevertheless, the conclusion that one can draw from the empirical literature is that less than half of the deterioration in the current account was associated with the relative strength of U.S. economic activity compared with that abroad, and more than half was associated with the loss of price competitiveness of U.S. goods and services, owing largely to the strong appreciation of the dollar in the first half of the 1980s.

The pace of economic activity at home and abroad as well as the course of the dollar were proximate causes only. Various econometric models indicate that expansionary U.S. fiscal policy coupled with restrictive fiscal policy in the major foreign industrial countries and the anti-inflation stance of U.S. monetary policy can explain a sizable amount of the developments in economic activity and exchange rates. There nevertheless remains a significant portion—perhaps one-third—of the rise in the dollar that remains unexplained, and which perhaps reflects a speculative bubble, and therefore some of the weakening in the U.S. current account is also unexplained.

The models also have been used to investigate the seemingly puzzling persistence of the current account deficit in the face of the dollar's steep decline since early 1985. Several points can be made with regard to the persistence of the deficit. First, in the absence of the dollar's fall, the nominal current account balance probably would have been weaker than the rates actually recorded. Second, the persistence is not too surprising in that the econometric models do not predict a rapid turnaround: trade volumes react with a fairly substantial lag (usually distributed over two years) to changes in prices, and the dollar prices of imports also respond with a lag (again typically distributed over two years) to changes in exchange rates. Moreover, much of the dollar's initial decline represented simply a reversal of its surge at the end of 1984 and early 1985, which probably was not reflected in prices or trade volumes anyway.

Finally, the dollar's depreciation between early 1985 and the end of 1987 was more-or-less continuous so that a series of so-called J-curve effects—a weakening of the current account as import prices in dollars rise before import volumes decline in response—would tend to mask the improvement in the underlying current account position for a while. There have been some special (and unpredicted) factors as well, such as the vagaries of the oil market.

Sustainability: The United States as a Debtor Nation

There are several statistical indicators or measures of a country's external debt "burden" or debt-servicing requirement. One common measure is the net external debt (D) to GNP (Y) ratio; another scales the debt by the value of a country's exports instead of national output. In either case, the rationale is that the denominator is related to a country's capacity to service its debt. In this paper, the debt-GNP ratio (d) is used as the indicator of the U.S. external debt burden.

The debt-GNP ratio is defined as:

$$(2) \qquad\qquad\qquad d = D/Y.$$

the debt-GNP ratio will continue to rise indefinitely as long as the economy is running a deficit on merchandise trade. Applying this result to the current U.S. situation, one could conclude that the U.S. external debt burden will continue to grow until the trade balance turns around and stops recording deficits.[8] (In 1988, the trade deficit was slightly less than the current account deficit—about $125 billion.) Since the debt-GNP ratio presumably cannot keep increasing forever, at some point the United States needs to stop registering trade deficits. (However, in principle, one could imagine the debt-GNP ratio increasing for a very long time, if its rate of growth were small enough.)

The question remains, however, when does the U.S. trade account have to switch to surplus (or at least a zero balance)? As mentioned in the first section of this paper, at the end of 1987 the U.S. net external debt—strictly speaking, the U.S. net international investment position with its sign reversed—was about 8 percent of GNP. Even making the pessimistic assumption that the U.S. current account deficits in 1988–1990 will average $150 billion, the debt-GNP ratio is likely to be less than 15 percent at the end of 1990. Debt-GNP ratios for "highly indebted" developing countries such as Argentina, Brazil, and Mexico are considerably larger—on the order of one-quarter to one-half of GNP.[9] Indeed, Canada's net external debt as a percentage of GNP was 40 percent in 1987—nearly three times the likely upper bound for the 1990 U.S. ratio.

Cross-country comparisons of debt ratios are not necessarily meaningful, since the sustainable debt-GNP ratio (debt burden) of a country is a function of many things that can vary across countries and over time. Moreover, a crisis of confidence among foreign investors cannot be ruled out no matter what the country's debt-GNP ratio might be. Nevertheless, the large discrepancy between the U.S. ratio, even using pessimistic assumptions about the next few years, and current Latin American ratios suggest that a U.S. "debt crisis" is not imminent. Several other considerations, not the least being the experience of Canada—an advanced industrial country with ready access to international financial markets—support this proposition. It does seem certain, however, based on the dynamics of debt accumulation that are reflected in equation 6, that at some point the U.S. trade balance must turn positive or at least nonnegative. Indeed, since early 1985, when the dollar's exchange value hit its peak, this seems to be the message that international financial markets have been conveying. The question of how the trade adjustment can or will take place is addressed in the next section of the paper.

Even after the United States stops recording trade deficits and the debt-GNP ratio levels off, the current account is likely to register sizable deficits, reflecting interest payments of the net external debt.

Closing the Gap

Feldstein and Horioka (1980) find a substantial degree of correlation between the country's domestic saving and domestic investment rates over the medium term and argue that this finding means that capital is not very mobile across national borders. Based on the Feldstein-Horioka study, one might argue that the question of how to close the U.S. current account deficit is not particularly interesting since the supposed international immobility of capital means that significant imbalances between domestic saving and domestic investment cannot persist. However, this argument is not compelling without an explanation of the mechanism by which current accounts tend to average near zero over time. To date, the literature has not provided a convincing explanation of this apparent empirical regularity. Even more worrisome is the fact that many of the explanatory stories offered by the literature entail explicit policy responses to widening current account imbalances that have the effect of keeping the current account balance near zero over time.[10] If indeed the Feldstein-Horioka proposition reflects past government policies of targeting on the current account, one cannot *rely* on the empirical regularity to exert itself and close the U.S. trade gap without an explicit policy mechanism or response.

In 1988, the U.S. nominal merchandise trade deficit was $2\frac{1}{2}$ percent of GNP. Econometric models can be used to get a rough indication of what adjustments in exchange rates and/or growth rates might be required to reduce the U.S. trade deficit from $2\frac{1}{2}$ percent of GNP to zero over a given time period. However, the models may not adequately reflect trade responses to large movements in exchange rates such as those experienced in the 1980s. In fact, some calculations of international competitiveness suggest that, based on purchasing power parity considerations alone, the dollar might not need to decline from its 1988 level in order eventually to close the U.S. trade deficit. Moreover, any substantive discussion of closing the U.S. external deficit requires attention to how changes in the proximate determinants of trade flows are put into place. For example, the different ways in which an exchange rate adjustment can be brought about can have different implications for economic activity and the external accounts, as witnessed earlier in the decade when first tight monetary policy and then expansionary fiscal policy exerted upward pressure on the dollar, with radically different implications for GNP growth and the U.S. current account.

To eliminate the U.S. trade deficit—and the corresponding rest-of-the-world trade surplus—more spending has to be directed toward U.S. exports and/or less toward U.S. imports. Such an outcome can be accomplished in either of two ways (or some combination of the two): "expenditure-changing" policies or events that affect the *level* of aggregate demand, and "expenditure-switching" policies or events that affect the *composition* of demand. The former is not very attractive—by itself—since it would involve a slowdown in U.S. economic output growth, which in turn would be responsible for the reduction in U.S. demand for imports. Lower U.S. demand also would imply a slowdown in foreign economic activity unless there were compensatory changes in foreign demand such as expansionary macroeconomic policy measures abroad. In fact, the reduction in U.S. spending conceivably could be combined with an increase in foreign demand sufficient to close the U.S. deficit without much of an effect on the pace of economic activity in the United States. Macroeconomic stimulus in foreign industrial countries might be appropriate, but just as the expenditure-reduction option involves serious risks of recession in the United States, expansion of foreign demand—at least on the scale likely to be necessary to close the U.S. external deficit—involves inflation risks in the key foreign industrial countries.

The more attractive alternative is that of expenditure switching; U.S. residents and foreigners are induced to direct more of their total spending (domestic demand) on U.S. products. The expenditure-switching option would boost domestic demand (that is, consumption plus domestic capital formation plus government spending) relative to output in foreign countries and reduce domestic demand relative to output in the United States. In principle, coupled with suitable changes in aggregate demand levels, expenditure switching need not affect the level of output in either the United States or its trading partners.

Any redirection of demand almost certainly would entail a reallocation of productive resources (labor and capital) within the economies involved, and such reallocations might well be painful in the short run. Macroeconomic policy can ease the transition during which foreign economies become less dependent on U.S. demand for their products, but nothing can negate the need for adjustment in the rest of the world if the United States is to adjust its external position. The simple fact is that by definition closing the U.S. external deficit means that the trading partners of the United States—taken as a group—have to close their external surplus.

A switch in world expenditures toward U.S. products can be achieved by a real depreciation of the dollar, that is, a nominal depreciation of the dollar in excess of the inflation rate differential. Another way of implementing an expenditure-switching policy is through trade policy—the imposition of tariffs and quantitative restrictions on trade flows. However, trade policy typically distorts the allocation of resources, and even a system of import tariffs and export subsidies that just duplicated the effects of an exchange rate depreciation almost certainly would evoke foreign retaliation.[11] Moreover, with flexible exchange rates, the tariffs and subsidies could be offset by a strengthening of the exchange rate in reaction to the trade policy actions. Thus it would appear that the preferred method for switching expenditures toward U.S. products is by means of a real depreciation of the dollar. How the depreciation takes place has important implications for subsequent economic developments.

One approach to the adjustment in the U.S. external accounts is to let international financial markets dictate its timing; that is, accept whatever exchange rate is needed to equilibrate private supply and demand at any particular moment on the markets for foreign exchange. This approach has some appeal, but it carries a significant risk: the eventual decline in the dollar could be precipitous, even by recent standards, and perhaps excessive as well. Such an outcome could exert a substantial amount of upward pressure on U.S. prices over a fairly short period and create a situation that might elicit a contractionary policy response on the part of the U.S. policymakers. (Symmetrical problems could arise abroad.) Thus, inflation and recession, along with external adjustment, might result owing to the sudden nature of the exchange rate fall. A more gradual depreciation of the dollar, which also is a possible market-dictated outcome, would lower the chances of the inflation/recession occurring, since the price-level effects of the exchange-rate adjustment could be assimilated more smoothly by the economy, without the disruptive effects of a sudden burst in the rate of change of prices.

Another approach to U.S. external adjustment is to use macroeconomic policy to "manage" the pace and impact of the adjustment process. Presumably some combination of macroeconomic policy measures in the United States and other countries (for example, a tightening of U.S. fiscal policy, an easing of U.S. monetary policy, and expansionary fiscal actions abroad) could in principle produce a lower dollar, an undisturbed level of economic activity, and a stronger U.S. trade balance. It is easy to exaggerate the precision with which a change in the macroeconomic policy mix could be used to influence the external adjustment process, but the idea would be to put the real exchange rate on a path that would be likely to be less disruptive than the path determined by the financial markets alone. This approach is especially appealing if the macroeconomic policy changes are viewed as desirable in their own right in any case.

As mentioned earlier in this paper, analyses of the causes of the U.S. current account deficit have tended to focus on the U.S. fiscal deficit as a primary factor. U.S. fiscal policy adjustment (contraction), undertaken for its own sake, would appear to represent a major channel through which the U.S. external deficit could be reduced. If, however, a U.S. fiscal correction proves to be unwarranted or infeasible on its own merits, it is not clear if any other policy measures aimed at the external imbalance would be appropriate.[12] Under such circumstances, the market-dictated path of the exchange rate might win by default.

[1] The current account balance is equal to the trade balance (merchandise exports minus merchandise imports) plus net service transactions plus net unilateral transfers, all expressed in nominal terms, that is, in current dollars. A convenient method of scaling this aggregate is to express it as a percentage of nominal GNP. However, for many purposes a better method of measuring the "real" or deflated balance is to express it in volume terms, that is, in constant dollars where the price deflators refer to the specific baskets of export and import goods (and services) rather than the general GNP deflator.

[2] The reasons for doubting the accuracy of the data include the use of book value rather than market value for direct investments and the interpretation of the statistical discrepancy in the balance of payments accounts. A large part of the stock of U.S. direct investment abroad was made before foreign direct investment activity in the United States became significant. Thus, presumably the book value of U.S. direct investment understates its true market value to a larger extent than does the book value of direct investment in the United States. If so, the U.S. net position is understated. On the other hand, unrecorded capital transactions are not estimated, they are simply omitted. Since the large positive statistical discrepancy in the U.S. balance of payments accounts that has been in evidence since 1978 may indicate large unrecorded net capital inflows into the United States, a significant amount of foreign assets in the United States may be inappropriately excluded. It also should be noted that despite the United States' supposedly large net external debt position in 1987, the country's net investment income was positive, reflecting a systematic (positive) differential between the rates of return earned on U.S. assets abroad and foreign assets in the United States, and, perhaps, an overstatement of the underlying U.S. net external debt position as well.

[3] See OECD (1987). Eichengreen (1987) discusses some earlier episodes of large deficits in Canada and the United Kingdom.

[5] U.S. exports to Latin America declined by some $17 billion (40 percent) between 1981 and 1983.

[6] Of course, the foreigners did not necessarily buy U.S. government securities directly, but, since funds are fungible, the capital inflow facilitated the financing of the budget deficit.

[8] In practice, a zero trade balance is not necessarily the break-even point, but the exposition is clearer if the simplifying assumptions presented in the above discussion are maintained.

[9] The debt ratios for the Latin American countries are not really comparable with that for the United States, in part because there are no reliable figures on the external assets of the Latin American private sector (often referred to as "capital flight"). The one quarter of GNP figure mentioned in the text reflects a net-debt concept, incorporating a rough estimate of private capital outflows, while the one half of GNP figure is a gross-debt concept.

[10]See Dooley, Frankel, and Mathieson (1987) for a survey of the proposed explanations—including one of their own—of the Feldstein-Horioka results.

[11]Efforts to open foreign markets to U.S. exports would aid the adjustment process, but closing U.S. markets to foreign goods would be, if anything, counterproductive even in the short run because of the retaliatory actions likely to be taken in foreign markets.

[12]The need for U.S. fiscal adjustment, independent of the problem of the current account deficit, is another matter and is beyond the scope of the present paper.

■ *This paper represents the views of the author and should not be interpreted as reflecting the views of the Board of Governors of the Federal Reserve System or other members of its staff. I would like to thank Richard Freeman, William Helkie, Dale Henderson, Peter Hooper, Karen Johnson, Linda Kole, Michael Leahy, Ellen Meade, Larry Promisel, Kenneth Rogoff, Carl Shapiro, Charles Siegman, Ralph Smith, Joseph Stiglitz, Timothy Taylor, and participants in the International Finance Division's Monday workshop for their helpful comments and suggestions.*

References

Bryant, Ralph C., Gerald Holtham, and Peter Hooper, eds., *External Deficits and the Dollar: The Pit and the Pendulum.* Washington D.C.: The Brookings Institution, 1988.

Bryant, Ralph C., Dale W. Henderson, Gerald Holtham, Peter Hooper, and Steven A. Symansky, eds., *Empirical Macroeconomics for Interdependent Economies.* Washington D.C.: The Brookings Institution, 1988.

Diamond, Peter A., "National Debt in a Neoclassical Growth Model," *American Economic Review*, December 1965, *55*, 1126–1150.

Dooley, Michael, Jeffrey Frankel, and Donald J. Mathieson, "International Capital Mobility: What Do Saving-Investment Correlations Tell Us?," *IMF Staff Papers*, September 1987, *34*, 503–530.

Eichengreen, Barry, "Trade Deficits in the Long Run," *NBER Working Paper* No. 2437, November 1987.

Feldstein, Martin, and Charles Horioka, "Domestic Saving and International Capital Flows," *Economic Journal*, June 1980, *90*, 314–329.

Helkie, William L., and Peter Hooper, "An Empirical Analysis of the External Deficit, 1980–86," in Bryant, Ralph C., Gerald Holtham, and Peter Hooper, eds., *External Deficits and the Dollar: The Pit and the Pendulum.* Washington D.C.: The Brookings Institution, 1988.

Hooper, Peter, and Catherine L. Mann, "The U.S. External Deficit: Its Causes and Persistence," *International Finance Discussion Papers*, No. 316, November 1987.

Krugman, Paul R., and Richard E. Baldwin, "The Persistence of the U.S. Trade Deficit," *Brookings Papers on Economic Activity*, 1987, 1, 1–43.

OECD, *Economic Outlook*, No. 42, December 1987.

Persson, Torsten, "Deficits and Intergenerational Welfare in Open Economies," *Journal of International Economics*, August 1985, *19*, 67–84.

Distinguished Lecture on Economics in Government: Thinking About International Economic Coordination

Martin S. Feldstein

I should perhaps begin these remarks by emphasizing that I am not opposed to international cooperation in economic affairs. We as economists recognize that conflict in international trade and the development of protectionist policies would reduce the standard of living around the world. Moreover, the immediate effect of a shift to protectionism could be a major worldwide recession.

The quiet exchange of macroeconomic forecasts and policy plans among government officials that occurs within the framework of the Bank for International Settlements, the OECD, the Group of 7 (the United States, Great Britain, France, Germany, Japan, Italy and Canada) and elsewhere plays an important role in the formulation of domestic economic policies. It is also important for maintaining friendly working relationships among governments that senior officials are not surprised by major policy shifts abroad.

I start with these obvious remarks and with the assertion that I am not opposed to international cooperation in all economic matters because I do not want to be misunderstood when, as in this lecture, I stress the counterproductive consequences of the international coordination of macroeconomic policy.

I do not deny that the economies of the world are linked in a way that makes the monetary and budget policies adopted in one country affect the economic performance of other countries. But I believe that many of the claimed advantages of cooperation and coordination are wrong, that there are substantial risks and disadvantages to the types of coordination that are envisioned, and that an emphasis on international coordination can distract attention from the necessary changes in domestic policy. Moreover, the attempt to pursue coordination in a wide range of macroeconomic policies is likely to result in disagreements and disappointments that reduce the prospects for cooperation in those more limited areas of trade, defense and foreign assistance where international cooperation is actually necessary.[1]

In stressing the limited scope for the international coordination of macroeconomic policy and exchange rates, I do not wish to imply that such action is never appropriate. Far from it. There are some small and very interdependent countries where such coordination should undoubtedly be the general rule. There are also some conditions when the potential gains from coordination are such that all countries could expect to benefit from participation. But the active coordination of the macroeconomic policies and of exchange rates among the United States, Japan and Germany will generally be inappropriate. Moreover, as I shall explain in these remarks, the United States is particularly unsuited to participate in an ongoing process of economic coordination.

■ Martin Feldstein is Professor of Economics, Harvard University, and President, National Bureau of Economic Research, both in Cambridge, Massachusetts.

The Management of Exchange Rates

After less than a decade of floating exchange rates, the sharp rise in the value of the dollar during the early 1980s caused a renewed interest in the possibility of the international management of exchange rates and even of a return to a system of fixed exchange rates. The rise in the real value of the dollar was the primary reason why the United States shifted from a trade surplus in 1981 to a massive trade deficit by 1986. It is not surprising, therefore, that American businesses and their workers in the wide range of industries hurt by the strong dollar called for government action to stop and reverse the dollar's rise.

Until September 1985, the Reagan Administration argued that the value of the dollar should be left to the market and that it was inappropriate to shift U.S. domestic economic policy or to intervene in currency markets in an attempt to alter the dollar's value. This was a continuing source of conflict with the European and Japanese governments that did not like the dollar's rise because of the inflationary pressures that it imparted to their own economies, the rising real interest rates that resulted from the capital outflow to the United States, and the increased support for protectionist trade policies that was developing in the United States because of the surging U.S. trade deficit.

The Plaza Hotel meeting of the finance ministers of the G-5 countries (United States, Great Britain, France, Germany and Japan) in September 1985 was a political watershed in this process. Faced with the reality that the dollar had been declining for more than six months, Treasury Secretary James Baker abandoned the previous Treasury position that the strong dollar was a measure of foreign investors' approval of the economic policies of the United States. He acknowledged publicly that the high value of the dollar was a serious problem for American industry. And, most surprisingly and significantly of all, he agreed to participate in coordinated exchange market intervention aimed at lowering the dollar's value.

Immediately after the Plaza meeting the United States did join with other countries in a major exchange market intervention, selling dollars and buying other currencies. The Japanese central bank also raised short-term interest rates temporarily in order to make yen denominated bonds a more attractive investment and thereby to stimulate the demand for the yen.

Exchange rate targeting and economic policy coordination aimed at achieving desired levels of the exchange rates have been a frequent theme of intergovernmental meetings since that time. The finance ministers of the G-7 countries met at the Louvre in February 1987 to assert their belief in macroeconomic coordination and to call for exchange rate stability. They reaffirmed this call at the June 1987 Venice summit and the September 1987 IMF-World Bank meeting. In more recent days (November and December 1987), European and Japanese government officials have repeated their case for coordinated actions to achieve a stable value of the dollar and a new G-7 communique calling for a stable dollar has been issued.

In contrast to these assertions, I believe that the dollar must continue to decline because the future trade deficit implied by the dollar's current level would be too large to finance otherwise. Experts estimate that without a further decline of the dollar the U.S. trade deficit will remain at more than $100 billion a year and the current account deficit will grow explosively because of the interest and dividends owed on the U.S. net borrowing from abroad. Only a decline of the dollar can achieve the change in the relative prices of American and foreign goods that can induce American consumers to import less and foreign consumers to buy more American-made goods. The more rapid growth in Japan and Europe that the finance ministers continually stress as an alternative to a dollar decline simply cannot be powerful enough to make a significant dent in the U.S. trade deficit. Similarly, while a decline of the American budget deficit would help to shrink the U.S. trade deficit, it would do so by lowering U.S. interest rates which in turn would reduce the value of the dollar; a decline in the budget deficit, while essential for other reasons, is not an alternative to a decline in the dollar as a means of shrinking the trade deficit. (A longer nontechnical discussion of why the dollar must decline is presented in Feldstein, 1987a.)

I believe that the pursuit of exchange rate goals is likely to be both futile and economically damaging, not just in the current circumstances but more generally as well. In the short term, as the experience of October 1987 painfully demonstrated, the expectation that monetary policy would tighten to defend artificial exchange rate levels can destabilize financial markets. The fear that the Fed would push rates even higher than they were in early October—to offset the downward pressure on the dollar that resulted from the unfavorable trade news of October 14th—was one of the key factors that triggered the stock market crash. Over an extended period of time, the primary risk in the pursuit of exchange rate targets is an increase in the rate of inflation in every country. A policy of targeting exchange rates can also hurt the process of capital formation, weaken the capital goods and construction industries, and delay the recovery of the manufacturing industries that are hurt by an overvalued exchange rate.

Nominal and Real Exchange Rates

To understand the likely effects of an exchange rate policy, it is crucial to distinguish between changes in nominal exchange rates and changes in real exchange rates. The change in the nominal exchange rate between two countries is the change in the actual exchange rate that prevails in the market. The change in the real exchange rate is equal to the change in nominal exchange rate adjusted for differences in the inflation rates in the two countries. It is, of course, the real value of the currency that influences the competitiveness of the country's products and thus its exports and imports. This point is worth emphasizing for two reasons.

First, the political discussion about exchange rate targets, target zones and exchange rate management are always in terms of the nominal exchange rates. Therefore even if the politically agreed upon exchange rate targets were achieved and maintained, the relative competitiveness of the countries could change substantially because differences in inflation rates would cause the real exchange rates to change. In short, exchange rate management is likely to be misguided because it focuses on the wrong target.

Second, economic policies that change a country's rate of inflation can easily alter nominal exchange rates without changing the real exchange rates. Therefore, there is a serious danger that an agreement to stabilize exchange rates would lead to increased inflation without any change in the real exchange rates that influence imports and exports.

Consider, for example, the sharp rise in the real value of the dollar that began in 1980 because of the massive increase in current and projected U.S. budget deficits. Reversing the budget deficit could have prevented the dollar's rise or caused it to decline at an earlier time. But on the basis of my experience as a participant in the making of American economic policy at that time, I do not believe that an exchange rate agreement would have produced such a change in budget policy. The Reagan administration was already trying to reduce the budget deficit by a strategy that combined major domestic spending cuts with a conditional tax increase. There is no reason to think that it would have taken a more conciliatory position with Congress in order to deal with the high dollar. Treasury Secretary Regan apparently believe that the budget deficit had no effect on the dollar. In addition, many experts both inside and outside the government argued that the strong dollar showed only that monetary policy was too tight and therefore argued in favor of depressing the dollar by a monetary expansion.

If the United States had agreed in 1983 to stop the dollar's rise, the easiest way would have been for the Federal Reserve to ease monetary policy. The easier monetary policy would have temporarily lowered real interest rates and that in turn would have caused a temporary decline in the real value of the dollar. More importantly, the easier monetary policy would produce inflation and the inflation would cause the dollar's nominal value to decline. In the end, there would have been no change in the real exchange rate or the trade deficit but a higher price level and a high rate of inflation.

Of course, there are two sides to every exchange rate and the relative value of the dollar could have been depressed by a tightening of monetary policy in Europe and Japan that lowered the inflation rates in those countries. There was in fact some tightening of monetary policy in Europe in response to the rising dollar, but that process was inevitably limited by the increased unemployment that resulted from such a monetary contraction. Political reality would inevitably have required that a change in monetary policy to stabilize the dollar be an inflationary easing by the United States rather than a deflationary tightening in the other countries of the world.

The current attempts to slow the rise of the yen and the German mark provide a further example of the risk that exchange rate coordination is likely to be inflationary. The process of intervention in both Germany and Japan has led to very rapid increases in the money supply and in overall liquidity. This had increased the fear of inflation and raised long-term interest rates in both countries. Although the governments of Germany and Japan have asked the United States to raise interest rates as an alternative way of maintaining the value of the dollar, the U.S. has been reluctant to do so in the context of a recovery that has already lasted five years and with an election this year. Although the German and Japanese intervention has not yet produced any significant rise in inflation, a continuation of the associated increases in money and overall liquidity for an extended period would undoubtedly begin to do so.

Gains and Losses of an Overstrong Dollar

There are of course some who believe that the real value of the dollar can be influenced by exchange market intervention alone. Before considering whether such a policy could be expected to work, it is useful to ask whether stabilizing the dollar would in itself have been desirable in today's world economy.

Stopping the rise in the dollar's real value in early 1983 would have reduced the subsequent U.S. trade deficit. Output and employment would have deteriorated less in our export industries and in those firms that compete with imports from abroad. But that is only half of the story. The reduced trade deficit would automatically have meant a reduced capital inflow from abroad. Real interest rates would have been higher in the United States. Investment in plant and equipment and housing construction would have been depressed. The pattern of employment would have been different, but there is no reason to suppose that total employment and output would have been higher. Moreover, the lower rate of capital formation would have reduced the growth of productivity.

In short, stopping the dollar's rise earlier would have had both good and bad effects on the American economy. There is no way to know whether the favorable effects on the export industries and firms that compete with imports would have outweighed the adverse effects on capital investment. I believe that in the absence of clear evidence or analysis to the contrary, it is best to assume that the market produces a better solution than government intervention. That is as true about exchange market intervention as it is about so many other aspects of government interference with the market economy.

The same principle is relevant today. If intervention per se could stop the dollar's fall at the present time, that would contribute to U.S. price stability and would maintain a flow of capital from abroad that dampens real interest rates and provides the funds to finance additional investment in housing and in plant and equipment. But the high dollar would also limit the improvement in the trade deficit, depressing activity in export industries and those that compete with imports from abroad. Ultimately, moreover, the dollar's adjustment would have to occur and would have to be larger because the dollar had contributed to a greater accumulation of net debt from the United States to the rest of the world.

Exchange Market Intervention

Although substantial past experience and economic logic both imply that sterilized exchange market intervention (i.e., currency intervention with no change in domestic monetary policy) cannot be expected to have a sustained effect on exchange rates, the fall of the dollar in the year after the G-5 finance ministers meeting at the Plaza Hotel in September 1985 and the relative stability of the dollar in the seven months after the Louvre meeting in February 1987 have led some government officials and others to attribute significant power to coordinated exchange rate intervention. I believe that conclusion is a misreading of the recent experience.

There is in fact no evidence that the G-5 Plaza meeting or the subsequent coordinated intervention had any lasting effect on the dollar's rate of decline. In the days immediately after the G-5 meeting there was a four percent decline in the dollar's value. But the rate of decline of the dollar during the subsequent year was no greater than it had been in the six months before the G-5 meeting.

Immediately after the Louvre meeting the central banks were able to prevent the dollar's continued decline by a combination of massive intervention and the threat of even more intervention in the future. But after a short time, continued stabilizing of the dollar required a significant rise in U.S. interest rates relative to interest rates in Japan and Germany. The resulting tight monetary policy in the United States and the fear of further Fed tightening in response to market pressure for a lower dollar were important causes of the stock market crash. As soon as the United States declared that monetary policy would no longer be directed at stabilizing the dollar, the dollar's value responded to market pressures and began to decline sharply. The experience in 1987 thus again demonstrates the inability of intervention to shift currency values for more than a very short time.

The Coordination of Macroeconomic Policies

Coordinated exchange rate intervention is only one aspect of the potential coordination of macroeconomic policies. Indeed there are many who accept that exchange rate intervention per se is powerless and who therefore argue for a more general coordination of monetary and budget policies. The Tokyo summit in May 1986 emphasized such macroeconomic coordination and called for a new "multi-lateral surveillance" procedure managed by the International Monetary Fund.

The first such multilateral surveillance session was held in conjunction with the IMF annual meetings in September 1986. The agenda was predictable. The United States called on Japan and the European countries to expand their economies more rapidly in order to increase their imports from the United States. The Europeans and Japan called on the United States to reduce its budget deficit and to slow the decline of the dollar relative to their currencies, an inherently self-contradictory request. No serious agreements were reached. The Germans explained that their economy was expanding rapidly, that their monetary policy was if anything too loose already, and that a tax cut was scheduled for 1988. The Japanese noted that they were moving gradually toward fundamental changes in their economy and Treasury Secretary Baker said the United States was committed to eliminating the budget deficit over the next five years as promised in the Gramm-Rudman-Hollings legislation. In short, every country said it would go on doing just what it had been doing. And, despite the subsequent pronouncements at the Louvre meeting and the Venice summit, each country continued to pursue what it saw as its own interest, generally unaffected by the "international coordination" process.

Only when the government of Japan became convinced in early 1987 that the sharp rise in the yen-dollar rate during 1986 would create a serious downturn for the Japanese economy did Japan abandon its goal of budget deficit reduction and adopt a package of fiscal and monetary stimulus. In contrast, Germany, despite its high unemployment and zero inflation rate, has not adopted any significant expansionary policies because of a government decision to give primacy to preventing inflation and to reducing domestic labor market rigidities. And the $70 billion decline in the U.S. budget deficit between 1986 and 1987 was not the result of international actions but of domestic politics and the peculiarities of budget accounting. This failure of the summit and other international coordination discussions to achieve any changes in domestic economic policies should not be seen as a surprise or as a reflection of the fact that the process of explicit coordination only began in 1986. It should be seen as the most likely outcome of all such meetings. The experience at and immediately after the September 1987 IMF-World Bank meetings again demonstrated the emptiness of the coordination process and the inclination of major governments to pursue their own self interests.

Constitutional Limits on American Participation

A primary reason why macroeconomic policy coordination cannot work as envisioned by its advocates is that the United States is constitutionally incapable of participating in such a negotiation. The separation of powers in the American form of government means that the Secretary of the Treasury cannot promise to reduce or expand the budget deficit or to change tax rules. This power does not rest with the president or the administration but depends on a legislative agreement between the president and the Congress. In this sense, the United States' participation in any macroeconomic coordination process is fundamentally different from the participation of a country with a parliamentary system in which the prime minister or the prime minister's representative can commit to a change in the nation's economic policy.

It is sometimes suggested that an American Treasury secretary or president, although incapable of promising the enactment of specific budget legislation, could promise that the American government would support a particular legislative pro-posal. Such a suggestion ignores the negotiating nature of the relation between the president and the Congress. The president cannot propose the legislative package that he expects Congress to enact and he cannot disclose the extent to which he is willing to compromise on specific issues.

Because it is impossible for the United States to reach an international agreement on specific budget, tax or spending policies, any actual agreement would have to call for a change in U.S. monetary policy. International economic coordination could thus be a recipe for the wrong policy change in the United States. For example, if the United States had entered into an agreement in 1983 or 1984 to shift policy in a way that reduced the value of the dollar, the agreement would have required an infla-tionary increase in the supply of money. At the present time, the finance ministers of other major industrial countries are urging the United States to defend the dollar by a tight monetary policy that could push the U.S. economy into an unnecessary recession. Moreover, even agreements on monetary policy would be beyond the legal authority of the Treasury secretary or the president since it would require the concurrence of the independent Federal Reserve.

Even if the United States could participate effectively in international macroeco-nomic coordination, I believe that the incentive for the United States and other major industrial countries to do so is more apparent than real. Uncertainties about the actual state of the international economy and uncertainties about the effects of one country's policies on the economies of other countries make it impossible to be confident that coordinated policy shifts would actually be beneficial. The Germans still remember and regret their agreement to serve as a "locomotive" for worldwide expansion after the 1978 Bonn summit meeting. Today the Germans argue that foreign pressure for more expansionary German policy exaggerates the potentially favorable effects of such a change on foreign economies and ignores both the underlying strength of German demand and the need to achieve structural reforms in the German labor market as a precondition for reduced unemployment. A few years ago U.S. Treasury Secretary Regan argued that foreign pressure for the United States to reduce its budget deficit was misplaced because budget deficits do not influence interest rates, exchange rates and capital flows. When there are fundamental disagreements about the way the world economy works, there is little reason to believe that coordinated policy will produce improved performance.

It is important to remember that to a very great extent a nation has the ability to achieve its economic goals by itself. Although the levels of demand, inflation, and interest rates in one country do affect the economies elsewhere, a country can manage its own monetary, budget and tax policies to offset many of the potential influences from abroad. Thus changes in domestic monetary policy can counteract the contrac-tionary or inflationary pressures from abroad and structural tax policies designed to encourage investment can offset the effects of a worldwide rise in real interest rates.

There is also a serious risk that economic summits and ministerial meetings will inhibit appropriate changes in national economic policies. Governments may not take the politically painful steps that they should because they believe that foreign actions will make such policies unnecessary or because they want to use their own lack of action as part of a bargaining strategy to induce desired policies on the part of foreign governments. Thus the assertion at the Louvre ministerial and at the Venice summit that the dollar would stop declining may have contributed to a complacency that reduced pressure on the German government to provide adequate domestic stimulus and that may even have contributed to the failure of the American Congress to make greater progress in reducing future budget deficits.

Concluding Remarks

It is unfortunately easy and often politically convenient to exaggerate the potential gains from international economic coordination and to understate the ability of a nation to guide its own economic future. Our politicians and those of other leading countries should not be allowed to escape their responsibilities by blaming poor domestic economic performance on the policies pursued abroad. Similarly, it would be a serious mistake if the pursuit of international coordination in exchange markets and in macroeconomic policy management became an excuse for not pursuing appropriate domestic policies.

Washington's explicit recognition of its responsibility for America's economic future would also reassure a nation that has become unnecessarily frightened by the prospect that international economic coordination will collapse. Unfortunately, ever since the May 1986 summit the U.S. administration and the governments of the other industrial countries have emphatically asserted that international economic cooperation is crucial to a healthy international economy in general and to continued U.S. growth in particular. Since such assertions are not justified by the extent of the actual interdependence of the industrialized nations, Americans have been inappropriately worried about whether policy coordination would continue.

Because foreign governments will inevitably pursue the policies that they believe are in their own best interests, it was inevitable that the process of international coordination would eventually collapse. This began with the actions of the German and Japanese governments in early October and was underscored by the statements of Secretary Baker just before the market crash. But the real problem contributing to the market decline was not the collapse of international macroeconomic coordination per se, but the false impression created by governments that healthy expansion requires such international coordination. Moreover, what appeared as cooperation by the European governments in reducing interest rates since late October was motivated by their desire to offset the contractionary effects of the worldwide stock market declines and the falling dollar, rather than as a gesture of cooperation with the United States.

The United States should now explicitly but amicably abandon the policy of international coordination of macroeconomic policy. We should continue to cooperate with other countries by exchanging information about current and future policy decisions, but we should recognize explicitly that Japan and Germany have the right to pursue the monetary and fiscal policies that they believe are in their own best interests.

It is frightening to the American public and upsetting to our financial markets to believe that the fate of our economy depends on the decisions made in Bonn and Tokyo. Portfolio investors, business managers and the public in general need to be reassured that we are not hostages to foreign economic policies, that the United States is the master of its own economic destiny, and that our government can and will do what is needed to maintain healthy economic growth.

Although international coordination of macroeconomic policy-making sounds like a way to improve international relations more generally, there is a serious risk that it will have the opposite effect. An emphasis on international interdependence instead of sound domestic policies makes foreign governments the natural scapegoats for any poor economic performance. Pressing a foreign government to alter its domestic economic policies is itself a source of friction and the making of unkeepable promises can only lead to resentment. It would in general be far better if the major industrial countries concentrated on the pursuit of sound domestic economic policies and reserved the pursuit of international cooperation for those subjects like international trade and national security in which cooperation is truly essential.

■ *This article is a condensed version of the 1987 Distinguished Lecture on Economics in Government, Joint Session of the American Economic Association and the Society of Government Economists, Chicago, December 28, 1987. A copy of the full lecture is available from the author.*

[1] My criticisms of international macroeconomic coordination were sketched first in an article that I wrote for the Economist magazine ("The World Economy Today," June 11, 1983). Earlier versions of the current lecture were presented as one of my two 1986 Horowitz Memorial Lectures of the Bank of Israel and as a lecture on the fiftieth anniversary of Nuffield College, Oxford (see Feldstein, forthcoming). The general subject of international economic cooperation (in macroeconomic policy, exchange rate policy, international trade and developing country debt management) was unexplored at an April 1987 conference of the National Bureau of Economic Research. The conference volume presents valuable survey papers, personal comments by individuals who have had significant experience in government and business, and an extensive bibliography that makes it unnecessary to provide such references in the current talk; my own views are summarized in an introductory chapter. The interested reader may also wish to see Feldstein (1987b; forthcoming a, b).

References

Feldstein, Martin, "Correcting the Trade Deficit," *Foreign Affairs*, Spring 1987a, 795–806.

Feldstein, Martin, *International Economic Cooperation: Summary Report*, National Bureau of Economic Research, 1987b.

Feldstein, Martin, "Rethinking International Economic Cooperation," Oxford Economic Papers, forthcoming.

Feldstein, Martin, *International Economic Cooperation*, Chicago: University of Chicago Press.

Is Growth Obsolete?

William Nordhaus
and James Tobin

A long decade ago economic growth was the reigning fashion of political economy. It was simultaneously the hottest subject of economic theory and research, a slogan eagerly claimed by politicians of all stripes, and a serious objective of the policies of governments. The climate of opinion has changed dramatically. Disillusioned critics indict both economic science and economic policy for blind obeisance to aggregate material "progress," and for neglect of its costly side effects. Growth, it is charged, distorts national priorities, worsens the distribution of income, and irreparably damages the environment. Paul Erlich speaks for a multitude when he says, "We must acquire a life style which has as its goal maximum freedom and happiness for the individual, not a maximum Gross National Product."

Growth was in an important sense a discovery of economics after the Second World War. Of course economic development has always been the grand theme of historically minded scholars of large mind and bold concept, notably Marx, Schumpeter, Kuznets. But the mainstream of economic analysis was not comfortable with phenomena of change and progress. The stationary state was the long-run equilibrium of classical and neoclassical theory, and comparison of alternative static equilibriums was the most powerful theoretical tool. Technological change and population increase were most readily accommodated as one-time exogenous shocks; comparative static analysis could be used to tell how they altered the equilibrium of the system. The obvious fact that these "shocks" were occurring continuously, never allowing the system to reach its equilibrium, was a considerable embarrassment. Keynesian theory fell in the same tradition, attempting rather awkwardly, though nonetheless fruitfully, to apply static equilibrium theory to the essentially dynamic problem of saving and capital accumulation.

Sir Roy Harrod in 1940 began the process, brought to fruition by many theorists in the 1950s, of putting the stationary state into motion. The long-run equilibrium of the system became a path of steady growth, and the tools of comparative statics could then be applied to alternative growth paths rather than to alternative stationary states. Neo-Keynesian macroeconomics began to fall into place as a description of departures from equilibrium growth, although this task of reinterpretation and integration is still far from a satisfactory completion.

By now modern neoclassical growth theory is well enough formulated to have made its way into textbooks. It is a theory of the growth of potential output, or output at a uniform standard rate of utilization of capacity. The theory relates potential output to three determinants: the labor force, the state of technology, and the stock of human and tangible capital. The first two are usually assumed to grow smoothly at rates determined exogenously by noneconomic factors. The accumulation of capital is governed by the thrift of the population, and in equilibrium the growth of the capital stock matches the growth of labor-*cum*-technology and the growth of output. Simple as it is, the model fits the observed trends of economic growth reasonably well.

The steady equilibrium growth of modern neoclassical theory is, it must be acknowledged, a routine process of replication. It is a dull story compared to the convulsive structural, technological, and social changes described by the historically oriented scholars of development mentioned above. The theory conceals, either in aggregation or in the abstract generality of multisector models, all the drama of the events — the rise and fall of products, technologies, and industries, and the accompanying transformations of the spatial and occupational distribution of the population. Many economists agree with the broad outlines of Schumpeter's vision of capitalist development, which is a far cry from growth models made nowadays in either Cambridge, Massachusetts, or Cambridge, England. But visions of that kind have yet to be transformed into a theory that can be applied in everyday analytic and empirical work.

In any case, growth of some kind is now the recognized economic norm. A symptom of the change in outlook can be found in business cycle semantics. A National Bureau *recession* was essentially a period in which aggregate productive activity was declining. Since 1960 it has become increasingly customary to describe the state of the economy by the gap between its actual output and its growing potential. Although the word recession is still a source of confusion and controversy, almost everyone recognizes that the economy is losing ground — which will have to be recaptured eventually — whenever its actual rate of expansion is below the rate of growth of potential output.

In the early 1960s growth became a proclaimed objective of government policy, in this country as elsewhere. Who could be against it? But like most value-laden words, growth has meant different things to different people and at different times. Often growth policy was simply identified with measures to expand aggregate demand in order to bring or keep actual output in line with potential output. In this sense it is simply stabilization policy, only more gap-conscious and growth-conscious than the cycle-smoothing policies of the past.

To economists schooled in postwar neoclassical growth theory, growth policy proper meant something more than this, and more debatable. It meant deliberate effort to speed up the growth of potential output itself, specifically to accelerate the productivity of labor. Growth policy in this meaning was not widely understood or accepted. The neoclassical model outlined above suggested two kinds of policies to foster growth, possibly interrelated: measures that advanced technological knowledge and measures that increased the share of potential output devoted to accumulation of physical or human capital.[1] Another implication of the standard model was that, unless someone could find a way to accelerate technological progress permanently, policy could not raise the rate of growth permanently. One-shot measures would speed up growth temporarily, for years or decades. But once the economy had absorbed these measures, its future growth rate would be limited once again by constraints of labor and technology. The level of its path, however, would be permanently higher than if the policies had not been undertaken.

Growth measures nearly always involve diversions of current resources from other uses, sacrifices of current consumption for the benefit of succeeding generations of consumers. Enthusiasts for faster growth are advocates of the future against the present. Their case rests on the view that in a market economy left to itself, the future would be shortchanged because too small a fraction of current output would be saved. We mention this point now because we shall return later to the ironical fact that the antigrowth men of the 1970s believe that it is they who represent the claims of a fragile future against a voracious present.

Like the enthusiasts to whom they are a reaction, current critics of growth are disenchanted with both theory and policy, with both the descriptive and the normative implications of the doctrines of the previous decade. The sources of disenchantment are worth considering today, because they indicate agenda for future theoretical and empirical research.

We have chosen to direct our attention to three important problems raised by those who question the desirability and possibility of future growth: (a) How good are measures of output currently used for evaluating the growth of economic welfare? (b) Does the growth process inevitably waste our natural resources? (c) How does the rate of population growth affect economic welfare? In particular, what would be the effect of zero population growth?

MEASURES OF ECONOMIC WELFARE

A major question raised by critics of economic growth is whether we have been growing at all in any meaningful sense. Gross national product statistics cannot give the answers, for GNP is not a measure of economic welfare. Erlich is right in claiming that maximization of GNP is not a proper objective of policy. Economists all know that, and yet their everyday use of GNP as the standard measure of economic performance apparently conveys the impression that they are evangelistic workshipers of GNP.

An obvious shortcoming of GNP is that it is an index of production, not consumption. The goal of economic activity, after all, is consumption. Although this is the central premise of economics, the profession has been slow to develop, either conceptually or statistically, a measure of economic performance oriented to consumption, broadly defined and carefully calculated. We have constructed a primitive and experimental "measure of economic welfare" (MEW), in which we attempt to allow for the more obvious discrepancies between GNP and economic welfare. A complete account is given in Appendix A. The main results will be discussed here and summarized in Tables 1 and 2.

In proposing a welfare measure, we in no way deny the importance of the conventional national income accounts or of the output measures based upon them. Our MEW is largely a rearrangement of items of the national accounts. Gross and net national product statistics are the economists' chief tools for short-run analysis, forecasting, and policy and are also indispensable for many other purposes.

Our adjustments to GNP fall into three general categories: reclassification of GNP expenditures as consumption, investment, and intermediate; imputation for the services of consumer capital, for leisure, and for the product of household work; correction for some of the disamenities of urbanization.

1. Reclassification of GNP Final Expenditures

Our purposes are first, to subtract some items that are better regarded as instrumental and intermediate than as final output, and second, to allocate all remaining items between consumption and net investment. Since the national accounts do not differentiate among government purchases of goods and services, one of our major tasks will be to split them among the three categories: intermediate, consumption, and net investment. We will also reclassify some private expenditures.

Intermediate products are goods and services whose contributions to present or future consumer welfare are completely counted in the values of other goods and services. To avoid double counting they should not be included in reckoning the net yield of economic activity. Thus all national income accounts reckon as final consumption the bread but not the flour and as capital formation the finished house but not the lumber. The more difficult and controversial issues in assigning items to intermediate or final categories are the following:

Capital Consumption. The depreciation of capital stocks is a cost of production, and output required to offset the depreciation is intermediate as surely as materials consumed in the productive process. For most purposes, including welfare indexes, NNP is preferable to GNP. Only the difficulties and lags in estimating capital consumption have made GNP the popular statistic.

However, NNP itself fails to treat many durable goods as capital, and counts as final their entire output whether for replacement or accumulation. These elementary points are worth repeating because some of our colleagues are telling the public that economists glorify wasteful "through-put" for its own sake. Focusing on NNP, and accounting for all durables as capital goods, would avoid such foolish paradoxes as the implication that deliberate efforts to make goods more perishable raise national output. We estimate, however, that proper treatment of consumer durables has little quantitative effect (see Table 1, lines 3 and 5).

The other capital consumption adjustments we have made arise from allowing for government capital and for the educational and medical capital embodied in human beings. In effect, we have reclassified education and health expenditures, both public and private, as capital investments.

Growth Requirements. In principle net national product tells how much consumption the economy could indefinitely sustain. GNP does not tell that; consuming the whole GNP in any year would impair future consumption prospects. But *per capita* rather than aggregate consumption is the welfare objective; neither economists nor other observers would as a rule regard sheer increase in the numbers of people enjoying the same average standard of living as a gain in welfare. Even NNP exaggerates sustainable *per capita* consumption, except in a society with stationary population—another example of the pervasiveness of the "stationary" assumption in the past. Per capita consumption cannot be sustained with zero net investment; the capital stock must be growing at the same rate as population and the labor force. This capital-widening requirement is as truly a cost of staying in the same position as outright capital consumption.[2]

This principle is clear enough when growth is simply increase in population and the labor force. Its application to an economy with technological progress is by no means clear. Indeed, the very concept of national income becomes fuzzy. Should the capital-widening requirement then be interpreted to mean that capital should keep pace with output and technology, not just with the labor force? If so, the implied sustainable consumption per capita grows with the rate of technological progress. This is the point of view which we have taken in what follows. On the other hand, a given level of consumption per capita could be sustained with a steady decline in the capital-output ratio, thanks to technological progress.[3]

The growth requirement is shown on line 7 of Table 2. This is clearly a significant correction, measuring about 16 per cent of GNP in 1965.

Our calculations distinguish between actual and sustainable per capita consumption. *Actual MEW* may exceed or fall short of *sustainable MEW*, the amount that could be consumed while meeting both capital consumption and growth requirements. If these requirements are met, per capita consumption can grow at the trend rate of increase in labor productivity. When actual MEW is less than sustainable MEW, the economy is making even better provision for future consumers; when actual MEW exceeds sustainable MEW, current consumption in effect includes some of the fruits of future progress.

Instrumental Expenditures. Since GNP and NNP are measures of production rather than of welfare, they count many activities that are evidently not directly sources of utility themselves but are regrettably necessary inputs to activities that may yield utility. Some consumer outlays are only instrumental, for example, the costs of commuting to work. Some government "purchases" are also of this nature — for example, police services, sanitation services, road maintenance, national defense. Expenditures on these items are among the necessary overhead costs of a complex industrial nation-state, although there is plenty of room for disagreement as to the necessary amounts. We are making no judgments on such issues in classifying these outlays as intermediate rather than final uses of resources. Nevertheless, these decisions are difficult and controversial. The issues are clearly illustrated in the important case of national defense.

We exclude defense expenditures for two reasons. First, we see no direct effect of defense expenditures on household economic welfare. No reasonable country (or household) buys "national defense" for its own sake. If there were no war or risk of war, there would be no need for defense expenditures and no one would be the worse without them. Conceptually, then, defense expenditures are gross but not net output.

The second reason is that defense expenditures are input rather than output data. Measurable output is especially elusive in the case of defense. Conceptually, the output of the defense effort is national security. Has the value of the nation's security risen from $0.5 billion to $50 billion over the period from 1929 to 1965? Obviously not. It is patently more reasonable to assume that the rise in expenditure was due to deterioration in international relations and to changes in military technology. The cost of providing a given level of security has risen enormously. If there has been no corresponding gain in security since 1929, the defense cost series is a very misleading indicator of improvements in welfare.

The economy's ability to meet increased defense costs speaks well for its productive performance. But the diversion of productive capacity to this purpose cannot be regarded simply as a shift of national preferences and the product mix. Just as we count technological progress, managerial innovation, and environmental change when they work in our favor (consider new business machines or mineral discoveries) so we must count a deterioration in the environment when it works against us (consider bad weather and war). From the point of view of economic welfare, an arms control or disarmament agreement which would free resources and raise consumption by 10 per cent would be just as significant as new industrial processes yielding the same gains.

In classifying defense costs — or police protection or public health expenditures — as regrettable and instrumental, we certainly do not deny the possibility that given the unfavorable circumstances that prompt these expenditures consumers will ultimately be better off with them than without them. This may or may not be the case. The only judgment we make is that these expenditures yield no direct satisfactions. Even if the "regrettable" outlays are rational responses to unfavorable shifts in the environment of economic activity, we believe that a welfare measure, perhaps unlike a production measure, should record such environmental change.

We must admit, however, that the line between final and instrumental outlays is very hard to draw. For example, the philosophical problems raised by the malleability of consumer wants are too deep to be resolved in economic accounting. Consumers are susceptible to influence by the examples and tastes of other consumers and by the sales efforts of producers. Maybe all our wants are just regrettable necessities; maybe productive activity does no better than to satisfy the wants which it generates; maybe our net welfare product is tautologically zero. More seriously, we cannot measure welfare exclusively by the quantitative flows of goods and services. We need other gauges of the health of individuals and societies. These, too, will be relative to the value systems which determine whether given symptoms indicate health or disease. But the "social indicators" movement of recent years still lacks a coherent, integrative conceptual and statistical framework.

We estimate that overhead and regrettable expenses, so far as we have been able to define and measure them, rose from 8 per cent to 16 per cent of GNP over the period 1929–65 (Table 2, line 4).

2. Imputations for Capital Services, Leisure, and Nonmarket Work

In the national income accounts, rent is imputed on owner-occupied homes and counted as consumption and income. We must make similar imputations in other cases to which we have applied capital accounting. Like owner-occupied homes, other consumer durables and public investments yield consumption directly, without market transactions. In the case of educational and health capital, we have assumed the yields to be intermediate services rather than direct consumption; that is, we expect to see the fruits of investments in education and health realized in labor productivity and earnings, and we do not count them twice. Our measure understates economic welfare and its growth to the extent that education and medical care are direct rather than indirect sources of consumer satisfaction.

The omission of leisure and of nonmarket productive activity from measures of production conveys the impression that economists are blindly materialistic. Economic theory teaches that welfare could rise, even while NNP falls, as the result of voluntary choices to work for pay fewer hours per week, weeks per year, years per lifetime.

These imputations unfortunately raise serious conceptual questions, discussed at some length in section A.3, below. Suppose that in calculating aggregate dollar consumption the hours devoted to leisure and nonmarket productive activity are valued at their presumed opportunity cost, the money wage rate. In converting current dollar consumption to constant dollars, what assumption should be made about the unobservable price indexes for the goods and services consumed during those hours? The wage rate? The price index for marketed con-

TABLE 1
Measures of Economic Welfare, Actual and Sustainable, Various Years, 1929–65
(billions of dollars, 1958 prices, except lines 14–19, as noted)

	1929	1935	1945	1947	1954	1958	1965
1 Personal consumption, national income and product accounts	139.6	125.5	183.0	206.3	255.7	290.1	397.7
2 Private instrumental expenditures	−10.3	−9.2	−9.2	−10.9	−16.4	−19.9	−30.9
3 Durable goods purchases	−16.7	−11.5	−12.3	−26.2	−35.5	−37.9	−60.9
4 Other household investment	−6.5	−6.3	−9.1	−10.4	−15.3	−19.6	−30.1
5 Services of consumer capital imputation	24.9	17.8	22.1	26.7	37.2	40.8	62.3
6 Imputation for leisure							
B	339.5	401.3	450.7	466.9	523.2	554.9	626.9
A	339.5	401.3	450.7	466.9	523.2	554.9	626.9
C	162.9	231.3	331.8	345.6	477.2	554.9	712.8
7 Imputation for nonmarket activities							
B	85.7	109.2	152.4	159.6	211.5	239.7	295.4
A	178.6	189.5	207.1	215.5	231.9	239.7	259.8
C	85.7	109.2	152.4	159.6	211.5	239.7	295.4
8 Disamenity correction	−12.5	−14.1	−18.1	−19.1	−24.3	−27.6	−34.6
9 Government consumption	0.3	0.3	0.4	0.5	0.5	0.8	1.2
10 Services of government capital imputation	4.8	6.4	8.9	10.0	11.7	14.0	16.6
11 Total consumption = actual MEW							
B	548.8	619.4	768.8	803.4	948.3	1,035.3	1,243.6
A	641.7	699.7	823.5	859.3	968.7	1,035.3	1,208.0
C	372.2	449.4	649.9	682.1	902.3	1,035.3	1,329.5
12 MEW net investment	−5.3	−46.0	−52.5	55.3	13.0	12.5	−2.5
13 Sustainable MEW							
B	543.5	573.4	716.3	858.7	961.3	1,047.8	1,241.1
A	636.4	653.7	771.0	914.6	981.7	1,047.8	1,205.5
C	366.9	403.4	597.4	737.4	915.3	1,047.8	1,327.0
14 Population (no. of mill.)	121.8	127.3	140.5	144.7	163.0	174.9	194.6

(continued)

Table 1 (concluded)

		1929	1935	1945	1947	1954	1958	1965
	Actual MEW per capita							
15	Dollars							
	B	4,506	4,866	5,472	5,552	5,818	5,919	6,391
	A	5,268	5,496	5,861	5,938	5,943	5,919	6,208
	C	3,056	3,530	4,626	4,714	5,536	5,919	6,832
16	Index (1929 = 100)							
	B	100.0	108.0	121.4	123.2	129.1	131.4	141.8
	A	100.0	104.3	111.3	112.7	112.8	112.4	117.8
	C	100.0	115.5	151.4	154.3	181.2	193.7	223.6
	Sustainable MEW per capita							
17	Dollars							
	B	4,462	4,504	5,098	5,934	5,898	5,991	6,378
	A	5,225	5,135	5,488	6,321	6,023	5,991	6,195
	C	3,012	3,169	4,252	5,096	5,615	5,991	6,819
18	Index (1929 = 100)							
	B	100.0	100.9	114.3	133.0	132.2	134.3	142.9
	A	100.0	98.3	105.0	121.0	115.3	114.7	118.6
	C	100.0	105.2	141.2	169.2	186.4	198.9	226.4
19	Per capita NNP							
	Dollars	1,545	1,205	2,401	2,038	2,305	2,335	2,897
	1929 = 100	100.0	78.0	155.4	131.9	149.2	151.1	187.5

Note: Variants A, B, C in the table correspond to different assumptions about the bearing of technological progress on leisure and nonmarket activities. See section A.3.2, below, for explanation.
Source: Appendix Table A.16.

sumption goods? Over a period of forty years the two diverge substantially; the choice between them makes a big difference in estimates of the growth of MEW. As explained in Appendix A, the market consumption "deflator" should be used if technological progress has augmented nonmarketed uses of time to the same degree as marketed labor. The wage rate should be the deflator if no such progress has occurred in the effectiveness of unpaid time.

In Tables 1 and 2 we provide calculations for three conceptual alternatives. Our own choice is variant B of MEW, in which the value of leisure is deflated by the wage rate; and the value of nonmarket activity, by the consumption deflator.

3. Disamenities of Urbanization

The national income accounts largely ignore the many sources of utility or disutility that are not associated with market transactions or measured by the market value of goods and services. If one of my neighbors cultivates a garden of ever-increasing beauty, and another makes more and more noise, neither my increasing appreciation of the one nor my growing annoyance with the other comes to the attention of the Department of Commerce.

Likewise there are some socially productive assets (for example, the environment) that do not appear in any balance sheets. Their services to producers and consumers are not valued in calculating national income. By the same token no allowance is made for depletion of their capacity to yield services in the future.

Many of the negative "externalities" of economic growth are connected with urbanization and congestion. The secular advances re-

TABLE 2
Gross National Product and MEW, Various Years, 1929–65
(billions of dollars, 1958 prices)

	1929	1935	1945	1947	1954	1958	1965
1. Gross national product	203.6	169.5	355.2	309.9	407.0	447.3	617.8
2. Capital consumption, NIPA	−20.0	−20.0	−21.9	−18.3	−32.5	−38.9	−54.7
3. Net national product, NIPA	183.6	149.5	333.3	291.6	374.5	408.4	563.1
4. NIPA final output reclassified as regrettables and intermediates							
a. Government	−6.7	−7.4	−146.3	−20.8	−57.8	−56.4	−63.2
b. Private	−10.3	−9.2	−9.2	−10.9	−16.4	−19.9	−30.9
5. Imputations for items not included in NIPA							
a. Leisure	339.5	401.3	450.7	466.9	523.2	554.9	626.9
b. Nonmarket activity	85.7	109.2	152.4	159.6	211.5	239.7	295.4
c. Disamenities	−12.5	−14.1	−18.1	−19.1	−24.3	−27.6	−34.6
d. Services of public and private capital	29.7	24.2	31.0	36.7	48.9	54.8	78.9
6. Additional capital consumption	−19.3	−33.4	−11.7	−50.8	−35.2	−27.3	−92.7
7. Growth requirement	−46.1	−46.7	−65.8	+5.4	−63.1	−78.9	−101.8
8. Sustainable MEW	543.6	573.4	716.3	858.6	961.3	1,047.7	1,241.1

NIPA = national income and product accounts.

Note: Variants A, B, C in the table correspond to different assumptions about the bearing of technological progress on leisure and nonmarket activities. Variant A assumes that neither has benefited from technological progress at the rate of increase of real wages; variant C assumes that neither has so benefited; variant B assumes that leisure has not been augmented by technological progress but other nonmarket activities have benefited. See section A.3.2, below, for explanation.

Source: Appendix Table A.17.

corded in NNP figures have accompanied a vast migration from rural agriculture to urban industry. Without this occupational and residential revolution we could not have enjoyed the fruits of technological progress. But some portion of the higher earnings of urban residents may simply be compensation for the disamenities of urban life and work. If so we should not count as a gain of welfare the full increments of NNP that result from moving a man from farm or small town to city. The persistent association of higher wages with higher population densities offers one method of estimating the costs of urban life as they are valued by people making residential and occupational decisions.

As explained in section A.4, below, we have tried to estimate by cross-sectional regressions the income differentials necessary to hold people in localities with greater population densities. The resulting estimates of the disamenity costs of urbanization are shown in Table 1, line 8. As can be seen, the estimated disamenity premium is quite substantial, running about 5 per cent of GNP. Nevertheless, the urbanization of the population has not been so rapid that charging it with this cost significantly reduces the estimated rate of growth of the economy.

The adjustments leading from national accounts "personal consumption" to MEW consumption are shown in Table 1, and the relations of GNP, NNP, and MEW are summarized in Table 2. For reasons previously indicated, we believe that a welfare measure should have the dimension *per capita*. We would stress the per capita MEW figures shown in Tables 1 and 2.

Although the numbers presented here are very tentative, they do suggest the following observations. First, MEW is quite different from conventional output measures. Some consumption items omitted from GNP are of substantial quantitative importance. Second, our preferred variant of per capita MEW has been growing more slowly than per capita NNP (1.1 per cent for MEW as against 1.7 per cent for NNP, at annual rates over the period 1929–65). Yet MEW has been growing. The progress indicated by conventional national accounts is not just a myth that evaporates when a welfare-oriented measure is substituted.

Note: We would like to express our appreciation to Walter Dolde, James Pugash, Geoffrey Woglom, Hugh Tobin, and especially Laura Harrison, for assistance in the preparation of this paper. We are grateful to Robin Matthews for pointing out some problems in our treatment of leisure in the first draft.

[1] The variety of possible measures, and the difficulty of raising the growth rate b more than one or two percentage points, have been explored by Edward Denison in hi influential study, *The Sources of Economic Growth in the United States and the Alte natives Before Us*, New York, Committee for Economic Development, January 196. Supplementary Paper No. 13.

[2] Consider the neoclassical model without technological change. When labor force is growing at rate g, the capital-labor ratio is k, gross product per worker is $f(k)$, net product per worker is $f(k) - \delta k$, then the net investment requirement is gk, and sustainable consumption per worker is $f(k) - \delta k - gk$. Denoting the capital-output ratio as $\mu = [k/f(k)]$, sustainable consumption per worker can also be written as $f(k)[1 - \mu(\delta + g)]$. Although NNP embodies in principle the depreciation deduction δk, it does not take account of the capital-widening requirement gk.

[3] As is well known, the whole concept of equilibrium growth collapses unless progress is purely labor-augmenting, "Harrod-neutral." In that case the rate g above is $n + \gamma$, where n is the natural rate of increase and γ is the rate of technological progress, and "labor force" means effective or augmented labor force. In equilibrium, output and consumption per natural worker grow at the rate γ, and "sustainable" consumption per capita means consumption growing steadily at this rate. Clearly, level consumption per capita can be sustained with smaller net investment than $g\mu f(k)$; so μ and k steadily decline. See section A.2.3, below.

The Case Against Economic Growth

Ezra J. Mishan

       . . . The notion of economic expansion as a process on balance beneficial to society goes back at least a couple of centuries, about which time, however, the case in favour was much stronger than it is today when we are not only incomparably wealthier but also suffering from many disagreeable by-products of rapid technological change. Yet so entrenched are the interests involved, commercial, institutional and scientific, and so pervasive the influence of modern communications, that economic growth has embedded itself in the ethos of our civilization. Despite the manifest disamenities caused by the post-war economic expansion, no one today seeking to advance his position in the hierarchy of government or business fails to pay homage to this sovereign concept.

II

The general conclusion of this volume is that the continued pursuit of economic growth by Western Societies is more likely on balance to reduce rather than increase social welfare. And some additional light on the pattern of arguments employed is shed by enumerating the set of conditions that, if met, would ensure a positive relation between economic growth and welfare.

First, that the economy be highly competitive in structure in all its branches, or else so organized that in all sectors the outputs of goods are such that their prices tend to equal their corresponding marginal costs.[1]

Second, that all the measurable effects on other people or firms arising in the production and use of any good – other than those effects which already register on the market mechanism in the form of alterations in product and factor prices – be brought into the cost calculus.

Third, that in increasing *per capita* output over time the process of economic growth does not bring about a less equitable distribution of income.

[1] Perhaps it should be repeated that these conditions are sufficient, though *not* necessary. Necessary conditions would be more difficult to specify. The allocative requirements, for instance, if expressed as a necessary condition in conjunction with the others, would state that any given technological advance, or increase in the stock of capital, should not be offset by a worsening of allocation. One cannot be more specific since there are an unlimited number of ways in which the allocation could be sufficiently worse (in the sense that notwithstanding technological advance or capital accumulation, the associated reallocation would be such that it would not be possible to redistribute the new set of outputs as to make everyone better off).

Though of theoretic interest, such difficulties need not detain us here. The choice of statement of any one sufficient condition, rather than another, is only incidental to the main object of drawing attention to the range of considerations that must be attended before one can draw any conclusion about the movement of social welfare.

Fourth, that the consuming public be fully conversant with the comparative qualities and performances of all new goods coming on to the market.

Fifth, that the public, regarded as producers, become no worse off in adapting themselves to new techniques of production.

Sixth, that the so-called relative income hypothesis does not hold; or, less stringently, that an over-all increase in real income *per capita* will have more than negligible effects in making some people feel better off without making others feel worse off.

Seventh, that the welfare experienced by men from sources other than goods produced by the economic system is small enough to be neglected.

Though it goes without saying that none of these conditions is likely to be met in today's wealthy societies, some of the conditions are more important than others. Observations, both slight and significant on each of the first six conditions, may be found in the professional literature. Since it lends itself to elegant formulation, the first condition is the one treated in most detail. Indeed, owing to the traditional presumption in favour of competition and free trade, measures of the degree of monopoly in the economy and, occasionally, of allocative waste associated therewith, are of continued interest to economists. Yet the scope for improvements in welfare by policies designed to increase competition is, I should think, very slight in comparison with the losses of welfare from neglect of the other conditions. The concern with external effects, relevant to the second condition, is hardly less pronounced. A good deal of the interest in these external effects, however, may be imputed to the intellectual fascination with optimality problems – not, alas, to universal alarm at what is happening to our environment. I have suggested that the potential contribution to social welfare of adopting a policy of correcting outstanding external diseconomies is vastly underrated, and this for several reasons: (i) because of the present difficulties of measurement; (ii) because of the mistaken view that the disamenities inflicted are limited, since there appear to be incentives to voluntary agreement for their control; and (iii) because of a sense of resignation induced by the slippery problems connected with hypothetical and actual compensation. To these professional reasons we may add the popular impression – which in consequence of the above reasons also appeals to many economists – that economic growth provides a more direct and certain means of advancing welfare. . . .

In illustrating some of the chief sources of external diseconomies no attempt was made to disguise the author's conviction that the invention of the private automobile is one of the great disasters to have befallen the human race. Given the absence of controls, the growth of population and its increased wealth and urbanization would, in any case, have produced overgrown cities. Commercial and municipal greed, coupled with architectural apathy, share the responsibility for a litter of shabby buildings. But it needed the motor-car to consummate these developments, to fill our days with clamour and fumes, to suburbanize the countryside and to subtopianize suburbia, and to ensure that any resort which became accessible should simultaneously become unattractive. The motor industry has come to dominate the economy as brazenly as its products dominate our physical environment, and our psychology. The common sight today, of street after street strewn thick with layabout cars, no longer dismays us.

The other two rapidly growing sources of disamenity used in illustrating the external diseconomies thesis were air-travel and tourism. No effective legislation putting the onus on airlines has been contemplated. The noise created is limited only by what the authorities believe people can be made to put up with. And the public may be conditioned over time to bear with increasing disturbance simply (i) because of the difficulties and cost of organizing protests; (ii) because of the apparent hopelessness of prevailing upon the authorities to put the claims of the residents before the claims of 'progress', that is, the airlines; and (iii) because of the timidity felt in pressing one's claims against so effective a retort as 'the national interest'. If there is a national interest, however, our discussion reveals the case for the Government's bearing the cost of its safeguard; not the unfortunate victims of aerial disturbance. The least that should be done to promote social welfare is to extend to the public some choice in the matter by legislating for wholly noise-free zones – zones that are, however, desirable in other respects and easily accessible.

As for the rapid destruction by mass-tourism of the world's dwindling resources of natural beauty, a small contribution towards preservation could be made by the prohibition of motorized vehicles within selected areas and by the discontinuing of air services to such areas. Once the public becomes aware of the spread of devastation, international agreement on more radical measures may be forthcoming – if by then there is anything left worth preserving.

In sum, the thesis of the first two parts of this essay is that if men are concerned primarily with human welfare, and not primarily with productivity conceived as a good in itself, they should reject economic growth as a prior aim of policy in favour of a policy of seeking to apply more selective criteria of welfare. Such a policy would involve (1) legislation recognizing the individual's right to amenity, which legislation would spearhead the attack on much of our post-war blight; and (2) a substantial diversion of investible resources from industry to the task of re-planning our towns and cities – in general, to direct our national resources and our ingenuity to recreating an environment that will gratify and inspire men. Finally, if public opinion cannot, for the present, be swung overwhelmingly towards this alternative view of the primary ends of policy, any regard at all to the declared doctrine of increasing the range of choices available to men warrants an extension to existing minorities of separate facilities in matters both large and small – though especially in respect of viable areas wherein a man of moderate means may choose to dwell unmolested by those particular features of modern technology that most disturb his equanimity.

III

If the moving spirit behind economic growth were to speak, its motto would be 'Enough does not suffice'. The classical description of an economic system makes sense in today's advanced economy only when stood on its head. Certainly the American economy presents us with a spectacle of growing resources pressing against limited wants. Moreover the pace of change in the patterns of people's wants destroys the base on which the economist's comparison of social welfare is raised: if all seven conditions mentioned were met, the mere fact of continually changing tastes alone would prevent the economist from inferring that economic growth *per capita* increased welfare. Moreoever, the vagaries of fashion can become burdensome and the multiplication of goods disconcerting.

Once we move away from the economist's frame of reference, other factors bearing on social welfare loom large. Expanding markets in conditions of material abundance depend upon men's dissatisfaction with their lot being perpetually renewed. Whether individual campaigns are successful or not, the institution of commercial advertising accentuates the materialistic tendencies in society and promotes the view that the things that matter most are the things money will buy – a view to which the young, who have plenty of need of the wherewithal, if they are to avail themselves of the widely advertised opportunities for fast living and cool extravagance, are peculiarly vulnerable, and which explains much of their vociferous impatience and increasing violence.

These and other informal considerations brought to bear in the digression of Part III lead to pessimistic conclusions. Technological innovations may offer to add to men's material opportunities. But by increasing the risks of their obsolescence it adds also to their anxiety. Swifter means of communications have the paradoxical effect of isolating people; increased mobility has led to more hours commuting; increased automobilization to increased separation; more television to less communication. In consequence, people know less of their neighbours than ever before in history.

The pursuit of efficiency, itself regarded as the lifeblood of progress, is directed towards reducing the dependence of people on each other, and increasing their dependence on the machine. Indeed, by a gradual displacement of human effort from every aspect of living, technology will eventually enable us to slip swiftly through our allotted years with scarce enough sense of physical friction to be certain we are still alive.[1]

Considerations such as these, which do not lend themselves to formal treatment, are crucial to the issue of human welfare. And the apparent inevitability of technological advance does not thereby render them irrelevant. Death too is inevitable. But one does not feel compelled to hurry towards it on that account. Once we descry the sort of world towards which technological growth is bearing us, it is well worth discussing whether humanity will find it more congenial or not. If, on reflection, we view the prospects with misgivings we are, at least, freed from the obligation to join in the frequent incantations of our patriotic growthmen. More positively, we have an additional incentive to support the policy of reducing industrial investment in favour of large-scale replanning of our cities, and of restoring and enhancing the beauty of many of our villages, towns and resorts.

[1] The recent electric-power breakdown in New York (1965), obviously to be deplored on grounds of efficiency, broke the spell of monotony for millions of New Yorkers. People enjoyed the shock of being thrown back on their innate resources and into sudden dependence upon one another. For a few hours people were freed from routine and brought together by the dark. Next-door strangers spoke, and gladdened to help each other. There was room for kindness.

The fault was repaired. The genie of power was returned to each home. And as the darkness brought them stumbling into each other's arms, so the hard light scattered them again. Yet someone was quoted as saying, 'This should happen at least once a month.'

The Limits to Growth

**Donella H. Meadows, Dennis L. Meadows,
Jorgen Randers, and William W. Behrens III**

INTRODUCTION

*I do not wish to seem overdramatic, but
I can only conclude from the information
that is available to me as Secretary-
General, that the Members of the United
Nations have perhaps ten years left in
which to subordinate their ancient
quarrels and launch a global partnership
to curb the arms race, to improve the
human environment, to defuse the population explosion, and to supply the
required momentum to development
efforts. If such a global partnership is
not forged within the next decade, then
I very much fear that the problems I
have mentioned will have reached such
staggering proportions that they will be
beyond our capacity to control.*
U THANT, 1969

The problems U Thant mentions—
the arms race, environmental deterioration, the population explosion, and economic stagnation—are often cited as the central, long-term problems of modern man. Many people believe
that the future course of human society, perhaps even the survival of human society, depends on the speed and effectiveness
with which the world responds to these issues. And yet only a
small fraction of the world's population is actively concerned
with understanding these problems or seeking their solutions.

HUMAN PERSPECTIVES

Every person in the world faces a series of pressures and problems that require his attention and action. These problems
affect him at many different levels. He may spend much of
his time trying to find tomorrow's food for himself and his
family. He may be concerned about personal power or the

344

Figure 1 HUMAN PERSPECTIVES

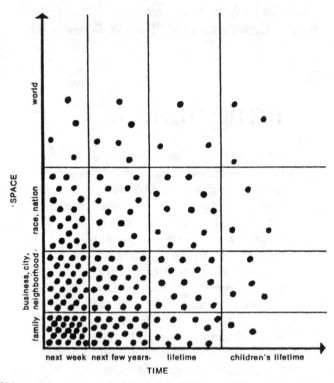

Although the perspectives of the world's people vary in space and in time, every human concern falls somewhere on the space-time graph. The majority of the world's people are concerned with matters that affect only family or friends over a short period of time. Others look farther ahead in time or over a larger area—a city or a nation. Only a very few people have a global perspective that extends far into the future.

power of the nation in which he lives. He may worry about a world war during his lifetime, or a war next week with a rival clan in his neighborhood.

These very different levels of human concern can be represented on a graph like that in figure 1. The graph has two dimensions, space and time. Every human concern can be located at some point on the graph, depending on how much geographical space it includes and how far it extends in time. Most people's worries are concentrated in the lower left-hand corner of the graph. Life for these people is difficult, and they must devote nearly all of their efforts to providing for themselves and their families, day by day. Other people think about and act on problems farther out on the space or time axes. The pressures they perceive involve not only themselves, but the community with which they identify. The actions they take extend not only days, but weeks or years into the future.

A person's time and space perspectives depend on his culture, his past experience, and the immediacy of the problems confronting him on each level. Most people must have successfully solved the problems in a smaller area before they move their concerns to a larger one. In general the larger the space and the longer the time associated with a problem, the smaller the number of people who are actually concerned with its solution.

There can be disappointments and dangers in limiting one's view to an area that is too small. There are many examples of a person striving with all his might to solve some immediate, local problem, only to find his efforts defeated by events occurring in a larger context. A farmer's carefully maintained fields can be destroyed by an international war. Local officials' plans can be overturned by a national policy. A country's economic development can be thwarted by a lack of world demand for its products. Indeed there is increasing concern today that most personal and national objectives may ultimately be frustrated by long-term, global trends such as those mentioned by U Thant.

Are the implications of these global trends actually so threatening that their resolution should take precedence over local, short-term concerns?

Is it true, as U Thant suggested, that there remains less than a decade to bring these trends under control?

If they are not brought under control, what will the consequences be?

What methods does mankind have for solving global problems, and what will be the results and the costs of employing each of them?

These are the questions that we have been investigating in the first phase of The Club of Rome's Project on the Predicament of Mankind. Our concerns thus fall in the upper right-hand corner of the space-time graph.

PROBLEMS AND MODELS

Every person approaches his problems, wherever they occur on the space-time graph, with the help of models. A model is simply an ordered set of assumptions about a complex system. It is an attempt to understand some aspect of the infinitely varied world by selecting from perceptions and past experience a set of general observations applicable to the problem at hand. A farmer uses a mental model of his land, his assets, market prospects, and past weather conditions to decide which crops to plant each year. A surveyor constructs a physical model—a map—to help in planning a road. An economist uses mathematical models to understand and predict the flow of international trade.

Decision-makers at every level unconsciously use mental models to choose among policies that will shape our future world. These mental models are, of necessity, very simple when compared with the reality from which they are abstracted. The human brain, remarkable as it is, can only keep track of a limited number of the complicated, simultaneous interactions that determine the nature of the real world.

We, too, have used a model. Ours is a formal, written model of the world.* It constitutes a preliminary attempt to improve our mental models of long-term, global problems by combining the large amount of information that is already in human minds and in written records with the new information-processing tools that mankind's increasing knowledge has produced—the scientific method, systems analysis, and the modern computer.

Our world model was built specifically to investigate five major trends of global concern—accelerating industrialization, rapid population growth, widespread malnutrition, depletion of nonrenewable resources, and a deteriorating environment. These trends are all interconnected in many ways, and their development is measured in decades or centuries, rather than in months or years. With the model we are seeking to understand the causes of these trends, their interrelationships, and their implications as much as one hundred years in the future.

The model we have constructed is, like every other model, imperfect, oversimplified, and unfinished. We are well aware of its shortcomings, but we believe that it is the most useful model now available for dealing with problems far out on the space-time graph. To our knowledge it is the only formal model in existence that is truly global in scope, that has a time horizon longer than thirty years, and that includes important variables such as population, food production, and pollution, not as independent entities, but as dynamically interacting elements, as they are in the real world.

Since ours is a formal, or mathematical, model it also has two important advantages over mental models. First, every assumption we make is written in a precise form so that it is open to inspection and criticism by all. Second, after the assumptions have been scrutinized, discussed, and revised to agree with our best current knowledge, their implications for the future behavior of the world system can be traced without error by a computer, no matter how complicated they become.

* The prototype model on which we have based our work was designed by Professor Jay W. Forrester of the Massachusetts Institute of Technology. A description of that model has been published in his book *World Dynamics* (Cambridge, Mass.: Wright-Allen Press, 1971).

We feel that the advantages listed above make this model unique among all mathematical and mental world models available to us today. But there is no reason to be satisfied with it in its present form. We intend to alter, expand, and improve it as our own knowledge and the world data base gradually improve.

In spite of the preliminary state of our work, we believe it is important to publish the model and our findings now. Decisions are being made every day, in every part of the world, that will affect the physical, economic, and social conditions of the world system for decades to come. These decisions cannot wait for perfect models and total understanding. They will be made on the basis of some model, mental or written, in any case. We feel that the model described here is already sufficiently developed to be of some use to decision-makers. Furthermore, the basic behavior modes we have already observed in this model appear to be so fundamental and general that we do not expect our broad conclusions to be substantially altered by further revisions.

It is not the purpose of this book to give a complete, scientific description of all the data and mathematical equations included in the world model. Such a description can be found in the final technical report of our project. Rather, in *The Limits to Growth* we summarize the main features of the model and our findings in a brief, nontechnical way. The emphasis is meant to be not on the equations or the intricacies of the model, but on what it tells us about the world. We have used a computer as a tool to aid our own understanding of the causes and consequences of the accelerating trends that characterize the modern world, but familiarity with computers is by no means necessary to comprehend or to discuss our conclusions. The implications of those accelerating trends raise issues that go far beyond the proper domain of a purely scientific document. They must be debated by a wider community than that of scientists alone. Our purpose here is to open that debate.

The following conclusions have emerged from our work so far. We are by no means the first group to have stated them. For the past several decades, people who have looked at the world with a global, long-term perspective have reached similar conclusions. Nevertheless, the vast majority of policymakers seems to be actively pursuing goals that are inconsistent with these results.

Our conclusions are:

1. If the present growth trends in world population, industrialization, pollution, food production, and resource depletion con-

tinue unchanged, the limits to growth on this planet will be reached sometime within the next one hundred years. The most probable result will be a rather sudden and uncontrollable decline in both population and industrial capacity.

2. It is possible to alter these growth trends and to establish a condition of ecological and economic stability that is sustainable far into the future. The state of global equilibrium could be designed so that the basic material needs of each person on earth are satisfied and each person has an equal opportunity to realize his individual human potential.

3. If the world's people decide to strive for this second outcome rather than the first, the sooner they begin working to attain it, the greater will be their chances of success.

These conclusions are so far-reaching and raise so many questions for further study that we are quite frankly overwhelmed by the enormity of the job that must be done. We hope that this book will serve to interest other people, in many fields of study and in many countries of the world, to raise the space and time horizons of their concerns and to join us in understanding and preparing for a period of great transition—the transition from growth to global equilibrium.

Is the End of the World at Hand?

Robert M. Solow

I was having a hard time figuring out how to begin when I came across an excerpt from an interview with my MIT colleague Professor Jay Forrester, who is either the Christopher Columbus or the Dr. Strangelove of this business, depending on how you look at it. Forrester said he would like to see about 100 individuals, the most gifted and best qualified in the world, brought together in a team to make a psychosocial analysis of the problem of world equilibrium. He thought it would take about ten years. When he was asked to define the composition of his problem-solving group, Forrester said: "Above all it shouldn't be mostly made up of professors. One would include people who had been successful in their personal careers, whether in politics, business, or anywhere else. We should also need radical philosophers, but we should take care to keep out representatives of the social sciences. Such people always want to go to the bottom of a particular problem. What we want to look at are the problems caused by interactions."

I don't know what you call people who believe they can be wrong about everything in particular, but expect to be lucky enough somehow to get it right on the interactions. They may be descendants of the famous merchant Lapidus, who said he lost money on every item he sold, but made it up on the volume. Well, I suppose that as an economist I am a representative of the social sciences; and I'm prepared to play out the role by talking about first principles and trying to say what the Growth vs. No-Growth business is really all about. This is going to involve me in the old academic ploy of saying over and over again what I'm not talking about before I ever actually say what I think I am talking about. But I'm afraid that some of those boring distinctions are part of the price you have to pay for getting it right.

First of all, there are (at least) two separate questions you can ask about the prospects for economic growth. You can ask: Is growth desirable? Or you can ask: Is growth possible? I suppose that if continued economic growth is not possible, it hardly matters whether or not it's desirable. But if it is possible, it's presumably not inevitable, so we can discuss whether we should want it. But they are separate questions, and an answer to one of them is not necessarily an answer to the other. My main business is with the question about the possibility of continued growth; I want to discuss the validity of the negative answer given by the "Doomsday Models" associated with the names of Forrester and Meadows (and MIT!) and, to a lesser extent, with the group of English scientists who published a manifesto called "Blueprint for Survival." The main concern of Dr. E. J. Mishan [whose article will appear in a later issue], on the other hand, was with the desirability of continued economic growth (and, at least by implication, with the desirability of past economic growth). If I spend a few minutes poaching on his territory, it is mainly because that seems like a good way to get some concepts straight, but also just to keep a discussion going.

Sorting out the issues

Arguments about the desirability of economic growth often turn quickly into arguments about the "quality" of modern life. One gets the notion that you favor growth if you are the sort of person whose idea of heaven is to drive at 90 miles an hour down a six-lane highway reading billboards, in order to pollute the air over some crowded lake with the exhaust from twin 100-horsepower outboards, and whose idea of food is Cocoa Krispies. On the other hand. to be against economic growth is to be a granola-eating, backpacking, transcendental-meditating canoe freak. That may even be a true statistical association, but I will argue that there is no necessary or logical connection between your answer to the growth question and your answer to the quality-of-life question. Suppose there were no issue about economic growth; suppose it were impossible; suppose each man or each woman were equipped to have only two children (one bomb under each wing); suppose we were stuck with the technology we have now and had no concept of invention, or even of increased mechanization through capital investment. We could still argue about the relative merits of cutting timber for building houses or leaving it stand to be enjoyed as forest. Some people would still be willing to breathe carbon monoxide in big cities in return for the excitement of urban life, while others would prefer cleaner air and fewer TV channels. Macy's would still not tell Gimbel's. Admen would still try to tell you that all those beautiful women are actually just looking for somebody who smokes Winchesters, thus managing to insult both men and women at once. Some people would still bring transistor radios to the beach. All or nearly all of the arguments about the quality of life would be just as valid if the question of growth never arose.

I won't go so far as to say there is no connection. In particular, one can argue that if population density were low enough, people would interfere much less with each other, and everyone could find a part of the world and style of civilization that suited him. Then differences of opinion about the quality of life wouldn't matter so much. Even if I grant the truth of that observation, it is still the case that, from here on out, questions about the quality of life are separable from questions about the desirability of growth. If growth stopped, there would be just about as much to complain about; and, as I shall argue later on, one can imagine continued growth that is directed against pollution, against congestion, against sliced white bread.

I suppose it is only fair to admit that if you get very enthusiastic about economic growth you are likely to be attracted to easily quantifiable and measurable things as objects of study, to point at with pride or to view with alarm. You are likely to pay less attention to important, intangible aspects of the standard of living. Although you can't know whether people are happier than they used to be, you can at least determine that they drink more orange juice or take more aspirin. But that's mere weakness of imagination and has nothing to do in principle with the desirability of economic growth, let alone with its possibility.

There is another practical argument that is often made; and although it is important, it sometimes serves as a way of avoiding coming to grips with the real issues. This argument says that economic growth, increasing output per person, is the only way we are likely to achieve a more equitable distribution of income in society. There is a lot of home truth in that. It is inevitably less likely that a middle-class electorate will vote to redistribute part of its own income to the poor than that it will be willing to allocate a slightly larger share of a growing total. Even more pessimistically, I might suggest that even a given relative distribution of income, supposing it cannot be made more nearly equal, for political or other reasons, is less unattractive if the absolute standard of living at the bottom is fairly high than it is if the absolute standard at the bottom is very low. From this point of view, even if economic growth doesn't lead to more equity in distribution, it makes the inequity we've got more tolerable. I think it is one of the lessons of history as recent as the McGovern campaign that this is a realistic statement of the prospects.

It is even clearer if one looks, not at the distribution of income within a rich country like the U.S., but at the distribution of income between the developed countries of the world and the undeveloped ones. The rich Western nations have never been able to agree on the principle of allocating as much as one percent of their GNP to aid undeveloped countries. They are unlikely to be willing to share their wealth on any substantial scale with the poor countries. Even if they were, there are so many more poor people in the world that an equally shared income would be quite low. The *only* prospect of a decent life for Asia, Africa, and Latin America is in more total output.

But I point this out only to warn you that it is not the heart of the question. I think that those who oppose continued growth should in honesty face up to the implications of their position for distributional equity and the prospects of the world's poor. I think those who favor continued growth on the grounds that only thus can we achieve some real equality ought to be serious about that. If economic growth with equality is a good thing, it doesn't follow that economic growth with a lot of pious talk about equality is a good thing. In principle, we can have growth with or without equity; and we can have stagnation with or without equity. An argument about first principles should keep those things separate.

What has posterity done for us?

Well, then, what *is* the problem of economic growth all about? (I'm giving a definition now, not stating a fact, so all I can say is that I think this way of looking at it contributes to clarity of thought.) Whenever there is a question about what to *do*, the desirability of economic growth turns on the claims of the future against the claims of the present. The pro-growth-man is someone who is prepared to sacrifice something useful and desirable right now so that people should be better off in the future; the anti-growth-man is someone who thinks that is unnecessary or undesirable. The nature of the sacrifice of present enjoyment for future enjoyment can be almost anything. The classic example is investment: We can use our labor and our resources to build very durable things like roads or subways or factories or blast furnaces or dams that will be used for a long time by people who were not even born when those things were created, and so will certainly have contributed nothing to their construction. That labor and those resources can just as well be used to produce shorter-run pleasures for us now.

Such a sacrifice of current consumption on behalf of the future may not strike you as much of a sacrifice. But that's because you live in a country that is already rich; if you had lived in Stalin's Russia, that need to sacrifice would be one of the reasons you would have been given to explain why you had to live without comfort and pleasures while the Ministry of Heavy Industry got all the play. If you lived in an underdeveloped country now you would face the same problem: What shall you do with the foreign currency earned by sales of cocoa or copper or crude oil—spend it on imports of consumer goods for those alive and working now, or spend it on imports of machinery to start build-

ing an industry that may help to raise the standard of living in 30 years' time?

There are other ways in which the same choice can be made, including, for instance, the direction of intellectual resources to the invention of things (like the generation of electricity from nuclear fusion) that will benefit future generations. Paradoxically, one of the ways in which the present can do something for the future is to conserve natural resources. If we get along with less lumber now so that there will be more forests standing for our grandchildren, or if we limit the present consumption of oil or zinc so that there will be some left for the twenty-first century, or if we worry about siltation behind dams that would otherwise be fun for fishermen and water-skiers, in all those cases we are promoting economic growth. I call that paradoxical because I think most people identify the conservation freak with the anti-growth party whereas, in this view of the matter, the conservationist is trading present satisfaction for future satisfaction, that is, he is promoting economic growth. I think the confusion comes from mixing up the quality-of-life problem with the growth problem. But it is nonetheless a confusion.

Why should we be concerned with the welfare of posterity, given the indubitable fact that posterity has never done a thing for us? I am not anthropologist enough to know how rare or common it is that our culture should teach us to care not only about our children but about their children, and their children. I suppose there are good Darwinian reasons why cultures without any future-orientation should fail to survive very long in the course of history. (But remember that they had a merry time of it while they lasted!) Moreover, we now enjoy the investments made by our ancestors, so there is a kind of equity in passing it on. Also, unless something terrible happens, there will be a lot more future than there has been past; and, for better or worse—probably worse—there will be more people at each future instant than there are now or have been. So all in all, the future will involve many more man-years of life than the present or the past, and a kind of intergenerational democracy suggests that all those man-years-to-be deserve some consideration out of sheer numbers.

On the other hand, *if* continued economic growth is possible—which is the question I'm coming to—then it is very likely that posterity will be richer than we are even if we make no special efforts on its behalf. If history offers any guide, then, in the developed part of the world at least, the accumulation of technological knowledge will probably make our great-grandchildren better off than we are, even if we make no great effort in that direction. Leaving aside the possibility of greater equality—I have already discussed that—there is hardly a crying need for posterity to be on average very much richer than we are. Why should we poor folk make any sacrifices for those who will in any case live in luxury in the future? Of course, if the end of the world is at hand, if continued economic growth is *not* possible, then we ought to care more about posterity, because they won't be so well off. Paradoxically, if continued growth is not possible, or less possible, then we probably ought to do more to promote it. Actually, there's no paradox in that, as every student of economics will realize, because it is a way of saying that the marginal return on investment is high.

Overshoot, collapse, doom

There is, as you know, a school of thought that claims that continued economic growth is in fact not possible anymore, or at least not for very long. This judgment has been expressed more or less casually by several observers in recent years. What distinguishes the "Doomsday Models" from their predecessors is that they claim to much more than a casual judgment: they deduce their beliefs about future prospects from mathematical models or systems analysis. They don't merely say that the end of the world is at hand—they can show you computer output that says the same thing.

Characteristically, the Doomsday Models do more than just say that continued economic growth is impossible. They tell us why: in brief, because (*a*) the earth's natural resources will soon be used up; (*b*) increased industrial production will soon strangle us in pollution; and (*c*) increasing population will eventually outrun the world's capacity to grow food, so that famine must eventually result. And, finally, the models tell us one more thing: the world will end with a bang, not a whimper. The natural evolution of the world economy is not at all toward some kind of smooth approach to its natural limits, wherever they are. Instead, it is inevitable—unless we make drastic changes in the

way we live and organize ourselves—that the world will overshoot any level of population and production it can possibly sustain and will then collapse, probably by the middle of the next century.

I would like to say why I think that the Doomsday Models are bad science and therefore bad guides to public policy. I hope nobody will conclude that I believe the problems of population control, environmental degradation, and resource exhaustion to be unimportant, or that I am one of those people who believe that an adequate response to such problems is a vague confidence that some technological solution will turn up. On the contrary, it is precisely because these are important problems that public policy had better be based on sound and careful analysis. I want to explain some of my reasons for believing that the global models don't provide even the beginnings of a foundation of that kind.

The first thing to realize is that the characteristic conclusion of the Doomsday Models is very near the surface. It is, in fact, more nearly an assumption than a conclusion, in the sense that the chain of logic from the assumptions to the conclusion is very short and rather obvious.

The basic assumption is that stocks of things like the world's natural resources and the waste-disposal capacity of the environment are finite, that the world economy tends to consume the stock at an increasing rate (through the mining of minerals and the production of goods), and that there are no built-in mechanisms by which approaching exhaustion tends to turn off consumption gradually and in advance. You hardly need a giant computer to tell you that a system with those behavior rules is going to bounce off its ceiling and collapse to a low level. Then, in case anyone is inclined to relax into the optimistic belief that maybe things aren't that bad, we are told: Imagine that the stock of natural resources were actually twice as big as the best current evidence suggests, or imagine that the annual amount of pollution could be halved all at once and then set to growing again. All that would happen is that the date of collapse would be postponed by T years, where T is not a large number. But once you grasp the quite simple essence of the models, this should come as no surprise. It is important to realize where these powerful conclusions come from, because, if you ask yourself "Why didn't I realize earlier that the end of the world was at hand?" the answer is not that you weren't clever enough to figure it out for yourself. The answer is that the imminent end of the world is an immediate deduction from certain assumptions, and one must really ask if the assumptions are any good.

It is a commonplace that if you calculate the annual output of any production process, large or small, and divide it by the annual employment of labor, you get a ratio that is called the productivity of labor. At the most aggregative level, for example, we can say that the GNP in 1971 was $1,050 billion and that about 82 million people were employed in producing it, so that GNP per worker or the productivity of a year of labor was about $12,800. Symmetrically, though the usage is less common, one could just as well calculate the GNP per unit of some particular natural resource and call that the productivity of coal, or GNP per pound of vanadium. We usually think of the productivity of labor as rising more or less exponentially, say at 2 or 3 percent a year, because that is the way it has in fact behaved over the past century or so since the statistics began to be collected. The rate of increase in the productivity of labor is not a constant of nature. Sometimes it is faster, sometimes slower. For example, we know that labor productivity must have increased more slowly a long time ago, because if we extrapolate backward at 2 percent a year, we come to a much lower labor productivity in 1492 than can possibly have been the case. And the productivity of labor has risen faster in the past 25 years than in the 50 years before that. It also varies from place to place, being faster in Japan and Germany and slower in Great Britain, for reasons that are not at all certain. But it rises, and we expect it to keep rising.

Now, how about the productivity of natural resources? All the Doomsday Models will allow is a one-time hypothetical increase in the world supply of natural resources, which is the equivalent of a one-time increase in the productivity of natural resources. Why shouldn't the productivity of most natural resources rise more or less steadily through time, like the productivity of labor?

Of course it does for some resources, but not for others. Real GNP roughly doubled between 1950 and 1970. But the consumption of primary and scrap iron increased by about 20 percent, so the productivity of iron, GNP per ton of iron,

increased by about 2.5 percent a year on the average during those 20 years. The U.S. consumption of manganese rose by 30 percent in the same period, so the productivity of manganese went up by some 70 percent in 20 years, a bit under 2.25 percent a year. Aggregate consumption of nickel just about doubled, like GNP, so the productivity of nickel didn't change. U.S. consumption of copper, both primary and secondary, went up by a third between 1951 and 1970, so GNP per pound of copper rose at 2 percent a year on the average. The story on lead and zinc is very similar, so their productivity increased at some 2 percent a year. The productivity of bituminous coal rose at 3 percent a year.

Naturally, there are important exceptions, and unimportant exceptions. GNP per barrel of oil was about the same in 1970 as in 1951: no productivity increase there. The consumption of natural gas tripled in the same period, so GNP per cubic foot of natural gas fell at about 2.5 percent a year. Our industrial demand for aluminum quadrupled in two decades, so the productivity of aluminum fell at a good 3.5 percent a year. And industrial demand for columbium was multiplied by a factor of 25: in 1951 we managed $2.25 million of GNP (in 1967 prices) per pound of columbium, whereas in 1970 we were down to $170 thousand of GNP per pound of columbium. On the other hand, it is a little hard to imagine civilization toppling because of a shortage of columbium.

Obviously many factors combine to govern the course of the productivity of any given mineral over time. When a rare natural resource is first available, it acquires new uses with a rush; and consumption goes up much faster than GNP. That's the columbium story, no doubt, and, to a lesser extent, the vanadium story. But once the novelty has worn off, the productivity of a resource tends to rise as better or worse substitutes for it appear, as new commodities replace old ones, and as manufacturing processes improve. One of the reasons the productivity of copper rises is because that of aluminum falls, as aluminum replaces copper in many uses. The same is true of coal and oil. A resource, like petroleum, which is versatile because of its role as a source of energy, is an interesting special case. It is hardly any wonder that the productivity of petroleum has stagnated, because the consumption of energy—

both as electricity for domestic and industrial use and in the automobile—has recently increased even faster than GNP. But no one can doubt that we will run out of oil, that coal and nuclear fission will replace oil as the major sources of energy. It is already becoming probable that the high-value use of oil will soon be as feed stock for the petrochemical industries, rather than as a source of energy. Sooner or later, the productivity of oil will rise out of sight, because the production and consumption of oil will eventually dwindle toward zero, but real GNP will not.

So there really is no reason why we should not think of the productivity of natural resources as increasing more or less exponentially over time. But then overshoot and collapse are no longer the inevitable trajectory of the world system, and the typical assumption-conclusion of the Doomsday Models falls by the wayside. We are in a different sort of ball game. The system might still burn itself out and collapse in finite time, but one cannot say with any honesty that it must. It all depends on the particular, detailed facts of modern economic life as well as on the economic policies we and the rest of the world pursue. I don't want to argue for any particular counterstory; all I want to say now is that the overshoot-collapse pattern is built into the models very near the surface, by assumption, and by implausible assumption at that.

Scarcity—and high prices

There is at least one reason for believing that the Doomsday story is almost certainly wrong. The most glaring defect of the Forrester-Meadows models is the absence of any sort of functioning price system. I am no believer that the market is always right, and I am certainly no advocate of laissez-faire where the environment is concerned. But the price system is, after all, the main social institution evolved by capitalist economies (and, to an increasing extent, socialist economies too) for registering and reacting to relative scarcity. There are several ways that the working of the price system will push our society into faster and more systematic increases in the productivity of natural resources.

First of all, let me go back to the analogy between natural resources and labor. We are not surprised to learn that industry quite consciously tries

make inventions that save labor, i.e., permit the same product to be made with fewer man-hours of work. After all, on the average, labor costs amount to almost three-fourths of all costs in our economy. An invention that reduces labor requirements per unit of GNP by 1 percent reduces all costs by about 0.75 percent. Natural resource costs are a much smaller proportion of total GNP, something nearer 5 percent. So industry and engineering have a much stronger motive to reduce labor requirements by 1 percent than to reduce resource requirements by 1 percent, assuming—which may or not be true—that it is about as hard to do one as to do the other. But then, as the earth's supply of particular natural resources nears exhaustion, and as natural resources become more and more valuable, the motive to economize those natural resources should become as strong as the motive to economize labor. The productivity of resources should rise faster than now—it is hard to imagine otherwise.

There are other ways in which the market mechanism can be expected to push us all to economize on natural resources as they become scarcer. Higher and rising prices of exhaustible resources lead competing producers to substitute other materials that are more plentiful and therefore cheaper. To the extent that it is impossible to design around or find substitutes for expensive natural resources, the prices of commodities that contain a lot of them will rise relative to the prices of other goods and services that don't use up a lot of resources. Consumers will be driven to buy fewer resource-intensive goods and more of other things. All these effects work automatically to increase the productivity of natural resources, i.e., to reduce resource requirements per unit of GNP.

As I mentioned a moment ago, this is not an argument for laissez-faire. We may feel that the private decisions of buyers and sellers give inadequate representation to future generations. Or we may feel that private interests are in conflict with a distinct public interest—strip-mining of coal is an obvious case in point, and there are many others as soon as we begin to think about environmental effects. Private market responses may be too uncoordinated, too slow, based on insufficient and faulty information. In every case there will be actions that public agencies can take and should take; and it will be a major political struggle to see that they are taken. But I don't see how one can have the slightest confidence in the predictions of models that seem to make no room for the operation of everyday market forces. If the forecasts are wrong, then so are the policy implications, to the extent that there are any realistic policy implications.

Every analysis of resource scarcity has to come to terms with the fact that the prices of natural resources and resource products have not shown any tendency to rise over the past half-century, relative to the prices of other things. This must mean that there have so far been adequate offsets to any progressive impoverishment of deposits—like improvements in the technology of extraction, savings in end uses, or the availability of cheaper substitutes. The situation could, of course, change; and very likely some day it will. If the experienced and expert participants in the market now believed that resource prices would be sharply higher at some foreseeable time, prices would *already* be rising, as I will try to explain in a moment. The historical steadiness of resource prices suggests that buyers and sellers in the market have not been acting as if they foresaw exhaustion in the absence of substitutes, and therefore sharply higher future prices. They may turn out to be wrong; but the Doomsday Models give us absolutely no reason to expect that—in fact, they claim to get whatever meager empirical basis they have from such experts.

Why is it true that if the market saw higher prices in the future, prices would already be rising? It is a rather technical point, but I want to explain it because, in a way, it summarizes the important thing about natural resources: conserving a mineral deposit is just as much of an investment as building a factory, and it has to be analyzed that way. Any owner of a mineral deposit owns a valuable asset, whether the owner is a private capitalist or the government of an underdeveloped country. The asset is worth keeping only if at the margin it earns a return equal to that earned on other kinds of assets. A factory produces things each year of its life, but a mineral deposit just lies there: its owner can realize a return only if he either mines the deposit or if it *increases in value*. So if you are sitting on your little pile of X and confidently expect to be able to sell it for a very high price in the year 2000 because it will be very scarce by then, you must be earning your 5 percent a year,

or 10 percent a year, or whatever the going rate of return is, each year between now and 2000. The only way this can happen is for the value of X to go up by 5 percent a year or 10 percent a year. And that means that anyone who wants to use any X any time between now and 2000 will have to pay a price for it that is rising at that same 5 percent or 10 percent a year. Well, it's not happening. Of course, we are exploiting our hoard of exhaustible resources; we have no choice about that. We are certainly exploiting it wastefully, in the sense that we allow each other to dump waste products into the environment without full accounting for costs. But there is very little evidence that we are exploiting it too fast.

Crowding on planet earth

I have less to say about the question of population growth, because it doesn't seem to involve any difficult conceptual problems. At any time, in any place, there is presumably an optimal size of population—with the property that the average person would be somewhat worse off if the population were a bit larger, and also worse off if the population were a bit smaller. In any real case it must be very difficult to know what the optimum population is, especially because it will change over time as technology changes, and also because it is probably more like a band or zone than a sharply defined number. I mean that if you could somehow plot a graph of economic welfare per person against population size, there would be a very gentle dome or plateau at the top, rather than a sharp peak.

I don't intend to guess what the optimal population for the United States may be. But I am prepared to hazard the guess that there is no point in opting for a perceptibly larger population than we now have, and we might well be content with a slightly smaller one. (I want to emphasize the likelihood that a 15 percent larger or 15 percent smaller population would make very little difference in our standard of well-being. I also want to emphasize that I am talking only about our own country. The underdeveloped world offers very special problems.) My general reason for believing that we should not want a substantially larger population is this. We all know the bad consequences of too large a population: crowding, congestion, excessive pollution, the disappearance of open space—that is why the curve of average well-being eventually turns down at large population sizes. Why does the curve ever climb to a peak in the first place? The generic reason is because of what economists call economies of scale, because it takes a population of a certain size and density to support an efficient chemical industry, or publishing industry, or symphony orchestra, or engineering university, or airline, or computer hardware and software industry, especially if you would like several firms in each, so that they can be partially regulated by their own competition. But after all, it only takes a population of a *certain* size or density to get the benefit of these economies of scale. And I'm prepared to guess that the U.S. economy is already big enough to do so; I find it hard to believe that sheer efficiency would be much served in the United States by having a larger market.

As it happens, recent figures seem to show that the United States is heading for a stationary population: that is to say, the current generation of parents seems to be establishing fertility patterns that will, if continued, cause the population to stabilize some time during the next century. Even so, the absolute size of the population will increase for a while, and level off higher than it is now, because decades of population growth have left us with a bulge of population in the childbearing ages. But I have already argued that a few million more or less hardly make a difference; and a population that has once stabilized might actually decrease, if that came to seem desirable.

At the present moment, at least for the United States, the danger of rapid population growth seems to be the wrong thing to worry about. The main object of public policy in this field ought to be to ensure that the choice of family size is truly a voluntary choice, that access to the best birth-control methods be made universal. That seems to be all that is needed. Of course, we know very little about what governs voluntary fertility, about why the typical notion of a good family size changes from generation to generation. So it is certainly possible that these recent developments will reverse themselves and that population control will again appear on the agenda of public policy. This remains to be seen.

In all this I have said nothing about the Doomsday Models because there is practically nothing that needs to be said. So far as we can tell, they make

one very bad mistake: in the face of reason, common sense, and systematic evidence, they seem to assume that at high standards of living, people want more children as they become more affluent (though over most of the observed range, a higher standard of living goes along with smaller families). That error is certainly a serious one in terms of the recent American data—but perhaps it explains why some friends of mine were able to report that they had run a version of the Forrester World Dynamics Model starting with a population of two people and discovered that it blew up in 500 years. Apart from placing the date of the Garden of Eden in the fifteenth century, what else is new?

There is another analytical error in the models, as Fred Singer has pointed out. Suppose resource exhaustion or increased pollution conspires to bring a reduction in industrial production. The model then says that birth rates will rise because, in the past, low industrial output has been associated with high birth rates. But there is nothing in historical evidence to suggest that a once-rich country will go *back* to high birth rates if (as I doubt will happen) its standard of living falls from an accustomed high level. Common sense suggests that a society in such a position would fight to preserve its standard of living by reducing the desired family size. In any case, this is another example of a poorly founded—or unfounded—assumption introduced to support the likelihood of overshoot-and-collapse.

Paying for pollution

Resource exhaustion and overpopulation: that leaves pollution as the last of the Doomsday Devils. The subject is worth a whole lecture in itself, because it is one of those problems about which economists actually have something important to say to the world, not just to each other. But I must be brief. Fine print aside, I think that what one gets from the Doomsday literature is the notion that air and water and noise pollution are an inescapable accompaniment of economic growth, especially industrial growth. If that is true, then to be against pollution is to be against growth. I realize that in putting the matter so crudely I have been unjust: nevertheless, that is the message that comes across. I think that way of looking at the pollution problem is wrong.

A correct analysis goes something like this. Excessive pollution and degradation of the environment certainly accompany industrial growth and the increasing population density that goes with it. But they are by no means an inescapable by-product. Excessive pollution happens because of an important flaw in the price system. Factories, power plants, municipal sewers, drivers of cars, strip-miners of coal and deep-miners of coal, and all sorts of generators of waste are allowed to dump that waste into the environment, into the atmosphere and into running water and the oceans, without paying the full cost of what they do. No wonder they do too much. So would you, and so would I. In fact, we actually do—directly as drivers of cars, indirectly as we buy some products at a price which is lower than it ought to be because the producer is not required to pay for using the environment to carry away his wastes, and even more indirectly as we buy things that are made with things that pollute the environment.

This flaw in the price system exists because a scarce resource (the waste-disposal capacity of the environment) goes unpriced; and that happens because it is owned by all of us, as it should be. The flaw can be corrected, either by the simple expedient of regulating the discharge of wastes to the environment by direct control or by the slightly more complicated device of charging special prices—user taxes—to those who dispose of wastes in air or water. These effluent charges do three things: they make pollution-intensive goods expensive, and so reduce the consumption of them; they make pollution-intensive methods of production costly, and so promote abatement of pollution by producers; they generate revenue that can, if desired, be used for the further purification of air or water or for other environmental improvements. Most economists prefer this device of effluent charges to regulation by direct order. This is more than an occupational peculiarity. Use of the price system has certain advantages in efficiency and decentralization. Imposing a physical limit on, say, sulfur dioxide emission is, after all, a little peculiar. It says that you may do so much of a bad thing and pay nothing for the privilege, but after that, the price is infinite. Not surprisingly, one can find a more efficient schedule of pollution abatement through a more sensitive tax schedule.

But this difference of opinion is minor compared with the larger point that needs to be made. The annual cost that would be necessary to meet decent pollution-abatement standards by the end of the century is large, but not staggering. One estimate says that in 1970 we spent about $8.5 billion (in 1967 prices), or 1 percent of GNP, for pollution abatement. An active pollution abatement policy would cost perhaps $50 billion a year by 2000, which would be about 2 percent of GNP by then. That is a small investment of resources: you can see how small it is when you consider that GNP grows by 4 percent or so every year, on the average. Cleaning up air and water would entail a cost that would be a bit like losing one-half of one year's growth, between now and the year 2000. What stands between us and a decent environment is not the curse of industrialization, not an unbearable burden of cost, but just the need to organize ourselves consciously to do some simple and knowable things. Compared with the possibility of an active abatement policy, the policy of stopping economic growth in order to stop pollution would be incredibly inefficient. It would not actually accomplish much, because one really wants to reduce the amount of, say, hydrocarbon emission to a third or a half of *what it is now*. And what no-growth would accomplish, it would do by cutting off your face to spite your nose.

The end of the world—
a matter of timing

In the end, that is really my complaint about the Doomsday school. It diverts attention from the really important things that can actually be done, step by step, to make things better. The end of the world *is* at hand—the earth, if you take the long view, will fall into the sun in a few billion years anyway, unless some other disaster happens first. In the meantime, I think we'd be better off passing a strong sulfur-emissions tax, or getting some Highway Trust Fund money allocated to mass transit, or building a humane and decent floor under family incomes, or overriding President Nixon's veto of a strong Water Quality Act, or reforming the tax system, or fending off starvation in Bengal—instead of worrying about the generalized "predicament of mankind."

ROBERT M. SOLOW is Professor of Economics at MIT. His paper, along with others presented at Lehigh University, will appear in *The Economic Growth Controversy*, to be published this spring by International Arts & Sciences Press, Inc.

Tax Policy and Economic Growth:
Lessons from the 1980s

Michael J. Boskin

Determinants of Growth

The power of compounding even modest increases in the growth rate is enormous. The United Kingdom, growing at only one percentage point per year less than the United States, France and Germany, transformed itself from the wealthiest society on earth to a relatively poor member of the Common Market in less than three generations.

As an illustration, consider two equally wealthy economies. In one, per capita income grows at 1.5 percent; in the other, at 2 percent. The more rapidly growing economy will be almost 30 percent more wealthy than the less rapidly growing economy in less than two generations, a difference in living standards that carries labels like "successful" and "sick," respectively. Thus, differences of *fractions of a percentage point* in the long run growth rate must be explained in attempting to assess growth performance. Increasing the growth rate (at minimal opportunity costs) by .2 or .3 percentage points is an enormous economic and social achievement.

Studies of economic growth usually attempt to decompose the rate of growth of real GNP (or some related output measure) into the contributions of various factors thought to explain it. These include such factors as increased labor input, increased capital input, improved resource allocation, and technical change.

The Empirical Evidence on Growth

As Table 1 demonstrates, real gross product and real product per hour worked in the United States have grown more rapidly in the period from 1981 through the first quarter of 1988 than from 1973 to 1981, but much slower than in the 1948–73 period.[1] Perhaps the quarter century after World War II should be thought of as an aberration, a special period of growth more rapid than is likely in the long run. What caused this history of rapid growth, a major slowdown, and the recent modest growth turnaround?

The usual growth accounting framework—based on the production function $F(K, L, t)$ where K is capital inputs, L is labor inputs, and t is time—asks how much could have been produced with the growth of inputs if technology was constant between two periods in time. The difference, the residual unexplained by input

■ *Michael J. Boskin is Wohlford Professor of Economics and Director, Center for Economic Policy Research, Stanford University, and Research Associate, National Bureau of Economic Research, all at Stanford, California.*

Table 1

Output and Productivity Growth in the U.S. Economy

(average annual percentage rates of growth)

Year	Real Gross Product	Real Product Per Employee Hour
1948:IV–1973:IV	3.7	2.8
1973:IV–1981:III	2.2	0.7
1981:IV–1988:I	3.3	1.3

Source: U.S. Dept. of Labor

growth, represents the shift in the production function, which is taken to represent technical change, organizational efficiency gains, entrepreneurship, improved resource allocation, and so on. Many strong assumptions are usually made to draw such inferences: for example, constant returns to scale, profit maximization and competitive markets to allow use of factor shares as weights, no aggregation errors, capital malleability, no unmeasured inputs, no deviations of marginal products from normalized input prices, no scale or learning effects, no measurement errors in capital or labor input prices or utilization rates. Each of these issues is the subject of much research and debate. The sources and the quantitative determinants of economic growth remain a source of major controversy. However, I think the existing literature does support this mild conclusion:

Lesson 1: The best empirical growth studies suggest that the rate of capital formation *and* technical change have been important determinants of long-run U.S. growth. These factors also help to explain differences in international productivity growth. Therefore, the effect of tax policy on investment *and* technical change is important in understanding the effects of tax policy on long-run growth.

When M. Abramovitz (1956) and R. Solow (1957) asked how much of the growth of output can be explained by the growth of inputs, their answer was precious little. Subsequent studies by E. Denison (1974), and others appeared to confirm this small contribution of increased labor and capital input to increased output. In particular, Denison (1979) places very little weight on the decline in the rate of growth of the capital-labor ratio as a contributing factor in the productivity growth slowdown. These authors placed a heavy emphasis on technological change as the *prime* determinant of economic growth. Jorgenson (1986) and others have questioned the Abramovitz-Solow-Denison finding, attributing a much greater share of postwar U.S. growth to increased capital input and much less to the unexplained residual "technical change."[2] In the work of Jorgenson and others, greater disaggregation and improved measures of labor quality seem to be a major reason for assigning greater weight to capital formation. As Lesson 1 states, I conclude from this evidence that both investment and innovation play a major role in determining productivity growth. In fact, as discussed below, I suspect investment and innovation are interdependent and that interdependence increases the elasticity of output with respect to capital inputs.[3]

Of course, saying that "innovation causes productivity" begs the question of what causes innovation. John Kendrick (1986) stresses the role of research and development. He estimates a typical lag of about six years between spending on R&D and its commercial application. He therefore attributes part of the decline in productivity growth in the 1973–81 period to a prior slowdown in R&D spending. Although R&D spending has increased recently, the lag involved in commercialization contributed to productivity growth being less strong in the 1981–86 period than otherwise.

Major efforts to incorporate R&D into the growth accounting framework (Griliches (1980) and his paper in this issue) conclude that changes in R&D spending explain only a modest part of the postwar productivity growth episodes. But R&D spending is not a sufficient proxy for innovation. Disembodied technical change and capital input growth (capital deepening and perhaps other effects discussed below) remain major foci for attention.

International growth rate comparisons also come to mixed conclusions on the relative (separate) importance of investment and technical change. Martin Baily and Alok Chakrabarti (1985) noted that while the absolute level of productivity in the United States is quite high, the rest of the world is catching up in productivity and industrialization. In the 1973–84 period, output per labor hour in the manufacturing sector grew 2 percent in the United States, but $3\frac{1}{2}$ times more rapidly in Japan and about twice as rapidly in France and Germany. R&D spending in these countries has risen faster than in the United States. Baily notes that the fraction of U.S. patents granted to foreigners had risen from 16 percent in 1960 to 41 percent by 1982. He stresses the importance of innovation and technical change to long-run growth, and with Denison, adopts the position that only 20 percent of U.S. productivity growth in this period was due to an increase in the capital/labor ratio.[4] The comparison with Japan, France, and Germany, however, could equally well highlight the very high cross-country correlation between investment and growth rates. These countries had investment and productivity growth rates two to three times those of the United States.[5] Kormendi and Meguire (1985) document the substantial contribution of differentials in investment rates to explaining cross-country differences in growth rates.

Distinguishing Permanent and Temporary Increases in the Growth Rate

Policies designed to alter the rate of economic growth tend to focus on enhancing technological advances, the quality of the labor force, and the level or rate of growth of capital per worker. It is important to note that the only way to raise the long-run growth rate permanently is to increase the rate of technical change or the rate of improvement in the quality of the labor force. A policy which increases the capital-labor ratio (for example, by increasing the rate of investment) can lead to permanently higher *levels* of income, but only a temporarily higher growth *rate* (unless it also leads to an increase in the rate of technical change). Here's why: real per capita income grows at the rate of technical change and labor quality improvement, given some capital-labor ratio. Now along comes a policy (perhaps tax policy) that increases the desired capital stock of firms (or perhaps more accurately, the desired wealth of the population, relative to levels of income). This policy leads to an investment boom for some years which will cause a spurt in the short-run growth rate as the economy moves to a new long-run growth path. Notice that the level of per capita income is permanently higher, but once the transition to the new growth path is complete, the rate of economic growth returns to the original rate given by the underlying factors of the rate of technical change and improvement in labor force quality. This basic conclusion of simple neoclassical growth theory is highly stylized, but it is now standard issue. However, the distinction between the level and rate of growth of income is often confused in policy debates.

It is important to note some potential interactions between the investment rate and the rate of technical change.[6] Learning-by-doing effects in investment may positively link the rates of investment and technical change. A society with a higher investment rate might not only have a temporarily higher growth rate in its transition to a higher growth path, but actually might also increase the long-run rate of growth. In the process of investment, people learn new production processes and discover new potential products. Thus, the rate of investment may positively feed back on the rate of technical change. At the micro level, consider the options opening up in the course of a major project: for example, oil exploration in the frozen tundra or the ocean depths, or space exploration. Just as new technologies arise—sometimes—to meet such challenges, the rate of technical advance may depend on the level of investment, and conversely.[7]

Will these effects be temporary or permanent? They may just take production to best practice more rapidly. But they may also expand the horizons of best practice. Since it is impossible to know what it is possible to know, I am content to consider the potential ultimate knowledge and engineering barriers as sufficiently distant to ignore for the sake of this argument.

While analytical and empirical research on the importance of learning and embodiment continues, I tentatively conclude that the investment rate does indeed affect the long term growth rate, not just the temporary (if lengthy) transition to a higher level of output with the same underlying growth rate. The empirical studies of Jorgenson (this issue), Kormendi and Meguire (1985) and Romer (1987) lend strong credence to this conclusion; otherwise, differences in rates of capital formation could be expected to have small, temporary effects on the growth rate and modest effects on the level of output. I suspect a primary source of this effect is the learning or other external economies generated in specific sectors of the economy, which leads to an aggregate increasing returns phenomenon.[8]

The policies which affect the generation of new technology and therefore long-term growth most directly probably occur one layer down from aggregate GNP, in the composition of spending in the economy. Government spending on research and development and physical and human investment can affect the rate of technical change and, of course, spending on human investment such as education may increase productivity directly. Probably the most important of these categories is direct government support of research and development. Table 2 presents some data on recent trends in federal government support of R&D and physical investment expenditures. As can be seen from the table, real government R&D spending and real government physical investment are both substantially lower as a percentage of GNP than in the 1960s, although defense investment and R&D have made something of a comeback in the last few years. (See Boskin, Robinson and Huber (1988) for estimates of government capital formation).

Tax policies make up a second set of policies that, by affecting the way in which the private sector utilizes its resources, can affect how new technology is generated. The structure of the tax system can substantially affect the rate of investment in the economy and the rate of R&D spending by changing the costs of such spending relative to their returns. The original 1981 tax reform was clearly pro-investment and pro-research and development, with the research and development tax credit and accelerated depreciation. The 1986 tax reform extended the research and development tax credit for three years, but reduced it to 20 percent while tightening eligibility. However, other investment incentives were severely restricted, and the reduction in tax rates only partly compensates for this tightening. The net effect is somewhat anti-

Table 2

Federal Outlays By Category, Selected Years

(billions of constant 1972 dollars; percentages of GNP in parentheses)

Fiscal Year	Physical Investment			R&D	
	Defense	Non-Defense	Grants-in-Aid	Defense	Non-Defense
1949	4.0	1.8	0.9	2.0	0.5
	(0.8)	(0.4)	(0.2)	(0.4)	(0.1)
1958	25.2	1.9	2.8	4.7	1.4
	(3.7)	(0.3)	(0.5)	(0.7)	(0.2)
1968	30.2	3.4	7.6	11.4	10.2
	(2.9)	(0.3)	(0.7)	(1.1)	(1.0)
1978	15.8	4.4	11.0	7.6	7.9
	(1.1)	(0.3)	(0.8)	(0.5)	(0.5)
1985	31.1	5.0	9.8	11.6	6.5
	(1.9)	(0.3)	(0.6)	(0.7)	(0.4)

Sources: Office of Management and Budget, Budget of the United States, selected years, and appendices.

investment.[9] Obviously, overall fiscal and monetary policy may also affect the allocation of resources to investment and R&D, and hence the level and perhaps growth rate of output.

[1] While the introduction of new products is a major source of increased economic well-being and is probably undervalued in the traditional GNP estimates, and numerous other measurement issues abound as well, I take the figures in Table 1 to be representative of the true trends. However, I have much sympathy with a Schumpeterian approach to growth emphasizing entrepreneurship. In the aggregate data, these gains are buried in investment, R&D, and other data.

[2] Before proceeding to examine growth theory, it is worth noting that since the trough of the 1981–82 recession, cumulative real GNP growth in the United States has substantially exceeded that in France, Italy, Germany, and the United Kingdom. Only Canada (whose economy is tied closely to the United States) and Japan have fared as well as the United States in the 1980s.

[3] See P. Romer (1987) for a provocative argument stressing the importance of externalities generated by capital input. B. Arthur (1987) develops some interesting implications of positive feedback mechanisms in economics.

[4] Of course, the rate of growth of the capital/labor ratio slowed and this was one of the reasons why productivity slowed, but this reason was not the only one, nor by some estimates the most important one.

[5] Trends in multifactor productivity growth are quite similar to the trends of labor productivity growth (the latter include increases due to a higher capital/labor ratio). If one focuses on what determines the rate of R&D expenditures and innovation, clearly there is some exogenous component. There is a demand for new technology that reflects the obsolescence and cycles of old products and production processes; technologies can mature, and while awaiting major breakthroughs a productivity growth slowdown may occur in the sector. However one divides up the credit for the productivity turnaround in the 1980s, the turnaround itself is not inconsequential.

[6] This and related issues are discussed in many of the papers in R. Landau and N. Rosenberg (1986).

[7] Embodiment of technical change may also do so, although I consider this potentially less important. The embodiment hypothesis entails the notion that it is much too expensive to embody new technology in old capital by converting it, and therefore that the rate at which new technology augments productivity depends upon the rate at which new capital is generated: that is, it depends on the investment rate. If technology is other than Cobb-Douglas, embodiment, like learning, creates a positive correlation between the investment and growth rates.

[8] Note that virtually all econometric growth studies assume constant returns; Denison's original famous study of long-run U.S. growth assumed (never estimated) slight increasing returns to scale; but that no single national time series study could possibly hope to identify separate scale and technical change effects.

[9] Large deficits also ultimately crowd out private investment and/or crowd-in foreign capital, as discussed below. We must also ask whether the increased borrowing is financing government investment or research and development or whether it is simply financing consumption. Monetary policy also can affect the composition of output and the level of aggregate demand in the economy, since it potentially affects the before-tax cost of capital (by affecting interest rates and their term structure), and thus the real cost of embarking on R&D and investment projects.

The United States and Economic Development

Council of Economic Advisers

AFTER WORLD WAR II, the United States in cooperation with other countries established the basic policies and institutions of the open system of world trade and investment that has since guided economic relations among nations. On the whole, the world has enjoyed an extraordinary record of economic progress under this system. Between 1950 and 1984, U.S. real per capita gross national product (GNP) rose at a 1.8 percent average annual rate, allowing nearly a doubling of average real living standards in 34 years. In the other nine largest Western industrial countries, real per capita income rose at a spectacular 3.7 percent average annual rate, implying that real living standards in these countries (as measured by real per capita GNP) rose by more than twice as much as they had in all of previous history. Despite disappointing economic performance of some developing countries, the average annual rate of growth of real per capita income for all developing countries was 2.8 percent between 1955 and 1984, implying more than a doubling of average real living standards in these countries in just 29 years.

The progress of developing countries over the past three decades is manifested in other important indicators of human welfare. Between 1955 and 1984, their population nearly doubled. Despite the problems of some developing countries, this increase in population was not accompanied by increasing human misery, as some feared, but rather by generally rising real living standards that were reflected in longer life expectancies, lower infant and child mortality rates, better nutrition and health care, and higher educational attainment. For example, between 1965 and 1983, average life expectancy rose by 9 years in lower income developing countries and by 8 years in middle-income developing countries.

This overall record of economic and social progress provides the context for this chapter's discussion of important economic problems that have recently afflicted a number of developing countries and of the policies that are needed to deal with these problems. The record of long-term economic success of many countries suggests that these problems can be successfully resolved. It also suggests that retention and refinement of the policies and institutions that helped to generate this success, together with reform of practices that have contributed to recent difficulties, is the appropriate prescription for restoring prosperity and reviving growth in countries that have suffered economic slowdown or stagnation.

Before embarking on this discussion, it is important to stress the interest of the United States in seeking more vigorous economic growth in both developed and developing countries. Beyond wishing its friends well, the United States has a strong national interest in the economic prosperity of its allies, and has an important national interest in economic prosperity of developing countries, including especially countries striving to strengthen their democratic institutions. The United States also has an economic interest in the prosperity of other countries. Economic growth appears to be a mutually reinforcing process. For example, the rapid recovery in the United States during the first six quarters of the current expansion contributed significantly to recovery and expansion in other countries and particularly to easing of some of the economic problems of developing countries. Conversely, as discussed in Chapter 1, relatively sluggish recovery of other industrial countries and recent economic problems in many developing countries are seen as factors contributing to the deterioration of the U.S. trade balance during the current recovery and perhaps also to the slowdown of that recovery since mid-1984. Thus, for economic as well as broader national purposes, the United States has an important interest in rapid and sustainable growth in other countries.

ECONOMIC PERFORMANCE AND PROBLEMS OF DEVELOPING COUNTRIES

Developing countries are the home of three-quarters of the world's population. Their aggregate national products in 1983 were more than half of that of the United States and nearly double that of Japan. Merchandise trade (exports plus imports) of the developing countries (including high-income oil exporters) in 1983 accounted for more than a quarter of total world merchandise trade and was more than twice the size of that of the United States, the world's largest trading country. The substantial and growing economic importance of developing countries is reflected specifically in the extent of trade between these countries and the United States and, especially during the past decade, in the flow of credit from the United States and other industrial countries to the developing countries.

TRADE BETWEEN DEVELOPING COUNTRIES AND THE UNITED STATES

The importance of trade with developing countries has been growing along with the general importance of international trade for the U.S. economy in the postwar period, especially during the past 20 years. In 1965 exports to and imports from developing countries were, respectively, 1.2 and 1.0 percent of U.S. GNP. They rose to 3.0 and 4.4 percent of U.S. GNP, respectively, in 1980. By 1984 the share of exports to developing countries in GNP fell to 2.0 percent, and the share of imports from such countries fell to 3.3 percent. The relatively small shares of exports and imports in U.S. GNP are somewhat deceiving because industries that account for about 70 percent of U.S. GNP produce either services that do not enter into international merchandise trade, or produce products that are largely nontradable. For the industries that account for the remaining 30 percent of U.S. GNP, international merchandise trade is of considerable importance. On average for these industries in 1984, exports to developing countries accounted for about 7 percent of annual product, and imports from developing countries accounted for about 11 percent of annual product.

Increased imports of some categories of manufactured goods from developing countries have been a particular cause of concern for and complaint by U.S. competitors. Without attempting to judge the merits of individual complaints, it should be noted that the United States has until recently had a trade surplus in manufactured goods with developing countries and still exports large amounts of such goods to these countries. In 1980 the United States exported $60 billion of manufactured goods to and imported $32 billion of such goods from developing countries, for a net export surplus of $28 billion. Although the magnitude of this surplus may have reflected temporary factors such as the weak dollar and the large borrowing of developing countries in 1980, the existence of such a surplus is consistent with past trends. By 1984 exports of manufactures to developing countries fell to $52 billion, while imports of manufactures from these countries rose to $64 billion, yielding a net export deficit of $12 billion. The deterioration in the net trade position in manufactured products with developing countries, however, is proportionately smaller than the deterioration of the overall U.S. net trade position between 1980 and 1984.

CREDIT FLOWS TO DEVELOPING COUNTRIES

The growing importance of financial relationships between developed and developing countries is apparent in the rapid growth of the real flow of financial resources to developing countries, as reported in Table 2-1. The net flow of funds to developing countries (in 1983 dollars), as estimated by the Organization for Economic Cooperation and Development (OECD), nearly doubled in real terms between 1970 and 1980, from $53.1 billion to $93.9 billion. After peaking in 1983 at $118.3 billion, this flow declined to $92.3 billion in 1984. The sources of these funds have shifted substantially over the past 15 years. In 1970 official development assistance accounted for 42 percent of the net flow of funds to developing countries, while lending by commercial banks accounted for only 15 percent of the total. By 1983 the share of official development assistance declined to 29 percent, while the share of bank lending (including rescheduling) rose to 46 percent. This trend was reversed in 1984, when the share of official development assistance rose to 39 percent of net lending and the share of commercial banks fell to 26 percent. More recent information indicates a further substantial decline in commercial bank net lending to developing countries in 1985.

By 1983 total external liabilities of developing countries reached an estimated $843 billion, equal to about one-third of the annual GNP of these countries and about 10 percent of the annual GNP of the developed countries. More than half of these liabilities were loans from commercial banks, and nearly a third of these bank loans were owed to U.S. financial institutions. The problems recently experienced by several of the high-debt countries in meeting their debt-service obligations, and the consequences of these problems for the

TABLE 2-1.—*Real net flow of funds to developing countries, selected years, 1970-84*

[Billions of 1983 dollars]

Type of receipt	1970	1975	1980	1981	1982	1983	1984
Official development assistance	22.2	31.6	36.1	36.2	33.7	33.8	35.8
Grants by private voluntary agencies	2.3	2.0	2.2	2.0	2.3	2.3	2.5
Nonconcessional flows	28.7	51.0	55.7	68.6	60.1	82.1	54.0
Official or officially supported flows	10.4	15.7	22.9	21.6	21.9	19.8	20.0
Private flows	18.3	35.4	32.8	47.0	38.2	62.3	34.0
Direct investment	9.7	16.9	9.9	16.8	11.8	7.8	9.5
Bank lending[1]	7.9	17.8	21.6	29.2	25.9	54.0	24.0
Bond lending	.8	.6	1.3	1.1	.5	.5	.5
TOTAL	53.1	84.6	93.9	106.8	96.1	118.3	92.3

[1] Includes for 1983 and 1984 significant amounts of rescheduled short-term debt.

Note.—Detail may not add to totals due to rounding

Source: Organization for Economic Cooperation and Development.

financial institutions that hold their obligations, have dramatized the deepening financial relationships between developing countries and the United States and other developed countries.

ECONOMIC PROBLEMS OF DEVELOPING COUNTRIES

Economic growth in developing countries has been rapid over the past 30 years, on average, as indicated in Table 2-2. Some countries, however, have not shared in this progress over the long run, and, in the past few years, a number of countries with relatively good long-run performance have experienced economic difficulties. The chronic economic problems of many quite poor countries in Sub-Saharan Africa, South Asia, and Latin America deserve treatment separate from the acute difficulties recently experienced by middle-income countries with large debt burdens.

The low-income developing countries (those with per capita incomes of less than $400 in 1983) had an average annual growth rate of real per capita GNP of 2.3 percent between 1955 and 1984. This result is dominated by the performance of China and India, which together account for three-quarters of the population of low-income developing countries and which had a combined average annual growth rate of real per capita GNP of 2.4 percent over this period. Interestingly, the combined growth performance of these two large countries has been improving recently as they have adopted more market-oriented, pro-growth economic policies. Some other low-income developing countries have also enjoyed vigorous growth, including some spectacularly successful countries that earlier adopted market-oriented, pro-growth economic policies and have now graduated to the class of middle-income developing countries. In many other low-income countries growth performance has not been very strong. Between 1965 and 1984, real per capita income in the low-income countries of Sub-Saharan Africa rose at only a 0.5 percent average annual rate.

The road to economic prosperity for many of the poorest countries will be a long and difficult one. In some extreme situations, such as the recent and continuing famine in Ethiopia, extraordinary external assistance has been essential to provide the bare requirements of

TABLE 2-2.—*Indicators of economic growth, 1955-84*

[Annual growth rate; percent]

Period	Population	Real GNP	Real GNP per capita
DEVELOPING COUNTRIES: [1]			
1955–70	2.2	5.4	3.1
1970–80	2.2	5.3	3.1
1980–84	2.0	3.1	1.1
Low-income countries:			
1955–70	2.1	3.7	1.6
1970–80	2.1	4.5	2.4
1980–84	1.8	6.7	4.9
Middle-income countries:			
1955–70	2.4	6.0	3.5
1970–80	2.4	5.6	3.1
1980–84	2.4	1.8	−.6
INDUSTRIAL MARKET COUNTRIES:			
1955–70	1.1	4.7	3.6
1970–80	.8	3.2	2.4
1980–84	.5	1.8	1.3

[1] Excludes the high-income oil exporters.

Source: International Bank for Reconstruction and Development.

human survival. The success of some formerly quite poor countries, however, gives hope that some of today's poorer countries will be able to graduate to the ranks of the middle-income developing countries by early in the next century.

The middle-income developing countries (those with per capita incomes between $400 and $7,000 in 1983) had good growth performance on average between 1955 and 1984. As a group, they recorded an average annual growth rate of real per capita income of 2.8 percent per year, enabling the real income of the average resident of these countries to rise by 123 percent in just 29 years. Some countries, of course, performed less well than the average, and a few even registered substantial declines in real per capita incomes over periods of two decades or longer. On the other hand, nine countries had growth rates of real per capita income of 5 percent per year or better between 1965 and 1983, implying an increase in real per capita income of more than 140 percent in just 18 years.

The early 1980s have been a period of sharp contrasts in the economic performances of developing countries. For all developing countries, excluding the high-income oil exporters, the average growth rate of real per capita income was only 1.1 percent per year between 1980 and 1984. Thanks primarily to the good performance and large weight of China and India, low-income developing countries registered a 4.9 percent average annual growth rate of real per capita income over these 4 years. Other low-income countries in Asia did about as well as China and India, on average, but low-income countries in Africa suffered a cumulative 8.7 percent decline in average real per capita income over these 4 years. For the middle-income developing countries, average real per capita incomes declined at a 0.6 percent annual rate between 1980 and 1984. Despite the recession in the industrial countries, some of these countries, especially in Asia, continued to enjoy strong real growth. Other middle-income developing countries, especially in Latin America, had enjoyed generally good growth during the 1960s and 1970s, but experienced economic stagnation or decline in the early 1980s.

EFFECTS OF EXTERNAL SHOCKS

For developing countries that experienced poor economic performance in the early 1980s, adverse external economic developments explain part, but only part, of this poor performance. Some countries whose national incomes depend heavily on revenues from oil exports saw their real national incomes decline because of the fall in world oil prices and in the volume of oil exports. However, some oil-exporting countries that saved some of their oil-export revenues in the 1970s have been able to draw on those savings to support domestic consumption and investment during a period of lower oil prices and export volumes. Other oil exporters that spent all of their export revenues and even borrowed from world capital markets to spend on consumption and domestic investment have faced a more difficult task in adjusting to lower oil exports and oil prices. The same is true for developing countries that experienced export booms for other commodities during the 1970s and failed to foresee that these booms might not last forever.

Moreover, evidence suggests that adverse external events are not primarily responsible for the recent poor economic performance of some developing countries. As previously mentioned, other developing countries that faced similar external circumstances continued to perform well in the early 1980s. Table 2–3 summarizes results from a World Bank study that compared the magnitude of external shocks to developing countries that needed to reschedule their external debts by the end of 1984 with countries that did not need to reschedule. The index of external shocks was calculated as the combined effects on a country's balance of payments of deteriorations in its terms of trade (the ratio of export prices to import prices), declines in world demand for its exports, and increases in interest rates on its outstanding external debt. In 1979–80 and 1981–82, the average adverse external shock was about the same for reschedulers and nonreschedulers. The average of annual growth rates of real gross domestic product (GDP) in 1979–83 for reschedulers, however, was only 0.9 percent, versus 4.3 percent for nonreschedulers.

External shocks did, of course, affect developing countries in the early 1980s. The disinflation of the early 1980s was associated with an unwinding of the effects of the inflation of the 1970s on relative commodity prices, including prices of some products exported by developing countries. The recession in the industrial countries in the early 1980s reduced demand for the exports of developing countries. The real burden of the external, dollar-denominated debt of many developing countries rose as the dollar appreciated in foreign exchange markets. Increased nominal and real interest rates, especially in 1981, increased the debt-service requirements of heavily indebted countries with large amounts of floating-rate loans. Countering these adverse developments have been the recovery in the industrial countries, especially the United States, and the decline in interest rates since 1982, plus the recent moderate decline of the dollar.

The effects of movements in interest rates and in the foreign exchange value of the dollar on debt-service burdens were important for developing countries that chose, as a consequence of the policies they pursued, to borrow large sums from international capital markets. The problems of these countries are best understood in the

TABLE 2-3.—*External shocks and real GDP growth in selected developing countries, 1979–83*

Country Category	Net external shocks as percent of GNP[1]		Growth of real GDP (percent)[2]
	1979–80	1981–82	1979–83
Reschedulers[3]	−2.6	−9.3	0.9
Nonreschedulers	−2.6	−8.4	4.3

[1] External shocks are defined as the impact on the balance of payments as a percentage of GNP of: (a) changes in the terms of trade, (b) a decline in the growth rate of world demand for a country's exports; and (c) increases in interest rates, averaged across countries.
[2] Averaged across countries and years.
[3] Countries that had rescheduled debt as of the end of 1984.

Sources: International Bank for Reconstruction and Development, *World Development Report, 1985,* and International Monetary Fund, *International Financial Statistics Yearbook, 1985.*

context of a general discussion of the role of international credit flows and the current international debt situation.

THE ROLE OF INTERNATIONAL CREDIT

The international flow of capital performs at least two important economic functions. It allows countries with more attractive investment opportunities than can be financed out of domestic saving to obtain resources from countries with excess savings. It also allows countries suffering temporary economic difficulties to borrow from world capital markets rather than institute sharp temporary reductions in consumption or costly cutbacks in investment.

International capital flows have performed these functions for many countries over a long span of time. In the 50 years prior to World War I, the United States, Canada, Australia, Argentina, and the Scandinavian countries financed domestic investments with substantial loans from Great Britain and other European countries. The evidence indicates that despite occasional defaults and other difficulties, the providers of this credit earned higher returns than those typically available on investments in their own countries. In most of the period since World War II, the United States has been a net supplier of capital to the rest of the world, especially through the mechanism of direct investment by U.S. firms in foreign countries. The generally higher real growth rates of other industrial countries up to 1975 and of developing countries up to 1980 suggest that this flow of capital out of the United States was generally in the direction of higher returns. During the current expansion, the United States has become a net borrower in world credit markets. This is consistent with the high rate of return on and rapid growth of investment in the United States, in comparison with other countries, and with the need to finance the Federal deficit. The suppliers of credit to the United States are primarily other industrial countries where desired saving rates exceed desired rates of domestic investment.

With the exception of some oil-exporting countries, developing countries have generally been recipients of net capital inflows in the postwar period. Evidence indicates that from the mid-1960s to the late 1970s, there was a generally positive relationship between the growth of external indebtedness of particular developing countries and the growth of investment in these countries. Evidence suggests a similarly positive relationship between the growth of external indebtedness and the growth rate of real gross domestic product. This is consistent with the notion that international capital flows were, on the whole, performing the desirable function of financing investment in countries with good growth opportunities. From 1979 to 1983, however, there is no significant relationship between growth of external indebtedness and growth of investment for developing countries, and there is a negative relationship between growth of external debt and growth of real domestic product.

In the 1960s and 1970s, a few developing countries experienced difficulties in meeting their debt-service obligations and had to reschedule their external debts. At least up to 1979, however, these problems affected no more than two or three countries in any year, and the total amount of debt rescheduled in any year did not exceed $2 billion. In 1979, 7 countries rescheduled $6.2 billion of external debts; in 1980, 6 countries rescheduled $3.7 billion; and in 1981, 13 countries rescheduled $5.8 billion. In 1982 reschedulings fell when 9 countries rescheduled $2.4 billion; but in 1983, 21 countries rescheduled $51 billion; and in 1984, 24 countries (many of them the same as in the preceding year) rescheduled $116 billion. Because rescheduling agreements are typically reached some time after a country begins to experience debt-servicing difficulties, it is reasonable to conclude that by 1982 many of the developing countries with large external debts were already in trouble.

THE INTERNATIONAL DEBT SITUATION

A stylized description of events leading up to the recent international debt crisis is the following. Starting in 1973, growth of balance of payments surpluses of some high-income oil-exporting countries stimulated expansion of the international banking system that recycled these surpluses. Increased availability of credit on attractive terms through the international banking system increased opportunities for many developing countries to become borrowers from that system in the mid-1970s. Initially, debt-service requirements did not rise relative to the export earnings of many of these countries because they enjoyed rapid economic growth and because the inflationary expansion of the 1970s contributed to a boom in demand for their exports. Moreover, nominal interest rates on dollar-denominated loans declined from 1974 to 1976 and rose modestly between 1976 and 1978. Real interest rates became increasingly negative during the late 1970s as inflation accelerated. In addition, depreciation of the dollar relative to the currencies of other industrial countries after 1976 reduced the value of the dollar-denominated debt of many countries, thereby making further borrowing seem even more attractive.

In 1981–83 difficulties arose for many developing countries that had borrowed extensively from the international banking system in the late 1970s and 1980. The recession in the industrial countries, the high level of nominal and real interest rates (especially from late 1980 through mid-1982), the strengthening of the U.S. dollar, and the declines in the dollar prices of many commodities exported by heavily indebted developing countries (associated with the undoing of the inflationary excesses of the 1970s) contributed to an increase in the debt-service requirements of these countries relative to their export earnings, especially for countries with large volumes of dollar-denominated, floating-rate loans. To meet rising debt-service requirements, many debtor nations increased external borrowing. These high levels of borrowing, together with deteriorating export earnings and slackening economic growth, caused concern among lenders about the longer run capacity of these countries to meet their external debt-service obligations.

Table 2-4 presents data for two groups of debtor countries that are useful in understanding the debt crisis. Group A consists of indebted developing countries that incurred external payments arrears between 1981 and 1983 or rescheduled their external debts between 1981 and mid-1984. The 57 countries in group A accounted for 42.8 percent of GDP and 59.5 percent of the external debt of all developing countries in 1980. Group B consists of those indebted developing countries that did not experience recent debt-servicing difficulties. The 66 countries in group B accounted for 43.2 percent of GDP and 40.5 percent of the external debt of all developing countries in 1980. These two groups had the same average annual growth rate of real GDP, 5.5 percent per year, from 1967 to 1976. Both groups enjoyed substantial growth between 1976 and 1980, although even by this stage, countries in group B (with generally lower external debt burdens) were growing somewhat more rapidly. The growth rate of real GDP for group A fell to 1.1 percent in 1981, to −0.1 percent in 1982, and to −1.9 percent in 1983, and was estimated to be only 2.0 percent in 1984. In contrast, group B continued to enjoy impressive growth rates of real GDP, with annual growth rates of 5.1 percent in 1981, 4.0 percent in 1982, 5.4 percent in 1983, and an estimated 5.7 percent in 1984.

Another important difference between these two groups is the behavior of their respective current account balances. On average, from 1967 to 1976, group A had a slightly larger current account deficit as a percentage of exports of goods and services than group B. By 1977 the current account deficit as a percentage of exports had risen to 25.5 percent for group A, while it was only 6.1 percent of exports for group B. In the late 1970s and early 1980s the current account deficit of group B remained modest, peaking at 14 percent of exports in 1981. For group A the current account deficit remained much larger, peaking in absolute size in 1981, and relative to exports at 33.3 percent in 1982. An important factor contributing to the larger current account deficit of group A was the interest they had to pay on their larger external debt.

A current account deficit implies an excess of national spending over national income that must somehow be financed. The primary means of finance for developing countries is usually external net borrowing. This is shown in Table 2-4 in the close relationship between net external borrowing as a percentage of exports and the current account balance as a percentage of exports for both groups of countries. Not surprisingly, debt-servicing difficulties are associated with countries that run large and persistent current account deficits that need to be financed by large and persistent net external borrowing.

Loss of confidence in a country's creditworthiness might be expected to affect internal as well as external creditors, leading to a flight of domestic capital. This is reflected in Table 2-4 in the behavior of net asset transactions plus errors and omissions in the balance of payments. As a percentage of exports, these items remain quite small for group B, which did not experience debt-servicing problems. For group A, however, these items grow quite large in 1980–82.

TABLE 2-4.—*Debt indicators for developing countries, 1967–84*

Indicator by country group [1]	1967–76 average	1977	1978	1979	1980	1981	1982	1983	1984 [2]
					Percent				
Growth of real GDP									
Group A	5.5	5.4	3.7	5.3	3.9	1.1	−0.1	−1.9	2.0
Group B	5.5	6.3	8.2	4.7	4.9	5.1	4.0	5.4	5.7
					Billions of U.S. dollars				
Exports of goods and services									
Group A		107.8	117.3	154.5	201.3	207.4	185.4	178.2	192.1
Group B		154.5	183.5	240.1	310.5	328.2	319.1	322.5	354.9
					Percent of exports of goods and services				
Current account balance									
Group A	−18.5	−25.5	−31.9	−25.3	−23.7	−32.2	−33.3	−14.4	−7.6
Group B	−13.3	−6.1	−10.6	−9.4	−9.4	−14.0	−12.9	−10.5	−6.5
Net external borrowing									
Group A		29.5	36.1	28.8	32.3	37.5	32.2	18.3	11.0
Group B		8.9	10.9	10.5	10.6	12.9	11.9	10.2	7.2
Net asset transactions plus errors and omissions									
Group A		−7.4	−5.9	−3.4	−10.0	−14.5	−16.7	−6.2	
Group B		−3.1	−1.6	−2.5	−2.2	−2.1	−2.2	−2.7	−2.2
External debt									
Group A		171.7	195.8	178.1	167.1	194.5	246.0	268.1	256.8
Group B		95.3	91.9	81.6	73.6	78.3	91.1	97.0	94.2
Debt-service payments									
Group A		22.3	29.6	30.2	26.9	33.8	41.6	36.2	36.6
Group B		10.0	11.8	11.7	11.0	12.7	14.6	14.4	14.9

[1] Group A: countries with recent debt-servicing problems.
Group B: countries without debt-servicing problems.
[2] Estimates.

Source: International Monetary Fund, *World Economic Outlook, 1985.*

Adverse external developments can contribute to a loss of confidence in creditworthiness. A decline in export earnings due to a decline in world market demand for a country's exports may cause creditors to worry about the security for their loans. For a country with a large amount of floating-rate debt, an increase in interest rates increases debt-service requirements. This tends to worsen the current account balance, thereby contributing to creditor worries. Such events did adversely affect many heavily indebted developing countries in the early 1980s. However, the extent of these effects depended on the size of a country's external debt. In Table 2-4, group A has a higher ratio of debt service to exports in both 1977 and 1982 and a larger increase in this ratio between 1977 and 1982 than group B. This is not because group A faced higher interest rates or a larger increase in interest rates. It is because they had a higher ratio of external debt to exports in 1977 and a larger increase in this debt ratio between 1977 and 1982. Especially in developing countries where most external debt is government debt, the effects of changing interest rates on debt-service problems are a mixture of the effects of external events and of past government policies.

When a country experiences debt-servicing difficulties, its creditors tend to want to reduce their exposure by collecting all interest and principal payments as they come due, while extending no new credit. This may be neither desirable nor feasible. For the countries that experienced debt-servicing difficulties to pay all of the interest and principal on their external debts in 1982, without any new gross external borrowing, they would have had to move from net external borrowing equal to 37.5 percent of exports in 1981 to net external lending equal to principal payments on outstanding external loans (probably about 20 percent of exports). This would have required these countries to improve their trade balances in 1982 by more than $100 billion, relative to actual performance. Engineering such a massive change in the trade position of these countries was probably not feasible in so short a time, and it certainly would have been very costly. Moreover, it is questionable whether the major creditor countries, including the United States, would have wished to see a deterioration of more than $100 billion in their own trade balances, which would have been the necessary counterpart of an improvement of similar magnitude in the trade balances of debtor countries. To deal with this problem, debtor countries and their creditors normally attempt to negotiate rescheduling arrangements under which the creditors agree to extend the time period for repayment of the principal and sometimes part of the interest on existing loans.

POLICIES FOR ECONOMIC GROWTH AND DEVELOPMENT

Achievement of a rapid rate of economic growth has been a key objective of economic policy in many older and newly emergent developing countries for the past three decades. Different countries at different times have pursued a wide array of different policies in their efforts to stimulate and sustain rapid rates of growth, and have enjoyed varying degrees of success in these efforts. From this wealth of experience, it is possible to learn a good deal about economic policies likely to support successful development and about policies likely to inhibit economic growth.

ESTABLISHING APPROPRIATE INCENTIVES THROUGH RELATIVE PRICES

One basic lesson is that the rules governing economic behavior in developing countries do not fundamentally differ from the rules governing such behavior in more economically advanced countries. Allowed the opportunity to pursue their own interests, individuals respond to the incentives implicit in the relative prices of products they consume and produce and of factor services they sell or employ. Hence, it is crucial that economic policies operate to confront individuals with relative prices of products and factors that accurately reflect their true values and allow them to respond appropriately to the incentives embodied in these prices.

The importance of this point has not always been recognized in either developing or developed countries. For example, policies that depress prices of agricultural commodities in many developing countries are often seen as benefiting low-income consumers, without much reducing agricultural production. Experience demonstrates the error of this supposition. When prices of cash crops are depressed by export taxes, overvalued exchange rates, or price controls, production declines as farmers shift to crops with higher market prices or shift back to subsistence agriculture, sometimes with disastrous consequences for the national food supply. The opposite side of this coin has been observed in many developed countries where programs to support prices of agricultural products have generated mountains of surplus grain, oceans of surplus dairy products, and enough sugar production to please even Mary Poppins.

Another recent example of this fallacy is the supposed lack of responsiveness of producers and consumers to changes in the price of energy. After 1973 the U.S. Government imposed controls on the prices paid to domestic producers of oil and natural gas and on standards for energy consumption, including fuel economy standards for automobiles. Part of the rationale for these controls was the supposition that allowing domestic energy prices to rise would redistribute income from energy consumers to domestic energy producers, but would have little effect on the quantities of energy produced and consumed. However, as discussed in Chapter 5, energy production in the United States responded strongly to the incentives provided by higher prices. Similarly, when consumers faced higher energy prices, they demanded higher gas mileage vehicles, better insulated homes and factories, and more energy-efficient equipment and applicances.

The relevance of this point is not limited to the United States. In some oil-exporting countries, domestic fuel prices were kept well below world market levels throughout the 1970s. When the economic situation of many of these countries deteriorated in the early 1980s, there was resistance to raising domestic fuel prices as a means of conserving a valuable resource because it was believed that price increases would reduce real incomes of fuel consumers without stimulating much conservation. Countries that raised domestic fuel prices, however, found that fuel consumption responded to the incentives created by higher prices.

MAINTAINING REASONABLE FISCAL DISCIPLINE

A second basic lesson from experiences with economic growth is the virtue of maintaining reasonable fiscal discipline. This requires that governments not run large and persistent fiscal deficits, especially deficits financed by inflationary money creation or by heavy foreign borrowing, and that the size of the public sector be limited.

The "reasonable" size of the fiscal deficit depends on the situation and circumstances of particular countries. A country that enjoys rapid economic growth can usually expand its money supply more rapidly without generating inflation than a country that suffers slower economic growth. A country with good credit standing can finance a temporary fiscal deficit by foreign borrowing, while a country with a poorer credit rating may not have this option. A country that devotes a large fraction of its income to productive and profitable investments can sustain a higher rate of foreign borrowing than a country that does not invest as much in its future growth. However, the experience of many developing countries in the international debt crisis of the early 1980s demonstrates the dangers and disadvantages of policies that lead to persistent, large-scale foreign borrowing.

More generally, experience indicates that countries whose governments run large and persistent fiscal deficits (sometimes exceeding 8 or 10 percent of national income) may enjoy rapid economic growth for a while, but sooner or later they suffer severe economic difficulties. These difficulties may become acute during periods when deficits are being curtailed, thereby complicating observed relationships between fiscal deficits and economic performance. The painful effects of reducing government deficits, however, should be attributed to their basic cause. We suffer hangovers not because we stop drinking, but because we drank too much in the first place.

For a country with a large public sector, it is especially important that the public sector be run efficiently. Public sector enterprises that provide services similar to those that might be provided by private firms (such as electricity or transportation) should meet the standards of efficiency and profitability normally expected of private sector enterprises. Some public sector enterprises may meet this performance criterion; many do not. Often, employment in public sector enterprises is artificially high and wage and benefit levels for workers and managers of such enterprises exceed levels generally prevailing in the private sector. As discussed in Chapter 5, public sector enterprises in the United States are less efficient than their private sector counterparts. Evidence suggests that public sector enterprises in developing countries also suffer from serious inefficiencies, implying that substantial gains can be made by making public sector enterprises behave more like private firms or, better still, by shifting their activities to private firms.

Restoring fiscal discipline is a politically painful exercise. The short-run effect of either a reduction in government spending or an increase in taxes may be a decline in economic activity. The longer run effect of higher taxes, which distort economic incentives, is likely to be a lower level of real income. Moreover, the beneficiaries of deficit spending see themselves harmed by spending cuts, by tax-rate increases, or by efforts to expand the tax base. There is an important asymmetry here. Recipients of subsidized public services, transfer payments, or special tax breaks frequently blame governments for reducing these benefits. They do not protest with similar intensity the failure to provide such benefits in the first place. Hence, to maintain reasonable fiscal discipline, it is important not to initiate programs that may become expensive and are likely to generate interest groups supporting their continuation.

RESTRAINING GENERAL PRICE INFLATION

A third basic lesson is that a rapid rate of price inflation is generally associated with relatively poor growth performance. For the industrial countries, the higher inflation period of the 1970s and early 1980s generally brought poorer economic performance than the lower inflation period of the 1950s and 1960s. Some developing countries with inflation rates in the range of 20 to 40 percent per year have enjoyed reasonably good real growth. When inflation rates have accelerated to 50 percent per year or higher, however, growth performance has generally been poor relative to lower inflation periods. Inflation rates of 100 percent per year or higher have frequently been associated with economic stagnation or decline. Successful efforts to reduce high inflation rates have usually been associated with higher real economic growth. Countries enjoying the highest real growth rates have generally had low or moderate inflation rates.

The causal linkage between high inflation and poor growth is complex. Because governments often resort to inflationary policies when their economies are not performing well, inflation can be a symptom as well as a cause of poor economic performance. In theory, a country could have a high and predictable rate of inflation, and could adjust its economic institutions (including its tax system) to such inflation. In practice, high inflation rates are usually variable and unpredictable. High and variable inflation rates tend to induce wide variations in relative prices that interfere with the signals concerning the appropriate allocation of resources. With high and variable inflation rates, economic agents divert time, effort, and resources from productive activities into socially unproductive efforts to profit or to avoid losses from inflation and its attendant effects. Inflation frequently interacts with other distortions of the economic system to impair economic performance. For example, taxation of interest and other returns from capital on a nominal rate of return basis produces high real effective rates of taxation in the presence of high inflation.

MAINTAINING AN OPEN POLICY TOWARD INTERNATIONAL TRADE

A fourth basic lesson is that an outward looking, open policy toward international trade tends to be conducive to rapid economic growth. The essence of such a policy is that internal relative prices of internationally traded goods are not forced to diverge too far from world market prices because of import tariffs or quotas, exports taxes or subsidies, multiple or misvalued exchange rates, or other government policies. An open policy toward international trade allows for relatively unrestricted importation of products cheaply available in world markets and for exportation of products in which a country has or can develop a comparative advantage.

This contrasts with the inward looking, import-substitution policies adopted by many developing countries early in the postwar period. The objective of these import-substitution policies was to stimulate economic growth by encouraging development of domestic industries to produce products (especially manufactured products) previously imported. The tools were high-import tariffs, restrictive import quotas, foreign exchange licensing schemes, and other protective devices. In a few extreme cases, domestic producers could even obtain absolute prohibitions of imports on the promise that they would supply domestic substitutes.

Many studies have shown that relatively open policies toward international trade provide a better environment for economic growth in developing countries than policies of import-substitution. The most rapidly growing countries generally have relatively open trade policies. Countries that have shifted from import substitution to more open policies have generally improved economic performance. In contrast, import-substitution policies have produced large distortions between the domestic relative prices of tradable goods and the true costs of these goods, as reflected in world market relative prices. As a result, resources were diverted from potential export activities into production of high-cost domestic substitutes for products that could be purchased more cheaply in world markets. In addition, smaller countries that adopted import-substitution policies lost economies of scale by attempting to produce a diversified range of products for a small domestic market, rather than concentrating on a more limited range of products to be produced for export as well as domestic consumption. In some cases, loss of productive efficiency was exacerbated by a decline in market discipline on domestic firms and their workers because these firms faced little internal competition and were shielded from foreign competition.

Some countries with relatively open policies toward international trade have provided temporary protection for some import-competing industries or have given direct or indirect export subsidies to some industries (including preferential tax treatment and favorable tariff rates on imported inputs used in these industries). In some cases, special privileges accorded to particular industries may merely offset other distortions that impair the exploitation of natural comparative advantage. Although there are a few examples of successful industrial targeting, there are also many examples of industries that have become successful exporters without benefit of specific targeting by government authorities. There are also examples of industries targeted for development that never proved especially successful. Worst of all are the examples of targeted industries that continue to require subsidies or protection long after they were initially selected for special assistance. The general lesson appears to be that industrial targeting may occasionally succeed when a government has the luck to select the right industries for development. But there is a danger that special government privileges will be supplied for long periods to industries with little development potential. Moreover, if private sector investors err in selecting an industry for development, they bear an important part of the cost of that mistake, rather than passing it on to the rest of society. For this reason, there is less danger that the private sector will prolong activities that prove unsuccessful.

Given that most countries will not pursue policies of complete free trade, it is important to recognize that some impediments to trade are worse than others. A uniform ad valorem import tariff applied to all imports is generally less distortionary than a tariff structure with the same average tariff rate but with wide variations in the tariffs applied to individual commodities. This is especially so when imported goods are used as inputs in producing other goods. In this situation, relatively small variations in nominal tariff rates can generate large differences in effective rates of protection for value added in different domestic production activities. Large differences in effective protection rates, in turn, imply large distortions of the incentives to devote domestic resources to different production activities.

In general, import tariffs are less harmful than import quotas that provide the same initial level of protection. Tariffs raise revenue for the government. The implicit revenue associated with an import quota is usually distributed to the private parties who receive quota allocations and who hence have an interest in preserving and enhancing the scarcity value of the right they have received. A tariff generally allows less latitude for the exercise of market power by domestic producers of import substitutes (or by suppliers of factors to such producers) than does an import quota. With an import tariff, the degree of protection for domestic producers relative to foreign competitors is fixed; domestic producers are therefore under pressure to match the efficiency gains of their foreign competitors. With an import quota, the discipline on domestic producers to remain efficient is often diminished because the level of protection rises to offset any deterioration in the efficiency of domestic producers relative to their foreign competitors. Systems of foreign exchange licenses, with different exchange rates for different classes of imports and exports and with complicated mechanisms for the allocation of licenses, share the disadvantages of import and export quotas and frequently offer even greater latitude for harmful manipulation.

MAINTAINING AN APPROPRIATELY VALUED EXCHANGE RATE

A fifth basic lesson from the growth experiences of developing countries is the importance of maintaining an appropriately valued exchange rate. The exchange rate is the price of domestic money in terms of foreign monies. The economically appropriate exchange rate establishes the correct relationship between internal nominal prices of goods and services in terms of domestic money and the nominal prices of goods and services in terms of foreign monies. For most developing countries that maintain some form of pegged exchange rate, the economically appropriate exchange rate is difficult to identify with great precision. However, there is little doubt that some developing countries have injured their export industries and their overall growth performances by maintaining substantially overvalued exchange rates. Frequently, this has happened because rapid domestic inflation has transformed an initially appropriate nominal exchange rate into a substantially overvalued exchange rate.

The initial effect of an overvalued exchange rate is often to enlarge a country's trade deficit beyond the level that can be financed by the normal equilibrium level of capital inflow. In the short run, to sustain the foreign exchange value of its currency, the government may intervene in the foreign exchange market by using its official reserves or reserves borrowed on the world capital market. Alternatively, a large-scale capital inflow resulting from either official foreign borrowing or from private capital inflows can contribute to overvaluation of the exchange rate by financing an excess of domestic spending over domestic income. To sustain an overvalued exchange rate and stem reserve losses, governments frequently resort to trade restrictions and foreign exchange controls. Although the reason for imposing these restrictions may not be a desire to engage in import substitution, the effect is the same—a distortion of the economically appropriate relationship between internal and external prices and a corresponding distortion of incentives for the efficient allocation of resources.

LIMITING DISTORTIONS OF DOMESTIC PRODUCT AND FACTOR MARKETS

A sixth basic lesson from the experiences of developed and developing countries is the importance of limiting distortions of domestic product and factor markets. Such distortions can arise from the activities of private economic agents, in particular through the exercise of market power. The appropriate role of government policy in this regard is not to facilitate the exercise of market power by supporting cartels or other anticompetitive practices but to promote competition. Even more important, the government should not allow its own policies to distort excessively the markets for domestic products and factors.

Some distortion of domestic product and factor markets is the inevitable consequence of taxes used to raise revenue to finance essential government operations. The harmful distortionary effects of taxation generally rise more than proportionately with the rate of taxation. They become especially acute when rates of taxation are highly variable across similar products or across different uses of the same factor of production. Hence, it is important to keep overall tax rates as low as possible and to keep tax rates relatively even across similar products and different uses of the same factor of production. Increasingly, experience suggests that low and even tax rates contribute to economic growth, presumably by maintaining incentives to work, save, and invest.

MAINTAINING POLITICAL STABILITY

A final general lesson from the growth experiences of many countries over a long span of time is the importance of maintaining reasonable political and economic stability. Economic growth requires current sacrifice to obtain future reward. A political and economic system that does not provide reasonable assurance that those who make the sacrifices will enjoy a fair share of the reward will almost inevitably fail to generate much growth. This is apparent in countries where the insecurity created by war or political turmoil has caused economic stagnation or decline.

Lessons from Korean Economic Growth

Susan M. Collins

In 1960, Korea was a poor developing country with a small manufacturing sector and heavily dependent on foreign aid. It had seemingly few prospects to increase and maintain high growth rates. However, between 1965 and 1979, Korea's real GDP growth averaged over 9 percent per year, with manufacturing growth of nearly 19 percent.

In 1981, Korea was the fourth largest debtor country in the world, behind Brazil, Mexico, and Argentina. Output had declined sharply in 1980. With a debt-to-GDP ratio of 50 percent, there were widespread concerns about Korea's ability to meet its debt obligations. However, Korea's economy was booming again by 1986, with a substantial trade surplus due to rapid export growth. In addition to meeting all debt service obligations, Korea had begun to repay the principal on its external debt.

Korea's impressive history of economic growth stands out from the experience of most developing countries that have borrowed heavily in international financial markets. A comparison of per capita income (PCI) growth rates from the World Bank presents the differences starkly. Over 1965-87, Korea's PCI grew at an average annual rate of 6.4 percent. Over the same period, PCI grew on average by just 2.0 percent in the 17 heavily indebted countries, by 2.5 percent in middle-income countries and by 3.1 percent in low-income countries. (In fact, only three World Bank member countries—Botswana, Oman, and Singapore—had faster annual PCI growth rates than Korea.)

As stated in the *World Development Report*, "for most of the highly indebted countries, the debt crisis has become a growth crisis as well" (1989, p. 17). The contrasts in

†*Discussant*: Andrei Shleifer, University of Chicago.

*Harvard University, Cambridge, MA 02138.

growth performance between these countries and Korea, since 1965 and particularly during the 1980s debt crisis recovery, are striking. This paper examines distinguishing aspects of Korea's economic growth and argues that these factors do contain lessons for policymakers in other countries struggling to revive stagnant economies.

I. Policy Stability

Korea's experience does not provide an example of "quick fix" policy packages, but of a long history of relatively consistent, stable, and sensible macroeconomic policies. At the same time, Korea's history is not completely devoid of policy mistakes. For example, the 1973-79 "Big Push" to develop heavy industry is widely recognized as having contributed to a real appreciation and loss of competitiveness and to distorting allocation of credit and other resources.[1] Instead, what stands out is that macroeconomic policies were adjusted before they became far out of line. The point could be made with a variety of policy indicators; budget deficits, real interest rates and real exchange rates are discussed below.[2]

First, budget deficits have been kept small in Korea, averaging just 2.3 percent, and ranging from 1.0 to 4.2. The average deficit was more than twice as large in Mexico and Argentina. The range between the smallest and the largest deficit was more than 10 percent of GNP in all three Latin American countries.

Korea has also maintained relatively stable real interest rates. Between 1977 and 1987, the real deposit rate (average nominal rate less *ex post* consumer price inflation) averaged 2.5 percent, compared to -2.3 percent in the Philippines, -13.4 percent in Mexico, and -22.3 percent in Argentina. While Korea's real deposit rates were not positive every year, they were negative in only two of eleven years, compared with five years of negative rates in the Philippines, six years in Argentina, and nine years in Mexico.

Relative to other countries, Korea's real exchange rate has remained stable as well. Although a fixed nominal exchange rate was maintained from December 1974 through January 1980, resulting in a 15 percent real appreciation, this appreciation is small when compared to the real appreciations of 23 percent in Mexico during 1977–81, and the 81 percent in Argentina during 1977–80. The standard deviation in Korea's real exchange rate during 1975–85 was just 6.5, less than half of the 14.7 and 16.7 standard deviations in Brazil and Argentina.

II. Breathing Space for Policy Reforms

In 1980, Korea was in the midst of an economic crisis. Real output declined by 4.8 percent and inflation had doubled to 28.7 percent from 14.4 percent in 1978. The debt/GNP ratio had jumped from 28 to 45 percent and the current account deficit had ballooned to 9 percent of GNP. Years of the Big Push to heavy industry had resulted in growing price controls, import restrictions, and regulations distorting financial markets. Korea needed a combination of macroeconomic stabilization policies, trade and financial market liberalization, and economic restructuring. Korea's recovery from this crisis was striking and rapid. Real growth averaged over 7 percent during 1981–84 and, by 1984, inflation had been cut to 2.3 percent, the current account deficit was less than 2 percent of GNP, and there was little remaining concern about Korea's creditworthiness.

Should we believe that other countries could implement the same policy package to rapidly restore creditworthiness and growth? My response has three parts. First, Korea's policy package is a sound one for other countries. However, Korea's history of relatively stable, sensible macroeconomic policies, high rates of investment, and strong growth also played a role in the rapid turnaround. In this sense, Korea's short-lived economic crisis was less severe than the difficulties faced by many heavily indebted countries. The second point, therefore, is that Korea's policies are unlikely to result in as quick and as impressive a recovery in countries with a history of policy reversals and inconsistencies, and which have had low investment rates since 1982.

The third point is that many observers omit a key part of Korea's recovery package. Korea did not implement macroeconomic stabilization and restructuring measures, nor did it revive growth at the same time that it reversed its dependence on foreign borrowing. Instead, Korea had the breathing space of large continued capital inflows (together with some special circumstances) during the first years of its recovery which enabled it to revive growth *before* undertaking restrictive monetary and fiscal policy actions. Korea does *not* provide an example of how to stabilize and restructure an economy, shift from receiving capital inflows to making large resource transfers abroad and raise living standards, all at the same time.

Table 1 provides economic indicators for Korea during 1979–84. It is useful to divide the recovery into two periods: 1980–82 and 1983–84. In the early period, Korean policymakers devalued, liberalized price controls and many import restrictions, and initiated tax reforms. Although monetary and fiscal policies were initially to be restrictive, the tight stance was relaxed because of concerns over flagging investment in 1981, and to bail firms out after a financial crisis in 1982. In fact, fiscal policy was quite expansionary, accommodated by strong money growth. Korea continued to borrow heavily to finance imports and investment. Also, a good harvest (following extremely poor harvests in 1978 and 1980) helped to expand output while reducing food imports.

The 1981–82 measures set the Korean economy up to take advantage of stronger world growth in 1983–84. It was not until exports and output were booming that the government reversed its expansionary macroeconomic policies, and the debt-to-GNP ratio stabilized.

Korea's phased policy response, with its initial breathing period, contrasts sharply with the attempts in many heavily indebted countries (for example, in Latin America) to do everything at once. In these countries, trade deficits were quickly transformed to surpluses after 1982 through cuts in imports and investment. This approach has not produced adjustment with growth.

Korea is not the only example that breathing space facilitates a growth recovery from a debt crisis. Turkey, during 1980–82, and Indonesia, during the mid-1960s, also received generous capital inflows as they were implementing their adjustment packages. Like Korea, these countries both got into

TABLE 1 — KOREAN ECONOMIC INDICATORS

	1979	1980	1981-82	1983-84
GNP Growth Rate	7.0	-4.8	6.0	10.2
Current Account	-6.8	-8.8	-5.4	-1.9
Fixed Investment	33.2	32.3	29.6	31.3
Domestic Saving	28.1	23.5	23.8	29.1
M2 Growth Rate	24.6	26.9	26.0	11.5
Budget Deficit	-1.4	-3.2	-4.6	-1.5
External Debt	32.5	45.0	53.5	52.3
External Debt (billions $)	$20.3	$27.2	$37.1	$43.1

Source: Economic Planning Board, Korea.
Notes: Percent of GNP, unless otherwise indicated; 1981-82 and 1983-84 data are annual averages, except for external debt, which is end of period.

trouble *before* the 1982 widespread debt crisis, and both benefited from favorable borrowing conditions in international financial markets. However, breathing space is not a panacea. There are also examples of countries that received large capital inflows, but did not implement necessary reforms, and therefore did not engineer a recovery to sustainable growth and creditworthiness.

III. Investment and Growth

A related feature that distinguishes Korea's adjustment from the experience in many Latin American countries is that Korea maintained high rates of investment. This investment, concentrated in export industries, helps to account for Korea's rapid growth during the 1960s and 1970s, and also for the quick recovery in the 1980s. Korea's gross domestic investment grew at an average annual rate of 15.9 percent during 1965-80 and 10.0 percent during 1980-1987. In contrast, investment growth in the 17 highly indebted countries fell from 8.6 percent during 1965-80 to -5.1 percent during 1980-87. Many analysts have expressed grave concern about their ability to revive growth as the capital stock erodes. External borrowing helped to finance Korea's investments in 1980-82. It was not until the 1983 surge in growth that domestic savings began to rebound, reducing the need for foreign financing. Breathing space contributed significantly to Korea's ability to maintain high rates of investment.

What are the underlying sources of Korea's growth, and how important was capital accumulation? A Denison growth accounting analysis by K. S. Kim and J. K. Park (1985) decomposes Korean growth during 1963-82. They show that factor inputs, and especially capital accumulation, played an increasingly central role. During 1963-72, increased quantity and quality of capital and labor accounted for about half of average annual growth, or 4.2 percent per year. During 1972-82, factor inputs accounted for nearly 80 percent of Korean growth, or 5.6 percent per year. In particular, increased nonresidential structures and equipment augmented growth by 1.5 percent per year more during 1963-72 than during 1972-82, offsetting a decline in factor productivity growth that followed the first oil price shock. On the labor input side, increased work hours and improved education helped to offset slower employment growth. The importance of physical and especially human capital accumulation distinguish Korea's growth history from that of countries which industrialized prior to 1973.

IV. Concluding Remarks

What, then, are the lessons from Korea's economic growth? First, a stable policy environment provides a solid stage for adjusting to internal and external shocks. Although difficult to quantify, there can be little doubt that Korea's policy history was an important stabilizing factor in the quick 1981-84 recovery. Second, investment in both physical and human capital is a key to economic growth, In Korea, increased factor inputs alone accounted for an average annual growth rate of over 5 percent during the 1970s.

It is against this backdrop that a third, important lesson emerges. Even in Korea, where policies have been stable and high rates of investment have been maintained, breathing space in the form of continued capital inflows played a key role in reviving and sustaining growth after 1980. Korea's experience should not be construed as an example that a country in the midst of a prolonged economic crisis, with a depleted capital stock and a history of policy reversals and mistakes, can simultaneously undertake structural adjustments together with restrictive macroeconomic policies, transfer resources abroad and revive stagnant growth rates.

[1] See my paper with Won-Am Park (1989, especially pp. 191-98) for further discussion of Korea's Big Push and also for additional references.
[2] Data on central budget deficits and real interest rates come from the International Monetary Fund. Real exchange rate data are from Morgan Guaranty.

Organizing Debt Relief: The Need for a New Institution

Peter B. Kenen

When Mexico suspended debt-service payments in August 1982, creditor countries, led by the United States, responded promptly. Animated by concern about confidence in the banking system, not mere solicitude for the banks, they extended large short-term credits to Mexico, then put pressure on the banks to reschedule Mexican debt and lend more to Mexico, once the International Monetary Fund had endorsed the policies that Mexico would follow to deal with its problems. This was the birth of the case-by-case approach to the debt problem. It was predicated implicitly on the belief that debtors faced a short-term problem arising from an unusual combination of worldwide recession and high interest rates brought on by a shift in the policy stance of the major industrial countries. On this view, it was eminently sensible for debtors to take on more debt temporarily in order to pay interest on their existing debts.[1]

The problem was still with us three years later, however, and the case-by-case approach was in trouble. The world economy was growing again and interest rates had fallen, but the debtor's export earnings were not growing, and their governments were increasingly reluctant to deal with the IMF, which was asking for more austerity but providing less Fund credit. The banks were willing to reschedule larger amounts of debt for longer intervals but would put up new money only for the largest debtors.

The Baker and Brady Plans

In October 1985, at the annual IMF-World Bank meeting in Seoul, the U.S. Secretary of the Treasury, James Baker, proposed a three-part "program for sustained growth" to deal with the debt problem:

First and foremost, the adoption by principal debtor countries of comprehensive macroeconomic and structural policies, supported by the international financial institutions, to promote growth and balance of payments adjustment, and to reduce inflation.

Second, a continued central role for the IMF, in conjunction with increased and more effective structural adjustment lending by the multilateral development banks ...

Third, increased lending by the private banks in support of comprehensive economic adjustment programs.

■ *Peter B. Kenen is Walker Professor of Economics and International Finance and Director of the International Finance Section, Princeton University, Princeton, New Jersey.*

Austerity would fight inflation and produce the trade surpluses needed by the debtors to make their debt-service payments. Structural reforms and new lending would generate the growth needed to reduce the burden of those payments. Secretary Baker went on to ask that the multilateral institutions and commercial banks adopt specific targets for new lending to the 15 highly indebted countries listed in Table 1.

The banks fell far short of those targets, however, and actually reduced their claims on some debtor countries. In mid-1987, moreover, major U.S. banks, led by Citicorp, set aside larger loan-loss reserves against their exposure to the debtor countries.[2] Secretary Baker came back to the banks in 1987, to ask that they develop a "menu" of new instruments and methods to step up their lending. But the whole debt strategy began to change in 1988, even as the banks were adopting the menu approach, most notably in a new agreement with Brazil.[3]

At the economic summit in Toronto, the seven major industrial countries had agreed to grant debt relief to low-income countries, mainly in Africa, but had pointedly excluded middle-income debtors, mainly in Latin America. At the IMF-World Bank meeting in Berlin, however, the IMF Interim Committee proposed that the menu approach be broadened to include "voluntary market-based techniques which . . . reduce the stock of debt without transferring risk from private lenders to official creditors." The aim of the menu approach was shifted from raising to reducing debt: a late but fundamental change in the official interpretation of the debt problem.

In March 1989, the new U.S. Secretary of the Treasury, Nicholas Brady, endorsed the change in strategy, calling for a three-year waiver of clauses in existing loan agreements that stand in the way of debt reduction "to accelerate sharply the pace of debt reduction and pass the benefits directly to the debtor nations," and called on the IMF and World Bank to use some of their policy-based lending to aid the debt-reducing process; some of it could be used to collaterize debt-for-bond exchanges at significant discounts and replenish reserves following cash buybacks of debt, and some could be used to underwrite the interest payments on new or modified debt contracts.

Events moved rapidly thereafter. The IMF and World Bank adopted guidelines to implement the Brady plan, and the IMF extended new credits to Mexico, Costa Rica, and the Philippines in accordance with those guidelines. Japan agreed to provide $4.5 billion in supplementary lending (and has recently raised its pledge to $10 billion). Commercial banks began to negotiate an agreement with Mexico, which would reduce its interest payments to the banks by as much as 35 percent if every bank participated fully.[4]

Is there anything left to argue about? Unhappily, yes. Some economists, such as Bulow and Rogoff (1988, 1989), argue that debtors are wrong to use reserves or

Table 1

Discounts on the debts of fifteen heavily indebted countries

Argentina	$82\frac{1}{2}$	Ecuador	$86\frac{1}{2}$	Peru	97
Bolivia	89	Ivory Coast	94	Philippines	$50\frac{1}{2}$
Brazil	$70\frac{1}{2}$	Mexico	$58\frac{1}{2}$	Uruguay	45
Chile	$35\frac{1}{2}$	Morocco	$56\frac{1}{2}$	Venezuela	$62\frac{1}{4}$
Colombia	43	Nigeria	$76\frac{1}{2}$	Yugoslavia	49

Source: Salomon Brothers, July 1989; discounts are for cash bids.

borrow to buy back debt, even at large discounts. Advocates of debt relief, such as Sachs (1989a) and myself, maintain that the Brady plan will not go far enough. It relies too heavily on debtors and creditors to strike mutually beneficial bargains; it does not provide enough resources to generate the deep debt reductions that debtors need to solve their problems; and it does not shift risk forthrightly enough from private lenders to official creditors. I would correct the defects of the Brady plan by creating a new international institution to manage and finance the debt-reducing process or assign the task to an existing institution but give it enough resources to get the job done.

The Case for Debt Relief

Krugman (1989) argues that debt reduction can raise economic efficiency in a heavily indebted country, and thus raise the debtor's real income, reducing the probability of default. Therefore, a debt buyback can raise the present value of the remaining debt, and can raise it sufficiently to compensate creditors for selling debt on terms that benefit the debtor. Even outright debt forgiveness can benefit both parties.

A large debt overhang reduces economic efficiency in two ways. First, high debt-service payments require high tax rates that discourage capital formation and the repatriation of flight capital; see Krugman (1989) and Sachs (1988, 1989b). Second, the government is the main maker of debt-service payments in most of the heavily indebted countries, and its payments figure in its budget. Hence, they can prevent a devaluation from improving the trade balance, because a devaluation raises the domestic-currency cost of servicing foreign-currency debt, increasing the budget deficit, raising the growth of the money supply, and raising the inflation rate; see, e.g., Dornbusch (1988). Therefore, debtors must use less efficient methods to produce the trade surpluses required to make debt-service payments.

When these and other inefficiencies are powerful, creditors confront what Krugman calls the Debt Relief Laffer Curve—an apt but unfortunate name, because it should be taken more seriously than its namesake. If a debtor's obligations get very large, their expected value begins to fall. The income-depressing effects of the debt make it more likely that the debtor will default when an adverse shock arrives. By reducing that vulnerability, debt relief raises the expected value of the debt. The debtor is better off in "good states" because it keeps the incremental income produced by debt reduction, but creditors are better off in "bad states" because the debtor is more likely to meet its obligations.

Krugman believes that the small debtor countries are on the downward-sloping side of the Debt Relief Laffer Curve. He is less sure about large debtors. But he understates the strength and generality of the case for debt relief, which may apply most aptly to large debtors. Use of the conventional stochastic framework, with good and bad states, makes the shape of the Debt Relief Laffer Curve depend entirely on the strength of the inefficiencies associated with a big debt overhang. Use of a different framework frees it from that limitation.[5]

Consider the framework used by Eaton and Gersovitz (1981), where repudiation is voluntary and can benefit the debtor unambiguously. This is the most appropriate framework for analyzing the behavior of a sovereign debtor, which never faces insolvency in a strict balance-sheet sense but must weigh the costs of continuing to service its debt against the costs of repudiation.

When a country can look forward to borrowing and growing, it is apt to reject repudiation. When it cannot expect to borrow more, its decision will depend on the advantages of halting debt-service payments and the strength of the inefficiencies examined earlier, compared to the size of the penalties that creditors and their governments are likely to impose if the debtor repudiates. These may include the seizure of reserves, the penalty stressed in the current literature, but the debtor must also disguise its exports to keep creditors from seizing them and must pay for its imports with cash when trade-credit lines are cut. In effect, it can experience a deterioration in its terms of trade.

Repudiation will be beneficial to the debtor when its debt is large compared to the present value of the penalties. By implication, debt reduction can be mutually beneficial, because it reduces the debtor's obligations but raises the expected value of the creditors' claims by reducing the debtor's incentive to repudiate. The Debt Relief Laffer Curve comes into being, not because of the inefficiencies produced by a debt overhang but because debt reductions can tilt the debtor's cost-benefit calculation against repudiation.

There is no way to know a priori whether a particular country is on the downward-sloping side of the curve. That will depend in part on the nature of the penalties that creditors can be expected to impose. But these may not vary across countries in proportion to their debts, which means that large debtors are more likely to be on the downward-sloping side.

Unfortunately, large debtors are least likely to receive outright debt forgiveness. Their creditors are reluctant to accept the large accounting losses involved in reducing substantially the face value of their claims on Mexico, Brazil, and Argentina. And though they would have to reduce them by less than the amount of debt forgiveness, because it would raise the expected value of their remaining claims, it is hard to persuade accountants, regulators, and securities analysts that lower book values can mean larger economic values. When Citicorp and other U.S. banks set aside larger loan-loss reserves, their stock prices rose; investors were ready to reward the banks for being more realistic. But investors who were eager to accept the tax-policy implications of the original Laffer Curve are less eager to accept the more valid implications of the Debt Relief Laffer Curve.

The Mechanics of Debt Relief

There is a secondary market for sovereign debt in which it can be shifted from bank to bank or to other institutions. Most countries' debts sell there at large discounts, reflecting the creditors' belief that debtors will not meet their obligations fully. Representative discounts are shown in Table 1. When the Interim Committee endorsed voluntary, market-based debt reduction, it had in mind transactions based on these discounts.

Such transactions can involve purchases of debt with currently available resources or purchases with future resources made by exchanging new debt for old. The second method is known as defeasance (which sounds pejorative, but isn't). Their benefits and costs depend in part on the values that debtors and creditors attach to the existing debt—which need not coincide precisely with those represented by the discounts quoted in the secondary market.[6]

Purchases with currently available resources have taken two forms: buybacks with cash and debt-equity swaps, which may be deemed to represent an exchange of debt for an entrepreneurial opportunity. Buybacks with cash have been debated extensively, and I have already reviewed the main issues, but these transactions have been rare. Debtor countries do not have the cash needed to buy back their debts, even at deep discounts. The Bolivian example is cited frequently but was very special; the money was provided by official donors expressly for the purpose of debt reduction.[7]

Several debtor countries have experimented with debt-equity swaps, but Chile is the only one that encouraged them enthusiastically. Difficulties arise on three fronts. First, many debtor countries are ambivalent about foreign direct investment of any sort. Second, they wonder whether they are attracting additional investments or merely subsidizing what would take place anyway on normal commercial terms. Third, they worry about inflationary side effects, because external debt must be exchanged for domestic currency before it can be used for equity investment, and the domestic currency is usually supplied by the central bank, expanding the money supply, as the government is usually running a budget deficit and cannot put up the money.

This brings us to the use of future resources to buy back debt. What can be done by defeasance? A small number of governments have offered "exit bonds" to small and medium-sized banks interested in opting out of debt reschedulings and concerted lending. The problem of subordination, discussed below, does not arise in connection with these issues; the bonds do not take precedence over other obligations but were thought to be potentially attractive because buyers would not have to increase their exposure. Hence, the holders of old debt would not be adversely affected financially, and were expected to benefit indirectly, because the creditors' coalition would become more compact and cohesive.

Yet experience has not been encouraging. Argentina tried to issue exit bonds in 1987, but the terms were not attractive. Mexico was somewhat more successful in 1988, but it used reserves to guarantee its promise to repay. It bought zero-coupon U.S. Treasury securities, which were used to back the principal of the Mexican bonds issued in exchange for Mexican debt. Yet Mexico's sales were smaller than expected, presumably because the interest payments were not guaranteed, and the promise to pay interest on the bonds was not more credible than the promise to pay interest on the debt. Exit bonds appeared in the menu of financial options listed in the 1988 agreement between Brazil and its bank creditors. Although they were not guaranteed, Brazil sold more than $1 billion to more than 100 banks (Rhodes, 1988), but it has not reached its $5 billion target.

It is sometimes suggested that debtors should subordinate old debt to new, to market the new debt successfully. But that cannot be done without the unanimous consent of those who hold the old debt, and this produces a paradox. If enough new debt is issued to retire much of the old debt, those who continue to hold the old debt may not accept subordination, even if the exercise sharply reduces the debtor's obligations and thus raises the expected value of the whole debt; the buyers of the new debt will be seen to appropriate most of the gain. But if the issue is cut back to reduce the redistribution of rights from holders of old debt to holders of new debt, the exercise will not reduce the debtor's obligations by enough to make subordination meaningful —to raise the value of the whole debt by enhancing the debtor's ability and willingness to service it.

When the problem of defeasance is viewed this way, the function of a new institution becomes very clear. It would guarantee new debt, whether by issuing its own obligations or backing new bonds issued by the debtor countries.

The Functioning of a New Institution

I suggested the creation of a new institution soon after the debt crisis erupted (Kenen, 1983).[8] An International Debt Discount Corporation (IDDC) would be established by the governments of the major industrial countries. It could be an independent entity or an affiliate of the IMF or World Bank. Its capital would be subscribed by its sponsors and used exclusively to guarantee its own obligations. Subscriptions might be made in proportion to the sponsors' shares in the capital of the World Bank or quotas in the IMF. The IDDC would issue its own long-term obligations to commercial banks in exchange for their claims on developing countries. (The claims would be those issued or guaranteed by debtor governments, not those of private entities, and limited to those having an original maturity longer than one year.)

In 1983, when my plan appeared, there was no secondary market for sovereign debt. That is why I did not suggest that the IDDC might buy up debt at market prices. Nevertheless, that approach raises some serious problems. Market rates would begin to reflect expectations about IDDC operations even before it came into being, and they would cease to serve as independent benchmarks (Fischer, 1989). Furthermore, debtors should not be given incentives to threaten repudiation—explicitly or by following imprudent policies—to force down the prices at which the IDDC could buy up their debts in the market and thus raise the amounts of debt relief that it would pass on to them (Corden, 1988b). Hence, the IDDC should choose in advance the rate at which it will discount debt, say 40–50 percent. A case can be made for using several discount rates and letting each debtor choose the one for its own obligations. This would be particularly sensible if larger discounts were linked to tighter policy conditions.

Commercial banks would not be required to do business with the IDDC, but those that do would be subject to certain restrictions. First, banks should not be allowed to sell their claims on some debtors and keep their claims on others; a bank wanting to discount claims on any debtor country doing business with the IDDC should be required to discount a uniform fraction of its total claims on all such countries. Second, banks would have only a limited period, perhaps six months to a year, to decide whether they will turn to the IDDC.

Debtor countries would not have to deal with the IDDC, either, and it would deal only with those countries that agreed to enter into suitable arrangements with the IMF and World Bank concerning the debtors' policies. During the time that banks are deciding whether they will sell to the IDDC, the debtor governments would have to decide whether they will do business with the IDDC; the discount window would be opened at the end of that period.

Sponsoring governments would agree to make changes in their banking laws and regulations if such changes are required for their banks to deal with the IDDC. Furthermore, they would permit their banks to amortize gradually some of the losses incurred by discounting debt with the IDDC. Bonds issued by the IDDC might be amortized over a 30-year period, starting five years after issue, and bear an interest rate slightly higher than the then-current rate on long-term U.S. government bonds. The bonds should be marketable, and the IDDC should encourage the development of a secondary market for them. Furthermore, it should be empowered to redeem them by issuing new ones to holders of maturing bonds and in the open market.

Claims discounted by the IDDC would be converted into long-term debt at or slightly above the discounted value of those claims. The difference between the face value of the new debt and the discounted value of the old would yield a "profit" that the IDDC might hold as a reserve or use for selective interest-rate relief. Debt to the IDDC might be amortized over a 25-year period, after a 5-year grace period. It should bear an interest rate 50 basis points above the average rate on the IDDC's own bonds.

Many permutations of this plan have appeared recently. The boldest is by Robinson (1988), in which the new institution would issue consols. In that case, of course, it would be guaranteeing interest payments rather than principal, which would be eminently sensible. The present value of the institution's obligations would be the same whether its bonds were amortized or not, but its exposure to cash-flow problems would be reduced.

Another variant would use the new institution to guarantee bonds issued directly by the debtors, rather than its own.[9] This option has one disadvantage. It would produce a large number of new bonds, each with its own market, rather than one issue by the IDDC with a single market, and the latter would probably function more efficiently. Furthermore, the terms of existing debt contracts allow banks to block bond issues by debtors, but they could not be invoked as easily to block bond issues by the IDDC. The point is important because the success of the debt-conversion exercise will depend on the ability of the IDDC to make banks an offer they cannot refuse or block.

Answering the Critics

Critics of an international agency invoke a litany of difficulties—adverse selection, moral hazard, and the free-rider problem.

The first says that the IDDC will gather in the debt that is least likely to be honored. This problem is minimized by the requirement that banks sell baskets of debt to the IDDC, offering some or all of their claims on all participating debtor countries. The problem could be eliminated by requiring all debtors countries to participate, but that would be impractical and unfair. Some debtor countries, like Korea, have worked hard to preserve their creditworthiness; they should not have to damage it.

The moral hazard argument says that the scheme would invite debtor countries to pursue irresponsible policies and would lead eventually to a new round of overborrowing.

The first part of this assertion says that debtor governments would be less concerned to achieve domestic stability and promote economic growth if their debts were reduced. In other words, it rejects the main rationale for debt relief, that debtors have failed to achieve their policy objectives because the debt overhang prevents them from doing so. (Alternatively, it may say that the debtors would take their obligations to the IDDC less seriously than their obligations to the commercial banks. That is unlikely. No country has kept up its debt-service payments to the banks but suspended its payments to the IMF or World Bank, but several have done the opposite.)

The second part of the assertion predicts that debt relief will cause another debt crisis by removing reminders of this one. There may be another debt crisis eventually, but its timing is less likely to reflect the manner of settling this one than the speed at which institutional memories fade. Many governments that strive today to meet their countries' obligations are not the ones that took them on, and they will not be around at the start of the next century to make new mistakes. Furthermore, the IDDC will not "bail out" the banks, though the banks are likely to do better than by letting the debt problem drag on.

The free-rider problem needs to be taken more seriously. If one bank believes that the rest will grant debt relief, bilaterally or through an IDDC, improving the debtor's ability to meet its remaining obligations, it has an incentive to hang back.

The obvious solution, mandatory participation by the banks, is not politically feasible. It is hard enough to shift risk from private to official creditors, let alone to shift from voluntary to mandatory debt reduction. But the problem may be less serious than commonly supposed.

Although debt reduction will raise the debtors' ability to meet their remaining obligations, some of the benefits will accrue to the IDDC. In fact, banks that hang back may be hurt, because debtor governments may be less concerned to meet their obligations to those banks than to the IDDC, and the governments sponsoring the IDDC will not be particularly interested in upholding the claims of banks that decline to do business with it. In other words, it may be possible to subordinate old debt to new debt when the new debt is owed to the IDDC, not formally by abrogating existing debt contracts, but informally by casting doubt on the likelihood that those contracts will be honored.

Finally, the sponsors of the IDDC can limit the free-rider problem by offering incentives for banks to participate and penalizing those that don't. Participants can be allowed to amortize their losses, as proposed above. Nonparticipants can be required to mark remaining debt to market and thus acknowledge larger losses.[10] In short, the sponsors and debtors can make sure that the IDDC appropriates most of the increase in the value of the debt resulting from debt relief and thus reduce the value of the old debt still outstanding.

Critics have been slow to spot another problem. They endorse the view that participating debtors be subject to some form of conditionality—that they have a bargain with the IMF or take structural-adjustment loans from the World Bank. It may be very hard, however, to condition debt relief. IMF drawings and World Bank structural-adjustment loans are disbursed in tranches, not in a lump sum, and disbursements can be halted if policy commitments are not met. It is rather difficult to do this with debt relief. It would be foolish, indeed, to withdraw debt relief from governments that fail to meet their policy commitments, as that would merely make it harder for them to do so. It may make sense, however, for the IDDC to grant relief provisionally and modestly at first, so that debtors are made to meet their policy commitments to qualify for permanent, full-scale relief. This argues for providing provisional relief by reducing the interest rate payable to the IDDC, then moving to permanent relief by writing down the claims themselves by more than the counterpart of the initial interest-rate reduction.

Two questions remain: Would the creation of an IDDC interfere with the resumption of voluntary lending? Why should the U.S. taxpayer get involved?

The first is easily answered. Most of the numbers suggest that the heavily indebted countries are farther from returning to creditworthiness than they were at the start of the debt crisis. There has been no concerted lending to small debtors for some years, and the large debtors have continued to qualify only because banks have been reluctant to acknowledge the losses they would face if Argentina, Brazil, and Mexico could not borrow enough to keep on paying interest. If the IDDC can facilitate large-scale debt relief, the debtors will be able to manage their economies more effectively, and this will hasten, not delay, the return to creditworthiness.

The second question has two answers. First, the risks assumed by the sponsoring countries and their taxpayers are not large insofar as debtors lie on the downward-sloping side of the Debt Relief Laffer Curve. Debt relief reduces the risk by raising the value of the debt. Second, taxpayers are already involved. They take on risks directly whenever the World Bank makes another loan to one of the heavily indebted countries, and they take them on indirectly whenever the commercial banks engage in additional concerted lending. But there are larger issues. The taxpayers are involved because the debt problem impinges on foreign policy, the prospects for democracy in the debtor countries, and the outlook for reducing imbalances in the world economy. Much has been said about the need for the newly industrialized countries of Asia to liberalize their trade regimes and thus help to reduce the U.S. trade deficit. The debtor countries could make an equally important contribution if their foreign-exchange earnings were not eaten by their interest payments and their economies could grow more rapidly.

[1]This view is best represented in Cline (1984). The literature on debt is vast and space in this journal is precious, so I do not cite all of the relevant sources. Good bibliographies are found in Cohen (1989) and Dornbusch (1988), which also supplies a compact history of the debt problem; the theoretical literature is surveyed by Eaton, Gersovitz, and Stiglitz (1986).

[2]For reasons and possible results, see Guttentag and Herring (1988).

[3]On the early evolution of the menu approach, see World Bank (1988); on the Brazilian agreement, see Lamdany (1988a).

[4]Under the agreement announced in July 1989, banks will have three main options: (1) To swap Mexican debt for new long-term bonds at a 35 percent discount; Mexico will buy zero-coupon U.S. Treasury securities to guarantee the principal. (2) To switch from floating-rate debt, paying about 10 percent when the agreement was announced, to new fixed-rate debt paying $6\frac{1}{4}$ percent, without any change in face value; the interest rate will rise after 1996 if higher oil prices raise Mexico's oil revenues in real terms. (3) To retain their present claims but make new loans to Mexico over the next four years by enough to raise those claims by 25 percent; they will thus capitalize some of Mexico's debt-service payments. Interest payments under the first two options will be covered by a rolling 18-month guarantee, backed by Mexican deposits in escrow accounts. The agreement has to be ratified by individual banks, and some time will pass before we know how much of Mexico's debt will be covered by each option. Bankers forecast that those holding about 60 percent of the debt will take the first option, with the rest divided evenly between the other two. In light of experience with earlier debt-for-bond swaps, cited later in this paper, the 60 percent figure seems high. Even if the forecast is accurate, however, the whole package will reduce the face value of the debt by just 16 percent (the 35 percent reduction in face value ×60 percent participation *less* the 25 percent increase in exposure ×20 percent participation), and it will reduce the present value of the debt by only 23 percent (if the interest rate cut on the other 20 percent is treated as being roughly equivalent to a 35 percent reduction in face value).

[5]The argument that follows is based on the model in Kenen (1989). A similar argument is made by Corden (1988a). The analysis depends crucially on one assumption. The penalties imposed when a debtor repudiates get weaker if they are delayed. Otherwise, the debtor would repudiate sooner rather than later. The use of the framework developed in the text also helps to answer the objections raised by Bulow and Rogoff (1988, 1989). Their case against debt buybacks is based on two premises: (1) Debtors and creditors hold identical views about the future, so that prices prevailing in the secondary market represent debtors' valuations of their obligations, as well as creditors' valuations of their claims. Under this assumption, a buyback at the market price cannot benefit a debtor unless the debtor can expect to raise its real income by reducing the inefficiencies associated with a large debt overhang. (2) If those inefficiencies reflect unexploited investment opportunities, a debtor would do better to use its scarce resources for capital formation than for debt reduction. In Kenen (1989), however, valuations by debtors and creditors differ, because the costs of repudiation borne by debtors do not directly raise the value of the creditors' claims, and I go on to show that a buyback at the market price can be mutually beneficial even under conditions resembling those embodied in the Bulow-Rogoff model. It can raise the debtor's income even when the opportunity costs of using scarce resources to buy back debt are larger at the margin than the costs of being in debt, including the income-depressing effects of a large debt overhang.

[6]There are at least two reasons for differences between the market's valuations and those at which debtors and creditors will do business with each other. (1) If creditors believe that they can seize the debtor's assets in the event of default or repudiation, the market price will reflect the present value of the gross debt *plus* the value of the assets that creditors can seize in the event of repudiation—and the debtor's assets do not change when creditors swap debt in the secondary market. But the debtor's assets fall when it uses some of its assets to buy back debt, and creditors will want to be compensated for the fall in the stock of assets that they can expect to seize if the debtor repudiates the rest of its debt; Froot (1989) and Kenen (1989). (2) The price at which the debtor can buy back debt for cash or trade it for new debt depends on both parties' expectations, whereas the market price depends on the creditors' expectations. All creditors do not have the same expectations, which is indeed one reason for the existence of a secondary market. Corden (1988b)

studies the implications of differences between debtors' and creditors' expectations; Williamson (1989) examines the implications of heterogeneity in the creditors' expectations.

[7]Lamdany (1988b) points out, however, that some of the money was official aid earmarked for Bolivia, so the Bolivians had to act as though they were using their own resources. Sachs (1988) reports that banks agreed to a very large discount in the Bolivian case only under pressure from U.S. regulators. (It should perhaps be noted that Mexico may have to lay out some $7 billion to implement its new agreement with the banks—$3 billion for zero-coupon bonds to guarantee principal and $4 billion more to fund the escrow accounts that back up the rolling interest-payment guarantee. These figures reflect the assumption in Note 4 that banks holding 80 percent of Mexico's debt will take the debt-reducing options and thus cut the present value of their claims on Mexico by 35 percent. To buy back 80 percent of the debt at a 35 percent discount, Mexico would have to lay out some $28 billion. Buybacks are expensive.)

[8]The proposal was introduced earlier (Kenen, 1982), but so was its main rival. Felix Rohatyn published a similar plan early in 1983, but an early version appeared some months before (Rohatyn, 1982, 1983). Credit or blame may really belong to G. C. Rodney Leach, then General Manager of the Trade Development Bank in London, whose proposal appears in a letter circulated late in 1982, and his plan had some features that have come up again. Banks would be shareholders in his institution, as in the one proposed by Robinson (1988). A revised version of my own plan was circulated privately in 1985, and another revision was published in Kenen (1988); it is the one described in the text.

[9]The newest version of this variant comes from L. William Seidman, chairman of the Federal Deposit Insurance Corporation, who would elicit the required capital from the IMF, the World Bank, governments, and commercial banks, but would charge the banks an annual premium to insure their holdings of the debtor's bonds (*The New York Times*, July 10, 1989). An earlier version by Rotberg (1988) was designed initially to encourage new bank lending but could be adapted to insure bond issues by the debtors.

[10]Corden (1988b) makes the same suggestion, and it is my reason for reversing the position I took in earlier presentations that banks should not be made to write down their remaining claims.

References

Bulow, Jeremy, and Kenneth Rogoff, "The Buyback Boondoggle," *Brookings Papers on Economic Activity*, 1988, *2*, 675–98.

Bulow, Jeremy, and Kenneth Rogoff, "Sovereign Debt Repurchases: No Cure for Overhang," Working Paper 2850. Cambridge: National Bureau of Economic Research, February 1989.

Cline, William R., *International Debt: Systemic Risk and Policy Response*. Washington: Institute for International Economics, 1984.

Cohen, Benjamin J., "LDC Debt: A Middle Way," *Essays in International Finance, 173*. Princeton: International Finance Section, Princeton University, 1989.

Corden, W. Max, "Debt Relief and Adjustment Incentives," *International Monetary Fund Staff Papers*, December 1988a, *35*, 628–43.

Corden, W. Max, "An International Debt Facility?," *International Monetary Fund Staff Papers*, September 1988b, *35*, 401–21.

Dornbusch, Rudiger, "Our LDC Debts," in Feldstein, Martin, ed., *The United States in the World Economy*. Chicago: University of Chicago Press for The National Bureau of Economic Research, 1988.

Eaton, Jonathan, and Mark Gersovitz, "Debt with Potential Repudiation," *Review of Economic Studies*, March 1981, *48*, 289–309.

Eaton, Jonathan, Mark Gersovitz, and Joseph E. Stiglitz, "The Pure Theory of Country Risk," *European Economic Review*, June 1986, *30*, 481–513.

Fischer, Stanley, "Resolving the International Debt Crisis," in Sachs, Jeffrey, ed., *Developing Country Debt and Economic Performance*. Chicago: University of Chicago Press, 1989.

Froot, Kenneth A., "Buybacks, Exit Bonds, and the Optimality of Debt and Liquidity Relief," *International Economic Review*, February 1989, *30*, 49–70.

Guttentag, Jack, and Richard Herring, "Provisioning, Charge-Offs, and the Willingness to Lend," *Essays in International Finance, 172*. Princeton: International Finance Section, Princeton University, 1988.

Kenen, Peter B., "National Economic Policy, International Adjustment, and Exchange Rates," *Foreign Exchange Service Conference Proceedings*. Philadelphia: Wharton Econometric Forecasting Associates, Fall 1982.

Kenen, Peter B., "Third-World Debt: Sharing the Burden. A Bailout Plan for the Banks," *The New York Times*, March 6, 1983.

Kenen, Peter B., "A Proposal for Reducing Debt Burdens for Developing Countries," in Denoon, David B. H., ed., *Changing Capital Markets and the Global Economy*. Philadelphia: Global Interdependence Center, 1988.

Kenen, Peter B., "Debt Buybacks and Forgiveness in a Model with Voluntary Repudiation," Working Paper 89-1. Princeton: International Finance Section, Princeton University, July 1989.

Krugman, Paul R., "Market-Based Debt-

Reduction Schemes." In Frenkel, Jacob A., Michael P. Dooley, and Peter Wickham, eds., *Analytical Issues in Debt*. Washington D.C.: International Monetary Fund, 1989.

Lamdany, Ruben, "The Brazil Financing Package: Main Components and Lessons for the Future," unpublished manuscript, September 1988a.

Lamdany, Ruben, "Bolivia, Mexico, and Beyond...," unpublished manuscript, June 1988b.

Rhodes, William R., "An Insider's Reflection on the Brazilian Debt Package," *The Wall Street Journal*, October 14, 1988.

Robinson, James D., "A Comprehensive Agenda for LDC Debt and World Trade Growth," *Amex Bank Review Special Papers, 13*. London: American Express Bank, March 1988.

Rohatyn, Felix G., "The State of the Banks," *New York Review of Books*, November 4, 1982.

Rohatyn, Felix G., "A Plan for Stretching Out Global Debt," *Business Week*, February 28, 1983.

Rotberg, Eugene H., *Toward a Solution to the Debt Crisis*. New York: Merrill Lynch & Co., May 1988.

Sachs, Jeffrey, "Comprehensive Debt Retirement: The Bolivian Example," *Brookings Papers on Economic Activity*, 1988, *2*, 705–13.

Sachs, Jeffrey, "Making the Brady Plan Work," *Foreign Affairs*, Summer 1989a, *68*, 87–104.

Sachs, Jeffrey, "Conditionality, Debt Relief, and the Developing Country Debt Crisis," in Sachs, Jeffrey, ed., *Developing Country Debt and Economic Performance*. Chicago: University of Chicago Press, 1989b.

Williamson, John, "Voluntary Approaches to Debt Relief," *Policy Analyses in International Economics, 25*, Revised Edition. Washington D.C.: Institute for International Economics, 1989.

World Bank, *Market-Based Menu Approach*. Washington D.C.: World Bank Debt Management and Financial Advisory Services Department, September 1988.

Cleaning up Third World Debt Without Getting Taken to the Cleaners

Jeremy Bulow
and Kenneth Rogoff

Should taxpayers of wealthy countries finance a leveraged buyout of third world debt? The case for establishing an international debt discount facility rests on the belief that the overhang of foreign commercial bank debt is stifling growth in the Highly Indebted Countries,[1] and that coordination problems among private sector banks are blocking efficiency-enhancing debt reduction schemes.[2] Thus there is scope for a multilateral government agency to step in, buy up the debts, and pass on the efficiency gains to struggling debtors. True, wealthy-country taxpayers would ultimately be liable for paying off the "junk" bonds issued to finance the leveraged buyout but the risks would be minimal, at least so the advocates say. Because the debt facility would buy up the debts at discount, it would be able to forgive a large enough fraction so that debtors could afford to repay the remainder.

Our contention is that a debt discount facility would in fact be a black hole for aid funds, and would yield only minimal efficiency benefits. First, the costs of buying up the debt would considerably exceed estimates based on current secondary market prices. Experiences such as the 1988 Bolivian buyback and the 1989 Mexican debt deal have shown that it is not at all easy to coerce all banks into selling at discount, and that otherwise the presence of an official buyer tends to bid up prices sharply. Second, if the track records of existing official lenders such as the World Bank are any guide, one has to doubt whether the debtor countries would continue to make any significant *net* repayments once their obligations passed into official hands. That is, sovereign debts worth $100 billion in the hands of hard-bargaining private banks may be worth only $10 billion once taken over by a lenient multilateral agency. Admittedly, our view contrasts with the conventional wisdom that multilateral lending institutions are hard money lenders and senior creditors to private banks, but the evidence on World Bank and International Monetary Fund loans during the 1980s supports us.

We also take issue with the presumption that the debt overhang is the primary cause of the growth slowdown in the Highly Indebted Countries. Indeed, the debt problem is better viewed as a symptom of poor growth rather than its primary cause. Many of the debtor countries have been hammered by adverse terms of trade shocks, and all have suffered long periods of poor economic management. In any event, it is questionable whether increased participation by creditor-country governments would expedite an efficient settlement. One can argue that it is precisely the presence of

■ *Jeremy Bulow is Professor of Economics, Graduate School of Business, Stanford University, Stanford, California. Kenneth Rogoff is Professor of Economics, University of California, Berkeley, California.*

deep-pocketed creditor-country governments in debt negotiations which has led to the present impasse, and that efficiency would best be served by having less official involvement, not more.

Our assessment of the debt crisis suggests a very different approach. Development aid should be divorced from debt negotiations and instead should be tied to countries' performance in areas such as environmental policy, drug interdiction and population control. Future aid allocations should not be disguised as loan guarantees, and the massive bond obligations of existing multilateral lenders ought to be placed on the books. Finally, we recommend reversing a number of legal and regulatory changes made in the 1970s that served to encourage the loans in the first place.

Costs of a Debt Discount Facility

As of mid-1989, the Highly Indebted Countries owed roughly $300 billion to commercial banks in government and government-guaranteed debt. These debts trade at huge discounts; e.g., Chile 36 percent, Philippines 50 percent, Brazil 70 percent, Argentina 83 percent, Peru 97 percent. Evaluated at these prices, the total market value of the bank debt is less than $100 billion.

The most optimistic assessments of the taxpayer cost of a debt discount facility are based on the assumption that (a) the new government-backed institution would only have to pay $100 billion to buy up the debt, and (b) once two-thirds of their debt is forgiven, the Highly Indebted Countries will pay off the remaining debt like clockwork. Thus the agency will generate enough income to pay off most or all of the interest on the bonds issued to finance the repurchase. Wealthy-country taxpayers would at most be responsible for putting up an initial $10 billion to capitalize the institution. Unfortunately, these calculations rest on some shaky assumptions.

How Much Would Banks Be Paid?

Before asking what price a multilateral debt facility would have to pay banks in a buyout, it's helpful to consider first what happens when a highly indebted country repurchases a portion of its own debt on the open market. Many countries have experimented with this approach over the past three years and buybacks are an important element of the current official approach to debt, the so-called Brady plan.

Open market buybacks are superficially appealing. What can go wrong if a country such as Peru, whose debt trades at less than five cents on the dollar, uses $1 worth of aid money to buy back $20 worth of debt? The basic problem is that the value to a highly indebted country of retiring a marginal dollar of its debt is generally far less than its market price. To consider an extreme example, consider a country which owes $1 billion, but with certainty will only be able to pay $100 million. In this case, the debtor would not benefit at all from a repurchase which knocks its debt down to $500 million; all that will happen is that the price of its remaining debt will rise to 20 cents. Indeed, this is also the price the country will have to pay in the buyback.

In fact, one can argue that this is precisely what happened in March 1988 when Bolivia repurchased roughly half of its $670 million dollar debt. Prior to the repurchase, Bolivia's $670 million in debt traded at 6 cents for a total market value of $40.2 million. After expending $34 million to buy back $308 million of its debt, the remaining $362 million traded at 11 cents, for a total market value of $39.8 million. (See Bulow and Rogoff, 1988a.)

Realistically, of course, there is generally some positive probability that the debtor country will repay the reduced debt in full. One also has to consider factors such as the benefits of reducing debt overhang, and the returns to alternative investments. For most of the Highly Indebted Countries, however, taking these factors into account does not appear to reverse the basic conclusion that open-market buybacks dissipate resources. (See Bulow and Rogoff, 1988a.) This criticism generalizes to all forms of open-market repurchases including debt-for-equity swaps and even debt-for-nature swaps. (In the latter, a conservation group repurchases some of the country's debt and swaps it back for local currency bonds. The interest from the bonds is then designated for funding domestic conservation programs. The implication of our analysis is that it is more efficient for a conservation group to donate funds directly to the country.)

A debt discount facility would face very similar problems to those described above. Banks will know that the new multilateral agency plans to forgive part of the debt it buys up, so that any remaining debt will appreciate. Thus, to induce them to tender voluntarily, the debt discount facility will have to pay banks a large premium. One way to finesse this problem, of course, would be for creditor country governments to jointly coerce the banks into selling at a low price. It is extremely unclear whether this is possible, however, given that private banks have both significant legal rights and substantial political clout in most creditor countries. Note that the United States could not accomplish much by acting unilaterally. Its banks hold only a quarter of the debt; even in the case of Latin America, they hold only a third.

Another approach would be to make the debt discount facility's claims senior to those of any private creditors who refuse to sell. Many advocates of a debt discount facility seem to see this as a real possibility. After all, aren't the debts of the existing multilateral institutions already senior to private debt?

The conventional view that the International Monetary Fund and the World Bank are senior debtors is based on the observation that few countries have ever explicitly defaulted on their loans from these institutions. But then few borrowers have ever been required to make repayments over any sustained period. During 1982–1987, for example, multilateral official creditors re-lent $1.29 to the Highly Indebted Countries for every dollar repaid (World Bank, 1988). Few debtors will default on repayments from creditors who are always relending all repayments, and doling out new "loans" beside.

Over the same period when the multilateral institutions were receiving negative net repayments, the commercial banks succeeded in extracting net repayments of more than 50 cents for every dollar owed. Given their experience with existing multilateral institutions, it will not be easy to convince bankers that their claims will be junior to those of the new debt facility. Thus we conclude that the facility would probably have to pay considerably in excess of $100 billion for the initial buyback.

How Much Will Debtors Repay the Debt Discount Facility?

Our views on the seniority of IMF and World Bank debt translate into similar skepticism about the odds of seeing the developing countries make substantial net repayments to a multilateral debt discount facility. In all likelihood, creditor-country taxpayers would find themselves having to pay off the facility's bonds, a sum far exceeding their initial capital contribution.

Stripping away debt accounting conventions, it is simply hard to imagine that funds will flow from developing-country governments to industrialized-country governments for any extended period. In the past, the developing countries have consistently succeeded in extracting positive net intergovernmental transfers. The mere creation of some paper claims will not change the fundamental bargaining factors which govern relations between the governments.

Private banks have proven to be much tougher bargainers than public lending institutions. Thus debt worth $100 billion in the hands of private banks would likely be worth much less in the hands of a multilateral debt discount facility.

Is Public Intervention into Debt Efficiency-Enhancing?

Most of the debate on developing-country debt is not over whether creditor country governments should intervene, but how they should do it. Since the onset of the debt crisis in 1982, academics, bankers and statesmen have advanced literally hundreds of financial engineering schemes for resolving the problem. The common presumption is that subsidies from industrialized country taxpayers are needed to induce banks and debtor countries to make mutually beneficial, efficiency-enhancing deals.

The fact is that the International Monetary Fund, the World Bank and the industrialized country governments have been deeply enmeshed in private debt negotiations for almost eight years, and that they have already kicked in tens of billions of dollars in aid money. Far from speeding compromise, the presence of official creditors has tended to ossify the negotiating position of the banks and countries.[3]

Consider what happens when an owner and a buyer try to agree on the price of a house. The owner may ask for $205,000 while the buyer may offer $195,000. If there were no parties involved in the negotiations, the two sides might quickly settle on a sale price of $200,000. But what if there is a real estate broker involved? Each party would have an incentive to take a more intransigent posture, hoping that the broker can be convinced to kick in part of the commission to sweeten the deal. The presence of an outside party with a vested interest can actually complicate negotiations.

Of course, North-South relations transcend the debt crisis. It may be a practical impossibility for creditor-country governments to stay out of negotiations, even if they want to. Still, the less creditor-country governments are involved in the bargaining over private debt, the better.

Debt Overhang

What about the view that the overhang of foreign debt is stifling growth in the Highly Indebted Countries, and that alleviating the overhang would lead to an investment boom? This theory suggests that once a large fraction of their debt is forgiven, debtor countries will easily generate enough income to pay off (more precisely, to be willing to pay off) their remaining obligations, and our estimates of the costs of a debt discount facility are overblown. Our assessment of the post-1982 debt crisis is that it is a symptom of the HICs' growth problems, not the principal cause. Several observations should help support this latter view.

It is often overlooked that a large fraction of the growth shortfall in the Highly Indebted Countries occurred from 1980 to 1983, *before* the countries were required to make any significant debt repayments. The worldwide recession of 1980–82, caused in part by a steep rise in world interest rates, was a disaster for the HICs. Their real per capita GDP plummeted by 9.7 percent between 1980 and 1983 (International Monetary Fund, 1989, Table A6). This period also marked the onset of a prolonged deterioration in the terms of trade for developing countries. After climbing by 5.5 percent per year during the 1970s, the terms of trade for the Highly Indebted Countries fell by 3.7 percent annually between 1980 and 1988.[4]

The debt crisis began only after almost three years of dismal growth. Indeed, during 1980–1982, the Highly Indebted Countries were still receiving substantial net resource transfers from abroad; they received $24 billion more in new long-term loans than they were required to repay in principal and interest. Even as late as 1983, the HICs made net repayments on government and government-guaranteed long term debt of .02 percent of GDP (World Bank, 1988). Substantial net transfers abroad began only in 1984, averaging 2.5 percent of GDP from 1984–1988. It is true that real growth in per capita GDP has averaged an unsatisfactory 0.5 percent since then, but on the other hand the HICs' terms of trade deteriorated about as rapidly between 1983 and 1988 as between 1980 and 1983 (International Monetary Fund, 1989, Table A6).

Another seldom-noted fact is that in comparison with earlier periods, the current level of investment in the HICs is not extraordinarily low. Consider the case of Latin America, which accounts for well over half the problem loans. During the 1960–73 era, before the debt buildup began in earnest, Latin American investment averaged roughly 20 percent of GDP. The ratio for 1987 was roughly two points lower, at 18.2 percent. But the investment ratio for industrialized countries has fallen even more sharply, from over 24 percent in 1960–73 to 20.7 in 1987.[5] It is only relative to the peaks of the late 1970s that Latin American investment today looks so low. Moreover, the difference between periods may be exaggerated. As Carlos Diaz-Alejandro (1984) and others have emphasized, the investment data for the 1970s includes an exceptionally large amount of government consumption.

Also, it would be wrong to blame any investment shortfall solely on the unwillingness of private banks to invest in the region. Latin America's own citizens have the resources needed to increase investment if profitable opportunities are available. Several years before the debt crisis began, Latin citizens began moving tremendous sums of money out of their countries (Cumby and Levich, 1987). Estimates of total capital flight, including money diverted to foreign direct investment such as corporate stock and Florida real estate, actually exceed the book value of the countries' government and government-guaranteed foreign bank debt, as shown in Table 1. Table 2 shows that by the end of 1988, the $100 billion-plus of Latin American *bank deposits alone* held in the North approximated the market value of this debt (World Bank, 1989b). Thus if one aggregates the government and private sectors, some "highly indebted" Latin American countries may even be net creditors!

Given that so much capital flight preceded the debt crisis, one should be reluctant to accept the popular view that the banks' demands for debt repayment were the major factor contributing to capital flight. We offer an alternative story. High interest rates abroad, combined with low commodity prices and misguided economic policies discouraged Latin citizens from making domestic investments. This made bank loans less secure and precipitated demands for repayment.

At a casual level, it is certainly difficult to detect a strong relationship between the amount a highly indebted country has devoted to debt repayment and its growth rate. Chile, perhaps Latin America's most conscientious repayer in recent years, saw real per capita GDP grow by 3.5 percent per year from 1983–1988 (Latin Finance, 1989). In contrast, Argentina stopped making debt repayments entirely in April 1988 and experienced a near total collapse of its economy over the next 18 months. Peru, which stopped repaying debt in 1986, did enjoy two years of solid growth until it ran out of foreign currency reserves. After that, however, its economy deteriorated sharply (Dornbusch, 1989). Of course, the Republic of Korea, considered by many a problem debtor at the onset of the debt crisis, enjoyed tremendous growth while making the largest debt payments in the world from 1986 to 1987.

Table 1
Capital Flight
(In billions of 1987 dollars)

	Flight Capital Assets	As Percentage of Long Term Public and Publicly Guaranteed Debt
Argentina	$46	111%
Bolivia	2	178
Brazil	31	46
Chile	2	17
Colombia	7	103
Ecuador	7	115
Ivory Coast	0	0
Mexico	84	114
Morocco	3	54
Nigeria	20	136
Peru	2	27
Philippines	23	188
Uruguay	4	159
Venezuela	58	240
Yugoslavia	6	79
Total	295	103

Sources: Flight Capital, Morgan Stanley as cited in "The International Economy," July/August 1989. Debt, World Debt Tables, 1988–89 edition. Data refer to external debt to private creditors.

The Dubious Equity Grounds for a Debt Bailout

Northern policy makers should not be swayed by "moral" arguments that they should contribute to wiping out the debt. The average per capita income in the 17 Highly Indebted Countries was $1430 in 1987. This compares with $470 in developing East Asia and $290 in South Asia; booming Thailand's per capita GNP was only $850. While South Korea's per capita income (measured in dollars) caught up to Argentina's in 1986, many nontraded goods such as housing are far more expensive in Korea, and the average worker toils longer and harder. Even Bolivia, South America's basket case, has twice the per capita income of India (World Bank, 1989a).

Another consideration which dictates against increasing aid to Latin America at the expense of other regions is that incomes in Latin America are much less evenly distributed than in Asia. If the 1970s are any guide, the poorer half of the Latin American population will receive only a meager share of the benefits of any new net flows to the region.

Fundamentally, decisions about where to provide foreign aid in the 1990s should not be straightjacketed by the decisions commercial bank lending officers made in the 1970s. Why should wealthy Brazil, which borrowed to finance pharaonic investments in the 1970s, receive scarce aid funds that might otherwise go to poor but growing Thailand or impoverished Africa?

Table 2
Net Northern commercial bank claims on developing countries
(In millions of dollars)

Country	Commercial Bank Claims (1)	Market Value of Bank Claims (2)	Commercial Bank Liabilities (3)
Argentina	35,090	7,369	11,735
Bolivia	424	42	568
Brazil	75,891	30,356	16,181
Chile	11,011	6,276	4,292
Colombia	6,946	3,994	5,795
Costa Rica	866	104	276
Ecuador	4,874	609	1,237
Ivory Coast	3,177	731	2,218
Jamaica	613	245	557
Mexico	69,315	29,632	24,466
Morocco	5,081	2,439	1,411
Nigeria	8,869	2,040	2,975
Peru	4,555	228	2,723
Philippines	12,267	6,011	3,984
Uruguay	2,019	1,201	3,547
Venezuela	25,523	10,401	15,907
Yugoslavia	9,013	4,056	3,806
17 HICs	275,534	105,734	101,678

Sources: Columns (1) and (3), World Bank, *Quarterly Review* (June 1989). Column (2), computed by multiplying column (1) by prices from Salomon Brothers, "Indicative Prices for Less Developed Country Bank Loans," December 22, 1988. Market value may be underestimated because of the greater value of trade credits. Commercial bank liabilities consist of Latin deposits held in foreign commercial banks, including both government and private deposits.

Aid and Debt in the 1990s

We believe that the main focus of aid to developing countries should be to encourage responsible policies towards the environment, population growth, and other areas where third world actions create major externalities. Mexico's population explosion, Colombia's drug enforcement program, and Brazil's policies towards deforestation will have a far greater impact on northern welfare in the next century than any policies these countries might adopt towards their foreign bank debts. The industrialized countries can ill afford to tie up huge quantities of aid resources in grandiose debt reduction schemes at a time when funds are urgently needed for negotiating solutions to far more important problems.

A concrete method for rechanneling aid would be to create an International Citizenship Fund as a new grant-making arm of the World Bank. Aid from the ICF would be completely independent of a country's performance in "repaying" its existing World Bank and IMF loans. Industrialized country contributions to the new facility could be based on similar criteria to those used for making grants to developing countries. For example, industrialized countries might be given incentives to reduce the burning of fossil fuels, and to curtail the production of chlorofluorocarbons and other halons. Contributions to drug eradication programs could be based on industrialized country drug use. Subjecting the industrialized countries to requirements parallel to those for developing countries would surely make the ICF more politically palatable in the third world.

Restructure Official Debt

To help avoid having ICF aid become entangled with existing IMF and World Bank loans, it is important to reform the financial structure of these agencies. In many respects, the World Bank is capitalized like the U.S. savings and loan associations of the 1980s. That is, it borrows most of its money from private sources using member-country government guarantees as collateral. Little of the World Banks's subscribed capital is paid in directly; for example, of the $74.8 billion capital increase approved in April 1988, only 3 percent is to be paid in capital. The remainder will be "callable" capital, which the member countries must pay only if the World Bank cannot meet its financial obligations.[6]

Since most outstanding official loans will never really be repaid anyway, these debts should be written down. This would force the World Bank's sponsors to assume the Bank's bond liabilities directly, and put these costs "on the books." Policymakers and taxpayers would then have a clearer picture about the amount of aid they are providing, and the IMF and World Bank staff would be able to focus on development issues without becoming entangled in debt accounting.

Leave Private Debt Hanging

Our debt plan focuses on restructuring official "lending." Of course, debtors would be free to use aid money to negotiate efficient debt reduction deals with the private creditors. (We are assuming that the incentive payments required to induce countries to conform with their citizenship targets would considerably exceed countries' net internal costs.) With the decks cleared of official creditors, there would be nothing blocking the very competent country and bank negotiators from designing their own efficient debt reduction plans. However, since our approach enables debtors to threaten to use their funds for other purposes, it should allow them to bargain for better terms than when aid funds are tied to buybacks.

In fact, we suspect that few debtors would divert substantial resources to debt reduction, and that most of the private debt would be left hanging. Though some third-world leaders find it politically popular to blame all their countries' problems on foreign debt, most realize that debt elimination would be no cure-all, and that other issues deserve equal or greater attention.

Reform the Laws on Private Lending

There is a tendency to think of the 1970s as the halcyon days of sovereign lending, when developing countries were able to borrow vast sums in world capital markets. Back then, many creditor-country governments considered banks' efforts to "recycle" petrodollars praiseworthy and enacted legal changes to help the market develop. The United States, for example, passed the Foreign Sovereign Immunities Act in 1976, and Great Britain passed the similar State Immunity Act of 1978. These laws made it easier for foreign sovereigns to borrow under the umbrella of the industrialized countries' legal systems, by strengthening and clarifying the rights of a sovereign's creditors in default. The main weapon creditors have is the ability to seize assets abroad; this allows them to make it difficult for a country to default and still enjoy the full benefits of integration into world goods and financial markets.[7]

The expansion of the sovereign debt market in the 1970s was really quite dramatic. As of 1970, Argentina, Brazil, and Mexico combined owed their foreign private creditors roughly $6 billion in principal. By 1982, however, the annual interest bill for Mexico alone had topped $10 billion. Table 3 should give an idea of the explosive growth of third world debt from 1970 to 1982.

Table 3

The explosive growth of Third World debt

(In millions of dollars)

	1970		1982	
	Interest	*Principal*	*Interest*	*Principal*
Argentina	88	1,494	1,167	15,846
Brazil	81	2,224	5,373	50,087
Chile	39	886	485	4,063
Mexico	156	2,047	5,754	44,683
Venezuela	20	362	1,611	11,930
17 HICs	512	10,228	17,971	174,296

Source: World Debt Tables, 1988–89 edition, volumes 1 and 2. Data refer to public and publicly guaranteed long term debts to private creditors.

In the sober light of the 1990s, it is far from clear whether official policy should have encouraged these loans. Though some did go to finance worthwhile investment projects, a very large percentage went to finance conspicuously unpromising government investment projects and capital flight. Indeed as we discussed above, over much of the period wealthy Latin citizens were "re-recycling" the loan money out of their countries as fast as the banks were recycling it in. In other cases, bank loans were used to temporarily support unpopular dictatorships, such as in Argentina or the Philippines.

The experience of the 1970s suggests that in the future, industrialized countries should try to steer adjudication of developing-country loans into debtor-country courts. Foreign creditors would then presumably have the same types of recourse in default as domestic creditors now have. To accomplish this end, some of the legal changes adopted in the 1970s must be reversed.

Conclusions

Many of our criticisms of an international debt facility apply with equal force to the March 1989 plan of Treasury Secretary Nicholas Brady. Under the Brady blueprint, governments of the industrialized countries are planning to devote at least $30 billion to $40 billion over the next three years to help buy back third world debt at discount. Recent academic research on buybacks suggest that a very substantial fraction of these funds will end up in the hands of private banks, without benefiting debtors. Even if this were not the case, it is hard to see why such a large fraction of world aid budgets should necessarily go to middle-income countries with large bank debts.

In contrast, the premise of our debt strategy is that most aid money should be devoted to environmental problems, population control, and other issues in North-South relations that involve externalities. By offering a flow of funds conditional on meeting environmental targets, rather than the large one-time commitment payment needed for a leveraged buyout of debt, donors will have more power to enforce agreements with aid recipients. Creating a new grant-making arm of the World Bank, an International Citizen Fund, is one way to accomplish this goal. It would also help divorce official aid payments from negotiations between debtor nations and private banks, and so streamline the bargaining process.

Any excess foreign exchange countries earn by meeting their international citizenship targets could be spent in whatever manner they think best. If a country does decide to use its aid to negotiate a debt reduction deal, its ability to redirect funds to other areas should enable it to negotiate more attractive terms.

Finally, by preventing countries from forfeiting their sovereign immunity status when they negotiate future loans, our plan will effectively make new debt contracts enforceable only in debtor country courts. Investors will only lend if they perceive that there will be a strong political consensus to repay. Current leaders will not be able to indenture the income of future generations quite so easily, and the imprudent borrowing policies of the 1970s could not be repeated.

■ *The authors are grateful to Carl Shapiro, Joseph Stiglitz, Lawrence Summers, and Timothy Taylor for helpful comments, and to the National Science Foundation, the Sloan Foundation, and Bradley Foundation for financial support.*

[1]The World Bank's list of 17 Highly Indebted Countries includes Argentina, Bolivia, Brazil, Chile, Colombia, Costa Rica, Côte d'Ivoire, Ecuador, Jamaica, Mexico, Morocco, Nigeria, Peru, Philippines, Uruguay, Venezuela and Yugoslavia.

[2]The term International Debt Discount Facility was coined by Peter Kenen in his pioneering 1983 proposal; since then dozens of related plans have been advanced.

[3]Bulow and Rogoff (1988b) present a dynamic bargaining-theoretic model of the three way negotiations between creditor banks, debtor countries and creditor country taxpayers.

[4]International Monetary Fund, *World Economic Outlook* (April 1989), table A28, P. 154. Implicitly, we are treating the Highly Indebted Countries, which are small in comparison with the industrialized countries, as price takers in world markets. Of course, if a debtor country has monopoly power, then the transfer problem becomes an issue.

[5]See International Monetary Fund, *International Financial Statistics*, 1988 Yearbook pp. 168–169, and World Bank, *World Development Report 1989,* table A7, p. 149. Data for 1960–73 includes all Western Hemisphere developing countries.

[6]Of course, since the guarantees of some member states like the Highly Indebted Countries can hardly be considered "money in the Bank," the World Bank must keep its borrowings somewhat below its total callable capital.

[7]For a more detailed discussion of creditors' legal rights and the probable costs to a country of evading them, see Bulow and Rogoff (1989a). For a discussion of reputational factors underpinning sovereign loans, see Bulow and Rogoff (1989b).

References

Bulow, Jeremy, and Kenneth Rogoff, "The Buyback Boondoggle," *Brookings Papers on Economic Activity,* 1988a, *2,* pp. 675–698.

Bulow, Jeremy, and Kenneth Rogoff, "Multilateral Sovereign Debt Reschedulings," *International Monetary Fund Staff Papers,* December 1988b, *35,* pp. 644–57.

Bulow, Jeremy, and Kenneth Rogoff, "A Constant Recontracting Model of Sovereign Debt," *Journal of Political Economy,* February 1989a, *97,* pp. 155–78.

Bulow, Jeremy, and Kenneth Rogoff, "Sovereign Debt: Is to Forgive to Forget?" *American Economic Review,* March 1989b, *79,* pp. 43–50.

Cumby, Robert, and Richard M. Levich, "On the Definition and Magnitude of Recent Capital Flight," National Bureau of Economic Research Working Paper No. 2275, June 1987.

Diaz-Alejandro, Carlos F., "Latin American Debt: I Don't Think We Are in Kansas Anymore," *Brookings Papers on Economic Activity,* 1984, *2,* pp. 335–389.

Dornbusch, Rudiger, "It's Coup Time in Peru," *The International Economy,* January/February 1989, pp. 46–49.

International Monetary Fund, "International Financial Statistics: 1988 Yearbook," Washington, D.C., 1989.

International Monetary Fund, *World Economic Outlook*, Washington, D.C., April 1989.

Kenen, Peter B., "A Bailout Plan for the Banks," *New York Times*, March 6, 1983.

Latin Finance Data Bank, *Latin Finance*, June 1989, United Nations Economic Commission for Latin America and the Caribbean, table, p. 64.

Miller, Michelle B., "The World Bank: An Investor's Perspective," Salomon Brothers, New York, July 18, 1989.

World Bank, *World Debt Tables: External Debt of Developing Countries*, 1988–89 ed., Volumes 1, 2, and 3, Washington, D.C., 1988.

World Bank, *World Development Report 1989*, Washington, D.C., 1989a.

World Bank, *Quarterly Review*, June 1989b, Table 3, p. 18.

Problem 1:
National Income Accounting:
Product and Income Approaches

Name_____

Section_____

Problem 1 is designed to provide drill on the principles underlying the construction of national income accounts. Each question highlights a particular aspect of the problem of measuring national output.

1. Some of the items listed below would be counted in Net National Product when it is computed by the product approach; some would be counted in NNP as measured by the income (or earnings) approach; some should not be counted in NNP at all. In the blank following each item; write one of the letters P, Y, or N to denote the following:

P = counted in NNP as measured by the flow-of-product approach.

Y = counted in NNP as measured by the income approach.

N = not counted in NNP.

Keep in mind the difference between <u>intermediate</u> and <u>final</u> goods and services.

a. Interest payments on corporate bonds received by bond holders._____

b. A new automobile bought for pleasure driving._____

c. A new auto bought by a firm for use by salesmen._____

d. Gasoline used for pleasure driving._____

e. Gasoline used for trucks and buses._____

f. Wages of a tobacco-picker._____

g. Tobacco leaf used by a cigarette manufacturer._____

h. Increases in inventory of tobacco leaf._____

i. Tobacco leaf exported to Canada._____

j. Excise taxes on cigarettes._____

k. Fees paid to an advertising agency by a cigarette manufacturer._____

l. Salaries of employees of the advertising agency._____

m. A new atomic submarine built for the U.S. Navy._____

n. Paper clips purchased by the U.S. Treasury._____

o. Paper clips purchased by General Motors for office use. _____

Problem 1 (continued):

    p.   Land purchased as a site for a new apartment house._____

    q.   New common stock sold by a realty corporation to finance the construction of the new apartment building._____

    r.   The apartment house constructed on the site._____

    s.   Rents paid by tenants of the apartment house._____

    t.   Rents paid by tenants of a medical office building._____

    u.   Net rental income of the landlord of an office building._____

    v.   Profits of a monopolist._____

    w.   Net gains from the sale of common stock out of an individual's portfolio. _____

    x.   Inheritance of a building by an individual._____

    y.   Relief payments from the government to individuals._____

    z.   Haircuts paid for out of relief checks._____

2.   Clearly, some items are counted on the product side and other items are counted on the income side. Then why must we in principle arrive at the same total of Net National Product whether we measure from the product side or from the income side?

3.   Of the items which are counted in NNP from the product side, how do we distinguish between a consumption item and an investment item? Give an example of each from the list above.

Problem 1 (continued):

4. a. What is an <u>intermediate good</u>? an <u>intermediate service</u>? Give an example of each from the list above.

    b. Show why the counting of intermediate goods and services in NNP would lead to <u>double-counting</u>.

5. If a suit is manufactured in 1983 and sold to a consumer in 1984, is it double-counted? (That is, would it be counted on the product side of NNP in both 1983 and 1984?) Explain briefly.

6. Is it double-counting to include in NNP both the value of an apartment building constructed early in 1983 and the rents paid by tenants during the year? Explain briefly.

Problem 1 (continued):

7. a. For certain purposes, Net National Product is a more meaningful concept of the nation's output than Gross National Product. Why?

    b. Then why do official statistics stress Gross National Product (rather than NNP?)

8. Why is the item <u>indirect business taxes</u> an entry on the income side of NNP when no other taxes are so entered?

9. a. The Dept. of Commerce uses 1972 as the "base year" for measuring real national product. The price index for 1972 is therefore_____.

    b. In 1972, GNP was $1,186 billion. In 1973 GNP was $1329 billion, while the price index was about 106. Therefore, from 1972 to 1973, real GNP (rose, fell) by about (one, four, six, nine) percent.

    c. In 1980, GNP was $2633 billion, while the price index was 179. Therefore, <u>real</u> GNP for 1980 amounted to_____ billions of 1972 dollars.

    d. In 1978, GNP was $2164 billion and the price index was 150. In 1979, GNP was $2418 billion and the price index was 163. Therefore, real GNP (rose, fell) by about_____percent, from 1978 to 1979.

    e. The population of the United States rose by about 1.1 percent between 1978 and 1979. Therefore, <u>real</u> GNP <u>per capita</u> (rose, fell) by_____per-cent between 1978 and 1979.

Problem 2:   Name _____
Saving, Consumption, and Investment   Section _____

This problem deals with the nature of the propensity-to-consume of individual households and the relationship between it and the aggregate propensity-to-consume of the whole household sector. It serves to emphasize the point that all macroeconomic variables are aggregated from individual consumers, firms, and markets.

1. All families in community A have identical propensity-to-consume schedules, which are as follows:

Disposable Y	C	MPC	S	MPS
$ 0	$ 700		_____	
2000	2500	_____	_____	_____
4000	4000	_____	_____	_____
6000	5300	_____	_____	_____
8000	6500	_____	_____	_____

   a. Fill in the blanks above to show the marginal propensity-to-consume (MPC), personal saving (S), and the marginal propensity to save (MPS) at various income levels of families in community A.

   b. In this community, as a family's income rises:

      1) its expenditure on consumption (rises, falls, remains constant.)

      2) its saving (rises, falls, remains constant.)

      3) the fraction of its income spent on consumption. i.e. its average propensity-to-consume, APC, (rises, falls, remains constant.)

      4) its MPC (rises, falls, remains constant)

   c. On Figure 2-1 below plot the five points given and join them with a smooth curve to show the propensity-to-consume schedule graphically.

      Label the Schedule A. Indicate on the graph the consumption and saving of a family with an income of $8,000.

410

Problem 2 (continued):

Figure 2-1

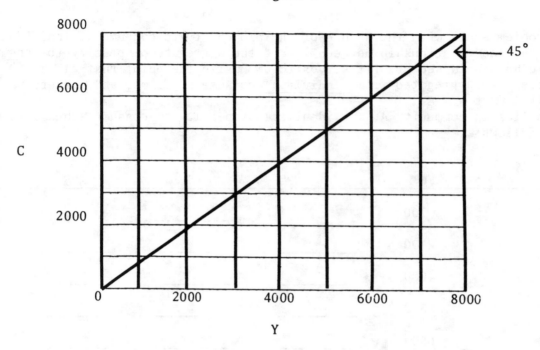

2. In community B, all families have the following propensity-to-consume schedule:

Disposable Y	Consumption	MCP
$ 0	$ 700	
2000	2300	_____
4000	3900	_____
6000	5500	_____
8000	7100	_____

a. Fill in the blanks to show the marginal propensity-to-consume.

b. In this community, as a family's income rises:

    1) its expenditure on consumption (rises, falls, remains constant.)

    2) its saving (rises, falls, remains constant.)

    3) its APC (rises, falls, remains constant)

    4) its MPC (rises, falls, remains constant.)

Problem 2 (continued):

    c. On Figure 2-1 above, draw the propensity-to-consume schedules for families in this community and label the schedule B. Geometrically, how is B different from A?

3. There are four families in A and four families in B. Aggregate disposable income is $16,000 in each community. Consider three alternative ways in which income might be distributed.

    Distribution I   - each family has an income of $4,000.

    Distribution II - two families have $2,000 each and two have $6,000 each.

    Distribution III - two families have zero income and two have $8,000 each.

    a. In community A, aggregate consumption would be:

      1) $_____with Distribution I.

      2) $_____with Distribution II.

      3) $_____with Distribution III.

    b. In community B, aggregate consumption would be:

      1) $_____with Distribution I.

      2) $_____with Distribution II.

      3) $_____with Distribution III.

    c. What do you conclude concerning the influence of income distribution on aggregate consumption in community A? In community B? Explain the differences.

Problem 2 (continued):

4. List several factors--other than psychological differences in "thriftiness"--
    which are likely to account for different levels of consumer spending by
    various families at the same level of disposable income. Explain.

5. Economists emphasize the difference between savings and investment. These two
    functions are usually performed for different reasons, by different people. A
    clearer understanding of this important proposition can be obtained by considering
    possible exceptions. Can you name a kind of household in our economy which is
    motivated to save by a desire to invest?

Problem 3:
National Income Determination

Name_____

Section_____

Consider an economy in which net corporate saving, net government receipts, and government purchases of goods and services are all always equal to zero. In such an economy, the total of consumption goods (and services) and investment goods is equal to the value of national income. Futhermore, the level of purchases by the household sector of the economy for consumption is largely determined by the level of total income for the sector. These statements along with the notion of equilibrium constitute the core of the theory of national income determination. Problem III explores the implications of equilibrium and these statements through various numerical examples.

In the economy described above, Disposal Income equals Net National Product and Personal Saving is the only form of saving. The full-employment level of NNP is $100 billion. Intended consumption varies with the level of NNP according to the following schedule (figures are billions of dollars):

NNP (or Disp. Y)	Consumption	Saving
0	10	_____
20	25	_____
40	40	_____
60	55	_____
80	70	_____
100	85	_____
120	100	_____

1. Fill in the blanks in the saving column above to show how much households would wish to save at various levels of NNP.

2. Between the 0 and $20 levels of NNP, the marginal propensity to consume is _____, and the marginal propensity to save is _____. As NNP rises, the marginal propensity to consume (rises, falls, remains constant), and the marginal propensity to save (rises, falls, remains constant). As NNP rises, the average propensity to consume (rises, falls, remains constant), while the average propensity to save (rises, falls, remains constant).

3. Using these data, plot and label on the graph below:

a) the consumption function (C)

b) the saving function (S)

Problem 3 (continued):

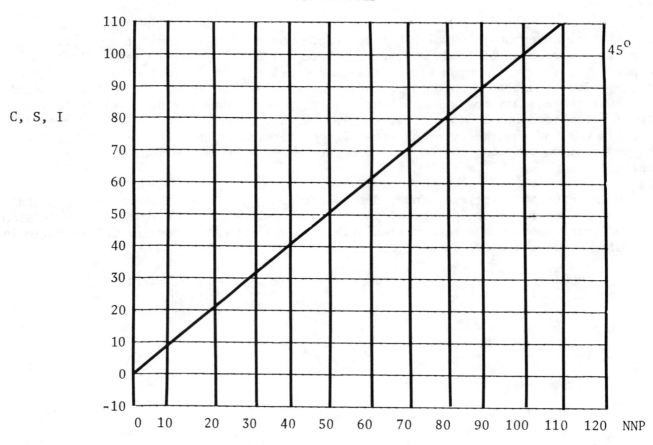

Figure 3-1

4. Assuming that intended investment is $10 at all levels of income, plot and label:

a) the investment function (I)

b) the aggregate demand function (consumption plus investment, C + I)

5. On the diagram above, the equilibrium level of NNP can be located in two ways:

a) The level of NNP at which intended saving equals intended investment.

b) The level of NNP at which intended consumption plus intended investment equals NNP.

Show the two equilibrium points on the graph; label them E_a and E_b respectively. (Be sure you understand why the two methods must yield identical results.)

6. The equilibrium level of NNP you have found should be $80. Suppose, however, that producers were misinformed and overly optimistic so they began producing at a rate of $100. With NNP at $100, aggregate demand (i.e., the sum of intended consumption and intended investment) would be $_____. Thus, firms would find that they had sold less than they produced by an amount equal to $_____; this amount would be unintended investment (i.e., including the unintended portion) would be $_____. From this situation firms would find it desirable to (expand output, contract output, leave output unchanged).

Problem 3 (continued):

7. Suppose instead that firms were overly pessimistic and therefore decided to produce at a rate of $60. Then intended consumption would be $_____; intended saving would be $_____; intended investment would be $_____; and aggregate demand would be $_____.

   a) In order to fill all orders, firms would have to engage in unintended inventory disinvestment amounting to $_____. In that event, realized saving would amount to $_____ and realized investment would be $_____.

   b) Suppose that, with output at $60, firms were unable (or unwilling) to reduce inventories and that they filled orders amounting only to $60, including all $10 of orders for investment goods. In that event, realized consumption would be $50, so unintended saving would amount to $_____. Total realized saving would be $_____, and realized investment would be $_____.

   In both case a) and case b), firms will find it desirable to (expand output, contract output, leave output unchanged).

8. a) The investment multiplier in this economy is_____.

   b) If the MPC were larger, the multiplier would be (larger, smaller, unchanged).

   c) Present a brief explanation in common sense terms of why the size of the multiplier is related to the size of MPC.

   d) With a given value of the MPC, suppose that intended investment rises when income rises (instead of being constant at all levels of income). How does the presence of induced investment alter the multiplier? Explain briefly.

9. Return to the original assumptions and suppose the economy is initially in equilibrium with NNP at $80, then:

   a) A rise in intended consumption of $1 at all levels of income will (raise by $_____, lower by $_____, leave unchanged) the equilibrium level of NNP.

Problem 3 (continued):

9. b) A rise in intended saving of $1 at all levels of income will (raise by
        $_____, lower by $_____, leave unchanged) the equilibrium
        level of NNP.

    c) A rise in intended investment of $1 at all levels of income will (raise by
        $_____, lower by $_____, leave unchanged) the equilibrium
        level of NNP.

    d) A technical innovation which raises full-employment NNP by $1 and does not
        alter intended investment will (raise by $_____, lower by $_____,
        leave unchanged) the equilibrium level of NNP.

Note on Gaps

The inflationary and deflationary gaps as used in this problem set are defined as
follows:

    Inflationary gap: If at full employment NNP, the planned C + I + G expendi-
    tures (a) would be greater than the full employment level of NNP (b) then the
    inflationary gap is (a) - (b).

    Deflationary gap: If at full employment NNP, the planned C + I + G expendi-
    tures (a) would be less than full employment NNP, (b) then the deflationary gap
    is (b) - (a).

10. Suppose that full employment NNP in this economy is $100. Given the aggregate
    demand function (C + I) that you graphed in Figure 3-1, the economy has (an in-
    flationary gap of $_____, a deflationary gap of $_____, no gap).
    The gap would be eliminated and equilibrium NNP would rise to the full-employment
    level of $100, if:

    a) intended consumption at all levels of income (rose, fell) by $_____.

    or b) intended saving at all levels of income (rose, fell) by $_____.

    or c) intended investment at all levels of income (rose, fell) by $_____.

11. Suppose equilibrium NNP does in fact rise to the full-employment level as a result
    of one of the possible autonomous changes listed in 10.

    a) Could any further change in intended consumption, intended saving, or intend-
        ed investment raise real NNP? Explain briefly.

Problem 3 (continued):

11. b) Would a rise in aggregate demand which was accompanied by a rise in the full-employment level of real NNP raise the level of real NNP?

     c) Could a change in the full-employment level of real NNP--with no change in aggregate demand--raise the equilibrium level of NNP?

     d) What then is needed to produce a rise in real NNP over time when the economy is initially at full-employment equilibrium?

12. a) If the economy has an inflationary gap of $5 with the consumption and saving functions as originally given, and a full-employment NNP at $100, intended investment must be $_____.

     b) In this case, why is it perhaps not appropriate to speak of an equilibrium level of NNP?

Problem 3 (continued):

12. c) What will happen in the economy as a result of the inflationary gap?

     d) What changes would eliminate the inflationary gap so as to produce equili-
         brium at the full-employment level of NNP?

Problem 4: Name_____

Fiscal Instruments and National Income Section_____

This problem deals with fiscal policy. Part III of this problem summarized what should have been learned from the numerical exercises. See if you can write down some of the important conclusions which emerge from the exercises before you read the four paragraphs of Part III.

Assumptions:

In a certain economy there is no foreign trade. The full employment level of national income is $300. (All dollar sums in this problem are to be interpreted as billions of dollars per year.) At the full employment level of income the government initially collects $50 in lump-sum personal taxes; there are no other taxes. Initially, government expenditures on goods and services are $50 and transfer payments are zero. At a disposable income of $150, consumers save zero, the marginal propensity to consume is 3/4 at all levels of disposable income.

I. Anti-Inflationary Fiscal Policy

Planned Investment is $31 at all levels of income.

A. In line A of Table I below fill in the amount of disposable income which would exist at a full employment level of output. Then enter the volume of consumption associated with that level of disposable income. Finally, add C, I, and G to obtain aggregate demand.

There is an inflationary gap of $_____.

B. Since taxes are constant at all levels of income, a reduction in government expenditures on goods and services (G) by one dollar would lower the level of aggregate demand associated with the full employment level of income by $_____. Thus, the inflationary gap can be eliminated and full employment equilibrium can be attained through a reduction in G by $_____.

Fill in the blanks of line B in Table I to show the value of the various items when full employment equilibrium is attained through a reduction in G.

C. With G constant, a rise in taxes (T) of one dollar lowers the disposable income at full employment national income by $_____; therefore the dollar rise in T lowers consumption and hence aggregate demand at full employment national income by $_____. In order to eliminate the initial inflationary gap, with G held at initial level of $50, the government must raise T by $_____.

Fill in line C of Table I to show the results of this method of attaining full employment equilibrium.

D. Now suppose instead that both G and T are reduced by equal amounts from their initial levels. A one dollar drop in T raises consumption at the full employment level of national income by $_____. If G simultaneously drops by one dollar, the combined effect of the changes in G and T of one dollar each lowers aggregate demand (C + I + G) by $_____. In order to

420

Problem 4 (continued):

    D. (continued):

eliminate the initial inflationary gap by this "balanced budget" method, both G and T must be reduced by $_____.

    Show the results of the "balanced budget" method by filling line D of Table I.

TABLE I

	Natl. Y or NNP	Taxes	Disp. Y	C	I	G	Aggregate D C + I + G
A	300	50	_____	_____	31	50	_____
B	300	50	_____	_____	31		_____
C	300	_____	_____	_____	31	50	_____
D	300	_____	_____	_____	31	_____	_____

    E. From Table I, find the Government Surplus in each case:

        A $_____   B $_____   C $_____   D $_____

II. Anti-Deflationary Fiscal Policy

    In another year planned investment in this economy is $15 at all levels of income. In all other respects, the economy is exactly as described in the assumption above.

    A. In this case there is a deflationary gap of $_____. Since the value of the multiplier is _____, the equilibrium level of national income is $_____ below the full employment level; thus the equilibrium level of national income is $_____.

        Enter the equilibrium level of national income, and the level of disposable income and of consumption at equilibrium in line A of Table II below.

    B. Applying the results of B, C, and D of Part I to a deflationary gap situation in the same economy, one may conclude that:

Problem 4 (continued):

    1. A rise in G of $1 would reduce the size of a deflationary gap by $_____, and increase the equilibrium level of income by $_____.

    2. A reduction in T of $1 would reduce the size of a deflationary gap by $_____, and increase the equilibrium level of income by $_____.

    3. A rise in both G and T of $1 would reduce the size of a deflationary gap by $_____, and increase the equilibrium level of income by $_____.

    4. The effects of a rise in transfer payments on disposable income and hence on aggregate demand will be identical to those of an equal reduction in taxes. Therefore, a rise in transfer payments of $1 would reduce the size of a deflationary gap by $_____.

C. A rise in G of $10 with T constant at $50 would reduce the deflationary gap by $_____; the equilibrium level of national income rises by $_____. The new equilibrium level of income is $_____.

    Show the effects of the rise in G by filling in line C of Table II with the values of the items in the new equilibrium situation.

D. A reduction in T by $10 with G at its initial level of $50 would reduce the size of the deflationary gap by $_____; it would therefore raise the equilibrium level of income by $_____ to a new equilibrium level of $_____.

    Show the new equilibrium situation achieved by this tax reduction of $10 by filling in line D of Table II.

E. A rise of both G and T by $10 each would reduce the deflationary gap by $_____, and would therefore raise the equilibrium level of national income by $_____ to $_____.

    Show the new equilibrium situation achieved by a $10 rise in the size of a balanced budget by filling in line E of Table II.

Problem 4 (continued):

TABLE II

	Natl. Y or NNP	Taxes	Disp. Y	C	I	G	Aggregate D C + I + G
A	_____	50	_____	_____	15	50	_____
C	_____	50	_____	_____	15	60	_____
D	_____	40	_____	_____	15	50	_____
E	_____	60	_____	_____	15	60	_____

F. The initiation of programs whereby the government makes $10 of transfer payments, with T and G each at the $50 level, would raise the equilibrium level of national income by $_____ to a new equilibrium level of $_____.

Show the new equilibrium situation by filling the blanks in the line below.

Natl. Y or NNP	Taxes	Transfers	Disp. Y	C	I	G	Aggregate D C + I + G
_____	50	10	_____	_____	15	50	_____

III. Summary

The numerical exercises above are intended to demonstrate the effect of government fiscal operations on the level of economic activity of a simplified hypothetical economy. The results can be applied, if the proper qualifications are included, to the understanding of fiscal policy in the modern American economy. Some of the important conclusions which emerge from the exercise are summarized below.

1. One way to combat inflation is to reduce aggregate desired expenditure. This goal can be achieved by decreasing government expenditures on output: a reduction equal to the size of the inflationary gap will eliminate the gap.

2. Aggregate demand can also be reduced by legislation which raises the yield of taxes or lowers government transfer payments, since such legislation would lower disposable income and therefore reduce consumer expenditure. Because consumer spending at full employment would decrease by only a fraction (the MPC) of the rise in taxes (or fall in transfer), taxes must be increased by an amount greater than the inflationary gap in order to achieve full employment equilibrium.

3. Since the effect of a change in government purchases of output outweighs the effect of an equal change in taxes, an equal reduction of both government purchases and taxes will reduce the size of an inflationary gap, despite the fact that no government surplus is created.
   (Compare these statements with the numerical answers to Part I.)

4. Spending must be raised in order to combat a deflationary gap situation. Consequently, a reversal of the policy measures referred to above will reduce the size of a deflationary gap and raise the equilibrium level of national income. Such

Problem 4 (continued):

4. (continued)

anti-deflationary measures could take the form of a rise in government expenditures on output, or a lowering of tax yields, or an increase in transfer payment programs, or an equal increase in both taxes and government expenditure on output. (Compare the numerical results in Part II.)

424

Problem 5:
Deposit Creation

The fact that banks are not required to hold 100% reserves against their demand deposits gives rise to the process called " multiple expansion of bank deposits." Problem 5 provides drill in the mechanics of deposit creation.

1. <u>Check Clearence</u>

You are A. Jones, a student at Penn, and you have an account at the Philadelphia Bank. Your father, B. Jones, who banks at the Lancaster Bank, sends you a check for $100 which you deposit to your account.

1. The Philadelphia Bank then passes the check on to the Federal Reserve Bank of Philadelphia where the deposit balances of the Philadelphia Bank and Lancaster Banks are appropriately adjusted by bookkeeping entries. The Federal Reserve Bank then completes its services as a clearing house by sending the check to the Lancaster Bank.

2. Show on the T accounts the changes which occur in the balance sheet items of each bank.

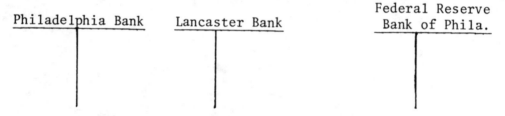

3. How would your answer to 2 have differed if you had cashed the check at the Philadelphia Bank instead of depositing it? (Assume that the Philadelphia Bank immediately replenishes its cash supply, passing the check on to the Federal Reserve Bank and receiving cash in return.

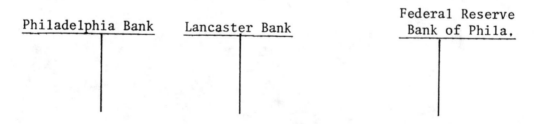

Although the technical aspects are somewhat different if the checks are cleared through local clearing houses, or if they are cleared between two Federal Reserve destricts, the results properly obtained are substantially the same as above.

Problem 5 (continued):

II. Bank Lending - Individual Bank

A. Below you are given a simplified balance sheet for a commercial bank. Assume the reserve requirement for this bank is 20 percent.

Philadelphia Bank

Loans	$650,000	Demand Deposits	$1,500,000
Gov't Securities	500,000	Capital Stock and Sur-	
Other Securities	150,000	plus	250,000
F. R. Reserves	450,000		
	$1,750,000		$1,750,000

B. Answer the following questions:

1. The amount of the required reserves is $_____.

2. The amount of the excess reserves is $_____.

In Question 3, 4, and 5, use T-accounts and enter changed from the original situation.

3. Suppose the bank now makes a commercial loan of $50,000. (The normal way for such a loan to be made is for the bank to open a checking account for the borrower.) What is the immediate effect of this loan on the balance sheet items shown above?

4. The borrower now uses the full amount of his loan to pay Smith who deposits it in the Chester State Bank. Show the effect of check clearance on the balance sheets of the Philadelphia and Chester Banks.

<u>Problem 5 (continued)</u>:

5.   Suppose that instead of making a loan, the Philadelphia Bank buys U.S. securities amounting to $50,000. The securities had been owned by Brown, who deposits his proceeds from the sale in the Chester State Bank. Show the effect of these transactions in terms of their effects on balance sheet items of the Philadelphia and Chester Banks.

6.   Suppose the bank had expanded its loans to $750,000. This would have increased Demand Deposits to $2,250,000 so that the F. R. Reserves would have been just 20% of demand deposits, the minimum required by law. However this would be very foolish banking policy. Explain why.

7.   The maximum amount the bank could <u>safely</u> expand its loans, or holdings of securities is $_____.

8.   If you have done your work carefully and correctly, you have just figured out the "why" of a very important banking principle: NO ONE BANK CAN EXPAND ITS DEMAND DEPOSITS THROUGH INCREASING ITS LOANS OR ITS HOLDINGS OF SECURITIES BY MORE THAN THE AMOUNT OF ITS EXCESS RESERVES. Explain in words how you reached this conclusion.

III. Bank Lending: Multiple Expansion Through a Banking System

  A.   Below you are given T-accounts for a very simple banking system. In B you are asked to make entries in these T-accounts. <u>Make all of your entries refer to changes from the initial situation rather than the immediately preceding situation</u>.

Problem 5 (continued):

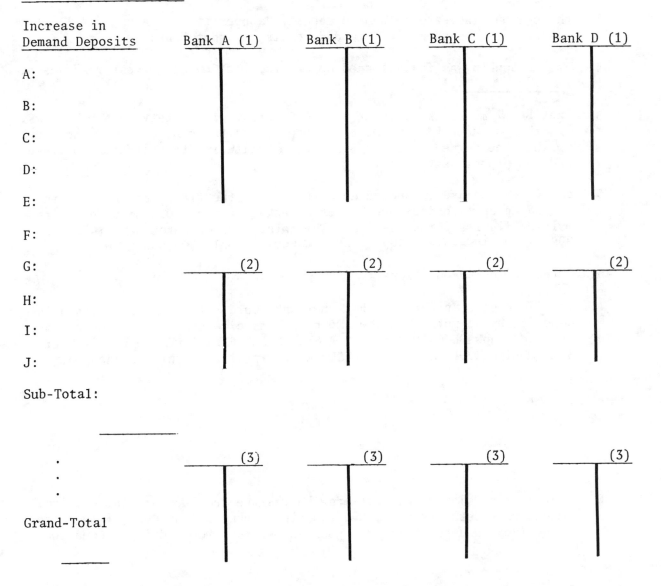

Increase in Demand Deposits — Bank A (1), Bank B (1), Bank C (1), Bank D (1)

A:

B:

C:

D:

E:

F:

G: (2)   (2)   (2)   (2)

H:

I:

J:

Sub-Total:

.   (3)   (3)   (3)   (3)

.

.

Grand-Total

B. Follow these instructions carefully and answer all questions. Assume a reserve requirement of 20%.

1. Assume Bank A is initially fully "loaned up" (i.e., has no excess reserves). It sells $100,000 of its holdings of government securities to the Federal Reserve Bank and receives deposit credit in exchange. Show in its "T" account (1) the changes and their sign in Bank A's balance sheet. Bank A's excess reserves are now $_____.

2. Bank A sold its 3 percent governmant bonds to increase its six percent loans so Bank A then makes the largest loan consistent with safety to Mr. Black. Enter the proper additional balance sheet changes in "T" account (2).

3. Mr. Black writes a check for the full amount of his account and gives it to Mr. Green who deposits it in Bank B. The check is cleared through the A's "T" account (3) and in Bank B's "T" account (1). Notice what the net effect has been for Bank A, by considering its 3 "T" accounts. Enter in

428

Problem 5 (continued):

B. 3. the column "Increase in demand deposits" opposite Bank A any final net change you have shown in demand deposits for that Bank.

   4. Assume Bank B was fully loaned up before. It now has excess reserves of $_____.

   5. Bank B now makes the largest loan consistent with safety to a Mr. Adams, and then so does Bank C, D, etc. Repeat for Banks B, C, and D the steps you have performed in 2 and 3 above, substituting the different borrowers and the proper bank letters.

   6. For the "Increase in demand deposits," show the final net increase in demand deposits experienced by each Bank, B through D. Compute the remaining figures for Banks E-J. The total should approximate $433,000, and if you included enough banks, it would equal $500,000.

C. Answer the following questions.

   1. You discovered in Part II that one bank could safely increase its demand deposits by no more than the amount of its excess reserves. Here you have seen how SEVERAL BANKS IN A SYSTEM CAN EXPAND DEMAND DEPOSITS BY SOME MULTIPLE OF THE EXCESS RESERVES. Explain why this can happen.

   2. What is the relationship between the reserve requirement, the original amount of excess reserves, and the final amount ($500,000) of increased money (demand deposits)? Put your answer in words and in an equation.

   3. How would the result have varied in the problem if the reserve requirements had been 25% instead of 20%? 10% instead of 20%?

<u>Problem 5 (continued)</u>:

C. 4. Why do we consider demand deposits as "money"?

5. This was very simplified. Suppose that instead of only Bank A gaining excess reserves, each bank had gained excess reserves by the sale of bonds to the Federal Reserve Banks as follows: Bank A, $30,000; Bank B, $10,000; Bank C, $40,000; and Bank D, $20,000. How would your final conclusion have differed? Why?

6. The $500,000 increase in money computed in this problem represents a theoretically possible maximum. This extreme limit is not likely ever to occur because the conditions necessary for the extreme expansion are not likely to be completely met in reality. List these conditions and explain how the incomplete fulfillment of each would affect the situation.

7. Suppose Bank A had to part with $100,000 of reserves to repay a loan it had previously taken from the Federal Reserve Bank. What effects would this have on the banking system? Explain, comparing results with the deposit expansion in III B above.

Problem 6:   Name _____
Monetary Policy   Section _____

    The primary instruments of Federal Reserve monetary policy are examined in this problem. The mechanics of open-market operations, with their effects, are covered in Part I. Control of the discount rate and the reserve requirements are treated more briefly in Part II.

I. Open-Market Operations

    A. Below you are given T accounts for three different institutions.

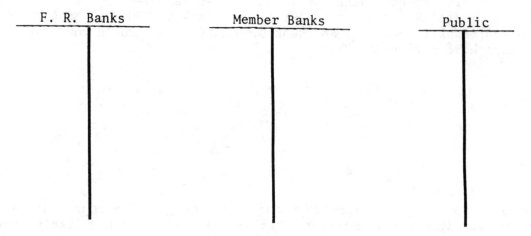

F. R. Banks   Member Banks   Public

    B. Follow the instructions below and answer the questions.

        1. In pursuit of an (anti-inflation, anti-deflation) policy, the Open-Market Committee decides the F.R. Banks should sell government securities to the public. Assume that at the beginning, the banks are fully loaned up.

        2. The F.R. Banks sell $100,000 in government bonds to the public. The public then makes payment by checks which are then cleared.

            a) Show the immediate changes and their signs in the above T accounts of all three institutions.

            b) What is the new reserve deficiency (i.e., negative excess reserves) of the Member Banks assuming a 20% required reserve? Put another way, given that they have just lost a substantial amount of deposits, by how much must Member Banks increase their reserves in order to support their remaining deposits? (Constructing a more specific example for yourself may help you to understand.)

            c) The volume of excess reserves of all Member Banks depends on the size of 1) Total F.R. Reserves and 2) Demand Deposits. Therefore, any measures by which the banks may regain an adequate reserve position must ultimately be reflected in an (increase, decrease) in total reserves or in an (increase, decrease) in demand deposits. (Circle the correct word in each case.)

Problem 6 (continued):

    d) If Member Banks wish to eliminate the reserve deficiency by borrowing from the F. R. Banks, they will need to borrow \$_____. In that event, what will be the net effect of the open market sale on 1) Total F. R. Reserves and 2) Demand Deposits?

    e) Suppose instead that Member Banks eliminate the reserve deficiency you found in b) by reducing their loans to the public or by selling securities to the public. In that event, the maximum required reduction in loans and security-holdings would be \$_____. What then will be the total net effect of the open market sale on 1) Total F. R. Reserves and 2) Demand Deposits?

    f) Why are the results in part d- and e- above so markedly different?

3. a) At any given moment of time, there is a given stock of bonds in existence. When the Federal Reserve Banks reduce their holdings of U.S. bonds they are increasing the supply of bonds available for the public to hold. Since there is no reason to expect the public's demand curve for bonds to shift, the increase in the supply of bonds must (raise, lower) the price of bonds. This is necessarily equivalent to a (rise, fall) in the yield or interest rate on existing bonds.

    b) To the extent that the Member Banks respond to the reserve deficiency by selling securities, this will lead to further (rise, fall) in the price and, therefore, (rise, fall) in the interest rate on bonds. To the extent that Member Banks reduce their loans, they are likely to (raise, lower) the rate of interest and (increase, reduce) the availability of such loans.

    c) Suppose Member Banks eliminate the reserve deficiency by selling securities and reducing loans. Then, because of the open-market sale by the F. R. Banks and the resulting actions of the Member Banks, the non-bank public now holds (more, less) money than initially and (more, fewer) bonds, and owes (more, less) to the commercial banks. What has made the public willing to alter its portfolio in this fashion?

Problem 6 (continued):

4. The open market policy above was undertaken to combat an inflationary gap.

    a) This policy would tend to (increase, reduce) the ease of obtaining loans for consumer installment credit and to (raise, lower) the interest costs of such loans.

    b) How would the above tend to influence consumer spending? What kind of consumer purchases would most likely be affected?

    c) If monetary policy were effective in the manner indicated in b), the inflationary gap would be reduced by

        1) a rise in the full employment level of output.
        2) a reduction in the amount of disposable income associated with full employment NNP.
        3) A downward shift of the consumption function.
        4) a reduction of investment demand.
        (Circle the number designating the proper alternative.)

    d) The open market policy would tend to (increase, reduce) the availability and (increase, reduce) the interest costs of bank loans to business to finance inventory accumulation and sales on credit. Therefore, inventory investment would be (stimulated, depressed).

    e) How might the monetary policy affect investment spending by altering the ease and cost of financing business plant and equipment purchases through new security issues?

Problem 6 (continued):

    f) Why should actions of the banking system alter conditions in corporate security markets when the banks do not themselves hold an appreciable volume of such securities?

    g) If monetary policy was effective in the ways indicated in d) and e), the inflationary gap would be reduced by:

       1) a rise in the full-employment level of output.
       2) a reduction in the amount of disposable income associated with full employment NNP.
       3) a downward shift of the consumption function.
       4) a reduction of investment demand.
       (Circle the number designating the proper alternative.)

C. Follow the instructions below and answer the questions:

    1. The economic situation in the country is just the reverse of the above, and the Open-Market Committee decides that the F. R. Banks should buy bonds.

    2. The F. R. Banks buy $150,000 worth of Government bonds from the public and make payment by checks which are then deposited in Member Banks. The checks are cleared. Show the immediate changes and their signs in the T Accounts below:

F. R. Banks	Member Banks	Public
	Demand Deposits 1,000,000	
	F. R. Reserves $200,000	

    3. What is the new reserve position (excess reserves) of the Member Banks assuming a 20% required reserve?

Problem 6 (continued):

4. What total net effect on the supply of money may occur as a maximum as a result of the Federal Reserve Banks' purchase?

5. Under what conditions would this maximum effect occur?

6. What is the minumum effect on the supply of money which one could reasonably expect to occur?

7. Under what conditions would the effect be minimal?

D. Suppose either policy of selling or buying a given amount of bonds could be pursued during appropriate economic conditions. Which of the two could you expect to be the more effective? Why?

Problem 6 (continued):

II. Other Federal Reserve Instruments

Follow the instructions below and answer the questions.

A. The following are the principal items in the consolidated balance sheets of the twelve F. R. Banks.

F. R. Banks, Dec. 30, 1981
(billions of dollars)

Gold Certificates	11.1	F. R. Notes Outstanding	132.6
U. S. Gov't. Securities	131.5	Member Bank Deposits	29.0
Loans to Member Banks	1.2	U. S. Treasury Deposits	3.4
Other (Special Drawing Rights,		Other Deposits	0.9
Fed. Agency Obligations,		Miscellaneous Liabilities	9.2
uncollected items, and		Net Worth	2.9
miscellaneous cash assets)	34.2		

Total Assets	178.0	Total Liabilities and Net Worth	178.0

B. When a Member Bank borrows from a F. R. Bank, the Member Bank is given deposit credit; and, when it repays its loan, the deposit balance is correspondingly reduced.

1. If the discount rate were raised to so high a level that member-bank borrowing fell to zero, total member-bank reserves would fall by $_____ billion, according to the balance sheet above.

2. What would be the maximum effect on the money supply as a result of such an action? (Assume a 20% required reserve).

C. Say demand deposits of all member banks are currently about $100 billion.

1. A rise in the reserve requirement by five percentage points would, therefore, raise required reserves by $_____ billion.

Problem 6 (continued):

2. Suppose the reserve requirement were raised from 20% to 25% in pursuit of an anti-inflationary policy. If the Member Banks are initially loaned up and if total reserves cannot be increased, what maximum change in the money supply can occur as a result of this policy?

3. Compare your results above with those that would follow from an open market sale of $5 billion where the reserve requirement was left at 20%.

4. Why is it usually argued that a change of reserve requirements is likely to be less effective as anti-deflationary policy than as anti-inflationary policy?

5. Is it possible that a reduction of reserve requirements in deflation will fail entirely to increase the money supply?

Problem 7
IS-IM Analysis

Name _____
Section _____

This problem analyzes the joint determination of the equilibrium interest rate and output level.

Suppose that an economy is described by the following relationships:

$$C = 10 + .75 \, Y_D$$

$$I = 15 - 1/2 \, r$$

$$G = 18$$

$$T = 18$$

$$M^S = 44$$

$$M^D = 10 - .4r + .4Y$$

$$P = 1$$

where
C = Consumption
I = Investment
G = Government Spending
T = Taxes
M^S = Money Supply
M^D = Money Demand
P = Price Level
Y = NNP
Y_D = Disposable Income
r = Interest Rate

I. <u>LM Curve</u>

The LM Curve is the set of combinations of NNP and the interest rate that result in money market clearing. Thus, along the LM Curve, the demand for real money balances is equal to the real money supply.

A. Derive the LM Curve for this economy. Plot it below. Label the curve LM_A.

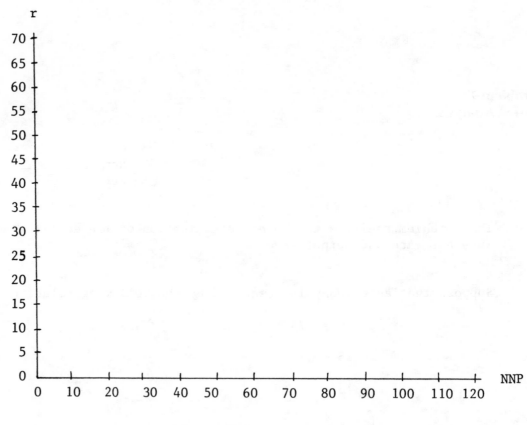

Figure 7-1

B. Suppose that the nominal money supply is increased by 6. Find the new LM curve. Plot it on the same diagram. Label the curve LM_B. Holding prices constant, how does an increase in the nominal supply of money affect the LM curve?

C. Now suppose that this increase in the money supply causes the price level to increase to 10/9. Find the new LM curve. Plot it with the others. Label the curve LM_C. Holding the nominal money supply constant, how does an increase in the price level affect the LM curve?

II. IS Curve

The IS curve is the set of combinations of NNP and the interest rate which result in goods market clearing.

A. Begin with the (closed economy) National Income Accounting identity Y= C +I +G. Derive the IS curve for this economy. Plot it on the diagram below. Label the curve IS_A.

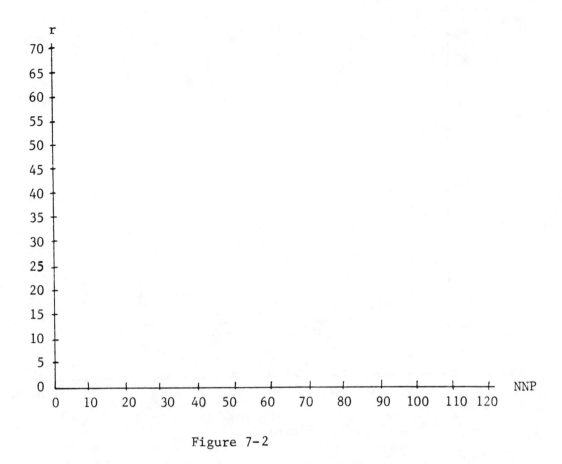

Figure 7-2

B. Suppose that Government spending increases by 5. Find the new IS curve.
    Plot it with IS$_A$. Label this curve IS$_B$. How does an increase in
    government spending affect the IS curve?

III. <u>Equilibrium Determination</u>

Equilibrium occurs when both the goods and money markets clear. Thus, the
equilibrium output level and interest rate pair must be on both the IS and
LM curves.

If M^S= 44, P= 1, and G= 18, find the equilibrium output level and interest rate.
Plot the appropriate IS and LM curves below. Show the equilibrium in this
diagram.

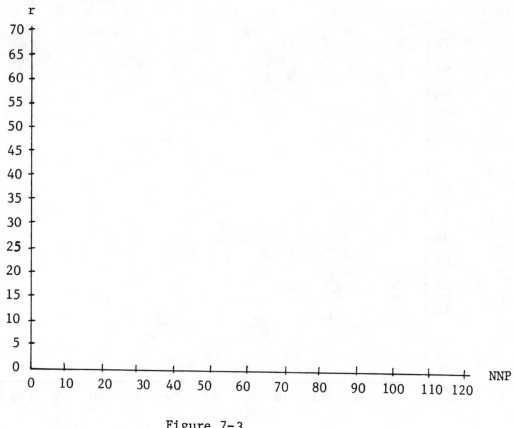

Figure 7-3

Problem 8
International Trade, Fiscal and
Monetary Policies, and Economic
Development

Name_____

Section_____

A country's attempt to secure the advantages of full employment, price stability, and growth may be complicated by the Balance of Payments effects of the fiscal and monetary policies it follows. This problem touches on some of the difficulties.

Assumptions:

1. Below is the national product account for Alertia in year one:

Consumption	1000
Net Domestic Investment	0
Net Foreign Investment	0
Exports 300	
Less Imports 300	
Government Purchases	0
Net National Product	1000

2. The economy is in equilibrium at full employment during year one.

3. The marginal propensity to consume is 4/5 at all levels of income.

4. Taxes are zero in year one, so disposable income is equal to NNP initially.

5. The quantity of imports demanded is entirely autonomous: it is affected neither by income changes nor price changes.

A. Changes in Export Demand

1. In year two, there is a reduction in the demand of the United States for Alertia's goods. As a result, exports fall to 225, with prices assumed constant. This creates a deflationary gap of _____.

2. The gap can be eliminated by the initiation of government expenditures of _____ while taxes remain zero. Fill in the blanks of row A2 below assuming that the gap is closed in this way. While the expansionary fiscal policy can maintain full employment equilibrium, it fails to solve the balance of payments problem since the Net Foreign Balance on current account is _____.

	NNP	Disp. Y	C	G	Exports	Imports
A2.	1000	_____	_____	_____	225	300

Problem 7 (continued):

3. Assuming that exchange rates are <u>fixed</u>, what is likely to happen to Alertia's holdings of gold and foreign currency in year two under these circumstances? Why is this a matter of concern to Alertia?

4. What would happen to Alertia's currency relative to other currencies if exchange rates were <u>not</u> fixed?

5. Alternatively, the inflationary gap you found in A1. above can be eliminated if the government takes measures to lower imports by _____. Show the results of this method by filling in the blanks of row A4. below. In this case, the Net Foreign Balance on current account is _____.

NNP	Disp. Y	C	G	Exports	Imports
1000	_____	_____	_____	225	_____

6. What are the disadvantages of such a policy of restricting imports?

B. The Effects of a Development Program

1. Again, return to the initial situation. Now, suppose that Alertia embarks on a program of economic development in year two. By making attractive loans and granting concessions to enterprises, the government stimulates a demand of 100 for capital goods. In the absence of any other measures, this program creates an inflationary gap of _____.

Problem 7 (continued):

2. The inflationary gap can be eliminated through the imposition of taxes amounting to _____. In that event, show the national accounts for year two by filling the blanks below.

	NNP	Taxes	Disp. Y	C	Net. Priv Dom. I	Exports	Imports
B2	1000	_____	_____	_____	100	300	300

3. Alternatively, if the government can successfully stimulate import demand, the inflationary gap can be eliminated by a rise of _____ in imports while taxes remain zero. Fill the blanks below to show how full employment equilibrium can be attained by this policy.

	NNP	Taxes	Disp. Y	C	NPDI	Exports	Imports
B3	1000	0	_____	_____	100	300	_____

4. Two ways of curbing inflation are suggested by B2. and B3. What are the relative merits of these alternative policies?

5. As a result of the net domestic investment undertaken in year two, the capital stock of Alertia is 100 higher at the start of year three. Therefore, the productive capacity of the economy is higher. Suppose that each dollar increase in the stock of capital raises the full employment level of output by fifty cents. In that case, full employment NNP for year three is_____.

6. Net Private Domestic Investment is kept at 100 in year three. Assume that, as in B3., taxes are to remain zero while full employment equilibrium is maintained by the adjusting of import demand through public policy. Then, for year three, the required deficit in the Net Foreign Balance on current account is _____. Fill in the blanks below to show the national accounts for year three in this case.

NNP	Taxes	Disp. Y	C	NPDI	Exports	Imports
___	0	_____	_____	100	300	_____

Problem 7 (continued):

7. Suppose that net domestic investment is maintained at a constant annual
    rate of 100. Then, for year twelve, under the above assumptions, full
    employment NNP is _____. Show that, in year twelve, neither
    anti-inflationary fiscal policy nor a deficit in the Net Foreign Balance
    is required to maintain full employment equilibrium.

Answers to Problem 1

1.

a – Y	h – P	o – N	v – Y
b – P	i – P	p – N	w – N
c – P	j – Y	q – N	x – N
d – P	k – N	r – P	y – N
e – N	l – Y	s – P	z – P
f – Y	m – P	t – N	
g – N	n – P	u – Y	

2. All payments for final products are distributed as factor payments (where profits are a residual item among the latter).

3. A consumption item satisfies wants of the current accounting period, while an investment item satisfies wants, at least in part, in a future period. (Note that by this definition, durable consumer goods such as washing machines should be considered investment items, but in the accounts they are included with the consumption items.) Consumption Items: b, d, s, z. Investment Items: c, h, r.

4. a. An intermediate good (or service) is a good (or service) used in the current accounting period in the production of other goods or services. Intermediate goods: e, g, o. Intermediate services: k, t.

    b. The value of a final good or service includes the value of all intermediate goods and services used in its production. Hence counting intermediate goods and services in NNP would be double-counting.

5. No. It enters in 1983 as investment (i.e., increase in inventories). It enters in 1984 as consumption and as disinvestment (i.e., reduction in inventories), and thus cancels out in the 1984 NNP.

6. No. The value of the apartment is included in 1983 as investment and the rents paid by tenants during the year (and, likewise, for subsequent years) are included as the consumption of the services of the apartment. Over time depreciation charges offset the original investment item.

7. a. For purposes associated with the measurement of growth, net product is more meaningful than gross product, because it excludes that part of output used to replace capital used up ("depreciated") in the production process.

    b. Depreciation is difficult to measure. Moreover the available measures change systematically so that changes in measured NNP are similar to those in measured GNP.

8. Other taxes (such as the personal income tax) are included in the factor payments, but indirect business taxes (such as sales taxes) are not.

9. a - 100. b - rose, six %. c - 1471. d - rose, 2.8%.

    e - rose, 1.7% $\left[\left(\dfrac{GNP_{1979}}{Pop_{1979}} \Big/ \dfrac{GNP_{1978}}{Pop_{1978}} - 1 \right) \cdot 100 = \left(\dfrac{GNP_{1979}}{GNP_{1978}} \cdot \dfrac{P_{1978}}{P_{1979}} - 1 \right) \cdot 100 \right.$

    $\left. = \left(\dfrac{1.028}{1.011} - 1 \right) \cdot 100 = 1.7\% \right]$

Answers to Problem 2

1. a)

Y	C	MPC	S	MPS
$ 0	$ 700		-700	
2000	2500	.9	-500	.1
4000	4000	.75	0	.25
6000	5300	.65	700	.35
8000	6500	.60	1500	.40

b)
1) rises
2) rises
3) falls
4) falls

c)

Figure 2-1

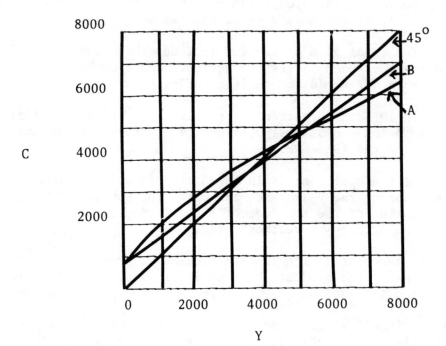

2. a.

MPC
.8
.8
.8
.8

b.
1) rises
2) rises
3) falls
4) remains constant

c.   B is a straight line (constant slope) but A is a curve
with a decreasing slope.

Answers to Problem 2 (continued):

3. a.   1) $16,000
                    2)   15,600
                    3)   14,400

    b.   1)   15,600
                    2)   15,600
                    3)   15,600

    c.   Income distribution changes aggregate consumption in community A because MPC depends on the level of income. Income distribution does not change aggregate consumption in community B because MPC is constant at all income levels.

4.   Family size, accumulated wealth, family age, "keeping up with the Jones'" effect, past history and future expectations in regard to disposable incomes.

5.   Unincorporated family business (including farms).

Answers to Problem 3

1.   Saving: -10,   -5,   0,   5,   10,   15,   20

2.   .75   .25,   remains constant, remains constant, falls, rises.

3-5 see Figure 3-1 below:

Figure 3-1

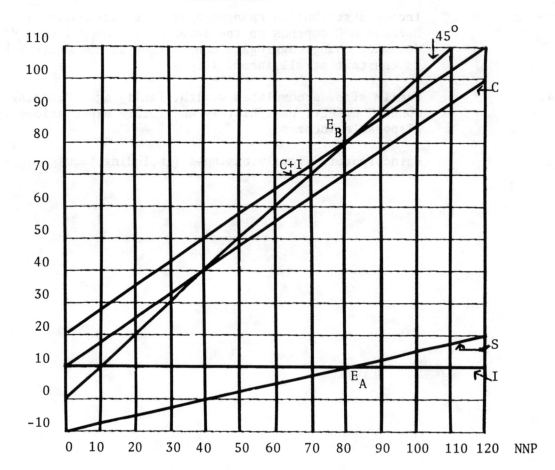

C, S, I

6. $95, $5, $15, $15,   contract output

7. $55, $5, $10, $65

        a) $5, $5, $5

        b) $5, $10, $10
            expand output

8.   a) 4
        b) larger
        c) The more people spend of their extra income each round (i.e.,
            the higher is the MPC) the more demand increases, and the more
            income therefore rises as a result of a given increase in an
            autonomous expenditure such as investment.

Answers to Problem 3 (continued):

        d) The multiplier is increased at each stage since the rise in income referred to in the previous answer induces an additional increase in investment and therefore in income.

$$\text{Multiplier} = 1/(1-MPC-MPI)$$

9.   a) raise by $4
        b) lower by $4
        c) raise by $4
        d) leave unchanged

10.   Deflationary gap of $5

        a) rose by $5
        b) fell by $5
        c) rose by $5

11.   a) In the short run, no, because the full employment level gives the maximum sustainable real production. Therefore, in the short run, prices would probably rise. (If an increase in intended investment resulted in an increase in real net investments, however, the full-employment level would increase in subsequent years as the capital stock grew.

        b) Yes.

        c) No.

        d) To increase both the production capacity of the economy (and hence its full employment level) and aggregate demand.

12.   a) $20
        b) It can not be achieved. The maximum level of real NNP is $100.
        c) Prices will be bid up.
        d) Reduction in desired investment or consumption; increase in desired savings.

Answers to Problem 4

I. A. 6
    B. 1, 6
    C. 1, .75, 8
    D. .75, .25, 24

Table I

	NNP	Taxes	Disp. Y	C	I	G	C+I+G
A.	300	50	250	225	31	50	306
B.	300	50	250	225	31	44	300
C.	300	58	242	219	31	50	300
D.	300	26	274	243	31	26	300

E. A. 0, B. 6, C. 8, D. 0.

II. A. 10, 4, 40, 260
    B. 1. 1, 4
        2. .75, 3
        3. .25, 1
        4. .75
    C. 10, 40, 300
    D. 7.5, 30, 290
    E. 2.50, 10, 270
    F. 30, 290

Table II

	NNP	Disp. Y	C	C+I+G
A.	260	210	195	260
C.	300	250	225	300
D.	290	250	225	290
E.	270	210	195	270
F.	290	250	225	290

Answers to Problem 5

I. 2.

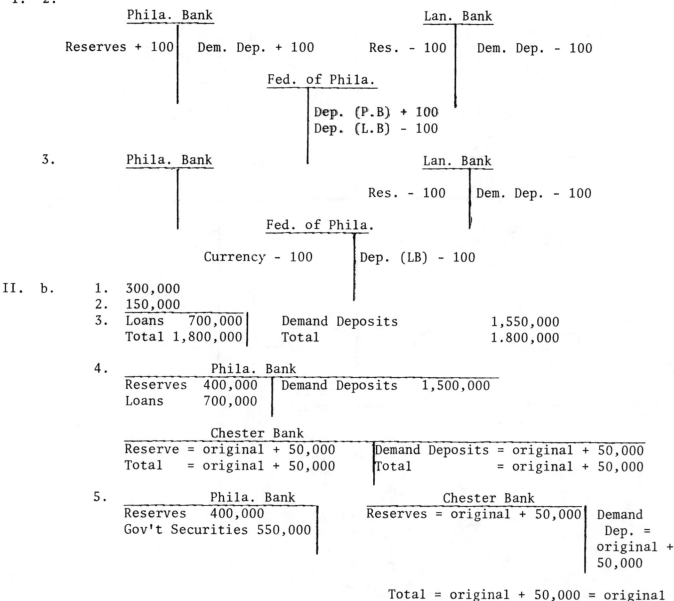

           Phila. Bank   Lan. Bank

      Reserves + 100 | Dem. Dep. + 100   Res. - 100 | Dem. Dep. - 100

                        Fed. of Phila.

                          Dep. (P.B) + 100
                          Dep. (L.B) - 100

    3.   Phila. Bank   Lan. Bank

                                            Res. - 100 | Dem. Dep. - 100

                        Fed. of Phila.

              Currency - 100 | Dep. (LB) - 100

II. b.   1. 300,000
         2. 150,000
         3. Loans   700,000 | Demand Deposits   1,550,000
            Total 1,800,000 | Total   1.800,000

         4.   Phila. Bank
            Reserves 400,000 | Demand Deposits   1,500,000
            Loans   700,000 |

                       Chester Bank
            Reserve = original + 50,000 | Demand Deposits = original + 50,000
            Total   = original + 50,000 | Total   = original + 50,000

         5.   Phila. Bank   Chester Bank
            Reserves   400,000 | Reserves = original + 50,000 | Demand
            Gov't Securities 550,000 | Dep. =
                                                                        original +
                                                                        50,000

                        Total = original + 50,000 = original
                                                  + 50,000

    6. This policy does not allow for losses of reserves due to withdrawal
       of loans for their use.

    7. $150,000

    8. Each bank must be prepared for withdrawal of money lent out and
       therefore it can lend only what it has in excess reserves.

Answers to Problem 5 (continued):

III. A.

Bank A(1)	
R + 100,000	
GS - 100,000	

(2)	
L + 100,000	D + 100,000

(3)	
R 0	D 0

Bank B(1)	
R + 100,000	D + 100,000

(2)	
L + 80,000	D + 180,000

(3)	
R + 20,000	D + 100,000

Bank C(1)	
R + 80,000	D + 80,000

(2)	
L + 64,000	D + 144,000

(3)	
R + 16,000	D + 80,000

Bank D(1)	
R + 64,000	D + 64,000

(2)	
L + 51,200	D + 115,000

(3)	
R + 12,800	D + 64,000

Increase in
Demand Deposits

A: 0
B: 100,000
C: 80,000
D: 64,000
E: 51,200
F: 40,960
G: 32,768
H: 26,214
I: 20,971
J: 16,177

Total ≅   433,000

B. 1. 100,000
    4.   80,000

C. 1. When excess reserves leave one bank (say, as loans), they go to
        another (for example as new deposits). Part of these new deposits are
        newly created excess reserves for the second bank, and can be loaned
        out by that bank, thus creating new deposits elsewhere in the system,
        etc.

Answers to Problem 5 (continued):

C. 2. The final increase in money (demand deposits) is the original amount of excess reserves times the inverse of the reserve ratio.

$$\text{Final amount} = \frac{\text{original excess reserves}}{\text{reserves ratio}}$$

3. 25% $ 400,000
    10% $1,000 000

4. Because demand deposits generally are accepted as a means of payment.

5. In the aggregate, no difference because

$$\frac{30,000}{.2} + \frac{10,000}{.2} + \frac{40,000}{.2} + \frac{20,000}{.2} = \frac{100,000}{.2}$$
$$= 500,000$$

6. a) No leakage into domestic currency holdings
    b) No leakage abroad
    c) All banks fully loaned up.
              1) Bankers willing to expand loans
              2) Borrowers available

    The failure to meet these conditions will result in a lower expansion of the money supply.

7. Contractions of $500,000. Process is same as above, only in reversed direction.

Answers to Problem 6

I. a.   <u>F.R. Banks</u>

Securities - 100,000 | Mem. bank
                       deposits - 100,000

<u>Member Banks</u>

Reserves - 100,000 | Demand
                     Deposits - 100,000

<u>Public</u>

Securities
    + 100,000

Demand
Deposits
    - 100,000

   b. 1. anti-inflation

       2. a) (See above)
           b)   80,000
           c) increase, decrease
           d)   80,000. Total F. R. reserves down by $20,000. Demand
               deposits down by $100,000.
           e) $400,000, -100,000, -500,000
           f) In d) F.R. Banks put $80,000 back into the system, but not in e).

       3. a) lower, rise
           b) fall, rise, raise, reduce
           d) less, more, less. Change in price of securities (and therefore
               in price of loans) has made the public willing to so alter its
               portfolio.

       4. a) reduce, raise
           b) The above probably would tend to reduce consumer spending,
               especially on items (such as durables) for which credit pur-
               chases are relatively common.
           c) 3
           d) reduce, increase, depressed
           e) Because of the higher interest rate required to sell bond issues
               it would be more difficult and/ or more costly to finance business
               plant and equipment purchases through new security issues, therefore
               less such financing probably would occur.
           f) Because for many portfolios corporate and government securities
               are substitutes so when a change occurs in the market for the latter
               the market for the former also is affected.
           g) 4

Answers to Problem 6 (continued):

c. 2.   F. R. Banks

Securities + 150,000 | Member bank
                       Deposits + 150,000

                    Member Banks

                                    Demand deposits
                                        1,000,000
                                        + 150,000

          F.R. Reserves
              200,000
            + 150,000

                    Public

          Securities
            - 150,000

          Demand
          Deposits
            + 150,000

    3. $120,000
    4. 750,000
    5. If there are no leakages (i.e., if currency holdings do not
        increase) and if all banks are fully loaned up.
    6. $150,000
    7. If banks make no new loans
    8. Selling, because once banks are down to their minimum reserve
        level, they have to take actions which contract the money
        supply in the multiple process. If the F.R. buys, on the
        other hand, banks can choose just to hold the excess reserves
        (see 6 and 7 above).

II. b. 1. 1.2
         2. -6 billion

     c. 1. 5
         2. -20 billion
         3. The contraction would be $5 billion greater in the case of the
             open market sale.
         4. There is no guarantee that banks will make use of excess re-
             serves due to lowering of reserve requirements as part of an anti-
             deflationary policy, but if reserve requirements are increased
             sufficiently as part of an anti-inflationary policy banks must
             respond to their resulting shortage of reserves by taking con-
             tracting actions.
         5. Yes, since banks may be satisfied with simply holding their in-
             creased reserves.

456

I.   A.   The LM curve is derived by equating real money demand, M^D, to the real money supply, M^S/P. The equation for LM_A is $r= Y - 85$.

     B.   The equation for LM_B is $r= Y - 100$. Holding the price level constant, an increase in the money supply shifts the LM curve to the right.

     C.   The equation for LM_C is $r= Y - 87.5$. Holding the nominal money supply constant, an increase in the price level shifts the LM curve to the left.

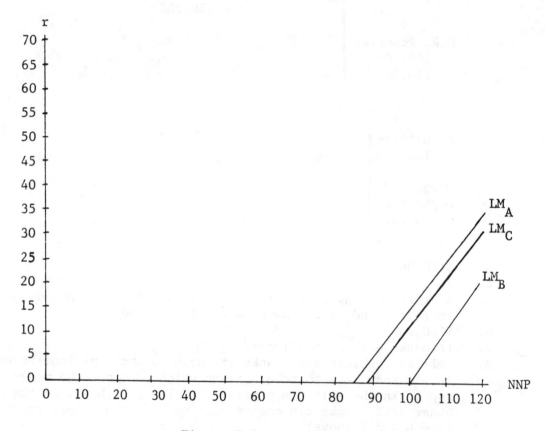

Figure 7-1

II. A.   The IS curve is derived from the identity $Y= C + I + G$. Substitution of the consumption and investment function into this identity, given $G= T = 18$, results in the following expression for IS_A: $r = 59 - 1/2\,Y$.

     B.   The equation for IS_B is $r= 69 - 1/2\,Y$. An increase in government spending shifts the IS curve to the right.

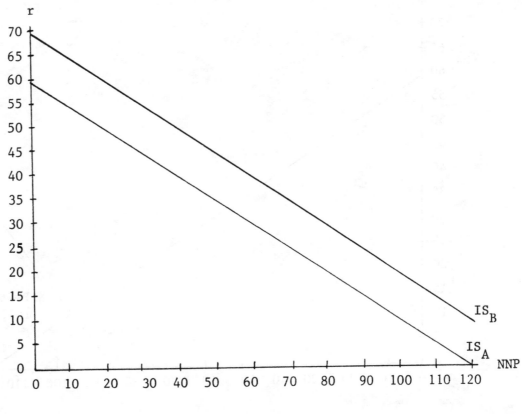

Figure 7-2

III.   If $M^S = 44$, P= 1, and G= 18, then the LM curve is LM_A and the IS curve is IS_A. The equation for LM_A is r= Y- 85, and the equation for IS_A is r= 59- 1/2 Y. Thus, the equilibrium level of NNP must satisfy Y- 85 = 59- 1/2 Y, or Y= 96. If Y= 96, then r= 11. These are the equilibrium levels of NNP and r.

458

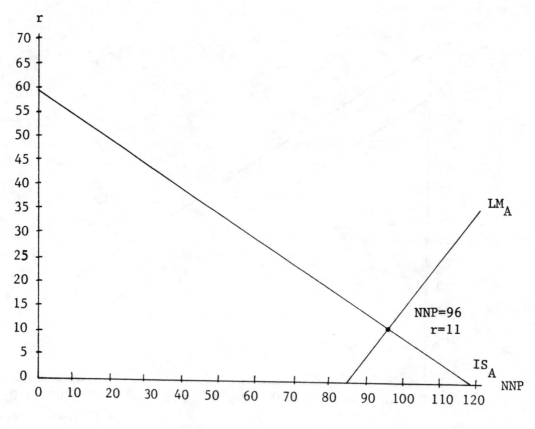

Figure 7-3

Answers to Problem 8

A. Changes in Export Demand:

   1. 75
   2. 75, -75
       A2. 1000,   1000,   1000,   75,   225,   300
   3. Alertia's holdings of gold and foreign currency are likely to be reduced, which -- if such reductions continue -- eventually will deplete such international reserves and Alertia will not be able to import.
   4. It would fall in value relative to other currencies.
   5. 75, 0
       A4. 1000,   1000,   1000,   0,   225,   225
   6. The benefits of trade and specialization are lessened if imports are restricted. Moreover the probability of retaliation in the form of restrictions on the importation of Alertia's exports into other countries is increased.

B. The Effects of a Development Program:

   1. 100
   2. 125
       B2. 1000,   125,   875, 900,   100,   300,   300
   3. 100
       B3. 1000, 0, 1000,   1000, 100,   300,   400
   4. The use of taxes has the merit of not creating a balance of payments problem and the possible merit of creating a government surplus, but also has the disadvantage of creating disincentives. The use of increased imports does not create short run disincentives and has the advantage of increased short run consumption, but has the disadvantage of creating a balance of payments problem and of utilizing foreign exchange in part for consumer imports which may have a high opportunity cost in respect to the development goals of the country.
   5. 1050
   6. 90
       1050, 0, 1050,   1040,   100,   300,   390
   7. 1500

Economics 2
1st Midterm Examination

Instructions:

1. Write all answers in blue books. Show all work.
2. Answer every part. In determining the grade, the weight assigned to each part is proportional to the time allowed for it.
3. This examination is given under the rules of the University of Pennsylvania Honor System.
4. Write your name, your instructor's name, and your section number on every blue book you use.
5. This is a 60 minute exam.
6. Illustrate your answers with carefully labelled diagrams where appropriate.

Part I (24 minutes)

Evaluate 6 of the following 7 statements. State whether the statement is true, partly true, or false; be sure to explain WHY. Explanation determines grade.

1. If the (CPI) Consumer Price Index at the end of 1988 was 300 and at the end of 1989 the index was 320, the rate of inflation over the period was about 6.7 percent.

2. A sum of $300 received by an American airline from a Greek passenger who flies from Athens to Paris is not included in the GNP of the United States.

3. The purchase of 100 shares of IBM stock is an investment which is included in GNP.

4. The multiplier is always equal to (1/MPS) where MPS is the marginal propensity to save.

5. Nordhaus and Tobin argue that GNP is a good measure of social welfare.

6. If a student graduates from College and begins to look for a job, the unemployment rate increases.

7. It is impossible to have a rise in the general price level and unemployment occurring together.

Part II   (24 minutes)

Consider this model of a closed economy in which prices are fixed:

$C = 100 + .75Y_d$ (Intended Consumption)
$I = 125$ (Intended Investment)
$G = 100$ (Government Expenditure on goods and services)
$T = 100$ (Amount of Tax Revenue)
Y_d = Disposable Income

a) Calculate the value of equilibrium income (Y). What is consumption expenditure at equilibrium?

b) Calculate the effect on equilibrium income of an increase in intended investment of 25.

c) Suppose Y_f - full employment income - is equal to 200. At what level should the government set its spending in order to restore full employment?

d) Alternatively, at what level should the government set (lump sum) taxes in order to restore full employment?

e) Explain the difference between your answers to sections (c) and (d) above.

Part III   (12 minutes)

Assume an economy where prices and wages can gradually adjust to achieve long-run equilibrium. The rate of unemployment is way above the natural rate.

a) Illustrate this situation using AS-AD curves.

b) What policies could the government use to move the economy to full employment? Show the effects of one such policy in an AS-AD graph.

c) If the government does not intervene how would the economy adjust? Show the adjustment in a graph, and explain it in words.

Economics 2
First Term Examination

Instructions:

1. Write all answers in blue books. Show all work to get full credit.

2. Answer every part. In determining the grade, the weight assigned to each
part is proportional to the time allowed for it.

3. This examination is given under the rules of the University of Pennsylvania
Honor System.

4. Write your name, your instructor's name, and your section number on every
blue book you use.

5. This is a 60 minute exam.

6. Illustrate your answers with carefully labelled diagrams where appropriate.

Part I (25 minutes)

Evaluate five of the following six statements. State whether the statement is
true, partly true, or false; be sure to explain WHY.

1. The value-added approach to calculating GNP adds up the value of all
intermediate goods in the economy.

2. Intended expenditure must equal intended output only in equilibrium.

3. A $1,000 increase in intended investment will result in a less than $1,000
increase in national income (NNP) if the MPS is greater than the MPC.

4. Equilibrium real output will always equal potential real output.

5. Rudolph Penner, in his article "Fiscal Management," holds that the
ambivalence of the general voter has contributed to an upward bias in
government spending.

6. The Laffer curve reflects the view that lower marginal tax rates will
always lead to higher government revenue.

<u>Part II</u>   (20 minutes)

Consider the following model of the closed economy:

$$C = 0.8Y_d$$
$$I = 50$$
$$G = 100$$
$$T = 150$$

where: C = Intended Consumption

I = Intended Net Investment

G = Government Expenditure on Goods/Services

T = Amount of Tax Revenues

Y_d = Disposible Income

Y = Net National Product

Assume prices are constant.

Section 1

1) Calculate the equilibrium level of Net National Product (Y) and the value of the multiplier.

2) Calculate the level of savings at the equilibrium level of Y that you calculated in (1) above.

Section 2

Let the 'full employment level of Y' (Y_f) be 250.

1) Given the equilibrium level of Y as calculated in section 1, state if this economy is experiencing an inflationary or a deflationary gap. Calculate the size of the relevant gap.

2) Calculate the amount of change in G (ΔG) that is needed to close the deflationary/inflationary gap as calculated in (1) above; also calculate ΔT, i.e. change in T needed to close the same gap. Explain any differences in your answers.

<u>Part III</u>   (15 minutes)

Use aggregate demand and aggregate supply analysis to demonstrate the impact on the equilibrium price level and equilibrium national output, in each of the cases (a) and (b) below. Use separate graphs, appropriately labeled, to illustrate your discussion of each case.

a) A reduction of the marginal tax rate

b) A technological break-through.

Economics 2

2nd Midterm Examination

Instructions:

1. Write all answers in blue books. Show all work.
2. Answer every part. In determining the grade, the weight assigned to each part is proportional to the time allowed for it.
3. This examination is given under the rules of the University of Pennsylvania Honor System.
4. Write your name, your instructor's name, and your section number on every blue book you use.
5. This is a 60 minute exam.
6. Illustrate your answers with carefully labelled diagrams where appropriate.

Part I: (25 minutes)

Evaluate 5 of the following 6 statements. State whether the statement is true, partly true, or false; be sure to explain WHY. Explanation determines grade.

1. Paper money cannot be used as a standard of value because it has no intrinsic value.

2. According to T. Mayer in "A Symposium: Incomes Policy" incomes policies in the U.S. have not been successful in restraining inflation.

3. M. Feldstein in "Inflation and Supply Side Economics" points out that by increasing productivity, supply side strategies can eliminate inflation.

4. According to the quantity theory of money, there is no necessary relationship between the money supply and nominal national output.

5. Transactions demand for money increases as interest rates increase.

6. Rational expectations theory is inconsistent with the Phillips curve.

Part II: (20 minutes)

1. The money supply (M_1) is currently $600 million, the amount of currency held by the public is $200 million, and the commercial banks are loaned up, given a current legal reserve ratio of 20%.

   Produce the balance sheet of the banking system. You should assume that the banks hold no assets other than loans and reserves, and that the banks have zero net worth.

2. Given the situation in (1), the Federal Reserve now buys $50 million worth of government securities from the public. After all adjustments have taken place, and assuming that the public continues to hold $200 million in currency, demonstrate what happens to:

   a) the balance sheet of the banks;
   b) the money supply; and
   c) the money market (use a graph).

3. Given the situation in (1), now assume that the reserve ratio changes from 20% to 25%. Demonstrate what happens to:

   a) the balance sheet of the banks;
   b) the money supply; and
   c) the interest rate.

Part III (15 minutes)

Consider the IS/LM model of Net National Product determination.

a) What is the LM curve? Explain its derivation. Is the LM curve upward or downward sloping? Why?

b) Under what conditions would you expect the LM curve to be very flat? Very steep? Why?

c) Suppose that the LM curve is relatively steep. Discuss the relative effectiveness of both fiscal and monetary policy.

Economics 2
2nd Midterm Examination

Instructions:

1. Write all answers in blue books. Show all work.
2. Answer every part. The weight of each answer in your grade is proportional to the time allowed.
3. This examination is given under the rules of the University of Pennsylvania Honor System.
4. Write your name and your instructor's name in every blue book that you use.
5. This is a 60 minute exam.
6. Illustrate your answers with carefully labelled diagrams where appropriate.

Part I (25 minutes)

Discuss 5 of the following 6 statements, indicating whether you agree or disagree with the statement.

1. The crowding out effect of government spending refers to the tendency of increased government spending to displace private consumption expenditures.

2. Because he believes that monetary policy is more effective than fiscal policy, a monetarist such as Milton Friedman would advocate using monetary policy to achieve a government desired stabilization policy.

3. If I withdraw $100 from my checking account and hold it as cash, I have increased the level of the money supply (using the M1 definition.

4. The real interest rate is the nominal interest rate divided by the price level.

5. A reduction of the discount rate affects member banks' reserves in the same way as an open market purchase of government securities.

6. The Stagflation of the 1970's is seen by many as evidence against the simple Keynesian model.

Part II (15 minutes)

The following is the consolidated balance sheet of all commercial banks for December 31, 1989 in millions of $.

Assets		Liabilities	
Reserves	40	Deposits	200
Loans	160		
	200		200

The required reserve ratio is: r - 0.2. The money stock on this date is M1 - $300 millions.

1. What is the amount of currency held by consumers?

2. Suppose that the consumer preferences change and they want to increase their currency holding by $20 million.

   a) What will be the value of M1 after the above change in preferences? (Assume that the commercial banks are "fully loaned up" i.e, their ER = 0.) Assuming no action taken by the Fed.

   b) Assume now that the Fed, in order to accomodate the change in consumers' preferences (as described above) simultaneously buys $20 million worth of government securities. What will happen to the money supply, M1, as a result? Show the consolidated balance sheet of all the banks.

Part III   (20 minutes)

1. Define the IS curve. Explain why the IS curve is upward or downward sloping. Explain how the magnitude of the slope of the IS curve depends on the size of the multiplier (m) and the sensitivity of investment to changes in the interest rate: $I = \bar{I} - bi$

2. Define the LM curve. Explain why it slopes upward or downward, and why the magnitude of its slope depends upon the sensitivity of real money demand to changes in the level of the nominal interest rate or the nominal level of output: $L = kY - hi$.

3. Assume that the real demand for money is given by $L = kY - hi$, where Y is nominal output and i is the nominal interest rate. Assume that the real money supply increases by 100. Show how the curves would shift and by how much. Discuss the effect on the equilibrium levels of national income, the interest rate, investment, and consumption.

Economics 2
Final Examination

Instructions

1. Write all answers in blue books. Show all work.
2. Answer every part. The weight of each answer in your grade is proportional to the time allowed.
3. This examination is given under the rules of the University of Pennsylvania Honor System.
4. Write your name and your <u>instructor's</u> name on every blue book that you use.
5. This is a 120 minute exam.
6. Illustrate your answers with <u>carefully labelled</u> diagrams where appropriate.

Part I (40 minutes)

Explain briefly why or in what respects the following statements are true, partly true, or false. (Choose 8 out of 9 of these statements.)

1. According to rational expectations theorists, people come to learn how policy is made, and only unanticipated policy changes can have a substantial effect on employment and output.

2. If Americans demand more Brie cheese, Burgundy wine, and other French goods and services, this will cause both the demand curve and the supply curve for French francs to shift to the right.

3. If the marginal propensity to save is 0.15 and taxes are imposed so consumers must pay $3 billion to the government at each level of NNP, consumption expenditure at each level of NNP will be $450 million less than before the imposition of the taxes.

4. If a New York contractor buys a piece of land in the Bronx, the purpose being to build an apartment house on this site next year, this would be included in gross private domestic investment.

5. John Doe pays back a $1,000 loan from his father; he also pays back a $1,000 loan from the Chase Manhattan Bank. Both of these transactions have the same effect on the money supply.

6. The monetarists at times have argued that the LM curve is very steep (close to vertical); thus, they have concluded that the crowding-out effect is small.

7. If the Federal Reserve buys government bonds, it tends to push the aggregate demand curve to the right. To offset the resulting inflationary pressures, the government should lower taxes, since this will enhance incentives for work, thus shifting the aggregate supply curve to the right.

8. According to the Council of Economic Advisers, the debt problem of the less developed countries seems to be one of liquidity rather than one of solvency.

9. We need not worry about government debt, since the view that debt represents a burden on future generations is mistaken.

Part II (40 minutes)

A small economy has the following structure:

$$C = 100 + .8D$$

$$I = 200$$

$$G = 100$$

$$T = 150$$

$$X = 200$$

$$U = .1Y,$$

where C — consumption expenditure   T — tax revenue
       I — investment expenditure   X — exports
       G — government expenditure   U — imports
                                         D — disposable income

1. What is the equilibrium value of NNP?

2. If the full-employment value of NNP is 1,800, and if it is politically impossible to change government expenditure, should taxes be lowered if the government wants to attain full employment? If so, by how much?

3. If the government is committed to a balanced budget (and if it is no longer impossible to change government expenditure), at what level should government expenditures (and taxes) be set to reach full employment?

4. Criticize the above model of this economy. What important aspects of the economy are omitted? What additional sorts of equations would you like to have; and if you had them, how would you use them to help solve the government's problem of achieving full employment with a balanced budget?

<u>Part III</u> (40 minutes)

1. In their 1989 Annual Report, President Reagan's Council of Economic Advisers stated: "At the beginning of the year economic forecasters saw two major impediments to growth in 1988. One was the stock market crash in October 1987....The other...was the...large inventory [increase]."

a. Explain in detail why the stock market crash was expected to retard the increase in NNP in 1988.

b. Explain in detail why the large inventory increase was expected to retard the increase in NNP in 1988.

c. If sales during 1988 grew less rapidly than in 1987, what effect would you expect that this would have on investment?

d. What factors will determine the rate of growth of per capita output in the United States in the next 20 years?

2.   a. Prove that the U.S. trade deficit equals the budget deficit plus the difference between investment and saving.

b. Does this fact help to explain why the United States has a substantial trade deficit at present?

c. According to the Council of Economic Advisers, this trade deficit was due partly to the very strong dollar (that is, the high value of the dollar relative to other currencies) in the early 1980's. Does this seem reasonable? Why or why not?

d. Does the fact that the United States has a balance of trade deficit mean that we must have a balance-of-payments deficit? Explain.

e. During the early 1980's, the inflation rate fell substantially. What effect would this be expected to have on the exchange rate between the dollar and other currencies? Explain.

Economics 2
Final Examination

Instructions:
1.   Write your name, your <u>instructor's</u> name, and your section number on every blue book you use.
2.   This examination is given under the rules of the University of Pennsylvania Honor System. Do not give or receive information during the exam.
3.   Show all your work in your blue books! Partial credit can only be given if you show your work.
4.   Answer every part. The weight of each answer in your grade is proportional to the time allowed for the question.
5.   This is a 120 minute (two hour) examination.
6.   Illustrate your answers with <u>carefully</u> <u>labelled</u> diagrams where appropriate.

Part I (40 minutes)
     Explain briefly why or in what respects the following statements are true, partly true, or false. Your explanation determines your grade.
     Choose 8 of the 10.

1. When a country's currency is devalued, its exports fall.

2. The Great Leap Forward period in China in the late 1950's was one of rapid growth in income per capita and in the fraction of output produced in relatively "high tech" industries such as electronics.

3. Under freely floating exchange rates, the current account is always balanced.

4. Rational expectations theory suggests that a decrease in the rate of monetary growth will cause the inflation rate to rise because unemployment does not adjust.

5. Monetarists believe that small changes in the interest rate will result in large changes in the quantity of money demanded as well as the quantity of money supplied.

6. If autonomous savings increases by 100 and simultaneously autonomous investment increases by 100, the IS curve shifts to the right by 100 times the multiplier.

7. Unemployment would be costless--at least to the overall economy--if workers were given sufficient unemployment compensation.

8. When the stock market rises, people's incomes rise. Thus GNP measured from the income side rises.

9. Poor countries have "shared poverty"--i.e. their income distributions are quite equitable relative to those of the developed economies.

10. Robert Solow believes that the price system cannot deal effectivly with the problems of the environment and overpopulation.

Part II (45 minutes)

Assume an open economy under fixed exchange rates with the following features:

$$C = 250 + 0.7Y_d \qquad \text{(Consumption)}$$
$$I = 100 + 0.1Y \qquad \text{(Investment)}$$
$$G = 325 \qquad \text{(Government Spending)}$$
$$T = 250 \qquad \text{(Taxes)}$$
$$X = 200 \qquad \text{(Exports)}$$
$$M = 0.2Y \qquad \text{(Imports)}$$

A. Calculate the equilibrium values of the following variables. Show your work!
   1. NNP
   2. Private savings.
   3. Budget deficit.
   4. Domestic Investment.
   5. Trade balance.

B. Show and explain carefully the relationship between the budget deficit, the trade deficit, and private savings and investment (leakages and injections). Show that this relationship holds for your answers to part A.

C. Assume that the full employment level of NNP is $Y_f=2000$. By how much does G have to change to move output to its full employment level?. What is the new level of the trade deficit? Explain why it has changed.

D. The functions for X and M given above are for a particular fixed exchange rate. Qualitatively, what will be the effect on X, M, and Y of a devaluation of the country's currency? Explain carefully.

Part III (35 minutes)

Consider a closed economy operating with unemployment higher than the natural rate. The government wants to use expansionary policy to get the economy to full employment. Economist A suggests a reduction in income taxes paid by households. Economist B suggests that the government should expand the money supply. In each case the magnitude of the policy change will be chosen to get the economy to full employment.

A. Use the IS-LM model to show how each of the suggested policies would affect the interest rate. Label your diagrams carefully!

B. Which policy yields a higher level of consumption in the new equilibrium? Which policy yields a higher level of investment? Explain your answers carefully.

C. How would these policies affect the future level of potential output (Y_f)? Why should people care which policy is pursued?

D. Assume now that the economy is an open one. What are the effects of the two policies on the demand for and supply of foreign currency? Explain carefully.

The Handywoman's Guide
to the Maintenance and Repair of Small Heat-Producing Electrical Appliances

The Handywoman's Guide
to the Maintenance and Repair of Small Heat-Producing Electrical Appliances

by Michael Squeglia

Illustrated by Carl Bryant

HENRY REGNERY COMPANY

CHICAGO

It's nice, of course, to have a handyman around the house, but it seems that he's never there when the steam iron won't steam or the toaster won't toast. So this book is written for and dedicated to the housewife who needs a repair manual on hand for those all too many fix-it jobs— especially those that occur among the vast array of small electrical appliances.

Edited by the staff of Vocational Horizons, Inc.